THE POCKET

GAELIC–ENGLISH,

ENGLISH–GAELIC

DICTIONARY

THE POCKET GAELIC–ENGLISH, ENGLISH–GAELIC DICTIONARY

Angus Watson

BIRLINN

First published in 2015 by
Birlinn Limited
West Newington House
10 Newington Road
Edinburgh
EH9 1QS

www.birlinn.co.uk

Copyright © Angus Watson 2015

ISBN: 978 184158 809 7

British Library Cataloguing-in-Publication Data
A catalogue record for this book is available from the British Library

Designed and typeset by Sharon McTier
Printed and bound by Grafica Veneta, Italy

Contents

Abbreviations   vii

Gaelic–English
Layout of the Entries, Gaelic–English Section   3

English–Gaelic
Layout of the Entries, English–Gaelic Section   111

The Forms of the Gaelic Article   265
The More Common Forms of the Gaelic Irregular
    and Defective Verbs   266
Constructions Using Bi as an Auxiliary Verb   278
The Gaelic Prepositional Pronouns   279

Abbreviations

abbrev	abbreviation	*f*	feminine
abstr	abstract	*fam*	familiar
acc	accusative	*fig*	figurative, figuratively
adj	adjective, adjectival	*fin*	financial, financially
admin	administration	*freq*	frequent, frequently
adv	adverb, adverbial	*fut*	future
agric	agriculture, agricultural	*gen*	genitive case
alt	alternative	*geog*	geography, geographical
anat	anatomy	*gram*	grammar, grammatical
approx	approximate,	*hist*	history, historical
	approximately	*hort*	horticulture, gardening
arch	archaeology	*imper*	imperative (case)
art	article	*incl*	including
Bibl	Bible, Biblical	*infin*	infinitive
biol	biology	*inter*	interrogative
bot	botany, botanical	*irreg*	irregular
chem	chemistry, chemical	*IT*	information technology,
cf	compare		computing
coll	collective	*lang*	language
comp	comparative	*lit*	literally
con	concrete	*Lit*	literature, literary
conj	conjunction	*m*	masculine
cons	consonant	*med*	medical
corres	correspondence,	*mil*	military
	corresponding	*misc*	miscellaneous
dat	dative case	*mus*	music, musical
def	defective	*n*	noun
derog	derogatory	*nec*	necessarily
dimin	diminutive	*neg*	negative
ed	education, educational	*nf*	noun, feminine
elec	electric, electrical	*nm*	noun, masculine
emph	emphasis, emphatic	*nmf*	noun, masculine &
Eng	English		feminine
engin	engineering	*nom*	nominative case
esp	especially	*num(s)*	numeral(s), numerical
excl(s)	exclamation(s)	*obs*	obsolete
expr(s)	expression(s), expressing	*occas*	occasionally

Abbreviations (continued)

orthog	orthography	*pt*	part
past part	past participle	*rel*	relative
PC	politically correct	*relig*	religion, religious
pej	pejorative	*Sc*	Scots (language), Scottish
pers pron	personal pronoun		
philo	philosophy, philosophical	*sing*	singular
		sing coll	singular collective
phys	physical, physically	*sp*	spelling
pl	plural	*sup*	superlative
poet	poetry, poetic(al)	*topog*	topography
pol	politics, political	*trad*	traditional, traditionally
poss	possessive	*typog*	typography
prep	prepositional	*usu*	usual, usually
pron	pronoun	*v*	verb, verbal
pres	present	*veg*	vegetable
pres part	present participle	*vi*	verb intransitive
pron	pronoun	*vt*	verb transitive
prov	proverb	*vti*	verb transitive & intransitive
psych	psychology, psychological		
		voc	vocative, vocative case

GAELIC–ENGLISH

Layout of the Entries, Gaelic–English Section

Within this section all Gaelic material is in bold type. Italics are used for all text in English that is not translation of the Gaelic material, ie abbreviations, instructions and all notes, comments, explanatory material and grammatical information. Where appropriate the different senses or usages a headword may have are subdivided into numbered sections, separated by semi-colons. The Gaelic spelling used corresponds to up-to-date norms.

NOUNS

When the headword is a noun the forms normally given are the nominative singular (also called the radical), the genitive singular and the nominative plural, unmarked for case, and in that order. Nouns are marked for masculine or feminine gender. Some nouns are marked as having both genders, a situation that typically came about when neuter nouns in the older language took on different genders in different dialects as the neuter went out of use.

VERBS

In the case of verbs, it should be explained that in Gaelic the basic form that is given in grammar books etc corresponds to the second person singular imperative, rather than to the infinitive, which is the form usually given for English verbs. The verbal forms given in the entries are the imperative form, followed by the present participle. It is important to know whether a verb can be used transitively or intransitively, that is, whether it can be used with or without a direct object, and this is conveyed by the abbreviations *vt, vi* and *vti* given immediately after the imperative of the verb.

A

a *particle*
a *voc*
a *poss adj*
a *rel pron*
a¹ *prep (for* **de**) of
a² *prep (for* **do**) to
a' *art*
a' (*sign of the pres part*)
à *prep* from
ab/aba, *gen* **aba,** *pl* **abachan** *nm* abbot
abachadh, *gen* **abachaidh** *nm* ripening
abaich *adj* mature, ripe
abaich *vti,* ripen, mature
abaid, abaide, abaidean *nf* abbey
abair *vt irreg, pres part* **ag ràdh** say
abairt, abairte, abairtean *nf* phrase, expression
àbhacas/àbhachdas, *gen* **àbhac(hd)ais** *nm* mirth, ridicule
àbhachd *nf* humour, amusement
àbhachdach *adj* amusing, humorous
abhag, abhaig, abhagan *nf* terrier
abhainn, aibhne, aibhnichean *nf* river
àbhaist, àbhaiste, àbhaistean *nf* habit, custom
àbhaisteach *adj* usual
a' bhòn-dè *adv* day before yesterday
abhlan, abhlain, abhlanan *nm* wafer
a' bhòn-raoir *adv* night before last
a' bhòn-uiridh *adv* year before last
a-bhos *adv* here, over here
ablach, ablaich, ablaichean *nm* carcase, wretch
abstol, abstoil, abstolan *nm* apostle
aca *prep pron* at them, their
acadaimigeach *adj* academic
acadamh, acadaimh, acadamhan *nmf* academy
acaid, acaide, acaidean *nf* stabbing pain, stitch
acair(e)¹, *gen* **acaire/acrach,** *pl* **acraichean** *nmf* anchor
acair(e)², *gen* **acaire/acrach,** *pl* **acraichean** *nmf* acre
acarsaid, acarsaide, acarsaidean *nf* anchorage, harbour

acfhainn, *gen* **acfhainne,** *pl* **acfhainnean** *nf* 1 equipment; 2 set of tools; 3 harness; 4 rigging
ach *conj* but
achadh, achaidh, achaidhean *nm* field
a-chaoidh *adv* always, forever
achd, achd, achdannan *nf* (*pol*) act, **Achd Pàrlamaid**
a-cheana/cheana, *adv* already
a chionn *prep* because of
achlais, achlaise, achlaisean *nf* 1 armpit; 2 arm
achlasan, *gen & pl* **achlasain** *nm* armful
achmhasan, *gen & pl* **achmhasain** *nm* reproach
acrach *adj* hungry
acraich *vt, pres part* **ag acrachadh** anchor, moor
acras, *gen* **acrais** *nm* hunger
acrasach *adj* hungry
ad, aide, adan *nf* hat
adag, adaig, adagan *nf* haddock
àdha, àdha, àinean *nm* (*anat*) liver
adhaltraiche, adhaltraiche, adhaltraichean *nm* adulterer
adhaltranas, *gen* **adhaltranais** *nm* adultery
adhar, *gen* **adhair** *nm* sky, air
adharc, adhairc, adharcan *nf* horn
adharcach *adj* horny
adhart, *gen* **adhairt** *nm, in expr* **air adhart** *adv* forwards
adhartach *adj* progressive
adhartas, *gen* **adhartais** *nm* progress
adhbhar, *gen* **adhbhair,** *pl* **adhbharan** *nm* 1 reason; 2 materials
adhbharaich *vt, pres part* **ag adhbharachadh,** cause
adhbrann, adhbrainn, adhbrainnean *nmf* ankle
adhradh, adhraidh, adhraidhean *nm,* worship
Afganach *gen & pl* **Afganaich** *nm,* Afghan, *also adj* **Afganach** Afghan
Afraga *nf* Africa
Afraganach, *gen & pl* **Afraganaich** *nm* African, *also adj* **Afraganach** African

ag *with following verbal noun forms pres part*

agad (*emph* **agadsa**), **againn** (*emph form* **againne**), **agaibh** (*emph form* **agaibhse**), *prep prons, see* **aig**

agallamh, agallaimh, agallamhan *nm* **1** interview; **2** conversation

agam (*emph* **agamsa**) *prep pron* at me

àgh & **àigh**, *gen* **àigh** *nm* joy

agh, aighe, aighean *nf* heifer

aghaidh, aghaidhe, aghaidhean *nf* **1** face; **2** cheek, nerve; **3** *in expr* **an aghaidh** *prep* against; **4** *in expr* **air aghaidh** *adv* forward(s)

aghaidh-choimheach, aghaidh-coimhich, aghaidhean-coimheach *nf* mask

aghann, aigh(ain)ne, aghannan *nf* (frying) pan

agus *conj* and

aibidil, aibidile, aibidilean *nf* alphabet

aice (*emph* **aicese**) *prep pron* at her

àicheadh, *gen* **àicheidh** *nm* denial, renunciation

àicheidh *vt, pres part* **ag àicheadh** deny, renounce

aideachadh, aideachaidh, aideachaidhean *nm* admitting, confession

aidich *vti, pres part* **ag aideachadh**, confess, admit

aifreann, *gen* **aifrinn** *nm* (*relig*) Mass

aig *prep* at

àigeach, *gen* & *pl* **àigich** *nm* stallion

aige (*emph* **aigesan**) *prep pron* at him

aighear, *gen* **aigheir** *nm* joy

aighearach *adj* cheerful

aigne *nf* mind, disposition

ailbhinn, *gen* **ailbhinne** *nf* flint

àile, *also* **àileadh, fàile** & **fàileadh**, *gen* **(f)àileidh**, *pl* **(f)àileachan, fàilean** & **fàilidhean** *nm* **1** air, atmosphere; **2** smell

aileag, aileig, aileagan *nf* hiccups (*with art*)

àill *nf* **1** desire; **2** *in expr* **B' àill leibh?** Pardon?

àilleag, àilleig, àilleagan *nf* jewel

aillse *nf* cancer

ailseag, ailseig, ailseagan *nf* caterpillar

ailtire, ailtire, ailtirean *nm* architect

ailtireachd *nf* architecture

aimhreit, aimhreite, aimhreitean *nf* disturbance

aimsir, aimsire, aimsirean *nf* weather

aindeoin *nf* **1** reluctance; **2** *in expr* **a dh'aindeoin** (*with gen*) in spite of

aineolach *adj* ignorant

aineolas, *gen* **aineolais** *nm* ignorance

aingeal, aingil, ainglean *nm* angel

aingidh *adj* wicked

ainm, *gen* **ainme**, *pl* **ainmean** & **ainmeannan** *nm* name

ainmeachadh, *gen* **ainmeachaidh** *nm* naming, mentioning

ainmear, ainmeir, ainmearan *nm* noun

ainmeil *adj* famous

ainmhidh, ainmhidhe, ainmhidhean *nm* animal

ainmich *vt, pres part* **ag ainmeachadh** name, mention

ainneamh *adj* unusual, scarce

ainneart, *gen* **ainneirt** *nm* violence

aintighearna, aintighearnan *nm* tyrant

air *prep* on

air ais *adv* back(wards)

air b(h)all *adv* at once

air beulaibh *prep* in front of

air choreigin *adj* some or other

air cùlaibh *prep* behind (*with gen*)

àird(e), àirde, àirdean *nf* **1** high place; **2** promontory; **3** compass point **4** *in expr* **an-àird** *adv* up

àirde *nf* height

aire *nf* mind, attention, care

àireamh, àireimh, àireamhan *nf* number

air feadh *prep* through(out)

airgead, *gen* **airgid** *nm* **1** money; **2** silver

airidh *adj* worthy, deserving

àirigh, àirighe, àirighean *nf* sheiling

àirneis *nf* furniture

air neo *conj* or (else)

airson *prep* for

aiseag, aiseig, aiseagan *nm* ferry (crosssing)

aiseal, aiseil, aisealan *nf* axle

aisean, *gen* **aisne**, *pl* **aisnean, aisnichean** & **asnaichean** *nf* rib

aiseirigh *nf* resurrection

Àisia *nf* Asia

Àisianach, *gen* & *pl* **Àisianaich** *nm* Asian, *also adj* **Àisianach** Asian

aisling, aislinge, aislingean *nf* dream

aiste, aiste, aistidhean *nf* essay, article

àite, *gen* **àite**, *pl* **àiteachan, àitichean** & **àiteannan** *nm* place

àiteach, *gen* **àitich** *nm* cultivation

àiteachadh, *gen* **àiteachaidh** *nm* **1** cultivating; **2** occupation

àiteachas, *gen* **àiteachais** *nm nf* agriculture

aiteal, *gen* & *pl* **aiteil** *nm* glimpse

aiteamh, *gen* **aiteimh** *nm* thaw(ing)

àiteigin *nm* somewhere

aithghearr *adj* **1** short, brisk; **2** *in expr* **a dh'aithghearr** *adv* soon, shortly

aithghearrachd *nf* **1** abbreviation; **2** short cut

aithisg, aithisge, aithisgean *nf* report

aithne *nf* acquaintance

aithneachadh & **faithneachadh**, *gen* **(f)aithneachaidh** *nm* knowing

aithnich/faithnich, *vt*, *pres part* **ag aithneachadh** & **a' faithneachadh**, know

aithreachas, *gen* **aithreachais** *nm* repentance, remorse

aithris *vt*, *pres part* **ag aithris, 1** recount; **2** recite

aithris, aithrise, aithrisean *nf* **1** account; **2** recitation

àitich *vt*, *pres part* **ag àiteachadh, 1** cultivate; **2** inhabit

aitreabh, aitreibh, aitreabhan *nm* building

àl, *gen* **àil** *nm* litter, brood

àlainn *adj* **1** lovely

Alba, *gen* **Alba**, *nf* Scotland

Albàinia *nf* Albania

Albàinianach *gan* & *pl* **Albàinianaich** *nm* Albanian, *also adj* Albanian

Albais, *gen* **Albaise** *nf* Scots

Albannach, *gen* & *pl* **Albannaich** *nm* Scotsman

allaban, *gen* **allabain** *nm* wandering

allaidh *adj* wild (*not domesticated*)

allt, *gen* & *pl* **uillt** *nm* (mountain) stream, burn,

alt, uilt, altan *nm* **1** (*anat*) joint; **2** method; **3** (*gram*) **an t-alt** the article; **4** *in expr* **an altan a chèile/an altaibh a chèile** together

altachadh, *gen* **altachaidh** *nm* grace (*before meals etc*)

altair, altarach, altairean *nf* altar

altraim *vt*, *pres part* **ag altram** & **ag altramas, 1** foster; **2** nurse

altram, *gen* **altraim, 1** fosterage, fostering; **2** nursing

am *poss adj see* **an** *poss adj*

am *art see* **an** *art*

àm, ama, amannan *nm* time

a-mach *adv* **1** out (*motion*)

amadan, *gen* & *pl* **amadain** *nm*

amaideach *adj* foolish

amaideas, *gen* **amaideis** *nm* foolishness, nonsense

a-màireach *adv* tomorrow

amais *vti*, *pres part* **ag amas** (at **air**) **1** aim; **2** *in expr* **amais air** hit upon

amar, amair, amaran *nm* basin, pool

amas, amais, amasan *nm* aim

Ameireaga(idh) *nf* America

Ameireaganach, *gen* & *pl* **Ameireaganaich** *nm* American, *also adj* **Ameireaganach** American

amh *adj* raw, unripe

amha(i)ch, amhaiche, amhaichean *nf* neck, throat

a-mhàin *adv* only

àmhainn, àmhainne, àmhainnean *nf* oven

amhairc *vi*, *pres part* **ag amharc**, look

amharas, *gen pl* **amharais** *nm* suspicion, doubt

amharasach *adj* suspicious, doubting

amharc, *gen* **amhairc** *nm* sight, view

am measg *prep* among

a-muigh *adv* outside (*position*)

an *art* the

an (**am** *before b, f, m, p*) *poss adj* their

an (**am** *before b, f, m, p*) *prep* in

an (**am** *before b, f, m, p*), *with neg v*, **nach**, *inter particle*

ana- (**an-** *before a vowel*) a negativising *prefix*

anabarrach *adj* extreme

anail, analach, anailean *nf* breath

a-nall *adv* here (*movement*), hither

anam, anma, anman *nm* soul

anart, anairt, anartan *nm* linen

an ath-bhliadhna *adv* next year

an ath-oidhch(e) *adv* tomorrow night

an-ceart(u)air *adv* just now; shortly

an comhair *prep* in the direction of

an-còmhnaidh *adv* always

an-dè *adv* yesterday

an dèidh & **às dèidh**, **1** *prep* after; **2 an dèidh sin** *adv* nevertheless

an-diugh *adv* today

an-dràsta *adv* just now

an-earar *adv* the day after tomorrow

an-fhoiseil *adj* restless

an impis *prep* about to

a-nis(e) *adv* now

anmoch *adv* late

ann an (**ann am** *before b,f, m, p*) in

annas, annais, annasan *nm* rarity, novelty

annasach *adj* unusual

a-nochd *adv* tonight

an seo, ann an s(h)eo *advs* here

an sin, ann an s(h)in *advs* there

an siud, ann an s(h)iud *advs* there

a-nuas *adv* down

an-uiridh *adv* last year

a-null *adv* there (*movement*), thither

aodach, aodaich, aodaichean *nm* cloth(es)

aodann, aodainn, aodainnean *nm* face

aoibhneach *adj* pleasant, happy

aoidion, aoidiona, aoidionan *nm* (*tap etc*) leak

aoigh, aoigh, aoighean *nm* guest

aoigheachd, *nf* hospitality

aoir, aoire, aoirean *nf* satire

aois, aoise, aoisean *nf* (old) age

aol, *gen* **aoil** *nm* (*mineral*) lime

aom *vi, pres part* **ag aomadh** bend, incline

aomadh, *gen* **aomaidh** *nm* **1** bending, tending; **2** tendency, inclination,

aon *n and num adj* one

aon *nmf* **1** one; **2** (*cards*) **an t-aon** the ace

aonach, aonaich, aonaichean *nm* moorland

aonachadh, *gen* **aonachaidh** *nm* **1** uniting, combining; **2** coalition

aonad, aonaid, aonadan *nm* unit

aonadh, aonaidh, aonaidhean *nm* union

aonaich *vti, pres part* **ag aonachadh,** unite, combine, merge

aonaichte *adj & past part* united

aonan *adj & pron* one

aonar, *gen* **aonair** *nmf,* (*in phrase* **nad aonar**) **1** one person; **2** aloneness

aonaran, aonarain, aonaranan *nm* hermit

aon(a)ranach *adj* lonely

aon(a)ranachd *nf* loneliness

aon-deug 1 *n & adj* eleven

aonta & **aontadh,** *gen* **aontaidh,** *pl* **aontaidhean** *nm* agreement, assent

aontachadh, *gen* **aontachaidh** *nm* agreeing

aontaich *vi, pres part* **ag aontachadh,** agree

aosmhor *adj* ancient

aosta aged, elderly

aotrom *adj* light

aotromachadh, *gen* **aotromachaidh** *nm* lightening

aotromaich *vt, pres part* **ag aotromachadh, 1** lighten; **2** unload

aotroman, *gen & pl* **aotromain** *nm* (*anat*) bladder

aparan, aparain, aparanan *nm* apron

ar (**ar n-** *before vowel*) *poss adj* our

àr, àir, àir *nm* slaughter

àra, àrann, àirnean *nf* (*anat*) kidney

Arabach, *gen & pl* **Arabaich** Arab, *also adj* **Arabach** Arab, Arabic

Arabais *nf* (*lang*) Arabic

àrach, *gen* **àraich** *nm* raising, upbringing, rearing

àrachas, *gen* **àrachais** *nm* insurance

àradh/fàradh, *gen* **(f)àraidh,** *pl* **(f)àraidhean** *nm* ladder

Aràbia *nf* Arabia

àraich *vt, pres part* **ag àrach,** raise, rear

àraid *adj* particular, peculiar

àraidh *adj* particular, unusual

àrainneachd *nf* environment

ar-a-mach *nm* rebellion

aran, *gen* **arain** *nm* bread

a-raoir *adv* last night

arbhar, *gen* **arbhair** *nm* corn

àrc, àirce, àrcan *nf* cork

Arcach, *gen & pl* **Arcaich** *nm* Orcadian, *also adj,* **Arcach** Orcadian

Arcaibh *nm* Orkney

arc-eòlaiche, arc-eòlaiche, arc-eòlaichean *nm* archaeologist

àrd *adj* **1** (*person etc*) high, tall; **2** (*sound*) loud

àrdachadh, *gen* **àrdachaidh** *nm* **1** increasing; **2** promotion

àrdaich *vt, pres part* **ag àrdachadh, 1** increase; **2** promote

àrdaichear, àrdaicheir, àrdaichearan *nm* elevator

àrdan, *gen* **àrdain** *nm* arrogance

àrd-sgoil, àrd-sgoile, àrd-sgoiltean *nf* high school

àrd-ùrlar, àrd-ùrlair, àrd-ùrlaran *nm* (*theatre etc*) stage, platform

a rèir *prep* 1 according to; 2 *as adv* accordingly

argamaid, argamaide, argamaidean *nf* argument, discussion

argamaidich *vi, pres part* **ag argamaid,** argue

a-riamh *adv* 1 ever, always; 2 *with neg verb*, never

a-rithist *adv* again

arm *gen & pl* **airm** *nm* army

arsa *def verb* said

àrsaidh *adj* ancient, archaic

Artach *adj* Arctic

Artaig, *gen* **Artaige** *nf, used with art,* **an Artaig** the Arctic

asal, asail, asalan *nf, also* **aiseal, aiseil, aisealan** *nm* donkey

às aonais *prep* without, in the absence of

asgaidh, asgaidhe, asgaidhean *nf* 1 gift; 2 *in exprs* **an-asgaidh** free

a-staigh *adv* within

astar, *gen & pl* **astair** *nm* 1 distance; 2 speed

a-steach *adv* into

Astràilia *nf* Australia

Astràilianach, *gen & pl* **Astràilianaich** *nm* Australian, *also adj* **Astràilianach** Australian

at, at, atan *nm* swelling

at *vi, pres part* **ag at(adh)**

ath *adj* next

àth, àtha, àthan *nf* kiln

àth, àth, àthan *nm* ford

ath- *prefix usu corres to Eng* re-

ath- *prefix corres to Eng* after-

athair, athar, athraichean *nm* father

atharrachadh, atharrachaidh, atharrachaidhean *nm* changing

atharraich *vti, pres part* **ag atharrachadh,** change

atharrais *nf* imitation

atharrais *vt, pres part* **ag atharrais air,** imitate

ath-bheothachadh, *gen* **ath-bheothachaidh** *nm* reviving, revival

ath-bheothaich *vt, pres part* **ag ath-bheothachadh,** revive

ath-chruthaich *vt, pres part* **ag ath-chruthachadh,** recreate

ath-chuairtich, *pres part* **ath-chuairteachadh,** recycle

athchuinge, athchuinge, athchuingean *nf* entreaty, petition

ath-dhìol *vt, pres part* **ag ath-dhìoladh,** repay

ath-leasachadh, ath-leasachaidh, ath-leasachaidhean *nm* reforming

ath-leasaich *vt, pres part* **ag ath-leasachadh,** reform

ath-nuadhachadh, *gen* **ath-nuadhachaidh** *nm* renewal

ath-nuadhaich *vt, pres part* **ag ath-nuadhachadh,** renew

ath-sgrìobh *vt, pres part* **ag ath-sgrìobhadh,** re-write

ath-sgrùdadh, ath-sgrùdaidh, ath-sgrùdaidhean *nm* 1 re-appraisal; 2 (*education etc*) revision

B

babhstair, babhstair, babhstairean *nm*
1 bolster; 2 mattress

bac, *gen* **baca** & **baic,** *pl* **bacan** *nm*
1 hindrance; 2 hollow, bend; 3 peat-bank;
4 sandbank

bac *vt, pres part* **a' bacadh,** prevent

bacach *adj* 1 lame, crippled

bacach, *gen* & *pl* **bacaich** *nm* cripple

bacadh, bacaidh, bacaidhean *nm*
obstacle

bacan, *gen* & *pl* **bacain** *nm* tether post

bachall, bachaill, bachallan *nm* crozier

bachlach & **bachallach** *adj* curly

bachlag, bachlaig, bachlagan *nf* 1 curl;
2 (*of plant etc*) shoot, sprout

bad, baid, badan *nm* 1 place, spot; 2 tuft;
3 flock; 4 thicket; 5 *in exprs* **anns a'**
bhad immediately

badan, *gen* & *pl* **badain** *nm* nappy

baga, *gen* **baga,** *pl* **bagannan** &
bagaichean *nm* bag

bagaid, bagaide, bagaidean *nf* bunch

bagair *vti, pres part* **a' bagairt** & **a'**
bagradh, 1 threaten; 2 (*vi*) bluster

bagairt, bagairt, bagairtean *nf* &
bagradh, bagraidh, bagraidhean *nm*
threatening, blustering

bàgh, *gen* **bàigh,** *pl* **bàghan** &
bàghannan *nm* bay

bàidh, *gen* **bàidhe** *nf* 1 affection, fondness;
2 good turn

bàidheil *adj* kindly

baidhsagal, baidhsagail, baidhsagalan
nm bicycle

baile, baile, bailtean *nm* 1 (*crofting*)
township; 2 *esp with* **beag,** village, small
town; 3 *in expr* **aig baile** at home

bàillidh, bàillidh, bàillidhean *nm*
1 bailiff; 2 factor

bàinidh *nf* madness, fury

bainne, *gen* **bainne** *nm* milk

bàirneach, bàirnich, bàirnich *nf*
barnacle, limpet

baist *vt, pres part* **a' baisteadh,** baptise

Baisteach, Baistich, Baistich *nm* Baptist

baisteadh, baistidh, baistidhean *nm*
baptism

bàl, *gen* & *pl* **bàil** *nm* ball (*dance*)

bàla, bàla, bàlaichean *nm* (*for games*
etc) ball

balach, *gen* & *pl* **balaich** *nm* boy

balbh *adj* 1 dumb, mute; 2 silent; 3 (*place*
etc) peaceful

balg & **bolg,** *gen* & *pl* **builg** *nm* 1 (*anat*)
abdomen; 2 blister

balgair, balgaire, balgairean *nm* 1 fox;
2 rogue

balgam, balgaim, balgaman *nm* sip,
swig

balgan-buachair, *gen* & *pl* **balgain-**
buachair *nm* mushroom

ball[1], *gen* & *pl* **buill** *nm* 1 (*anat*) limb,
organ; 2 member; 3 item of; 4 rope; 5 *in*
exprs **ball-àbhachdais** laughing-stock,
air ball immediately

ball[2], *gen* & *pl* **buill** *nm* ball (*games*)

balla, *gen* **balla,** *pl* **ballachan** &
ballaichean *nm* wall

ballach *adj* spotted, speckled

ballan, ballain, ballanan *nm* tub

ball-coise, *gen* & *pl* **buill-coise** *nm*
football

ball-dòbhrain, *gen* & *pl* **buill-dòbhrain**
nm mole (*on skin*)

ball-maise, *gen* & *pl* **buill-maise** *nm*
ornament

ballrachd, *gen* **ballrachd** *nf* membership

bàn[1] *adj* 1 fallow; 2 blank

bàn[2] *adj* white, fair (*colouring*)

bana- & **ban-** *prefix, corres to Eng* female,
woman, -ess

banacharaid, banacharaide,
banachàirdean *nf* (female, woman)
friend or relative

banachdach, *gen* **banachdaich** *f*
vaccination

bànag, bànaig, bànagan *nf* sea-trout

banais, bainnse, bainnsean *nf* wedding

banaltram, banaltraim, banaltraman
nf nurse

banc & **banca,** *gen* **banca,** *pl*
bancaichean & **bancan** *nm* bank

bancair, bancair, bancairean *nm*
banker

bancaireachd *nf* banking

bann, bainne, bannan *nm* **1** strip (*material etc*); **2** bandage; **3** hinge

ban(n)trach, ban(n)traich, ban(n)traichean *nf* widow(er)

banrigh, banrighe, banrighrean *nf* queen

baoit *nf also* **baoiteag**, *gen* **baoiteige** *nf* bait

baoth *adj* foolish

barail, baraile, barailean *nf* opinion

baraille, baraille, baraillean *nm* barrel

bàrd, *gen & pl* **bàird** *nm* bard, poet

bàrdachd *nf* poetry

bargan, *gen* **bargain**, *pl* **bargain** & **barganan** *nm* bargain

bàrr, barra, barran *nm* **1** top; **2** (*agric etc*) crop; **3** *in expr* **thoir** *v* **bàrr air** top, cap or beat something; **4** *in expr* **bhàrr** & **far** *prep* (*for* **de bhàrr**) *plus noun in gen* from, from off, down from

barrachd *nf* more; **2** *in expr* **barrachd air** *prep* more than; **3** *in expr* **a bharrachd (air)** in addition (to), as well (as), besides

barraichte *adj* top-class

barrall, barraill, barraillean *nm* shoe-lace

barrantaich *vt, pres part* **a' barrantachadh**, **1** guarantee; **2** commission

bar(r)antas, bar(r)antais, bar(r)antasan *nm* pledge, security

bas/bois, *gen* **boise**, *pl* **basan** & **boisean**, *nf* palm of the hand

bàs, *gen* **bàis** *nm* **1** death; **2** *in expr* **a' dol bàs** dying out, fading away; **3** *in expr* **faigh bàs** die

bàsachadh, *gen* **bàsachaidh** *nm* dying

bàsaich *vi, pres part* **a' bàsachadh**, die

Basgach, *gen & pl* **Basgaich** *nm* Basque, *also adj* Basque

basgaid, basgaide, basgaidean *nf* basket

Basgais *nf* Basque (*language*)

bàsmhor *adj* **1** mortal; **2** deadly, fatal

bata, bata, bataichean *nm* stick

bàta, bàta, bàtaichean *nm* boat

bataraidh, bataraidh, bataraidhean *nmf* (*elec*) battery

bàth *vt, pres part* **a' bàthadh**, drown

bàthach, bàthcha, bàthchannan *nf* & **bàthaich, bàthaich, bàthaichean** *nm* byre

bàthadh, *gen* **bàthaidh** *nm* drowning

bathais, bathais, bathaisean *nf* **1** forehead; **2** impudence

bathar, *gen* **bathair** *nm* *coll* wares

beachd, beachda, beachdan *nm* **1** idea, opinion; **2** *in expr* **bi am beachd a . . .** be thinking of . . . ; **3** *in expr* **rach** *v* **às mo (etc) b(h)eachd** lose my (etc) mind

beachdaich *vi, pres part* **a' beachdachadh**, consider

beag *adj, comp* **(n)as** (*etc*) **lugha**, **1** small; **2** slight; **3** *in expr* **rud beag** *adv* somewhat; **4** *in expr* **is beag orm** I don't like

beagan *adv* slightly,

beagan, *gen* **beagain** *nm* little of, a few

bealach, *gen & pl* **bealaich** *nm* **1** mountain pass; **2** top of pass; **3** detour

bealaidh *nm* (*bot*) broom

Bealltainn, *gen* **Bealltainne** *nf* May Day

bean, *gen* **mnà**, *dat* **mnaoi**, *pl* **mnathan**, *gen pl* **ban** *nf* **1** wife; **2** woman

bean *vi, pres part* **a' beantainn 1** (*with* **ri** & **do**) touch, handle; **2** (*with* **ri**) brush against; **3** (*with* **ri**) deal with

bean-ghlùine, mnà-glùine, mnathan-glùine *nf* midwife

beannachadh, beannachaidh, *pl* **beannachaidhean** *nm* **1** blessing; **2** greeting, farewell

beannachd, beannachd, beannachdan *nf* blessing; **2** compliments, regards

beannaich *vti, pres part* **a' beannachadh**, bless

bean-taighe, mnà-taighe, mnathan-taighe *nf* housewife, lady of the house

beàrn, *gen* **bèirn/beàirn**, *pl* **beàrnan** *nmf* gap

beàrnan-brìde, *gen & pl* **beàrnain-bhrìde** *nm* dandelion

beàrr *vt, pres part* **a' bearradh** shear, shave

bearradh[1], *gen* **bearraidh** *nm* shaving, shearing

bearradh[2], *gen* **bearraidh**, **bearraidhean** *nm* cliff, precipice

beart/beairt, *gen* **beairt**, *pl* **beartan** & **beairtean** *nf* **1** a machine; **2** loom

beartach/beairteach *adj* rich, wealthy

beartas/beairteas, *gen* **beartais** & **beairteis** *nm* wealth

beatha, beatha, beathannan *nf* **1** life; **2** *in expr* **'s e do bheatha** you're welcome; **3** *in expr* **mar mo** (etc) **b(h) eatha** for dear life

beathach, beathaich, beathaichean *nm* beast, animal

beathachadh, *gen* **beathachaidh** *nm* feeding, maintaining

beathaich *vt, pres part* **a' beathachadh**, feed, maintain

beic, beice, beiceannan *nf* curtsey, **dèan** *v* **beic** curtsey

bèicear, bèiceir, bèicearan *nm* baker

Beilg *nf, used with art,* **a' Bheilg** Belgium

Beilgeach, *gen & pl* **Beilgich** *nm* Belgian, *also adj* **Beilgeach** Belgian

being, beinge, beingean *nf* bench

beinn, *gen* **beinne**, *pl* **beanntan**, *gen pl* **beann** mountain

beir *vti, pres part* **a' breith**, **1** (*vt*) bear, give birth to; **2** (*vi*) *with* **air**, overtake, catch up with, catch; **3** (*vi*) *with* **air**, seize, take hold of

beirm, *gen* **beirme** *nf* yeast

beithe *nf* birch(-tree)

beò *adj* **1** alive, animate; **2** life

beòshlaint, beòshlainte, beòshlaintean *nf* livelihood

beothachadh, *gen* **beothachaidh** *nm* reviving

beothaich *vti, pres part* **a' beothachadh**, revive

beothail *adj* lively

beuc, beuc, beucan *nm* roar, bellow

beuc *vi, pres part* **a' beucadh**, roar, bellow

beucadh, *gen* **beucaidh** *nm* roaring, bellowing

beud, beud, beudan *nm* loss *in expr* **is mòr am beud (e)** it's a great shame/pity

beul, *gen & pl* **beòil** *nm* mouth

beulaibh *nm* front part

beum, *gen* **beuma**, *pl* **beuman** & **beumannan** *nm* **1** stroke, blow; **2** taunt

Beurla *nf* English language

beus, beusa, beusan *nf* **1** moral character; **2** behaviour

beus *adj* (*music*) bass

bhidio, bhidio, bhidiothan *nmf* video

bho/o *prep* from

bhòt(a), bhòt(a), bhòtaichean *nf* vote

bhòt *vi, pres part* **a' bhòtadh**, vote

biadh, *gen* **bìdh** & **bidhe**, *pl* **biadhan** *nm* **1** food; **2** meal

bian, *gen & pl* **bèin** *nm* **1** fur; **2** skin, hide

biast/bèist, *gen* **bèiste**, *pl* **biastan** & **bèistean** *nf* beast

biath *vt, pres part* **a' biathadh**, feed

biathadh, *gen* **biathaidh** *nm* feeding

bìd, bìde, bìdean *nm* **1** (*bird*) cheep; **2** (*human*) sound, word

bìd *vt, pres part* **a' bìdeadh**, bite

bìdeadh, bìdidh, bìdidhean *nm* biting

bìdeag, bìdeig, bìdeagan *nf* fragment, bit

bidh *pt of irreg v* **bi**

bile, bile, bilean *nf* **1** lip, rim

bile, bile, bilean *nm* (*parliament*) bill

bileag, bileig, bileagan *nf* **1** petal; **2** blade (*grass*); **3** bill; **4** ticket; **5** label; **6** leaflet

billean, billein, billeanan *nm* billion

binid, *gen* **binide** *nf* rennet

binn *adj* **1** (*sound*) sweet, melodious

binn, *gen* **binne** *nf* judgement

binnean, *gen & pl* **binnein** *nm* pinnacle

binneas, *gen* **binneis** *nm* (*sound*) sweetness

bìoball, *gen* **bìobaill**, *pl* **bìobaill** & **bìoblaichean** *nm* bible

bìobhar, bìobhair, bìobharan *m* beaver

bìodach *adj* tiny

biodag, biodaig, biodagan *nf* dagger

biodh, *pt of irreg v* **bi**

bìog, bìoga, bìogan *nf* cheep

bìog *vi, pres part* **a' bìogail**, (*bird*) cheep

biolair, *gen* **biolair** *nf* watercress

biona, biona, bionaichean *nmf* bin

bior, biora, bioran *nm* **1** point (*stick etc*); **2** prickle

biorach *adj* **1** pointed, prickly

bioran, *gen & pl* **biorain** *nm* pointed stick

biorra-crùidein, biorra-crùidein, biorrachan-crùidein *nm* kingfisher

biotais *nm* beet

birlinn, birlinn, birlinnean *nf* galley

bith *nf* **1** life, existence; **2** the world

bìth, *gen* **bìthe** *nf* **1** tar; **2** gum

bitheag, bitheige, bitheagan *nf* microbe

bitheanta *adj* common

bithibh, bithidh, bithinn *pts of irreg v* **bi**

bithis, bithis, bithisean *nf* (*joinery*) screw

blais *vt, pres part* **a' blasad(h)**, taste

blàr, blàir, blàran *nm* **1** plain;
2 battle(field)

blas, *gen* **blais** *nm* **1** taste; **2** (*language*)
accent

blasad, *gen* **blasaid** *nm* tasting; **2** taste

blasaich *vt, pres part* **a' blasachadh,**
flavour

blasta *adj* tasty

blàth *adj* warm

blàth, blàith, blàthan *nm* **1** blossom;
2 flower

blàthachadh, *gen* **blàthachaidh** *nm*
warming

blàthaich *vt, pres part* **a' blàthachadh,**
warm

blàths, *gen* **blàiths** *nm* warmth

bleideag, bleideig, bleideagan *nf* flake

bleith, *gen* **bleithe** *nf* grinding

bleith *vt, pres part* **a' bleith,** grind

bleoghain(n) *vt, pres part* **a'**
bleoghan(n), milk

bleoghann *nf* milking

bliadhna, *gen* **bliadhna,** *pl*
bliadhnachan & **bliadhnaichean** *nf*
year

bliadhnach, *gen* & *pl* **bliadhnaich** *nm*
yearling

bliadhnail *adj* annual

blian *vi, pres part* **a' blianadh,** sunbathe

blianadh, *gen* **blianaidh** *nm* sunbathing

blobhsa, blobhsa, blobhsaichean *nm*
blouse

bloigh & **bloidh,** *gen* **bloighe,** *pl*
bloighean *nf* fragment, fraction

bloighd, bloighd, bloighdean *nf*
fragment, splinter

bloinigean-gàrraidh, *gen* **bloinigein-**
gàrraidh *nm* spinach

blonag, *gen* **blonaig** *nf* lard, fat

bò, *gen* **bà,** *dat* **boin** & **bò,** *pl* **bà,** *gen pl*
bò *nf* cow

bobhla, bobhla, bobhlaichean *nm* bowl

bòc *vi, pres part* **a' bòcadh,** swell

bòcadh, bòcaidh, bòcaidhean *nm*
swelling

boc, *gen* & *pl* **buic** *nm* **1** billygoat;
2 roebuck

bòcan, *gen* & *pl* **bòcain** *nm* **1** spectre;
2 bog(e)y-man

bochd *adj* **1** poor; **2** unfortunate; **3** poorly

bochdainn, *gen* **bochdainne** *nf*
1 poverty; **2** misfortune

bod, *gen* & *pl* **buid** & **boid** *nm* penis

bodach, *gen* & *pl* **bodaich** *nm* old man

bodhaig, bodhaige, bodhaigean *nf*
(*human*) body

bodhair *vt, pres part* **a' bòdhradh,**
deafen

bodhar *adj* deaf

bòdhradh, *gen* **bòdhraidh** *nm* deafening

bodraig *vti, pres part* **a' bodraigeadh,**
bother

bodraigeadh, *gen* **bodraigidh** *nm*
bothering

bog *adj* **1** soft; **2** tender; **3** moist; **4** limp

bog, buig, bogachan *nm* **1** bog; **2** *in expr*
air bhog floating

bog *vti, pres part* **a' bogadh,** **1** dip; **2** *vi*
(*tail*) wag

bogachadh, *gen* **bogachaidh** *nm* wetting

bogadaich *nf* bouncing

bogadh, *gen* **bogaidh** *nm* **1** soaking;
2 immersion

bogaich *vti, pres part* **a' bogachadh**
1 (*vt*) wet; **2** (*vti*) soften

bogha, bogha, boghachan *nm* **1** bow;
2 arch

boghadair, boghadair, boghadairean
nm archer

bogha-frois, bogha-fhrois/bogha-
froise, boghachan-frois *nm* rainbow

boglach, boglaich, boglaichean *nf* bog

bogsa, *gen* **bogsa,** *pl* **bogsaichean** *nm*
box

bòid, bòide, bòidean *nf* oath

bòideachadh, *gen* **bòideachaidh** *nm*
vowing

bòidhchead, *gen* **bòidhcheid** *nf* beauty

bòidheach, *comp* **(n)as** (etc) **bòidhche**
adj beautiful

bòidich *vi, pres part* **a' bòideachadh**
vow, swear

boile *nf* madness, passion

boillsg, boillsge, boillsgean *nm* gleam

boillsg *vi, pres part* **a' boillsgeadh,** gleam

boillsgeach *adj* gleaming

boillsgeadh, *gen* **boillsgidh** *nm* gleaming

boinne, *gen* **boinne,** *pl* **boinnean** &
boinneachan *nmf* drop (*liquid*)

boireann *adj* female, feminine

boireannach, *gen* & *pl* **boireannaich** *nm*
woman, (*human*) female

boiteag, boiteig, boiteagan *nf* worm

boladh, bolaidh, bolaidhean *nm* smell

bolgan, *gen* **bolgain,** *pl* **bolgain &**
bolganan *nm* bulb

boltrach, *gen & pl* **boltraich** *nm* scent

boma, boma, bomaichean *nm* bomb

bonaid, bonaide, bonaidean *nmf*
bonnet

bonn, *gen & pl* **buinn** *nm* **1** base; **2** coin;
3 medal

bonnach, *gen & pl* **bonnaich** *nm*
1 bannock; **2** cake; **3** scone

borb *adj* savage

bòrd, *gen & pl* **bùird** *nm* **1** table; **2** board

bòst, bòsta, bòstan *nm* a boast

bòstail *adj* boastful

botal/buideal, *gen & pl* **botail** *nm* bottle

bòtann, bòtainn, bòtannan *nmf* boot

bothan, *gen & pl* **bothain** *nm* **1** cottage;
2 hut; **3** bothy; **4** shebeen

bracaist, bracaiste, bracaistean *nf*
breakfast

brach *vti, pres part* **a' brachadh,**
1 ferment; **2** (*vi*) (*boil, spot etc*) gather

brachadh, brachaidh, brachaidhean
nm **1** fermenting; **2** pus

bradan, *gen & pl* **bradain** *nm* salmon

brag, *gen* **braig** *nm* bang

bragail *adj* **1** boastful; **2** cheeky

braich, *gen* **bracha** *nf* malt

braid(e), *gen* **braide** *nf* theft

bràigh¹, *gen* **bràighe/bràghad,** *pl*
bràigheachan *nm* upper part of anything

bràigh², bràighe, bràighdean *nmf* a
prisoner

braighdeanas, *gen* **braighdeanais** *nm*
captivity

braim, brama, bramannan *nm* fart

braisead, *gen* **braiseid** *nf* impetuosity,
intrepidity

bràiste, bràiste, bràistean *nf* brooch

bràithreil *adj* brotherly

bràmair, bràmair, bràmairean *nm*
girlfriend/boyfriend

branndaidh *nf* brandy

braoisg, braoisge, braoisgean *nf* grin,
grimace

braon, *gen & pl* **braoin** *nm* **1** drop;
2 drizzle

bras *adj* **1** impetuous; **2** intrepid;
3 precipitous

brat, brata, bratan *nm* **1** covering;
2 cloak; **3** mat

bratach, brataich, brataichean *nf*
banner

bràth, *gen* **bràtha** *nm* **1** doom; **2** *in expr*
gu bràth forever

brath, *gen* **bratha** *nm* **1** knowledge;
2 (unfair) advantage; **3** betrayal

bràthair, bràthar, bràithrean *nm*
brother

breab, breaba, breaban *nmf* kick

breab *vti, pres part* **a' breabadh,** kick

breabadair, breabadair,
breabadairean *nm* **1** weaver; **2** daddy-
longlegs

breabadh, *gen* **breabaidh** *nm* kicking

breac *adj* speckled

breac¹, *gen & pl* **bric** *nm* trout

breac², *gen* **brice** *nf* (*with art*) **a' bhreac**
smallpox

breacag, breacaig, breacagan *nf* **1** cake;
2 bannock

breacan, *gen* **breacain,** *pl* **breacain &**
breacanan *nm* **1** plaid; **2** tartan

brèagha *adj* fine, lovely

Breatainn *nf* Britain; **A' Bhreatainn**
Bheag Britanny

Breatannach, *gen & pl* **Breatannaich**
nm Briton, *also adj* **Breatannach** British

Breatnais *nf* (*lang*) Breton

brèid, brèide, brèidean *nm* **1** kerchief;
2 patch; **3** cloth

brèig, brèige, brèigichean *nf* brake

breige, breige, breigichean *nmf* brick

breigire, breigire, breigirean *nm*
bricklayer

breisleach, *gen* **breislich** *nmf* confusion,
delirium

breisleachadh, *gen* **breisleachaidh** *nm*
confusing, raving

breislich *vti, pres part* **a' breisleachadh,**
1 (*vt*) confuse; **2** (*vi*) rave

breith¹, *nf* birth

breith² *nf* judgement

breithneachadh, *gen* **breithneachaidh**
nm judging

breithnich *vti, pres part* **a'**
breithneachadh, judge

breug, brèige, breugan *nf* lie

breugach *adj* false

breugnaich *vt, pres part* **a'**
breugnachadh, 1 refute; **2** falsify

breugaire, breugaire, breugairean *nm*
liar

breun *adj* putrid, vile

briathar, briathair, briathran *nm*
(*language*) term

briathrach *adj* wordy

briathrachas, *gen* **briathrachais** *nm*
1 verbosity; 2 terminology

brìb, *gen* **brìbe,** *pl* **brìbean** &
brìbeachan *nf* bribe

brìb *vt, pres part* **a' brìbeadh,** bribe

brìbeadh, *gen* **brìbidh** *nm* bribing

brìgh *nf* 1 meaning; 2 virtue; 3 pith; 4
strength; 5 *prep* **do bhrìgh** because of

brìodail *vt, pres part* **a' brìodal,** 1 caress;
2 flatter; 3 woo

brìodal, *gen* **brìodail** *nm* 1 caressing;
2 flattery

briogais, briogais, briogaisean *nf*
trousers

brìoghmhor *adj* sappy, energetic

briosgaid, briosgaide, briosgaidean *nf*
biscuit

brisg *adj* 1 crisp; 2 brittle

brisgean, brisgein, brisgean *nm*
1 silverweed; 2 (potato) crisp

bris(t) *vti, pres part* **a' bris(t)eadh,** break

briste *adj* broken

bris(t)eadh, *gen* **bris(t)idh** *nm* breaking

bris(t)eadh-cridhe, bris(t)idh-cridhe,
bris(t)idhean-cridhe *nm* heartbreak

bris(t)eadh-dùil, bris(t)idh-dùil,
bris(t)idhean-dùil *nm* disappointment

bris(t)eadh-là, bris(t)idh-là,
bris(t)idhean-là (*also* **bris(t)eadh**
an là) *nm* daybreak

britheamh, *gen* **britheimh,** *pl*
britheamhan *nm* judge

broc, *gen* & *pl* **bruic** *nm* badger

brochan, *gen* & *pl* **brochain** *nm* porridge,
gruel

brod, bruid, brodan *nm* 1 goad; 2 the
best part of/the pick of

brod *vt, pres part* **a' brodadh,** goad,
stimulate

brodadh, *gen* **brodaidh** *nm* 1 goading;
2 masturbation

bròg, bròige, brògan *nf* shoe, boot

broilleach, *gen* **broillich,** *pl*
broilleachan & **broillichean** *nm* breast

broinn, *dat of* **brù,** *nf* 1 belly; 2 interior

bròn, *gen* **bròin** *nm* 1 sadness;
2 mourning,

brònach *adj* sad, sorrowful

brosnachadh, *gen* **brosnachaidh** *nm*
encouraging

brosnachail *adj* encouraging

brosnaich *vt, pres part* **a' brosnachadh,**
encourage

brot, brota, brotan *nm* broth, soup

broth, brotha, brothan *nm* rash

brù, *gen* **bronn** & **broinne,** *dat* **broinn,**
pl **brùthan** *nf* 1 womb; 2 belly; 3 bulge

bruach, bruaich, bruaichean *nf* bank
(*river etc*)

bruadair *vi, pres part* **a' bruadar** & **a'**
bruadarachd, dream

bruadar, bruadair, bruadaran *nm*
dream(ing)

bruaillean, *gen* **bruaillein** *nm* trouble,
confusion

brùchd, brùchda, brùchdan *nm* belch

brùchd *vi, pres part* **a' brùchdadh,**
1 belch; 2 burst out

bruich *adj* cooked, boiled

bruich *nf* boiling, cooking

bruich *vt, pres part* **a' bruich,** cook, boil

bruicheil *adj* (*of weather*) sultry

brùid, brùide, brùidean *nmf* brute

brùidealachd *nf* brutality

brùideil *adj* brutal

bruidhinn, *gen* **bruidhne** *nf* speaking,
talk(ing)

bruidhinn *vti, pres part* **a' bruidhinn,**
speak

bruidhneach *adj* talkative

bruis, bruise, bruisean *nf* brush

bruisig *vt, pres part* **a' bruisigeadh,**
brush

bruisigeadh, *gen* **bruisigidh** *nm*
brushing

brùite *adj* bruised, crushed

brùth *vt, pres part* **a' bruthadh,** 1 bruise;
2 push, press

bruthach, bruthaich, bruthaichean
nmf 1 slope; 2 bank (*river etc*)

bruthadh, *gen* **bruthaidh** *nm* 1 bruising,
pushing; 2 pressure

bruthainneach *adj* (*weather*) sultry

buachaille, buachaille, buachaillean
nm herdsman

buachailleachd *nf* herding

buachaillich *vt, pres part* **a'
buachailleachd**, herd
buachar, *gen* **buachair** *nm* cowdung
buadh, buaidh, buadhan *nf* **1** attribute;
2 virtue
buadhair, buadhair, buadhairean *nm*
adjective
buadhmhor *adj* effective
buaic, buaice, buaicean *nf* wick
buaidh, buaidhe, buaidhean *nf*
1 victory; **2** influence; **3** effect
buail *vt, pres part* **a' bualadh,** hit
buaile, buaile, buailtean *nf* sheep-fold,
cattle-fold
buailteach *adj* liable, apt
buailteachd *nf* tendency
buain, *gen* **buana** *nf* reaping
buain *vt, pres part* **a' buain**, reap
buair *vt, pres part* **a' buaireadh,**
1 disturb; **2** tempt
buaireadh, buairidh, buairidhean *nm*
1 disturbing; **2** temptation
buaireas, buaireis, buaireasan *nm*
trouble
buaireasach *adj* troublesome
buaireasachd *nf* turbulence
bualadh, *gen* **bualaidh** *nm* hitting
buan *adj* lasting
buannachadh, *gen* **buannachaidh** *nm*
winning
buannachd, buannachd, buannachdan
nf profit, advantage
buannachdail *adj* advantageous
buannaich *vti, pres part* **a'
buannachadh**, win
buar, *gen & pl* **buair** *nm* herd (*esp cattle*)
bucaid, bucaide, bucaidean *nf* bucket
bucas, *gen & pl* **bucais** *nm* box
bugair, bugaire, bugairean *nm* bugger
buidhe *adj* **1** yellow; **2** fortunate
buidhe *nm* yellow
buidheach *adj* grateful
buidheachas, *gen* **buidheachais** *nm*
gratitude
buidheagan, *gen & pl* **buidheagain** *nf*
egg-yolk
buidheann, buidhne, buidhnean *nmf*
1 group; **2** company
buidhinn *vti, pres part* **a' buidhinn**, win
buidhre *nf* deafness
buidseach, buidsich, buidsichean *nmf*
wizard

bùidsear, bùidseir, bùidsearan *nm*
butcher
buidseat, buidseit, buidseatan *nm*
budget
buige *nf* **1** softness; **2** moistness;
3 humidity; **4** limpness
buil, *gen* **buile** *nf* **1** consequence;
2 completion
buileach *adj used as adv, also* **gu
buileach** *adv*, completely
buileann, builinn, buileannan *nf* loaf
builgean, builgein, builgeanan *nm*
bubble
builgeanach *adj* bubbly
builich *vt, pres part* **a' buileachadh**,
bestow
buille, buille, *pl* **buillean** & **builleannan**
nf **1** blow, stroke; **2** emphasis, stress
buin *vi, pres part* **a' buntainn**, **1** belong;
2 be related to; **3** interfere with; **4** be
relevant
buinneach, *gen* **buinnich** *nf, with art*, **a'
bhuinneach** diarrhoea
buinnig & **buintig**, *vi, pres part* **a'
buintig**, win
buinteanas, buntainneas & **buntanas**,
gen **buinteanais** *nm* **1** link(s);
2 relevance
buirbe *nf* barbarity
bùirdeasach *adj* bourgeois
bùirdeasach, *gen & pl* **bùirdeasaich** *nm*
bourgeois
bùirdeasachd *nf, usu with art*, **a'
bhùirdeasachd** the bourgeoisie
Bulgàrianach, *gen & pl* **Bulgàrianaich**
Bulgarian, *also adj* **Bulgàrianach**
Bulgarian
Bulgàrais *nf* (*lang*) Bulgarian
bumailear, bumaileir, bumailearan *nm*
fool, blockhead
bun, *gen* **buna** & **buin**, *pl* **buin** & **bunan**
nm base; **2** *in expr* **bun-os-cionn** upside-
down; **3** root; **4** mouth of river/stream
bunai(l)teach *adj* **1** stable; **2** fundamental
bunait, bunaite, bunaitean *nmf* basis
bunasach *adj* basic
bun-sgoil, bun-sgoile, bun-sgoiltean *nf*
primary school
buntainn, *gen* **buntainne** *nm* belonging,
interfering with
buntainneach *adj* relevant
buntàta *nm* potato

bùrach, *gen* **bùraich** *nm* shambles
bùrn, *gen* **bùirn** *nm* water
burraidh, burraidh, burraidhean *nm*
  1 fool; **2** bully
bus¹, bus, busaichean *nm* bus

bus², buis, busan *nm* **1** mouth; **2** grimace;
  3 *in expr* **a-mach air a bhus le . . .**
  overflowing with . . .
bùth, *gen* **bùtha,** *pl* **bùthan, bùithean** &
  bùithtean *nmf* shop

C

cab, *gen & pl* caib *nm* gob
cabach *adj* talkative
cabadaich, *gen* cabadaiche *nf* chattering
càball, càbaill, càballan *nm* cable
cabar, *gen & pl* cabair *nm* 1 antler; 2 pole;
3 caber
cabhag, *gen* cabhaig *nf* hurry
cabhagach *adj* 1 hurried; 2 urgent
cabhlach, cabhlaich, cabhlaichean *nm*
fleet
cabhsair, cabhsair, cabhsairean *nm*
pavement, causeway
cac, *gen* caca *nm* excrement
cac *vi*, *pres part* a' cac & a' cacadh,
defecate
càch, *gen* càich & chàich *pron* other
people
cachaileith, cachaileithe,
cachaileithean *nf* gateway
cadal, *gen* cadail *nm* sleep
cadalach *adj* sleepy
cafaidh, cafaidh, cafaidhean *nmf* café
cagailt, cagailte, cagailtean *nf* hearth
cagainn *vt*, *pres part* a' cagnadh, chew,
gnaw
cagair *vti*, *pres part* a' cagar, a'
cagarsaich & a' cagartaich, whisper
cagar, cagair, cagairean *nm* 1 whisper;
2 secret
cagnadh, *gen* cagnaidh *nm* chewing,
gnawing
caibe, caibe, caibeachan *nm* 1 spade;
2 mattock
caibeal, caibeil, caibealan *nm* chapel
caibideil, caibideil, caibideilean *nmf*
chapter
caidil *vi*, *pres part* a' cadal, sleep
caidreabhas, *gen* caidreabhais *m*
alliance
càil, càile, càiltean *nf* desire, appetite
càil *nm* 1 thing; 2 *with verb in neg or inter*
anything
cailc, cailce, cailcean *nf* chalk
caileag, caileige, caileagan *nf* 1 girl
cailin, cailin, cailinean *nf* girl
caill *vti*, *pres part* a' call, 1 lose; 2 miss

cailleach, cailliche, cailleachan *nf* 1 old
woman; 2 (*esp* cailleach-dhubh) a nun;
3 ha
cailleach-oidhche, caillich-oidhche,
cailleachan-oidhche *nf* owl
caime, caime, caimean *nf* curve
càin, *gen* cànach & càine, *pl* càintean *nf*
1 taxation 2 fine
càin *vt*, *pres part* a' càineadh, 1 criticise;
2 slander
cainb, *gen* cainbe *nf* 1 hemp; 2 canvas
càineadh, *gen* càinidh *nm* 1 criticising;
2 (verbal) abuse
caineal, *gen* caineil *nm* cinnamon
cainnt, cainnte, cainntean *nf* speech,
language
caiptean, caiptein, caipteanan *nm*
captain
càirdeach *adj* related
càirdeas, *gen* càirdeis *nm* 1 kinship;
2 friendship
càirdeil *adj* friendly
càirdineal, càirdineil, càirdinealan *nm*
cardinal
càirean, càirein, càireinean *nm* gum(s),
palate
cairidh, cairidh, cairidhean, *also*
caraidh, caraidh, caraidhean *nf* weir
cairgein, *gen* cairgein *nm*, *also*
carraigean, *gen* carraigein *nm*
carrageen
càirich (*also* càir), *vt*, *pres part.* a'
càradh, mend
cairt¹, cartach, cairtean *nf* 1 card;
2 chart; 3 charter; 4 tree bark
cairt², cartach, cairtean *nf* cart
cairt *also* cart *vt*, *pres part* a' cartadh,
1 tan; 2 clean out
cairteal, cairteil, cairtealan *nm*
quart(er)
caisbheart, *gen* caisbheirt *nf* footwear
caise *nf* 1 irritability; 2 steepness
càise, càise, càisean *nmf* cheese
caisead, *gen* caiseid *nm* steepness
Càisg, *gen* Càisge *nf*, *used with art*, a'
Chàisg Easter

18

caisg *vti, pres part* **a' casgadh, 1** prevent; **2** (*vi*) subside

caismeachd, caismeachd, caismeachdan *nf* **1** alarm; **2** march; **3** beating time

caisteal, caisteil, caistealan *nm* castle

càite (*before a vowel* **càit**) *inter adv* where

caith *vt, pres part* **a' caitheamh, 1** wear out; **2** (*time*) pass; **3** squander; **4** throw

caitheamh, *gen* **caitheimh** *nf* **1** wearing, spending ; **2** (*with art*) **a' chaitheamh** tuberculosis; **3** (*business etc*) consumption

caitheamh-beatha *nm* lifestyle

caithte *adj* **1** worn out; **2** (*gram*) past

caith(t)each *adj* wasteful

Caitligeach, *gen & pl* **Caitligich** *nm* Catholic, *also adj*

càl, *gen & pl* **càil** *nm* cabbage, kail

cala(dh), cala(idh), calaidhean *nm* harbour

càl-colaig, *gen & pl* **càil-cholaig** *nm* cauliflower

calg, *gen* **cuilg** *nm* **1** prickle; **2** bristle

calg-d(h)ìreach *adv* directly

call, *gen* **calla** *nm* **1** losing, missing; **2** loss; **3** waste

calla *&* **callda** *adj* **1** tame; **2** domesticated

callachadh, *gen* **callachaidh** *nm* taming, domesticating

callaich, *vt, pres part* **a' callachadh,** tame, domesticate

callaid, callaide, callaidean *nf* **1** hedge; **2** fence

Callainn, *gen* **Callainne** *nf, used with art,* **a' Challainn** New Year's Day

calltainn, *gen* **calltainne** *nm* hazel

calma *adj* stout, sturdy

calman, *gen* **calmain,** *pl* **calmain** *&* **calmanan** *nm* dove, pigeon

calpa[1]**, calpa, calpannan** *nm* calf (*of leg*)

calpa[2]**, calpa, calpannan** *nm* (*fin*) capital

calpachas, *gen* **calpachais** *nm* capitalism

cam *adj* bent, curved

camag, camaig, camagan *nf* **1** curl; **2** (*typog*) bracket

camagach *adj* curled

caman, *gen* **camain,** *pl* **camain** *&* **camanan** *nm* **1** shinty stick; **2** golf club; **3** (*mus*) quaver

camanachd *nf* shinty

camara, camara, camarathan *nm* camera

camas, *gen & pl* **camais** *nm* **1** bay; **2** bend in river

càmhal, *gen & pl* **càmhail** *nm* camel

camhana(i)ch, *gen* **camhanaich** *nf* **1** dawn; **2** twilight

campa, campa, campaichean *nm* camp

campachadh, *gen* **campachaidh** camping

campaich *vi, pres part* **a' campachadh,** camp

can *vti def pres part* **a' cantainn** *&* **a' cantail** say

cana, cana, canaichean *nm* can

canabhas, *gen* **canabhais** *nm* canvas

canach, *gen* **canaich** *nm* (bog)-cotton

Canada *nf* Canada

cànain, cànaine, cànainean *nf &* **cànan,** *gen & pl* **cànain** *nm* language

cànanach *adj* linguistic

canastair, canastair, canastairean *nm* can

Canèidianach, *gen & pl* **Canèidianaich** *nm* Canadian, *also adj* **Canèidianach** Canadian

caochail *vi, pres part* **a' caochladh, 1** change; **2** (*person*) die

caochladh, caochlaidh, caochlaidhean *nm* **1** changing, dying ; **2** change; **3** variety

caochlaideach *adj* changeable

caog *vi, pres part* **a' caogadh,** blink, wink

caogad, caogaid, caogadan *nm* fifty

caogadh, *gen* **caogaidh** *nm* blinking, winking

caoidh, *gen* **caoidhe** *nf* lament(ing)

caoidh *vi, pres part* **a' caoidh,** lament

caoin *adj* (*esp of character*) gentle, mild

caoin *vi, pres part* **a' caoineadh, 1** lament; **2** weep

caoineadh, *gen* **caoinidh** *nm* lamenting, weeping

caol *adj* **1** thin; **2** (*angle*) acute

caol, *gen* **caoil,** *pl* **caoil** *&* **caoiltean** *nm* **1** strait, narrows; **2** narrow part

caolan, *gen* **caolain,** *pl* **caolain** *&* **caolanan** *nm* intestine

caolas, *gen & pl* **caolais** *nm* strait

caol-shràid, caol-shràide, caol-shràidean *nf* alley, lane

caomh *adj* **1** kind; **2** beloved, *cf* **ionmhainn**; **3** *in expr* **is caomh leam** I like

caomhain *vt, pres part* **a' caomhnadh**, economise

caomhnadh, *gen* **caomhnaidh** *nm* economising

caon *adj* wily

caora, *gen* **caorach**, *dat* **caora**, *pl* **caoraich**, *gen pl* **chaorach** *nf* sheep

caorann, *gen* **caorainn** *nmf* rowan

car, cuir, caran *nm* twist, turn, movement, trick

càr, càir, càraichean *nm* car

car(a)bhaidh, car(a)bhaidh, car(a)abhaidhean *nm* boyfriend

carach *adj* 1 wily; 2 changeable

carachadh, *gen* **carachaidh** *nm* moving

carachd *nf* wrestling

caractar, caractair, caractairean *nm* character

càradh, *gen* **càraidh** *nm* 1 repair(ing); 2 state, condition

caraich *vti, pres part* **a' carachadh**, move

caraiche, caraiche, caraichean *nm* wrestler

caraid, caraid, càirdean *nm* 1 friend; 2 relative

càraid, càraide, càraidean *nf* 1 pair

caran *dimin of* **car** *nm, used adverbially*, a little, a bit

carbad, carbaid, carbadan *nm* carriage

Carghas, *gen* **Carghais** *nm* (*used with art*), **An Carghas** Lent

cargu/carago, *gen* **carago**, *pl* **caragothan** *nm* cargo

càrn, *gen* **càirn** & **cùirn**, *pl* **càirn** & **cùirn** *nm* 1 cairn; 2 hill

càrn *vt, pres part* **a' càrnadh**, heap

càrnadh, *gen* **càrnaidh** *nm* heaping

càrnaid, càrnaide, càrnaidean *nf* carnation

càrnan, càrnain, càrnanan *nm* cockroach

càrr, *gen* **càrra** *nf, also* **càir**, *gen* **càire** *nf*, 1 scab; 2 dandruff

carragh, carraigh, carraighean *nf* 1 pillar; 2 standing stone

carraig, carraige, carraigean *nf* rock

carson *inter adv* why

cartadh, *gen* **cartaidh** *nm* 1 tanning; 2 mucking out

carthannachd *nf* & **carthannas**, *gen* **carthannais** *nm* 1 kindness; 2 charity

cas *adj* 1 steep; 2 fast-flowing; 3 (*person*) irritable

cas, *gen* **coise**, *dat* **cois**, *pl* **casan** *nf* 1 foot; 2 leg; 3 handle; 4 *in expr* **an cois** near; 5 *in expr* **cuir** *v* **air chois** set up

càs, càis, càsan *nm* predicament

casad, casaid, casadan *nm* cough

casadaich *nf* coughing

casa-gòbhlach *adj* & *adv* astride

casaid, casaide, casaidean *nf* accusation

cas-chrom, cois(e)-cruim(e), casan-croma *nf* foot plough

casg, *gen* **caisg** *nm* prevention

casgadh, *gen* **casgaidh** *nm* 1 subsiding, preventing

casgair *vt, pres part* **a' casgairt** & **a' casgradh**, slay

casgairt *nf, also* **casgradh**, *gen* **casgraidh** *nm*, slaying, slaughter

casgan, *gen* **casgain**, *pl* **casgain** & **casganan** *nm* 1 brake; 2 condom

cat, *gen* & *pl* **cait** *nm* cat

Catalanach, *gen* & *pl* **Catalanaich** *nm* Catalan, *as adj* **Catalanach** Catalan

Catalanais *nf* (*lang*) Catalan

cath, *gen* **catha**, *pl* **cathan** & **cathannan** *nm* battle

càth, *gen* **càtha** *nf* chaff

cathadh, cathaidh, cathaidhean *nm* snowstorm

cathag, cathaig, cathagan *nf* jackdaw

cathair, cathrach, cathraichean *nf* 1 chair; 2 city

cathraiche, cathraiche, cathraichean *nm* chairperson

cèaban, cèabain, cèabainean *nm* cabin

cead *nm* 1 permission; 2 licence; 3 farewell

ceadachadh, *gen* **ceadachaidh** *nm* permitting, licensing

ceadachail *adj* permissive

ceadachas, *gen* **ceadachais**, *nm* permissiveness

ceadaich *vti, pres part* **a' ceadachadh**, 1 allow; 2 license

ceadaichte *adj* permitted

ceàird, ceàirde, ceàirdean *nf* trade, craft

cealg, *gen* **ceilge** *nf* deceit

cealgach *adj* deceitful

cealgair(e), cealgair(e), cealgairean *nm* hypocrite

cealla, cealla, ceallan *nf* (*biol*) cell

ceanalta *adj* 1 pretty; 2 kind

ceangail *vt, pres part* **a' ceangal**, link

ceangal, ceangail, ceanglaichean *nm* 1 linking; 2 connection

ceangaltach *adj* (*promise etc*) binding

ceann, *gen & pl* **cinn** *nm* 1 head; 2 end of anything; 3 *in expr* **an ceann** *prep* after

ceannach, *gen* **ceannaich** *nm* buying

ceannaich *vt, pres part* **a' ceannach(d)**, buy

ceannaiche, ceannaiche, ceannaichean *nm* 1 purchaser; 2 merchant

ceannard, ceannaird, ceannardan *nm* head, boss

ceannbheart, *gen* **ceannbheairt** *nf* headgear

ceann-bliadhna, *gen & pl* **cinn-bliadhna** *nm* a birthday

ceann-cinnidh, *gen & pl* **cinn-chinnidh** *nm also* **ceann-feadhna**, *gen & pl* **cinn-fheadhna** *nm* a clan chief

ceann-là, *gen & pl* **cinn-là** *nm* (*calendar*) date

ceann-pholan, ceann-pholain, ceann-pholanan *nm also* **ceann-simid, ceann-simide, ceann-simidean** *nm* tadpole

ceannsachadh, *gen* **ceannsachaidh** *nm* conquering

ceannsaich *vt, pres part* **a' ceannsachadh**, conquer, repress, tame

ceannsaiche, ceannsaiche, ceannsaichean *nm* conqueror

ceannsaichte *adj* conquered, tamed

ceannsal, *gen* **ceannsail** *nm* rule

ceannsalach *adj* authoritative, dictatorial

ceann-simid *see* **ceann-pholan**

ceann-suidhe, *gen & pl* **cinn-suidhe** *nm* president

ceann-uidhe, *gen & pl* **cinn-uidhe** *nm* destination

ceap, *gen* **cip**, *pl* **ceapan** & **ceapannan** *nm* block

ceap, ceapa, ceapan *nm* cap

ceapach, *gen & pl* **ceapaich** *nmf* (*hort*) plot

ceapaire, ceapaire, ceapairean *nm* sandwich

cearb, cirbe, cearban *nf* 1 rag; 2 defect

cearbach *adj* 1 awkward; 2 ragged

cearc, circe, cearcan *nf* hen

cearcall, *gen* **cearcaill**, *pl* **cearcaill** & **cearcallan** *nm* circle

cearclach *adj* circular

ceàrd, *gen* **ceàird**, *pl* **ceàrdan** *nm* 1 tinker; 2 smith

ceàrdach, ceàrdaich, ceàrdaichean *nf* smithy, forge

ceàrn, *gen* **ceàrnaidh**, *pl* **ceàrnaidhean** & **ceàrnan** *nm* area

ceàrnach *adj* square

ceàrnag, ceàrnaig, ceàrnagan *nf* square

ceàrnagach *adj* square

ceàrr *adj* 1 wrong; 2 left

ceàrrachas, *gen* **ceàrrachais**, *also* **ceàrrachadh**, *gen* **ceàrrachaidh** *nm* gambling

ceàrraiche/cèarraiche, *gen* **ceàrraiche**, *pl* **ceàrraichean** *nm* gambler

ceart *adj* 1 correct; 2 just; 3 same, very; 4 right-hand; 5 *as adv* **a cheart cho** just as; 6 *used as noun*, right

ceartachadh, ceartachaidh, ceartachaidhean *nm* correction

ceartaich *vt, pres part* **a' ceartachadh**, correct

ceartas, *gen* **ceartais** *nm* justice

ceas, ceasa, ceasaichean *nm* (suit)case

ceasnachadh, ceasnachaidh, ceasnachaidhean *nm* questioning

ceasnachail *adj* inquisitive

ceasnaich *vti, pres part* **a' ceasnachadh**, question

ceathrad, ceathraid, ceathradan *nm* forty

ceathramh *num adj* fourth

ceathramh, ceathraimh, ceathramhan *nm* quarter

ceathrar *nm* foursome

cèic, cèice, cèicean *nmf* cake

cèidse, cèidse, cèidsichean *nf* cage

ceil *vt, pres part* **a' ceileadh, a' cleith** & **a' ceiltinn**, hide

cèile *nmf* 1 spouse; 2 counterpart

ceileadh, *gen* **ceilidh** *nm, also* **ceiltinn** *nf* & **cleith**, *gen* **cleithe** *nmf* hiding

ceileir *vi, pres part* **a' ceileireadh**, warble

cèilidh, cèilidh, cèilidhean *nmf* 1 visit; 2 ceilidh

ceilp, *gen* **ceilpe** *nf* kelp

Ceilteach, *gen & pl* **Ceiltich** *nm* Celt, *also adj* **Ceilteach** Celtic

ceimig, ceimig(e), ceimigean *nf* chemical

ceimigeachd *nf* chemistry

ceimigear, ceimigeir, ceimigearan *nm* chemist

cèin *adj* **1** foreign; **2** faraway

cèir, *gen* **cèire** *nf* wax

cèis, cèise, cèisean *nf* frame, envelope

cèiseag, cèiseig, cèiseagan *nf* cassette

ceist, ceiste, ceistean *nf* question

ceistear, ceisteir, ceistearan *nm* **1** questioner; **2** catechist

Cèitean, *gen* **Cèitein** *nm* May

ceithir *n and num adj* four

ceithir-deug *n & adj* fourteen

ceò, ceò, ceothannan *nm* **1** mist; **2** fog; **3** smoke

ceòl, *gen* **ciùil** *nm* music

ceòlmhor *adj* musical

ceòthach/ceòthar *adj* **1** misty; **2** foggy

ceud, ceud, ceudan *nm* hundred

ceudameatair, ceudameatair, ceudameatairean *nm* centimetre

ceudamh *num adj* hundredth

ceudna *adj* **1** same; **2** *in expr* **mar an ceudna** also, as well

ceum, *gen* **ceuma** *&* **cèim,** *pl* **ceuman** *&* **ceumannan** *nm* **1** step; **2** track; **3** degree

ceumnachadh, ceumnachaidh, ceumnachaidhean *nm* **1** pacing; **2** graduating

ceumnaich *vi, pres part* **a' ceumnachadh, 1** pace; **2** graduate

ceus *vt, pres part* **a' ceusadh,** crucify

ceusadh, ceusaidh, ceusaidhean *nm* crucifixion

cha (*before a vowel, or fh followed by a vowel,* **chan**), *neg particle expressing concepts* 'not', 'No'

chaidh *pt of irreg v* **rach**

chì, chitheadh, chithinn *pts of irreg vb* **faic**

chluinn, chluinneadh, chluinneas, chluinninn, chluinntinn *pts of irreg v* **cluinn**

cho *adv* **1** so; **2** *in comparisons* **cho . . . sin** as . . . as that

chuala *pt of irreg v* **cluinn**

chun *prep* towards

ciad *adj* first, *used with art*

ciall, *gen* **cèille,** *dat* **cèill** *&* **ciall,** *pl* **ciallan** *nf* **1** sense; **2** reason; **3** meaning;

4 *in expr* **cuir an cèill** express; **5** *excl* **a chiall!** goodness!

ciallach *adj* sensible, sane

ciallaich *vt, pres part* **a' ciallachadh,** mean

ciamar *inter adv* how

cia mheud/co mheud, *inter adv* how many

cian *adj* **1** distant; **2** long, weary

cian, *gen* **cèin** *nm* distance

cianail *adj* **1** sad; **2** terrible

cianalas, *gen* **cianalais** *nm* **1** sadness; **2** homesickness; **3** nostalgia

ciar *adj* dark

ciar *vi, pres part* **a' ciaradh,** darken

ciaradh, *gen* **ciaraidh** *nm* dusk

ciatach *adj* pleasant

cidhe, cidhe, cidhean *nm* quay

cidsin, cidsin, cidsinean *nm* kitchen

cileagram, cileagraim, cileagraman *nm* kilogram

cilemeatair, cilemeatair, cilemeatairean *nm* kilometre

cill, *gen* **cille,** *pl* **cillean** *&* **cilltean** *nf* **1** holy site; **2** kirkyard

cineal, cineil, cinealan *nm* race, species

cinealtach *adj* racist

cinealtas, *gen* **cinealtais** *nm* racism

cinn *vi, pres part* **a' cinntinn,** grow

cinneach, *gen & pl* **cinnich** *nm* heathen

cinneadail *adj* clannish, racial

cinneadh, cinnidh, cinnidhean *nm* **1** clan; **2** race, tribe; **3** surname

cinneas, *gen* **cinneis** *nm* growth

cinnt, *gen* **cinnte** *nf* certainty

cinnteach *adj* certain

cinntinn *nm* growing

cìobair, cìobair, cìobairean *nm* shepherd

cìoch, cìche, cìochan *nf* breast, nipple

cìochag, cìochaig, cìochagan *nf* valve

ciod *inter pron* what

ciomach, *gen & pl* **ciomaich** *nm* prisoner

ciomachas, *gen* **ciomachais** *nm* imprisonment

cion *nm* **1** lack; **2** desire

cionnas *conj* how

ciont(a), ciont(a), ciontan *nm* **1** guilt; **2** transgression

ciontach *adj* guilty

ciontach, *gen & pl* **ciontaich** *nm* offender

ciontachadh, *gen* **ciontachaidh** *nm* offending

ciontaich *vi, pres part* **a' ciontachadh**, offend

ciorram, ciorraim, ciorraman *nm* disability

ciorramach *adj* disabled

ciorramach, *gen & pl* **ciorramaich** *nm* disabled person

ciotach *adj* left-handed

cipean, cipein, cipeanan *nm* **1** stake; **2** tether post

cìr, cìre, cìrean *nf* **1** comb; **2** cud

cìr *vt, pres part* **a' cìreadh**, comb

cìreadh, *gen* **cìridh** *nm* combing

cìrean, *gen* **cìrein**, *pl* **cìrein** & **cìreanan** *nm* comb, crest

cìs, cìse, cìsean *nf* tax, duty

ciste, ciste, cisteachan *nf* (*household*) chest

ciùb, ciùb, ciùban *nm* cube

ciùbach *adj* cubic

ciùbhran/ciùthran, *gen & pl* **ciùbhrain**, *also* **ciuthrach**, *gen & pl* **ciuthraich**, *nm* drizzle

ciudha, ciudha, ciudhaichean *nf* queue

ciùin *adj* mild

ciùineachadh, *gen* **ciùineachaidh** *nm* quietening

ciùineas, *gen* **ciùineis** *nm* calm, quiet

ciùinich *vti, pres part* **a' ciùineachadh**, quieten

ciùrr *vt, pres part* **a' ciùrradh**, **1** torture; **2** harm

ciùrradh, ciùrraidh, ciùrraidhean *nm* hurting

ciùrrte *adj* hurt

clabhstair, clabhstair, clabhstairean *nm* cloister

clach, cloiche, clachan *nf* **1** stone; **2** testicle

clach *vt, pres part* **a' clachadh**, stone

clachach *adj* stony

clachadh, *gen* **clachaidh** *nm* stoning

clachair, clachair, clachairean *nm* stonemason

clachan, *gen & pl* **clachain** *nm* **1** kirktoun; **2** hamlet; **3** kirkyard

cladach, cladaich, cladaichean *nm* shore, beach

cladh, *gen* **cladha** & **claidh**, *pl* **cladhan** *nm* churchyard, cemetery

cladhach, *gen* **cladhaich** *nm* digging

cladhaich *vi, pres part* **a' cladhach**, dig

cladhaire, cladhaire, cladhairean *nm* coward

cladhaireach *adj* cowardly

cladhaireachd *nf* cowardice

clag, *gen & pl* **cluig** *nm* bell

clagarsaich *nf* clinking, rattling

claidheamh, claidheimh, claidhnean *nm* sword

claigeann, claiginn, claignean *nm* skull

clàimhean, clàimhein, clàimheanan *nm* door latch

clais, claise, claisean *nf* **1** ditch; **2** drain; **3** furrow; **4** rut; **5** groove

claisneachd & **claisteachd** *nf* hearing

clamhan, *gen & pl* **clamhain** *nm* buzzard

clann, *gen* **cloinne** *nf* **1** children; **2** clan

claoidh *nf* & **claoidheadh** *gen* **claoidhidh** *nm* exhausting

claoidh *vt, pres part* **a' claoidh** & **a' claoidheadh**, exhaust, vex

claoidhte *adj* exhausted

claoin *vi, pres part* **a' claoineadh** (*of verbs*), decline

claon *adj* **1** awry; **2** sloping; **3** perverse

claon, *vti, pres part* **a' claonadh**, **1** slope; **2** go astray; **3** (*vt*) pervert; **4** veer

claonadh, *gen* **claonaidh** *nm* **1** inclining; **2** slant; **3** obliqueness; **4** squint; **5** perversion; **6** prejudice

clàr, clàir, clàran *nm* **1** board; **2** register; **3** map; **4** disc

clàrachadh, *gen* **clàrachaidh** *nm* recording, registering

clàraich *vti, pres part* **a' clàrachadh**, register, record

clàrc, *gen & pl* **clàirc** *nm* clerk

clàr-fhiacail, clàr-fhiacail, clàr-fhiaclan *nf* (*tooth*) incisor

clàrsach, clàrsaich, clàrsaichean *nf* harp

clàrsair, clàrsair, clàrsairean *nm* harper

clas, clas, clasaichean *nm* (*school etc*) class

clasaigeach *adj* classical

cleachd *vti, pres part* **a' cleachdadh**, **1** (*vt*) use; **2** (*vt*) accustom

cleachdadh, cleachdaidh, cleachdaidhean *nm* **1** using; **2** custom; **3** practice

cleachdte *adj* used, accustomed
cleamhnas, *gen* **cleamhnais** *nm*
  1 relationship by marriage; **2** sex
cleas, **cleasa**, **cleasan** *nm* **1** exploit;
  2 trick; **3** playing
cleasachd *nf* **1** playing; **2** conjuring;
  3 juggling
cleasaich *vi, pres part* **a' cleasachd**, play
cleasaiche, **cleasaiche**, **cleasaichean**
  nm **1** actor; **2** comedian; **3** conjurer; **4**
  juggler
clèir, *gen* **clèire** *nf* **1** clergy; **2** presbytery
clèireach *adj* presbyterian
clèireach, *gen & pl* **clèirich** *nm*
  1 clergyman; **2** clerk; **3** Presbyterian
clèireachail *adj* clerical
cleòc, **cleòca**, **cleòcan** *nm* cloak.
clì *adj* left
cliabh, *gen & pl* **clèibh** *nm* **1** pannier;
  2 creel; **3** thorax; **4** (*mus*) a stave
cliamhainn, **cleamhna**, **cleamhnan** *nm*
  son-in-law
cliath, **clèithe**, **cliathan** *nf* **1** grid;
  2 harrow
cliath *vti, pres part* **a' cliathadh** harrow
cliatha(i)ch, **cliathaich**, **cliathaichean**
  nf side
cliathan, **cliathain**, **cliathanan** *nm*
  sternum
clìomaid, **clìomaide**, **clìomaidean** *nf*
  climate
clis *adj* nimble
cliseachd *nf* nimbleness
clisg, *pres part* **a' clisgeadh**, start, jump
clisgeach *adj* **1** jumpy; **2** timid
clisgeadh, **clisgidh**, **clisgidhean** *nm*
  1 start, jump, fright
clisgear, **clisgeir**, **clisgearan** *nm* (*gram*)
  exclamation
cliù *nm* **1** fame; **2** praise
cliùiteach *adj* famous
clò¹, *gen* **clò(tha)**, *pl* **clòitean &**
  clòithean *nm* **1** cloth; **2** tweed
clò²/clòdh, *gen* **clòdha**, *pl* **clòdhan** *nm*
  1 print; **2** printing press; **3** imprint
clòbha, **clòbha**, **clòbhan** *nf* clove
clobha, **clobha**, **clobhan** *nm* tongs
clòbhar, *gen* **clòbhair** *nm* clover
clobhd, **clobhda**, **clobhdan** *nm* cloth
clobhsa, **clobhsa**, **clobhsaichean** *nm* (*in
  tenement etc*) close

clò-bhuail *vt, pres part* **a' clò-bhualadh**,
  print
clò-bhualadair, **clò-bhualadair**, **clò-
  bhualadairean** *nm* printer
clò-bhualadh, **clò-bhualaidh**, **clò-
  bhualaidhean** *nm* printing
clò-chadal, *gen* **clò-chadail** *nm* doze
clochar, **clochair**, **clocharan** *nm* convent
cloga(i)d, **clogaide**, **clogaidean** *nmf*
  helmet
clòimh, *gen* **clòimhe** *nf* wool
clòimhteachan, *gen & pl*
  clòimhteachain *nm* eiderdown
closach, **closaich**, **closaichean** *nf*
  carcase
clòsaid, **clòsaide**, **clòsaidean** *nf* closet
clua(i)n, *gen* **cluaine**, *pl* **cluainean &**
  cluaintean *nf* meadow, pasture
cluaineas, *gen* **cluaineis** *nm* retirement
cluaran, **cluarain**, **cluaranan** *nm* thistle
cluas, **cluaise**, **cluasan** *nf* **1** ear; **2** handle
cluasag, **cluasaig**, **cluasagan** *nf* pillow
club, **club**, **clubaichean** *nm* club
clùd, **clùid**, **clùdan** *nm* **1** rag; **2** cloth
cluich & cluiche, *gen* **cluiche**, *pl*
  cluichean & cluicheannan *nm* **1** play;
  2 game
cluich *vti, pres part* **a' cluich(e)**, play
cluicheadair, **cluicheadair**,
  cluicheadairean *nm* player
cluinn, *vt irreg, pres part* **a' cluinntinn**,
  hear
cluinneadh, **cluinneam**, **cluinneamaid**,
  cluinnibh *pts of irreg v* **cluinn**
cluinntinn *nf* hearing
cnag, **cnaig**, **cnagan** *nf* **1** knock; **2** peg;
  3 knob; **4** plug; **5** *in expr* **cnag na cùise**,
  the nub/crux of the matter
cnag *vti, pres part* **a' cnagadh**, **1** (*vi*)
  crunch; **2** (*vti*) knock
cnàimh, *gen* **cnàmha**, *pl* **cnàmhan &**
  cnàimhean *nm, also* **cnàmh**, **cnàimh**,
  cnàmhan *nm* bone
cnàimhneach, *gen & pl* **cnàimhnich** *nm*
  skeleton
cnàimhseag, **cnàimhseig**,
  cnàimhseagan *nf* pimple
cnàmh², *gen* **cnàimh** *nm* potato blight
cnàmh *vt, pres part* **a' cnàmhadh & a'
  cnàmh**, **1** chew; **2** digest; **3** *in expr* **a'
  cnàmh na cìre**, chewing the cud
cnàmhach *adj* bony

cnàmhadh, *gen* **cnàmhaidh** *nm* chewing
cnap, cnaip, cnapan *nm* **1** lump; **2** knob
cnapach *adj* lumpy, knobby
cnap-starra(dh) *nm* obstruction
cnatan, *gen & pl* **cnatain** *nm* a cold, *used with art*
cnead, cneada, cneadan *nm* groan
cnèadachadh, *gen* **cnèadachaidh** *nm* caressing
cnèadaich & **cniadaich** *vt, pres part* **a' cnèadachadh,** caress
cnò, *gen* **cnò** & **cnotha,** *pl* **cnothan** *nf* nut
cnoc, *gen & pl* **cnuic** *nm* hill
cnocan, *gen & pl* **cnocain** hillock
cnuasaich/cnuas *vti, pres part* **a' cnuasa(cha)dh,** **1** chew; **2** (*vi*) ruminate
cnuimh, cnuimhe, cnuimhean *nf* **1** maggot; **2** worm
cò *inter pron* who, which
co- *a prefix often corres to Eng* co-, con-, fellow-
cobhair, *gen* **cobhrach** & **coibhre** *nf* help
cobhan, cobhain, cobhanan (*also* **cobhan-airgid**) *nm* cash register
cobhar, *gen* **cobhair** *nm* foam, froth
cobhartach, *gen* **cobhartaich** *nmf* **1** booty; **2** prey
còcaire, còcaire, còcairean *nm* cook
còcaireachd *nf* cooking, cookery
cochall, *gen & pl* **cochaill** *nm* **1** husk; **2** hood
cofaidh, cofaidh, cofaidhean *nmf* coffee
cofhurtachadh, *gen* **cofhurtachaidh** *nm* comforting
cofhurtachd *nf* comfort
cofhurtaich *vt, pres part* **a' cofhurtachadh,** comfort
cofhurtail *adj* comfortable
cogadh, cogaidh, cogaidhean *nm* war
cogais, cogaise, cogaisean *nf* conscience
cogaiseach *adj* conscientious
co-ghnìomhair, co-ghnìomhair, co-ghnìomhairean *nm* (*gram*) adverb
coibhneas, *gen* **coibhneis** *nm* kindness
coibhneil *adj* kind
coidse, *gen* **coidse,** *pl* **coidseachan** *nf* (*transport*) coach
còig *n and num adj* five
còig-deug *adj* fifteen
còigeamh *adj* fifth
còignear *nm* fivesome

coigreach, *gen & pl* **coigrich** *nm* **1** foreigner; **2** stranger; **3** incomer
coileach, *gen & pl* **coilich** *nm* cock (*bird*)
coilean *pres part* **a' coileanadh** *vt,* accomplish
coileanadh, *gen* **coileanaidh** *nm* accomplishing
coileanta *adj* **1** accomplished; **2** perfect
coilear, coileir, coilearan *nm* collar
coill *nf* **1** guilt, sin; **2** *in expr* **fon choill** outlawed
coille, coille, coilltean *nf* wood, forest
coilleag, coilleig, coilleagan *nf* cockle
coillear, coilleir, coillearan *nm* woodcutter
coillteachadh, *gen* **coillteachaidh** *nm* afforestation
coilltear, coillteir, coilltearan *nm* forester
coilltearachd *nf* forestry
coimeas, *gen* **coimeis** *nm* comparison
coimeas *vt, pres part* **a' coimeas,** compare
coimheach *adj* unfamiliar
coimheach, *gen & pl* **coimhich** *nm* **1** foreigner; **2** stranger
coimhead, *gen* **coimhid** *nm,* watching, looking
coimhead *vti, pres part* **a' coimhead,** watch, look
coimhearsnach, *gen & pl* **coimhearsnaich** *nm* neighbour
coimhearsnachd *nf* community
coimhleapach *also* **coileapach,** *gen & pl* **coi(mh)leapaich** *nmf* bidie-in
coimisean, coimisein, coimiseanan *nm* commission
coimpiutair, coimpiutair, coimpiutairean *nm* computer
coineanach, *gen & pl* **coineanaich** *nm* rabbit
còinneach, *gen* **còinnich** *nf* (*bot*) moss
coinneachadh, *gen* **coinneachaidh** *nm* (*act of*) meeting
coinneal, coinnle, coinnlean *nf* candle
coinneamh, coinneimh, coinneamhan *nf* **1** meeting; **2** *in expr* **mu choinneimh** opposite; **3** *in expr* **an coinneimh** towards
coinnich *vi, pres part* **a' coinneachadh,** meet

coinnlear, coinnleir, coinnlearan *nm* candlestick

co-ionann & **co-ionnan,** *adj* identical, equal

còir *adj* 1 decent; 2 dear

còir, *gen* **còire** & **còrach,** *pl* **còraichean** *nf* 1 obligation; 2 right; 3 *in expr* **tuilleadh 's a' chòir** more than enough; 4 justice

coirb *vt, pres part* **a' coirbeadh,** corrupt

coirbte *adj* corrupt

coirce *nm* oats

coire[1]**, coire, coireannan** *nf* 1 offence; 2 blame

coire[2]**, coire, coireachan** *nm* 1 kettle; 2 cauldron; 3 corrie

coireach *adj* 1 guilty; 2 responsible

coireach, *gen* & *pl* **coirich** *nm* offender

coireachadh, *gen* **coireachaidh** *nm* blaming

coireachail *adj* censorious

coirich *vti, pres part* **a' coireachadh,** blame

coiseachd *nf* walking

coisich *vi, pres part* **a' coiseachd,** walk

coisiche, coisiche, coisichean *nm* walker

coisinn *vt, pres part* **a' cosnadh,** 1 earn; 2 win

còisir(-chiùil), *gen* **còisre(-ciùil)** & **còisire(-ciùil),** *pl* **còisirean(-ciùil)** *nf* choir

coisrig *vt, pres part* **a' coisrigeadh,** 1 consecrate; 2 devote; 3 (*book etc*) dedicate

coisrigeadh, coisrigidh, coisrigidhean *nm* consecration

coisrigte *adj* consecrated

coitcheann *adj* 1 communal; 2 general

coiteachadh, *gen* **coiteachaidh** *nm* pressing

coitheanal/coithional, *gen* **coitheanail,** *pl* **coitheanalan** *nm* congregation

coitich *vt, pres part* **a' coiteachadh,** press, urge

col, *gen* **cola** *nm* incest

colach *adj* incestuous

co-labhairt *nf* conference

co-là-breith, co-là-breith, co-làithean-breith *nm* birthday

cola-deug *nm* fortnight

colaiste, *gen* **colaiste,** *pl* **colaistean** *nmf* college

colann, *gen* **colainn** & **colna,** *pl* **colainnean** *nf* body

colbh, *gen* & *pl* **cuilbh** *nm* column

co-leagh *vti, pres part* **co-leaghadh,** fuse, amalgamate

collaidh *adj* 1 sensual; 2 lewd

coltach *adj* 1 likely, probable

coltachadh, *gen* **coltachaidh** *nm* comparing

coltachd *nf* likelihood

coltaich *vt, pres part* **a' coltachadh,** compare

coltas, *gen* **coltais** *nm* appearance

com, *gen* & *pl* **cuim** *nm* 1 bosom; 2 trunk (*of human body*)

coma *adj* indifferent

comain, comain, comainean *nf* obligation

comanachadh, comanachaidh, comanachaidhean *nm* Communion

comanaiche, comanaiche, comanaichean *nm* communicant

comann *gen* & *pl* **comainn** *nm* association, commune, fellowship

comar, comair, comaran *nf* a confluence

comas, comais, comasan *nm* ability, capacity

comasach *adj* capable

combaist, combaiste, combaistean *nf* compass

comhachag, comhachaig, comhachagan *nf* owl

comhair *nf* 1 direction; 2 *in expr* **fa chomhair** *prep* opposite

comhairle, comhairle, comhairlean *nf* 1 advice; 2 council

comhairleach, *gen* & *pl* **comhairlich** *nm* adviser

comhairleachadh, *gen* **comhairleachaidh** *nm* advising

comhairlich *vt, pres part* **a' comhairleachadh,** advise

comhairliche, comhairliche, comhairlichean *nm* councillor

comharrachadh, *gen* **comharrachaidh** *nm* marking

comharra(dh), comharraidh, comharraidhean *nm* 1 mark; 2 symptom

comharraich *vt, pres part* **a' comharrachadh,** mark

comhart, comhairt, comhartan *nm* bark (*dog*)

comhartaich *nf* barking (*dog*)

còmhdach, còmhdaich, còmhdaichean *nm* cover

còmhdaich *vt, pres part* a' **còmhdach(adh)**, cover

còmhdaichte *adj* covered

còmhdhail, còmhdhalach, còmhdhailean *nf* **1** transport; **2** congress, conference

co-mheadhanach *adj* concentric

co-m(h)easgachadh, *gen* **co-m(h)easgachaidh** *nm* mixing

co-mheasgaich, *also* **co-measgaich** & **coimeasgaich,** *vti, pres part* a' **co-m(h)easgachadh**, mix

còmhla(dh) *adv* together

còmhla, *gen* **còmhla** & **còmhlaidh**, *pl* **còmhlan, còmhlaidhean** & **còmhlaichean** *nmf* **1** door; **2** shutter

còmhlan, *gen* & *pl* **còmhlain** *nm* band, group

còmhnaich *vi, pres part* a' **còmhnaidh**, live (*in a place*), inhabit

còmhnaidh, còmhnaidhe, còmhnaidhean *nf* dwelling; **2** *in expr* **an-còmhnaidh** *adv* always

còmhnard *adj* (*surface etc*) **1** flat; **2** horizontal

còmhnard, còmhnaird, còmhnardan *nm* plain, level

còmhradh, còmhraidh, còmhraidhean *nm* conversation

còmhrag, còmhraig, còmhragan *nf* combat

còmhraideach *adj* talkative

còmhstri, còmhstri, còmhstrithean *nf* strife, competition

com-pàirt, com-pàirte, com-pàirtean *nf* (*mus*) accompaniment

com-pàirteachadh, *gen* **com-pàirteachaidh** *nm* accompanying

com-pàirtich *vti, pres part* a' **com-pàirteachadh,** **1** participate; **2** accompany

companach, *gen* & *pl* **companaich** *nm* companion, associate

companaidh, companaidh, companaidhean *nmf* company

companas, *gen* **companais** *nm* companionship

comraich, comraiche, comraichean *nf* sanctuary

còn, còn, cònaichean *nm* (*geometry etc*) a cone

cònail *adj* coniferous

conair(e), conair(e), conairean *nf* rosary

conaltrach *adj* (*of person*) social

conaltradh, *gen* **conaltraidh** *nm* **1** conversation; **2** company; **3** sociability; **4** communication

conasg, *gen* **conaisg** *nm* gorse

con(a)stabal, con(a)stabail, conastabalan *nm* constable

connadh, *gen* **connaidh** *nm* fuel

connadh-làmhaich, *gen* **connaidh-làmhaich** *nm* ammunition

connlach, *gen* **connlaich** *nf* straw, fodder

connrag, connraig, connragan *nf* consonant

connsachadh, *gen* **connsachaidh** *nm* arguing

connsachail *adj* quarrelsome

connsaich *vi, pres part* a' **connsachadh,** argue

connspeach, connspeach, connspeachan *nf* hornet, wasp

connspaid, connspaide, connspaidean *nf* controversy

connspaideach *adj* controversial

con(n)traigh, con(n)traighe, con(n)traighean *nf* neap tide

consal, consail, consalan *nm* consul

consan, *gen* & *pl* **consain** *nm* consonant

co-obrachadh, co-obrachaidh, co-obrachaidhean *nm* co-operation

co-obraich *vi, pres part* a' **co-obrachadh,** co-operate

co-obraiche, *gen* **co-obraiche,** *pl* **co-obraichean** *nm* colleague

co-ogha, *gen* **co-ogha,** *pl* **co-oghachan** & **co-oghaichean** *nm* cousin

cop, *gen* **coip** & **cuip** *nm* foam, froth

copach *adj* frothy, foaming

copag, copaig, copagan *nf* (*bot*) dock

copan, copain, copanan *nm* cup

copar, *gen* **copair** *nm* copper

cor, coir, cuir *nm* **1** condition; **2** method

còrcair/corcair *adj* purple

corcais, corcais, corcaisean *nf* cork

còrd, *gen* & *pl* **cùird** *nm* cord

còrd *vi, pres part* a' **còrdadh,** agree with

còrdadh, còrdaidh, còrdaidhean *nm* agreement

co-rèir *nf* accordance

còrn, *gen & pl* **cùirn** *nm* **1** horn; **2** corn (*on foot*)

còrnair, còrnair, còrnairean *nm* corner

corp, *gen & pl* **cuirp** *nm* **1** body; **2** corpse

corpailear, corpaileir, corpailearan *nm* corporal

corp-eòlaiche, corp-eòlaiche, corp-eòlaichean *nm* anatomist

corp-eòlas, *gen* **corp-eòlais** *nm* anatomy

corporra *adj* corporeal

còrr *adj* odd (*ie not even*)

còrr *nm* **1** *in expr* **còrr is,** more than; **2** *with art* **an còrr,** the rest; **3** *with art* **an còrr,** anything else

corra *adj* odd, occasional

corra-biod *nm, in expr* **air do chorra-biod** on tiptoe

corrach *adj* **1** unsteady; **2** steep, rough

corrag, corraig, corragan *nf* finger

corra-ghritheach, corra-grithich, corrachan-gritheach *nf* heron

corran, *gen & pl* **corrain** *nm* **1** sickle; **2** crescent

còs, còis, còsan *nm* (*topog*) hollow

còsach *adj* hollow

cosamhlachd, cosamhlachd, cosamhlachdan *nf* parable

cosg *nm* **1** (*also* **cosgadh,** *gen* **cosgaidh**) cost(ing); **2** waste

cosg *vt, pres part* **a' cosg** & **a' cosgadh,** **1** cost; **2** spend; **3** waste

cosgail *adj* expensive

cosgais, cosgaise, cosgaisean *nf* cost

co-sheirm, *gen* **co-sheirme** *nf* harmony

co-shìnte *adj* parallel

cosnadh, cosnaidh, cosnaidhean *nm* **1** earning; **2** employment; **3** work

costa, costa, costaichean *nm* coast

còta, còta, còtaichean *nm* coat

cotan, *gen* **cotain** *nm* cotton

cothrom *adj* even (*not odd*)

cothrom, cothruim, cothroman *nm* **1** opportunity; **2** *in expr* **chan eil cothrom air** it can't be helped; **3** balance

cothromach *adj* fair, just

cothromachadh, *gen* **cothromachaidh** *nm* balancing

cothromaich *vt, pres part* **a' cothromachadh,** balance

co-thuit *vi, pres part* **a' co-thuiteam,** coincide

co-thuiteamas, co-thuiteamais, co-thuiteamasan *nm* coincidence

cràbhach *adj* devout

cràbhadh, *gen* **cràbhaidh** *nm* piety

cràdh, *gen* **cràidh** *nm* pain, torture

craiceann, *gen* **craicinn** & **craicne,** *pl* **craicnean** *nm* skin

cràidh *vt, pres part* **a' cràdh,** torment

crài(dh)teach *adj* grievous, painful

cràin, cràine, cràintean *nf* sow

crann, *gen & pl* **crainn** & **croinn** *nm* **1** tree; **2** mast; **3** bar; **4** plough; **5** (*engin*) bolt; **6** crane, a derrick; **7** saltire; **9** *in expr* **cuir** *v* **crainn** draw lots

crannag, crannaig, crannagan *nf* **1** pulpit; **2** milk churn; **3** crannog

crann-ceusaidh, *gen & pl* **crainn-cheusaidh** & **croinn-cheusaidh** *nm* cross (*for crucifixion*)

crannchur, crannchuir, crannchuran *nm* casting or drawing of lots

crann-sgaoilidh, *gen & pl* **crainn-sgaoilidh** *nm* transmitter

craobh, craoibhe, craobhan *nf* tree

craobh-sgaoil *vti, pres part* **a' craobh-sgaoileadh** broadcast

craobh-sgaoileadh, *gen* **craobh-sgaoilidh** *nm* broadcasting

craos, craois, craosan *nm* **1** maw; **2** gluttony

craosach *adj* gluttonous

craosaire, craosaire, craosairean *nm* glutton

crasg, craisg, crasgan *nf* crutch

crasgag & **crosgag,** *gen* **crasgaig,** *pl* **crasgagan** *nf* starfish

crath *vti, pres part* **a' crathadh,** shake, sprinkle

creach, creiche, creachan *nf* **1** booty; **2** ruination

creach *vti, pres part* **a' creachadh,** **1** rob; **2** ruin

creachadh, *gen* **creachaidh** *nm* **1** robbing; **2** ruining

creachan(n), creachain(n), creachan(n)an *nm* scallop

crèadh/criadh & **crè,** *gen* **creadha** & **creadhadh** *nf* clay

crèadhadair, crèadhadair, crèadhadairean *nm* potter

crèadhadaireachd *nf* pottery

creag, creige, creagan *nf* 1 rock, cliff; 2 hill

creagach *adj* rocky

creamh, *gen* creamha *nm* garlic

creamh-gàrraidh *nm* leek

creapan, *gen & pl* creapain *nm* stool

creathail (*also* creathall), *gen* creathaile & creathlach, *pl* creathailean *nf* cradle

creid *vti, pres part* a' creidsinn & a' creids, believe

creideamh, creideimh, creideamhan *nm* belief, religion

creideas, *gen* creideis *nm* 1 trust; 2 belief

creidsinn *nm* believing

creim/criom *vti, pres part* a' creimeadh, nibble, gnaw

creimeach, creimich, creimich *nm* rodent

creimeadh/criomadh, *gen* creimidh *nm* nibbling

crèis, *gen* crèise *nf* grease

crèiseach *adv* greasy

creithleag, creithleig, creithleagan *nf* horsefly

creuchd, creuchda, creuchdan *nf* a wound

creud, creuda, creudan *nf* creed

creutair, creutair, creutairean *nm* creature

criathar, criathair, criatharan *nm* sieve

criathraich *vt, pres part* a' criathradh & a' criathrachadh, sieve

cridhe, cridhe, cridheachan *nm* 1 heart; 2 courage

cridhealas, *gen* cridhealais *nm* heartiness,

cridheil *adj* (*person, atmosphere etc*) hearty

crìoch, crìche, crìochan *nf* 1 end; 2 boundary

crìoch(n)ach *adj* finite, neo-chrìoch(n)ach infinite

crìochnachadh, *gen* crìochnachaidh *nm* finishing

crìochnaich *vt, pres part* a' crìochnachadh, finish

crìochnaichte *adj* finished

criomag, criomaige, criomagan *nf* bit, crumb

crìon *adj* 1 tiny; 2 insignificant; 3 withered

crìon *vti, pres part* a' crìonadh, wither

crìonadh, *gen* crìonaidh *nm* withering

crioplach & cripleach, *gen & pl* crioplaich *nm* cripple

crios, criosa, criosan *nm* belt

Crìosdachd *nf, with art* A' Chrìosdachd Christendom

Crìosdaidh, Crìosdaidh, Crìosdaidhean *nm* Christian

Crìosdaidheachd *nf* Christianity

Crìosdail/Crìosdaidh *adj* Christian

criostal, criostail, criostalan *nm* crystal

crith, crithe, crithean *nf* trembling

crith *vi, pres part* a' crith, tremble

critheanach *adj* 1 shaky; 2 scary

crò, *gen* cròtha, *pl* cròithean & cròthan *nm* pen, fold

croch *vt, pres part* a' crochadh, hang

crochadair, crochadair, crochadairean *nm* hangman, hanger

crochadh, *gen* crochaidh *nm* 1 hanging; 2 *in expr* an crochadh air *prep* depending on

crochte *adj* hung, hanged

crodh, *gen* cruidh *nm* cattle

crò-dhearg *adj* crimson

cròg, cròige, crògan *nf* paw, fist

cròic, cròice, cròicean *nf* antler

croich, croiche, croichean *nf* gallows

cròileagan, *gen & pl* cròileagain *nm* playgroup

crois, croise, croisean *nf* cross

croit/cruit, *gen* croite, *pl* croitean *nf* 1 croft; 2 hump (*on back*)

croitear/cruitear, *gen* croiteir, *pl* croitearan *nm* crofter

croitearachd *nf* crofting

croitse, croitse, croitseachan *nf* crutch

crom *adj* bent

crom *vti, pres part* a' cromadh, 1 (*vt*) bend; 2 (*vi*) *in expr* crom air set to; 3 (*vti*) bend; 4 (*vi*) descend

cromadh, *gen* cromaidh *nm* bending

cromag, cromaig, cromagan *nf* 1 hook; 2 shepherd's crook; 3 comma

cron, *gen & pl* croin *nm* 1 harm; 2 fault

cronachadh, *gen* cronachaidh *nm* rebuking

cronachail *adj* censorious

cronaich *vt, pres part* a' cronachadh, rebuke

cronail *adj* harmful

crònan, *gen* crònain *nm* 1 humming;
2 bellowing

crost(a) *adj* 1 cross; 2 naughty

crotach *adj* hump-backed

crotal, *gen* crotail *nm* lichen

cruach, cruaiche, cruachan *nf* 1 heap;
2 hill

cruach *vt, pres part* a' cruachadh, heap

cruachann, cruachainn, cruaichnean
nf hip

cruadal, *gen* cruadail *nm* 1 hardship;
2 intrepidity

cruadalach *adj* 1 difficult; 2 intrepid

cruadhaich *vti, pres part* a'
cruadhachadh, harden

cruadhachadh, *gen* cruadhachaidh *nm*
hardening

cruaidh *adj* hard, hardy

cruaidh, *gen* cruaidhe *nf* steel

cruaidh-chàs, cruaidh-chàis, cruaidh-
chàsan *nm* 1 emergency; 2 tight corner

cruan, *gen* cruain *nm* enamel

cruas, *gen* cruais *nm* 1 hardness;
2 cruelty; 3 hardiness

crùb *vi, pres part* a' crùbadh, 1 crouch;
2 stoop; 3 cringe; 4 crawl

crùbach *adj* 1 lame

crùbadh, *gen* crùbaidh *nm* crouching *etc*

crùbag, crùbaig, crùbagan *nf* crab

crùdh *vt, pres part* a' crùidheadh, shoe
(*horse*)

crudha, cruidhe, cruidhean *nm*
horseshoe

cruinn *adj* 1 round; 2 accurate;
3 assembled

cruinne (*m*), *gen* cruinne (*f*), *pl*
cruinnean (*m*) *nmf* 1 roundness;
2 sphere; 3 (*with art*) an cruinne the
world; 4 accuracy

cruinneachadh, cruinneachaidh,
cruinneachaidhean *nm* 1 gathering;
2 collection

cruinnead *nf* roundness

cruinne-cè (*m*), *gen* cruinne-cè (*f*), *nmf*,
used with art, an cruinne-cè, 1 the
world; 2 the universe

cruinneil *adj* global

cruinn-eòlas, *gen* cruinn-eòlais *nm*
geography

cruinnich *vti, pres part* a'
cruinneachadh, gather

cruinn-leum, cruinn-lèim, cruinn-
leuman *nm* standing jump

crùisgean, crùisgein, crùisgeanan *nm*
cruisie

cruit, cruite, cruitean *nf* harp

cruitheachd, cruitheachd,
cruitheachdan *nf* creation

cruithear, cruitheir, cruithearan *nm*
creator

Cruithneach, *gen & pl* Cruithnich *nm*
Pict, *also adj* Cruithneach Pictish

cruithneachd & cruineachd *nf* wheat

crùn, crùin, crùintean *nm* crown

crùn *vt, pres part* a' crùnadh, crown

crùnadh, crùnaidh, crùnaidhean *nm*
crowning, coronation

cruth, *gen* crutha, *pl* cruthan &
cruthannan *nm* shape, form

cruthachadh, *gen* cruthachaidh *nm*
1 creating

cruthachail *adj* creative

cruthaich *vt, pres part* a' cruthachadh,
create

cù, *gen & pl* coin, *gen pl* chon *nm* dog

cuach, cuaich, cuachan *nf* 1 bowl; 2 cup,
quaich

cuagach *adj* 1 bent; 2 lame

cuaille, cuaille, cuaillean *nm* a cudgel

cuain, cuaine, cuainean *nf* (*animals*)
litter

cuairt, cuairte, cuairtean *nf* 1 circuit;
2 stroll; 3 tour

cuan, cuain, cuantan *nm* sea, ocean

cuaraidh, cuaraidh, cuaraidhean *nmf*
quarry

cuaran, *gen* cuarain, *pl* cuarain &
cuaranan *nm* sandal

cuartachadh & cuairteachadh, *gen*
cuartachaidh *nm* 1 surrounding;
2 circulation

cuartaich & cuairtich *vti, pres part* a'
cuartachadh, 1 surround; 2 circulate

cùbaid, cùbaide, cùbaidean *nf* pulpit

cubhaidh *adj* fitting

cùbhraidh *adj* fragrant

cucair, cucair, cucairean *nm* cooker

cudrom/cuideam, *gen* cudruim &
cuideim *nm* 1 weight; 2 importance

cudromach *adj* 1 heavy; 2 important

cugallach *adj* precarious

cuibheas, cuibheis, cuibheasan *nm*
average

cuibheasach *adj* average
cuibhle, cuibhle, *pl* **cuibhlean &**
cuibhlichean, *also* **cuibheall, cuibhle,**
cuibhleachan, *nf* wheel
cuibhreach, cuibhrich, cuibhrichean
nm chain
cuibhreachadh, *gen* **cuibhreachaidh**
nm chaining
cuibhreann, *gen* **cuibhrinn,** *pl*
cuibhrinnean & **cuibhreannan** *nm*
1 portion; **2** allocation; **3** instalment
cuibhrich *vt, pres part* **a'**
cuibhreachadh, chain
cuibhrig, cuibhrige, cuibhrigean *nmf*
quilt
cuid, codach, codaichean *nf* **1** share;
2 some; **3** *in expr* **an dà chuid** both; **4** *in*
expr **aon chuid . . . no** neither . . . nor; **5**
in expr **an dara cuid . . . no** either . . . or
cuideachadh, *gen* **cuideachaidh** *nm*
helping
cuideachail *adj* helpful
cuideachd *adv* also
cuideachd, cuideachd, cuideachdan *nf*
company
cuideachdail *adj* sociable
cuideigin *nmf* someone
cuide ri *prep* with
cuidhteag/cùiteag, *gen* **cuidhteig,** *pl*
cuidhteagan *nf* whiting
cuidhteas, cuidhteis, cuidhteasan *nm*
1 receipt; **2** *in expr* **faigh** *v* **cuidhteas**
get rid of; **3** *in expr* **cùm cuidhteas** keep
clear of
cuidhtich, *pres part* **a' cuidhteachadh** *vt*
compensate
cuidich *vti, pres part* **a' cuideachadh,**
help
cuidiche, cuidiche, cuidichean *nm* a
helper
cuid-oidhche *nf* night's lodging
cùil, cùile, cùiltean *nf* **1** corner; **2** nook
cuilbheart, cuilbheirt, cuilbheartan
nf trick
cuilc, cuilce, cuilcean *nf* **1** reed; **2** cane
cuileag, cuileig, cuileagan *nf* fly
cuilean, cuilein, cuileanan *nm* **1** puppy;
2 cub, whelp
cuileann, *gen* **cuilinn** *nm* holly
cuimhne *nf* memory
cuimhneachadh, *gen* **cuimhneachaidh**
nm remembering

cuimhneachan, *gen & pl*
cuimhneachain *nm* **1** memorial;
2 souvenir; **3** memorandum
cuimhnich *vi, pres part* **a'**
cuimhneachadh, remember
cuimir *adj* **1** succinct; **2** shapely
Cuimreach, *gen & pl* **Cuimrich** *nm*
Welshman, *also adj* **Cuimreach** Welsh
Cuimrigh *nf, used with art,* **a'**
Chuimrigh Wales
Cuimris *nf (lang), usu with art,* **a'**
Chuimris Welsh
cuimseachadh, *gen* **cuimseachaidh** *nm*
aiming
cuimsich *vti, pres part* **a'**
cuimseachadh, aim
cuine & **cuin** *inter adv* when
cuing[1]**, cuinge, cuingean** *nf* yoke
cuing[2]**,** *gen* **cuinge** *nf (with art)* **a' chuing**
asthma
cuingealaich & **cuingich** *vt, pres part* **a'**
cuingealachadh & **a' cuingeachadh,**
restrict
cuinneag, cuinneige, cuinneagan *nf*
bucket, pail
cuinnean, cuinnein, cuinneanan *nm*
nostril
cuip, *gen* **cuipe,** *pl* **cuipean &**
cuipeachan *nf* whip
cuip *vt, pres part* **a' cuipeadh,** whip
cuipeadh, *gen* **cuipidh** *nm* whipping
cuir *vti, pres part* **a' cur** put
cuireadh, cuiridh, cuiridhean *nm*
invitation
cuirm, cuirme, cuirmean *nf* **1** feast;
2 treat
cuirmeach *adj* festive
cùirt, cùirte, cùirtean *nf* court
cùirtean, cùirtein, cùirteanan, *also*
cùirtear, cùirteir, cùirtearan *nm*
curtain
cùirteil *adj* courteous, courtly
cùis, cùise, cùisean *nf* **1** matter, affair;
2 *(legal)* case; **3** cause; **4** *in expr* **dèan** *v*
a' chuis air manage; **6** *in expr* **nì sin a'**
chùis! that'll do!
cùis-bheachd, cùis-bheachd, cùis-
bheachdan *nf* abstraction
cùisear, cùiseir, cùisearan *nm* subject
cuisle, cuisle, cuislean *nf* **1** vein;
2 artery; **3** pipe
cuislean, cuislein, cuisleanan *nm* flute

cùl, cùil, cùiltean *nm* 1 back; 2 *in expr*
air cùl *prep* behind

cùlaibh *nm* back part of anything, cùlaibh
air beulaibh back to front, vice versa

culaidh, culaidhe, culaidhean *nf*
1 garment; 2 suit of clothes; 3 costume;
4 butt

cùlaist, cùlaiste, cùlaistean *nf* scullery

cularan, cularain, cularanan *nm*
cucumber

cùl-chàin *vt, pres part* a' cùl-chàineadh,
slander

cùl-chàineadh, *gen* cùl-chàinidh *nm*
slander(ing)

cullach, *gen & pl* cullaich *nm* 1 boar;
2 tom-cat

cùl-mhùtaire, cùl-mhùtaire, cùl-
mhùtairean *nm* smuggler

cùl-mhùtaireachd *nf* smuggling

cultar, cultair, cultaran *nm* culture

cultarach *adj* cultural

cum *vt, pres part* a' cumadh, shape, form

cùm *vt, pres part* a' cumail, 1 keep;
2 continue; cùm a-mach assert

cumadh, cumaidh, cumaidhean *nm*
1 shaping; 2 shape

cumail, *gen* cumalach *nf* keeping

cuman, *gen & pl* cumain *nm* pail

cumanta *adj* common

cumantas, *gen* cumantais *nm* normality,
in exprs an cumantas *adv* usually

cumha¹, cumha, cumhachan *nf*
1 stipulation; 2 *in expr* air chumha is gu
. . . on condition that . . .

cumha², cumha, cumhachan *nm* elegy

cumhach *adj* conditional

cumhachd *nmf* power

cumhachdach *adj* powerful

cumhang *adj* narrow

cùmhnant, cùmhnaint, cùmhnantan
nm contract, condition

cunbhalach *adj* 1 regular; 2 tidy

cungaidh, cungaidh, cungaidhean *nf*
1 stuff; 2 tool

cunnart, cunnairt, cunnartan *nm*
danger

cunnartach *adj* dangerous

cunnradh, cunnraidh, cunnraidhean
nm 1 contract; 2 deal

cunnt *vti, pres part* a' cunntadh, count

cunntachail *adj* accountable

cunntadh, *gen* cunntaidh, *also*
cunntais, *gen* cunntais *nm* counting

cunntas, cunntais, cunntasan *nm*
1 arithmetic; 2 account; 3 invoice; 4
description

cunntasachd *nf* accountancy

cunntasair, cunntasair, cunntasairean
nm accountant

cuntair (*also* cunntair), cuntair,
cuntairean *nm* counter

cùp, cùpa, cùpannan *nm* cup

cupa, cupannan *nm* cup

cuplachadh, *gen* cuplachaidh *nm*
copulation

cuplaich *vi, pres part* a' cuplachadh,
copulate

cùpon, cùpoin, cùponan *nm* coupon

cur, *gen* cuir *nm* putting

curach, curaich, curaichean *nf* curach,
coracle

curaidh, curaidh, curaidhean *nm* hero

cùram, cùraim, cùraman *nm* 1 care;
2 (*relig*) conversion

cùramach *adj* 1 careful; 2 anxious

cur na mara *nm* sea-sickness

curracag, curracaig, curracagan *nf*
lapwing

curran, *gen* currain, *pl* currain &
curranan *nm* carrot

cùrsa, cùrsa, cùrsaichean *nm* course

cùrsair, cùrsair, cùrsairean *nm* cursor

cur-seachad, cuir-seachad, cur-
seachadan *nm* pastime

cur-sìos *adj* derogatory

cus, *gen* cuis *nm* excess

cusbainn *nf* customs (*duty*)

cusp, cusp, cuspan *nf* chilblain

cuspair, cuspair, cuspairean *nm*
1 subject; 2 object

cuspaireach *adj* (*gram*) accusative

cut *vti, pres part* a' cutadh, gut

cutair, cutair, cutairean *nm* gutter

cuthach, *gen* cuthaich *nm* 1 madness;
2 rage

cuthag, cuthaig, cuthagan *nf* cuckoo

D

dà *adj* **a dhà** *n* two
dà-bhitheach *adj* amphibious
dachaigh, dachaigh(e), dachaighean *nf* home
dà-chànanach *adj* bilingual
dad *nf* 1 anything; 2 *in expr* **dad ort!** never mind
dadaidh, dadaidh, dadaidhean *nm* Daddy
dadam, *gen & pl* **dadaim** *nm* 1 atom; 2 tiny piece
dà-dheug *n & adj* twelve
dà-fhillte *adj* 1 two-fold; 2 binary
dag(a) & dag, *gen* **daige**, *pl* **dagan & dagaichean** *nm* pistol
dail, dalach, dailean *nf* 1 meadow; 2 dale
dàil, dàlach, dàlaichean *nf* delay; 2 (*fin*) credit
dalma *adj* blatant
dàimh, *gen* **dàimhe** *nmf* relationship, link
dàimheach *adj* relative
dàimheil *adj* friendly, affectionate
daingeann *adj* firm, solid
daingneach, daingnich, daingnichean *nf* fort, stronghold
daingneachadh, *gen* **daingneachaidh** *nm* fortifying, confirming
daingnich *vt*, *pres part* **a' daingneachadh**, 1 fortify; 2 confirm
dàir, *gen* **dàra** *nf* (*cattle*) coupling
dall *adj* blind
dall *vt*, *pres part* **a' dalladh**, 1 blind; 2 delude
dalladh, *gen* **dallaidh** *nm* 1 blinding; 2 delusion
dàmais *nf* draughts (*game*)
damh, *gen & pl* **daimh** 1 *nm* stag; 2 ox; 3 bullock
dàmhair, dàmhair, dàmhairean *nf* 1 rutting; 2 (*with art*) **An Dàmhair** October
damaiste, damaiste, damaistean *nf* damage
damhan-allaidh, *gen & pl* **damhain-allaidh** *nm* spider
dàn¹, *gen* **dàin** *nm* fate

dàn², *gen* **dàin**, *pl* **dàna & dàin** *nm* 1 poem; 2 song
dàna *adj* 1 bold; 2 impudent; 3 arrogant
dànachd *nf* poetry
dànadas, *gen* **dànadais** *nm* 1 boldness; 2 impudence; 3 arrogance
Danmhairg *nf*, *used with art*, **an Danmhairg** Denmark
Danmhairgeach, Danmhairgich, Danmhairgich *nm* Dane, *also adj*, **Danmhairgeach** Danish
danns *vti*, *pres part* **a' dannsa(dh)**, dance
dannsa, dannsa, dannsaichean *nm* dance
dannsadh, *gen* **dannsaidh** *nm* dancing
dannsair, dannsair, dannsairean *nm* dancer
daoimean, daoimein, daoimeanan *nm* diamond
daolag, daolaig, daolagan *nf* beetle, **daolag-bhreac-dhearg** ladybird
daonna/daonda *adj* human(e)
daonnachd *nf* humanity
daonnan *adv* always
daor *adj* expensive
daorach, *gen* **daoraich** *nf* 1 drunkenness; 2 spree
daorachail *adj* intoxicating
daorsa *nf* captivity
dara & dàrna *adj* 1 second; 2 (*in contrast to* **eile**) one; 3 *in expr* **an dara cuid**, either
darach, *gen & pl* **daraich** *nm* oak
dara-deug *adj* twelfth
da-rìribh *adv* 1 *in expr* **ann an da-rìribh** in earnest; 2 *in expr* **math dha-rìribh** excellent
dà-sheaghach *adj* ambiguous
dà-sheaghachd *nf* ambiguity
dàta *nm* data
dath *vt*, *pres part* **a' dathadh**, 1 colour; 2 dye
dath, datha, dathan *nm* 1 colour; 2 dye
dathail *adj* colourful
dà-thaobhach *adj* bilateral
dathte *adj* coloured; dyed

dè *pron* 1 what; 2 *in constr* **dè cho . . . agus/'s a . . . ?** how . . . is it?; 3
de & **dhe** *prep* from, made of
deacair *adj* difficult
deach, deachaidh *pts of irreg v* **rach**
deachd *vti, pres part* **a' deachdadh**, dictate
deachdadh, deachdaidh, deachdaidhean *nm* dictation
deachdaire, deachdaire, deachdairean *nm* dictator
deachdaireachd *nf* dictatorship
deadhan, *gen & pl* **deadhain** *nm* dean
deagh *adj* good, well
dealachadh, dealachaidh, dealachaidhean *nm* parting, separation, segregation, insulation
dealaich *vti, pres part* **a' dealachadh**, separate, insulate
dealan, *gen* **dealain** *nm* electricity
dealanach, *gen & pl* **dealanaich** *nm* lightning
dealanaich *vt, pres part* **a' dealanachadh**, electrify
dealanair, dealanaire, dealanairean *nm* electrician
dealan-dè, dealain-dè, dealanan-dè *nm* butterfly
dealantach *adj* electronic
dealas, *gen* **dealais** *nm* eagerness
dealasach *adj* eager
dealbh, *gen* **dealbha** & **deilbh**, *pl* **dealbhan, deilbh** & **dealbhannan** *nmf* 1 picture; 2 painting; 3 photograph; 4 drawing; 5 form, shape
dealbh *vt, pres part* **a' dealbhadh**, 1 picture; 2 shape; 3 design
dealbhadh, *gen* **dealbhaidh** *nm* picturing, shaping, planning
dealg, deilg, dealgan *nf* 1 prickle, thorn; 2 skewer; 3 pin
deàlrach *adj* 1 shining
deàlradh, *gen* **deàlraidh** *nm* 1 shining
deàlraich *vi, pres part* **a' deàlradh** shine
dealt, *gen* **dealta** *nmf* dew
deamhais, deamhais, deamhaisean *nmf* shears
deamhan, *gen & pl* **deamhain** *nm* demon
deamocrasaidh, deamocrasaidh, deamocrasaidhean *nm* democracy
deamocratach *adj* democratic

deamocratach, *gen & pl* **deamocrataich** *nm* democrat
dèan *vt irreg, pres part* **a' dèanamh**, 1 do; 2 make; 3 compose
dèanadach *adj* industrious
dèanadas, *gen* **dèanadais** *nm* industriousness
dèanadh, dèanaibh, dèanainn, dèanam, dèanamaid *pts of irreg v* **dèan**
dèanamh, *gen* **dèanaimh** *nm* 1 doing, making; 2 form, physique
deann, deanna, deannan *nf* 1 force; 2 haste
dearbh *adj* 1 very, same; 2 *as adv* **gu dearbh** indeed
dearbh *vt, pres part* **a' dearbhadh**, 1 prove; 2 test
dearbhadh, dearbhaidh, dearbhaidhean *nm* 1 proving; 2 proof; 3 test
dearbhte, *also* **dearbhta**, proven
dearc, dearc, dearcan *nf, also dimin* **dearcag, dearcaig, dearcagan** *nf*, berry
dearg *adj* 1 red; 2 *with other colours*, reddish-, reddy-; 3 *as pej intensifying element*, complete; 4 *as adv* completely
deargad, deargaid, deargadan *nf* & **deargann, deargainn, deargannan** *nf* flea
deargnaich *vt, pres part* **a' deargnachadh**, redden
dearmad, dearmaid, dearmadan *nm* neglect
dearmadach *adj* neglectful
dearmaid *vt, pres part* **a' dearmad**, neglect
deàrrs *vi, pres part* **a' deàrrsadh**, *also* **deàrrsaich** *vi, pres part* **a' deàrrsachadh**, shine
deas *nf* & *adj* 1 south; 2 *in expr* **an làmh dheas**, right
deas *adj* 1 ready; 2 quick
deasachadh, *gen* **deasachaidh** *nm* 1 preparing; 2 editing
deasaich *vt, pres part* **a' deasachadh**, 1 prepare; 2 edit
deasbad, deasbaid, deasbadan *nmf* discussion, debate
deasg, deasga, deasgan *nm* desk
deas-ghnàth, deas-ghnàith, deas-ghnàthan *nm* ceremony

deatach, deataiche, deataichean *nf*
smoke, vapour

deataich *vi, pres part* **a' deatachadh**
evaporate

deatamach *adj* crucial

deich *n & adj* ten

deicheach *adj* decimal

deichead, deicheid, deicheadan *nm*
decade

deicheamh, *gen* **deicheimh** *nm*
1 decimal; **2** tenth

deicheamh *adj* tenth

deichnear *nmf* tensome

dèideadh, *gen* **dèididh** *nm* toothache

dèideag, dèideig, dèideagan *nf* **1** toy;
2 pebble

dèidh, dèidhe, dèidhean *nf* **1** wish;
2 fondness

dèidheil *adj* fond

dèile, *gen* **dèilidh,** *pl* **dèilean** &
dèileachan *nf* plank

dèilig *vi, pres part* **a' dèiligeadh,** deal

deimhinn(e), *also* **deimhinnte** *adj* sure

dèine *nf* eagerness

dèirc, dèirce, dèircean *nf* charity

dèirceach *adj* charitable

dèirceach, *gen & pl* **dèircich** *nm* beggar

deireadh, deiridh, deiridhean *nm*
1 end; **2** *in expr* **air dheireadh** *adv*
behind; **3** *in expr* **air deireadh** *adv* last,
late; **4** *in expr* **mu dheireadh** *adj* last,
adv at last

deireannach *adj* final

deisciobal, *gen & pl* **deisciobail** *nm*
disciple

deise, deise, deiseachan *nf* suit (*clothes*)

dèiseag, dèiseige, dèiseagan *nf* smack

deiseil *adj* **1** ready; **2** finished; **3** handy
(*convenient*); **4** *adv* clockwise; **5** *adv*
sunwise

deit, deite, deitichean *nf* (*fruit*) date

deò *nf* **1** breath; **2** life

deoch, dighe, deochannan *nf* drink

deothail, *also* **deoghail,** *vti, pres part* **a'**
deothal, suck

deothal, *gen* **deothail** *nm* sucking

deòin, *gen* **deòine** *nf* willingness

deònach *adj* willing

deuchainn, deuchainne,
deuchainnean *nf* examination, test,
experiment, trial

deudach *adj* dental

deug *num suffix* -teen

deugaire, deugaire, deugairean *nm*
teenager

deur, *gen & pl* **deòir** *nm* tear(drop)

deurach *adj* tearful

dha, *with sing art* **dhan,** *for* **do,** to

dha (*emph form* **dhàsan**) *prep pron, see*
do *prep*

dhachaigh *adv* home

dhaibh (*emph form* **dhaibhsan**) *prep*
pron, see **do**

dhèanadh, dhèanainn *pts of irreg v*
dèan

dheth *adv* off

dheth (*emph form* **dhethsan**) *prep pron,*
see **de** *prep*

dhi (*emph form* **dhìse**) *prep pron, see* **do**
prep

dhibh (*emph form* **dhibhse**), **dhinn**
(*emph form* **dhinne**), **dhìom** (*emph*
form **dhìomsa**), **dhìot** (*emph form*
dhìotsa), **dhith** (*emph form* **dhithse**),
dhiubh (*emph form* **dhiubhsan**) *prep*
prons, see **de** *prep*

dhomh (*emph form* **dhòmhsa**), **dhuibh**
(*emph form* **dhuibhse**), **dhuinn** (*emph*
form **dhuinne**), **dhu(i)t** (*emph form*
dhu(i)tsa) *prep prons, see* **do** *prep*

dia, dè, diathan *nm* god

diabhal, diabhail, diabhail & **diabhlan**
nm devil

diabhlaidh *adj* diabolical

diadhachd *nf* **1** deity; **2** theology;
3 godliness

diadhaidh *adj* **1** devout; **2** divine

diadhaire, diadhaire, diadhairean *nm*
theologian

dian *adj* **1** eager; **2** intense

Diardaoin *nm* Thursday

dias, dèise, diasan *nf* ear (corn)

diathad, diathaid, diathadan *nf* **1** meal;
2 *with art* dinner

dibhearsan, *gen* **dibhearsain** *nm* fun

dìblidh *adj* vile, abject, weak

dìcheall, *gen* **dìchill** *nm* diligence

dìcheallach *adj* diligent

dì-cheannachadh, *gen* **dì-**
cheannachaidh *nm* decapitating

dì-cheannaich *vt, pres part* **a' dì-**
cheann(ach)adh, decapitate

Diciadain *nm* Wednesday

Didòmhnaich *nm* Sunday

didseatach *adj* digital

dìg, dìge, dìgean *nf* ditch

Dihaoine *nm* Friday

dìle, *gen* **dìleann** & **dìlinn** *nf* **1** downpour; **2** flood

dìleab, dìleib, dìleaban *nf* legacy, heritage

dìleas *adj* faithful

dìlseachd *nf* loyalty

Diluain *nm* Monday

Dimàirt *nm* Tuesday

dìmeas *nm* disrespect

dìnichean *npl* jeans

dinn *vti, pres part* **a' dinneadh,** cram

dinnear, *gen* **dinneir** & **dinnearach,** *pl* **dinnearan** *nf* dinner

dìobair *vt, pres part* **a' dìobradh,** desert, abandon

dìobhair *vti, pres part* **a' dìobhairt,** vomit

dìobhairt *nm* vomit(ing)

dìobradh, *gen* **dìobraidh** *nm* abandoning

dìochuimhne *nf* forgetfulness

dìochuimhneach *adj* forgetful

dìochuimhneachadh, *gen* **dìochuimhneachaidh** *nm* forgetting

dìochuimhnich, *vt, pres part* **a' dìochuimhneachadh,** forget

diofar, *gen* **diofair** *nm, also* **difir** *nm* & **deifir,** *gen* **deifire** *nf* difference

diof(a)rach, *also* **deifrichte** & **diofaraichte,** *adj* different

diog, diog, diogan *nm* (*time*) second

diogail *vti, pres part* **a' diogladh,** tickle

diogalach *adj* ticklish

dìoghail & **dìol** *vt, pres part* **a' dìo(gh)ladh, 1** repay; **2** take revenge

dìoghaltas, *gen* **dìoghaltais** *nm* revenge

dìo(gh)ladh, *gen* **dìo(gh)laidh** *nm* repaying

dìoghras, *gen* **dìoghrais** *nm* zeal

dìoghrasach *adj* zealous

dìolain *adj* illegitimate

dìollaid & **diallaid,** *gen* **dìollaide,** *pl* **dìollaidean** *nf* saddle

diomb *nm* displeasure

diombach *adj* **1** out of sorts; **2** annoyed

diombuan *adj* transient

dìomhain *adj* **1** vain; **2** idle

dìomhair *adj* **1** secret; **2** mysterious

dìomhaireachd *nf* **1** secrecy; **2** mystery

dìomhanas, dìomhanais, dìomhanasan *nm* vanity

dìon, *gen* **dìona** *nm* protection

dìon *vt, pres part* **a' dìon** & **a' dìonadh,** protect

dìonach *adj* **1** secure; **2** waterproof

dìonadh, *gen* **dìonaidh** *nm* protecting

dìorrasach *adj* keen

dìosail *nm* & *adj* diesel

dìosgan, *gen* **dìosgain** *nm* creaking

diosgo *nm* disco

dìreach *adj* & *adv* **1** straight; **2** upright; **3** (*as adv*) just; **4** *as excl* **dìreach!** exact▌

dìreachadh, *gen* **dìreachaidh** *nm* straightening

dìreadh, *gen* **dìridh** *nm* climbing

dìrich[1] *vti, pres part* **a' dìreachadh,** straighten

dìrich[2] *vt, pres part* **a' dìreadh,** climb

Disathairne *nm* Saturday

dìsinn *nm* & **dìsne** *nmf, gen* **dìsne,** *pl* **dìsnean,** die

dìt *vt, pres part* **a' dìteadh** condemn

dìteadh, dìtidh, dìtidhean *nm* condemning

dìth, *gen* **dìthe** *nm* **1** lack; **2** *in expr* **a** (*fo* **de**) **dhìth** lacking

dithis, dithis, dithisean *nf* **1** two; **2** pair

dìthreabh, dìthreibh, dìthreabhan *nf* wilderness

diùc, diùc, diùcan *nm* duke

diùid *adj* shy

diùide *nf* shyness

diùlt *vti, pres part* **a' diùltadh, 1** refuse; **2** deny

diùltadh, *gen* **diùltaidh** *nm* **1** refusing; **2** denial

diùraidh, diùraidh, diùraidhean *nm* jury

dleas, dleasa, dleasan *nm* due, duty

dleastanas/dleasnas, *gen* **dleas(ta)nais,** *pl* **dleas(ta)nasan** *nm* duty

dlighe *nf* **1** right

dligheach *adj* lawful

dlùth, *gen* **dlùtha** *nm* warp

dlùth *adj* **1** close; **2** dense

dlùthachadh, *gen* **dlùthachaidh** *nm* approaching

dlùthaich *vi, pres part* **a' dlùthachadh,** approach

dlùths *nm* density

do *poss adj* (*sometimes found as* **t'** *before a vowel or before* **fh** *followed by a vowel*), your

do *verbal particle used in some neg & inter contexts*

do *prep* to, for

do- *a prefix corres to Eng* un-, in-, im-,

dòbhran, *gen & pl* **dòbhrain** *nm* otter

doca, doca, docannan *nm* dock (*seaport etc*)

docair, docair, docairean *nm* docker

dòcha *comp adj* 1 probable; 2 *in expr* **'s dòcha** *adv* perhaps

dochainn *vt, pres part* **a' dochann**, hurt, harm

dochann, dochainn, dochannan *nm* hurt, harm

dòchas, dòchais, dòchasan *nm* hope

dòchasach *adj* hopeful

do(c)tair, do(c)tair, do(c)tairean *nm* doctor

dòigh, dòighe, dòighean *nf* 1 way; 2 *in pl* customs; 3 condition; 4 mood; 5 *in expr* **air dhòigh is gu/nach . . .** *conj* so that . . .

dòigheil *adj* proper, well

dòil *nm* dole

doille *nf* blindness

doilleir *adj* dark

doilleirich *vti, pres part* **a' doilleireachadh**, darken

doimhne *nf usu with art* **an doimhne** the Deep

doimhneachd *nf* depth

doimhnich *vti, pres part* **a' doimhneachadh**, deepen

doineann, doininn, doineannan *nf* storm, tempest

doineannach *adj* stormy

doirbh *adj* difficult

doire, *gen* **doire**, *pl* **doirean** & **doireachan** *nmf* grove

dòirt *vti, pres part* **a' dòrtadh** 1 (*vt*) pour; 2 (*vi*) flow; 3 (*vt*) spill

dol *nm* going, happening

dolaidh *nf* harm, deterioration

dolair, dolair, dolairean *nm* dollar

dol-air-adhart *nm* behaviour

dol-a-mach *nm* 1 *same as* **dol-air-adhart** *above*; 2 *in expr* **sa chiad dol-a-mach** at first, in the first instance

dòlas, *gen* **dòlais** *nm* grief

dòmhail & **dùmhail**, *adj* 1 congested; 2 dense

domhainn *adj* deep

domhan, *gen* **domhain** *nm* universe

dona *adj, comp* **(n)as** (*etc*) **miosa**, bad

donas, *gen* **donais** *nm* 1 badness; 2 *with art* **an Donas** the Devil

donn *adj* brown

donnal, donnail, donnalan *nm* howl

donnalaich, *gen* **donnalaiche** *nf* howling

dòrainn, dòrainne, dòrainnean *nf* anguish

dòrainneach *adj* anguished

doras, dorais, dorsan *nm* door

dorch(a) *adj* dark

dorchadas, *gen* **dorchadais** *nm* darkness

dòrlach, *gen & pl* **dòrlaich** *nm* 1 handful; 2 batch

dòrn, *gen & pl* **dùirn** *nm* fist

dòrn *vt, pres part* **a' dòrnadh**, thump

dorsair, dorsair, dorsairean *nm* doorman

dòrtadh, *gen* **dòrtaidh** *nm* spilling

dos, *gen* **dois**, *pl* **dois** & **dosan** *nm* 1 bush; 2 drone (of bagpipe)

dosgainn, dosgainn, dosgainnean *nf* calamity

dòth *vt, pres part* **a' dòthadh**, scorch

dòthadh, *gen* **dòthaidh** *nm* scorching

drabasta & **drabasda** *adj* obscene

drabastachd & **drabasdachd** *nf* obscenity

dràbhail *adj* grotty

dràc, dràic, dràcan *nm* drake

dragh, dragha, draghannan *nm* 1 trouble; 2 annoyance; 3 worry

draghail *adj* worrying

dràibh *vti, pres part* **a' dràibheadh**, *also* **dràibhig** *vti, pres part* **a' dràibhigeadh**, drive

dràibhear, dràibheir, dràibhearan *nm* driver

dram, drama, dramannan *nmf, also* **drama, drama, dramaichean** *nm* dram

dràma, dràma, dràmathan *nmf* drama

dranndan, *gen & pl* **dranndain** *nfm,* snarling

dranndanach *adj* snappy, irritable

draoidh, draoidh, draoidhean *nm* 1 druid; 2 wizard

draoidheachd *nf* magic

draoidheil *adj* magic

draosta *adj* obscene

draostachd & **draosdachd** *nf* obscenity

drathair/drabhair, drathair, dràthraichean *nm* drawer

drathais/drathars *nf* underpants

dreach, dreacha, dreachan *nm*
1 appearance; 2 complexion

dreachd, dreachd, dreachdan *nf* draft

dreachd *vt, pres part* **a' dreachdadh,** draft

dreachmhor *adj* handsome

dreag, dreige, dreagan *nf* meteor

dreallag, dreallaige, dreallagan *nf* swing

drèana, drèana, drèanaichean *nf*
1 drain; 2 ditch

dreasa, dreasa, dreasaichean *nf* dress

dreasair, dreasair, dreasairean *nm* dresser

dreathan-donn, dreathain-duinn, dreathain-donna *nm* wren

drèin, drèine, drèinean *nf* scowl

dreuchd, dreuchd, dreuchdan *nf* occupation, profession

dreuchdail *adj* professional

driamlach, driamlaich, driamlaich(ean) *nmf* fishing line

drile, drile, drilichean *nf* drill

drioftair, drioftair, drioftairean *nm* drifter

drip, *gen* **dripe** *nf* bustle

dripeil *adj* busy

dris, drise, drisean *nf* bramble, brier

drithleann, *gen* & *pl* **drithlinn** *nm* sparkle

dr(i)ùchd, dr(i)ùchd, dr(i)ùchdan *nmf* dew

dròbh, dròibh, dròbhan *nmf* drove (*cattle*)

dròbhair, dròbhair, dròbhairean *nm* cattle drover

droch *adj* bad (*precedes the noun*)

drochaid, drochaide, drochaidean *nf* bridge

droga, droga, drogaichean *nf* drug

droigheann, *gen* **droighinn** *nm* thorntree

droighneach *adj* thorny

droman, *gen* & *pl* **dromain** *nm* elder tree

drùdhag, drùdhaig, drùdhagan *nf* drop

druid, druid, druidean *nf* a starling

drùidh *vti, pres part* **a' drùidheadh,**
1 penetrate; 2 affect

drùidheadh, *gen* **drùidhidh** *nm*
1 penetrating; 2 impression

drùidhteach *adj* impressive

druim, droma, dromannan *nm* 1 back;
2 ridge

drùis, *gen* **drùise** *nf* lust

drùiseach *adj* & **drùiseil** *adj* lustful

druma, druma, drumaichean *nmf* drum

drumair, drumair, drumairean *nm* drummer

duais, duaise, duaisean *nf* 1 wages;
2 prize

dual¹, duaile, dualan *nm* birthright

dual², duail, dualan *nm* 1 curl; 2 plait

dualachadh, *gen* **dualachaidh** *nm* curling

dualaich *vt, pres part* **a' dualachadh,**
1 curl; 2 plait

dualchainnt, dualchainnte, dualchainntean *nf* dialect

dualchas, *gen* **dualchais** *nm* 1 heritage, tradition; 2 inheritance

dualchasach *adj* traditional

dual(t)ach *adj* innate

duan, *gen* & *pl* **duain** *nm* 1 poem; 2 song

duanaire, duanaire, duanairean *nm* anthology (*poetry*)

dùbailte *adj* double, dual

dubh *adj* 1 black; 2 *with other colours,* dark; 3 *as intensifying element,* very

dubh, *gen* **duibh** *nm* 1 black; 2 ink;
3 pupil (*eye*)

dubh *vti, pres part* **a' dubhadh,** blacken

dubhach *adj* 1 sad; 2 moody

dubhadh, dubhaidh, dubhaidhean *nm*
1 blackening; 2 (*astronomy*) eclipse

dubhag, dubhaig, dubhagan *nf* (*anat*) kidney

dubh-aigeann *nm* 1 ocean; 2 abyss

dubhan, *gen* & *pl* **dubhain** *nm* hook

dubhar, *gen* **dubhair** *nm* shade, shadow

Dùbhlachd & **Dùdlachd** *nf used with art,*
an Dùbhlachd December

dùbhlan *nm* challenge

dùbhlanach *adj* challenging

dùblaich *vti, pres part* **a' dùblachadh,** double

dùdach, dùdaiche, dùdaichean *nmf* &
dùdag, dùdaig, dùdagan *nf* 1 bugle;
2 hooter

duibhre *nf* dusk

duibhreachadh, *gen* **duibhreachaidh**
  nm shading

duibhrich *vti, pres part* **a'**
  duibhreachadh, shade

dùil[1], **dùile**, **dùilean** *nf* 1 hope;
  2 expectation

dùil[2], *gen* **dùile**, *pl* **dùil(t)ean**, *gen pl* **dùl**
  nf 1 creature; 2 (*chemistry etc*) element

duileasg, *gen* **duilisg** *nm* dulse

duilgheadas, **duilgheadais**,
  duilgheadasan *nm* difficulty

duilich *adj* 1 difficult; 2 sorry; 3 *in expr*
  tha sin duilich! that's a pity

duilleach, *gen* **duillich** *nm* foliage

duille, **duille**, **duillean** *nf* sheath

duilleachan, *gen & pl* **duilleachain** *nm*
  leaflet

duilleag, **duilleige**, **duilleagan** *nf* 1 leaf
  (*tree etc*); 2 sheet (*paper*); 3 page

dùin *vti, pres part* **a' dùnadh**, close

duine, **duine**, **daoine** *nm* 1 man;
  2 person; 3 husband; 4 *in pl* one's folks;
  5 *in excl* **dhuine! dhuine!** oh dear! oh
  dear!

duinealas, *gen* **duinealais** *nm*
  1 manliness; 2 decisiveness

duineil *adj* 1 manly; 2 mannish; 3 decisive

dùinte *adj* 1 closed; 2 introvert

dùisg *vti, pres part* **a' dùsgadh**, wake

Duitseach, *gen & pl* **Duitsich** *nm*
  Dutchman, *also adj* **Duitseach** Dutch

dùn, *gen* **dùin**, *pl* **dùin** & **dùintean** *nm*
  1 heap; 2 fortress; 3 hill

dùnadh, **dùnaidh**, **dùnaidhean** *nm*
  closing, cadence

dùnan, *gen & pl* **dùnain** *nm, dimin of*
  dùn, dung-heap

dup *vti, pres part* **a' dupadh**, dip (*sheep*)

dùr *adj* 1 stubborn; 2 stolid

dùrachd, **dùrachd**, **dùrachdan** *nm*
  1 earnestness; 2 good will

dùrachdach *adj* 1 serious; 2 eager

dùraig *vi, pres part* **a' dùraigeadh**, dare

durcan, *gen & pl* **durcain** *nm* pine cone

dùrdail, *gen* **dùrdaile** *nf* cooing

dùsal, *gen & pl* **dùsail** *nm* snooze

dusan, *gen & pl* **dusain** *nm* dozen

dùsgadh, *gen* **dùsgaidh** awakening

duslach, *gen* **duslaich** *nm* dust

dust *nm* dust

dustach *adj* dusty

dustaig *vti, pres part* **a' dustaigeadh**,
  dust

dustair, **dustair**, **dustairean** *nm* duster

dùthaich, **dùthcha**, **dùthchannan** *nf*
  1 country; 2 homeland; 3 countryside

dùthchail *adj* rural

dùthchas, *gen* **dùthchais** *nm* 1 ancestral
  land; 2 cultural inheritance

dùthchasach *adj* 1 native; 2 hereditary

dùthchasach, *gen & pl* **dùthchasaich**
  nmf native

E

e *pron m* he, him

eabar, *gen* eabair *nm* mire, mud

eabarach *adj* muddy

Eabhra *nf (lang)* Hebrew

Eabhrach *adj* Hebrew

eacarsaich, eacarsaiche,
eacarsaichean *nf* exercise

each, *gen & pl* eich *nm* horse

each-aibhne, *gen & pl* eich-aibhne *nm*
hippopotamus

eachdraiche, eachdraiche,
eachdraichean *nm* historian

eachdraidh, eachdraidhe,
eachdraidhean *nf* history

eachdraidheil *adj* historical

eachraidh *nm* cavalry

eaconamachd *nf* economics

eaconomaidh, eaconomaidh,
eaconomaidhean *nmf* economy

eaconomair, eaconomair,
eaconomairean *nm* economist

Eadailteach, *gen & pl* Eadailtich *nm*
Italian, *also adj* Eadailteach Italian

Eadailt *nf, used with art,* an Eadailt Italy

Eadailtis *nf, used with art, (lang)* an
Eadailtis Italian

eadar *prep* 1 between; 2 among; 3 both; 4
in compounds inter-

eadarach *adj* interim

eadar-aghaidh, eadar-aghaidhe,
eadar-aghaidhean *nf* interface

eadaraibh, eadarainn *prep prons, see*
eadar

eadar-dhealachadh, eadar-
dhealachaidh, eadar-
dhealachaidhean *nm* 1 distinguishing;
2 difference

eadar-dhealaich *vt, pres part* ag eadar-
dhealachadh, differentiate

eadar-dhealaichte *adj* distinct

eadar-lìon, eadar-lìn, eadar-lìontan
nm, usu with art, an t-eadar-lìon the
internet

eadar-nàiseanta *adj* international

eadar-sholas, *gen & pl* eadar-sholais
nm twilight

eadar-theangachadh, eadar-
theangachaidh, eadar-
theangachaidhean *nm* translation

eadar-theangaich *vt, pres part* ag
eadar-theangachadh, translate

eadar-theangair, eadar-theangair,
eadar-theangairean *nm* translator

èadhar, *gen* èadhair *nf* air

eadhon *adv* even

eag, eige, eagan *nf* notch

eagach *adj* notched

eagal/feagal, *gen* (f)eagail *nm* fear, fright

eagalach *adj* 1 fearful; 2 terrible

eaglais, eaglaise, eaglaisean *nf* church

eala, eala(idh), ealachan *nf* swan

èalaidh *vi, pres part* ag èala(i)dh, creep,
sneak

ealain, *gen* ealaine, *pl* ealain(ean), *gen
pl* ealain *nf* art

ealamh *adj* nimble

ealanta *adj* 1 artistic; 2 expert

ealantach, *gen & pl* ealantaich *nm* expert

eallach, *gen & pl* eallaich *nm* burden

ealt(a), ealta, ealtan *nf* flock

ealtainn, ealtainne, ealtainnean *nf*
razor

eanchainn, eanchainne, eanchainnean
nmf brain

eangarra *adj* irritable

eanraich, *gen* eanraiche *nf* soup

ear *nf* east

earalachadh, earalachaidh,
earalachaidhean *nm* 1 exhorting;
2 caution

earalaich *vt, pres part* ag earalachadh,
1 exhort; 2 caution

earalas, *gen* earalais *nm* caution

earb *vti, pres part* ag earbsa(dh), 1 (*vi*)
trust; 2 (*vt*) entrust

earb(a), earba, earbaichean *nf* roe-deer

earball, *gen & pl* earbaill *nm* tail

earbsa *nf* trust

earbsach *adj* 1 trusting; 2 trustworthy

eàrlas, *gen & pl* eàrlais *nm (fin)* advance

earrach, *gen & pl* earraich *nm (season)*
spring

arrann, earrainn, earrannan *nf*
1 section; 2 (*fin*) share,

arranta *adj* limited

as, easa, easan *nm* waterfall

as(-) *prefix corres to Eng* in-, un-, dis- *etc*

asag, easaig, easagan *nf* pheasant

as-aonta, eas-aonta, eas-aontan *nf*
disagreement

asbaig, easbaig, easbaigean *nm* bishop

asbaigeach, *gen & pl* **Easbaigich** *nm*
Episcopalian

asbhaidh, easbhaidhe, easbhaidhean
nf 1 lack; 2 defect

asbhaidheach *adj* 1 needy; 2 defective

ascaraid *m* a foe

as-chruthach *adj* abstract

asgaidh *adj* active, willing

asgann, easgainn, easgannan *nf* eel

as-umhail *adj* disobedient

as-urramach *adj* dishonourable

atarra (*also* **eatorra**) *prep pron, see*
eadar

athar, eathair, eathraichean *nmf, also*
eithear, eithir, eithrichean *nmf,* boat

ibhinn *adj* funny

ibhleag, èibhleige, èibhleagan *nf*
ember

ideadh, èididh, èididhean *nm* dress

idheann, *gen* **eidhne** *nf* ivy

ifeachd *nf* effect

ifeachdach *adj* effective

ifeachdas, *gen* **èifeachdais** *nf* efficiency,
effectiveness

igeantach *adj* compulsory

igh, èighe, èighe(ach)an *nf* shout

igh, *gen* **eighe** *nf, also* **eighre,** *gen*
eighre *nf, also* **deigh,** *gen* **deighe** *nf* ice

ighe, eighe, eigheachan *nf* (*metalwork*
etc) file

igh & èibh *vi, pres part* **ag èigheach(d),**
shout

igheachd *nf* shouting

igin *a suffix corres to Eng* some-,
appended to nouns

ginn *nf* 1 difficulty; 2 necessity;
3 violence; 4 *in expr* **air èiginn** hardly

ginneach *adj* difficult, desperate

gneachair, èigneachair,
èigneachairean *nm* rapist

gnich *vt, pres part* **ag èigneachadh,**
1 force; 2 rape

Eilbheis *nf, used with art,* **an Eilbheis**
Switzerland

Eilbheiseach, *gen & pl* **Eilbheisich** *nm*
Swiss, *also adj* **Eilbheiseach** Swiss

èildear, èildeir, èildearan *nm* (church)
elder

eile *adj* other, another, else

eileamaid, eileamaide, eileamaidean
nf element

eilean, eilein, eileanan *nm* island

eileanach, *gen & pl* **eileanaich** *nm*
islander

eilid, èilde, èil(i)dean *nf* hind (*deer*)

eilthireach, *gen & pl* **eilthirich** *nm*
1 foreigner; 2 exile; 3 pilgrim

eilthireachd *nf* 1 exile; 2 emigration

einnsean, einnsein, einnseanan *nm*
engine

einnseanair, einnseanair,
einnseanairean *nm* engineer

Èipheit *nf, used with art,* **an Èipheit**
Egypt

Èipheiteach, *gen & pl* **Èipheitich,**
Egyptian, *also adj* **Èipheiteach** Egyptian

eireachdail *adj* handsome

eireag, eireig(e), eireagan *nf* pullet

Èireannach, *gen & pl* **Èireannaich** *nm*
Irishman, *also adj,* **Èireannach** Irish

èirich *vi, pres part* **ag èirigh,** 1 get up;
2 rise up; 3 happen

eiridinn *nm* nursing

eiridnich *vt, pres part* **ag**
eiridneachadh, nurse

èirig, èirige, èirigean *nf* payment
(*reparation*)

èirigh *nf* rising

Èirinn, *gen* **(na h-) Èireann** *nf* Ireland

eirmseach *adj* 1 witty; 2 intelligent

eisimeil, *gen* **eisimeile** *nf,* dependence

eisimeileach *adj* dependent

eisimeileachd *nf* dependence

eisimpleir, eisimpleir, eisimpleirean
nm example

èist *vi, pres part* **ag èisteachd,** listen

èisteachd *nf* 1 listening, hearing;
2 audience

eitean, *gen* **eitein & eitne,** *pl* **eitnean** *nm*
1 kernel; 2 core

eòlach *adj* 1 knowledgeable; 2 acquainted

eòlaiche, eòlaiche, eòlaichean *nm*
1 expert; 2 scientist; 3 savant

eòlas, eòlais, eòlasan *nm* **1** knowledge; **2** acquaintance

eòrna *nm* barley

Eòrpa *nf* Europe, *usu* **an Roinn Eòrpa** Europe

Eòrpach, *gen & pl* **Eòrpaich** *nm* European, *also adj* **Eòrpach** European

eu(-), *occas* **ao(-),** *negating prefix, can corres to Eng* in-, un-, dis-, -less

euchd, euchd, euchdan *nm* **1** feat; **2** achievement

eucoir, eucorach, eucoirean *nf* **1** crime; **2** wrong

eu-coltach *adj* unlikely, dissimilar

eucorach, *gen & pl* **eucoraich** *nm* criminal

eud *nm* **1** jealousy; **2** zeal

eudach *adj* jealous

eudach *gen* **eudaich** *nm* jealousy

eudail/feudail, *gen* **eudail/eudalach,** *∕* **eudailean** *nf* **1** treasure, cattle; **2** *in address or excl* **m' eudail!** my darling!

eudmhor *adj* **1** jealous; **2** zealous

eu-dòchas, *gen* **eu-dòchais** *nm* hopelessness, lack of hope

eu-domhainn *adj* shallow

eug, *gen* **èig** *nm* death

eug *vi, pres part* **ag eugadh,** die

eun, *gen & pl* **eòin** *nm* bird

eun-eòlas, *gen* **eun-eòlais** *nm* ornithology

eunlaith *nf pl coll* birds

euslaint(e), euslainte, euslaintean *nf* illness

euslainteach *adj* ill, unhealthy

euslainteach, *gen & pl* **euslaintich** *nm* invalid, patient

F

fàbhar, fàbhair, fàbharan *nm* favour
fàbharach *adj* favourable
faca *pt of irreg v* **faic**
fabhra, fabhra, fabhran *nm* **1** eyelash;
2 eyelid
facal, gen facail, pl facail & faclan *nm*
1 word; **2** saying
faclach *adj* wordy
facladair, facladair, facladairean *nm*
word processor
facladaireachd *nf* word processing
faclair, faclair, faclairean *nm* dictionary
faclaireachd *nf* lexicography
facs, facsa, facsaichean *nm* fax
factaraidh, factaraidh, factaraidhean
nf factory
fad, gen faid *nm* **1** length; **2** *in expr* **air**
fad *adv* all, completely; **3 fhad is a** *conj*
while
fàd, fàid, fàdan *nm* peat
fad(a) *adj* **1** long, far, (*of people*) tall; **2** *in*
comparative exprs **fada nas fheàrr,**
fada nas sine far/much better, far/much
older; **3** *in expr* **fad' às** distant, remote; **4**
in compounds long-
fadachd *nf, also* **fadal, gen fadail** *nm,*
1 longing; **2** weariness
fadalach *adj* **1** late; **2** tedious
fadhail, gen fadhail & fadhlach, pl
fadhlaichean *nf* tidal ford
fàg *vt, pres part* **a' fàgail,** leave
fàgail, fàgaile *nf* leaving
faic *vt irreg, pres part* **a' faicinn,** see
faiceall, gen faicill *nf* care, caution
faiceallach *adj* careful
faiceadh, faiceam, faiceamaid *pts of*
irreg v **faic**
faiche, faiche, faichean *nf* meadow, lawn
faicinn *nf* seeing
faicsinneach *adj* visible
faide *nf* length
fàidh, fàidhe, fàidhean *nm* prophet
fàidheadaireachd, fàidheadaireachd,
fàideadaireachdan *nf* prophecy
faidhir, faidhreach, faidhrichean *nf*
fair

faidhle, gen faidhle, pl faidhlean &
faidhlichean *nm* (*document*) file
faigh *vt irreg, pres part* **a' faighinn & a'**
faotainn, 1 get, obtain; **2** find; **3 faigh**
a-mach find out; **4** *in expr* **faigh**
seachad air get over; **5** *in expr* **faigh**
air manage to
faigheadh, faigheam, faigheamaid *pts*
of irreg v **faigh**
faighean, faighein, faigheanan *nm*
vagina
faighinn *nf & faotainn* *nf* getting, finding
faighneach/faighneachail *adj* inquisitive
faighneachd *nf* asking
faighnich *vi, pres part* **a' faighneachd,**
ask
fail, faile, failean *nf* (*agric*) sty
failc *vti, pres part* **a' failceadh,** bathe
faileas, faileis, faileasan *nm* **1** shadow;
2 reflection
faileasach *adj* shadowy
faillean, faillein, failleanan *nm* eardrum
fàillig *vti, pres part* **a' fàilligeadh,** fail
fàilligeadh, fàilligidh, fàilligidhean *nm*
failing
fàillinn, fàillinne, fàillinnean *nf* failing
failm/ailm, gen (f)ailme, pl (f)ailmean
nf (boat's) tiller
failmean/falman, gen failmein, pl
failmeanan *nm* kneecap
fail-mhuc, fail-mhuc, failean-mhuc *nf*
pigsty
fàilte, fàilte, fàiltean *nf* **1** welcome;
2 greeting, salute
fàilteach & fàilteachail *adj* welcoming
fàilteachadh, gen fàilteachaidh *nm*
welcoming, greeting
fàiltich *vt, pres part* **a' fàilteachadh,**
welcome, salute
fàiltiche, fàiltiche, fàiltichean *nm*
receptionist
faing, fainge, faingean *nf, also* **fang,**
faing, fangan *nm*, **1** sheepfold; **2** fank
fàinne, fàinne, fàinneachan *nmf* ring
fàinne-solais, fàinne-solais,
fàinneachan-solais *nf* halo
fairche, fairche, fairchean *nm* mallet

faire, faire, fairean *nf* **1** guarding, watching; **2** guard

fàire, fàire, fàirean *nf* **1** horizon; **2** *in expr* **faigh** *v* **fàire air** catch sight of

faireachdainn, faireachdainne, faireachdainnean *nf* feeling

fàireag, fàireig, fàireagan *nf* gland

fairge, *gen* **fairge,** *pl* **fairgeachan** & **fairgeannan** *nf* ocean, sea

fairich *vti, pres part* **a' faireachdainn** & **a' faireachadh, 1** (*vti*) feel; **2** (*vt*) smell

fairtlich *vi, pres part* **a' fairtleachadh,** *also* **faillich** *vi, pres part* **a' faillicheadh,** overcome, defeat

faisg *adj* near, close

fàisg *vt, pres part* **a' fàsgadh,** squeeze

faisge *nf* nearness

fàisneachd *nf* prophecy

fàisnich *vti, pres part* **a' fàisneachadh,** prophesy

faite, faite, faitichean *nf* smile

fàitheam, fàitheim, fàitheaman *nm* hem

faitich *vi, pres part* **a' faiteachadh,** smile

fàl, *gen* & *pl* **fàil** *nm* **1** hedge; **2** divot

falach, *gen* **falaich** *nm* hiding

falach-fead *nm* hide-and-seek

falachd *nf* feud

falaich *vti, pres part* **a' falach** & **a' falachadh,** hide

falaichte *adj* hidden

falaid, *gen* **falaide** *nm* varnish

falamh *adj* **1** empty; **2** hollow

fal(a)mhachd *nf* **1** emptiness; **2** void

falbh *vi, pres part* **a' falbh,** go, depart

fallain *adj* healthy

fallas, *gen* **fallais** *nm* sweat

fallasach *adj* sweaty

fallsa *adj* false

falmadair, falmadair, falmadairean *nm* helm (*boat*)

falmhachadh, *gen* **falmhachaidh** *nm* emptying

falmhaich *vti, pres part* **a' falmhachadh,** empty

falt, *gen* **fuilt** *nm* hair (*human head*)

famh, faimh, famhan *nmf* mole (*animal*)

famhair, famhair, famhairean *nm, also* **fuamhaire, fuamhaire, fuamhairean** *nm,* **1** giant; **2** hero

fan *vi, pres part* **a' fantainn, a' fantail** & **a' fanachd, 1** wait; **2** live, stay

fanaid, *gen* **fanaide** *nf* mockery

fànas, fànais, fànasan *nm* **1** space (*extraterrestrial*); **2** void

fa-near *adv* **1** *in expr* **fa-near dhut** on your mind; **2** *as noun, in expr* **thoir** *v* **fa-near (do)** notice

fann *adj* weak, feeble, faint

fannachadh, *gen* **fannachaidh** *nm* weakening

fannaich *vti, pres part* **a' fannachadh, 1** weaken; **2** (*vi*) faint

fanntaig *vi, pres part* **a' fanntaigeadh,** faint

faobhar, faobhair, faobharan *nm* edge (*blade etc*)

faobharachadh, *gen* **faobharachaidh** *nm* sharpening

faobharaich *vt, pres part* **a' faobharachadh,** sharpen

faochag, faochaig, faochagan *nf* whelk, winkle

faod *vti def, no pres part,* may, can

faoighe *nf* cadging

faoileag, faoileig, faoileagan *nf* seagull

faoilidh *adj* **1** hospitable; **2** frank

Faoilleach, *gen* **Faoillich** *nm, also* **Faoilteach,** *gen* **Faoiltich** *nm, used with art* **am Faoilleach, am Faoilteach** January

faoin *adj* **1** silly; **2** futile

faoineas, *gen* **faoineis** *nm* **1** silliness; **2** futility

faoinsgeul, *gen* & *pl* **faoinsgeòil** *nm* **1** myth; **2** idle talk

faoisid, faoiside, faoisidean *nf* confession

faoisidich *vti, pres part* **a' faoisidich,** confess

faol, *gen* & *pl* **faoil** *nm* wolf

faothachadh/faochadh, *gen* **fao(tha)chaidh** *nm* relief

faothaich *vti, pres part* **a' fao(tha)chadh,** alleviate

far a *conj* where

faradh, faraidh, faraidhean *nm* fare, charge

far-ainm, *gen* **far-ainme,** *pl* **far-ainmean** & **far-ainmeannan** *nm* nickname

faram, *gen* **faraim** *nm* loud noise

faramach *adj* noisy

archluais, *gen* **farchluaise** *nf* eavesdropping

àrdach, fàrdaich, fàrdaichean *nf* 1 dwelling; 2 lodging

armad, *gen* **farmaid** *nm* envy

armadach *adj* envious

arpais, farpaise, farpaisean *nf* competition

arpaiseach *adj* competitive

arpaiseach, *gen & pl* **farpaisich** *nm* competitor

arranaich *vt, pres part* **a' farranachadh**, 1 tease; 2 vex

arsaing *adj* 1 wide

arsaingeachd *nf* 1 breadth; 2 extent, area; 3 *in expr* **san fharsaingeachd** generally

arspag/arspag, *gen* **(f)arspaig**, *pl* **(f)arspagan** *nf* great black-backed gull

às *adj* 1 empty; 2 uncultivated

às, *gen* **fàis** *nm* 1 growing, becoming

às *vi, pres part* **a' fàs**, grow

àsach, fàsaich, fàsaichean *nmf* 1 desert; 2 wilderness

àsachadh, *gen* **fàsachaidh** *nm* emptying, depopulating

àsaich *vt, pres part* **a' fàsachadh**, empty, depopulate

àsail *adj* desolate

asan, fasain, fasanan *nm* fashion, custom

asanta *adj* fashionable

asgach *adj* sheltering, sheltered

asgadh, fasgaidh, fasgaidhean *nm* shelter

àsgadh, *gen* **fàsgaidh** *nm* squeezing

asgain *vt, pres part* **a' fasgnadh**, winnow

astachadh/fastadh, *gen* **fastachaidh/ fastaidh** *nm* hiring

astaich/fastaidh, *vt, pres part* **a' fastachadh & a' fastadh**, hire, employ

astaidhear, fastaidheir, fastaidhearan *nm* employer

àth *nm* 1 cause; 2 opportunity; 3 *in expr* **gabh** *v* **fàth air** take (unfair) advantage of

athann, *gen & pl* **fathainn** *nm* rumour

eabhas, *gen* **feabhais** *nm* improvement, excellence, *in expr* **rach** *v* **am feabhas** improve, get better

eachd, feachd, feachdan *nf* army, force

ead, fead, feadan *nf* whistle (*noise*)

ead *vi, pres part* **a' feadail**, whistle

feadag, feadaige, feadagan *nf* 1 whistle (*instrument*); 2 plover

feadaireachd *nf, also* **feadalaich** *nf, &* **feadarsaich** *nf* whistling

feadan, feadain, feadanan *nm* 1 chanter; 2 tube, pipe, spout

feadarail *adj* federal

feadhainn, *gen* **feadhna** *nf* some

feàirrde *adj* better, made better, *in expr* **is fheàirrde e** (*etc*) he (*etc*) is the better for

fealladh, feallaidh, feallaidhean *nm* foul play

fealla-dhà *nf* joking

feall-fhalach, feall-fhalaich, feall-fhalaichean *nm* an ambush

feallsanach, *gen & pl* **feallsanaich** *nm* philosopher

feallsanachd, feallsanachd, feallsanachdan *nf* philosophy

feallsanachd-maise *nf* aesthetics

fealltach *adj* fraudulent

feamainn, *gen* **feamann, feamnach &** **feamad**, *nf* seaweed

feannag¹, feannaige, feannagan *nf* crow

feannag², feannaige, feannagan *nf* rig, lazybed

feanntag, feanntaige, feanntagan *nf, &* **deanntag, deanntaige, deanntagan** *nf*, nettle

feansa, feansa, feansaichean *nmf* fence

feansaig *vti, pres part* **a' feansaigeadh**, fence

fear, *gen & pl* **fir** *nm* 1 man; 2 *representing a m sing n*, one

fearachas, *gen* **fearachais** *nm* virility

fearail *adj* manly

fearalachd *nf* manliness

fearann, *gen* **fearainn** *nm* land

fearas-chuideachd, *gen* **fearais-chuideachd** *nf* fun, pastime

fearas-feise *nf* homosexuality

fear-brèige, *gen & pl* **fir-bhrèige** *nm* puppet

fearg, *gen* **feirge** *nf* anger

feargach *adj* angry

feàrna *nf* alder

feàrr *adj* 1 better; 2 *usu with v* is, *eg* **an tè as** (*for* **a is**) **fheàrr** the best one; 3 *in expr* **b' fheàrr dhomh** (etc) . . . I (etc) had better . . .

feart¹ & feairt, *gen* **feirt**, *pl* **feartan** *nf* attention

feart², **fearta**, **feartan** *nm* attribute

feasgar, *gen* **feasgair**, *pl* **feasgair** & **feasgaran/feasgraichean** *nm* afternoon, evening

fèath, **fèatha**, **fèathan** *nmf* (*weather*) calm

fèichear, **fèicheir**, **fèichearan** *nm* debtor

fèileadh & **èileadh** (*also* **(f)èile**), *gen* **(f)èilidh**, *pl* **(f)èilidhean** (*also* **(f)èilichean** & **(f)èileachan**) *nm* kilt

fèill, **fèille**, **fèill(t)ean** *nf* 1 festival; 2 fair; 3 market; 4 (*economics*) demand

fèin *reflexive pron* (*usu lenited as* **fhèin**, *after* **mi** & **sinn** *often becomes* **fhìn**) 1 *corres to Eng* -self; 2 *emphasising identity*, **rinn mi fhìn e** I (*emph*) did it; 3 own; 4 even; 5 same; 6 *as emphasising element*; 7 *as noun* **am fèin** the self

fèin-eachdraidh, **fèin-eachdraidhe**, **fèin-eachdraidhean** *nf* autobiography

fèinealachd *nf* selfishness

fèineil *adj* selfish

fèin-ghluaiseach *adj* automatic

fèis, **fèise**, **fèisean** *nf* festival

feis(e), *gen* **feise** *nf* sexual intercourse

fèist, **fèiste**, **fèistean** *nf* feast

feiste, **feiste**, **feistean** *nf* tether

fèistear, **fèisteir**, **fèistearan** *nm* entertainer

fèisteas, *gen* **fèisteis**, *nm* entertainment

feith *vi, pres part* **a' feitheamh**, 1 wait; 2 stay

fèith, **fèithe**, **fèithean** *nf* 1 muscle; 2 sinew; 3 vein

fèith(e), **fèithe**, **fèitheachan** *nf* bog

fèitheach *adj* 1 muscular; 2 sinewy

feitheamh, *gen* **feithimh** *nm* waiting

feòil, *gen* **feòla(dh)** *nf* 1 meat; 2 flesh

feòladair, **feòladair**, **feòladairean** *nm* butcher

feòlmhor *adj* fleshy, carnal

feòlmhorachd *nf* sensuality

feòrag, **feòraig**, **feòragan** *nf* squirrel

feòrachadh, *gen* **feòrachaidh** *nm* asking

feòraich *vi, pres part* **a' feòrachadh**, ask

feuch, *vti, pres part* **a' feuchainn** 1 try; 2 behold

feudar *n* 1 possibility; 2 *in expr* **'s fheudar dhomh** (*etc*) I (*etc*) must

feum, *gen* **feuma** & **fèim** *nm* 1 need; 2 use, good; 3 *in expr* **dèan** *v* **feum** be useful

feum *vti def, no pres part*, 1 must; 2 (*vt*) need

feumach *adj* needy

feumail *adj* 1 useful; 2 necessary

feumalachd *nf* usefulness

feur, *gen* **feòir** *nm* 1 grass; 2 hay

feurach *adj* grassy

feurach, *gen* **feuraich** *nm* grazing

feuraich *vt, pres part* **a' feurachadh**, graze

feusag, **feusaig**, **feusagan** *nf* beard

feusgan, *gen* & *pl* **feusgain** *nm* mussel

fhathast *adv* 1 yet; 2 still; 3 again

fhuair *pt of irreg v* **faigh**

fiabhras, **fiabhrais**, **fiabhrasan** *nm* fev◖

fiacail(l), **fiacla**, **fiaclan** *nf* tooth

fiach *adj* worthwhile

fiach, **fèich**, **fiachan** *nm* 1 value; 2 debt

fiaclach *adj* 1 toothed, dental

fiaclair(e), **fiaclaire**, **fiaclairean** *nm* dentist, **ionad fiaclaire** *m* a dental surgery

fiadh, *gen* & *pl* **fèidh** *nm* deer

fiadhaich *adj* wild

fial & **fialaidh** *adj* 1 generous; 2 liberal

fiamh, *gen* **fiamha** *nm* 1 hue; 2 fear; 3 (*transient*) look

fianais, **fianais**, **fianaisean** *nf* 1 witnessing; 2 evidence; 3 sight; 4 presence

fiar *adj* 1 bent; 2 oblique; 3 squinting; 4 wily

fiar & **fiaraich** *vti, pres part* **a' fiaradh**, 1 bend; 2 distort

fiaradh, *gen* **fiaraidh** *nm* 1 bending; 2 a squint (*in eye*); 3 slant

fiathaich *vt, pres part* **a' fiathachadh**, invite

fichead, **fichid**, **ficheadan** *nm* twenty

ficheadamh *adj* twentieth

ficsean, *gen* **ficsein** *nm* fiction

fìdeag, **fìdeig**, **fìdeagan** *nf* whistle

fidheall, *gen* **fìdhle**, *dat* **fidhill**, *pl* **fìdhlean** *nf* fiddle

fidhlear, **fìdhleir**, **fìdhlearan** *nm* fiddl◖

fidir *vti, pres part* **a' fidreadh**, appreciat◖

figear, **figeir**, **figearan** *nm* figure

figearail *adj* digital

figh *vti, pres part* **a' fighe(adh)**, 1 weave 2 knit

fighe *nf* 1 weaving; 2 knitting

ìgheachan, *gen & pl* **fìgheachain** *nm* pigtail

ìgheadair, **fìgheadair**, **fìgheadairean** *nm* **1** weaver; **2** knitter

ìghte *adj* **1** woven; **2** knitted

ìleanta *adj* eloquent, fluent

ìlidh, **filidh**, **filidhean** *nm* poet

ìll *vt, pres part* **a' filleadh**, **1** fold; **2** braid, plait; **3** wrap (up)

ìlleadh, *gen* **fillidh**, *pl* **filltean** & **filleachan** *nm* folding, pleating, braiding

ìllte *adj* **1** folded, pleated, plaited; **2** implicit

ìlm, **film**, **filmichean** *nm* film

ìne, **fine**, **fineachan** *nf* **1** tribe; **2** clan

ìnealta *adj* elegant

ìodh, *gen* **fiodha** *nm* wood, timber

ìodhrach, *gen* **fiodhraich**, *nm* timber, wood

ìogais, **fìogais**, **fìogaisean** *nf, also* **fìge**, **fìge**, **fìgean** *nf* fig

ìolan, **fiolain**, **fiolanan** *nm, also* **fiolan-gòbhlach**, **fiolain-ghòbhlach**, **fiolanan-gòbhlach** *nm*, earwig

ìon, *gen* **fìona** *nm* wine

ìonan, *gen & pl* **fìonain** *nm* vine

ìon-dhearc, **fìon-dhearc**, **fìon-dhearcan** *nf* grape

ìon-geur, *gen* **fìon-ghèir** *nm* vinegar

ìonn *adj* white

ìonnach *adj* hairy

ìonnadh, *gen* **fionnaidh** *nm* hair (*animal*)

ìonnairidh *nf* evening

ìonnan-feòir, *gen & pl* **fionnain-fheòir** *nm* grasshopper

ìonnar *adj* cool

ìonnarachadh, *gen* **fionnarachaidh** *nm* **1** cooling; **2** refrigeration

ìonnaraich *vti, pres part* **a' fionnarachadh**, cool, refrigerate

ìonnlainn *nf, used with art* **an Fhionnlainn** Finland

ìonnsgeul, *gen & pl* **fionnsgeòil** *nm* legend

ìor *adj* **1** true; **2** real; **3** *as emphasising element*; **4** *in expr* **mas fhìor** pretending

ìos, *gen* **fiosa** *nm* **1** knowledge; **2** *in expr* **tha fios agam (etc)** I (*etc*) know; **3** information; **4** *in expr* **tha fios** obviously; **5** *in expr* **gun fhios nach** *conj* lest

fiosaiche, **fiosaiche**, **fiosaichean** *nm* **1** prophet; **2** fortune teller

fiosrach *adj* knowledgeable

fiosrachadh, **fiosrachaidh**, **fiosrachaidhean** *nm* information

fireann *adj* masculine, male

fireann-boireann *adj* androgynous

fireannach, *gen & pl* **fireannaich** *nm* male

fireannta *adj* masculine

fìrinn, **fìrinne**, **fìrinnean** *nf* **1** truth; **2** fact

fìrinneach *adj* truthful, true

fitheach, *gen & pl* **fithich** *nm* raven

fiù *nm* **1** worth; **2** *in expr* **fiù agus/is** even, as much as

fiùdalach *adj* feudal

flaitheas, *gen* **flaitheis** *nm* heaven, paradise

flanainn, **flanainne**, **flanainnean** *nf* flannel

flat, **flat**, **flataichean** *nm* **1** flat (*dwelling*); **2** saucer

fleadh, **fleadha**, **fleadhan** *nm* feast

fleadhach *adj* festive

fleasgach, *gen & pl* **fleasgaich** *nm* **1** youth; **2** bachelor

fleisg, **fleisge**, **fleisgean** *nf* flex

fleòdradh, *gen* **fleòdraidh** *nm* floating

flin, **flinne** *nm* sleet

fliuch *adj* wet

fliuch *vt, pres part* **a' fliuchadh**, wet

fliuchadh, *gen* **fliuchaidh** *nm* wetting

flùr¹, **flùir**, **flùraichean** *nm* flower

flùr², *gen* **flùir** *nm* flour

flùranach *adj* flowery

fo *prep* under, affected by

fodar, *gen* **fodair** *nm* fodder

fògair *vt, pres part* **a' fògradh** & **a' fògairt**, exile

fògarrach/fògrach, *gen & pl* **fòg(ar)raich** *nm* exile

foghain *vi, pres part* **a' fòghnadh**, suffice

foghar, **foghair**, **fogharan** *nm* **1** harvest; **2** autumn

foghlaim *vt, pres part* **a' foghlam**, educate, learned

foghlaimte, *also* **foghlaimichte**, *adj* educated

foghlam, *gen* **foghlaim** *nm* education, learning, scholarship

fòghnadh, *gen* **fòghnaidh** *nm* sufficiency,

fòghnan, fòghnain, fòghnanan *nm* thistle

fògradh, *gen* **fògraidh** *nm, also* **fògairt** *nf* banishment

fòid & **fòd,** *gen* **fòide,** *pl* **fòidean** *nf* 1 sod; 2 clod; 3 peat

foighidinn, *gen* **foighidinne** *nf* patience

foighidneach *adj* patient

foileig, foileig, foileagan *nf* pancake

foill, *gen* **foille** *nf* 1 deceit; 2 cheating; 3 fraud

foilleil *adj* 1 deceitful; 2 treacherous; 3 fraudulent

foillseachadh, *gen* **foillseachaidh** *nm* 1 publishing; 2 revealing

foillsear, foillseir, foillsearan *nm* (*IT*) monitor

foillsich *vt, pres part* **a' foillseachadh** 1 publish; 2 reveal

foillsichear, foillsicheir, foillsichearan *nm* publisher

foinne, foinne, foinnean *nm* wart

foireann, foirinn, foireannan *nm* 1 gang; 2 personnel

foirfe *adj* perfect

foirfeach, *gen* & *pl* **foirfich** *nm* elder (*of church*)

foirfeachd *nf* perfection

foirm, foirm, foirmean *nm* form (*document*)

foirmeil *adj* formal

fòirneart, *gen* **fòirneirt** *nm* violence

fois, *gen* **foise** *nf* rest

foiseil *adj* restful

fo-lèine, fo-lèine, fo-lèintean *nf* vest

follais *nf* evidentness

follaiseach *adj* 1 evident; 2 public

fòn, fòn, fònaichean *nmf* phone (call)

fòn *vi, pres part* **a' fònadh,** *also* **fònaig** *vi, pres part* **a' fònaigeadh** (*with* **gu**), phone

fonn, *gen* & *pl* **fuinn** *nm* 1 tune; 2 mood

fonnmhor *adj* tuneful

for *nm* attention

fo-rathad, fo-rathaid, fo-rathaidean *nm* underpass

forc(a), *gen* **forca,** *pl* **forcan** & **forcaichean** *nf* fork

fòrladh, *gen* **fòrlaidh** *nm* furlough

forsair, forsair, forsairean *nm* forester

fortan, *gen* **fortain** *nm* fortune

fortanach *adj* lucky

for-thalla, for-thalla, for-thallachan *nm* foyer

fosgail *vti, pres part* **a' fosgladh,** open

fosgailte *adj* 1 open; 2 public

fosgailteachd *ni* openness

fosgarra *adj* (*of person*) 1 frank; 2 approachable

fosgladh *gen* **fosglaidh** *nm* opening

fosglair, fosglair, fosglairean *nm* opener

fo-sgrìobhadh, fo-sgrìobhaidh, fo-sgrìobhaidhean *nm* 1 postscript; 2 a subscription

fradharc, fradhairc *nm* sight

Fraing *nf, used with art* **an Fhraing** France

Fraingis *nf, usu with art,* (*lang*) **an Fhraingis** French

Frangach, *gen* & *pl* **Frangaich** *nm* Frenchman, *also adj,* **Frangach** French

fraoch, *gen* **fraoich** *nm* heather

fraoidhneas, fraoidhneis, fraoidhneasan *nm* fringe

fras, froise, frasan *nf* 1 shower; 2 (*coll*) seed

fras *vi, pres part* **a' frasadh,** shower

frasair, frasair, frasairean *nm* (*bathroom*) shower

freagair *vti, pres part* **a' freagairt,** 1 answer; 2 suit; 3 match

freagairt, freagairt, freagairtean *nf* answer(ing)

freagarrach *adj* suitable

frèam, frèama, frèamaichean *nm* frame

freastail, *vti, pres part* **a' freastal,** attend

freastal, *gen* **freastail** *nm* 1 attending; 2 providence

freiceadan, freiceadain, freiceadanan *nm* watch, guard

freumh, freumha, freumh(aiche)an *nm* root

frìde, frìde, frìdean *nf, also* **meanbh-fhrìde** *nf,* insect

frids, frids, fridsichean *nm* fridge

frighig *vt, pres part* **a' frighigeadh,** fry

frioghan, *gen* & *pl* **frioghain** *nm* bristle

frionas, *gen* **frionais** *nm* 1 annoyance; 2 touchiness

frionasach *adj* 1 fretful; 2 irritable; 3 vexing

frìth, frìthe, frìthean *nf* 1 deer forest; 2 moor

frith-ainm, *gen* **frith-ainme**, *pl* **frith-ainmean** & **frith-ainmeannan** *nm* nickname

frithealadh, *gen* **frithealaidh** *nm* attending

frithearra *adj* touchy

fritheil *vti*, *pres part* **a' frithealadh**, serve

frith-rathad, frith-rathaid, frith-rathaidean *nm* path, track

froga, *gen* **froga**, *pl* **frogaichean** *nm* frock

fuachd, fuachd, fuachdan *nmf* cold

fuadachadh, *gen* **fuadachaidh** *nm*, *also* **fuadach, fuadaich, fuadaichean** *nm*, banishing

fuadaich *vt*, *pres part* **a' fuadachadh** & **a' fuadach**, banish, exile

fuadain *adj* artificial

fuadan, *gen* **fuadain** *nm* **1** wandering, **air fhuadan** *adv* wandering

fuaigh/fuaigheil *vti*, *pres part* **a' fuaigheal**, sew, stitch, seam

fuaigheal, *gen* **fuaigheil** *nm* sewing, stitching, seaming

fuaighte *adj* **1** sewn, stitched; **2** connected

fuaim, fuaime, fuaimean *nmf* noise

fuaimeadair, fuaimeadair, fuaimeadairean *nm* megaphone

fuaimneach *adj* noisy

fuaimnich *vt*, *pres part* **a' fuaimneachadh**, (*lang*) pronounce

fuaimneachadh, *gen* **fuaimneachaidh** *nm* (*lang*) pronunciation

fuaimreag, fuaimreig, fuaimreagan *nf* vowel

fual, *gen* **fuail** *nm* urine

fuamhaire *see* **famhair**

fuar *adj* cold

fuarachadh, *gen* **fuarachaidh** *nm* cooling

fuaradair, fuaradair, fuaradairean *nm* fridge

fuaraich *vti*, *pres part* **a' fuarachadh**, cool

fuaraidh *adj* chilly, damp

fuaran, *gen* **fuarain**, *pl* **fuarain** & **fuaranan** *nm* spring, well

fuasgail *vt*, *pres part* **a' fuasgladh**, **1** liberate; **2** untie; **3** solve

fuasgladh, *gen* **fuasglaidh** *nm* loosening, solving

fuath, fuatha, fuathan *nm* hate

fuathach *adj* hateful

fuathachadh, *gen* **fuathachaidh** *nm* hating

fuathaich *vt*, *pres part* **a' fuathachadh**, hate

fuidheall, *gen* **fuidhill** *nm* **1** relic **2** balance, remainder

fuidhleach, *gen* **fuidhlich** *nm* rubbish, refuse

fuil, *gen* **fola** & **fala**, *nf* blood

fuilear *adv* **1** too much; **2** *in expr* **chan fhuilear dhut** you need …

fuiling/fulaing *vti*, *pres part* **a' fulang**, **1** (*vi*) suffer; **2** (*vt*) bear

fuil-mìos(a), *gen* **fala-mìos(a)** *nf* menstruation

fuil(t)each *adj* bloody

fuiltean, fuiltein, fuilteana(n) *nm* (single) hair (*of head*)

fuin *vt*, *pres part* **a' fuine(adh)**, **1** bake; **2** knead

fuineadair, fuineadair, fuineadairean *nm* baker

fuineadh, *gen* **fuinidh** *nm*, *also* **fuine** *nf* baking, kneading

fuireach(d), *gen* **fuirich** *nm* staying, waiting

fuirich *vi*, *pres part* **a' fuireach(d)**, **1** stay; **2** dwell

fùirneis, fùirneis, fùrneisean *nf* furnace

fulang, *gen* **fulaing** *nm* **1** suffering; **2** endurance

fulangach *adj* **1** hardy; **2** passive

fulangas, *gen* **fulangais** *nm* **1** tolerance; **2** endurance

fulmair, fulmaire, fulmairean *nm* fulmar

furachail *adj* attentive

furan, *gen* & *pl* **furain** *nm* hospitality

furasta, *comp* **(n)as** (etc) **fhasa**, *adj* easy

furm, fuirm, fuirm(ean) *nm* **1** form, bench; **2** stool

furtachadh, *gen* **furtachaidh** *nm* consoling

furtachd *nf* consolation

furtaich *vi*, *pres part* **a' furtachadh**, console, relieve

G

gabh *vt, pres part* **a' gabhail 1** take; **2** go; **3** give, perform, deliver; **4** can, **cha ghabh sin dèanamh** that can't be done

gàbhadh, gàbhaidh, gàbhaidhean *nm* **1** danger; **2** crisis

gàbhaidh *adj* dangerous

gabhail, gabhalach, gabhalaichean *nmf* **1** taking; **2** lease; **3** a course, tack (*boat etc*); **4** welcome, reception

gabhaltach *adj* infectious

gabhaltas, *gen* **gabhaltais** *nm* **1** rented land; **2** tenancy

gach *adj* **1** each, every; **2** *in expr* **gach cuid** both

gad, goid, gadan *nm* withy

gadaiche, gadaiche, gadaichean *nm* a thief

gagach *adj* stammering

gagachd *nf* stammering

gagaire, gagaire, gagairean *nm* stammerer

Gàidheal, *gen & pl* **Gàidheil** *nm* **1** Gael; **2** Highlander

Gàidhealach, *adj* **1** Gaelic; **2** Highland

Gàidhealtachd, *nf, with art* **a' Ghàidhealtachd** the Highlands

Gàidhlig, *gen* **Gàidhlig(e)** *nf* (*lang*) Gaelic

gailbheach *adj* stormy

gailearaidh, *gen* **gailearaidh**, *pl* **gailearaidhean** *nm* gallery

gailleann, gaillinn, gailleannan *nf* storm

gainmheach, *gen* **gainmhich** *nf* sand

gainmheil *adj* sandy

gainne *nf, also* **gainnead** *nm* scarcity

gàir, gàir, gàirean *nm* cry, call

gàir *vi, pres part* **a' gàireachdainn**, laugh

gairbhe *nf, also* **gairbhead**, *gen* **gairbheid** *nm* roughness

gàirdeachas, *gen* **gàirdeachais** *nm* joy

gàirdean, gàirdein, gàirdeanan *nm* arm (*person, chair*)

gàire *nmf* laugh

gàireachdaich *nf* **1** laughing; **2** laughter

gairge *nf* fierceness

gairm, gairme, gairmean(nan) *nf* **1** calling; **2** crow (*sound*); **3** cry, call; **4** vocation; **5** proclamation

gairm *vi, pres part* **a' gairm**, **1** call, cry; **2** (*cock etc*) crow

gairmeach *adj* vocative

gàirnealair, gàirnealair, gàirnealairean *nm* gardener

gàirnealaireachd *nf* gardening

gaiseadh, *gen* **gaisidh** *nm, used with art*, **an gaiseadh** potato blight

gaisge *nf, also* **gaisgeachd** *nf* bravery, heroism

gaisgeach, *gen & pl* **gaisgich** *nm* hero

gaisgeil *adj* heroic

galan, galain, galanan *nm* gallon

galar, galair, galaran *nm* disease

Gall, *gen & pl* **Goill** *nm* **1** foreigner; **2** Lowlander

galla, galla, gallachan *nf* **1** bitch; **2** *as a swear*, damned, bloody

gallan, *gen* **gallain**, *pl* **gallain** & **gallanan** *nm 1* branch; **2** youth; **3** standing stone

gall-chnò, gall-chnotha, gall-chnothan *nf* walnut

Gallta *adj* Lowland

Galltachd *nf, used with art*, **a' Ghalltachd** the Lowlands

gàmag, gàmaig, gàmagan *nf* (*music*) octave

gamhainn, *gen & pl* **gamhna** & **gaimhne** *nm* stirk

gamhlas, *gen* **gamhlais** *nm* malice

gamhlasach *adj* spiteful

gann *adj* **1** scarce; **2** *in expr* **is gann** scarcely

gànraich *vt, pres part* **a' gànrachadh**, soil

gaoid, gaoide, gaoidean *nf* blemish

gaoir, gaoire, gaoirean *nf* **1** cry; **2** thrill

gaoisid/gaosaid, *gen* **gaoiside** *nf* **1** hair (*of animals*); **2** pubic hair

gaol, *gen* **gaoil** *nm* **1** love; **2** *in voc expr* **a ghaoil** (my) love

gaolach *adj* **1** loving; **2** beloved

gaoth, *gen* **gaoithe**, *pl* **gaothan** & **gaoithean** *nf* 1 wind; 2 *with art*, **a' ghaoth** flatulence

gaothach, *also* **gaothar**, *adj* 1 windy; 2 flatulent

gaotharan, gaotharain, gaotharanan *nm* fan

garaids, garaids, garaidsean *nf* garage

garbh *adj* 1 rough; 2 uncouth; 3 *as intensifying adv* very, terribly

garg *adj* fierce

gàrradh, gàrraidh, gàrraidhean *nm* 1 stone dyke; 2 garden

gartan, *gen* **gartain**, *pl* **gartain** & **gartanan** *nm* 1 tick (insect); 2 garter

gas, *gen* **gaise**, *pl* **gasan** & **gaisean** *nf* stalk, stem

gas, *gen* **gais** *nm* gas

gasta *adj* 1 handsome; 2 great

gath, gatha, gathan(nan) *nm* 1 dart, sting, barb; 2 spear; 3 ray, beam

ge *conj* 1 though; 2 *in expr* **ge b 'e** whatever, however

gèadh, *gen* & *pl* **geòidh** *nmf* goose

geal *adj* white

geal, *gen* **gil** *nm* white

gealach, gealaich, gealaichean *nf*, *used with art*, **a' ghealach** the moon

gealachadh, *gen* **gealachaidh** *nm* whitening

gealagan, *gen* & *pl* **gealagain** *nm* egg white

gealaich *vti*, *pres part* **a' gealachadh**, 1 whiten; 2 bleach

gealbhonn, gealbhuinn, gealbhonnan *nm* sparrow

geall, *gen* & *pl* **gill** *nm* 1 bet; 2 promise

geall *vti*, *pres part* **a' gealltainn**, promise

gealladh, geallaidh, geallaidhean *nm* promise

gealltanach *adj* 1 promising; 2 auspicious

gealtach *adj* cowardly

gealtachd *nf* cowardice

gealtaire, gealtaire, gealtairean *nm* coward

gèam(a)/geam(a), *gen* **gèama** & **geama**, *pl* **geamannan, geamachan** & **geamaichean** *nm* game

geamair, geamair, geamairean *nm* gamekeeper

geamhrachail *adj* wintry

geamhradh, geamhraidh, geamhraidhean *nm* winter

gean, *gen* **geana** *nm* mood, humour

geanmnachd *nf* chastity

geanmnaidh *adj* chaste

geansaidh, geansaidh, geansaidhean *nm* jersey

gearain *vi*, *pres part* **a' gearan**, complain

gearaineach & **gearanach** *adj* complaining

gearan, gearain, gearanan *nm* complaining

gearastan, *gen* **gearastain**, *pl* **gearastanan** *nm* garrison

Gearmailt *nf*, *used with art* **a' Ghearmailt** Germany

Gearmailteach, *gen* & *pl* **Gearmailtich** *nm* German, *also adj* **Gearmailteach** German

Gearmailtis *nf*, *used with art* **a' Ghearmailtis** (*lang*) German

geàrr *adj* short

geàrr, gearra, gearran *nf* hare

geàrr *vt*, *pres part* **a' gearradh**, 1 cut; 2 castrate

gearradh, gearraidh, gearraidhean *nm* 1 cutting; 2 cut; 3 sarcasm

Gearran, *gen* **Gearrain** *nm*, *with art*, **an Gearran** February

gearran, *gen* & *pl* **gearrain** *nm* 1 gelding; 2 garron

geàrr-chunntas, geàrr-chunntais, geàrr-chunntasan *nm* 1 summary; 2 (*meeting*) minute(s)

geas, *gen* **geasa** & **geis**, *pl* **geasan** *nf*, 1 enchantment 2 *in expr* **fo gheasaibh** spellbound

geata, geata, geataichean *nm* gate

ged, *conj* though

gèile, *gen* **gèile**, *pl* **gèilean** & **gèileachan** *nm* gale

gèill *vi*, *pres part* **a' gèilleadh**, yield

gèilleadh, *gen* **gèillidh** *nm* yielding

geimheal, geimheil, geimhlean *nm* shackle

geimhlich *vt*, *pres part* **a' geimhleachadh**, shackle

geinn, geinne, geinnean *nm* 1 chunk; 2 wedge

geir, *gen* **geire** *nf* 1 suet; 2 fat

gèire *nf* sharpness

geòcach *adj* gluttonous

geòcaire, geòcaire, geòcairean *nm* glutton

geòcaireachd *nf* gluttony

geodha, geodha, geodhaichean *nmf* cove

geòla, geòla(dh), geòlachan *nf* yawl

geòlas, *gen* **geòlais** *nm* geology

ge-tà *adv* though, however

geug, gèige, geugan *nf* branch (*of tree*)

geum, *gen* **geuma/gèime,** *pl* **geuman** *nm* (*cattle*) bellowing,

geum *vi, pres part* **a' geumnaich,** bellow, moo

geur *adj* **1** sharp; **2** bitter; **3** acerbic

geurachadh, *gen* **geurachaidh** *nm* sharpening

geuraich *vt, pres part* **a' geurachadh,** sharpen

gheibh, gheibheadh, gheibhinn *pts of irreg v* **faigh**

giall, *gen* **gialla/gèille,** *pl* **giallan** *nf* jaw

gibht, gibht, gibhtean *nf* gift

Giblean, *gen* **Giblein** *nm, also* **Giblinn,** *gen* **Giblinne** *nf, used with art,* **an Giblean/a' Ghiblinn** April

gidheadh *adv* nevertheless

gilb, gilbe, gilbean *nf* chisel

gile *nf, also* **gilead,** *gen* **gilid** *nm* whiteness

gille, gille, gillean *nm* **1** servant; **2** lad

gille-brì(gh)de, gille-bhrì(gh)de, gillean-brì(gh)de *nm* oystercatcher

gin *pron* any, *with neg v* none

gin *vti, pres part* **a' gineadh** *also* **a' gineamhainn** beget, conceive

gine, gine, gineachan *nf* gene

gineadair, gineadair, gineadairean *nm* **1** progenitor; **2** generator

gineal, gineil, ginealan *nmf* offspring

ginealach, *gen & pl* **ginealaich** *nm* generation

gineamhainn *nm* **1** breeding; **2** conception

ginean, ginein, gineanan *nm* foetus

ginideach *adj* genitive

ginidich *vi, pres part* **a' ginideachadh,** germinate

giodar, *gen* **giodair** *nm* sewage, dirt

gìodhar, gìodhair, gìodhraichean *nm* gear (*machinery*)

giomach, *gen & pl* **giomaich** *nm* lobster

gioma-goc, gioma-goc, gioma-gocan *nm* piggy-back

gionach *adj* greedy

gionaiche *nm* greed

giorrachadh, giorrachaidh, giorrachaidhean *nm* shortening

giorrad, *gen* **giorraid** *nm* shortness

giorraich *vt, pres part* **a' giorrachadh,** shorten

gìosg *vt, pres part* **a' gìosgail,** gnash

giotàr, giotàir, giotàran *nm* guitar

giùlain *vt, pres part* **a' giùlan, 1** carry; **2** wear (*clothing*); **3** behave

giùlan, giùlain, giùlanan *nm* **1** carrying; **2** transport; **3** behaviour

giùran, giùrain, giùranan *nm* **1** gill (*fish*); **2** barnacle

giuthas, *gen* **giuthais** *nmf* pine

glac *vt, pres part* **a' glacadh,** catch

glac, glaice, glacan *nf* **1** hollow; **2** palm (hand)

glacadh, *gen* **glacaidh** *nm* **1** catching; **2** grasp

glacte *adj* caught

glagadaich, *gen* **glagadaiche** *nf* clattering, rattling

glaine *nf* cleanliness

glainne *gen* **glainne,** *pl* **glainneachan & glainnichean** *nf* glass

glais *vt, pres part* **a' glasadh,** lock

glaiste *adj* locked

glam & **glamh** *vt, pres part* **a' glam(h)adh,** gobble, 'wolf'

glan *adj* **1** clean; **2** fine, grand

glan *vt, pres part* **a' glanadh,** clean

glanadh, *gen* **glanaidh** *nm* cleaning

glaodh¹, glaoidh, glaodhan *nm* call, cry

glaodh², glaoidh, glaodhan *nm* glue

glaodh¹ *vi, pres part* **a' glaodha(i)ch,** call, cry

glaodh² *vt, pres part* **a' glaodhadh,** glue

glaodhadh, *gen* **glaodhaidh** *nm* glueing

glaodha(i)ch *nm* calling, crying

glaodhaire, glaodhaire, glaodhairean *nm* loudspeaker

glaodhan, *gen* **glaodhain** *nm* **1** pulp; **2** paste

glas *adj* **1** grey; **2** green

glas, glaise, glasan *nf* (*door etc*) lock

glas-làmh, glais-làmh, glasan-làmh *nf* handcuff

glasraich *nf* vegetable(s)

glè *adv* very

gleac, *gen* **gleaca** *nm* 1 struggle;
2 wrestling

gleac *vi, pres part* **a' gleac(adh),**
1 struggle; 2 wrestle

gleacadair, gleacadair, gleacadairean
nm wrestler

gleacadh, *gen* **gleacaidh** *nm* struggling,
wrestling

gleadhar, gleadhair, gleadharan *nm*
uproar

**gleadhraich, gleadhraich,
gleadhraichean** *nf* din

gleann, *gen* **glinn(e),** *pl* **glinn &
gleanntan** *nm* glen

gleans, *gen* **gleansa** *m* shine, a lustre

glèidh *vt, pres part* **a' gleidheadh,** 1 hold;
2 save; 3 keep

gleidheadh, *gen* **gleidhidh** *nm* keeping,
saving

glèidhte *adj* kept

glèidhteach *adj* conservative

glèidhteachas, *gen* **glèidhteachais** *nm*
conservation

gleoc/cloc/cleoc, *gen* **gleoca,** *pl*
gleocaichean *nm* clock

gleus *vt, pres part* **a' gleusadh,** 1 prepare;
2 (*machines etc*) adjust, service; 3 (*music*)
tune

gleus, *gen* **gleusa/gleòis,** *pl* **gleusan &
gleois** *nmf* 1 (*of objects*) condition; 2 (*of
people*) mood; 3 (*music*) key

gleus *vt, pres part* **a' gleusadh,** 1 prepare;
2 (*machines etc*) adjust; 3 (*musical
instruments*) tune

gleusadh, *gen* **gleusaidh** *nm* preparing,
adjusting

gleusta & gleusda, *adj* 1 prepared;
2 (*person*) in good trim; 3 (*person*) handy

glic *adj* 1 wise; 2 clever; 3 sensible

gliocas, *gen* **gliocais** *nm* 1 wisdom;
2 cleverness

gliog, glioga, gliogan *nm* a drip, dripping
(*sound*)

gliong, glionga, gliongan *nm, also*
gliongartaich *nm* clinking, tinkling

gloc, *gen* **gloic** *nm, also* **glocail** *nf* cackle

gloc *vi, pres part* **a' glocail,** cackle

glòir, *gen* **glòir(e) & glòrach** *nf* glory

glòirich *vt, pres part* **a' glòireachadh,**
glorify

glòrmhor *adj* glorious

gluais *vti, pres part* **a' gluasad** move

gluasad, gluasaid, gluasadan *nm*
1 moving; 2 motion; 3 gait; 4 agitation

glug, gluig, glugan *nm* gurgle

glugan, glugain, gluganan *nm* gurgle

glumag, glumaig, glumagan *nf* 1 pool;
2 puddle

glùn, glùin(e), glùin(t)ean *nf* knee

gnàth, gnàtha, gnàthan(nan) *nm, also*
gnàth(a)s, *gen* **gnàthais** *nm,* 1 custom;
2 convention

gnàthach *adj* customary, normal

gnàthaich *vt, pres part* **a' gnàthachadh,**
1 use; 2 accustom

gnè *nf* 1 kind, sort; 2 species; 3 gender

gnè(i)theach & gnè(i)theasach *adj*
sexual

gnìomh, gnìomha, gnìomhan *nm*
1 action; 2 function

gnìomhach *adj* active

gnìomhachadh, *gen* **gnìomhachaidh**
nm acting, processing

gnìomhachail *adj* industrial

gnìomhachas, *gen* **gnìomhachais** *nm*
1 industry; 2 business

gnìomhaich *vti, pres part* **a'
gnìomhachadh,** 1 (*vi*) act; 2 (*vt*) effect

**gnìomhaiche, gnìomhaiche,
gnìomhaichean** *nm* 1 executive;
2 activist

gnìomhair, gnìomhair, gnìomhairean
nm verb

gnog *vt, pres part* **a' gnogadh,** 1 knock;
2 nod (head)

gnogadh, *gen* **gnogaidh** *nm* 1 knocking;
2 nod (head)

gnothach, gnothaich, gnothaichean
nm 1 business; 2 affair; 3 errand; 4 *in
expr* **gabh gnothach ri** get involved
in; 5 *in expr* **a dh'aon ghnothach**
adv deliberately; 6 *in expr* **dèan** *v* **an
gnothach air** get the better of; 7 *in expr*
nì sin an gnothach! that'll do!

gnù *adj* surly

gnùis, gnùise, gnùisean *nf* face,
complexion

gob, *gen & pl* **guib** *nm* 1 beak, bill; 2 point;
3 gob

gobach *adj* prattling

gobaireachd *also* **gabaireachd** *nf* prattle

gobha, gobhainn, goibhnean *nm*
(black)smith

gobhal & **gabhal**, *gen* **gobhail** & **goibhle**, *pl* **goibhlean** *nm* 1 fork (*angle*); 2 crutch (*groin*)

gobhar, *gen* **goibhre** & **gobhair**, *pl* **goibhrean**, **gobhraichean** & **gobhair** *nmf* goat

gòbhlach *adj* forked

gòbhlag, **gòbhlaig**, **gòbhlagan** *nf* 1 pitchfork; 2 earwig

gòbhlan-gaoithe, **gòbhlain-ghaoithe**, **gòbhlanan-gaoithe** *nm* swallow (*bird*)

goc, *gen* **goca**, *pl* **gocan** & **gocaichean** *nm* tap, stopcock

gogail *nf* cackling

goid, *gen* **goide** *nf* thieving, theft

goid *vt, pres part* **a' goid**, steal

goil *vti, pres part* **a' goil** boil

goile, **goile**, **goilea(cha)n** *nf* stomach

goileach *adj* boiling

goileam, *gen* **goileim** *nm* prattle

goireas, **goireis**, **goireasan** *nm* resource, amenity, convenience

goireasach *adj* convenient, handy

goirid (*comp* **(n)as** (*etc*) **giorra**) *adj* 1 short; 2 (*as n*) **o chionn ghoirid** recently

goirt *adj* 1 painful; 2 sour; 3 bitter

goirteachadh, *gen* **goirteachaidh** *nm* hurting

goirtich *vt, pres part* **a' goirteachadh**, hurt

goistidh, **goistidh**, **goistidhean** *nm* 1 godfather; 2 sponsor; 3 gossip

gòrach *adj* stupid, silly

gòraiche, *nf* stupidity, silliness

gorm *adj* 1 blue; 2 green

gort, *gen* **gorta** *nf* famine

gràbhail *vt, pres part* **a' gràbhal(adh)**, engrave

grad *adj* 1 sudden; 2 quick

gràdh, *gen* **gràidh** *nm* 1 love; 2 *in expr* **a ghràidh**, (my) love

gràdhach *adj* loving

graf, **grafa**, **grafaichean** *nm* graph

gràg, **gràig**, **gràgan** *nm* croak, caw

gràgail *nf* croaking, cawing

graide *nf* suddenness

gràin, *gen* **gràine** *nf* 1 hate; 2 disgust

gràineag, **gràineig**, **gràineagan** *nf* hedgehog

gràineil *adj* 1 hateful; 2 disgusting

gràinne, **gràinne**, **gràinnean** *nf* (*single*) grain

gràinneach *adj* granular

gràinnean, **gràinnein**, **gràinneanan** *nm* grain

gràisg, **gràisge**, **gràisgean** *nf* mob

gràisgealachd *nf* yobbishness

gràisgeil *adj* yobbish

gram, **grama**, **graman** *nm* gram(me)

gramail & **greimeil** *adj* persistent

gràmar, *gen* **gràmair** *nm* grammar

gràmarach *adj* grammatical

gràn, *gen* & *pl* **gràin** *nm* 1 cereal; 2 (*coll*) grain

granaidh, **granaidh**, **granaidhean** *nf* granny

grànda *adj* 1 ugly; 2 vile

gràpa, **gràpa**, **gràpan** *nm* graip

gràs, **gràis**, **gràsan**, *nm* grace

gràsmhor *adj* gracious

greadhnach *adj* gorgeous

greallach, *gen* **greallaiche** *nf* entrails

greannach *adj* 1 ill-tempered; 2 (*weather*) gloomy

greannmhor *adj* cheerful

greas *vti, pres part* **a' greasad**, 1 hurry; 2 urge on

grèata, **grèata**, **grèataichean** *nm* a grate

greideal, *gen* **greideil** & **greidealach**, *pl* **greidealan** *nf* griddle

Grèig *nf, used with art* **a' Ghrèig** Greece

greigh, **greighe**, **greighean** *nf* herd, flock, stud

greigheach *adj* gregarious

grèim, **greime**, **greimean(nan)** *nm* 1 grip, hold; 2 bite, bit; 3 (*needlework*) stitch

greimich *vi, pres part* **a' greimeachadh**, seize, grasp

greimire, **greimire**, **greimirean** *nm* 1 (table) fork; 2 pliers

greis, **greise**, **greisean** *nf* while

grèis, *gen* **grèise** *nf* needlework

greiseag, **greiseig**, **greiseagan** *nf* whilie

Greugach, *gen* & *pl* **Greugaich** *nm* Greek, *also adj* **Greugach** Greek

Greugais *nf, used with art* **a' Ghreugais** Greek (*language*)

greusaiche, **greusaiche**, **greusaichean** *nm* cobbler

grian, **grèine**, **grianan** *nf, used with art* **a' ghrian** the sun

grinn *adj* 1 elegant; 2 pretty

grinneal, *gen* **grinneil** *nm* **1** gravel;
2 bottom of sea, river or well

grinneas, *gen* **grinneis** *nm* elegance

grìogag, grìogaig, grìogagan *nf* bead (*on necklace etc*)

Grioglachan, *gen* **Grioglachain** *nm*, *used with art*, **an Grioglachan** the Pleiades

grìos, grìosa, grìosachan *nm* grill (*cooking*)

grìosaich *vt*, *pres part* **a' grìosachadh**, (*cookery*) grill

griù(th)lach & **griù(th)rach**, *gen* **griùlaich** *nf*, *used with art*, **a' ghriùlach** (the) measles,

grod *adj* rotten

grod *vi*, *pres part* **a' grodadh**, rot

grodach *adj* grotty

grodadh, *gen* **grodaidh** *nm* rotting

gròiseid, gròiseide, gròiseidean *nf* gooseberry

grosair, grosair, grosairean *nm* grocer

gruag, gruaig, gruagan *nf* **1** hair (*human*); **2** wig

gruagach, gruagaich(e), gruagaichean *nf* maid

gruagaire, gruagaire, gruagairean *nm* hairdresser

gruaidh, gruaidhe, gruaidhean *nf* cheek

gruaim, *gen* **gruaime** *nf* **1** gloom; **2** scowl;
3 sulk; **4** grumpiness

gruamach *adj* **1** gloomy; **2** scowling;
3 sulky; **4** grumpy

grùdair(e), grùdaire, grùdairean *nm* brewer

grùdaireachd *nf* brewing

grùid, *gen* **grùide**, *nf* **1** lees, dregs

grunn, *gen* **gruinn** *nm* **1** crowd; **2** many

grunnan, grunnain, grunnanan *nm* group, few

grunnd, *gen* **gruinnd** & **grunnda**, *pl* **grunndan** *nm* **1** bottom; **2** ground

grùnsgal, *gen* **grùnsgail** *nm* growling

gruth, *gen* **grutha** *nm* curd(s)

grùthan, grùthain, grùthanan *nm* (*anat*) liver

gu¹ *particle placed before an adj to form an adv, eg* **gu mòr** greatly

gu² *prep* **1** towards; **2** for (*with implication of intention*); **3** almost

gu³ & **gus** *prep* until

gual, *gen* **guail** *nm* coal

gualan, gualain, gualanan *nm* carbon

gualann/gualainn, *gen* **gualainn/ guailne**, *pl* **guailnean/guaillean** *nf* shoulder

gual-fiodha, *gen* **guail-fhiodha** *nm* charcoal

guanach *adj* **1** giddy; **2** coquettish

gucag, gucaig, gucagan *nf* **1** (*botany*) bud; **2** bubble

gucag-uighe, gucaig-uighe, gucagan- uighe *nf* egg-cup

gu dearbh *adv* **1** certainly, definitely; **2** *as intensifying element* **gu dearbh fhèin** extremely

guga, guga, gugaichean *nm* young gannet

guidh *vi*, *pres part* **a' guidhe**, **1** beg;
2 wish; **3** pray

guidhe, guidhe, guidheachan *nmf* **1** beseeching; **2** entreaty; **3** wish; **4** prayer

guil *vi*, *pres part* **a' gul**, *also* **gail** *vi*, *pres part* **a' gal**, weep, cry

guilbneach, *gen* & *pl* **guilbnich** *nmf* curlew

guin, guin, guinean *nm* **1** sting; **2** pang

guin *vt*, *pres part* **a' guineadh**, sting

guineach *adj* **1** sharp; **2** stinging

guineadh, *gen* **guinidh** *nm* stinging

guir *vti*, *pres part* **a' gur** (*vi*, *of hen etc*) brood, (*vti*), hatch (*eggs*)

guirean, guirein, guireanan *nm* pimple

gul, *gen* **guil** *nm*, *also* **gal**, *gen* **gail** *nm* weeping, crying

gun *conj*, **gum** *before b, f, m, p, also in forms* **gu**, **nach** (*neg*) & (*with v* **is**) **gur** & **guma** (*see examples*), that

gun *prep* (*takes nom, lenites following cons except for d, n & t*) **1** without; **2** *in neg verbal exprs* **dh'iarr e orm gun a bhith mì-mhodhail** he asked me not to be rude; **3** *in conj* **gun fhios nach** in case

gùn, gùin, gùintean *nm* gown

gunna, gunna, gunnaichean *nm* gun

gunnair, gunnair, gunnairean *nm* gunner

gurraban, *gen* **gurrabain** *nm* crouching

gu ruige *prep* (*with nom*) **1** (*of distance, space*) as far as; **2** (*of time*) until

gus¹, gus am, gus an, gus nach, *conj* to, in order to

gus², gus am, gus an, gus nach, *conj* until

guth, gutha, guthan *nm* **1** voice; **2** news;
3 mention

H

hàidraidean, *gen* **hàidraidein** *nm*
hydrogen
halò *excl* hello
heactair, heactair, heactairean *nm*
hectare

**heileacopta(i)r, heileacoptair,
heileacoptaran** *nm* helicopter
hòro-gheallaidh *nm* **1** ceilidh; **2** *in expr*
cha toir mi hòro-gheallaidh
I don't give a damn

i *pron f sing, emph form* **ise**, she, her

iad *pron m & f pl, emph form* **iadsan**, they, them

iadh-shlat & **iath-shlat**, *gen* **iadh-shlait** *nf* honeysuckle

iall, èille, iallan *nf* thong, leash

ialtag, ialtaig, ialtagan *nf* bat (*animal*)

iar *nf* west

iar- 1 *prefix corres to Eng* under-, vice-; 2 *prefix corres to Eng* post-; 3 (*in family relationships*) great-

iarann, iarainn, iarannan *nm* iron

iargalt(a) *adj* churlish

iarla, iarla, iarlan *nm* earl

iarmad, iarmaid, iarmadan *nm* remnant

iarmailt, iarmailt, iarmailtean *nf, used with art,* **an iarmailt** the firmament

iarnaich *vti, pres part* **ag iarnachadh**, *also* **iarnaig** *vti, pres part* **ag iarnaigeadh**, iron

iarnachadh *gen* **iarnachaidh** *nm, also* **iarnaigeadh** *gen* **iarnaigidh** *nm,* ironing

iarr *vt, pres part* **ag iarraidh,** 1 want, require; 2 request; 3 invite; 4 *in expr* **rach** *v* **a dh'iarraidh rudeigin** go to get something

iarraidh, iarraidh, iarraidhean *nmf* 1 wanting; 2 request; 3 invitation

iarr(a)tas, iarr(a)tais, iarr(a)tasan *nm* 1 request; 2 application (*job etc*)

iasad, iasaid, iasadan *nm* borrowing, loan

iasg, *gen & pl* **èisg** *nm* fish

iasgach, *gen* **iasgaich** *nm* fishing

iasgaich *vt, pres part* **ag iasgach(d),** fish

iasgair, iasgair, iasgairean *nm,* fisherman

iath *vt, pres part* **ag iathadh,** surround

idir *adv* at all

ifrinn, ifrinn, ifrinnean *nf* hell

ifrinneach *adj* hellish

im, *gen* **ime** *nm* butter

imcheist, imcheist, imcheistean *nf* 1 anxiety; 2 perplexity

imcheisteach *adj* anxious, perplexed

imich *vi, pres part* **ag imeachd,** go

imleag, imleige, imleagan *nf* navel

imlich, *gen* **imliche** *nf* licking

imlich *vt, pres part* **ag imlich,** lick

imnidh, *gen* **imnidhe,** *nf* solicitude

impidh, impidhe, impidhean *nm* entreaty

impidheach *adj* urging

imrich, imriche, imrichean *nf* 1 flitting; 2 migration

imrich *vi, pres part* **ag imrich(d)** & **ag imreacheadh,** 1 flit; 2 migrate

inbhe, inbhe, inbhean *nf* 1 status; 2 maturity

inbheach *adj* adult

inbheach, *gen & pl* **inbhich** *nm* adult

inbheil *adj* eminent

inbhidh *adj* adult

inbhidheachd *nf* puberty

inbhir, inbhir, inbhirean *nm* confluence

inc *nmf* ink

ine, ine, inean *nf* 1 nail (*finger, toe*); 2 claw; 3 hoof

inneal, inneil, innealan *nm* 1 machine; 2 tool

innealach *adj* mechanical

innean, innein, inneanan *nm* anvil

inneir & **innear,** *gen* **innearach** *nf* manure

innidh *nf* bowel(s)

innis, innse, innsean *nf* 1 island; 2 meadowland

innis *vti, pres part* **ag innseadh** & **ag innse,** tell, inform

Innis Tìle *nf* Iceland

innleachadh, *gen* **innleachaidh** *nm* inventing

innleachd, innleachd, innleachdan *nf* 1 ingenuity; 2 artfulness; 3 intelligence; 4 stratagem; 5 machine

innleachdach *adj* 1 ingenious; 2 resourceful; 3 intelligent

innleadair, innleadair, innleadairean *nm* engineer

innleadaireachd *nf* engineering

innlich *vt, pres part* **ag innleachadh,** invent, devise

innse(adh), *gen* **innsidh** *nm* telling, informing

Innseachan *nmpl, used with art* **Na h-Innseachan** India, *also* the Indies

innte (*emph form* **inntese**) *prep pron, see* **an** *prep*

inntinn, inntinn, inntinnean *nf* mind

inntinneach *adj* **1** interesting; **2** intellectual

inntrig *vi, pres part* **ag inntrigeadh**, enter

inntrigeadh, inntrigidh, inntrigidhean *nm* **1** entering; **2** entrance

ìobair *vt, pres part* **ag ìobradh** sacrifice

ìobairt, ìobairte, ìobairtean *nf* sacrifice

ìoc, *gen & pl* **ìce** *nm* payment

ìoc *vti, pres part* **ag ìocadh**, pay

iochd *nf* compassion, mercy

ìochdar, ìochdair, ìochdaran *nm* bottom

ìochd(a)rach *adj* (*opposite of* **uachd(a)rach**), **1** lower; **2** inferior

ìochdaran, *gen & pl* **ìochdarain** (*opposite of* **uachdaran**), **1** inferior; **2** (*monarchy etc*) subject

ìochdaranachd *nf* inferiority

iochdmhor *adj* merciful, compassionate,

ìocshlaint, ìocshlainte, ìocshlaintean *nf* medicine, remedy

iodhal, iodhail, iodhalan *nm* idol

iodhlann, iodhlainn, iodhlannan *nf* stackyard

iolach, *gen & pl* **iolaich** *nf* shout, cheer

iolair(e), iolaire, iolairean *nf* eagle

iolra, iolra, iolran *nm, also adj* **iolra**, (*gram*) plural

ioma- *a prefix corres to Eng* multi-, poly-

iomadach *adj* many

iomadaich, *pres part* **ag iomadachadh**, *vt* multiply

iomadh *adj* many

iomagain, iomagaine, iomagainean *nf* **1** anxiety; **2** solicitude

iomagaineach *adj* **1** worried; **2** worrying

iomain, *gen* **iomaine** *nf* shinty

iomain *vt, pres part* **ag iomain**, drive, propel

iomair *vti, pres part* **ag iomramh**, row (*boat*)

iomair *vt, pres part* **ag iomairt**, employ, wield

iomairt, iomairte, iomairtean *nf* **1** employing, wielding (*see* **iomair** *vt*); **2** endeavour, campaign

iomall, iomaill, iomallan *nm* **1** edge; **2** a rim

iomallach *adj*, remote

iomchaidh *adj* **1** suitable; **2** fitting; **3** advisable

iomchair *vt, pres part* **ag iomchar**, bear, carry, transport

iomchar, *gen* **iomchair** *nm* bearing

ìomhaigh, ìomhaigh, ìomhaighean *nf* **1** image; **2** idol

iomlaid, iomlaid, iomlaidean *nf* **1** barter; **2** change (*money*)

iomlan *adj* complete, absolute

iompachadh, iompachaidh, iompachaidhean *nm* converting

iompachan, *gen & pl* **iompachain** *nm* convert

iompaich *vt, pres part* **ag iompachadh**, **1** convert; **2** persuade

ìompaire, ìompaire, ìompairean *nm* emperor

ìompaireachd, ìompaireachd, ìompaireachdan *nf* empire

ìompaireil *adj* imperial

iomradh, iomraidh, iomraidhean *nm* **1** mention; **2** report

iomraiteach *adj* renowned

iomrall, iomraill, iomrallan *nm* **1** error; **2** wandering

iomrallach *adj* mistaken

iomramh, *gen* **iomraimh** *nm* rowing (*boat*)

ion- **1** *a prefix corres to Eng* -able, -; **2** *occas corres to Eng* worthy of

ionad, ionaid, ionadan *nm* **1** place; **2** centre

ionadail *adj* local

ionaltair *vi, pres part* **ag ionaltradh**, graze

ionaltradh, ionaltraidh, ionaltraidhean *nm* grazing

ionann & **ionnan** *adj* same

iongantach *adj* wonderful

iongantas, iongantais, iongantasan *nm* wonder

iongnadh, iongnaidh, iongnaidhean *nm* **1** wonder; **2** surprise

ionmhainn *adj* beloved

ionmhas, ionmhais, ionmhasan *nm*
  1 treasure; **2** wealth; **3** finance
ionmhasair, ionmhasair,
  ionmhasairean *nm* treasurer
ionnanach *adj* equal
ionndrainn *vt, pres part* **ag ionndrainn**,
  miss, long for
ionnlad, *gen* **ionnlaid** *nm* bathing
ionnlaid *vti, pres part* **ag ionnlad**, bathe
ionnsachadh, *gen* **ionnsachaidh** *nm*
  learning
ionnsaich *vti, pres part* **ag ionnsachadh**,
  1 learn; **2** teach
ionnsaichte *adj* educated
ionnsaigh, ionnsaigh, ionnsaighean
  nmf **1** attack; **2** attempt; **3** *in prep* **a**
  dh'ionnsaigh to, towards
ionnsramaid, ionnsramaide,
  ionnsramaidean *nf* instrument
ionracas, *gen* **ionracais** *nm* **1** honesty;
  2 justice
ionraic *adj* **1** honest; **2** just
ìoran(t)as, *gen* **ìoran(t)ais** *nm* irony
ìoranta *adj* ironic(al)
iorghail, iorghail, iorghailean *nf* tumult
iorghaileach *adj* tumultuous
ìosal & **ìseal** *adj* low(ly)
Iosarail & **Israel**, *nf* Israel
Iosaraileach, *gen* & *pl* **Iosarailich**, also
  Israeleach, *gen* & *pl* **Israelich**, *nm,*
  Israeli, Israelite, *also adj* **Iosaraileach** &
  Israeleach Israeli
Ioslamach *adj* Islamic
ìota(dh), *gen* **ìotaidh** *nm* thirst
ìotmhor *adj* parched
ìre *nf* **1** level; **2** maturity; **3** *in expr* **an ìre**
  mhath *adv* quite, just about; **4** *in expr*
  gu ìre bhig all but
iriosal *adj* humble
irioslachadh, irioslachaidh,
  irioslachaidhean *nm* humbling,
  humiliating
irioslachd *nf* **1** lowliness; **2** humility

irioslaich *vt, pres part* **ag irioslachadh**,
  humble, humiliate
iris, iris, irisean *nf* magazine
is *conj and*
is (*inter* **an**, *neg* **cha(n)**, *neg inter* **nach**,
  past & conditional **bu**) *v irreg & def*, is,
  are
ìsbean, ìsbein, ìsbeanan *nm* sausage
isean, isein, iseanan *nm* **1** chick;
  2 young; **3** brat
ìsleachadh, *gen* **ìsleachaidh** *nm*
  1 lowering; **2** humiliation
ìslich *vti, pres part* **ag ìsleachadh**, lower
isneach, isnich(e), isnichean *nf* rifle
ist *pl* **istibh**, *also* **èist** *pl* **èistibh**, *excl*
  hush!
ite, ite, itean *nf* **1** feather; **2** fin (*fish*)
iteach *adj* feathered
iteach, *gen* **itich** *nm* plumage
iteachan, *gen* **iteachain**, *pl* **iteachain** &
  iteachanan *nm* bobbin
iteag, iteig, iteagan *nf* (*dimin of* **ite**)
  1 feather; **2** flight
iteagach *adj* feathered
itealaich *vi, pres part* **ag itealaich** & **ag**
  itealachadh, fly
itealan, *gen* & *pl* **itealain** *nm* aeroplane
iteileag, iteileig, iteileagan *nf* kite (*flying*
  structure)
ith *vti, pres part* **ag ithe(adh)**, eat
iubhar, iubhair, iubharan *nm* yew
iuchair, iuchrach, iuchraichean *nf* key
Iuchar, *gen* **Iuchair** *nm*, *used with art,* **an**
  t-Iuchar July
Iùdhach, *gen* & *pl* **Iùdhaich** *nm* Jew, *also*
  adj **Iùdhach** Jewish
iùil-tharraing, *gen* **iùil-tharrainge** *nf*
  magnetism
iùil-tharraingeach *adj* magnetic
iùl, iùil, iùilean *nm* **1** (*boat etc*) course;
  2 guidance; **3** landmark
iutharn(a), *gen* **iutharna** *nf* hell

L

là & **latha**, *gen* **là** & **latha**, *pl* **làithean**, **lathachan** & **lathaichean** *nm* day

labhair *vi, pres part* **a' labhairt**, speak, talk

labhairt *nf* **1** speaking, talking; **2** speech,

labhar *adj* loud

lach, lacha, lachan *nf* duck

lachdann *adj* **1** dun, tawny, khaki; **2** swarthy

ladar, ladair, ladaran *nm* **1** ladle; **2** scoop

ladarna *adj* bold, shameless

ladhar, *gen* **ladhair** & **ladhra**, *pl* **ladhran** *nm* hoof

lag *adj* weak, feeble

lag, *gen* **laig** & **luig**, *pl* **lagan** *nmf* **1** hollow, pit

lagaich *vti, pres part* **a' lagachadh**, weaken

lagachadh, *gen* **lagachaidh** *nm* weakening

lagh, lagha, laghannan *nm* law

laghach *adj* nice, kind

laghail *adj* lawful, legal

laghairt, laghairt, laghairtean *nmf* lizard

Laideann, *gen* **Laidinne** *nf* Latin

Laidinneach *adj* Latin

làidir *adj* strong, potent

laigh *vi, pres part* **a' laighe**, **1** lie (down); **2** land, settle

laighe *nmf* lying (down)

laigse, laigse, laigsean *nf* **1** weakness, infirmity; **2** faint

làimhseachadh, *gen* **làimhseachaidh** *nm* **1** handling; **2** treatment

làimhsich *vt, pres part* **a' làimhseachadh**, **1** handle; **2** treat; **3** wield

laimrig, laimrige, laimrigean *nf* landing-place

lainnir, *gen* **lainnire** *nf* sparkle; radiance

lainnireach *adj* sparkling, radiant

làir, *gen* **làiridh** & **làireadh**, *pl* **làiridhean** *nf* mare

làitheil *adj* daily

làmh, *gen* **làimh(e)**, *dat* **làimh**, *pl* **làmhan** *nf* **1** hand; **2** captivity, arrest; **3** handle

làmhainn, làmhainn, làmhainnean *nf* glove

làmh-lèigh, làmh-lèigh, làmh-lèighean *nm* surgeon

làmh-sgrìobhaidh, làmh-sgrìobhaidh, làmh-sgrìobhaidhean *nmf* handwriting

làmh-sgrìobhainn, làmh-sgrìobhainn, làmh-sgrìobhainnean *nmf* manuscript

lampa, lampa, lampaichean *nmf* lamp

làn *adj* **1** full; **2** *as adv* fully

làn, *gen* & *pl* **làin** *nm* **1** fullness; **2** tide

langa, langa, langan *nf* (*fish*) ling

lànachd *nf* fulness

langanaich *vi, pres part* **a' langanaich** bellow, low

langasaid, langasaide, langasaidean *nf* sofa, couch

lann¹, *gen* **lanna** & **lainne**, *pl* **lannan** *nf* **1** blade; **2** (*of fish etc*) scale

lann², **lainn, lannan** *nf* **1** enclosure; **2** fence; **3** (*in compounds*) repository

lanntair, lanntair, lanntairean *nmf* lantern

laoch, *gen* & *pl* **laoich** *nm* hero, warrior

laogh, laoigh, laoghan *nm* **1** calf; **2** (*as term of endearment*) **a laoigh!** (my) love!

laoidh, laoidhe, laoidhean *nmf* **1** song, poem, lay; **2** hymn; **3** anthem

lapach *adj* **1** numb; **2** weak

làr, làir, làran *nm* **1** (the) ground; **2** floor

làrach, làraich, làraichean *nmf* **1** vestige; **2** site

làraidh, làraidh, làraidhean *nf* lorry

làrna-mhàireach *adv* (on) the morrow

las *vti, pres part* **a' lasadh**, **1** light; **2** (*vi*) blaze

lasachadh, *gen* **lasachaidh** *nm* loosening

lasadair, lasadair, lasadairean *nm* match (*for lighting*)

lasadh, *gen* **lasaidh** *nm* lighting, blazing

lasaich *vti, pres part* **a' lasachadh**, **1** loosen; **2** ease

lasair, *gen* **lasrach** & **lasair**, *pl* **lasraichean** *nf* **1** flame; **2** flash

lasanta *adj* inflammable; hot-blooded
lasgan, *gen & pl* **lasgain** *nm* outburst
lasrach *adj* flaming, flashing
lastaig *nf* elastic
làthair, *gen* **làthaire** *nf* presence
làthaireachd *nf* presence
le *prep* with, by, belonging to
leabaidh, *gen* **leapa(ch)**, *pl* **leapannan** & **leapaichean** *nf* bed
leabhar, **leabhair**, **leabhraichean** *nm* book
leabharlann, **leabharlainn**, **leabharlannan** *nmf* library
leabhrachan, **leabhrachain**, **leabhrachanan** *nm* & **leabhran**, **leabhrain**, **leabhranan** *nm* booklet
leac, **lic(e)**, **leacan** *nf* slab, ledge
leacach *adj* flat
leacag, **leacaig**, **leacagan** *nf* tile
leag *vt, pres part* **a' leagail**, **1** knock down; **2** lower; **3** lay down; **4** drop
leagail, *gen* **leagalach** *nf* knocking down, lowering etc
leagh *vti, pres part* **a' leaghadh**, **1** melt, thaw; **2** dissolve
leaghadh, *gen* **leaghaidh** *nm* melting, thawing, dissolving
leamh *adj* exasperating
leamhachadh, *gen* **leamhachaidh** *nm* exasperating
leamhaich *vt, pres part* **a' leamhachadh**, exasperate
leamhan, *gen* **leamhain** & **leamhna** *nm* elm
lean *vti, pres part* **a' leantainn** & **a' leantail**, **1** follow; **2** understand; **3** continue; **4** stick, adhere
leanabail *adj* childish, infantile
leanaban, **leanabain**, **leanabanan** *nm* baby
leanabas, *gen* **leanabais** *nm* childhood
leanabh, **leanaibh**, **leanabhan**, **leanaban** *nm* baby, child
leanailteach *adj* **1** continuous; **2** adhesive
leann, **leanna**, **leannan**, **leanntan** *nm* beer, ale
leannan, **leannain**, **leannain**, **leannanan** *nm* lover, sweetheart
leannanach *adj* amorous
leannanachd *nf* courtship, courting
leannra, **leannra**, **leannran** *nm* sauce

leantainneach *adj* **1** continuous; **2** persevering
leas, *nm* **1** benefit, advantage
leas- *prefix (in family relationships)* step-
leasachadh, **leasachaidh**, **leasachaidhean** *nm* **1** developing; **2** improvement; **3** remedy; **4** fertiliser
leasaich *vt, pres part* **a' leasachadh**, **1** improve, develop; **2** remedy; **3** fertilise
leasaiche, **leasaiche**, **leasaichean** *nm* therapist
leasan, **leasain**, **leasanan** *nm* lesson
leasbach, *gen & pl* **leasbaich** *nf* a lesbian, *also adj* **leasbach** lesbian
leathad, **leathaid**, **leathaidean** *nm* slope, hillside
leathann *adj* broad, wide
leathar, *gen* **leathair** & **leathrach** *nm* leather
leatrom, *gen* **leatruim** *nm* pregnancy
leig *vt, pres part* **a' leigeil** & **a' leigeadh**, **1** permit; **2** leave, entrust; **3** & **leig às** let go; **4** **leig le** leave alone; **5** **leig de** & **leig seachad** cease; **6** **leig air** pretend
leigeadh, *gen* **leigidh** *nm*, *also* **leigeil**, *gen* **leigealach** *nf* letting, dropping
leigheas, **leigheis**, **leigheasan** *nm* **1** healing; **2** cure
leighis *vt, pres part* **a' leigheas**, cure, heal
lèine, **lèine**, **lèintean** *nf* shirt
lèir *adj* visible, evident
lèir-chlais(tin)neach *adj* audio-visual
lèirmheas *nm* review
lèirsinn *nf* **1** sight; **2** perceptiveness
lèirsinneach *adj* **1** visible; **2** perceptive
leis, **leise**, **leisean** *nf* thigh
leisg *adj* **1** lazy; **2** reluctant
leisg(e), *gen* **leisge** *nf* **1** laziness; **2** reluctance
leisgeadair, **leisgeadair**, **leisgeadairean** *nm* lazybones
leisgeul, **leisgeil**, **leisgeulan** *nm* excuse
leiteas, **leiteis**, **leiteisean** *nf* lettuce
lèith, **lèithe**, **lèithean** *nf (anat)* nerve
leitheach *adv* half, semi-
leithid, **leithide**, **leithidean** *nf* the like of
leitir, **leitire**, **leitirean** *nf* slope
leòinteach, *gen & pl* **leòintich** *nm* casualty, victim
leòm, *gen* **leòim(e)** *nf* pride, conceit
leòman, *gen & pl* **leòmain** *nm* moth

leòmhann, *gen & pl* **leòmhainn** *nmf* lion

leòn, **leòin**, **leòntan** *nm* wound, hurt, injury

leòn *vt, pres part* **a' leònadh** wound, hurt, injure

leònadh, *gen* **leònaidh** *nm* wounding, hurting, injuring

leònta & **leònte**, *adj* wounded, hurt, injured

leòr *nf* enough, sufficiency

leth *nm* **1** side; **2** *as adv expr* **air leth** apart, exceptional; **3** half; **4** one of a pair; **5** *in expr* **às leth** *prep* on behalf of; **6** *in expr* **cuir** *v* **às leth** accuse; **7** *in expr* **fa leth** *adv* separate

lethbhreac, **lethbhric**, **lethbhreacan** *nm* **1** equal; **2** copy

lethcheann, *gen & pl* **lethchinn** *nm* **1** cheek; **2** temple

leth-cheud & **lethcheud**, *gen* **leth-cheud**, *pl* **leth-cheudan** *nm* fifty

leud, *gen* **leòid** *nm* breadth, width

leudachadh, **leudachaidh**, **leudachaidhean** *nm* **1** extending; **2** extension

leudaich *vti, pres part* **a' leudachadh**, extend

leudaichte *adj* **1** extended; **2** flattened

leug, **lèig**, **leugan** *nf* jewel

leugh *vti, pres part* **a' leughadh**, read

leughadair, **leughadair**, **leughadairean** *nm* reader

leughadh, *gen* **leughaidh** *nm* reading

leum, **lèim**, **leuman(nan)** *nm* jump(ing)

leum *vti, pres part* **a' leum** *also* **a' leumadh**, **a' leumnaich** & **a' leumadaich**, **1** jump; **2** (*of nose*) bleed

leum-sròine, **lèim-sròine**, **leumannan-sròine** *nm* nose bleed

leum-uisge, **lèim-uisge**, **leumannan-uisge** *nm* waterfall

leus, *gen & pl* **leòis** *nm* **1** light; **2** torch; **3** blister

leusair, **leusair**, **leusairean** *nm* laser

liagh, **lèigh**, **liaghan** *nf* **1** ladle; **2** scoop

liath *adj* **1** grey; **2** (pale) blue

liath *vti, pres part* **a' liathadh**, grey

liathadh, *gen* **liathaidh** *nm* greying

liath-reothadh, *gen* **liath-reothaidh** *nm* hoar frost

libearalach *adj* liberal

lìbhrig *vt, pres part* **a' lìbhrigeadh**, deliver

lìbhrigeadh, **lìbhrigidh**, **libhrigidhean** *nm* delivering

lide, **lide**, **lidean** *nm* syllable

lighiche, **lighiche**, **lighichean** *nm* (medical) doctor

lili(dh), **lili(dh)**, **lilidhean** *nf* lily

lìnig *vt, pres part* **a' lìnigeadh**, line

lìnigeadh, **lìnigidh**, **lìnigidhean** *nm* lining

linn, **linn**, **linntean** *nmf* **1** age, time, era; **2** generation; **3** century

linne, *gen* **linne**, *pl* **linneachan** & **linntean** *nf* **1** pool; **2** waterfall

liomaid, **liomaide**, **liomaidean** *nf* lemon

lìomh, *gen* **lìomha** *nf* polish, gloss

lìomh *vt, pres part* **a' lìomhadh**, polish, shine

lìomharra *adj* polished, glossy

lìon *vti, pres part* **a' lìonadh**, fill

lìon, **lìn**, **lìontan** *nm* **1** net, web; **2** lint, flax

lìonadh, *gen* **lìonaidh** *nm* filling

lìonmhor *adj* numerous, abundant

lìonmhorachd *nf* abundance

lionn, **lionna**, **lionntan** *nm* liquid

lionsa, **lionsa**, **lionsaichean** *nf* lens

lìonta *adj* filled

liopard, **liopaird**, **liopardan** *nm* leopard

lios, *gen* **liosa** & **lise**, *pl* **liosan** *nmf* **1** garden; **2** enclosure

liosda *adj* boring, tedious

liosta, **liosta**, **liostaichean** *nf* list (*of items*)

liotach *adj* lisping

liotachas, *gen* **liotachais** *nm* lisp

liotair, **liotair**, **liotairean** *nm* litre

lip, **lipe**, **lipean** *nf* lip

lite *nf* porridge

litearra *adj* literate

litearrachd *nf* literacy

litir, **litreach**, **litrichean** *nf* letter

litireil *adj* literal

litreachadh, *gen* **litreachaidh** *nm* spelling

litreachail *adj* literary

litreachas, *gen* **litreachais** *nm* literature

litrich *vti, pres part* **a' litreachadh**, spell

liùdhag, **liùdhaig**, **liùdhagan** *nf* doll

liut, *gen* **liuit** *nf* knack, flair

lobh *vi, pres part* **a' lobhadh**, rot, putrefy

lobhadh, *gen* **lobhaidh** *nm* rotting, putrefaction

lobhar, *gen & pl* **lobhair** *nm* leper

lobht(a), **lobhta**, **lobhtaichean** *nm* **1** (*in tenement etc*) storey; **2** loft (*roofspace*)

lobhte *adj* putrid, rotten

locair, **locair**, **locairean** *nf also* **locar**, *gen* **locair**, *pl* **locaran** & **locraichean** *nmf* (*carpentry*) plane

lòcast, *gen & pl* **lòcaist** *nm* locust

loch, **locha**, **lochan** *nm* loch, lake

lochan, **lochain**, **lochanan** *nm* lochan

lochd, **lochda**, **lochdan** *nm* **1** fault, blame; **2** harm

lochdach *adj* harmful

Lochlann, *gen* **Lochlainn** *nf* **1** Scandinavia; **2** Norway

Lochlannach, *gen & pl* **Lochlannaich** *nm* **1** Scandinavian; **2** Norwegian; **3** Norseman, Viking

Lochlannach *adj* **1** Scandinavian; **2** Norwegian; **3** Norse, Viking

lòchran, *gen & pl* **lòchrain** *nm* lamp, lantern

lof, **lofa**, **lofaichean** *nmf* loaf

loidhne, **loidhne**, **loidhnichean** *nf* line

loingeas & **luingeas**, *gen* **loingeis** *nm* **1** shipping; **2** fleet, navy

lòinidh *nmf, with art,* **an lòinidh** rheumatism

loisg *vti, pres part* **a' losgadh**, **1** burn; **2** fire, shoot (*firearm*)

loisgte *adj* burnt

lòistear/loidsear, *gen* **lòisteir**, *pl* **lòistearan** *nm* lodger

lòistinn, **lòistinn**, **lòistinnean** *nm* lodging(s)

lom *adj* **1** bare, naked, nude; **2** bleak; **3** thin, threadbare; **4** (*weight etc*) net

lom *vt, pres part* **a' lomadh**, **1** bare, strip; **2** shave; **3** (*lawn, grass*) mow

lomadair, **lomadair**, **lomadairean** *nm* shearer

lomadh, *gen* **lomaidh** *nm* baring, shearing

loma-làn *adj* full up

lomnochd *adj* naked

lòn[1], *gen* **lòin** *nm* **1** sustenance; **2** meal

lòn[2], **lòin**, **lòintean** *nm* **1** pool; **2** puddle; **3** meadow

lònaid, **lònaide**, **lònaidean** *nf* lane

lon-dubh, **loin-duibh**, **loin-dubha** *nm* blackbird

long, **luinge**, **longan** *nf* ship

lorg, **luirge**, **lorgan** *nf* **1** looking for, finding; **2** trace, mark; **3** *in expr* **faigh** *v* **lorg air** find, locate

lorg *vt, pres part* **a' lorg** & **a' lorgadh**, **1** look for; **2** find

los *nm* **1** intention; **2** *in expr* **los gu(n)** *conj* so that

lòsan, *gen & pl* **lòsain** *nm* pane (glass)

losgadh, **losgaidh**, **losgaidhean** *nm* burning

losgann, **losgainn**, **losgannan** *nm* frog

lot[1], **lota**, **lotaichean** *nf* holding (land), croft

lot[2], **lota**, **lotan** *nm* wound

lot *vti, pres part* **a' lotadh**, wound

lotadh, *gen* **lotaidh** *nm* wounding

loth, **lotha**, **lothan** *nmf* **1** filly; **2** foal

luach *nm* worth, value

luachachadh, **luachachaidh**, **luachachaidhean** *nm* evaluating

luachaich *vt, pres part* **a' luachachadh**, evaluate

luachair, *gen* **luachrach** *nf* rush (*plant*)

luachmhor *adj* valuable, precious

luadhadh, *gen* **luadhaidh** *nm* waulking, fulling

luaidh[1] *nm* praising, mentioning

luaidh[2], **luaidhe**, **luaidhean** *nmf, often in voc,* **a luaidh!** love!

luaidh[1] *vt, pres part* **a' luaidh**, **1** praise; **2** mention

luaidh[2] *vti, pres part* **a' luadhadh**, waulk

luaidhe *nmf* lead

luaineach *adj* restless, changeable

luaisg *vi, pres part* **a' luasgadh**, rock, sway, toss

luaithre *nf, also* **luath**, *gen* **luaith** & **luatha(inn)** *nf* ash(es)

luamhan, *gen* **luamhain**, *pl* **luamhain** & **luamhanan** *nm* lever

luas & **luaths**, *gen* **luai(th)s** *nm* **1** speed; **2** agility

luasgadh, *gen* **luasgaidh** *nm* rocking etc

luasgan, *gen* **luasgain** *nm* **1** a rocking, shaking etc; **2** giddiness, dizziness

luath *adj* **1** fast, quick; **2** *in expr* **cho luath agus/is** as soon as; **4** *in expr* **luath no mall** sooner or later, eventually

luathachadh, *gen* **luathachaidh** *nm*
accelerating

luathaich *vti, pres part* **a' luathachadh**,
1 accelerate; **2** *as vt* hurry (on)

lùb, lùib, lùban *nf* **1** bend, curve; **2** loop,
noose; **3** *in expr* **an lùib** (*with gen*)
involved in

lùb *vti, pres part* **a' lùbadh**, bend, bow

lùbach *adj* **1** bending; **2** flexible; **3** winding

lùbadh, *gen* **lùbaidh** *nm* bending, curving
etc

lùbte *adj* bent, bowed

luch, *gen* **lucha** & **luchainn**, *pl* **luchan** &
luchainn *nf* mouse

lùchairt, lùchairte, lùchairtean *nf*
palace

luchd¹, luchda, luchdan *nm* cargo, load

luchd² *nm* people

luchdachadh, *gen* **luchdachaidh** *nm*
loading

luchdaich *vt, pres part* **a' luchdachadh**,
load

luchdmhor *adj* capacious

luchraban, *gen* & *pl* **luchrabain** *nm*
dwarf, midget

Lucsamburg *nf, also* **Lugsamburg**,
Luxembourg

Lucsamburgach, *gen* & *pl*
Lucsamburgaich *nm* Luxembourger,
also adj **Lucsamburgach** Luxembourger

lùdag, lùdaig, lùdagan *nf* **1** little finger;
2 hinge

lugha *comp adj, in comp exprs* **(n)as** (etc)
lugha smaller *etc*

lùghdachadh, *gen* **lùghdachaidh** *nm*
1 lessening; **2** reduction

lùghdaich *vti, pres part* **a' lùghdachadh**,
lessen, shrink, abate

luibh, luibhe, luibhean *nmf* herb, plant,
weed

luibheach *adj* botanical

luibhre *nf* leprosy

luideach *adj* **1** shabby, scruffy; **2** silly

luideag, luideig, luideagan *nf* rag

luidhear, luidheir, luidhearan *nm*
funnel, chimney

luime *nf* nakedness, bleakness

luinneag, luinneig, luinneagan *nf* ditty

Lùnastal, *gen* **Lùnastail** *nm, used with
art,* **an Lùnastal** August

lurach *adj* pretty, nice; beloved

lurgann, *gen* **lurgainn**, *pl* **lurgannan** &
luirgnean *nf* shin

lus, *gen* **luis** & **lusa**, *pl* **lusan** *nm* **1** herb;
2 plant, weed

lùth, *gen* **lùtha** *nm, also* **lùths**, *gen* **lùiths**
nm, **1** movement; **2** agility; **3** energy

lùthmhor *adj* **1** strong; **2** agile;
3 energetic

M

ma *conj* if

màb *vt, pres part* **a' màbadh**, vilify

màbadh, *gen* **màbaidh** *nm* abusing etc

mac, *gen & pl* **mic** *nm* son

macanta *adj* meek

machair(e), **machrach**, **machraichean** *nmf* **1** machair; **2** plain

machlag, **machlaig**, **machlagan** *nf* womb, uterus

mac-meanmna, *gen* **mic-meanmna** *nm* imagination

mac-meanmnach *adj* **1** imaginary; **2** imaginative

mac-samhail, *gen & pl* **mic-samhail** *nm* **1** replica; **2** equal, match

madadh, **madaidh**, **madaidhean** *nm* **1** dog; **2** (*esp* **madadh-ruadh**) fox; **3** (*esp* **madadh-allaidh**) wolf

madainn, **maidne**, *pl* **maidnean** & **madainnean** *nf* morning

màg, **màig**, **màgan** *nf* paw

mag *vi, pres part* **a' magadh**, mock

magadh, *gen* **magaidh** *nm* mockery

magail *adj* mocking, jeering

magairle, **magairle**, **magairlean** *nmf* testicle

maghar, **maghair**, **maghairean** *nm* **1** fly (*fishing*); **2** bait

maide, **maide**, **maidean** *nm* **1** wood, timber; **2** stick

maids(e), **maidse**, **maidsichean** *nm* match

màidsear, **màidseir**, **màidsearan** *nm* major

Màigh, *gen* **Màighe** *nf, with art* **a' Mhàigh** May

maighdeann, *gen* **maighdinn**, *pl* **maighdeannan** & **maighdinnean** *nf* **1** maiden; **2** virgin; **3** spinster; **4** *in formal address, corres,* Miss

maighdeannas, *gen* **maighdeannais** *nm* virginity, maidenhood

maigheach, **maighiche**, **maighichean** *nf* hare

maighstir, **maighstir**, **maighstirean** *nm* **1** master; **2** *in formal address, corres,* (*abbrev* **Mgr**) Mister, Mr

màileid, **màileide**, **màileidean** *nf* suitcase, briefcase, bag

maille *nf* **1** slowness; **2** delay

mailleachadh, *gen* **mailleachaidh** *nm* procrastinating

maille ri *prep* with

maillich *vti, pres part* **a' mailleachadh**, procrastinate

mair *vi, pres part* **a' mairsinn**, *also* **a' maireann** & **a' maireachdainn**, last, continue

maireann (*adj, & obs pres part/ verbal noun of* **mair** *v*) **1** *in expr* **rid mhaireann** during your lifetime; **2** *in expr* **nach maireann** the late . . .

maireannach *adj* **1** eternal; **2** durable; **3** long-lived

mairg *adj* pitiable

màirnealach *adj* **1** slow; **2** boring

màirnealaich *vi, pres part* **a' màirnealachadh**, procrastinate

mairtfheoil, *gen* **mairtfheòla** *nf* beef

maise *nf* beauty

maiseach *adj* beautiful

maiseachadh, **maiseachaidh**, **maiseachaidhean** *nm* decorating, embellishment

maisich *vt, pres part* **a' maiseachadh**, **1** decorate, beautify; **2** make up (*with cosmetics*)

màithreil *adj* motherly, maternal

màl, *gen & pl* **màil** *nm* rent

mala, **mala**, **malaichean** *nf* **1** eyebrow; **2** brow

malairt, **malairt**, **malairtean** *nf* **1** trade, business; **2** barter

malairteach *adj* commercial

malairtich *vi, pres part* **a' malairteachadh**, **1** trade; **2** barter

màlda *adj* coy, bashful

mall *adj* slow, tardy

mallachadh, *gen* **mallachaidh** *nm* cursing

mallachd/mollachd, *gen* **mallachd**, *pl* **mallachdan** *nf* a curse

mallaich *vt, pres part* **a' mallachadh**, curse

mallaichte *adj* cursed, damned

mamaidh, mamaidh, mamaidhean *nf* mammy

manach, *gen & pl* **manaich** *nm* monk

manachainn, manachainne, manachainnean *nf* monastery

manadh, manaidh, manaidhean *nm* omen

manaidsear, manaidseir, manaidsearan *nm* manager

Manainneach, *gen & pl* **Manainnich** *nm* Manxman, *also adj* **Manainneach** Manx

mang, mainge, mangan *nf* fawn

maodal, maodail, maodalan *nf* paunch

maoidh *vi, pres part* **a' maoidheadh**, 1 threaten; 2 bully

maoidheadh, maoidhidh, maoidhidhean *nm* 1 threatening; 2 bullying

maoidhear, maoidheir, maoidhearan *nm* bully

maoil, maoil, maoilean *nf* forehead, brow

maoile *nf, also* **maoilead**, *gen* **maoileid** *nm*, baldness

maoin, maoine, maoinean, *nf* 1 goods; 2 wealth

maol *adj* 1 blunt; 2 bald

maol, *gen & pl* **maoil** *nm* 1 cape, promontory; 2 rounded hill

maor, *gen & pl* **maoir** *nm* bailiff, factor, officer

maorach, *gen* **maoraich** *nm* shellfish

maoth *adj* 1 soft; 2 tender(-hearted)

maothachadh, *gen* **maothachaidh** *nm* softening

maothaich *vti, pres part* **a' maothachadh**, soften

mapa, mapa, mapaichean *nm* map

mar 1 *prep* like, as; 2 *in expr* **mar sin** so, *also in leave-taking* **mar sin leat/leibh!** 'bye, then!, 'bye just now!; 3 *in exprs* **mar sin** & **mar sin air adhart** and so on; 4 **mar ri** *prep* with; 6 *in expr* **mar an ceudna** *adv* likewise

mar a *conj* as

mar gun/nach *conj* as if/not

marag, maraig, maragan *nf* 1 pudding; 2 haggis

maraiche, maraiche, maraichean *nm* sailor, seafarer

marbh *adj* dead

marbh *vt, pres part* **a' marbhadh**, kill

marbhadh, *gen* **marbhaidh** *nm* killing

marbhaiche, marbhaiche, marbhaichean *nm* killer, murderer

marbhan, marbhain, marbhanan *nm* corpse

marbhtach *adj* deadly, fatal

marcachadh, *gen* **marcachaidh** *nm, also* **marcachd** *nf* 1 riding; 2 horsemanship

marcaich *vi, pres part* **a' marcachd** & **a' marcachadh**, ride

marcaiche, marcaiche, marcaichean *nm* rider, horseman

margadh, margaidh, margaidhean *nmf* market

margarain *nm* margarine

màrmor, *gen* **màrmoir** *nm* marble

màrsail, *gen* **màrsaile** *nf* marching, march

Màrt, *gen* **Màirt** *nm* 1 Mars; 2 *with art* **am Màrt** March

mart, *gen & pl* **mairt** *nm* beef animal

mar-thà, *adv* already

màs, màis, màsan *nm* 1 buttock; 2 backside

masg, masg, masgan *nm* mask

maslach *adj* disgraceful, shameful

maslachadh, *gen* **maslachaidh** *nm* disgracing etc

masladh, maslaidh, maslaidhean *nm* disgrace, shame

maslaich *vt, pres part* **a' maslachadh**, disgrace, shame

matamataig *nm* mathematics

math *adj* good

math, *gen* **maith** *nm* good

math & **maith** *vi, pres part* **a' mathadh**, forgive

mathachadh, *gen* **mathachaidh** *nm* manure, fertilizer

mathadh, *gen* **mathaidh** *nm* forgiving

mathaich *vt, pres part* **a' mathachadh**, manure, fertilize

màthair, màthar, màthraichean *nf* 1 mother; 2 (*esp in compounds*) origin

màthaireachd *nf* motherhood, maternity

mathan, mathain, *pl* **mathain** & **mathanan** *nm* bear

mathanas, *gen* **mathanais** *nm* forgiveness, pardon

mathas, *gen* **mathais** *nm* goodness

meadhan, meadhain, meadhanan
nm **1** middle, centre; **2** average, mean;
3 medium, mechanism; **4** waist

meadhanach *adj* **1** middling, average,
so-so; **2** middle

meal *vt, pres part* **a' mealadh & a'
mealtainn**, enjoy, *esp in exprs* **meal do
naidheachd!** congratulations!

mealadh, *gen* **mealaidh** *nm, also*
mealtainn *nm* enjoying

meal-bhucan, meal-bhucain, *pl* **meal-
bhucain & meal-bhucanan** *nm* melon

meall, *gen & pl* **mill** *nm* **1** lump; **2** lumpy
hill; **3** shower; **4 meall an sgòrnain**
adam's apple

meall *vt, pres part* **a' mealladh**, **1** deceive;
2 entice

meallach *adj* beguiling, bewitching

mealladh, *gen* **meallaidh** *nm* deceit,
deception, enticement

meallta(ch) *adj* deceitful, cheating,
deceptive

meallta *adj* deceived, cheated

mealltair, mealltair, mealltairean *nm*
cheat, deceiver

mean *adj* little, tiny, *in expr* **mean air
mhean** little by little, gradually

mèanan, mèananaich *see* **mèaran,
mèaranaich**

meanbh *adj* little, tiny

meang, *gen* **meanga & meing**, *pl*
meangan *nf* **1** fault, flaw; **2** abnormality

meangach *adj* abnormal

meang(l)an, *gen* **meang(l)ain**, *pl*
meang(l)ain & meang(l)anan *nm*
branch, bough

meann, *gen & pl* **minn** *nm* kid (*young
goat*)

mear *adj* animated, jolly

mearachd, mearachd, mearachdan *nf*
a mistake

mearachdach *adj* wrong, erroneous

mèaran & mèanan, *gen* **mèarain**, *pl*
mèaranan *nm* yawn

mèaranaich/mèananaich, *gen*
mèaranaiche *nf* yawning

mèarrsadh, *gen* **mèarrsaidh** *nm*
marching, march

meas¹ *nm* **1** respect, esteem; **2** valuation,
assessment

meas², measa, measan *nm* fruit

meas *vti, pres part* **a' meas(adh)**, **1** think;
2 esteem, value; **3** estimate

measach *adj* fruity

measadh, *gen* **measaidh** *nm* considering,
esteeming, valuing *etc*

measail *adj* **1** respectable, respected,
valued; **2** fond

measarra *adj* moderate, temperate

**measgachadh, measgachaidh,
measgachaidhean** *nm* mixing, mixture

measgaich *vt, pres part* **a'
measgachadh**, **1** mix, mingle; **2** combine

**measgaichear, measgaicheir,
measgaichearan** *nm* mixer

meata *adj* faint-hearted, feeble

meatailt, meatailte, meatailtean *nf*
metal

meatair, meatair, meatairean *nm* metre

meatrach *adj* metric

meidh, meidhe, meidhean *nf* **1** scales;
2 equilibrium

meil *vti, pres part* **a' meileadh**, mill,
grind

meileabhaid, *gen* **meileabhaide** *nf*
velvet

meileachadh, *gen* **meileachaidh** *nm*
chilling, numbing

mèilich *nf* bleat, bleating

meilich *vti, pres part* **a' meileachadh**,
chill, numb

mèinn, *gen* **mèinne** *nf* **1** temperament;
2 appearance

mèinn(e), mèinne, mèinnean *nf* **1** ore;
2 mine

**mèinneadair, mèinneadair,
mèinneadairean** *nm* miner

mèinneach & mèinneil *adj* mineral

mèinnear, mèinneir, mèinnearan
nm, also **mèinnearach**, *gen & pl*
mèinnearaich *nm*, mineral

mèinnearachd *nf* **1** mineralogy; **2** mining

mèinn-eòlas, *gen* **mèinn-eòlais** *nm*
mineralogy

meirg, *gen* **meirge** *nf* rust

meirg *vti, pres part* **a' meirgeadh**,
also **meirgich** *vti, pres part* **a'
meirgeachadh**, rust

meirgeach *adj* rusty

mèirle *nf* theft

mèirleach, *gen & pl* **mèirlich** *nm* thief

meomhair, *gen* **meomhair(e)**, *pl*
meomhairean *nf* memory

meòrachadh, *gen* **meòrachaidh** *nm*
remembering, meditating

meòraich *vi, pres part* **a' meòrachadh**, **1** meditate; **2** memorise; **3** remember

meud *nm* **1** size, extent; **2** amount; **3** *in expr* **cò/cia mheud** how many

meudachadh, meudachaidh, meudachaidhean *nm* **1** increasing ; **2** enlargement

meudachd *nf* magnitude

meudaich *vti, pres part* **a' meudachadh**, increase, enlarge

meur, *gen & pl* **meòir** *nf* **1** finger; **2** (*piano etc*) key; **3** branch

meuran, *gen* **meurain**, *pl* **meurain** & **meuranan** *nm* thimble

mi, *emph form* **mise**, *pers pron* I, me

mì- *a common neg prefix corres to Eng* un-, in-, dis-, mis-, -less *etc*

mial, miala, mialan *nf* **1** louse; **2** tick (*parasite*)

mial-chù, *gen & pl* **mial-choin** *nm* greyhound

mialaich *nf, also* **miamhail** *nf* mewing, miauing

miann, miann, miannan *nmf* desire, longing, wish

miannachadh, *gen* **miannachaidh** *nm* desiring *etc*

miannaich *vt, pres part* **a' miannachadh**, desire

mias, *gen* **mias** & **mèise**, *pl* **miasan** *nf* **1** basin; **2** platter

miastachd *nf* hooliganism

miastadh *gen* **miastaidh** *nm* **1** harm, damage; **2** hooliganism

mì-ghnàthaich, *pres part* **a' mì-ghnàthachadh** misuse

mil, meala(ch), mealan *nf* honey

mìle¹, mìle, mìltean *nm* thousand

mìle², mìle, mìltean *nmf* mile

milis *adj* sweet

mill *vti, pres part* **a' milleadh**, spoil, ruin

milleadh, *gen* **millidh** *nm* spoiling, ruining

millean, millean, milleanan *nm, also* **muillean, muillean, muilleanan** *nm*, million

millte *adj* spoilt, damaged

millteach *adj* destructive

milltear, millteir, milltearan *nm* vandal

mìlseachd *nf* sweetness

mìlsean, gen mìlsein, pl mìlsein & **mìlseanan** *nm* dessert, pudding

mì-mhodhail *adj* rude, ill-mannered

mìn *adj* **1** smooth, soft; **2** dainty, fine

min, *gen* **mine** *nf* **1** meal; **2** flour

mìneachadh¹, mìneachaidh, mìneachaidhean *nm* explanation, interpretation

mìneachadh², *gen* **mìneachaidh** *nm* smoothing

mìneachail *adj* explanatory

mìnich¹ *vt, pres part* **a' mìneachadh**, explain, interpret

mìnich² *vt, pres part* **a' mìneachadh**, smoothe

minig *adj* frequent

minig *vt, pres part* **a' minigeadh**, mean

ministear, ministeir, ministearan *nm* minister

ministrealachd, ministrealachd, ministrealachdan *nf* ministry

miodal, *gen* **miodail** *nm* flattery, fawning

mìog, mìoga, mìogan *nf* smirk

mìogadaich *nf* bleating, bleat

mion *adj, usu used as prefix* **1** small, minute; **2** detailed, punctilious; **3** minority

mionach, mionaich, mionaichean *nm* **1** entrails, guts; **2** belly

mionaid, mionaide, mionaidean *nf* minute

mionaideach *adj* thorough, detailed

mionn, mionna, mionnan *nmf* oath, curse

mionnachadh, *gen* **mionnachaidh** *nm* swearing

mionnaich *vi, pres part* **a' mionnachadh**, swear

mìorbhail, mìorbhaile, mìorbhailean *nf* **1** marvel; **2** miracle

mìorbhaileach *adj* **1** marvellous; **2** miraculous

mìos, mìosa, mìosan *nmf* month

mìosach/mìosail *adj* monthly

mìosachan, *gen & pl* **mìosachain** *nm* calender

miotag, miotaig, miotagan *nf* **1** glove; **2** mitten

mìr, mìre, mìrean *nm* bit, particle, scrap

mire(adh) *adj* mirth, light-heartedness

mìrean, *gen & pl* **mìrein** (*dimin of* **mìr**) *nm* particle

mì-reusanta *adj* unreasonable

mì-reusantachd *nf* unreasonableness

miseanaraidh, miseanaraidh, miseanaraidhean *nm* missionary

misg, *gen* **misge** *nf* drunkenness, intoxication

misgeach *adj* intoxicated; drunken

misgear, misgeir, misgearan *nm* drunkard, boozer

misneach, *gen* **misnich** *nf, also* **misneachd** *nf* **1** courage; **2** confidence

misneachadh, *gen* **misneachaidh** *nm* encouragement

misneachail *adj* **1** courageous; **2** spirited; **3** encouraging

misnich *vt, pres part* **a' misneachadh, 1** inspire; **2** encourage

miste *adj,* worse, the worse, *esp in expr* **is miste thu** . . . You are the worse for . . . ,

mithich *adj* timely

mo *poss adj* my

moch *adj, adv,* early

mòd, mòid, mòdan *nm* **1** court; **2** Mod

modh, modha, modh(ann)an *nmf* **1** manner, mode; **2** *in expr* **air mhodh eile** otherwise; **3** manners; **4** (*gram*) mood

modhail *adj* polite, well-bred

modhalachd *nf* politeness, courtesy

mogan, *gen* **mogain,** *pl* **moganan** *nm* slipper

Mohamadanach, *gen & pl* **Mohamadanaich,** Mohammedan, *also adj* **Mohamadanach** Mohammedan

mòine, *gen* **mòna, mònadh & mònach,** *nf* peat

mòinteach, mòintich, mòintichean *nf* moor, moorland

moit, *gen* **moite** *nf* pride

moiteil *adj* proud

mol, *gen* **moil & mola,** *pl* **molan** *nm* **1** shingle; **2** shingly beach

mol *vt, pres part* **a' moladh, 1** praise; **2** recommend

molach *adj* **1** hairy, rough

moladh, molaidh, molaidhean *nm* **1** praise; **2** recommendation

moll, *gen* **muill** *nm* chaff

molldair, molldair, molldairean *nm* mould

mòmaid, mòmaide, mòmaidean *nf* moment

monadail *adj* hilly, mountainous

monadh, monaidh, monaidhean *nm* moorland, moor, hill land

monmhar, monmhair, monmharan *m* murmuring

mòr *adj, comp* **(n)as** (etc) **mò/motha,** big, great

mòrachd *nf* greatness, grandeur, majesty

morair, morair, morairean *nm* lord

mòran, *gen* **mòrain** *nm* many; much

mòrchuis, *gen* **mòrchuise** *nf* pride, conceit

morgaidse, morgaidse, morgaidsean *nm* mortgage

morghan, *gen* **morghain** *nm* **1** gravel; **2** shingle,

mosach *adj* **1** nasty, scruffy; **2** niggardly

mosg, mosga, mosgan *nm* mosque

mosgail *vti, pres part* **a' mosgladh,** awake, wake, rouse

mosgladh, *gen* **mosglaidh** *nm* awakening

motair, motair, motairean *nm* motor

mothachadh, *gen* **mothachaidh** *nm* **1** noticing; **2** feeling; **3** consciousness

mothachail *adj* **1** aware, observant; **2** sensitive; **3** conscious

mothaich *vt, pres part* **a' mothachadh, 1** notice; **2** feel, experience

mu *prep* around/concerning

muc, muice, mucan *nf* pig

mùch *vt, pres part* **a' mùchadh, 1** extinguish, quench, smother; **2** strangle; **3** repress

mùchadh, *gen* **mùchaidh** *nm* **1** extinguishing; **2** suffocation; **3** repression

muc-mhara, muice-mara, mucan-mara *nf* whale

muga, *gen* **muga,** *pl* **mugannan & mugaichean** *nmf* (*drinking*) mug

mùgach *adj* **1** morose; **2** surly

muidhe, *gen* **muidhe,** *pl* **muidhean & muidheachan** *nm* churn

mùig, mùig, mùigean *nm* frown, scowl

muileann, *gen* **muilinn,** *pl* **muilnean & muileannan** *nmf, also* **muilinn, muilne, muilnean** *nf,* mill

muile-mhàg, muile-mhàg, muileacha-màg *nf* toad

muillear, muilleir, muillearan *nm* miller

muime, muime, muimeachan *nf* step-mother

muin *nf* **1** back; **2** top of something

mùin *vi, pres part* **a' mùn,** urinate

muinchill & muinichill, *gen*
muin(i)chill, *pl* muin(i)chillean *nm*,
also muil(i)cheann, muil(i)chinn,
muil(i)chinnean *nm* sleeve
muineal, muineil, muinealan *nm* neck
muing, muinge, muingean *nf* mane
muinntir, *gen* muinntire *nf* people,
followers
muir, mara, marannan *nmf* sea
muir-làn, *gen & pl* muir-làin *nm* high
tide
mulad, *gen* mulaid *nm* grief, sadness
muladach *adj* sad
mullach, mullaich, mullaichean *nm*
1 top; 2 roof
mult/molt, *gen & pl* muilt, wether
muiltfheòil *gen* muiltfheòla *nf* mutton

mùn, *gen* mùin *nm* urine
mùnadh, *gen* mùnaidh *nm* urinating
muncaidh, muncaidh, muncaidhean
nm monkey
mùr, mùir, mùirean *nm* wall, rampart
murt, *gen & pl* muirt, *nm* murder
murt *vt, pres part* a' murt(adh), murder
murtadh, *gen* murtaidh *nm*, murdering
murtair, murtair, murtairean *nm*,
murderer
mus/mun *conj* 1 before; 2 lest
mùth *vi, pres part* a' mùthadh, 1 change,
deteriorate; 2 mutate
mùthadh, mùthaidh, mùthaidhean
nm 1 changing; 2 change; 3 mutation; 4
(*phys*) corruption, decay

N

na *neg imper particle* don't, do not
na *conj* than
na *rel pron* that, what, (all) that which, (all) those which
na *form of art*
na *prep pron*
na b' (*in comp constrs*) *see* **na** *rel pron*
nàbaidh, nàbaidh, nàbaidhean *nm* neighbour
nàb(aidhe)achd *nf* neighbourhood
nàbaidheil *adj* neighbourly
nach *neg particle that not*
nàdar, *gen* **nàdair** *nm,* nature; temperament
nàdarra(ch) *adj* natural
naidheachd, naidheachd, naidheachdan *nf* news; anecdote **na naidheachdan** the news
naidheachdair, naidheachdair, naidheachdairean *nm* journalist
nàidhlean, *gen* **nàidhlein** *nm* nylon
nàimhdeas, *gen* **nàimhdeis** *nm* enmity, hostility
nàimhdeil *adj* hostile, inimical
nàire *nf* 1 shame, ignominy; 2 bashfulness; 3 embarassment
nàisean, nàisein, nàiseanan *nm* nation
nàiseanta *adj* national
nàiseantach, *gen & pl* **nàiseantaich** *nm* nationalist, *also adj* **nàiseantach**
nàiseantachd *nf* 1 nationalism; 2 nationhood
naisgear, naisgeir, naisgearan *nm* conjunction
nàmhaid, nàmhad, nàimhdean *nm* enemy
nan *conj* (**nam** *before b, f, m, p*) if
nan (**nam** *before b, f, m, p*) *form of art*
nan *prep pron*
naoi/naodh *n and num adj* nine
naoidheamh/naodhamh *num adj* ninth
naoidhean, naoidhein, naoidheanan *nm* infant, baby
naoinear/naodhnar *nmf* people numbering nine
naomh, *gen & pl* **naoimh** *nm* saint
naomh *adj* holy, sacred, saintly

naomhachd *nf* 1 saintliness; 2 holiness
nàr *adj* shameful, disgraceful
nar *prep pron*
nàrach & nàireach *adj* 1 shamefaced; 2 bashful
nàrachadh, *gen* **nàrachaidh** *nm* shaming
nàraich *vt, pres part* **a' nàrachadh**, shame
nas (*in comp exprs*) more than
nathair, nathrach, nathraichean *nf* 1 adder; 2 snake, serpent
neach *nm* person; one, someone
neach-cathrach *nm* chairperson
neach-ciùil *nm* musician
neach-ionaid, *pl* **luchd-ionaid** *nm* replacement, agent
neach-labhairt *nm* spokesperson
neach-obrach *nm* worker
neactar, *gen* **neactair** *nm* nectar
nead, *gen & pl* **nid** *nm* nest
nèamh, nèimh, nèamhan *nm* heaven(s)
nèamhaidh *adj* heavenly, celestial
neapaigear, neapaigeir, neapaigearan *nm* handkerchief
neapaigin, neapaigine, neapaiginean *nf* napkin
nèarbhach *adj* nervy, nervous
neart, *gen* **neirt** *nm* strength, might; vigour
neartachadh, *gen* **neartachaidh** *nm* strengthening
neartaich *vti, pres part* **a' neartachadh**, strengthen
neartmhor *adj* (*phys*) strong; mighty
neas, neasa, neasan *nf* 1 weasel; 2 stoat; 3 ferret
neasgaid/niosgaid, neasgaide, neasgaidean *nf* a boil, ulcer, abscess
nèibhi(dh), nèibhi(dh), nèibhidhean *nmf* a navy
neo- *prefix corres to Eng* un-, in-, -less *etc*
neo-àbhaisteach *adj* unusual
neo-chomasach *adj* incapable, incompetent
neo-chùramach *adj* irresponsible
neodrach *adj* neuter
neo-eisimeileachd *f* independence
neoichiontach *adj* guiltless, innocent

neòinean, *gen* **neòinein**, *pl* **neòinein** &
neòineanan *nm* daisy
neòinean-grèine sunflower
neo-iomlan *adj* incomplete
neònach *adj* strange, curious
neoni *nf* nothing, nought
neonithich *vt, pres part*
neonitheachadh, cancel; annihilate
neo-phàirteach *adj* impartial
neo-thruacanta *adj* pitiless
neul, *gen & pl* **neòil** *nm* 1 cloud;
2 complexion; 3 faint
neulach *adj* cloudy
neulaich *vti, pres part* **a' neulachadh**,
cloud
nì, **nì**, **nithean** *nm* 1 thing; 2 circumstance,
matter; 3 *in expr* **(an) Nì Math** God
nì *pt of irreg v* **dèan**
Nic- *prefix found in surnames* female
descendant
nigh *vt, pres part* **a' nighe**, wash
nighe *nm* washing
nigheadair, **nigheadair**, **nigheadairean**
nm washer, washing machine
nigheadaireachd *nf* washing
nighean, gen **nighinne** & **ìghne**, *pl*
nigheanan & **ìghnean** *nf* 1 girl; 2 young
woman; 3 daughter

nimh & **neimh**, *gen* **n(e)imhe** *nm*
1 poison; 2 malice
nimheil *adj* 1 poisonous; 2 malicious
Nirribhidh *nf* Norway
nitheil *adj* concrete, actual
niuclasach *adj* nuclear
no (*also* **neo**) *conj* or
nobhail, **nobhaile**, **nobhailean** *nf* novel
nochd *vti, pres part* **a' nochdadh**, 1 (*vt*)
show; 2 (*vi*) appear
Nollaig, **Nollaige**, **Nollaigean** *nf*
Christmas, **Nollaig Chridheil!** Merry
Christmas!
norradaich, *gen* **norradaiche** *nf* nap
(*sleep*)
norrag, **norraig**, **norragan** *nf* nap,
snooze
nòs, **nòis**, **nòsan** *nm* 1 a custom; 2 way,
style
nota, **nota**, **notaichean** *nf* note
nuadh *adj* new
nuadhachadh, *gen* **nuadhachaidh** *nm*
renovation
nuadhaich *vt, pres part* **a'**
nuadhachadh, renovate
nuallaich *vi, pres part* **a' nuallaich**, howl,
roar, bellow
nurs, **nurs**, **nursaichean** *nf* nurse

O

o (*also* **bho**) *prep* **1** from; **2** *as conj*, since

òb, *gen* **òba** & **òib**, *pl* **òban** *nm* bay, creek

obair, *gen* **obrach** & **oibre**, *pl* **obraichean** *nf* **1** work(ing); **2** job, employment

obann *adj* sudden

obh *excl, usu as* **obh! obh!** oh dear!

obraich (*occas* **oibrich**) *vti, pres part* **ag obrachadh**, work, function

obraiche (*occas* **oibriche**), **obraiche**, **obraichean** *nm* worker

och *excl* alas

ochd *n and num adj* eight

ochdad *nm* eighty

ochdamh *num adj* eighth

ochdnar *nmf* eightsome

o chionn *also* **bho chionn** *prep* **1** ago; **2** since

odhar *adj* **1** dun; **2** sallow

òg *adj* young

ògan, **ògain**, **òganan** *nm* (*plants etc*) shoot, tendril

òganach, *gen* & *pl* **òganaich** *nm* **1** young man; **2** adolescent

ogha, *gen* **ogha**, *pl* **oghachan** & **oghaichean** *nm* grandchild

Ògmhios *nm, with art* **an t-Ògmhios** June

ogsaidean, *gen* **ogsaidein** *nm* oxygen

oide, **oide**, **oidean** *nm* **1** step-father; **2** tutor

oideachas, *gen* **oideachais** *nm* learning, instruction

oidhche, **oidhche**, **oidhcheannan** *nf* night **Oidhche Challainn** New Year's Eve, Hogmanay, **Oidhche Shamhna** Halloween

oidhirp, **oidhirpe**, **oidhirpean** *nf* **1** attempt, try; **2** effort

oifig, **oifige**, **oifigean** *nf, also* **oifis**, **oifise**, **oifisean** *nf* office

oifigeach, *gen* & *pl* **oifigich** *nm, also* **oifigear**, **oifigeir**, **oifigearan** *nm* officer; official

òige *nf* youth (*abstr*)

òigeachd *nf* adolescence

òigear, **òigeir**, **òigearan** *nm* youngster, adolescent

òigh, **òighe**, **òighean** *nf* **1** virgin; **2** maiden

òigheil *adj* virginal, maidenly

oighre, **oighre**, **oighreachan** *nm* heir, inheritor

oighreachd, **oighreachd**, **oighreachdan** *nf* **1** inheritance; **2** estate

òigridh *nf coll* young people

oilbheum, **oilbheim**, **oilbheuman** *nm* offence

oilbheumach *adj* offensive

oileanach, *gen* & *pl* **oileanaich** *nm* student

oileanachadh, *gen* **oileanachaidh** *nm* training, instructing

oileanaich *vt, pres part* **ag oileanachadh**, train, instruct

oillt, **oillte**, **oilltean** *nf* terror; horror

oillteil *adj* horrible; dreadful, frightful

oilltich *vt, pres part* **ag oillteachadh**, terrify, horrify

oilthigh, **oilthigh**, **oilthighean** *nm* university

òinseach, **òinsiche**, **òinsichean** *nf* idiot, fool

oir, **oire**, **oirean** *nf* **1** edge, margin; **2** rim

oir *conj* for

òirdheirc *adj* **1** magnificent; **2** llustrious

òirleach, *gen* & *pl* **òirlich** *nmf* inch (*measurement*)

oirthir, **oirthire**, **oirthirean** *nf* coast, seaboard

oisean, **oisein**, **oiseanan** *nm, also* **oisinn**, **oisne**, **oisnean** *nf*, corner

oiteag, **oiteig**, **oiteagan** *nf* breeze

òl *vti, pres part* **ag òl**, drink

ola, **ola**, **olaichean** *nf* oil

Òlaind *nf, used with art* **an Òlaind** Holland

olann, *gen* **olainn** *nf* wool

olc, *comp* **(n)as** (*etc*) **miosa**, *adj* evil, wicked

olc, *gen* **uilc** *nm* evil, wickedness

ollamh, **ollaimh**, **ollamhan** *nm* **1** learned man; **2** (non-medical) doctor; **3** professor

òmar, *gen* **òmair** *nm* amber

on a & **bhon a** *conj* since

onair, onaire, onairean *nf* 1 honour, **air m' onair!** honestly!; 2 esteem; 3 honesty

onarach *adj* 1 honourable; 2 honorary; 3 honest

onarachadh, *gen* **onarachaidh** *nm* honouring

onaraich *vt, pres part* **ag onarachadh,** honour

opairèisean, opairèisein, opairèiseanan *nmf* operation (*medical*)

òr, *gen* **òir** *nm* gold; **òir** *adj* gold(en)

òraid, òraide, òraidean *nf* speech, lecture, address

òraidiche, òraidiche, òraidichean *nm* speaker, lecturer

orains *adj* orange

orainsear, orainseir, orainsearan *nm* orange

òran/amhran, *gen & pl* **òrain** *nm* song

orc, *gen* **oirc** *nm, used with art,* **an t-orc** (*muscular*) cramp

òrd, *gen* **ùird,** *pl* **ùird** & **òrdan** *nm* hammer

òrdachadh, *gen* **òrdachaidh** *nm* ordering

òrdag, òrdaig, òrdagan *nf* 1 thumb; 2 toe

òrdaich *vti, pres part* **ag òrdachadh,** 1 (*vi*) order, command; 2 (*vti*) order; 3 organise, tidy; 4 prescribe

òrdail *adj* 1 orderly; 2 ordinal

òrdugh, òrduigh, òrduighean *nm* 1 order, command; 2 sequence

òrgan, òrgain, òrganan *nm* (*mus*) organ

òrraiseach *adj* squeamish

ortha, ortha, orthannan *nf* spell, charm

os *prep* 1 above, *now usu in compound prep* **os cionn** above; 2 *as prefix corres to Eng* super- etc

osan, *gen* **osain,** *pl* **osain** & **osanan** *nm* stocking, hose

osna (*nf*) & **osnadh** (*nm*), *gen* **osnaidh,** *pl* **osnaidhean** *nmf, also* **osann,** *gen & pl* **osainn** *nm,* 1 sigh; 2 breeze

osnaich, *gen* **osnaiche** *nf, also* **osnachadh,** *gen* **osnachaidh** *nm* sighing

osnaich *vi, pres part* **ag osnaich** & **ag osnachadh,** sigh

ospadal, ospadail, ospadalan *nm* hospital

ospag, ospaig, ospagan *nf* 1 sigh; 2 breath of wind

òstair & **òsdair,** *gen* **òstair,** *pl* **òstairean** *nm* hotelier, landlord, licensee

Ostair, *gen* **Ostaire** *nf, used with art* **an Ostair** Austria

Ostaireach, *gen & pl* **Ostairich** *nm* Austrian, *also adj* **Ostaireach** Austrian

othail, othaile, othailean *nf* hubbub, uproar

othaisg, *gen* **othaisge,** *pl* **othaisgean** *occas* **òisgean** *nf* hogg

òtrach, òtraich, òtraichean *nm* dunghill, midden

P

paca, paca, pacannan *nm* pack **paca clòimhe** pack of wool, **paca chairtean** a pack of cards

pacaid, pacaide, pacaidean *nf* a packet

pàganach, *gen & pl* **pàganaich** *nm* pagan, *also adj* **pàganach** pagan

Pagastan *nf,* Pakistan

paidhir, *gen* **paidhir** *(m)* & **paidhreach** *(f), pl* **paidhrichean** *nmf* pair

paidir, paidire, paidrichean *nf, used with art,* **a' phaidir** the Paternoster

paidirean, paidirein, paidirean *nm* **1** (*relig*) rosary; **2** necklace

pàigh *nm* pay

pàigh *vt, pres part* **a' pàigheadh,** pay

pàigheadh, *gen* **pàighidh** *nm* paying

pàileis, pàileis, pàileisean *nf* palace

pàillean, pàillein, pàilleanan *nm* **1** pavilion; **2** tent

pailt *adj* plentiful

pailteas, *gen* **pailteis** *nm* plenty

pàipear, pàipeir, pàipearan *nm* paper

pàirc(e), pàirce, pàircean *nf* field, park

paireafain *nm* paraffin

pàirt, pàirt, pàirtean *nmf* part

pàirtich *vt, pres part* **a' pàirteachadh,** share

pàirtiche, pàirtiche, pàirtichean *nm* partner

paisg *vt, pres part* **a' pasgadh,** wrap (up); fold (up)

pàiste, *gen* **pàiste,** *pl* **pàistean** *nm* infant, baby

pàiteach *adj* thirsty

pana, pana, panaichean *nm* pan

pannal, pannail, pannalan *nm* panel

Pàp(a), *gen* **Pàpa,** *pl* **Pàpan** & **Pàpachan** *nm* Pope

Pàpanach, *gen & pl* **Pàpanaich** *nm* papist, *also adj* **pàpanach** papist, popish, Catholic

pàrant, pàrant, pàrantan *nm* parent

pàrlamaid, pàrlamaide, pàrlamaidean *nf* parliament

pàrlamaideach *adj* parliamentary

pàrras, *gen* **pàrrais** *nm* paradise

parsail, parsail, parsailean *nm* parcel

pàrtaidh, pàrtaidh, pàrtaidhean *nm* party

partan, partain, partanan *nm* a crab (*edible*)

pasgadh, *gen* **pasgaidh** *nm* packing

pasgan, *gen & pl* **pasgain** *nm* bundle, package

pastra *nf* pastry

pathadh, *gen* **pathaidh** *nm* thirst

pàtran, pàtrain, pàtranan *nm* pattern

peacach *adj* sinful

peacach, *gen & pl* **peacaich** *nm* sinner

peacadh, peacaidh, peacaidhean *nm* sin

peacaich *vi, pres part* **a' peacachadh,** sin

peanas, peanais, peanasan *nm* punishment, penalty

peanasachadh, *gen* **peanasachaidh** *nm* punishing

peanasaich *vt, pres part* **a' peanasachadh,** punish

peann, *gen & pl* **pinn** *nm* pen

peansail, peansail, peansailean *nm* pencil

peant *vti, pres part* **a' peantadh,** paint

peant(a), *gen* **peanta,** *pl* **peantan** & **peantaichean** *nm* paint

peantadh, *gen* **peantaidh** *nm* painting

peantair, peantair, peantairean *nm* painter

pearraid, pearraide, pearraidean *nf* parrot

pearsa, pearsa, pearsachan *nm* **1** person; **2** (*in novel etc*) character

pearsanta *adj* personal

pearsantachd *nf* personality

pears-eaglais, *gen* **pears-eaglais,** *pl* **pearsan-eaglais** & **pearsachan-eaglais** *nm* clergyman

peasair, peasrach, peasraichean *nf* pea (*vegetable*)

peasan, peasain, peasanan *nm* brat

peata, *gen* **peata,** *pl* **peatan** & **peatachan** *nm* pet

peathrachas, peathrachais, peathrachasan *nm* sisterhood peatrail, *gen* peatrail *nm, also* peatroil, *gen* peatroil *nm* petrol

peighinn, peighinne, peighinnean *nf* 1 penny; 2 pennyland

peile, peile, peilichean *nm* pail

pèileag, pèileig, pèileagan *nf* porpoise

peilear/peileir, *gen* peileir, *pl* peilearan/peileirean *nm* bullet

peinnsean, peinnsein, peinnseanan *nm* pension

peirceall, *gen* peircle & peircill, *pl* peirclean/peirceallan *nm* 1 jaw; 2 jawbone

pèist, pèiste, pèistean *nf* reptile

peitean, peitein, peiteanan *nm* 1 vest; 2 waistcoat

peitseag, peitseig, peitseagan *nf* peach

peur, peura, peuran *nf* pear

pian, pèin, piantan *nmf* pain

pian *vt, pres part* a' pianadh, 1 pain, distress; 2 torture

piàna *also* piàno, *gen* piàna, *pl* piànathan *nm* piano

pianadh, *gen* pianaidh *nm* 1 paining, tormenting; 2 torture

pianail *adj* painful

pic, pice, picean *nm* (*tool*) pick

picil, *gen* picile *nf* pickle

pile, *gen* pile, *pl* pilichean & pileachan *nf* pill

pìleat, pìleat, pìleatan *nm, also* poidhleat, poidhleit, poidhleatan *nm* pilot

pillean, pillein, pilleanan *nm* 1 cushion; 2 pillion

pinc *adj* pink

pinnt, pinnt, pinntean *nm* pint

pìob, pìoba, pìoban *nf* pipe, tube

pìobaire, pìobaire, pìobairean *nm* piper

pìobaireachd *nf* 1 piping; 2 pibroch

piobar, *gen* piobair *nm* pepper

piobraich *vt, pres part* a' piobrachadh, 1 add pepper to; 2 pep up

pioc *vti, pres part* a' piocadh, peck, nibble

pìos, pìos, pìosan *nm* piece

piseach, *gen* pisich *nm* 1 progress, improvement; 2 luck

piseag, piseig, piseagan *nf* kitten

pit, pite, pitean *nf* vulva

piuthar, *gen* peathar, *dat* piuthair, *pl* peathraichean *nf* sister

plaide, plaide, plaidean *nf* blanket

plàigh, plàighe, plàighean *nf* 1 plague, infestation; 2 nuisance

plàigheil *adj* pestilential

plana, plana, planaichean *nm* plan

planaid, planaide, planaidean *nf* planet

planaig *vti, pres part* a' planaigeadh, plan

planaigeadh, *gen* planaigidh *nm* planning

plangaid, plangaide, plangaidean *nf* blanket

plaoisg *vt, pres part* a' plaosgadh, shell, peel, skin

plaosg, plaoisg, plaosgan *nm* shell, skin, peel, husk

plap *nm* fluttering

plap *vi, pres part* a' plapail, flutter

plàst, *gen* plàsta, *pl* plàst(aidhe)an *nm* (sticking) plaster

plastaig, plastaige, plastaigean *nf* plastic

plathadh, plathaidh, plathaidhean *nm* 1 glance, glimpse; 2 instant

pleadhag, pleadhaig, pleadhagan *nf* paddle

pleadhagaich *vti, pres part* a' pleadhagaich, paddle

plèana, plèana, plèanaichean *nmf* plane

ploc, pluic, plocan *nm* 1 clod, turf, a divot; 2 block; 3 lump

plosg, ploisg, plosgan *nm* 1 gasp; 2 palpitation, throb

plosg *vi, pres part* a' plosgadh *also* a' plosgail & a' plosgartaich, 1 gasp, pant; 2 palpitate, throb

plosgadh, *gen* plosgaidh *nm, also* plosgail *nf* & plosgartaich *nf* gasping, palpitating

plub, pluba, pluban *nm* splash, plop

plubraich *vi, pres part* a' plubraich, *also* plub *vi, pres part* a' plubadaich & a' plubarsaich, splash, plop, slosh

plubraich, *gen* plubraiche *nf* splashing, sloshing *etc*

plucan, plucain, plucanan *nm* 1 a pimple; 2 plug (*for sink etc*)

pluic, pluice, pluicean *nf* cheek

plumair, plumair, plumairean *nm* plumber

poball, pobaill, poballan *nm* people

poblach *adj* public

poblachd, poblachd, poblachdan *nf* republic

poca, poca, pocannan *nm* 1 bag; 2 sack
pòcaid, pòcaide, pòcaidean *nf, also*
  pòca, pòca, pòcan(nan) *nm* pocket
pòg, pòige, pògan *nf* kiss
pòg *vti, pres part* **a' pògadh,** kiss
poidsear, poidseir, poidsearan *nm*
  poacher
poileas, *gen* **poilis** *nm,* police, policeman
poileasaidh, poileasaidh,
  poileasaidhean *nm* policy
poileasman, *gen & pl* **poileasmain** *nm*
  policeman
poilitigeach *adj* political
poilitigs *nf* politics
poit, poite, poitean *nf* pot
poit-dhubh *nf* (*whisky*) still
poitean, *gen* **poitein** *nm* poteen
pòitear, pòiteir, pòitearan *nm* drinker,
  boozer
pòitearachd *nf* tippling, boozing
pòla, pòla, pòlaichean *nm* pole
Pòlach, *gen & pl* **Pòlaich** *nm* Pole, *also*
  adj **Pòlach** Polish
Pòlainn *nf, used with art* **a' Phòlainn**
  Poland
poll, *gen & pl* **puill** *nm* 1 mud; 2 bog; 3 *esp*
  poll-mòna(ch) peat bank
pònaidh, pònaidh, pònaidhean *nm*
  pony
pònair, *gen* **pònarach** *nf* bean(s)
pong, puing, pongan *nm* (*music*) note
pongail *adj* 1 punctilious; 2 concise;
  3 punctual
pòr, pòir, pòran *nm* 1 seed; 2 crops;
  3 growth
port¹, *gen & pl* **puirt** *nm* tune **port-à-beul**
  mouth music
port², *gen & pl* **puirt** *nm* port, harbour
  port-adhair airport
Portagail *nf, used with art* **a' Phortagail**
  Portugal
Portagaileach, *gen & pl* **Portagailich**
  nm Portuguese, *also adj* **Portagaileach**
  Portuguese
portair, portair, portairean *nm* porter
pòs *vti, pres part* **a' pòsadh,** marry
pòsadh, pòsaidh, pòsaidhean *nm*
  marriage
post¹, *gen & pl* **puist** *nm* post
post², *gen & pl* **puist** *nm* stake, stob **post-**
  seòlaidh signpost
post(a), posta, postaichean *nm* postman
pòsta *adj* married

prabar, prabair, prabairean *nm* rabble,
  mob
prais, praise, praisean *nf* (cooking) pot
pràis, *gen* **pràise** *nf* brass
pràiseach *adj* brass
preantas, preantais, preantasan *nm*
  apprentice
preas¹, *gen* **pris,** *pl* **pris & preasan** *nm*
  bush, shrub
preas², preasa, preasan *nm, also*
  preasadh, preasaidh, preasaidhean
  nm wrinkle
preas *vt, pres part* **a' preasadh,** 1 crease;
  2 corrugate; 3 crush
preas(a), *gen* **pris,** *pl* **pris & preasan** *nm*
  cupboard
preasach *adj* 1 wrinkly, wrinkled;
  2 corrugated
preasag, preasaig, preasagan *nf* crease,
  wrinkle
prìne, prìne, prìnichean *nm* pin
priob *vti, pres part* **a' priobadh,** wink,
  blink
priobadh, priobaidh, priobaidhean *nm*
  1 winking, blinking
prìobhaideach *adj* private
prìomh *adj* main, foremost, principal
prìomhaire, prìomhaire,
  prìomhairean *nm* prime minister
prionnsa, prionnsa, prionnsan *nm*
  prince
prionnsapal, prionnsapail,
  prionnsapalan *nm* 1 principle;
  2 principal
prìosan, prìosain, prìosanan *nm* prison
prìosanach, *gen & pl* **prìosanaich** *nm*
  prisoner
prìs, prìse, prìsean *nf* price
prìseil *adj* precious, valuable
pròbhaist, pròbhaiste, pròbhaistean
  nm provost
prògram, prògraim, prògraman *nm*
  programme
proifeasair, proifeasair,
  proifeasairean *nm* professor
pròis, *gen* **pròise** *nf* pride
pròiseact, *pl* **pròiseactan** *nmf* project
pròiseil *adj* proud
pronn *adj* mashed, pulverised
pronn *vt, pres part* **a' pronnadh,** 1 mash,
  pulverise; 2 bash, beat up
pronnadh, *gen* **pronnaidh** *nm* mashing,
  bashing *etc*

pronnasg, *gen* **pronnaisg** *nm* sulphur, brimstone

prosbaig, prosbaig, prosbaigean *nf* **1** binoculars; **2** telescope

Pròstanach, *gen & pl* **Pròstanaich** *nm* a Protestant, *also adj* **Pròstanach** Protestant

prothaid, prothaide, prothaidean *nf* profit

puball & **pùball**, *gen* **pubaill**, *pl* **puballan** *nm* marquee

pùdar/fùdar, *gen* **pùdair**, *pl* **pùdaran** *nm* powder

pùdaraich & **fùdaraich** *vt, pres part* **a' pùdarachadh**, powder

puing, puinge, puingean *nf* **1** point; **2** (*typog*) stop, mark

puinnsean, puinnsein, puinnseanan *nm* poison

puinnseanach *also* **puinnseanta** *adj* poisonous

puinnseanaich *vt, pres part* **a' puinnseanachadh**, poison

pumpa, pumpa, pumpaichean *nm* pump

punnd, *gen & pl* **puinnd** *nm* pound

purgadair, *gen* **purgadaire** *nm* purgatory

purpaidh *adj* purple

purpar & **purpur**, *gen* **purpair** *nm* purple

put, puta, *pl* **putan** & **putaichean** *nm* buoy

put *vti, pres part* **a' putadh**, **1** push; **2** jostle

putadh, *gen* **putaidh** *nm* pushing, jostling

putan, putain, putanan *nm* button

R

rabaid, rabaide, rabaidean *nf* rabbit

rabhadh, rabhaidh, rabhaidhean *nm* warning

rabhd, *gen* **rabhda** *nm, also* **ràbhart**, *gen* **ràbhairt** *nm*, **1** idle talk; **2** obscene talk

ràc, ràic, ràcan *nm* drake

ràc *vti, pres part* **a' ràcadh** (*gardening etc*) rake

racaid, racaide, racaidean *nf* (*tennis etc*) racket

ràcan, ràcain, ràcanan *nm* (*tool*) rake

rach *vi, pres part* **a' dol**, **1** go; **2** happen; **3** become; **4** *in expr* **rach agam** (*etc*) **air** manage to, succeed in; **5** *used to expr passive*

radan, *gen & pl* **radain** *nm* rat

ràdh *nm* **1** saying

rag *adj* **1** stiff; **2** stubborn

ragaich *vti, pres part* **a' ragachadh**, stiffen

raidhfil, raidhfil, raidhfilean *nf* rifle

raineach, *gen* **rainich** *nf* bracken

ràinig *pt of irreg v* **ruig**

ràith, ràithe, ràithean *nf* **1** season, quarter (*of year*); **2** while

ràitheachan, *gen & pl* **ràitheachain** *nm* (*publishing*) quarterly, periodical

ràmh, *gen & pl* **ràimh** *nm* oar

ràn, *gen & pl* **ràin** *nm* roar, yell

ràn *vi, pres part* **a' rànail** & **a' rànaich**, **1** roar, yell; **2** weep

rànail *nm* **1** roaring, yelling; **2** weeping

rann, *gen* **rainn**, *pl* **rannan** & **ranntaichean** *nf* **1** poetry; **2** (*single*) verse

rannaigheachd *nf* versification, metre, metrics

rannsachadh, *gen* **rannsachaidh** *nm* **1** searching, rummaging etc; **2** research

rannsaich *vti, pres part* **a' rannsachadh**, **1** search; **2** rummage; **3** research; **4** explore; **5** ransack

raon, *gen* **raoin**, *pl* **raontan** & **raointean** *nm* **1** field; **2** (*fig*) field (*of knowledge etc*)

rapach *adj* slovenly, scruffy

ràsanach *adj* boring, tedious

rath, *gen* **ratha** *nm* luck, good fortune, prosperity

rathad, *gen* **rathaid** & **rothaid**, *pl* **rathaidean** & **ròidean** *nm* **1** road; **2** way

rathail *adj* auspicious

rè *nf* time, period

rè *prep* during, through(out)

reachd *nm* rule, command, law

reamhar *adj* fat

reamhraich *vti, pres part* **a' reamhrachadh**, fatten

reic *nm* selling, sale

reic *vt, pres part* **a' reic**, sell

reiceadair, reiceadair, reiceadairean *nm* **1** seller, vendor; **2** auctioneer

rèidh *adj* **1** level; **2** smooth; **3** cleared; **4** *in expr* **bi rèidh ri cuideigin** get on well with someone

rèidhlean, rèidhlein, rèidhleanan *nm* meadow, green

rèidio, rèidio, rèidiothan *nm* radio

rèile, rèile, rèilichean *nf* rail

rèilig, rèilige, rèiligean *nf* a kirkyard

rèis, rèise, rèisean *nf* (*sports etc*) race

rèiseamaid, rèiseamaide, rèiseamaidean *nf* regiment

rèite, rèite, rèitean *nf* **1** agreement; **2** reconciliation; **3** atonement; **4** betrothal

rèiteach, rèitich, rèitichean *nm* betrothal

rèiteachadh, *gen* **rèiteachaidh** *nm* conciliating, settling etc

rèitear, rèiteir, rèitearan *nm* (*sport*) referee

reithe, reithe, reitheachan *nm* tup, ram

rèitich *vt, pres part* **a' rèiteachadh**, **1** reconcile, appease; **2** (*situations, relationships etc*) settle; **3** disentangle; **4** clear

reoth *vti, pres part* **a' reothadh**, freeze

reòiteag, reòiteig, reòiteagan *nf* ice cream

reòthta *adj* frozen

reothadair, reothadair, reothadairean *nm* freezer, deep freeze

reothadh, *gen* **reothaidh** *nm* frost

reotha(i)rt, reothairt, reothartan *nmf* spring-tide

reub *vti, pres part* **a' reubadh**, tear, rend, rip, lacerate, mangle

reubadh, reubaidh, reubaidhean *nm* rip, rent

reubalach, *gen & pl* **reubalaich** *nm* rebel

reudan, reudain, reudanan *nm* wood-louse

reul, rèil, reultan *nf* star **an reul-iùil** the pole star

reuladair, reuladair, reuladairean *nm* astronomer

reultag, reultaig, reultagan *nf* (*typog*) asterisk

reusan, *gen* **reusain** *nm* reason; sanity

reusanta *adj* **1** reasonable, sensible; **2** reasonable, fair

ri, *prep* to, against, during, engaged in activity

riabhach *adj* **1** brindled; **2** grizzled, drab, dun

riadh, *gen* **rèidh** *nm* (*fin*) interest

riaghail *vti, pres part* **a' riaghladh**, *also* **riaghlaich** *vti, pres part* **a' riaghlachadh**, **1** rule, govern; **2** regulate, manage

riaghailt, riaghailte, riaghailtean *nf* **1** rule, regulation; **2** system, order

riaghailteach *adj* regular, systematical

riaghailteachd *nf* orderliness, regularity

riaghailtich *vt, pres part* **a' riaghailteachadh**, regularise, regulate

riaghaltas, riaghaltais, riaghaltasan *nm* government

riaghladair, riaghladair, riaghladairean *nm* **1** a ruler, governor; **2** regulator

riaghladh, *gen* **riaghlaidh** *nm* **1** governing; **2** administration, management

rian, rian, rianan *nm* **1** orderliness, system; **2** reason; **4** (*music*) arrangement

rianachd *nf* administration

rianadair, rianadair, rianadairean *nm* **1** (*music*) arranger; **2** computer

rianaich *vt, pres part* **a' rianachadh**, administer

rianail *adj* methodical

rianaire, rianaire, rianairean *nm* administrator

riarachadh, *gen* **riarachaidh** *nm* **1** pleasing; **2** dividing

riaraich *vt, pres part* **a' riarachadh**, **1** please; **2** divide, (*cards*) deal

riaraichte *adj* pleased, satisfied

riatanach *adj* essential

rib *vt, pres part* **a' ribeadh**, trap, ensnare

ribe, ribe, ribeachan *nmf* snare, trap

ribheid, ribheide, ribheidean *nf* reed

rìbhinn, rìbhinne, rìbhinnean *nf* maiden, girl

ridire, ridire, ridirean *nm* knight

rìgh, rìgh, rìghrean *nm* **1** king

rìghinn *adj* (*materials etc*) tough

rinn, rinne, rinnean *nm* point, promontory

rioban, riobain, riobanan *nm* ribbon

riochd, riochda, riochdan *nm* form, likeness, appearance

riochdachadh, riochdachaidh, riochdachaidhean *nm* representation

riochdaich *vt, pres part* **a' riochdachadh**, **1** represent; **2** portray, impersonate

riochdair, riochdair, riochdairean *nm* pronoun

riochdaire, riochdaire, riochdairean *nm* **1** representative; **2** (*film etc*) producer

rìoghachadh, rìoghachaidh, rìoghachaidhean *nm* reigning, reign

rìoghachd, rìoghachd, rìoghachdan *nf* a kingdom

Rìoghachd Aonaichte *nf, used with art* **an Rìoghachd Aonaichte** the United Kingdom

rìoghaich *vi, pres part* **a' rìoghachadh**, reign

rìoghail *adj* royal; kingly, regal

rìomhach *adj* beautiful, splendid

rionnach, *gen & pl* **rionnaich** *nm* mackerel

rionnag, rionnaig, rionnagan *nf* star

ro *adv* **1** too, excessively; **2** *as prefix* **ro-** over-; **3** *as intensifying element* very, extremely

ro, *prep* before, in front of

ro-, *prefix corres to Eng* pre-, fore-

ro-aithris *f* forecast

ro-aithris, *pres part* **a' ro-aithris** *vti*, forecast, foretell

robach *adj* **1** shaggy, hairy; **2** slovenly

roc, *gen & pl* **ruic** *nf* wrinkle

rocaid, rocaide, rocaidean *nf* rocket

ròcail, *gen* **ròcaile** *nf* croak(ing), caw(ing)

ròca(i)s, **ròcais**, **ròcaisean** *nf*, rook,
   bodach-ròcais *m* scarecrow
ro-chraiceann, *gen* **ro-chraicinn**, *pl* **ro-chraicnean** *nm* foreskin
roghainn, **roghainn**, **roghainnean** *nmf*
   choice, preference
roghnachadh, *gen* **roghnachaidh** *nm*
   choosing
roghnaich *vti, pres part* **a' roghnachadh**,
   choose
roilig *vti, pres part* **a' roiligeadh**, roll
roimhear, **roimheir**, **roimhearan** *nm*
   preposition
ròineag, **ròineig**, **ròineagan** *nf* (single)
   hair
roinn, **roinne**, **roinnean** *nf* **1** division;
   2 share; **3** department; **4** region; **5**
   continent
roinn *vt, pres part* **a' roinneadh**, **1** divide
   (up); **2** divide (*cards*) deal
ròist *vt, pres part* **a' ròstadh** & **a'
   ròsdadh**, **1** roast; **2** fry
ro-làimh *adj* advance
ròlaist, **ròlaist**, **ròlaistean** *nm* romantic
   novel
ro-leasachan, *gen & pl* **ro-leasachain** *nm*
   (*gram*) prefix
ròm *nmf* pubic hair
ròmach *adj* **1** woolly, hairy, shaggy;
   2 bearded
ròmag, **ròmaig**, **ròmagan** *nf* female
   genitals
Ròmàinia *nf* Romania
Ròmàinianach, *gen & pl* **Ròmàinianaich**
   nm Romanian, *also adj* **Ròmàinianach**
   Romanian
ròn, *gen & pl* **ròin** *nm* seal (*sea creature*)
rong[1], *gen* **roinge** & **ronga**, *pl* **rongan**
   nf, also **rongas**, *gen & pl* **rongais** *nm*,
   1 rung; **2** spar; **3** hoop
rong[2], *gen & pl* **roing** *nm* vital spark
ronn, **roinn**, **ronnan** *nm* mucus, phlegm
ro-òrdachadh, *gen* **ro-òrdachaidh** *nm*
   predestination
ro-phàigheadh, *gen* **ro-phàighidh** *nm*
   pre-payment
ròp(a), *gen* **ròpa**, *pl* **ròpaichean** &
   ròpannan *nm* rope
ro-ràdh, *gen* **ro-ràidh**, *pl* **ro-ràidhean**
   nm foreword, preamble
ròs, **ròis**, **ròsan** *nm* rose
rosg[1], **ruisg**, **rosgan** *nm* prose

rosg[2], **ruisg**, **rosgan** *nm* eyelash
rosgrann *f* (*gram*) sentence
ròsta & **ròsda** *adj* **1** roasted; **2** fried
roth, **rotha**, **rothan** *nmf* wheel
rothach *adj* wheeled
ro-thaghadh, *gen* **ro-thaghaidh** *nm* pre-
   selection
rothar, **rothair**, **rotharan** *nm* bicycle
ruadh *adj* red, red-haired, ginger
ruagadh, *gen* **ruagaidh** *nm* chasing, routing
rua(i)g *vt, pres part* **a' ruagadh**, **1** chase;
   2 (*military*) rout
ruaig, **ruaige**, **ruaigean** *nf* **1** chase;
   2 (*military etc*) flight
ruamhair *vi, pres part* **a' ruamhar**, **1** dig;
   2 rummage
rubair, **rubair**, **rubairean** *nm* rubber
rubha, **rubha**, **rubhaichean** *nm* (*topog*)
   point, promontory
rùchd, **rùchda**, **rùchdan** *nm* **1** grunt;
   2 belch; **3** retching
rùchd *vi, pres part* **a' rùchdail**, **1** grunt;
   2 belch; **3** retch
rud, **rud**, **rudan** *nm* **1** thing; **2** fact;
   3 matter, affair
rùda, **rùda**, **rùdan** *nm* ram, tup
rudail *adj* concrete, real, actual
rùdan, *gen* **rùdain**, *pl* **rùdain** & **rùdanan**
   nm knuckle, finger-joint
rudeigin 1 *pron* something, anything; **2** *as
   adv* somewhat
rudhadh, *gen* **rudhaidh** *nm* blush(ing),
   flush(ing)
ruidhle, **ruidhle**, **ruidhlea(cha)n** *nm*
   reel
ruig *vti irreg, pres part* **a' ruigsinn**, (*vi*)
   arrive, (*vt*) arrive at, reach
ruighe, **ruighe**, **ruighean** *nmf* **1** forearm;
   2 (*topog*) hillslope
ruigsinneach *adj* accessible
rùilear, **rùileir**, **rùilearan** *nm* rule(r)
   (*measuring*)
ruisean, *gen* **ruisein** *nm*, lunch
Ruiseanach, *gen & pl* **Ruiseanaich** *nm*
   Russian, *also adj* **Ruiseanach** Russian
Ruiseanais *nf* (*lang*) Russian
rùisg *vt, pres part* **a' rùsgadh**, **1** bare,
   strip; **2** shear, fleece; **3** peel; **4** chafe
rùisgte *adj* stripped, shorn, peeled
Ruisia *nf, also* **an Ruis** *nf* Russia
ruiteach *adj* **1** ruddy; **2** blushing,
   flushed

ruith, ruithe, ruithean *nf* **1** running;
2 (*military etc*) pursuit, rout **3** rate, pace;
4 sequence

ruith *vti, pres part* **a' ruith, 1** run; **2** flow;
3 chase

rùm, rùim, rumannan *nm* room

rùn, rùin, rùintean *nm* **1** love, affection;
2 secret; **3** ambition, purpose; wish; **4** *in*
expr **a dh'aon rùn (gu)** deliberately

rùnachadh, *gen* **rùnachaidh** *nm* wishing,
intending

rùnaich *vi, pres part,* **a' rùnachadh,** wish,
desire, resolve

rùnaire, rùnaire, rùnairean *nm*
secretary

rùrachadh, *gen* **rùrachaidh** *nm*
rummaging, exploring etc

rùraich *vi, pres part* **a' rùrachadh,**
1 rummage, grope; **2** *vti* explore

rus, *gen* **ruis** *nm* rice

rùsg, rùisg, rùsgan *nm* (*fruit etc*) peel,
skin, husk, (*sheep*) fleece, (*wood*) bark

rùsgadh, *gen* **rùsgaidh** *nm* baring,
shearing etc

S

's *conj* (*for* agus & **is**) and

sa¹ (*for* **anns a'**) in the

sa² *corres to* **seo**, this

-sa *a suffix used to emphasise poss adj*

Sàbaid/Saboin(n)d *etc*, **Sàbaid**, **Sàbaidean** *nf*, sabbath **Là na Sàbaid** the Sabbath

sabaid, **sabaide**, **sabaidean** *nf* fighting, brawling, scrap

sabaid *vi, pres part* **a' sabaid**, *also* **sabaidich** *vi, pres part* **a' sabaidich**, fight, scrap, brawl

sàbh, *gen* **sàibh**, *pl* **sàbhan** & **sàibh** *nm* saw

sàbh *vti, pres part* **a' sàbhadh**, saw

sàbhail *vt, pres part* **a' sàbhaladh**, **1** save, rescue; **2** economise

sàbhailte *adj* safe

sabhal, *gen* **sabhail**, *pl* **sabhalan** & **saibhlean** *nm* barn

sàbhaladh, *gen* **sàbhalaidh** *nm* **1** rescuing; **2** (*relig*) salvation; **3** (*fin*) savings

sabhs, **saibhse**, **sabhsan** *nm* sauce

sac, *gen* **saic**, *pl* **sacan** & **saic** *nm* **1** sack; **2** *with art*, **an sac** asthma

sagart, **sagairt**, **sagartan** *nm* priest

saibhear/sàibhear, *gen* **saibheir**, *pl* **saibhearan** *nm* **1** culvert; **2** sewer

saideal, **saideil**, **saidealan** *nm* satellite

saidhbhir *adj* wealthy, affluent

saidhbhreas, *gen* **saidhbhreis** *nm* wealth, affluence

saidheans, **saidheans**, **saidheansan** *nm* science

saighdear, **saighdeir**, **saighdearan** *nm* soldier

saighead, **saighde**, **saighdean** *nf* arrow

sail, **saile**, **sail(th)ean** *nf* (*building*) beam, joist

sàil, **sàile**, **sàil(t)ean** *nf* heel

sailead, **saileid**, **saileadan** *nm* salad

saill, *gen* **saille** *nf* fat, grease

saill *vt, pres part* **a' sailleadh**, **1** salt; **2** season

saillear, **sailleir**, **saillearan** *nf* salt-cellar

saillte *adj* salty, salted, salt

saimeant *nm* cement, concrete

sal, *gen* **sail** *nm* **1** filth; **2** dross; **3** stain

sàl, *gen* **sàil(e)** *nm* brine

salach *adj* dirty, filthy, foul

salachadh, *gen* **salachaidh** *nm* dirtying, defiling

salaich *vt, pres part* **a' salach(adh)**, **1** dirty, soil; **2** defile, sully

salann, *gen* **salainn** *nm* salt

salchar, *gen* **salchair** *nm* dirt, filth

salm, *gen* & *pl* **sailm** *nmf* psalm

salmadair, **salmadair**, **salmadairean** *nm* psalter, psalmist

saltair *vt, pres part* **a' saltairt**, tread, trample

sàmhach *adj* **1** quiet, silent; **2** peaceful, tranquil

samhail, **samhla**, **samhailean** *nm* match, likeness

Samhain, *gen* **Samhna** *nf* **1** Hallowtide, All Souls'/Saints' Day **Oidhche Shamhna** Halloween; **2** *with art*, **an t-Samhain** November

sàmhchair, *gen* **sàmhchaire** *nf* **1** quiet(ness), silence; **2** tranquillity

samhla(dh), **samhlaidh**, **samhlaidhean** *nm* **1** resemblance; **2** symbol, sign; **3** simile, comparison; **4** allegory, parable

samhlaich *vti, pres part* **a' samhlachadh**, (*vt*) compare, liken (**ri** to)

samhradh, **samhraidh**, **samhraidhean** *nm* summer

sanas, **sanais**, **sanasan** *nm* **1** announcement, notice; **2** hint

sanasaich *vti, pres part* **a' sanasachadh**, advertise

sannt, *gen* **sannta** *nm* avarice, covetousness

sanntach *adj* greedy, avaricious

sanntaich *vt, pres part* **a' sanntachadh**, covet

saobh *adj* foolish, wrong-headed **saobh-shruth** *m* eddy, **saobh-chràbhadh** *m* superstition

saobhaidh, **saobhaidh**, *pl* **saobhaidhean** *nf* den, lair

saoghal, saoghail, *pl* **saoghail** & **saoghalan** *nm* **1** world; **2** life, lifetime

saoghalta *adj* **1** wordly; **2** materialistic

saoil *vi, pres part* **a' saoilsinn,** think, suppose, believe

saor *adj* **1** free, at liberty; **2** cheap

saor, *gen & pl* **saoir** *nm* joiner, carpenter

saor *vt, pres part* **a' saoradh, 1** free; **2** save, redeem

saoradh, *gen* **saoraidh** *nm* **1** saving *etc*; **2** liberation, deliverance, absolution

saorsa *nf, also* **saorsainn,** *gen* **saorsainne** *nf,* **1** freedom; **2** redemption

saothair, saothrach, saothraichean *nf* labour, toil

saothrachadh, *gen* **saothrachaidh** *nm* labouring, manufacturing

saothraich *vti, pres part* **a' saothrachadh, 1** labour, toil; **2** manufacture

saothraichte *adj* manufactured

sàr *adv, adj & prefix,* very, extremely, true *etc*

sàrachadh, *gen* **sàrachaidh** *nm* **1** oppressing, vexing *etc*; **2** oppression

sàraich *vt, pres part* **a' sàrachadh, 1** oppress; **2** vex, weary, distress

sàraichte *adj* boring, tedious

sàs, *gen* **sàis** *nm* **1** *in expr* **an sàs** caught, stuck, involved in; **2** *in expr* **bi** *v* **an sàs ann an cuideigin** nag, natter, pester someone

sàsachadh, *gen* **sàsachaidh** *nm* **1** pleasing, satisfying; **2** satisfaction

sàsaich *vt, pres part* **a' sàsachadh, 1** content, satisfy; **2** satiate

sàsaichte *adj* **1** contented, satisfied; **2** sated

Sasainn *nf* England

Sasannach, *gen & pl* **Sasannaich** *nm* Englishman, *also adj* **Sasannach** English

sàsar, sàsair, sàsaran *nm* saucer

sàth, *gen* **sàith** *nm* one's fill

sàth *vti, pres part* **a' sàthadh, 1** stab; **2** thrust, push

sàthadh, sàthaidh, *pl* **sàthaidhean** *nm* stab(bing), thrust(ing), push(ing)

seabhag, seabhaig, seabhagan *nmf* hawk, falcon

seac/seachd, *reinforcing adverbial element, eg* **seac àraidh** (*adv*) especially

seacaid, seacaide, seacaidean *nf* jacket

seach *prep* **1** instead of, rather than; **2** in comparison; **3** (*esp of sequence*) after **4** *adv & prep* past, by

seachad *adv* **1** past; **2** over, finished

seachain *vt, pres part* **a' seachnadh,** avoid, shun, abstain from

seachanta *adj* avoidable

seachd *n and num adj* seven

seachdad, seachdaid, seachdadan *nm* seventy

seachdain, seachdaine, seachdainean *nf* week

seachdamh *num adj* seventh

seachdnar *nmf* septet

seachnadh, *gen* **seachnaidh** *nm* avoiding, shunning **àite-seachnaidh** *m* passing place

seachran, *gen* **seachrain** *nm* **1** wandering; **2** going astray

seach-rathad, seach-rathaid, seach-rathaidean *nm* bypass

seada, seada, seadaichean *nmf* shed

seadag, seadaig, seadagan *nf* grapefruit

seadh (*v* **is** *plus obs neuter* **eadh**) *adv, expr non-affirmative* yes, *in expr* **seadh dìreach!** absolutely!

seagal, *gen* **seagail** *nm* rye

seagh *occas* **seadh,** *gen* **seagha,** *pl* **seaghan** *nm* sense, meaning

seàla, seàla, seàlaichean *nf* shawl

sealbh, *gen* **seilbh** *nm* **1** luck, fortune; **2** providence, heaven

sealbhach *adj* **1** lucky; **2** (*gram*) possessive

sealg, seilge, sealgan *nf* hunt(ing)

sealg *vti, pres part* **a' sealg,** hunt

sealgair, sealgair, sealgairean *nm* hunter, a huntsman, **an Sealgair Mòr** (*constellation*) Orion

seall *vti, pres part* **a' sealltainn, 1** see, look; **2** (*vt*) show; **3** watch over, *usu in excls,* **gu sealladh (Dia/Sealbh) orm!** My Goodness!

sealladh, seallaidh, seallaidhean *nm* **1** sight, eyesight, **an dà shealladh** second sight; **2** look; **3** view

seamrag, seamraig, seamragan *nf* **1** shamrock; **2** clover

sean, *before d, s, t, l, n or r* **seann,** *lenites exc for d, s & t, comp* **(n)as sine** (*in past tense*) **(n)a bu shine,** *adj* **1** old; **2** former; **3** *as noun in expr* **o shean** of old; **4** *as prefix,* **sean(n)-** old-

seana- *adj prefix* old

seanailear, seanaileir, seanailearan *nm* general

seanair, seanar, seanairean *nm* **1** grandfather; **2** ancestor, forebear

seanchaidh, seanchaidh, seanchaidhean *nm* **1** tradition-bearer; **2** shenachie

seanchas, seanchais, seanchasan *nm* **1** traditional lore; **2** chat, gossip, news

seanfhacal, seanfhacail, *pl* **seanfhacail** & **seanfhaclan** *nm* proverb, saying, adage

seang *adj* slim, skinny, lank, thin

seangan, *gen* **seangain,** *pl* **seanganan** & **seangain** *nm* ant

seanmhair, seanmhar, seanmhairean *nf* grandmother

seantans, seantans, seantansan *nm* (*gram*) sentence

sear *adj* & *adv, corres to* **an ear** (*see* **ear**), east, eastern

sèar, sèair, sèaraichean *nm* (*stock market*) share

searbh *adj* **1** (*esp tastes*) bitter, sour, acrid, harsh, pungent; **2** disagreeable; **3** sarcastic, sharp; **4** acid

searbhadair, searbhadair, searbhadairean *nm* towel

searbhag, searbhaig, searbhagan *nf* acid

searbhagach *adj* acid(ic)

searbhanta, searbhanta, searbhantan *nmf* servant

searg *vti, pres part* **a' seargadh,** (*vti*) dry up, shrivel, wither, (*vt*) blight

seargach *adj* deciduous

seargadh, *gen* **seargaidh** *nm* **2** decay(ing); **3** blight(ing)

searmon, searmoin, searmonan *nm* sermon

searmonaich *vi, pres part* **a' searmonachadh,** preach

searrach, *gen* & *pl* **searraich** *nm* colt, foal

searrag, searraig, searragan *nf* **1** bottle; **2** flask

seas *vti, pres part* **a' seasamh, 1** (*vi*) stand; **2** (*vt*) stand by, support; **3** (*vi*) last

seasamh, *gen* **seasaimh** *nm* **1** standing position; **2** footing; **3** stance; **4** status; **5** *in expr* **an seasamh nam bonn** on the spot

seasg *adj* **1** barren, sterile; **2** (*animals*) dry

seasgad, seasgaid, seasgadan *nm* sixty

seasgair *adj* **1** cosy, snug; **2** comfortably off

seasmhach *adj* (*phys* & *morally*) **1** firm, stable, reliable; **2** enduring, durable

seatlair, seatlair, seatlairean *nm* settler

seic, seice, seicichean *nf* cheque

Seic, *gen* **Seice** *nf, used with art,* **an t-Seic** the Czech Republic

Seiceach, *gen* & *pl* **Seicich** *nm* Czech, *also adj* **Seiceach** Czech

seiche, seiche, seicheannan *nf* skin, pelt, hide

sèid *vti, pres part* **a' sèideadh, 1** (*vi*) blow; **2** (*vi*) swell, puff up

seilbh (*also* **sealbh** *nm*), *gen* **seilbhe,** *pl* **seilbhean** *nf* property, possession

seilbheach/sealbhach *adj* (*gram*) possessive

seilbheadair/sealbhadair, *gen* **seilbheadair,** *pl* **seilbheadairean** *nm* owner, proprietor

seilbhich *vt, pres part* **a' seilbheachadh,** own, possess

seilcheag, seilcheig, seilcheagan *nf* **1** snail; **2** slug

seile *nm* saliva, spittle

seileach, seilich, seileachan *nm* willow

seillean, *gen* **seillein,** *pl* **seilleanan** & **seillein** *nm* bee, **seillean-mòr** bumble-bee

sèimh *adj* (*person, weather etc*) calm, mild, gentle, **an Cuan Sèimh** the Pacific Ocean

sèimhe *nf* calm(ness), mildness, gentleness

sèimheachadh, *gen* **sèimheachaidh** *nm* (*gram*) lenition

seinn, *gen* **seinne** *nf* **1** singing; **2** playing (*instrument*)

seinn *vti, pres part* **a' seinn, 1** sing; **2** play (*musical instrument*)

seinneadair, seinneadair, seinneadairean *nm* singer

seirbheis, seirbheise, seirbheisean *nf* **1** service; **2** favour

seirbheiseach, *gen* & *pl* **seirbheisich** *nm* servant

seirc, *gen* **seirce** *nf* **1** love, affection; **2** (*Bibl*) charity

seirm *vti, pres part* **a' seirm,** ring (out), sound

seis(e), seise, seisean *nm* **1** like(s) of; **2** equal, match

seisean, seisein, seiseanan *nm* session

sèist¹, sèist, sèistean *nmf* siege

sèist², sèist, sèistean *nmf* refrain, chorus

sèithear, sèithir, sèithrichean *nm* chair

seo *adj/pron* this

seòd, *gen & pl* **seòid** *nm* hero

seòl¹, *gen & pl* **siùil** *nm* sail

seòl², *gen & pl* **siùil** *nm* **1** method, means; **2** course

seòl *vti, pres part* **a' seòladh, 1** (*vi*) sail; **2** (*vt*) navigate, steer; **3** (*vt*) guide, direct, manage, govern

seòladair, seòladair, seòladairean *nm* sailor, seaman

seòladh, seòlaidh, seòlaidhean *nm* **1** sailing, navigating, directing; **2** address (*postal*)

seòlta *adj* **1** cunning; **2** resourceful, shrewd

seòmar, seòmair, seòmraichean *nm* room, **seòmar-cadail** & **seòmar-leapa** bedroom, **seòmar-ionnlaid** bathroom, **seòmar-mullaich** attic, garret

seòrsa, *gen* **seòrsa**, *pl* **seòrsaichean** & **seòrsachan** *nm* **1** sort, kind; **2** genus, species; **3** (social) class

seòrsachadh, *gen* **seòrsachaidh** *nm* classifying, sorting

seòrsaich *vt, pres part* **a' seòrsachadh**, classify, sort

seud, *gen* **seòid**, *pl* **seudan** & **seòid** *nm* jewel, gem

seumarlan, *gen & pl* **seumarlain** *nm* **1** factor, land-agent; **2** chamberlain

Seumasach, *gen & pl* **Seumasaich** *nm* Jacobite, *also adj* **Seumasach** Jacobite

seun, seuna, seun(t)an *nm* **1** spell, charm; **2** amulet

seunta *adj* enchanted, spellbound

sgadan, *gen & pl* **sgadain** *nm* herring

sgàil *vt, pres part* **a' sgàileadh**, shade, darken, veil, mask, eclipse

sgailc, sgailce, sgailcean *nf* **1** slap, smack; **2** sharp sound; **3** swig; **4** baldness

sgailc *vt, pres part* **a' sgailc(eadh)**, slap, smack

sgàil(e), sgàile, sgàilean *nf* **1** shade, shadow, covering; **2** ghost, spectre

sgàileadh, *gen* **sgàilidh** *nm* shading, masking

sgàilean, sgàilein, sgàileanan *nm* **1** umbrella; **2** (*IT, TV etc*) screen

sgàin *vti, pres part* **a' sgàineadh**, burst, crack, split

sgàineadh, sgàinidh, sgàinidhean *nm* split, crack

sgàird, *gen* **sgàirde** *nf, with art,* **an sgàird** diarrhoea

sgairt¹, sgairte, sgairtean *nf* diaphragm

sgairt², sgairte, sgairtean *nf* **1** yell; **2** activity, gusto, vigour

sgairteil *adj,* **1** brisk, active, bustling, enthusiastic; **2** (*weather*) blustery

sgait, sgaite, sgaitean *nf* skate (*fish*)

sgal, sgala, sgalan *nm* **1** outburst; **2** yell, squeal

sgal *vi, pres part* **a' sgaladh**, yell, squeal

sgàl, *gen & pl* **sgàil** *nm* tray

sgàla, sgàla, sgàlaichean *nf* (*music*) scale

sgaladh, *gen* **sgalaidh** *nm* yelling, squealing

sgalag, sgalaig, sgalagan *nf* **1** farm servant; **2** skivvy

sgalanta *adj* (*sound*) shrill

sgall, *gen* **sgaill** *nm* **1** bald patch; **2** baldness

sgallach *adj* bald(-headed)

sgamhan, sgamhain, sgamhanan *nm* lung

sgaoil *nm* liberty, freedom, *esp in exprs* **fa/ ma/mu sgaoil** *adv* free, at liberty

sgaoil *vti, pres part* **a' sgaoileadh, 1** spread (out), stretch (out), disperse; **2** (*vt*) release

sgaoileadh, *gen* **sgaoilidh** *nm* **1** spreading, scattering, releasing; **2** dispersal

sgaoth, sgaotha, sgaothan *nm* **1** mass, multitude; **2** swarm

sgaothaich *vi, pres part* **a' sgaothachadh, 1** flock, mass; **2** swarm

sgap *vti, pres part* **a' sgapadh**, scatter

sgar *vti, pres part* **a' sgaradh**, separate, sever

sgaradh, sgaraidh, sgaraidhean *nm* separation, **sgaradh-pòsaidh** divorce

sgarbh, *gen & pl* **sgairbh** *nm* cormorant, **sgarbh an sgumain** shag

sgarfa, sgarfa, sgarfaichean *nmf* scarf

sgàrlaid *adj* scarlet

sgath *vt, pres part* **a' sgath(adh)**, cut off, prune

sgàth, sgàtha, sgàthan *nm* **1** shadow, protection; **2** fear; **3** *in expr* **air sgàth** *prep, with gen,* on account of, because of

sgàthan, sgàthain, *pl* sgàthain & **sgàthanan** *nm* mirror

sgeadachadh, *gen* **sgeadachaidh** *nm*
1 adorning; **2** embellishment

sgeadaich *vt, pres part* **a' sgeadachadh,**
1 adorn, embellish; **2** dress (up); **3** attend
to, trim

sgealb, sgeilb, sgealban *nf* chip, splinter,
fragment

sgealb *vti,* **1** split, shatter, chip; **2** carve

sgealbag, sgealbaig, sgealbagan *nf*
index finger

sgealp, sgealpa, sgealpan *nf* **1** slap,
smack; **2** sharp sound

sgeama, sgeama, sgeamaichean *nm*
scheme

sgeap, sgip, sgeap(aiche)an *nf* beehive

sgeilb, sgeilbe, sgeilbean *nf* chisel

sgeileid, sgeileide, sgeileidean *nf* skillet

sgeilp, sgeilp, sgeilpichean *nf* shelf

sgèimheach, sgiamhach *adj* beautiful,
elegant, graceful

sgèimheachadh, *gen* **sgèimheachaidh**
nm adorning, ornamenting

sgèimhich/sgiamhaich, *vt, pres part* **a'**
sgèimheachadh, adorn, ornament

sgeir, sgeire, sgeirean *nf* skerry

sgeith *vti, pres part* **a' sgeith(eadh),**
vomit

sgeul, *gen & pl* **sgeòil** *nm* **1** story; **2** news;
3 sign (*of something or someone*)

sgeulachd, sgeulachd, sgeulachdan *nf*
story

sgeulaiche, sgeulaiche, sgeulaichean
nm storyteller

sgeunach *adj* (*esp of animals*) **1** timid,
shy; **2** skittish, mettlesome

sgì, sgì(the), sgìthean *nf* ski

sgiamh, sgiamha, sgiamhan *nm* squeal,
shriek

sgiamh *vi, pres part* **a' sgiamhadh, a'**
sgiamhail & **a' sgiamhaich,** squeal,
shriek

sgian, *gen* **sgine** & **sgeine,** *dat* **sgithinn,**
pl **sgeinean** & **sgineachan** *nf* knife

sgiath, sgèithe, sgiathan *nf* **1** wing;
2 shield; **3** shelter; **4** *in expr* **fo sgèith**
under the auspices of

sgiathaich *vi, pres part* **a' sgiathadh,** fly

sgil, sgil, sgilean *nm* skill

sgileil *adj* skilful, skilled

sgillinn, sgillinne, sgillinnean *nf*
1 penny; **2** shilling Scots; **3** shilling-land

sgioba, sgioba, *pl* **sgioban, sgiobachan,**
sgiobaidhean *nmf* **1** crew; **2** team

sgiobair, sgiobair, sgiobairean *nm*
skipper, captain

sgiobalta *adj* **1** neat, tidy; **2** active, quick,
handy

sgioblachadh, *gen* **sgioblachaidh** *nm*
tidying

sgioblaich *vti, pres part* **a'**
sgioblachadh, tidy (up), put right/
straight

sgiorradh, sgiorraidh, sgiorraidhean
nm **1** accident; **2** slip, stumble

sgiort, sgiorta, *pl* **sgiortan** &
sgiortaichean *nf* skirt

sgìre, sgìre, sgìrean *nf* **1** district, area,
locality; **2** parish

sgìreachd, sgìreachd, sgìreachdan *nf*
parish

sgìth *adj* tired, weary

sgitheach, *gen & pl* **sgith(e)ich** *nm*
whitethorn; hawthorn

sgìtheachadh, *gen* **sgìtheachaidh** *nm*
tiring, wearying

sgìtheil *adj* tiring, wearisome

sgìthich *vti, pres part* **a' sgìtheachadh,**
tire, weary

sgithich *vi, pres part* **a' sgitheadh,** ski

sgìths *nf* tiredness, weariness

sgiùrs *vt, pres part* **a' sgiùrsadh,** scourge,
whip

sgiùrsair, sgiùrsair, sgiùrsairean *nm*
scourge, whip

sglàib *nf* (*building*) plaster

sglàibeadair, sglàibeadair,
sglàibeadairean *nm* (*building*) plasterer

sglèat, sglèata, sglèatan *nm* slate

sglèatair, sglèatair, sglèatairean *nm*
(*building*) slater

sgleog, sgleoig, sgleogan *nf* slap

sgob *vti, pres part* **a' sgobadh, 1** snatch;
2 sting; **3** peck

sgoch *vt, pres part* **a' sgochadh,** sprain

sgoil, sgoile, sgoiltean *nf* **1** school;
2 schooling

sgoilear, sgoileir, sgoilearan *nm*
1 pupil; **2** scholar

sgoilearach *adj* scholarly

sgoilearachd, sgoilearachd,
sgoilearachdan *nf* **1** scholarship;
2 bursary

sgoilt & **sgolt** *vti, pres part* **a' sgoltadh**, split, cleave, slit

sgoinneil *adj* great, smashing

sgol *vt, pres part* **a' sgoladh**, rinse

sgoltadh, sgoltaidh, sgoltaidhean *nm* split, cleft, slit, chink

sgona, sgona, sgonaichean *nmf* scone

sgonn, *gen* **sgoinn** & **sguinn,** *pl* **sgonnan** & **sguinn** *nm* lump, hunk

sgòr, sgòir, sgòraichean *nm* (*games etc*) score

sgòrnan, sgòrnain, sgòrnanan *nm* gullet, throat, windpipe

sgoth, sgotha, sgothan *nf* skiff, sailing boat

sgòth, sgòtha, sgòthan *nf* cloud

sgòthach *adj* cloudy

sgraing, sgrainge, sgraingean *nf* frown, scowl

sgreab, sgreaba, sgreaban *nf* scab

sgread, sgreada, sgreadan *nm* scream, shriek

sgread *vi, pres part* **a' sgreadadh** & **a' sgreadail**, scream, screech

sgreadhail, sgreadhaile, sgreadhailean *nf* trowel

sgreamh, *gen* **sgreamha** & **sgreimhe** *nm* loathing, disgust

sgreamhail *adj* disgusting, loathsome

sgreataidh *adj* loathsome, nauseating

sgreuch, sgreucha, sgreuchan *nm* scream, screech

sgreuch *vi, pres part* **a' sgreuchail**, scream, screech

sgrìob, sgrìoba, sgrìoban *nf* 1 scratch, scrape; 2 furrow; 3 trip, excursion; 4 (*typog*) dash

sgrìob *vti, pres part* **a' sgrìobadh**, 1 scratch, scrape; 2 furrow

sgrìobadh, *gen* **sgrìobaidh** *nm* scratching, scraping etc

sgrìoban, sgrìobain, sgrìobanan *nm* hoe

sgrìobh *vti, pres part* **a' sgrìobhadh**, write

sgrìobhadair, sgrìobhadair, sgrìobhadairean *nm* writer

sgrìobhadh, sgrìobhaidh, sgrìobhaidhean *nm* writing

sgrìobtar, sgrìobtair, sgrìobtairean *nm* scripture

sgrios, sgriosa, sgriosan *nm* destruction, ruin

sgrios *vti, pres part* **a' sgrios** & **a' sgriosadh**, destroy, ruin

sgriosadh, *gen* **sgriosaidh** *nm* destroying etc

sgriosail *adj* 1 destructive; 2 pernicious; 3 terrible, dreadful

sgriubha, sgriubha, sgriubhaichean *nmf* (*joinery*) screw

sgriubhaire, sgriubhaire, sgriubhairean *nm* screwdriver

sgròb *vti, pres part* **a' sgròbadh**, scratch

sgrùd *vt, pres part* **a' sgrùdadh**, 1 scrutinize, investigate; 2 audit

sgrùdadh, sgrùdaidh, sgrùdaidhean *nm* 1 scrutiny, investigation; 2 audit

sguab, sguaibe, sguaban *nf* 1 brush, broom; 2 sheaf

sguab *vti, pres part* **a' sguabadh**, sweep, brush

sguabadair, sguabadair, sguabadairean *nm* hoover, vacuum-cleaner

sgud *vti, pres part* **a' sgudadh**, chop

sgudal, *gen* **sgudail** *nm* 1 rubbish, refuse; 2 nonsense

sguir *vi, pres part* **a' sgur**, stop, cease, desist

sgur, *gen* **sguir** *nm* stopping, ceasing

sgùrr, sgurra, sgurran *nm* peak, pinnacle

shìos *adv* down (*position*)

shuas *adj* up (*position*)

sia *n and num adj* six

siab *vti, pres part* **a' siabadh**, 1 wipe, rub; 2 *vi* (*snow etc*) drift

siabann, *gen* & *pl* **siabainn** *nm* soap

siach *vt, pres part* **a' siachadh**, sprain, strain

sia-deug *adj and num* sixteen

sia-deugach *adj* hexadecimal

sian, sìne, siantan *nf*, storm, blast

sianar *nmf* sestet

siar *adj* & *adv*, west, western

siathamh *num adj* sixth

sibh *emph* **sibhse**, *pron pl, also expr formal sing,* you

sìde *nf* weather

sil *vi, pres part* **a' sileadh**, (*liquids*) 1 drip, drop; 2 flow; 3 rain

sileadh, *gen* **silidh** 1 *nm* dripping, flowing etc; 2 rainfall

silidh *nm* **1** jam; **2** jelly

silteach *adj* fluid, dripping, dropping, flowing,

similear, simileir, similearan *nm* chimney

simpleachadh, *gen* **sìmpleachaidh**, *nm* **1** simplifying; **2** simplification

simplich *vt, pres part* **a' sìmpleachadh**, simplify

simplidh *adj* **1** simple, uncomplicated; **2** simple-minded

sin *adj* that, those

sin *pron* that

sin *vti, pres part* **a' sìneadh**, **1** stretch; **2** extend; **3** pass, hand

sinc *nm* zinc

sinc(e), since, sincean *nmf* sink

sine, sine, sinean *nf* nipple, teat

sineach, *gen & pl* **sinich** *nm* a mammal; *also adj*, **sineach** mammalian

sìneadh, *gen* **sìnidh** *nm* **1** stretching; **2** outstretched position

singilte *adj* **1** single; **2** (*gram*) singular

sinn *emph* **sinne**, *pron*, we

sinn- *prefix used in family relationships*, great-

sinnsear, sinnsir, sinnsirean *nm* ancestor, forefather

sìnteag, sìnteig, sìnteagan *nf* **1** hop; **2** stride; **3** stepping-stone

siobhag, siobhaig, siobhagan *nf* wick

siobhalta *adj* civil, polite

siobhaltair, sìobhaltair, sìobhaltairean *nm* civilian

sìoda, sìoda, sìodachan *nm* silk

sìol, *gen* **sìl** *nm coll* **1** seed; **2** race, progeny; **3** (*livestock etc*) breed

sìolachadh, *gen* **sìolachaidh** *nm* **1** engendering, seeding etc; **2** insemination

sìol(t)achan, *gen & pl* **sìol(t)achain** *nm* strainer, filter

sìoladh, *gen* **sìolaidh** *nm* subsiding, filtering etc

sìolaich *vti, pres part* **a' sìolachadh**, **1** engender, beget, propagate; **2** (*vi*) seed; **3** (*vt*) inseminate

sìolaidh *vti, pres part* **a' sìoladh**, **1** subside, settle; **2** filter, strain

sìolp *vi, pres part* **a' sìolpadh**, slip/steal away

sìoman, sìomain, sìomanan *nm* straw rope

sìon a thing, something, anything, (*in neg exprs*) nothing

Sìona *nf* China

Sìonach, *gen & pl* **Sìonaich** Chinaman, *also adj* **Sìonach** Chinese

sionnach, *gen & pl* **sionnaich** *nm* fox

sionnsar, sionnsair, sionnsaran bagpipe chanter

sìor- *a prefix corres to Eng* ever-

siorrachd, siorrachd, siorrachdan *nf also* **siorramachd** *nf* **1** sheriffdom; **2** county, shire

siorraidh, siorraidh, siorraidhean *nm & ***siorram, siorraim, siorraman** *nm* sheriff

sìorraidh *adj* everlasting, eternal

sìorraidheachd *nf* eternity

sìos *adv* down (*expr movement*)

siosar, siosair, siosaran *nmf* scissors

siosarnaich *nf* **1** hissing; **2** whispering; **3** rustling

sir *vt, pres part* **a' sireadh**, seek, search for, require

sireadh, *gen* **siridh** *nm* seeking etc

siris(t), siris(t), siris(t)ean *nf* cherry

siteag, siteig, siteagan *nf & ***sitig, sitig, sitigean** *nf* dunghill, midden

sìth *adj* fairy

sìth, *gen* **sìthe** *nf* peace; tranquillity

sìtheachadh, *gen* **sìtheachaidh** *nm* pacifying

sìthean, *gen & pl* **sìthein** *nm* fairy hill

sitheann, *gen* **sìthne** *& ***sithinn** *nf* **1** venison; **2** game

sìtheil/sìo(th)chail *adj* **1** tranquil; **2** peaceable

sìthich *vt, pres part* **a' sìtheachadh**, pacify

sìthiche, sìthiche, sìthichean *nm* fairy

sitir, *gen* **sitire** *nf* braying, neighing, whinnying

siubhail *vti, pres part* **a' siubhal**, **1** (*vi*) travel, travelling; **2** (*vt*) travel, cross; **3** (*vi*) die; **4** (*vt*) seek

siubhal, siubhail, siùbhlaichean *nm* **1** travel, travelling; **2** time, *in expr* **fad an t-siubhail** all the time

siùbhlach *adj* **1** speedy; **2** (*speech*) fluent, fluid; **3** transient

siùcar, siùcair, siùcairean *nm* **1** sugar; **2** *in pl* sweets, sweeties

siud *& ***sud** *pron* that, yonder

siuga, siuga, siugannan *nmf* jug

siùrsach, siùrsaich, siùrsaichean *nf* prostitute

siùrsachd *nf* prostitution

siuthad, *pl* **siuthadaibh** *imperatives* on you go! get on with it!

slabhraidh, slabhraidh, slabhraidhean *nf* chain

slaic *vt, pres part* **a' slaiceadh,** thrash, beat, thump, bruise, maul

slaiceadh, slaicidh, slaicidhean *nm, also* **slacadaich** *nf* thrashing *etc*

slaightear, slaighteir, slaightearan *nm* knave, rascal

slàinte *nf* 1 health; 2; 3 *in toasts etc,* **deoch-slàinte** *f* toast, **slàinte!** Good health!, cheers!, **slàinte mhath/mhòr!** the best of health!, **air do dheagh shlàinte!** (to) your very good health!

slaman, *gen* **slamain** *nm* curds, crowdie

slàn *adj* 1 healthy, well; 2 *in expr* **slàn leat!** goodbye!; 3 complete

slànachadh, *gen* **slànachaidh** *nm* healing, curing

slànaich *vti, pres part* **a' slànachadh,** heal, cure

slànaighear, *gen & pl* **slànaigheir** *nm* saviour

slaod, slaoid, slaodan *nm* sledge, **slaod-uisge** raft

slaod *vti, pres part* **a' slaodadh,** drag, haul

slaodach *adj* 1 slow; 2 boring, long-drawn-out

slaodadh, *gen* **slaodaidh** *nm* dragging *etc*

slaodair, slaodair, slaodairean *nm* (*transport*) trailer

slapag, slapaig, slapagan *nf* slipper

slat, slait, slatan *nf* 1 (*measure*) yard; 2 twig; 3 rod; 4 penis, cock

sleagh, sleagha, sleaghan *nf* spear, lance, javelin

sleamhainn *adj* slippy, slippery

sleamhnachadh, *gen* **sleamhnachaidh** *nm* sliding, slipping

sleamhnag, sleamhnaig, sleamhnagan *nf* slide

sleamhnaich *vi, pres part* **a' sleamhnachadh,** slide, slip

sleuchd *vi, pres part* **a' sleuchdadh,** 1 kneel; 2 prostrate

sleuchdadh, sleuchdaidh, sleuchdaidhean *nm* 1 kneeling; 2 prostration

sliabh, slèibh, slèibhtean *nm* 1 moor, moorland; 2 hill

sliasaid, sliasaide, sliasaidean *nf* thigh

slige, slige, slige(ach)an *nf* shell

slighe, slighe, slighean *nf* path, road, track, way, route

slinnean, slinnein, slinneanan *nm* shoulder, **cnàimh-slinnein** *m* shoulder blade

slìob *vt, pres part* **a' slìobadh,** *also* **slìog** *vt, pres part* **a' slìogadh,** stroke (*dog etc*

sliochd, sliochda, sliochdan *nm* descendants, lineage

slios, sliosa, sliosan *nm* side, flank

slis, slise, slisean *nf, & dimin* **sliseag, sliseig, sliseagan** *nf,* slice

slisnich *vt, pres part* **a' slisneadh,** slice

sloc, *gen* **sluic,** *pl* **slocan** *nm* 1 hollow; 2 pit

sloinn *vi, pres part* **a' sloinneadh,** trace family tree

sloinneadh, sloinnidh, sloinnidhean *nm* 1 tracing family tree; 2 surname; 3 patronymic

sluagh, *gen* **sluaigh,** *pl* **slòigh,** *gen pl* **slògh** *nm* 1 army, host; 2 people, populace; 3 crowd

sluagh-ghairm, sluagh-ghairme, sluagh-ghairmean *nf* 1 war-cry; 2 slogan

sluaghmhor *adj* populous

sluasaid, sluasaide, sluasaidean *nf* shovel

slugadh, slugaidh, slugaidhean *nm* swallow(ing), gulp(ing)

sluig & slug *vti, pres part* **a' slugadh,** swallow, gulp

smachd *nm* authority, control, discipline, rule

smachdaich *vt, pres part* **a' smachdachadh,** discipline

smachdail *adj* authoritative, commanding

smà(i)l *vt, pres part* **a' smàladh,** extinguish, quench

smal, smail, smalan *nm* stain, spot

smàladair, smàladair, smàladairean *nm* 1 firefighter; 2 candle-snuffers

smàladh, *gen* **smàlaidh** *nm* extinguishing

smalan, *gen* **smalain** *nm* gloom, melancholy

smaoin, smaoine, smaointean *nf &*
smuain, smuaine, smuaintean *nf*
thought, notion, idea
smaoin(t)eachadh, *gen*
smaoin(t)eachaidh *nm* thinking,
considering etc
smaoin(t)ich *vi, pres part* **a'**
smaointinn & a' smaoin(t)eachadh,
also **smuain(t)ich** *vi, pres part* **a'**
smuain(t)eachadh, 1 think, reflect;
2 consider
smàrag, smàraig, smàragan *nf* emerald
smèid *vi, pres part* **a' smèideadh,**
1 beckon; **2** wave
smèideadh, *gen* **smèididh** *nm* beckoning,
waving
smeòrach, smeòraich, smeòraichean
nf thrush
smeur, smeura, smeuran *nf* bramble,
blackberry
smeuradh, *gen* **smeuraidh** *nm* smearing
smid, smide, smidean *nf* word, syllable
smig, smig, smigean *nm & more usu*
smiogaid, smiogaid, smiogaidean
nm chin
smior, *gen* **smior & smir** *nm* **1** marrow;
2 best part; **3** (*esp inner or moral*)
courage, spirit; **4** manliness, vigour
smiorach *adj* pithy
smiorail *adj* **1** strong, spirited; **2** manly,
vigorous
smiùr *vt, pres part* **a' smiùradh,** *&*
smeur *vt, pres part* **a' smeuradh,**
smear, daub, grease
smoc *vti, pres part* **a' smocadh,** smoke
(*tobacco etc*)
smocadh, *gen* **smocaidh** *nm* smoking
smuais *vt, pres part* **a' smuaiseadh,**
smash, splinter
smùch *vi, pres part* **a' smùchadh,** snivel
smugaid, smugaide, smugaidean *nf*
spit, *in expr* **tilg** *v* **smugaid** spit
smùid, smùide, smùidean *nf* **1** steam,
vapour; **2** smoke, *esp in expr* **cuir** *v*
smùid smoke; **3** fumes; **4** drunkenness
smùid *vti, pres part* **a' smùideadh, 1** (*of*
chimney etc) smoke; **2** smash
smùr, *gen* **smùir** *nm* dust, dross
snàgadh, *gen* **snàgaidh** *nm, &* **snàgail,**
gen **snàgaile** *nf* stealing, creeping
snagan-daraich, snagain-daraich,
snaganan-daraich *nm* woodpecker

snaidhm, snaidhm, snaidhmean(nan)
nm knot
snàig *vi, pres part* **a' snàgail & a'**
snàgadh, 1 crawl; **2** creep
snaigh *vt, pres part* **a' snaigheadh,** hew,
carve
snàmh, *gen* **snàimh** *nm* **1** swimming; **2** *in*
expr **air snàmh** inundated, awash
snàmh *vi, pres part* **a' snàmh,** swim, float
snasail & snasmhor *adj* neat, trim
snàth & snàith, *gen* **snàith & snàtha,** *pl*
snàithean *nm coll* thread
snàthad, snàthaid, snàthadan *nf* needle
snàthainn, *gen* **snàithne & snàthainne,**
pl **snàithnean & snàthainnean** *nm*
(single) thread
sneachd(a), *gen* **sneachda** *nm* snow
snèap, snèip, snèapan *nf* a turnip, swede
snigh *vi, pres part* **a' snighe,** drip, seep
snighe *nm* dripping, seeping
snìomh *vti, pres part* **a' snìomhadh & a'**
snìomh, 1 spin; **2** twist, wring
snìomhadh, *gen* **snìomhaidh** *nm*
spinning, twisting, wringing
snìomhair(e), snìomhaire,
snìomhairean *nm* (*tools*) drill
snodha-gàire, snodha-gàire, snodhan-
gàire *nm* smile
snog *adj* **1** pretty; **2** nice
snuadh, *gen* **snuaidh** *nm* **1** appearance;
2 complexion
so- *prefix corres to Eng* -able, -ible
sòbair, *also* **sòbarr(a),** *adj* sober
sòbhrach, sòbhraich, sòbhraichean
nf (also **seòbhrach** *etc*), and **sòbhrag,**
sòbhraig, sòbhragan *nf,* primrose
socair *adj* **1** mild, tranquil; **2** at peace,
relaxed
socair, *gen* **socrach & socaire** *nf* comfort,
ease, leisure, **air do shocair!** take it easy!
socais, socais, socaisean *nf* sock
(*footwear*)
sochar, *gen* **sochair** *nf* **1** bashfulness,
shyness; **2** weakness, compliance,
indulgence
socharach *adj* **1** bashful; **2** soft, weak,
indulgent
socrach *adj* at ease, sedate, leisurely
socrachadh, *gen* **socrachaidh** *nm*
settling
socraich *vti, pres part* **a' socrachadh,**
1 settle; **2** set, fix

sodal, *gen* **sodail** *nm* adulation, fawning, flattery

sòfa, sòfa, sòfathan *nf* sofa

sògh, *gen* **sòigh** *nm* luxury

sòghail *adj* luxurious

soilire, *gen* **soilire** *nm* celery

soilleir *adj* 1 bright, clear; 2 obvious

soilleirich *vti, pres part* **a' soilleireachadh**, 1 brighten up; 2 (*vt*) clarify, explain

soillse *nm* light

soillseachadh, *gen* **soillseachaidh** *nm* 1 shining; 2 clarification, enlightenment

soillsich *vti, pres part* **a' soillseachadh**, shine, gleam

soineannta *adj* naive

soirbh *adj* easy

soirbheachail *adj* successful, prosperous

soirbheachas, *gen* **soirbheachais**, *nm* prosperity, success

soirbhich *vi, pres part* **a' soirbheachadh**, succeed, turn out well

sòisealach, *gen & pl* **sòisealaich** *nm & adj* socialist, *also adj* **sòisealach** socialist

sòisealta *adj* social

soisgeul, *gen* **soisgeil** *nm* gospel

soisgeulach *adj* evangelical

soisgeulaiche, soisgeulaiche, soisgeulaichean *nm* evangelist

soitheach, soithich, soithichean *nfm* 1 container, dish; 2 (*sailing*) vessel

soitheamh *adj* gentle, good-natured

sòlaimte *adj* solemn; ceremonious

solair *vt, pres part* **a' solar(adh)** purvey, supply

solas, *gen & pl* **solais** *nm* light

sòlas, *gen* **sòlais** *nm* 1 solace, consolation; 2 joy

sòlasach *adj* 1 comforting, consoling; 2 joyful

solt(a) *adj* meek, gentle

sona *adj* 1 happy, content; 2 lucky

sònrachadh, *gen* **sònrachaidh** *nm* distinguishing, specifying

sònraich *vt, pres part* **a' sònrachadh**, 1 distinguish; 2 specify; 3 point out; 4 allocate, allot

sònraichte *adj* 1 particular; 2 special

sop, *gen* **suip**, *pl* **sopan** & **suip** *nm* wisp

soraidh *nf & excl* 1 farewell, **soraidh leibh!** farewell; 2 greeting

spaid, spaide, spaidean *nf* spade

spaideil *adj* (*of dress etc*) smart

spai(s)dirich *vi, pres part* **a' spai(s)dearachd**, strut

spàin, spàine, spàin(t)ean *nf* spoon

spàirn, *gen* **spàirne** *nf* exertion, effort, struggle

spanair, spanair, spanairean *nm* spanner

spàrr, sparra, sparran *nm* 1 (*joinery etc*) joist; 2 roost (*for hens etc*)

spàrr *vt, pres part* **a' sparradh**, drive, thrust

sparradh, *gen* **sparraidh** *nm* driving, thrusting

speach, speacha, speachan *nf* wasp

speal, speala, spealan *nf* scythe

spealg, speilg, spealgan *nf* splinter, fragment

spealg *vti, pres part* **a' spealgadh**, splinter, smash

spealgadh, *gen* **spealgaidh** *nm* splintering, smashing

spèil, spèile, spèilean *nf* (ice-)skate

spèil *vi, pres part* **a' spèileadh**, skate (*on ice*)

spèis, *gen* **spèise** *nf* 1 love, affection; 2 regard

speuclairean *nm pl* spectacles

speur, speura, speuran *nm* 1 sky; 2 *esp in pl* **na speuran** the heavens; 3 space

speuradair, speuradair, speuradairean *nm* 1 astrologer; 2 cosmonaut

speuradaireachd *nf* astrology

speurair, speurair, speurairean *nm* spaceman, astronaut

spìc, spìce, spìcean *nf* spike

spideag, spideig, spideagan *nf* nightingale

spìocach *adj* mean, miserly

spìocaire, spìocaire, spìocairean *nm* miser

spìon *vt, pres part* **a' spìonadh**, 1 snatch, grab; 2 pluck

spìonadh, *gen* **spìonaidh** *nm* snatching, grabbing, plucking

spionnadh, *gen* **spionnaidh** *nm* energy, strength

spiorad, spioraid, spioradan *nm* spirit

spioradail *adj* spiritual

spìosradh, spìosraidh, spìosraidhean *nm* spice

spìosraich *vt, pres part* **a' spìosrachadh,** **1** spice; **2** embalm

spiris, spirise, spirisean *nf* perch, roosting

spleuchd, spleuchda, spleuchdan *nm* **1** a stare, a gaze, a 'gawping' expression; **2** a squint

spleuchd *vi, pres part* **a' spleuchdadh,** **1** stare, gape; **2** squint

spleuchdadh, *gen* **spleuchdaidh** *nm* staring, squinting, gaping

spliùchan, spliùchain, spliùchanan *nm* pouch

spòg, spòig, spògan *nf* **1** paw; **2** hand of clock/watch; **3** spoke

spong, spuing, spongan *nm* sponge

sporan, *gen & pl* **sporain** *nm* **1** purse; **2** sporran

spòrs, *gen* **spòrsa** *nf* **1** sport; **2** fun

spot, spot, spotan *nm* spot, stain

spoth *vt, pres part* **a' spoth & a' spothadh,** castrate

spothadh, *gen* **spothaidh** *nm* castrating

spreadh *vti, pres part* **a' spreadhadh,** **1** (*vi*) burst; **2** (*vti*) explode

spreadhadh, spreadhaidh, spreadhaidhean *nm* bursting, exploding

sprèidh, *gen* **sprèidhe** *nf* livestock

spreig *vt, pres part* **a' spreigeadh,** incite, urge

spreigeadh, *gen* **spreigidh** *nm* inciting, urging

sprùilleach, *gen* **sprùillich** *nm* **1** crumbs; **2** debris

sprùilleag, sprùilleig, sprùilleagan *nf* crumb

spùill *vt, pres part* **a' spùilleadh,** *also* **spùinn** *vt, pres part* **a' spùinneadh,** plunder, despoil

spùinneadair, spùinneadair, spùinneadairean *nm* plunderer, brigand, **spùinneadair-mara** pirate, buccaneer

spu(i)r, spuir, spuirean *nm* claw, talon

spùt, spùta, spùtan *nm* **1** spout, gush, spurt; **2** waterfall; **3** *with art,* **an spùt** diarrhoea

spùt *vti, pres part* **a' spùtadh,** spout, spurt, squirt

spùtadh, *gen* **spùtaidh** *nm* spouting, spurting, squirting

sràbh, sràibh, sràbhan *nm* straw

srac *vt, pres part* **a' sracadh,** tear, rip

sracadh, *gen* **sracaidh** *nm* tearing, ripping

sradag, sradaig, sradagan *nf* spark

sràid, sràide, sràidean *nf* street

sràidearaich *vi, pres part* **a' sràidearachd,** stroll, saunter

srainnsear, srainnseir, srainnsearan *nm* stranger

srann, srainn, srannan *nmf, also* **srannail** *nf* & **srannartaich,** *gen* **srannartaiche** *nf,* snoring, snore

srann *vi, pres part* **a' srannail,** snore

sreang, sreinge, sreangan *nf* string (*not of musical instrument*)

sreath, sreatha, sreathan *nmf* **1** row, line, rank; **2** layer; **3** series

sreothart, sreothairt, sreothartan *nm* sneeze, **dèan** *v* **sreothart** sneeze

sreothartaich, *gen* **sreothartaiche** *nf* sneezing

srian, *gen* **srèine,** *pl* **srèinean & sriantan** *nf* **1** bridle, rein(s); **2** streak, stripe

sròn, *gen* **sròine,** *pl* **srònan & sròintean** *nf* **1** nose; **2** (*topog*) ridge, point, promontory

sròn-adharcach, *gen & pl* **sròn-adharcaich** *nm* rhinoceros

srùb, srùib, srùban *nm* spout (*of container*)

srùb *vti, pres part* **a' srùbadh,** **1** spout, spurt; **2** slurp

srùbadh, *gen* **srùbaidh** *nm* spouting, sucking, slurping

srùbag, srùbaig, srùbagan *nf* **1** sip; **2** snack, cup of tea

srùban, *gen & pl* **srùbain** *nm* cockle

sruth, *gen* **sruith & srutha,** *pl* **sruthan** *nm* **1** stream, burn; **2** flow; **3** current

sruth *vi, pres part* **a' sruthadh,** flow, stream, run

sruthach *adj* streaming, running, flowing

sruthadh, *gen* **sruthaidh** *nm* flowing, streaming, running

stàball, stàbaill, stàballan *nm* stable

stad, stada, stadan *nm* **1** stop, halt, pause; **2** end

stad *vti, pres part* **a' stad(adh),** **1** stop, halt, pause; **2** cease

stad-phuing, stad-phuinge, stad-phuingean *nf* full stop

staid, staide, staidean *nf* state, condition

staidhir, staidhreach, staidhrichean *nf, &* **staidhre, staidhre, staidhrichean** *nf,* **1** stair; **2** staircase

stail, staile, stailean *nf* (whisky) still

stailc, stailc, stailcean *nf* (*industry etc*) strike

stàilinn, *gen* **stàilinne** *nf* steel

staing, stainge, staingean *nf* difficulty, tight corner, fix

stàirn, *gen* **stàirne** *nf* **1** crashing, clattering; **2** rumbling

stairs(n)each, stairs(n)ich, stairs(n)ichean *nf* threshold

stais, staise, staisean *nf* moustache

stàit, stàite, stàitean *nf* (*pol etc*) state

Stàitean Aonaichte *fpl, used with art* **Na Stàitean Aonaichte** the United States

stàiteil *adj* stately

stalc, *gen* **stailc** *nm* starch

stalcair(e), stalcaire, stalcairean *nm* fool, blockhead

stalcaireachd *nf* stupidity

stalla, stalla, stallachan *nm* precipice

stamag, stamaig, stamagan *nf* stomach

stamh, *gen* **staimh**, *pl* **staimh** & **stamhan** *nm* (*seaweed*) tangle

stamp *vti, pres part* **a'** **stampadh**, stamp

stamp(a), stampa, stampaichean *nf* stamp

staoig, staoige, staoigean *nf* steak

staoin, *gen* **staoine** *nf* tin

steall, still, steallan *nf* **1** outpouring, spout, spurt, gush; **2** swig, slug

steall *vti, pres part* **a'** **stealladh**, spout, squirt, spurt, gush

stealladh, *gen* **steallaidh** *nm* spouting, squirting, spurting, gushing

steallag, steallaig, steallagan *nf, dimin of* **steall** *n* slug, swig

steallair(e), steallaire, steallairean *nm* syringe

stèidh, stèidhe, stèidhean *nf* **1** base, foundation; **2** basis

stèidheachadh, *gen* **stèidheachaidh** *nm* **1** founding, establishing; **2** foundation, establishment

stèidhich *vt, pres part* **a'** **stèidheachadh**, found, establish

stèidhichte *adj* founded, established

stèisean, stèisein, stèiseanan *nm* (*transport, radio etc*) station

stiall, stèill, stiallan *nf* **1** streak, stripe; **2** tape, strip; **3** scrap, stitch (*clothing*)

stiall *vt, pres part* **a'** **stialladh**, stripe, streak

stialladh, *gen* **stiallaidh** *nm* striping *etc*

stìopall, *gen* & *pl* **stìopaill** *nm* steeple

stiùbhard, stiùbhaird, stiùbhardan *nm* steward

stiùir, stiùire(ach), *also* **stiùrach, stiùir(ich)ean** *nf* **1** rudder; **2** helm

stiùir *vt, pres part* **a'** **stiùireadh**, **1** steer; **2** direct, run, manage

stiùireadair, stiùireadair, stiùireadairean *nm* steersman, helmsman

stiùireadh, *gen* **stiùiridh** *nm* steering, directing, managing

stiùiriche, stiùiriche, stiùirichean *nm* director

stob, stuib, stoban *nm* **1** fence post, stake; **2** stump

stòbh(a), stòbha, stòbhaichean *nmf* stove

stoc¹, *gen* & *pl* **stuic** *nm* **1** trunk (*of tree*; **2** root(-stock); **3** livestock

stoc², *gen* & *pl* **stuic** *nm* scarf, cravat

stocainn, stocainne, stocainnean *nf* stocking

stoidhle, stoidhle, stoidhlichean *nf* style

stò(i)r *vt, pres part* **a'** **stòradh**, store

stòiridh (& stòraidh), *gen* **stòiridh**, *pl* **stòiridhean** *nmf* story

stoirm, stoirme, stoirmean *nmf* **1** storm

stòl, *gen* **stòil** & **stòla**, *pl* **stòil** & **stòlan** *nm* (*furniture*) stool

stòlda *adj* (*of temperament, behaviour*) sedate, serious, staid, sober

stòr, stòir, stòran *nm* store, riches

stòradh, *gen* **stòraidh** *nm* storing

stòras, *gen* **stòrais** *nm* riches, wealth

stràc, stràic, stràcan *nm* **1** stroke, a blow; **2** accent (*diacritic*); **3** (*lang*) stress

stràic, stràice, stràicean *nm* tawse, lochgelly

streap *vti, pres part* **a'** **streap(adh)**, climb

streap(adh), *gen* **streapaidh** *nm* climbing

strì *nf* **1** struggling, striving; **2** strife, struggle, contest

94

strì *vi, pres part* **a' strì**, struggle, strive, compete

strìoch, strìocha, strìochan *nf (typog)* hyphen

strìochag, strìochaig, strìochagan *nf (typog)* tick

strìochd *vi, pres part* **a' strìochdadh**, 1 surrender, yield; 2 cringe

strìochdadh, *gen* strìochdaidh *nm* 1 submitting, surrendering, yielding, cringing; 2 surrender

strìopach, strìopaiche, strìopaichean *nf* prostitute

strìopachas, *gen* strìopachais *nm* prostitution

stròc, stròic, stròcan *nm (med)* stroke

structair, structair, structairean *nm* structure

struidh *vt, pres part* **a' struidh** squander, dissipate

struidhear, struidheir, struidhearan *nm* wastrel, spendthrift

struidheil/stròdhail *adj* extravagant, prodigal

struth, strutha, struthan *nmf* ostrich

stuadh/stuagh, *gen* stuaidh, *pl* stuadhan(nan) *nf* 1 *(in sea etc)* wave; 2 gable *(of building)*

stuaim, *gen* stuaime *nf, also* stuamachd *nf* abstemiousness, moderation, temperance, sobriety

stuama *adj* abstemious, moderate, temperate, sober

stùiceach & stùirceach *adj* surly, morose

stuig *vt, pres part* **a' stuigeadh**, incite, urge

stuigeadh, *gen* stuigidh *nm* inciting, urging

stùr, *gen* stùir *nm* dust

stuth, stutha, stuthan *nm* material, stuff

suaicheantas, *gen & pl* suaicheantais *nm* 1 badge, emblem; 2 rarity

suaimhneach *adj* calm, quiet

suain, *gen* suaine *nf* sleep, slumber

suain *vt, pres part* **a' suaineadh**, wrap, entwine

Suain *nf, used with art* **An t-Suain**, Sweden

Suaineach, *gen & pl* Suainich *nm* a Swede, *also adj* Suaineach Swedish

suaineadh, *gen* suainidh *nm* wrapping, entwining

suairc(e) *adj* 1 affable; 2 kind; 3 courteous

suarach *adj* 1 insignificant, petty; 2 despicable

suarachas, *gen* suarachais *nm* insignificance, pettiness

suas *adv* up *(movement)*

suath *vti, pres part* **a' suathadh**, rub, wipe, massage

suathadh, *gen* suathaidh *nm* 1 rubbing, wiping; 2 friction; 3 massage

sùbailte *adj* supple, flexible

sùbh, sùibh, sùbhan *nm* berry, **sùbh-làir** strawberry

sùgan, sùgain, sùganan *nm* straw rope

sùgh, *gen* sùgha & sùigh, *pl* sùghan *nm* 1 juice; 2 sap

sùgh & sùigh *vti, pres part* **a' sùghadh**, absorb, suck (up)

sùghach *adj* absorbent

sùghadh, *gen* sùghaidh *nm* 1 absorbing; 2 suction

sùghmhor *adj* juicy, sappy

sùgradh, *gen* sùgraidh *nm* 1 mirth, merry-making; 2 lovemaking

suidh *vi, pres part* **a' suidhe**, sit (down)

suidhe, suidhe, suidhe(ach)an *nm* 1 sitting; 2 seat

suidheachadh, suidheachaidh, suidheachaidhean *nm* 1 settling, arranging; 2 situation

suidheachan, *gen & pl* suidheachain *nm* seat, stool, pew

suidhich *vt, pres part* **a' suidheachadh**, 1 place, seat; 2 settle, arrange; 3 appoint, establish

suidhichte *adj* 1 settled; 2 determined; 3 sedate

suidse, suidse, suidsichean *nf (elec)* switch

suigeart, *gen* suigeirt *nm* cheerfulness

sùighteach *adj* absorbent

sùil, sùla, sùilean *nf* 1 eye; 2 look, glance; 3 *in expr* **tha sùil aige . . . ri** . . . he expects

sùil-chritheach, *gen & pl* sùil-chrithich *nf* quagmire

suilbhir *adj* cheerful

sùilich *vi, pres part* **a' sùileachadh** expect

sùim, suime, suimeannan *nf* 1 regard; 2 attention; 3 amount, sum

suipear/suipeir, *gen* suipeire, *also* suipearach *pl* suipearan *nf* supper

suirghe & **suiridhe** *nf* courting,
  courtship
suiteas, *gen & pl* **suiteis** *nm* sweet
sùith(e), *gen* **sùithe** *nmf* soot
sùlaire, **sùlaire**, **sùlairean** *nmf* gannet,
  solan goose
sult, *gen* **suilt** *nm* (*bodily*) fat, fatness
Sultain, *gen* **Sultaine** *nf* & **Sultuine**
  nf, used with art, **an t-Sultain/an
  t-Sultuine** September
sultmhor *adj* **1** fat, plump; **2** in rude
  health, lusty; **3** wealthy, prosperous
sumainn, **sumainne**, **sumainnean** *nf*
  surge, swell (*of sea*)
sunnd *nm* **1** cheerfulness; **2** mood

sunndach *adj* lively, cheerful, in good
  spirits   **Suòmaidh** *nf* Finland
Suòmach, *gen & pl* **Suòmaich** *nm* Finn,
  also adj **Suòmach** Finnish
sùrd, *gen* **sùird** *nm* **1** cheerfulness;
  2 alacrity
sùrdag, **sùrdaig**, **sùrdagan** *nf* jump, skip
  bounce, caper
sùrdagaich *vi, pres part* **a' sùrdagaich**,
  jump, skip, bounce, caper
susbaint, *gen* **susbainte** *nf* substance
susbainteach *adj* substantial
suth, **sutha**, **suthan** *nm* embryo
sù, **sù**, **sùthan**, *also* **sutha**, **sutha**,
  suth(ach)an *nmf* zoo

T

tàbhachdach *adj* sound, substantial

tabhairteach, *gen & pl* **tabhairtich**
nm, also **tabhairtiche, tabhairtiche,**
tabhairtichean *nm*, donor, benefactor

tabhannaich, *gen* **tabhannaiche** *nf, also*
tabhann, *gen* **tabhainn** *nm* barking

tabhannaich *vi, pres part* **a'**
tabhannaich, *also* **tabhainn** *vi, pres*
part **a' tabhann**, bark

tabhartach *adj* 1 giving, liberal; 2 dative

tabhartas, tabhartais, tabhartasan *nm*
a donation, presentation, grant

taca *nf* 1 proximity; 2 *in expr* **an taca ri**
compared to, alongside

tacaid, tacaide, tacaidean *nf* 1 tack,
tacket; 2 drawing-pin

tacan, tacain, tacanan *nm* while

tachair *vi, pres part* **a' tachairt**,
1 happen; 2 *in expr* **tachair ri**, meet

tachais *vti, pres part* **a' tachas**, 1 scratch;
2 (*vi*) itch, tickle

tachartas, tachartais, tachartasan *nm*
happening, event, incident

tachas, *gen* **tachais** *nm* scratching,
itching, tickling

tachd *vt, pres part* **a' tachdadh**, smother,
choke, throttle

tachdadh, *gen* **tachdaidh** *nm* smothering,
choking, suffocation

tadhail *vti, pres part* **a' tadhal**, visit

tadhal, tadhail, tadhalaichean *nm*
1 visit(ing); 2 (*sport*) goal

tagair *vt, pres part* **a' tagairt** & **a'**
tagradh, 1 claim; 2 plead, argue

tagairt, tagairte, tagairtean *nf* claiming,
pleading *etc*

tagh *vt, pres part* **a' taghadh**, 1 choose;
2 elect

taghadh, taghaidh, taghaidhean *nm*
1 choosing; 2 choice; 3 election

taghta *adj* 1 chosen, selected, elected;
2 great!

tagradh, tagraidh, tagraidhean *nm*
plea, appeal

tagsaidh, *gen* **tagsaidh**, *pl* **tagsaidhean**
nmf taxi

taibhs(e), taibhse, taibhsean *nmf* ghost

taibhsearachd *nf* second sight

taic(e), *gen* **taice** *nf* 1 support, prop;
patronage; 2 contact, proximity; 3 (*esp*
music) accompaniment

taiceil *adj* supporting, supportive

taidhr, taidhre, taidhrichean *nf* tyre

taifeid, taifeid, taifeidean *nm* bowstring

taigeis, taigeise, taigeisean *nf* haggis

taigh, taighe, taighean *nm & tigh, tighe,*
tighean *nm* 1 (dwelling) house; 2 home,
in exprs **aig an taigh** at home

taigheadas, *gen* **taigheadais** *nm* housing

tàileasg, *gen* **tàileisg** *nm* 1 chess;
2 backgammon

tàillear, tàilleir, tàillearan *nm* tailor

taing, *gen* **tainge** *nf* 1 thanks, gratitude;
2 *in exprs* **mòran taing!** many thanks!

taingeil *adj* thankful, grateful

tàir, tàire, tàirean *nf* contempt,
disparagement

tairbhe *nf* advantage, profit, benefit

tairbheach & **tarbhach** *adj* advantageous,
beneficial, profitable

tairbhich *vi, pres part* **a' tairbheachadh**,
also **tarbhaich** *vi, pres part* **a'**
tarbhachadh, profit, gain, benefit

tàireil *adj* 1 contemptible; 2 contemptuous

tairg *vti, pres part* **a' tairgse**, offer,
propose, bid

tairgse, tairgse, tairgseachan *nf* offer

tàirneanach, *gen* **tàirneanaich** *nm*
thunder

tairsgeir, tairsgeir, tairsgeirean *nf* peat
iron, peat spade

tais *adj* damp, moist, humid

taisbean/taisbein *vt, pres part* **a'**
taisbeanadh, display, show, reveal,
exhibit, demonstrate

taisbeanach *adj* 1 clear, distinct; 2 (*gram*)
indicative

taisbeanadh, taisbeanaidh,
taisbeanaidhean *nm* exhibition, display,
demonstration

taisbeanlann, taisbeanlainn,
taisbeanlannan *nf* exhibition hall, art
gallery

taise/taiseachd *nf* moisture, dampness, humidity

taiseachadh, *gen* **taiseachaidh** *nm* dampening, moistening

taisg *vt, pres part* **a' tasgadh**, 1 store; 2 hoard; 3 invest, deposit

taisich *vt, pres part* **a' taiseachadh**, dampen, moisten

taitinn *vi, pres part* **a' taitinn** & **a' taitneadh**, (*with* **ri**), please

taitneach *adj* agreeable, pleasant

taitneadh, *gen* **taitnidh** *nm* pleasing

taitneas, taitneis, taitneasan *nm* 1 pleasure; 2 pleasantness

talachadh, *gen* **talachaidh** *nm* complaining, grumbling

tàladh, tàlaidh, tàlaidhean *nm* 1 soothing; 2 attraction; 3 allurement; 4 lullaby

talaich *vi, pres part* **a' talachadh**, complain, grumble

tàlaidh *vt, pres part* **a' tàladh**, 1 attract; 2 allure, tempt; 3 calm; 4 sing/rock to sleep

tàlaidheach *adj* attractive

talamh, talmhainn, talamhan *nm* (*f in gen sing*) 1 **an Talamh** the Earth; 2 earth, soil; 3 land

tàlann, tàlainn, tàlann(t)an *nm* talent

tàlantach *adj* talented

talla, talla, tallachan *nm* hall

talmhaidh *adj* 1 earthly; 2 worldly

tàmailt, tàmailte, tàmailtean *nf* 1 disgrace, shame; 2 insult

tàmailteach *adj* 1 scandalous, shameful; 2 insulting

tàmailtich *vt, pres part* **a' tàmailteachadh**, insult

tamall, tamaill, tamallan *nm* while, time

tàmh, *gen* **tàimh** *nm* 1 dwelling; 2 rest, peace; 3 idleness, inactivity

tàmh *vi, pres part* **a' tàmh**, 1 rest; 2 dwell, live

tàmhadair, tàmhadair, tàmhadairean *nm* tranquilizer

tana *adj* 1 thin; 2 (*of liquids*) runny; 3 shallow; 5 flimsy

tanaich *vti, pres part* **a' tanachadh**, thin

tancair, tancair, tancairean *nm* tanker

tannasg, *gen* & *pl* **tannaisg** *nm* ghost

taobh, taoibh, taobhan *nm* 1 side; 2 way, direction; 3 *in expr* **(a-)thaobh** (*with gen*) concerning, regarding; 5 *in expr* **a thaobh (is gun)** *prep* & *conj* because of

taois, taoise, taoisean *nf* dough

taom *vti, pres part* **a' taomadh**, 1 pour (out), flow (out), empty; 2 bale

taomadh, *gen* **taomaidh** *nm* pouring, emptying *etc*

tap, tapa, tapaichean *nmf* (water) tap

tapachd *nf* cleverness, sturdiness

tapadh, *gen* **tapaidh** *nm* 1 handiness, smartness, willingness; 2 *in expr* **tapadh leat/leibh!** thank you!

tapag, tapaig, tapagan *nf* slip of the tongue, exclamation

tapaidh *adj* clever, quick, sturdy, manly, active

tarbh, *gen* & *pl* **tairbh** *nm* bull

tarbh-nathrach, *gen* & *pl* **tairbh-nathrach** *nm* dragonfly

tarcais, *gen* **tarcaise** *nf*, & **tailceas**, *gen* **tailceis** *nm*, 1 contempt, disdain; 2 spite

tarcaiseach/tailceasach *adj* 1 contemptuous, reproachful; 2 spiteful

targaid, targaide, targaidean *nf* 1 target; 2 shield

tàrmachadh, *gen* **tàrmachaidh** *nm* begetting, breeding, propagating, producing

tàrmaich *vt, pres part* **a' tàrmachadh**, 1 beget; 2 breed, propagate; 3 produce

tàrr *vi, pres part* **a' tàrradh**, *also* **tàir** *vi, pres part* **a' tàireadh**, *usu in expr* **tàrr/tàir às** escape, make off

tàrradh, *gen* **tàrraidh** *nm* escaping, making off

tarraing, *gen* **tarrainge/tàirgne**, *pl* **tarraingean/tàirgnean** *nf* 1 drawing, pulling, attracting; 2 pull, tug; 3 draught (*liquids*); 4 (*spirits*) distillation; 5 mention, reference

tarraing *vti, pres part* **a' tarraing**, 1 draw, drag, pull; 2 draw (*liquids etc*); 3 approach; 4 attract; 5 (*artist*) draw; 6 *in expr* **tarraing à cuideigin** tease/kid someone; 7 (*spirits*) distil

tarraingeach *adj* attractive

tarrang, tàirnge, tàirngean *nf*, *also* **tarrag, tarraig, tarragan** *nf* & **tarran, tarrain, tàirnean** *nm*, (*joinery*) nail

tarsainn 1 *adv* across, over

tart, *gen* **tairt** *nm* thirst

tartmhor *adj* thirsty

tasgadh, gen **tasgaidh** nm **1** storing, depositing; **2** investment

tasglann, tasglainn, tasglannan nf archive

tasgaidh, tasgaidhe, tasgaidhean nf store, hoard

tastan, tastain, tastanan nm shilling

tàth vt, pres part **a' tàthadh,** join together, glue (together), cement, solder, weld

tathaich vi, pres part **a' tathaich,** frequent, visit; haunt

tàthan, tàthain, tàthanan nm (typog) hyphen

tè nf **1** one (denoting object or living thing having female gender, gram or phys); **2** woman, female

teachd vi defective **1** come; **2** fit

teachd nm arrival, coming

teachdail adj future

teachdaire, teachdaire, teachdairean nm **1** messenger; **2** missionary

teachdaireachd nf mission, message, commission

teadhair, teadhrach, teadhraichean nf tether

teagaisg vt, pres part **a' teagasg,** teach, instruct

teagamh, teagaimh, teagamhan nm **1** doubt, uncertainty; **2** as conj **theagamh** perhaps

teagasg, gen **teagaisg** nm teaching

teaghlach, teaghlaich, teaghlaichean nm family

teagmhach adj doubtful, sceptical

teallach, teallaich, teallaichean nm hearth, fireside, fireplace

teampall, gen & pl **teampaill** nm temple

teanchair, teanchair, teanchairean nm, also **teannachair, teannachair, teannachairean** nm, **1** vice, clamp; **2** pincers; **3** tongs

teanga, teangaidh, teangan nf **1** tongue; **2** language

teann vi, pres part **a' teannadh, 1** move, go, proceed; **2 teann air** approach; **3** begin

teann adj **1** tight, tense; **2** firm; **3** severe, strict; **4** close, near

teannachadh, gen **teannachaidh** nm **1** tightening, constricting etc; **2** constriction

teannaich vti, pres part **a' teannachadh, 1** tighten, tense; **2** constrict, squeeze

teanntachd-cuim nf constipation

teanta, teanta, teantaichean nf tent

tèarainte adj safe, secure

tèarainteachd nf security, safety

tearc adj scant, scarce, few

tèarmann, gen **tèarmainn** nm protection, refuge, sanctuary

teàrr, gen **tearra** nf tar, pitch

teas nm heat

teasach, teasaich, teasaichean nf fever

teasachadh, gen **teasachaidh** nm heating

teasaich vti, pres part **a' teasachadh,** heat

teasairg & **teasraig** vt, pres part **a' teasairginn** & **a' teasraiginn,** save, rescue

teas-mheidh, teas-mheidh, teas-mheidhean nf thermometer

teatha nf & **tì** nf tea

teich vi, pres part **a' teicheadh,** flee, escape

teicheadh, gen **teichidh** nm **1** running away etc ; **2** escape; **3** desertion

teicneòlach adj technological

teicneòlaiche, teicneòlaiche, teicneòlaichean nm technologist

teicneòlas, gen **teicneòlais** nm technology

teicnigeach adj technical

teine, teine, teintean nm fire

teinntean, gen & pl **teinntein** nm hearth, fireplace

teip, teip, teipichean nf tape

teirce nf scarceness, scarcity

teirinn & **teàrn** vti, pres part **a' teàrnadh, 1** come/go down; **2** alight, dismount, climb/get down

teirm, teirm, teirmichean nf term (period)

teis-meadhan, teis-meadhain, teis-meadhanan nm dead centre

teisteanas, teisteanais, teisteanasan nm **1** testimony, evidence; **2** certificate, diploma; **3** testimonial

telebhisean, telebhisein, telebhiseanan nm television

teòclaid/seòclaid, gen **teòclaid,** pl **teòclaidean** nmf chocolate

teòiridh, teòiridh, teòiridhean nf theory

teodhachd & **teothachd** nf temperature

teòma adj **1** expert, skilful, adept; **2** ingenious

teòthaich *also* **teothaich** *vti, pres part* **a' teòthachadh,** *also* **teòdh** *vti, pres part* **a' teòthadh,** warm

teth *comp* **(n)as** (*etc*) **teotha** *adj* hot

teud, *gen* **tèid** & **teuda,** *pl* **teudan** *nm* a string (*of musical instrument*)

thairis *adv* **1** (*usu expr movement*) across, over; **2** *as prep* **thairis air** across, over; **3** beyond

thall *adv* **1** over there, (over) yonder; **2** (*in exprs of time*) *expr idea* furthest, latter

thalla *pl* **thallaibh** *imper* go, be off

thar *prep* (*with gen*) **1** across, over; **2** over, beyond (*expr motion*); **3** *in expr* **thar a chèile** in a state of confusion, *also* at loggerheads

theab *v def,* **1** miss; **2** *in preterite,* almost, nearly

thig *vi irreg, pres part* **a' tighinn,** **1** come, approach; **2** arrive; **3** *in expr* **thig do** suit, please, fit

thoir & **tabhair** *vt* **1** give (**do** to); **2** **thoir seachad** give, give away; **3** take, bring; **4** *in expr* **thoir air** make, force

tiamhaidh *adj* melancholy, plaintive

tibhre, tibhre, tibhrean *nm* a dimple

tìde, tìde, tìdean *nf* **1** time; **2** weather; **3** *with art* **an tìde** the tide

tidsear, tidseir, tidsearan *nm* teacher

tighearna, tighearna, tighearnan *nm* lord

Tìleach, *gen* & *pl* **Tìlich** *nm* Icelander, *also adj* **Tìleach** Icelandic

tilg *vt, pres part* **a' tilgeadh** & **a' tilgeil,** **1** throw; **2** accuse of; **3** throw up; **4** fire

tilgeadh, tilgidh, tilgidhean *nm* **1** throwing, accusing etc; **2** throw

till *vi, pres part* **a' tilleadh,** return, come/go back

tilleadh, *gen* **tillidh** *nm* returning, return

tìm, tìme, tìmean *nf* time

timcheall **1** *adv* round, around; **2** *as prep* **timcheall** round, around; **3** *as prep* **timcheall air** round about; **4** *as prep* **mu thimcheall** about, concerning

timcheallan, *gen* & *pl* **timcheallain** *nm* roundabout

tinn *adj* ill, sick

tinne, *gen* **tinne,** *pl* **tinnean** & **tinneachan** *nm* link (*in chain*)

tinneas, tinneis, tinneasan *nm* illness, disease

tiodhlac, tiodhlaic, tiodhlacan *nm* gift, present

tiodhlacadh, tiodhlacaidh, tiodhlacadhan *nm* burial, funeral

tiodhlaic *vt, pres part* **a' tiodhlacadh,** **1** bury, inter; **2** donate, gift

tiomnadh, tiomnaidh, tiomnaidhean *nm* **1** will, testament; **2** bequest

tiomnaich *vt, pres part* **a' tiomnachadh,** bequeath

tiompan, *gen* **tiompain,** *pl* **tiompain** & **tiompanan** *nm* cymbal

tional *vti, pres part* **a' tional,** **1** (*vi*) assemble, congregate; **2** (*vt*) gather

tional, tionail, tionalan *nm* **1** assembling, gathering, collecting; **2** assembly, gathering

tionalach *adj* cumulative

tionndadh, tionndaidh, tionndaidhean *nm* turn(ing)

tionndaidh *vti, pres part* **a' tionndadh,** turn

tionnsgail/tionnsgain *vt, pres part* **a' tionnsgal/tionnsgain/tionnsgnadh,** devise, invent

tionnsgal, tionnsgail, tionnsgalan *nm* inventiveness, invention

tionnsgalach *adj* **1** inventive; **2** industrial

tionnsgalair, tionnsgalair, tionnsgalairean *nm* inventor

tìoraidh! *excl* cheerio!

tioram *adj* dry, thirsty

tiormachadh, *gen* **tiormachaidh** *nm* drying (up)

tiormachd *nf* dryness, drought

tiormadair, tiormadair, tiormadairean *nm* dryer

tiormaich *vti, pres part* **a' tiormachadh,** dry (up)

tiota, tiota, tiotaidhean *nm, also* **tiotan,** *gen* & *pl* **tiotain** *nm,* **1** (*clock time*) second; **2** instant, tick

tiotal, tiotail, tiotalan *nm* title

tìr, tìre, tìrean *nf* **1** land; **2** country; **3** area, region; **4** ground

tiugainn *imper* come on

tiugh, *comp* **(n)as** (*etc*) **tighe,** *adj* thick, dense, slow-witted

tiughad, *gen* **tiughaid** *nm* & **tighead,** *gen* **tigheid** *nm* density, thickness

tlachd *nf* **1** pleasure, enjoyment; **2** affection, liking

tlachdmhor *adj* **1** pleasant; **2** enjoyable; **3** likeable

tnù(th), *gen* **tnùtha** *nm* envy; malice

tobar, *gen* **tobair** (*m*) & **tobrach** (*f*), *pl* **tobraichean** *nmf* spring, well

tobhta, tobhta, tobhtaichean *nmf* ruin(s) (*building*)

tobhta, *gen* **tobhta**, *pl* **tobhtan** & **tobhtachan** *nmf* (*boat*) thwart

tocasaid/togsaid, *gen* **tocasaid**, *pl* **tocasaidean** *nf* barrel; hogshead

tòchd *nm* stink

tochradh, tochraidh, tochraidhean *nm* dowry

todha, todha, todhaichean *nm* (*tool*) hoe

todhaig *vti, pres part* **a' todhaigeadh**, hoe

todhair *vt, pres part* **a' todhar**, **1** manure; **2** bleach

todhar, *gen* **todhair** *nm* manure, dung

tog *vt, pres part* **a' togail**, **1** raise, lift, pick up; **2** build; **3** (*people*) raise, bring up; **4** stir, rouse, *in expr* **tog ort!** rouse yourself!

togail, *gen* **togalach** *nf* raising, building, rousing etc

togair *vti, pres part* **a' togradh**, wish for, covet

togalach, togalaich, togalaichean *nm* building

togradh, tograidh, tograidhean *nm* wish, desire

toibheum, toibheim, toibheuman *nm* blasphemy

toigh *adj* **1** pleasing; **2** *in expr* **is toigh leam** (*etc*) I (*etc*) like

toil, toile, toilean *nf* **1** will; **2** *in expr* **mas e do thoil/ur toil e!** please!

toileach *adj* **1** willing; **2** voluntary; **3** content, glad

toileachadh, *gen* **toileachaidh** *nm* **1** pleasing etc; **2** satisfaction

toileachas, *gen* **toileachais** *nm* contentment, gladness

toilich *vt, pres part* **a' toileachadh**, please, content

toilichte *adj* happy, pleased, satisfied

toil-inntinn, toil-inntinne, toil-inntinnean *nf* **1** pleasure; **2** peace of mind

toill *vt, pres part* **a' toilltinn**, deserve

toillteanach *adj* worthy of

tòimhseachan, *gen* & *pl* **tòimhseachain** *nm* puzzle, riddle

toinisg, *gen* **toinisge** *nf* common sense

toinisgeil *adj* **1** sensible; **2** intelligent

toinn *vti, pres part* **a' toinneadh**, twist, wind, twine

tòir, *gen* **tòrach/tòire**, *pl* **tòirichean/tòirean** *nf* pursuit

toirm, toirme, toirmean *nf* noise, din

toirmeasg, *gen* **toirmisg** *nm* **1** forbidding; **2** prohibition

toirmeasgach *adj* prohibitive

toirmisg *vt, pres part* **a' toirmeasg**, forbid, prohibit

toirt *nf* giving, taking, bringing etc

toiseach, toisich, toisichean *nm* **1** start, beginning; **2** front, van(guard); **3** *in expr* **air thoiseach air** *prep* ahead of

tòiseachadh, *gen* **tòiseachaidh** *nm* beginning, start(ing)

tòisich *vti, pres part* **a' tòiseachadh**, start

toit, toite, toitean *nf* **1** steam; **2** smoke

toitean, toitein, toiteanan *nm* cigarette

toll, *gen* & *pl* **tuill** *nm* **1** hole; **2** pit, hollow

toll *vti, pres part* **a' tolladh**, bore, hole, perforate, pierce

tolladh, *gen* **tollaidh** *nm* boring, perforating etc

toll-tòine, *gen pl* **tuill-tòine** *nm* arsehole

tolman, tolmain, tolmanan *nm* knowe, knoll

tom, tuim, tomannan *nm* **1** hillock; **2** thicket

tomadach & **tomaltach** *adj* **1** sizeable, bulky; **2** burly

tombaca, tombaca, tombacan *nm* tobacco

tomhais *vt, pres part* **a' tomhas**, **1** measure; **2** survey; **3** calculate; **4** guess

tomhas, *gen* **tomhais**, *pl* **tòimhsean** & **tomhasan** *nm* **1** measuring, surveying, guessing etc; **2** measurement; **3** calculation; **4** guess

tòn, tòine, tònan *nf* **1** anus, rectum; **2** arse, bum, backside; **3** back part of

tonn, *gen* **tuinn(e)**, *pl* **tuinn** & **tonnan** *nmf* wave

tonna/tunna, *gen* **tonna/tunna**, *pl* **tonnachan/tunnachan** *nm* ton, tonne

topag, topaig, topagan *nf* (sky)lark

torach *adj* **1** fruitful, productive, fertile; **2** pregnant, fecund, fertilised

torachadh, *gen* **torachaidh** *nm*
fertilisation

torachas, *gen* **torachais** *nm* fertility

toradh, toraidh, toraidhean *nm*
1 produce, fruit(s); **2** result, effect;
3 output

toraich *vt, pres part* **a' torachadh**,
fertilise

Tòraidh, Tòraidh, Tòraidhean *nm* Tory,
Conservative

Tòraidheach *adj* Tory

torc, *gen & pl* **tuirc** *nm* boar

torman, tormain, tormanan *nm*
1 murmur, droning, hum; **2** rumble

tòrr, torra, torran *nm* **1** heap, mound;
2 lots, heaps, loads; **3** hill

tòrradh, tòrraidh, tòrraidhean *nm*
funeral, burial

tosgaire, tosgaire, tosgairean *nm*
ambassador, envoy

tosgaireachd, tosgaireachd,
tosgaireachdan *nf* embassy

tost *nm* silence

tostach *adj* silent

tràchdas, *gen & pl* **tràchdais** *nm* thesis,
dissertation

tractar, tractair, tractaran *nm* tractor

trafaig, *gen* **trafaige** *nf* traffic

tràghadh, *gen* **tràghaidh** *nm* **1** draining,
subsiding; **2** (*engine*) exhaust

tràigh, *gen* **tràgha(d)/tràighe**, *pl*
tràighean *nf* **1** shore, beach; **2** tide

tràigh *vti, pres part* **a' tràghadh**, *also*
traogh *vti, pres part* **a' traoghadh**,
1 drain, empty, ; **2** (*vi*) subside, settle;
3 ebb

tràill, tràill(e), tràillean *nmf* **1** slave;
2 drudge; **3** addict

tràilleachadh, *gen* **tràilleachaidh** *nm*
enslaving

tràilleachd *nf & * **tràillealachd** *nf*
1 slavery; **2** drudgery; **3** addiction

tràillich *vt, pres part* **a' tràilleachadh**,
enslave

traisg *vi, pres part* **a' trasg(adh)**, fast

tràlair, tràlair, tràlairean *nm* trawler

trang *adj* busy

trannsa, trannsa, trannsaichean *nf*
corridor, passage

trasg, traisg, trasgan *nf & * **trasgadh,**
trasgaidh, trasgaidhean *nm* fasting,
fast

trastanach *adj* diagonal

tràth *adj & (esp) adv* **1** early; **2** *in expr* **mu**
thràth *adv* already

tràth, *gen* **tràith/tràtha**, *pl* **tràthan** *nm*
1 time, season, period, while; **2** (*gram*)
tense

tràthach, *gen* **tràthaich** *nm* hay

treabh *vt, pres part* **a' treabhadh**, plough

treal(l)aich, treal(l)aich, treal(l)aichean
nf **1** jumble etc; **2** odds and ends, stuff;
3 *in pl* **treal(l)aichean** luggage, bits and
pieces

trèan *vti, pres part* **a' trèanadh**, train

trèan(a), trèana, trèanaichean *nf* train

treas *num adj* third

trèig *vt, pres part* **a' trèigsinn**, abandon,
leave, relinquish

trèigsinn *nm* abandoning *etc*

treis, treise, treisean *nf* while, time

treiseag, treiseig, treiseagan *nf* whilie

treòrachadh, *gen* **treòrachaidh** *nm*
1 guiding, leading; **2** guidance

treòraich *vt, pres part* **a' treòrachadh**,
1 guide; **2** lead

treubh, *gen* **trèibh/treubha**, *pl*
treubhan *nf* tribe

treud, *gen* **trèid/treuda**, *pl* **treudan** *nm*
1 flock, herd; **2** (*people*) group; **3** gang,
crowd

treun, *comp* **(n)as** (*etc*) **trèine, treise/**
treasa, *adj* strong, stout

treun *nf* **1** strength, *in expr* **ann an treun**
do neirt in your prime

trì *n and num adj* three

triall *vti, pres part* **a' triall**, travel, journey

trian *nm* third

triath, triaith, triathan *nm* lord

tric *adj, usu as adv* **1** often, frequent(ly);
2 *in adv expr* **mar as trice** usually

tricead, *gen* **triceid** *nm* frequency

trì-cheàrnag, trì-cheàrnaig, trì-
cheàrnagan *nf* triangle

trìd 1 *prep* through; **2** *prefix corres to Eng*
trans-

trì-deug *n & adj* thirteen

trioblaid, trioblaide, trioblaidean *nf*
trouble

trìthead, trìtheid, trìtheadan *nm and*
num thirty

triubhas, triubhais, triubhasan *nm*
trews, trousers

triùir *nmf* three, threesome

triuthach, *gen* **triuthaich** *nf, used with art,* **an triuthach** whooping cough

tro/troimh *prep,* through; **2** *in expr* **troimh-a-chèile** at loggerheads, *also* upset, agitated

trobhad, *pl* **trobhadaibh** *imper of def verb.* **1** come, come here, come to me; **2** come along

tròcair, **tròcaire**, **tròcairean** *nf* mercy

tròcaireach *adj* merciful

trod, *gen & pl* **troid** *nm* **1** quarreling; **2** quarrel, row

troich, **troiche**, **troichean** *nmf* dwarf

troid *vi, pres part* **a' trod**, quarrel, row, squabble, fight

troigh, **troighe**, **troighean** *nf (measure)* foot

troighean, **troighein**, **troigheanan** *nm* pedal

trom *adj* **1** heavy; **2** serious, important; **3** depressed; **4** pregnant; **5** *(typog)* bold

tromalach, *gen* **tromalaich** *nf* preponderance, majority

trombaid, **trombaide**, **trombaidean** *nf* trumpet

trom-laighe, **trom-laighe**, **trom-laighean** *nmf* nightmare

trosg, *gen & pl* **truisg** *nm* cod

trotan, *gen* **trotain** *nm* trotting, trot

truacanta *adj* compassionate, humane

truacantas, *gen* **truacantais** *nm* compassion, pity

truagh *adj* **1** pitiable, abject; **2** sad; **3** *with* **v** **is**, sad, pity, shame, **is truagh sin!** that's a pity/shame!

truaghan, **truaghain**, **truaghanan** *nm* **1** wretch; **2** *as excl,* **a thruaghain!** poor man!

truaighe, **truaighe**, **truaighean** *nf* misery, woe

truaill *vt, pres part* **a' truailleadh**, **1** pollute; **2** defile, profane; **3** corrupt, pervert

truailleadh, *gen* **truaillidh** *nm* **1** polluting, defiling, corrupting etc; **2** pollution, corruption, defilement

truas, *gen* **truais** *nm* pity, compassion

truileis *nf* rubbish, junk

truimead, *gen* **truimeid** *nm* heaviness

truinnsear, **truinnseir**, **truinnsearan** *nm (dinner etc)* plate

tru(i)s *vt, pres part* **a' trusadh** & **a' truiseadh**, **1** truss, bundle up; **2** tuck up, roll up; **3** gather

trusadh, *gen* **trusaidh** *nm* bundling up, gathering *etc*

trusgan, **trusgain**, **trusganan** *nm* **1** clothes, clothing; **2** suit *(clothes)*

tuagh, **tuaigh(e)**, **tuaghan** *nf* axe

tuainealach *adj* dizzy, giddy

tuainealaich, *gen* **tuainealaiche** *nf* vertigo, dizziness

tuaiream, **tuaireim**, **tuaireaman** *nf,* & **tuairmeas**, **tuairmeis**, **tuairmeasan** *nm* guess, conjecture, **air thuaiream** at random

tuaireamach *adj* **1** random, arbitrary; **2** conjectural, speculative

tuairisgeul, **tuairisgeil**, **tuairisgeulan** *nm* description

tuar, **tuair**, **tuaran** *nm* complexion, hue, appearance

tuarastal, *gen* **tuarastail**, *pl* **tuarastalan** *nm* salary, wage(s); stipend; fee

tuasaid, **tuasaide**, **tuasaidean** *nf* **1** quarrel; **2** scrap, tussle

tuath[1] *nf & adj* north, northern

tuath[2], *gen* **tuatha** *nf* peasantry, tenantry

tuathal *adj* **1** anti-clockwise; **2** widdershins; **3** awry, wrong

tuathanach, *gen & pl* **tuathanaich** *nm* farmer

tuathanachas, *gen* **tuathanachais** *nm* farming

tuathanas, **tuathanais**, **tuathanasan** *nm* farm

tubaist, **tubaiste**, **tubaistean** *nf* accident, mishap

tubhailte, **tubhailte**, **tubhailtean** *nf* towel

tùch *vi, pres part* **a' tùchadh**, **1** make hoarse; **2** smother, extinguish

tùchadh, *gen* **tùchaidh** *nm* hoarseness

tùchanach *adj* hoarse

tudan & **tùdan**, *gen* **tudain**, *pl* **tudanan** *nm* **1** stack *(corn etc)*; **2** turd

tugh *vt, pres part* **a' tughadh**, thatch

tughadh, *gen* **tughaidh** *nm* thatch(ing)

tuig *vti, pres part* **a' tuigsinn**, understand

tuigse *nf* understanding, intelligence, judgement, sense

tuigseach *adj* understanding, sensible, intelligent

tuigsinn *nf* understanding etc

tuil, tuile, tuiltean *nf* flood, deluge

tuilleadh *nm* **1** more, additional; **2** *adv* again, any more; **3** *in expr* **a thuilleadh air** *prep* in addition to; **4** *in expr* **tuilleadh 's a' chòir** too much

tuineachadh, *gen* **tuineachaidh** *nm* settling, dwelling

tuinich *vi, pres part* **a' tuineachadh,** dwell, settle

Tuirc *nf, used with art* **an Tuirc** Turkey

tuireadh, tuiridh, tuiridhean *nm* mourning, lament

tùirse & **tùrsa** *nf* sorrow

tuiseal, tuiseil, tuisealan *nm* (*gram*) case

tuisleadh, tuislidh, tuislidhean *nm* stumbling, tripping, slipping

tuislich *vi, pres part* **a' tuisleachadh** & **a' tuisleadh,** stumble, trip, slip

tuit *vi, pres part* **a' tuiteam, 1** fall; **2** happen to

tuiteam, tuiteim, tuiteaman *nm* falling, befalling

tuiteamach *adj* accidental, chance

tuiteamas, tuiteamais, tuiteamasan *nm* **1** event, occurrence, incident; **2** accident; **3** epilepsy

tulach, *gen* **tulaich,** *pl* **tulaichean** & **tulachan** *nm* hillock, mound

tulg *vti, pres part* **a' tulgadh,** rock, lurch, swing, toss

tulgach *adj* **1** rocking; **2** unsteady, rocky

tulgadh, *gen* **tulgaidh** *nm* rocking etc

tum *vt, pres part* **a' tumadh,** dip, immerse, steep

tumadh, tumaidh, tumaidhean *nm* dipping, immersing, steeping

tunnag, tunnaig, tunnagan *nf* duck

tur *adj* **1** whole, complete; **2** *in expr* **gu tur** *adv* completely

tùr¹, *gen* **tùir** *nm* sense, understanding

tùr², *gen* & *pl* **tùir** *nm* tower

turadh, *gen* **turaidh** *nm* dry spell

turaid, turaide, turaidean *nf* tower, turret

tùrail *adj* sensible

turas, turais, tursan *nm* **1** journey, trip; **2** touring, tour; **3** time, **aon turas** once

turasachd *nf* tourism

Turcach, *gen* & *pl* **Turcaich** *nm* Turk, *also adj* **Turcach** Turkish

tursa, tursa, tursachan *nm* standing stone

tùrsach *adj* sorrowful

tùs, *gen* **tùis** *nm* **1** beginning, origin; **2** *in expr* **o/bho thùs** from, since/in the beginning, originally

tùsanach, *gen* & *pl* **tùsanaich** *nm* aborigine

tuthag, tuthaig, tuthagan *nf* patch (*material etc*)

U

uabhar, *gen* **uabhair** *nm* pride, haughtiness

uabhas, *gen* **uabhais**, *pl* **uabhasan** *nm* **1** dread, horror, terror; **2** atrocity

uabhasach *adj/adv* dreadful(ly), awful(ly), terrible, terribly

uachdar, **uachdair**, **uachdaran** *nm* **1** surface; **2** cream; **3** upland; **4** *in expr* **làmh-an-uachdair** the upper hand

uachdarach *adj* **1** upper; **2** superior; **3** superficial; **4** creamy

uachdaran, **uachdarain**, **uachdaranan** *nm* **1** superior; **2** landowner, laird

uachdar-fhiaclan, **uachdair-fhiaclan**, **uachdaran-fhiaclan** *nm* toothpaste

uaibhreach *adj* **1** proud; **2** haughty, arrogant

uaibhreas, *gen* **uaibhreis** *nm* **1** pride; **2** haughtiness, arrogance

uaigh, *gen* **uaighe** & **uaghach**, *pl* **uaighean** *nf* grave

uaigneach *adj* **1** (*person*) lonely, lonesome; **2** (*place etc*) solitary, lonely, secluded; **3** private, secret

uaim, *gen* **uaime** *nf* alliteration

uaimh/uamh, *gen* **uaimhe/uamha**, *pl* **uaimhean/uamhan** *nf* cave

uaine *adj* green

uainfheòil, *gen* **uainfheòla** *nf* lamb (*meat*)

uaipear, **uaipeir**, **uaipearan** *nm* botcher, bungler

uair, **uarach**, **uairean** *nf* **1** (*clock time*) hour; **2** (*as adv*); **3** time (*repetition*)

uaireadair, **uaireadair**, **uaireadairean** *nm* **1** timepiece; **2** clock; **3** watch

uaireannan *adv* sometimes

uaireigin *adv* (at) some time

uaisle *nf* nobility, gentility

uallach, *gen* & *pl* **uallaich** *nm* **1** burden, load; **2** responsibility; **3** (*psych*) stress; **4** worry

uamhann, *gen* **uamhainn** *nm* dread, horror

uan, *gen* & *pl* **uain** *nm* lamb

uasal *adj* **1** noble, aristocratic, **duine-uasal** gentleman; **2** (*in manners etc*) genteel; **3** precious, *esp in expr* **clach uasal** *f* precious stone

uasal, **uasail**, **uaislean** *nm* **1** gentleman; **2** *in pl, esp with art* **na h-uaislean** the nobility, the aristocracy

ubhal, **ubhail**, **ùbhlan** *nm* apple

ubhalghort, **ubhalghoirt**, **ubhalghoirtean** *nm* orchard

uchd, **uchda**, **uchdan** *nm* **1** breast, bosom; **2** lap; **3** *in expr* **ri uchd** at the point of

ud *adj* that, yonder

ud, ud! *excl*, tut, tut!

uèir, **uèir**, **uèirichean** *nf* wire

ugan, **ugain**, **ugannan** *nm* chest area

ugh, **uigh**, **uighean** *nm* egg

ughach *adj* oval

ughach, *gen* & *pl* **ughaich** *nm* oval

ughagan, *gen* & *pl* **ughagain** *nm* custard

ùghdar, **ùghdair**, **ùghdaran** *nm* author

ùghdarraich, *pres part* **ag ùghdarrachadh**, *vt* authorise

ùghdarraichte *adj* authorised

ùghdarras, **ùghdarrais**, **ùghdarrasan** *nm* authority, authorisation

ughlann, **ughlainn**, **ughlannan** *nf* ovary

ùidh, **ùidhe**, **ùidhean** *nf* **1** hope; fondness; **2** interest

uidh, *gen* **uidhe** *nf* **1** step, gradation; journey; **2** *in expr* **uidh air n-uidh** gradually; **3** *in exprs* **ceann-uidhe** *m* destination

uidheam, **uidheim**, **uidheaman** *nf* **1** equipment, gear, tackle; **2** furnishings, trappings; **3** harness; **4** rigging

uidheamachadh, *gen* **uidheamachaidh** **1** equipping etc **2** preparation

uidheamaich *vt, pres part* **ag uidheamachadh**, equip, fit out, get ready

uidheamaichte *adj* **1** equipped, fitted out; **2** (*person*) qualified

uile *adj* & *adv* **1** all; **2** *as* **a h-uile** every; **3** *as noun & pron* **na h-uile** everyone, everybody; **4** *as adv, esp in expr* **uile-gu-lèir** *adv* completely, totally, altogether; **5** *as prefix corres to Eng* all-, omni-

uileann/uilinn, *gen* **uilinn/uilne**, *pl*
uilnean/uileannan *nf* **1** angle; **2** corner;
3 elbow

uilebheist, uilebheist, uilebheistean
nmf monster

ùilleach *adj* oily

uilleagan, *gen & pl* **uilleagain** *nm* spoilt
brat

uillnich *vti, pres part* **ag uillneachadh**,
jostle, elbow

uimhir *nf* **1** number, amount, quantity;
2 certain amount of something, **na
h-uimhir de** certain amount of; **3** same
number, quantity etc; **4** (*also* **na
h-uimhir**) so much, so many

ùine *nf* **1** time; **2** while

uinneag, uinneige, uinneagan *nf*
window

uinnean, uinnein, uinneanan *nm* onion

uinnseann, *gen* **uinnsinn** *nm* (*tree &
wood*) ash

ùir, *gen* **ùire** & **ùrach** *nf* soil, earth

uircean, uircein, uirceanan *nm* piglet

uiread *nm* **1** certain amount; **2** same
number; **3** *in neg exprs*, **uiread is/agus**
even, so much as; **4** (*also* **na h-uiread**)
great number ; **5** (*arith etc*) times,
multiplied by

uireasbhach *adj* needy, lacking

uireasbhach, *gen & pl* **uireasbhaich** *nm*
needy person

**uireasbhaidh, uireasbhaidhe,
uireasbhaidhean** *nf* **1** need, indigence;
2 lack, shortage

uirsgeul/ùirsgeul, *gen* **uirsgeil**, *pl*
uirsgeulan *nm* **1** fable, legend, myth;
2 fiction

uirsgeulach *adj* **1** legendary; **2** fictional

uiseag, uiseig, uiseagan *nf* skylark

uisge, uisge, uisgeachan *nm* **1** water;
2 (*used with art*) **an t-uisge** rain

uisge-beatha, *gen* **uisge-bheatha** *nm*
whisky

uisgeachadh, *gen* **uisgeachaidh** *nm*
watering, irrigating

uisgich *vt, pres part* **ag uisgeachadh**,
1 water; **2** irrigate

ulaidh, ulaidhe, ulaidhean *nf* treasure,
precious object

ulbhag, ulbhaig, ulbhagan *nf* boulder

ulfhart, *gen & pl* **ulfhairt** *nm* howl(ing)

ullachadh, *gen* **ullachaidh** *nm*
1 preparing, providing etc; **2** preparation;
3 provision

ullaich *vt, pres part* **ag ullachadh**,
1 prepare; **2** provide

ullamh *adj* **1** ready; **2** finished; **3** handy

ultach, ultaich, ultaichean *nm* **1** load,
armful; **2** bundle

ùmaidh, ùmaidh, ùmaidhean *nm*
blockhead, dolt, fool

umha *nm* bronze

umha(i)l *adj* **1** humble, lowly; **2** obedient;
3 obsequious

ùmhlachadh, *gen* **ùmhlachaidh** *nm*
1 humiliating *etc*; **2** humiliation

ùmhlachd *nf* **1** humbleness, lowliness;
2 obedience **3** obsequiousness; **4** bow

ùmhlaich *vti, pres part* **ag ùmhlachadh**,
1 humble; **2** (*vt*) humiliate

Ungair *nf, used with art* **an Ungair**
Hungary

Ungaireach, *gen & pl* **Ungairich** *nm*
Hungarian, *also adj* **Ungaireach**
Hungarian

ùnnlagh, ùnnlagha, ùnnlaghan *nm* fine

unnsa, unnsa, unnsachan *nm* ounce

ùpag, ùpaig, ùpagan *nf* jostle, jab

ùpraid, ùpraide, ùpraidean *nf* **1** uproar;
2 confusion, dispute

ùpraideach *adj* rowdy, unruly

ùr *adj* **1** new, fresh, recent; **2** modern; **3** *in
expr* **às ùr** *adv* afresh, anew; **4** *occas as
prefix* new, newly, fresh, freshly

ur, *also* **bhur**, *poss adj, pl & formal* your

ùrachadh, *gen* **ùrachaidh** *nm* **1** renewal;
2 modernisation; **3** change

ùraich *vti, pres part* **ag ùrachadh**,
1 renew, refresh; **2** modernise

urchair, urchrach, urchraichean *nf*
1 shot (*from firearm*); **2** missile

urchasg, urchaisg, urchasgan *nm*
antidote

ùrlar, ùrlair, ùrlaran *nm* floor

ùrnaigh, ùrnaigh, ùrnaighean *nf*
praying, prayer

ùr-nodha *adj* brand new

urra, urra, urraidhean *nf* **1** person;
2 authority, responsibility; **3** *in expr* **an
urra ri** *prep* dependent on

urrainn *nf* **1** power, ability; **2** *in verbal
expr* **is urrainn do** can

urram, *gen* **urraim** *nm* **1** respect;
  2 honour
urramach *adj* **1** honourable; **2** honorary;
  3 Reverend, *used with art*
urras, **urrais**, **urrasan** *nm* **1** guarantee,
  a bond, surety; **2** bail; **3** insurance; **4** trust
urrasach *adj* trustworthy, sound

ursainn, **ursainn**, **ursainnean** *nf* **1** prop,
  support; **2** jamb
usgar, **usgair**, **usgaran** *nm* a jewel
  (*ornament*)
uspag, **uspaig**, **uspagan** *nf* start, (*horse
  etc*) shying
ùth, **ùtha**, **ùthan(nan)** *nm* udder

ENGLISH–GAELIC

Layout of the Entries, English–Gaelic Section

Within these entries all English material for translation into Gaelic is given in bold type. Italics are used for all other text in English, ie for abbreviations, instructions such as *see* and *cf*, and all notes, comments, explanatory material and grammatical information.

Gaelic nouns are given in the nominative singular (radical) case, followed by the abbreviated gender of the noun. Some Gaelic nouns have both genders and this is shown by the abbreviation *mf*.

The Gaelic equivalents for many headwords are followed by common expressions involving that headword.

Verbs are given in the second person singular imperative form. The abbreviation *vt* (*transitive verb*) indicates that, *in the sense concerned in the entry*, a given verb is used with a direct object, while *vi* (*intransitive verb*) shows that it is used without a direct object.

A

a.m. *adv* sa mhadainn
abandon *v* trèig *vt*
abandonment *n* trèigsinn *m*
abasement *n* ìsleachadh *m*
abash *v* nàraich *vt*
abashed *adj & past part* nàraichte, air do (*etc*) nàrachadh
abate *v* lùghdaich *vi*, rach *vi* sìos
abatement *n* lùghdachadh *m*
abattoir *n* taigh-spadaidh *m*
abbess *n* ban-aba *f*
abbey *n* abaid *f*
abbot *n* aba *m*
abbreviate *v* giorraich *vt*
abbreviation *n* giorrachadh *m*
abdicate *v* leig dheth (*etc*) an crùn
abdication *n* leigeil *mf* dheth (*etc*) a' chrùin
abduct *v* thoir *vt* air falbh
abduction *n* toirt air falbh *f*
abet *v* cuidich *vti*
abettor *n* pàirtiche *m*, neach-cuideachaidh *m*
abeyance *n* stad *m*
abhor *v*, **I ~ him/it** tha gràin *f* agam air
abhorrence *n* gràin *f*
abhorrent *adj* gràineil
abide *v* 1 (*tolerate*) fuiling *vti*; 2 (*dwell*) fuirich *vi*, còmhnaich *vi*
abiding *adj* (*enduring*) maireannach
ability *n* comas *m*
abject *adj* truagh, suarach
able *adj* comasach
-able *suffix* ion- *prefix*
able-bodied *adj* corp-làidir, fallain
ablutions *n* ionnlad *m*
abnormal *adj* 1 (*unusual*) neo-chumanta, às a' chumantas; 2 (*phys*) meangach
abnormality *n* 1 (*state of being unusual etc*) neo-chumantas *m*; 2 (*phys*) meang *f*
aboard *adj* air bòrd *m*
aboard *adv* air bòrd *m*
abode *n* àite-còmhnaidh *m*, àite-fuirich *m*
abolish *v* cuir *vi* às (do)
abolition *n* cur *m* às
abomination *n* 1 (*emotion*) mòr-ghràin *f*; 2 (*cause of ~*) cùis-ghràin *f*

aborigine *n* tùsanach *m*, dùthchasach *m*
aboriginal *adj* dùthchasach
abortion *n* casg-breith *m*, casg-leatruim *m*
abortive *adj* gun toradh, neo-tharbhach
abound *v* bi *vi irreg* pailt, bi lìonmhor, cuir *vi* thairis
about *adv* (*around*) mun cuairt
about *prep* 1 (*around*) mun cuairt & mu chuairt; 2 (*concerning*) mu dheidhinn *prep*; 3 (*concerning/around*) mu; 4 (*approximately*) timcheall air, mu
above *prep* (*position*) os cionn
abrasive *adj* sgrìobach
abridge *v* giorraich *vt*
abridged *adj & past part* giorraichte
abridgement *n* giorrachadh *m*
abroad *adv* 1 (*movement*) a-null thairis; 2 (*position*) thall thairis; 3 (*circulating*) mun cuairt
abrupt *adj* 1 (*sudden etc*) grad; 2 (*persons*) cas, aithghearr; 3 (*slope etc*) cas
abscess *n* neasgaid *f*
abscond *v* teich (air falbh) *vi*
absence *n* neo-làthaireachd *f*
absent *adj* neo-làthaireach
absent *v* cùm *vi* às an làthair, cùm *vi* air falbh
absentee *n* neach *m* (*etc*) neo-làthaireach
absent-minded *adj* dìochuimhneach
absolute *adj* 1 (*complete*) làn- *prefix*; 2 (*utter*) dearg, gu chùl
absolutely *adv* gu h-iomlan, uile-gu-lèir
absolution *n* saoradh *m*
absolve *v* saor *vt*
absorb *v* 1 (*liquids etc*) sùigh *vt*; 2 (*information*) gabh *vt* a-steach
absorbent *adj* sùighteach
absorption *n* sùghadh *m*
abstain *v* cùm bho *vi*, seachain *vt*
abstemious *adj* stuama
abstention *n* seachnadh-bhòtaidh *m*
abstinence *n* stuamachd *f*
abstinent *adj* stuama
abstract *adj* eas-chruthach
abstract *n* (*résumé*) geàrr-chunntas *m*
abstraction *n* (*concept*) cùis-bheachd *f*
abstruse *adj* deacair, iomadh-fhillte

absurd *adj* gòrach, amaideach; mì-reusanta

absurdity *n* gòraiche *f*, amaideas *m*; mì-reusantachd *f*

abundance *n* pailteas *m*, lìonmhorachd *f*

abundant *adj* lìonmhor; pailt

abuse *n* 1 (*verbal*) càineadh *m*, màbadh *m*; 2 (*phys*) droch-làimhseachadh *m*; 3 (*sexual*) truailleadh drùiseach *m*

abuse *v* 1 (*verbally*) màb *vt*, dèan anacainnt air *f*; 2 (*phys*) droch-làimhsich *vt*; 3 (*sexually*) truaill *vt*; 4 (*substances etc*) mì-ghnàthaich *vt*

abyss *n* àibheis *f*, dubh-aigeann *m*

academic *adj* sgoilearach, acadaimigeach

academic *n* sgoilear *m*; neach-teagaisg oilthigh *m*

academy *n* 1 (*school*) àrd-sgoil *f*, acadamaidh *m*; 2 (*institution*) acadamh *mf*

accelerate *v* luathaich *vti*

acceleration *n* luathachadh *m*

accent *n* 1 (*speech*) blas *m*; 2 (*stress*) stràc *m*

accent *v* (*lang*) cuir stràc air

accentuate *v* cuir stràc air, leig cudrom air

accept *v* gabh *vi* (*with prep* ri)

acceptable *adj* iomchaidh

access *n* 1 (*way in*) inntrigeadh *m*; 2 (*opportunity*) cothrom *m*

accessible *adj* 1 (*place*) ruigsinneach; 2 (*person*) fosgarra, fosgailte

accessibility *n* ruigsinneachd *f*

accident *n* tubaist *f*; tuiteamas *m*

accidental *adj* tuiteamach

acclaim, acclamation *n* 1 (*approbation*) caithream *mf*; 2 (*renown*) cliù *m*

accommodation *n* 1 (*dwelling*) àitefuirich *m*, lòistinn *m*; 2 (*agreement*) rèite *f*, còrdadh *m*

accompaniment *n* com-pàirt *f*, taic *f*

accompanist *n* neach-taice *m*, compàirtiche *m*

accompany *v* 1 rach *vi* còmhla ri; 2 (*mus*) com-pàirtich *vti*, thoir taic *f* do

accompanying *adj* (*associated with*) an cois *prep*, an lùib *prep* (*both with gen*)

accomplice *n* pàirtiche *m*

accomplish *v* thoir *vt* gu buil, coilean *vt*

accomplished *adj & past part* 1 (*achieved*) coileanta; 2 (*skilled*) ealanta

accord *n* co-aontachadh *m*, co-chòrdadh *m*

accordeon *n* bogsa-ciùil *m*

accordance *n, in expr* **in ~ with** ann an co-rèir *f* ri

according *adj* a rèir (*with gen*)

accordingly *adv* 1 (*as result*) o chionn sin, air sgàth sin; 2 (*proportionately*) a rèir

account *n* cunntas *m*

accountability *n* cunntachalachd *f*

accountable *adj* cunntachail

accountancy *n* cunntasachd *f*

accountant *n* cunntasair *m*

accounting *n* cunntasachd *f*

accoutrements *npl* uidheam *f*, acainn *f*

accredited *adj* barrantaichte

accumulate *v* càrn *vt*, cruinnich *vti*

accumulation *n* 1 (*action*) càrnadh *m*; 2 (*things accumulated*) cochruinneachadh *m*

accurate *adj* ceart, cruinn, grinn; (*of weapon*) amaiseach, cuimseach

accursed *adj* mallaichte

accusation *n* casaid *f*

accusative *adj* cuspaireach

accuse *v* 1 (*legal*) dèan casaid *f* an aghaidh; 2 (*general*) cuir *vi*, tilg *vi*, fàg *vi*, (air)

accused *adj & past part* fo chasaid *f*

accused *n* neach fo chasaid *m*

accuser *n* neach-casaid *m*

accustom *v* cleachd *vt*, gnàthaich *vt*

accustomed *adj & past part* cleachdte

ace *n* (*cards*), **the ~** an t-aon *m*

acerbic *adj* 1 (*taste etc*) geur; 2 (*remark etc*) guineach

ache *n* goirteas *m*

ache *v* bi goirt

achieve *v* thoir gu buil *f*, coilean *vt*

achieved *adj & past part* coileanta

achievement *n* euchd *m*

acid *n* searbhag *f*

acid *adj* searbhagach

acidity *n* searbhachd *f*

acknowledge *v* aidich *vti*

acknowledged *adj* aithnichte

acne *n* cnàimhseagan *fpl*

acquaintance *n* 1 (*abstr*) eòlas *m*; 2 (*person*) neach-eòlais *m*

acquainted *adj* eòlach

acquire *v* 1 faigh *vt*, (*purchase*) ceannaich *vt*; 2 (*learn*) tog *vt*

acquit *v* fuasgail *vt*

acre *n* acair *mf*

acrid *adj* searbh

acrimonious *adj* guineach

acrimony n guineachas m
acronym n acranaim m
across adv (movement) tarsainn, thairis
across prep (position/movement) tarsainn, thar (with gen), thairis
act n 1 (action) gnìomh m; 2 (pol) achd f; 3 (section of play) earrann f
act v 1 gnìomhaich vi; 2 (in play etc) cluich vti
acting adj (temporary) an gnìomh
action n 1 gnìomh m; 2 (law) cùis-lagha f
active adj (energetic) beothail, èasgaidh, tapaidh, deas; 2 (industrious) dèanadach, gnìomhach, dìcheallach; 3 (busy) an sàs ann an); 4 (gram) spreigeach
activeness n beothalachd f, tapachd f
activist n gnìomhaiche m
activity n 1 (abstr) gnìomhachd f; 2 (professional) dreuchd f; 3 (hobby) cur-seachad m
actor n actair m, cluicheadair m, cleasaiche m
actress n ban-actair f
actual adj 1 (not abstract) nitheil, rudail; 2 (real) fìor
acute adj 1 (faculties) geur; 2 (illness) dian
adage n ràdh m
Adam's apple, the n meall m an sgòrnain
add v cuir ri
adder n nathair f
addict n tràill mf
addicted adj & past part na (etc) thràill aig, an urra ri
addiction n tràilleachd f
addition n 1 (numerical) meudachadh m; 2 in expr in ~ to a thuilleadh air
additional adj (an) tuilleadh, a bharrachd
address n 1 (speech, talk) òraid f; 2 (postal) seòladh m
address v 1 (speak to) bruidhinn ri; 2 (give talk) thoir seachad òraid f; 3 (letter etc) cuir seòladh air; 4 (face) cuir aghaidh ri
adept adj sgileil, deas, tapaidh, teòma, ealanta
adhesive adj leanailteach
adjacent adj faisg, dlùth
adjective n buadhair m
adjourn v 1 (as vt) cuir an dàil; 2 (as vi) sgaoil vi
adjournment n cur m an dàil f, sgaoileadh m

adjust v 1 (machine etc) gleus vt, rèitich vt; 2 (clothing) socraich vt
adjustment n 1 (machine etc) gleusadh m, rèiteachadh m; 2 (clothing) socrachadh m
administer v riaghail vt, rianaich vt, seòl vt
administration n 1 (abstr) riaghladh m, rianachd f; 2 (con) luchd-riaghlaidh m
administrative adj rianachail
administrator n rianaire m, neach-riaghlaidh m
admissible adj (acceptable) ceadaichte
adolescence n òigeachd f
adolescent n òganach m, òigear m, deugaire m
adopt v 1 (child) uchd-mhacaich vt; 2 (plan etc) cuir an gnìomh
adoption n 1 (child) uchd-mhacachd f; 2 (plan etc) cur m an gnìomh
adorn v sgeadaich vt, sgèimhich vt
adroit adj 1 (intellectually) innleachdach, luath nad (etc) inntinn f; 2 (phys) deas, làmhach
adult adj inbhidh
adult n inbheach m
adulterer, -ess n adhaltraiche m, ban-adhaltraiche f
adulterous n adhaltranach
adultery n adhaltranas m
adulthood n inbhe f
advance adj 1 (in time) ro-làimh; 2 (army etc) toisich
advance n 1 (progress) adhartas m, piseach m, leasachadh m; 2 (fin) eàrlas m; 3 in expr in ~, ron là, ron àm, ro-làimh
advance v 1 (proceed) rach air adhart; 2 (improve) thoir air adhart, adhartaich vt
advantage n 1 (benefit) buannachd f, tairbhe f; 2 in expr take ~ of gabh brath/cothrom air
advantageous adj buannachdail, tairbheach/tarbhach
adverb n co-ghnìomhair m
adverbial adj co-ghnìomhaireil
adversary n 1 (enemy) nàmhaid m; 2 (opponent) co-chòmhragaiche m
adversity n cruadal m
advertise v sanasaich vti
advertisement n sanas(-reic) m
advice n comhairle f
advisable adj iomchaidh, glic
advisability n iomchaidheachd f

advise v comhairlich vti, thoir comhairle air/do

adviser n neach-comhairle m

advocate n neach-tagraidh m

adze n tàl m

aeroplane n plèana m, itealan m

aerospace n adhar-fhànas m

aesthetics n feallsanachd-maise f

affair n 1 (matter) cùis f, rud m, nì m, gnothach m

affect v drùidh vt air

affectation n leòm f

affection n gràdh m, rùn m, tlachd f

affectionate adj gaolach, gràdhach, maoth

afforestation n coillteachadh m

afloat adj, air flod m, air fleòdradh m, air bhog m

afraid adj fo eagal, eagalach

afresh adv às ùr

Africa n Afraga f

after conj an dèidh

after prep 1 (sequence) an dèidh, às dèidh (with gen); 2 (interval) an ceann; 3 in expr **one ~ the other** fear an dèidh fir, tè an dèidh tè; 4 (in pursuit of) an tòir air

afternoon n feasgar m

afterthought n 1 ath-smuain f; ath-bheachd m

again adv a-rithist, fhathast

against prep an aghaidh (with gen); ri

age n 1 aois f; 2 (period) linn mf

agency n 1 (service etc) ionad m

agenda n clàr-gnothaich m

agent n 1 (representative) neach-ionaid m; 2 (one who takes action) neach-gnìomha m

aggravate v 1 (make worse) dèan vt nas miosa; 2 (annoy) cuir dragh air

aggravating adj draghail

aggravation (annoyance) dragh m

agile adj 1 (esp phys) clis, grad; 2 (mentally) luath nad (etc) inntinn f

agility n cliseachd f, luas m, lùth m

agitate v 1 (shake) crath vt; 2 (stir up) gluais vt; 3 (incite) brod vt, spreig vt, stuig vt; 4 (upset) cuir vt troimh-a-chèile

agitated adj & past part (upset) troimh-a-chèile

agitation n 1 (stir) gluasad m; 2 (emotional) buaireas m

ago adv 1 o chionn & bho chionn

agree v 1 (be in ~ment) co-aontaich vi, co-chòrd vi; 2 in expr ~ **to** gabh ri

agreeable adj 1 (person) ciatach; 2 (situations) taitneach; 3 (acceptable) iomchaidh

agreeableness n taitneachd f, taitneas m

agreed adj & past part aontaichte

agreement n 1 (abstr & con) còrdadh m, aonta m, co-aontachadh m, co-chòrdadh m; 2 (contractual) cùnnradh m, cùmhnant m

agriculture n 1 (subject) àiteachas m; 2 (activity) tuathanachas m, àiteach m

ahead prep air thoiseach

aid n 1 (help) cuideachadh m, cobhair f; 2 (support) taic f; 3 (tool) uidheam-cuideachaidh f

aid v cuidich vti, thoir taic do

aide n neach-cuideachaidh

aide-mémoire n nota f

ail v bi vi ceàrr air

ailing adj tinn, bochd, meadhanach

aim n 1 (weapon) amas m; 2 (intention) amas m, rùn m

aim v 1 (weapon etc) cuimsich vti, amais vti; 2 (intend) bi vi irreg am beachd

air[1] n 1 (breathed) àile m; 2 (sky) adhar m

air[2] n (appearance) coltas m

air[3] n (tune) fonn m

aircraft, airliner n plèana mf, itealan m

airfield n raon-adhair m

airport n port-adhair m

airstrip n raon-adhair m

alarm n rabhadh m

alas! excl och!, mo thruaighe!

alcohol n 1 (drink) deoch-làidir f; 2 (substance) alcol m

alcoholic adj alcolach

alcoholic n tràill mf don deoch(-làidir)

alcoholism n tinneas m na dibhe

alder n feàrna f

ale n leann m

alert adj 1 (mentally) grad/geur nad inntinn f; 2 (sentry etc) furachail; 3 (aware) mothachail

alert n comharradh-rabhaidh m

alert v thoir rabhadh do, earalaich vt

alien n 1 neach m/creutair m à planaid f eile; 2 (foreigner) coigreach m

alienate v cuir vt nad (etc) aghaidh fhèin

alight v teirinn & teàrn vi

alike adj ionann, coltach ri chèile

alive *adj* beò

all *adj & adv* **1** (*without exception*) uile, air fad, gu lèir; **2** (*whole*) an t-iomlan *m*, air fad

all- *prefix* uile-

alleviate *v* (*pain*) faothaich *vti*

alleviation *n* (*of pain*) faothachadh *m*

alley *n* caol-shràid *f*

alliance *n* caidreabhas *m*

alliteration *n* uaim *f*

allocate *v* riaraich *vt*, sònraich *vt*

allocation *n* **1** (*abstr*) riarachadh *m*; **2** (*con*) cuibhreann *mf*

allot *v* riaraich *vt*, sònraich *vt*

allow *v* leig *vi* do/le, ceadaich *vti*

allowable *adj* ceadaichte

allowance *n* (*fin etc*) cuibhreann *mf*

allowed *adj & past part* ceadaichte

alloy *n* coimheatailt *f*

allude *v* thoir tarraing/iomradh/guth air

allure *v* tàlaidh *vt*, meall *vt*

allurement *n* tàladh *m*, mealladh *m*

alluring *adj* meallach

allusion *n* iomradh *m*, tarraing *f*, guth *m*

ally *n* caidreabhach *m*

almost *adv* **1** cha mhòr; **2** (*nearly completed*) gu bhith; **3** (*narrowly avoided*) theab *vi def*

alms *n* dèirc *f*

alone *adj & adv* nam (*etc*) aonar, leam (*etc*) fhìn/fhèin

along *adv* air adhart, air aghaidh

along *prep* **1** (*movement*) fad (*with gen*); **2** (*position*) shuas, shìos; **3** (*accompanying*) ~ **with** còmhla ri, maille ri

alongside *prep* ri taobh (*with gen*); **2** (*compared to*) an taca ri

alphabet *n* aibidil *f*

alphabetical *adj* aibidileach

already *adv* mu thràth, mar-thà, (a-)cheana

also *adv* cuideachd, mar an ceudna

alter *v* atharraich *vti*, mùth *vi*

alteration *n* atharrachadh *m*, mùthadh *m*

alternative *adj* eile, eadar-dhealaichte, eadar-roghnach

alternative *n* roghainn *f*

alternatively *adv* an àite sin, air mhodh eile

although *conj* ged

altitude *n* àirde *f*

altogether *adv* uile-gu-lèir, gu tur

always *adv* daonnan, gun sgur, an-còmhnaidh

amalgamate *v* **1** (*companies etc*) co-aonaich *vi*; **2** (*substances*) co-leagh *vti*, co-mheasgaich *vti*

amalgamation *n* (*companies etc*) co-aonachadh *m*

amaze *v* cuir mòr-iongnadh air

amazement *n* mòr-iongnadh *m*

amazing *adj* a chuireas mòr-iongnadh

ambassador *n* tosgaire *m*

amber *n* òmar *m*

ambiguity *n* dà-sheaghachd *f*

ambiguous *adj* dà-sheaghach

ambition *n* **1** (*for self-advancement*) miann-adhartais *m*, gionaiche *m*; **2** (*wish*) rùn *m*, miann *f*, glòir-mhiann *mf*

ambitious *adj* gionach, glòir-mhiannach

ambivalence *n* **1** (*ambiguity*) dà-sheaghachd *f*; **2** (*in two minds*) dà-bharaileachd *f*

ambivalent *adj* **1** (*ambiguous*) dà-sheaghach; **2** (*in two minds*) dà-bharaileach, ann an ioma-chomhairle *f*

ambulance *n* carbad-eiridinn *m*

ambush *n* feall-fhalach *m*

amenable *adj* fosgailte do

amend *v* **1** (*change*) atharraich *vt*; **2** (*improve*) leasaich *vt*

amendment *n* **1** (*change*) atharrachadh *m*; **2** (*improvement*) leasachadh *m*

amenity *n* goireas *m*

America *n* Ameireaga *f*

amiss *adj* ceàrr, air iomrall

ammunition *n* connadh-làmhaich *m*

amorous *adj* leannanach

amount *n* uimhir *f*, uiread *f*

amphibian *n* muir-thìreach *m*

amphibious *adj* dà-bheathach, muir-thìreach

ample *adj* **1** (*of quantity*) pailt; **2** (*person*) tomadach

amusement *n* **1** (*abstr*) àbhachd *f*; **2** (*fun etc*) spòrs *f*, dibhearsain *m*; **3** (*distraction*) caitheamh-aimsir *m*

amusing *adj* èibhinn

anachronism *n* **1** (*abstr*) às-aimsireachd *f*; **2** (*con*) rud às-aimsireil *m*

anachronistic *adj* às-aimsireil

anaemia *n* cion-fala *m*

analyse *v* sgrùd *vt*, mion-sgrùd *vt*

analysis *n* sgrùdadh *m*, mion-sgrùdadh *m*

anatomical *adj* **1** (*abstr*) corp-eòlach;
 2 (*pertaining to body*) corporra

anatomist *n* corp-eòlaiche *m*

anatomy *n* **1** (*abstr*) corp-eòlas *m*;
 2 (*body*) corp *m*, bodhaig *f*

anchor *n* acair(e) *mf*

anchorage *n* acarsaid *f*

anchored *adj & past part* aig acarsaid *f*

and *conj* agus, is

androgynous *adj* fireann-boireann

anecdote *n* **1** sgeul *m*, seanchas *m*; stòiridh
 mf, naidheachd *f*

anew *adv* às ùr

anger *n* fearg *f*

angle *n* uileann & uilinn *f*, ceàrn *mf*

angler *n* iasgair *m*

angling *n* breacach *m*, iasgach-slaite *m*

angry *adj* feargach, fiadhaich

anguish *n* dòrainn *f*; cràdh *m*

anguished *adj* dòrainneach

animate *adj* beò

animate *v* **1** (*bring to life*) beothaich *vt*;
 2 (*stir up*) brosnaich *vt*, brod *vt*

animated *adj* **1** (*lively*) beothail;
 2 (*excited*) mear

animation *n* **1** (*liveliness*) beothalachd *f*;
 2 (*bustle*) drip *f*; **3** (*spirits*) mearachas *m*

ankle *n* caol *m* na coise, adhbrann *m*

annihilate *v* cuir *vi* às do, neonithich *vt*

annotate *v* cuir notaichean ri

annoy *v* cuir dragh air

annoyance *n* dragh *m*, leamhadas *m*

annoying *adj* draghail; leamh

annual *adj* bliadhnail

annual *n* **1** (*book*) bliadhnachan *m*;
 2 (*flower*) flùr *m* aon-bhliadhnach

annul *v* cuir *vt* an neoni

anonymous *adj* gun urra *f*

another *adj* eile

answer *n* freagairt *f*

answer *v* freagair *vti*

Antarctic *n* an Antartaig *f*

anthem *n* laoidh *mf*

anthology *n* cruinneachadh *m*, co-
 chruinneachadh *m*, (*poetry*) duanaire *m*

anti-clockwise *adj* tuathal

antidote *n* urchasg *m*

antler *n* crò(i)c *f*, cabar *m*

anus *n* tòn *f*, toll *m*, toll-tòine *m*

anvil *n* innean *m*

anxiety *n* cùram *m*, dragh *m*, imcheist *f*,
 iomagain *f*

anxious *adj* cùramach, fo chùram, fo
 imcheist, fo iomagain, imcheisteach,
 iomagaineach

any *adj & pron* **1** gin *pron*; **2** (*no matter
 which*) sam bith

anybody, anyone *pron* **1** duine *m*; **2** (*no
 matter who*) duine sam bith

anything *n* **1** càil *f*, dad *f*, sìon *m*, rudeigin
 pron; **2** (*no matter what*) rud *m* sam bith,
 nì *m* sam bith

anyway *adv* co-dhiù

aorta *n*, *used with art*, a' chuisle-chinn *f*

apart *adj* **1** (*special*) air leth; **2** *in expr* ~
 from ach a-mhàin

apathy *n* cion-ùidhe *m*

aperture *n* fosgladh *m*

apolitical *adj* neo-phoilitigeach

apologise *v* dèan leisgeul

apology *n* leisgeul *m*

apostrophe *n* (*orthog*) asgair *m*

apparatus *n* uidheam *f*, acainn *f*

apparent *adj* follaiseach

apparently *adv* a rèir c(h)oltais *m*

appeal *n* **1** (*attractiveness*) tàladh *m*;
 2 (*request*) iarrtas (dian) *m*, guidhe *mf*;
 3 (*law etc*) tagradh *m*

appeal *v* **1** (*attract*) tarraing *vt*, tàlaidh *vt*;
 2 (*request*) iarr *vt* (gu dian); **3** (*law etc*)
 tagair *vt*

appear *v* **1** (*arrive*) nochd *vi*, thig *vi* am
 follais; **2** (*seem*) bi coltach (gu)

appearance *n* **1** (*abstr*) nochdadh *m*;
 2 (*aspect*) cruth *m*; **3** (*features*) tuar *m*;
 4 (*resemblance*) coltas *m*

appease *v* (*parties etc*) rèitich *vt*

appetite *n* càil *f*, càil-bìdh

apple *n* **1** ubhal *m*; **2** *in expr* ~ **of eye**
 clach *f* na sùla

appliance *n* uidheam *f*

applicant *n* neach-iarraidh, neach-tagraidh
 m

application *n* **1** (*job etc*) iarrtas *m*;
 2 (*diligence etc*) dìcheall *m*; **3** (*putting
 into practice*) cur *m* an gnìomh **4** (*IT*)
 cleachdadh *m*

apply *v* **1** (*job etc*) cuir a-steach iarrtas
 airson); **2** (*put into practice*) cuir *vt* an
 gnìomh **3** (*affect*) buin do

appoint *v* **1** (*select*) tagh *vt*, cuir *vt* an
 dreuchd *f*; **2** (*set up*) suidhich *vt*

appointed *adj & past part* (*selected*) air do (*etc*) t(h)aghadh

apportion *v* roinn *vt*, riaraich *vt*, pàirtich *vt*

apportionment *n* **1** (*abstr*) roinneadh *m*; **2** (*share*) cuibhreann *mf*, roinn *f*

appraisal *n* measadh *m*

appraise *v* meas *vt*, dèan measadh air

appreciate *v* **1** (*understand*) fidir *vt*, tuig *vt*; **2** (*be grateful*) bi *vi irreg* taingeil airson

appreciation *n* **1** (*gratitude*) taingealachd *f*; **2** (*understanding*) tuigse *f*, mothachadh *m*

appreciative *adj* **1** (*grateful*) taingeil airson; **2** (*valuing*) mothachail, tuigseach

apprehend *v* glac *vt*

apprentice *n* preantas *m*

approach *v* dlùthaich *vi* ri; teann *vi* ri

approachable *adj* (*person*) fosgarra, fosgailte

apron *n* aparan *m*

appropriate *adj* freagarrach, iomchaidh

appropriate *v* gabh seilbh air

approval *n* **1** (*agreement*) aonta *m*; **2** (*consent*) cead *m*

approve *v* **1** (*consent*) bi *vi irreg* airson; **2** (*allow*) ceadaich *vt*, ùghdarraich *vt*

approved *adj & past part* ceadaichte, ùghdarraichte

approximately *adv* timcheall air

April *n* Giblean *m*, Giblinn *f, used with art*, an Giblean, a' Ghiblinn

apt *adj* **1** (*appropriate*) freagarrach, iomchaidh; **2** (*liable*) buailteach, dualtach

aquaculture *n* tuathanachas-uisge *m*

Arab *n* Arabach *m*

Arabic *adj* Arabach

arable *adj* àitich

arbiter *n* neach-rèiteachaidh *m*

arbitrary *adj* **1** (*chance*) tuaireamach; **2** (*unreasonable etc*) neo-riaghailteach

arbitrate *v* (*between parties etc*) rèitich *vi*

arbitration *n* rèiteachadh *m*

arch *n* stuagh *f*, bogha *m*

archbishop *n* àrd-easbaig *m*

archaeological *adj* àrsaidheil

archaeologist *n* àrsair *m*, arc-eòlaiche *m*

archaeology *n* àrsaidheachd *f*, arc-eòlas *m*

archaic *adj* àrsaidh

archer *n* boghadair *m*

archetypal *adj* prìomh-shamhlach

archetype *n* prìomh-shamhla *m*

architect *n* ailtire *m*

architectural *adj* ailtireach

architecture *n* ailtireachd *f*

archive *n* tasglann *f*

archivist *n* tasglannaiche *m*

Arctic, the *n* An Artaig *f*, **the ~ Circle** Cearcall *m* na h-Artaig, *also* An Cearcall Artach

ardent *adj* dian

ardour *n* dèine *f*

area *n* **1** (*abstr*) farsaingeachd *f*; **2** (*locality*) ceàrn *mf*; **3** (*topic*) raon *m*

argue *v* **1** (*discuss*) connsaich *vi*, argamaidich *vi*; **2** (*legal etc*) tagair *vti*

argument *n* **1** (*disagreement*) connsachadh *m*, argamaid *f*; **2** (*discussion*) deasbad *mf*; **3** (*points etc*) argamaid *f*

argumentative *adj* connsachail, aimhreiteach

arid *adj* tioram

arise *v* èirich *vi*

aristocracy *n* **1** (*abstr*) uaisle *f*; **2** (*con*) **the ~** na h-uaislean *mpl*

aristocrat *n* duine-uasal *m*

aristocratic *adj* uasal

arithmetic *n* cunntas *m*, àireamhachd *f*

arm[1] *n* (*body*) gàirdean *m*

arm[2] *n* (*weapon*) ball-airm *m*

armchair *n* cathair-ghàirdeanach *f*

armful *n* achlasan *m*, ultach *m*

armour *n* armachd *f*

armoury *n* armlann *f*

armpit *n* achlais *f*, lag *mf* na h-achlaise

armrest *n* taic-uilne *f*

army *n* arm *m*

around *adv* timcheall, mun cuairt/mu chuairt (*with gen*)

around *prep* timcheall (air), mun cuairt air

arrange *v* **1** (*organise*) cuir *vt* air chois; **2** (*put in order*) sgioblaich *vt*, cuir *vt* an òrdugh, cuir *vt* air dòigh

arrangement *n* **1** (*state etc*) suidheachadh *m*; **2** (*settlement*) còrdadh *m*, rèite *f*; **3** (*mus*) rian *m*

arranger *n* (*mus*) rianadair *m*

arrest *v* cuir *vt* an làimh, cuir *vt* an sàs

arrival *n* teachd *m*

arrive *v* thig *vi*, ruig *vti*

arrogance *n* dànadas *m*, uaibhreas *m*, àrdan *m*

arrogant *adj* dàna, àrdanach

arrow *n* saighead *f*

arse *n* màs *m*, tòn *f*

arsehole *n* toll *m*, toll-tòine

art *n* ealain *f*

artery *n* cuisle *f*

artful *adj* innleachdach, carach

artfulness *n* innleachd *f*

arthritis *n* tinneas *m* nan alt

article *n* **1** (*object*) rud *m*; **2** (*journalism etc*) aiste *f*, alt *m*; **3** (*gram*) alt *m*

articulate *adj* fileanta, pongail

articulate *v* (*express*) cuir *vt* an cèill

artificial *adj* fuadain, brèige

artisan *n* neach-ceàirde *m*

artist *n* neach-ealain *m*

artistic *adj* ealanta

artistry *n* ealantas *m*

as *adv* **1** (*in comparisons*) cho; **2** *in expr* ~ **much** ~ uiread agus/is; **3** (*distance*) ~ **far** ~ gu ruige; **4** *in expr* ~ **for** (*concerning*) a thaobh (*with gen*)

as *conj* **1** mar; **2** (*because*) on a & bhon a; **3** *in expr* ~ **well** (*also*) cuideachd, mar an ceudna; **4** *in expr* ~ **well** ~ (*in addition to*) cho math ri, a bharrachd air

ascertain *v* faigh *vt* a-mach

ascribe *v* cuir *vt* às leth

ash *n* **1** (*tree & wood*) uinnseann *m*; **2** (*residue*) luaithre *f*, luath *f*

ashamed *adj* fo nàire *f*, nàraichte, air do (*etc*) nàrachadh

ashen *adj* bàn-ghlas

ashore *adv* **1** (*position*) air tìr *mf*; **2** (*movement*) gu tìr, air tìr

aside *adv* air leth, an dara taobh *m*

ask *v* **1** (*enquire*) faighnich *vi* de/do; **2** (*request*) iarr *vti* air; **3** (*invite*) iarr *vt*

askew *adj* claon

aslant *adj* fiar

asleep *adj* nad (*etc*) chadal

aspect *n* **1** (*appearance*) dreach *m*, cruth *m*; **2** (*facet etc*) taobh *m*; **3** (*geographical*) sealladh-aghaidh *m*

aspiration *n* (*ambition*) miann *mf*, mòr-mhiann *mf*, rùn *m*

aspire *v* bi *vi irreg* miannach air

assailant *n* neach-ionnsaigh *m*

assassin *n* murtair *m*

assassinate *v* murt *vt*

assassination *n* murt *m*

assault *n* **1** ionnsaigh *mf*; **2** (*legal*) droch-ionnsaigh *mf*

assault *v* thoir ionnsaigh air

assemble *v* **1** (*gather*) cruinnich *vti*, thig *vi* còmhla; **2** (*machinery etc*) cuir *vt* ri chèile

assembled *adj & past part* **1** (*put together*) co-dhèanta, air an (*etc*) c(h)ur ri chèile; **2** (*gathered*) cruinn

assembly *n* **1** cruinneachadh *m*, tional *m*; co-chruinneachadh *m*; **2** (*putting together*) cur *m* ri chèile

assent *n* **1** aonta *m*; **2** (*permission*) cead *m*

assent *v* thoir aonta do

assert *v* **1** (*argue*) cùm a-mach *vi*; **2** *in expr* ~ **authority** gabh smachd air

assess *v* meas *vt*

assessment *n* **1** (*abstr*) measadh *m*; **2** (*con*) meas *m*

assessor *n* neach-measaidh *m*

assets *n* maoin *f*, so-mhaoin *f*

assign *v* sònraich *vt*

assist *v* cuidich *vti*, dèan cobhair air

assistance *n* cuideachadh *m*, cobhair *f*; taic *f*

assistant *n* neach-cuideachaidh *m*

associate *n* companach *m*, (com-)pàirtiche *m*

associated *adj & past part* an cois, an lùib

association *n* **1** (*abstr*) cruinneachadh *m*, tighinn *f* còmhla; **2** *in expr* **in** ~ **with** an co-bhann/co-bhuinn ri; **3** (*club etc*) comann *m*

assortment *n* measgachadh *m*, taghadh *m*

assume *v* **1** (*take as fact*) gabh *vi* ris; **2** (*take on*) gabh *vt* os làimh, gabh *vt* ort fhèin

assumption *n* **1** (*hypothesis*) tuaiream *m*; **2** (*opinion*) barail *f*

assurance *n* **1** barantas *m*, gealladh *m*; **2** (*insurance*) àrachas *m*, urras *m*

assure *v* rach an urras do

asterisk *n* reultag *f*

asthma *n* (*used with art*) a' chuing *f*, an sac *m*

astonish *v* cuir *vt* mòr-iongnadh air

astonishment *n* mòr-iongnadh *m*

astray *adj & adv* air fhuadan, air seachran, air iomrall

astride *adj & adv* casa-gòbhlach

astrology *n* speuradaireachd *f*

astronaut *n* speur-sheòladair *m*

astronomer *n* reuladair *m*

astronomy *n* reul-eòlas *m*

asylum *n* (*abstr*) tèarmann *m*

at *prep* aig

athletic *adj* lùthmhor

Atlantic *n*, **the**, *used with art*, An Cuan *m* Siar

atmosphere *n* àile *m*

atom *n* dadam *m*

atomic *adj* atamach

atone *v*, dèan èirig/rèite

atonement *n* èirig *f*, rèite *f*

atrocious *adj* uabhasach, oillteil, eagalach

atrocity *n* uabhas *m*

attached *adj past part* **1** (*phys*) ceangailte ri; **2** (*emotionally*) measail/dèidheil air

attachment *n* **1** (*phys*) ceangal *m*; **2** (*friendship*) tlachd *f*, dèidh *f*, spèis *f*

attack *n* **1** ionnsaigh *mf*; **2** (*verbal* ~) càineadh *m*, màbadh *m*; **3** *in expr* **heart** ~ grèim-cridhe *m*, clisgeadh-cridhe *m*

attack *v* thoir ionnsaigh air

attacker *n* neach-ionnsaigh *m*

attain *v* faigh *vt*, ruig *vt*

attempt *n* oidhirp *f*

attempt *v* feuch *vti* ri, dèan oidhirp air

attend *v* **1** (*serve etc*) freastail/fritheil *vi* air); **2** (*be present*) bi *vi* an làthair, bi *vi* ann, fritheil *v*; **3** (*pay attention*) thoir (an) àire do

attendance *n* **1** (*service etc*) freastal *m*; **2** (*at event etc*) frithealadh *m*; **3** (*audience etc*) luchd-èisteachd *m*

attendant *adj* na c(h)ois, na lùib

attendant *n* neach-frithealaidh *m*

attention *n* aire *f*

attentive *adj* aireachail, furachail

attestation *n* teisteanas *m*

attitude *n* **1** (*phys*) seasamh *m*; **2** (*mental*) gleus-inntinn *mf*

attract *v* **1** (*person etc*) tarraing *vt*; **2** (*entice*) tàlaidh *vt*

attraction *n* tàladh *m*, tarraing *f*

attractive *adj* **1** tàlaidheach, tarraingeach; **2** (*personality*) tlachdmhor

attribute *n* feart *m*

attribute *v* cuir *vt* às leth

attrition *n* bleith *f*

auctioneer *n* reiceadair *m*

audacious *adj* (*pejorative*) ladarna

audience *n* **1** (*concert etc*) luchd-èisteachd *m*; **2** (*meeting*) coinneamh (phrìobhaideach), agallamh (prìobhaideach)

audio-visual *adj* lèir-chlaistinneach

audit *n* sgrùdadh *m*

audit *v* dèan sgrùdadh air

auditor *n* neach-sgrùdaidh *m*

auger *n* drile *f*, snìomhaire *m*

augment *v* meudaich *vt*

augmentation *n* meudachadh *m*

August *n* (*used with art*) an Lùnastal *m*

aunt *n*, **my** ~ (*on mother's side*) piuthar *f* mo mhàthar, (*on father's side*) piuthar *f* m' athar

au revoir! *excl* chì mi fhathast sibh/thu!

Aurora Borealis *n* (*used with art*) Na Fir Chlis *mpl*

auspices *npl*, *in expr* **under the** ~ fo sgèith (*with gen*)

Australia *n* Astràilia *f*

Australian *n & adj* Astràilianach *f*

auspicious *adj* rathail, gealltanach

Austria *n* (*used with art*) an Ostair *f*

Austrian *n & adj* Ostaireach

author *n* ùghdar *m*

authorisation *n* ùghdarras *m*, cead *m*

authorise *v* ùghdarraich *vt*, ceadaich *vt*

authorised *adj & past part* ùghdarraichte, ceadaichte

authoritarian *adj* ceannsalach

authoritative *adj* ùghdarrasail

authority *n* **1** (*control*) ceannsal *m*, smachd *m*; **2** (*council etc*) ùghdarras *m*

autobiography *n* fèin-eachdraidh *f*

automatic *n* fèin-ghluaiseach

autonomous *adj* neo-eisimeileach, fèin-riaghlach

autumn *n* foghar *m*

auxiliary *adj* taiceil

auxiliary *n* cuidiche *m*, taicear *m*

avail *n* èifeachd *f*, buannachd *f*, tairbhe *f*

avail *v* (*make use of*) cleachd *vt*, gabh cothrom air

available *adj* **1** (*to hand*) deiseil, ullamh; **2** (*to be had*) ri f(h)aighinn

average *adj* **1** meadhanach, cumanta; **2** (*maths*) cuibheasach

average *n* **1** meadhan *m*; **2** (*maths*) cuibheas *m*

awake *adj* nad (*etc*) dhùsgadh, nad dhùisg

awake, **awaken** *v* dùisg *vti*
awakening *n*, dùsgadh *m*, mosgladh *m*
award *n* duais *f*
aware *adj* mothachail air
awareness *n* mothachadh *m*
away *adv* on taigh, a' falbh, air falbh, às an làthair *f*

awful *adj* uabhasach, eagalach, sgriosail
awfully *adv* uabhasach
awkward *adj* cearbach
awry *adj* 1 (*slanting etc*) claon; 2 (*wrong*) tuathal
axe *n* tuagh *f*
axle *n* aiseal *mf*

B

baa, baaing *n* mèilich *f*
baa *v* dèan mèilich
babble, babbling *n* gobaireachd *f*
baby *n* leanabh *m*, pàiste *m*, leanaban *m*, naoidhean *m*
babysitter *n* freiceadan-cloinne *m*
bachelor *n* fleasgach *m*, seana-ghille *m*
back *adj* **1** (*rear*) cùil; **2** (*anatomical*) droma
back *adv* air ais
back *n* **1** (*phys*) druim *m*; **2** (*rear*) cùl *m*; **3** (*esp of animal*) muin *f*; **4** (*~ part*) tòn *f*; **5** (*of book*) còmhdach *m*; **6** *in expr* ~ **to front** cùlaibh air beulaibh
back *v* **1** (*support*) cùm taic *f* ri; **2** (*reverse vehicle etc*) rach *vi* an comhair do (*etc*) chùil; **3** (*bet*) cuir geall/airgead air
back-biting *n* **1** (*action*) cùl-chàineadh *m*; **2** (*remarks etc*) cùl-chainnt *f*
backbone *n* cnà(i)mh-droma *m*
backer *n* neach-taice *m*
backing *n* taic(e) *f*
backpack *n* màileid-droma *f*
backside *n* (*buttocks*) màs *m*, tòn *f*
backup *n* **1** (*support*) taic(e) *f*; **2** (*IT*) cùl-ghleidheadh *m*
backward *adj* deireannach
backwards *adv* an comhair do (*etc*) chùil
bad *adj*, **1** droch; **2** dona; **3** (*rotten*) lobhte, grod
badge *n* suaicheantas *m*, bràiste *f*
badger broc *m*
badly *adv* gu dona
bad-natured *adj* droch-nàdarrach
badness *n* donas *m*, olc *m*
baffle *v* fairtlich *vi* air
bag *n* **1** poca *m*, baga *m*; màileid *f*
baggage *n* treal(l)aichean *fpl*
bagpipe *n* pìob *f*, (*Highland ~*) pìob mhòr
bail *n* urras *m*
bailiff *n* maor *m*
baillie *n* bàillidh *m*
bait *n* (*for fishing*) maghar *m*, biathadh *m*
bake *v* fuin *vt*
baker *n* fuineadair *m*
bakery *n* taigh-fuine *m*
baking *n* fuineadh *m*, fuine *f*

balance *n* **1** (*equilibrium*) co-chothrom *m*, cothrom *m*, meidh *f*; **2** (*fin, abstr*) cothromachadh *m;* **3** (*fin, sum*) còrr *m*
balance *v* cuir *vt* air mheidh, cothromaich *vt*
balanced *adj & past part* **1** (*in equilibrium*) air mheidh; **2** (*fair, even-handed*) cothromach; **3** (*fin etc*) cothromaichte
bald *adj* maol
baldness *n* maoile *f*, maoilead *m*
bale *n* (*hay etc*) bèile *m*
bale *v* (*boat etc*) taom *vti*
baler *n* taoman *m*
ball[1] *n* (*dance*) bàl *m*
ball[2] (*for games etc*) bà(l)la *m*, ball *m*
ballad *n* bailead *m*
ballast *n* balaiste *mf*
ballot *n* **1** baileat *m*, taghadh *m*
balmy *adj* tlàth
bamboo *n* cuilc *f* Innseanach
ban *n* toirmeasg *m*
ban *v* toirmisg *vt*
band[1] *n* **1** (*of people*) còmhlan *m*, buidheann *mf*, treud *m*; **2** (*music*) còmhlan(-ciùil) *m*
band[2] *n* (*loop*) crios *m*, bann *m*
bandage *n* bann *m*
bandy-legged *adj* cama-chasach, crom-chasach
bang *n* cnag *f*, brag *m*
bang *v* cnag *vti*
banish *v* fuadaich *vt*, fògair *vt*
banishment *n* fuadach *m*, fuadachadh *m*, fògradh *m*
bank[1] *n* (*fin*) banca *m*
bank[2] *n* **1** (*river etc*) bruach *f*; **2** (*slope*) bruthach *mf*
bank *v* (*money*) cuir *vt* sa bhanca
banker *n* bancair *m*
banking *n* bancaireachd *f*
banknote *n* nota *f*
bankrupt *adj* briste
banned *adj & past part* toirmisgte
banner *n* bratach *f*
bannock *n* bonnach *m*
banquet *n* fèist *f*, fleadh *m*, cuirm *f*
baptise *v* baist *vt*

baptism *n* baisteadh *m*

Baptist *n & adj* Baisteach *m*

bar *n* **1** (*wood etc*) crann *m*; **2** (*obstacle*) bacadh *m*; **3** (*in pub etc*) bàr *m*; **4** (*music*) car *m*

bar *v* (*prevent*) bac *vt*, cuir bacadh air

barb *n* gath *m*

barbaric, **barbarous** *adj* borb

barbed *adj & past part* gathach, biorach

barber *n* borbair *m*, bearradair *m*

bard *n* bàrd *m*

bare *adj* **1** (*naked*) lomnochd; **2** (*uncovered*) rùisgte; **3** (*landscape etc*) lom

bare *v* rùisg *vt*, lom *vt*

bared *adj & past part* **1** (*stripped*) rùisgte; **2** (*showing*) ris *prep pron*

bare-faced *adj* ladarna, dàna

barefoot *adj* casruisgte

bare-headed *adj* ceannruisgte

barelegged *adj* casruisgte

barely *adv* **1** (*rarely*) is gann (*with conj* a); **2** (*hardly*) cha mhòr (*with conj* gun); **3** (*expr difficulty*) is ann air èiginn (*with conj* a)

bareness *n* luime *f*, lomnochd *f*

bargain *n* **1** (*legal etc*) cùmhnant *m*, cunnradh *m*; **2** (*buy etc*) bargan *m*

bark¹ *n* (*of dog*) comhart *m*

bark² *n* (*of tree*) rùsg *m*, cairt *f*

bark *v* dèan comhart *m*, tabhannaich *vi*

barking *n* comhartaich *f*, tabhannaich *f*

barley *n* eòrna *m*

barn *n* sabhal *m*, *in expr* ~ **owl** comhachag *f*

barnacle *n* giùran *m*, bàirneach *f*

barometer *n* glainne-sìde *f*

baron *n* baran *m*

barrel *n* baraille *m* tocasaid *f*

barren *adj* **1** (*land*) fàs; **2** (*woman*) neo-thorrach; **3** (*livestock etc*) seasg

barrenness *n* **1** (*land*) fàsachd *f*; **2** (*woman*) neo-thorrachd *f*, neo-thorraichead *f*; **3** (*livestock etc*) seasgachd *f*

barrier *n* bacadh *m*, cnap-starra *m*

barrister *n* neach-tagraidh *m*, tagarair *m*, tagraiche *m*

barter *n* malairt *f*

barter *v* malairtich *vi*, dèan malairt *f*

base *adj* suarach, tàireil

base *n* bonn *m*, bun *m*

bash *v* pronn *vt*

bashful *adj* diùid, nàrach

bashfulness *n* diùideachd *f*, diùide *f*, nàire *f*

basic *adj* bunaiteach

basin *n* mias *f*

basis *n* stèidh *f*, bunait *f*

basket *n* basgaid *f*

basketball *n* ball-basgaid *m*

bass *n* (*music*) beus *m*

bastard *n* neach *m* dìolain

bastard *adj* dìolain

bat¹ *n* (*animal*) ialtag *f*

bat² (*games*) slacan *m*, bat *m*

batch *n* dòrlach *m*

bath *n* amar *m*, ionnaltair *f*

bathe *v* ionnlaid *vti*, failc *vti*

bathing *n* ionnlad *m*

bathroom *n* seòmar-ionnlaid *m*, rùm-ionnlaid *m*

battalion *n* cath-bhuidheann *f*

batter *v* pronn *vt*, dochainn *vt*

battery *n* bataraidh *mf*

battle *n* cath *m*, blàr *m*, batail *m*

battle-axe *n* tuagh-chatha *f*

battlefield *n* blàr *m*, àr *m*

battleship *n* long-chogaidh *f*

bawdy *adj* drabasta, draosta

bawl *v* glaodh *vi*

bay *n* bàgh *m*, camas *m*, òb *m*

bayonet *n* bèigleid *f*

be *v* **1** bi *v irreg*

be *v* **2** is *v irreg & def, past tense* bu, *inter* an (am *before b, f, m, p*)

beach *n* tràigh *f*, cladach *m*, (*shingly*) mol *m*

bead *n* (*on necklace etc*) grìogag *f*

beak *n* gob *m*

beam *n* **1** (*ray*) gath *m*; **2** (*timber*) sail *f*, spàrr *m*

beam *v* (*facial expr*) dèan fàite-gàire mhòr

bean, **beans** *n* pònair *f*

bear *n* mathan *m*

bear *v* **1** (*suffer*) fuiling *vt* ; **2** (*carry*) giùlain *vt*, iomchair *vt*; **3** (*give birth to*) beir *vt*

beard *n* feusag *f*

bearded *adj* feusagach, ròmach

bearer *n* neach-giùlain *m*, neach-iomchair *m*, portair *m*

bearing¹ *n* (*compass* ~) gabhail *mf*, àird *f*

bearing² (*posture*) giùlan *m*

bearing³ (*engineering etc*) giùlan *m*

beast *n* ainmhidh *m*, beathach *m*, biast *f*, brùid *mf*, bèist *f*

beat *n* (*music*) buille *mf*

beat *v* **1** (*defeat*) fairtlich *vi*, dèan a' chùis air, dèan an gnothach air; **2** (*strike*) buail *vt*, slac *vt*

beating *n* (*thrashing*) slacadh *m*, pronnadh *m*

beautiful *adj* rìomhach, bòidheach, brèagha, maiseach

beautify *v* maisich *vt*, sgèimhich *vt*

beauty *n* maise *f*, bòidhchead *f*, àilleachd *f*

beaver *n* bìobha(i)r *m*

because *conj* a chionn is gu, a thaobh is gu

because of *prep* a chionn, a thaobh, air sgàth

beckon *v* smèid *vi* air/ri

become *v* **1** fàs *vi*; **2** (*onset of emotion etc*) thig air; **3** (*onset of emotion*) gabh *vt*; **4** (*adopt profession etc*) rach *vi* nad (*etc*); **5** (*befall*) tachair *vi*, èirich *vi* do; **6** (*suit*) thig *vi* do, freagair *vi* air

bed *n* **1** leabaidh *f*; **2** (*of sea*) grunnd *m*

bedclothes, **bedding** *n* aodach *m* leapa

bedfellow *n* coimhleapach *mf*

bedroom *n* seòmar-cadail *m*

bee *n* seillean *m*

beef *n* mairtfheoil *f*

beehive *n* sgeap *f*

beer *n* leann *m*

beet *n* biotais *m*

beetle *n* daolag *f*

befall *v* tachair *vi*, èirich *vi*, tuit *vi*

befit *v* **1** (*suit*) thig do; **2** (*be incumbent on*) is *v irreg def* cubhaidh do

befitting *adj* cubhaidh, iomchaidh

before *adv* roimhe

before *conj* mus & mun

before *prep* **1** (*space*) ro, fa chomhair; **2** (*time*) ro

beforehand *adv* ro-làimh

beg *v* **1** (*for money etc*) dèan faoighe; **2** (*plead*) guidh *vi* air

beget *v* gin *vt*

beggar *n* dìol-dèirce *m*, dèirceach *m*

begging *n* (*for gifts*) faoighe *f*

begin *v* tòisich *vi* air/ri), teann *vi* ri

beginning *n* **1** (*time*) toiseach *m*; **2** (*of process*) tòiseachadh *m*; **3** (*first stage*) tùs *m*

beguile *v* meall *vt*

beguiling *adj* meallach

beguiling *n* mealladh *m*

behalf *n*, *in expr* on ~ of às leth (*with gen*)

behave *v* **1** giùlain *vti*; **2** (*treat*) làimhsich *vt*, gnàthaich *vt*

behaviour *n* **1** (*conduct*) dol-a-mach *m*, giùlan *m*; **2** (*treatment*) làimhseachadh *m*, gnàthachadh *m*

behead *v* dì-cheannaich *vt*

beheading *n* dì-cheannadh *m*

behind *adv* **1** (*position*) air dheireadh, air chùl; **2** (*less advanced*) air dheireadh

behind *prep* air cùlaibh, air cùl (*with gen*)

being *n* **1** (*abstr*) bith *f*; **2** (*living thing*) creutair *m*

belch *n* rùchd *m*, brùchd *m*

belch *v* rùchd *vi*, brùchd *vi*, dèan brùchd *m*

Belgium *n* A' Bheilg *nf*

belief *n* **1** (*abstr*) creideas *m*; **2** (*relig*) creideamh *m*

believe *v* creid *vti* ann an, thoir creideas do

belittle *v* cuir *vt* an suarachas *m*

bell *n* clag *m*

belling *n* (*deer*) langanaich *f*

bellow *n* (*humans, cattle etc*) geum *m*, beuc *m*

bellow *v* **1** beuc *vi*, geum *vi*, ràn *vi*; **2** (*animals*) nuallaich *vi*; **3** (*esp deer*) langanaich *vi*

bellowing *n* **1** (*humans, cattle etc*) beucadh *m*; **2** (*deer*) langanaich *f*

belly *n* **1** (*abdomen*) balg *m*; **2** (*paunch*) brù *f*, maodal *f*, mionach *m*

belly-button *n* imleag *f*

bellyful *n* làn broinne *m*

belong *v* buin *vi* do, is *v irreg & def* le

belongings *n* treal(l)aichean *fpl*

beloved *adj* gaolach, ionmhainn

below *adv* fodha (*etc*) *prep pron*, shìos bho

below *prep* fo

belt *n* crios *m*

bench *n* being(e) *f*

bend *n* **1** lùb *f*; **2** (*in river*) camas *m*

bend *v* **1** (*object*) fiar & fiaraich *vti*, lùb *vti*; **2** (*body*) crom *vti*, lùb *vti*

bending, **bendy** *adj* lùbach

beneath *prep* fo

benediction *n* beannachadh *m*

benefactor *n* tabhartaiche *m*, tabhairteach *m*

beneficial *adj* tairbheach & tarbhach

benefit *n* **1** (*abstr*) tairbhe *f*; **2** (*fin*) prothaid *f*; **3** (*social security etc*) sochair *f*, dòil *m*

benefit *v* buannaich *vi*, tairbhich *vi*

bent *adj* crom, lùbte

bent[1] *n* (*ability*) tàlann *m*

bent[2] (*grass*) muran *m*

bequeath *v* tiomnaich *vt*

bequest *n* tiomnadh *m*, dìleab *f*

berry *n* dearc *f*, dearcag *f*

beseech *v* guidh *vi* air

beside *prep* ri taobh (*with gen*)

besides *prep* a bharrachd air, a thuilleadh air

besiege *v* cuir sèist air

best *sup adj* feàrr *in exprs* as fheàrr

best *sup adv* feàrr, *with v irreg & def* is & do

best *n* **1** (*effort*) dìcheall *m*; **2** *in expr* **at ~** aig a' char as fheàrr; **3** (*best part*) brod *m*, smior *m*

best *v* dèan an gnothach air, dèan a' chùis air

bet *n* geall *m*

bet *v* cuir geall *m*, rach *vi* an geall

betray *v* brath *vt*

betrayal *n* brathadh *m*

betrothal *n* gealladh-pòsaidh *m*, rèiteach *m*

better *comp adj* **1** feàrr, *in exprs* as fheàrr & nas fheàrr; **2** (*health/quality*) am feabhas

better *comp adv* feàrr, *with v irreg & def* is & do

better *n*, *in expr* **get the ~ of** fairtlich *vi*, faillich *vi*, dèan an gnothach air, dèan a' chùis air

betting *n* gealladh *m*

between *prep* eadar

bevvy *n* **1** (*spree*) daorach *f*; **2** (*booze*) deoch *f*, deoch-làidir *f*

bevvying *n* daorach *f*, pòitearachd *f*

bewitch *v* cuir *vt* fo gheasaibh

bewitched *adj & past part* fo gheasaibh, seunta

bewitching *adj* meallach

beyond *prep* thairis air, seachad air, thar

bi- *prefix* dà-

bias *n* claon-bhàidh *f*, taobh *m*

bible *n* bìoball *m*

biblical *adj* bìoballach

bibliography *n* leabhar-chlàr *m*

bicycle *n* baidhsagal *m*, rothar *m*

bid *n* **1** (*at sale etc*) tairgse *f*; **2** (*attempt*) oidhirp *f*

bid *v* **1** (*at sale etc*) tairg *vti*, thoir tairgse air; **2** (*request*) iarr *vt* air; **3** (*greetings etc*) *in exprs* **~ welcome** cuir fàilte air

bidie-in *n* coimhleapach *mf*

big *adj* mòr

bigger *comp adj* **1** mò/motha; **2** *in exprs* **grow/get ~** rach *vi* am meud, meudaich *vi*

bigwig *n* duine mòr cudromach *m*

bilateral *adj* dà-thaobhach

bilingual *adj* dà-chànanach

bilingualism *n* dà-chànanas *m*

bill[1] *n* **1** (*fin*) cunntas *m*, bileag *f*; **2** (*parliament*) bile *m*

bill[2] *n* (*bird*) gob *m*

binary *adj* dà-fhillte

bind *v* ceangail *vt*

binding *adj* ceangaltach

binoculars *n* prosbaig *f*

biodegradable *adj* so-chnàmhach

biographer *n* beath-eachdraiche *m*

biographical *adj* beath-eachdraidheil

biography *n* beath-eachdraidh *f*

biology *n* bith-eòlas *m*

biped *n* dà-chasach *m*

bird *n* eun *m*

birth *n* **1** breith *f*; **2** (*delivery*) asaid *f*

birthday *n* ceann-bliadhna *m*, co-là-breith *m*

birthright *n* dual *m*

bishop *n* easbaig *m*

bit *adv* car, caran, rudeigin, rud beag

bit[1] *n* **1** mìr *m*, criomag *f*; **2** (*IT*) bìdeag *f*

bit[2] *n* (*horse*) cabstair *m*

bitch *n* galla *f*, bidse *f*

bite *n* **1** bìdeadh *m*; **2** (*food*) grèim bìdh *m*

bite *v* bìd *vti*

biting *adj* geur, guineach

bitter *adj* searbh, geur, goirt

bitterness *n* **1** (*emotion, taste*) gèire *f*; **2** (*directed at person*) nimh/neimh *m*

bivouac *n* teanta bheag *f*

bivouac *v* campaich *vi* (ann an teanta bheag)

black *adj* dubh

black *n* dubh *m*

blackberry *n* **1** (*plant*) dris ; **2** (*fruit*) smeur *f*

blackbird *n* lon-dubh *m*

blackboard *n* bòrd-dubh *m*

blackcock *n* (*grouse*) coileach-dubh *m*

blacken *v* dubh *vti*

black-haired adj dubh, dorcha
blackhead n guirean dubh m
blackout n dubhadh m
black out v dubh vt às
blacksmith n gobha m
bladder n aotroman m
blade n lann f
blame n coire f, cron m
blame v coirich vt, cuir a' choire air, faigh cron do
bland adj **1** (food etc) neo-bhlasmhor, gun bhlas m; **2** (personality) gun smior m, gun bhrìgh f
blank adj bàn
blanket n plaide f, plangaid f
blarney n cabadaich f, goileam m
blasphemy n toibheum m
blast n **1** (wind) sian m, sgal m; **2** (noise) toirm f, lasgan m, iorghail f; **3** (explosion) spreadhadh m; **4** (oath) ~! an donas!
blast v **1** (blight) searg vt, crìon vi; **2** (row) càin/cronaich vt gu dian
blatant adj ladarna, dalma
blaze n lasair f
blaze v las vi
blazing adj lasrach
bleach v gealaich vti
bleaching n gealachadh m
bleak adj **1** (landscape) lom; **2** (situation) gun dòchas m
bleakness n (landscape) luime f, dìthreabhachd f
bleary-eyed adj prab-shùileach
bleat, bleating n (sheep) mèilich f, (goats) miogadaich f, meigeall m
bleat v (sheep) dèan mèilich f, (goats) dèan miogadaich f
bleed v **1** (general) caill fuil, cuir fuil, leum; **2** (draw blood) leig fuil à
blemish n (moral) fàillinn f, (moral/physical) meang f, gaoid f
blend n coimeasgachadh m
blend v coimeasgaich vti
bless v beannaich vt
blessed adj & past part beannaichte, naomh
blessing n beannachd f
blether n **1** (also ~ing) cabadaich f, cabaireachd f, goileam m; **2** (person) duine cabach
blether v bleadraig vi

blight n **1** (disaster etc) sgrios m; **2** in expr **potato** ~ cnàmh m, (used with art) an gaiseadh
blight v searg vi, crìon vi
blighted adj & past part **1** crìon; **2** (career etc) air (a etc) sgrios(adh)
blind adj dall
blind v dall vt
blinding adj (dazzling) boillsgeach
blinding n dalladh m
blindness n doille f
blink n priobadh m
blink v priob vi, caog vi
blister n leus m, balg m, builgean m
blizzard n cathadh-sneachda m
block n ceap m, cnap m
block v **1** (aperture etc) tachd vt; **2** (stop) caisg vt
blockage n tachdadh m
blockhead n bumailear m, ùmaidh m, stalcaire m
blond(e) adj bàn
blonde n tè bhàn, boireannach m bàn
blood n fuil f
bloodshed n dòrtadh-fala m
bloodstream n ruith f na fala
bloody adj fuil(t)each
bloom n blàth m, flùr m
blot n smal m
blot v **1** (cause blot) leig vt inc air; **2** (soak up) sùgh vt; **3** ~ **out** dubh vt às
blotting-paper n pàipear-sùghaidh m
blow n **1** (with fist etc) buille f; **2** (disappointment) bristeadh-dùil m
blow v **1** sèid vt; **2** in expr ~ **up** (explode) spreadh vti; **3** in expr ~ **up** (enlarge) meudaich vt
blowout n **1** (tyre) spreadhadh m; **2** (food) làn broinne (de bhiadh)
blubber n saill f (na) muice-mara
blubber v (weep) ràn vi
bludgeon n cuaille m
blue adj gorm
blue n gorm m
bluff n (relief feature) sròn f
bluff v mas fhìor
blunt adj **1** (not sharp) maol; **2** (person) aithghearr
blush n rudhadh m, rudhadh-gruaidhe m
blush v ruadhaich vi
blushing adj ruiteach
boar n torc m, cullach m

board[1] *n* **1** (*plank*) bòrd *m*, dèile *f*, clàr *m*;
2 (*notice ~*) bòrd *m*; **3** (*sign ~*) clàr *m*;
4 (*for games etc*) bòrd *m*

board[2] *n* (*body*) bòrd *m*

board *v* (*plane etc*) rach *vi* air bòrd

boast *n* bòst *m*

boast *v* dèan bòst *m*

boastful *adj* bòstail

boasting *n* bòstadh *m*

boat *n* **1** bàta *m*; **2** (*rowing boat*) eathar *mf*,
geòla *f*

bobbin *n* iteachan *m*, piorna *mf*

bodily *adj* corporra

body *n* **1** (*of creature*) corp *m*; **2** (*human
~*) bodhaig *f*, colann *f*; **3** (*dead ~: human*)
corp *m*, (*not human*) closach *f*; **4** (*person*)
creutair *m*; **5** (*group*) buidheann *mf*;
6 (*collection*) stòras *m*, cruinneachadh *m*

bog *n* boglach *f*, fèith(e) *f*

bog-cotton *n* canach *m* (an t-slèibh)

boil *n* neasgaid *f*

boil *v* goil *vti*

boiler *n* goileadair *m*

boiling *adj* goileach

bold *adj* **1** (*intrepid*) cruadalach, dàna;
2 (*impudent*) ladarna, dàna; **3** (*typog*)
trom

boldness *n* dànadas *m*

bolt *n* crann *m*

bond *n* **1** (*abstr*) ceangal *m*; **2** (*fin etc*)
urras *m*

bond *v* tàth *vt*

bondage *n* cuibhreachadh *m*, slaibhreas *m*,
braighdeanas *m*, tràilleachd *f*

bonding *n* tàthadh *m*

bone *n* cnà(i)mh *m*

bony *adj* cnàmhach

book *n* leabhar *m*

bookcase *n* preas-leabhraichean *m*

booklet *n* leabhran *m*, leabhrachan *m*

boot *n* **1** (*of foot*) bròg-mhòr *f*, bròg throm;
2 (*Wellington ~*) bòtann *mf*; **3** (*of car*)
ciste(-càir) *f*; **4** *in expr* **to** ~ cuideachd *adv*

booty *n* cobhartach *mf*, creach *f*

booze *n* deoch *f*, deoch-làidir *f*

boozer *n* pòitear *m*, drungair *m*

boozing *n* pòitearachd *nf*

border *n* **1** (*of territory etc*) crìoch *f*; **2** (*of
material etc*) oir *f*

bore[1] *v* (*~ hole etc*) toll *vti*

bore[2] *v* (*cause tedium*) is *v irreg def* liosda
le

bored *adj* bi *vi irreg* fadachd *f* air (*etc*)

boredom *n* fadachd *f*, fadal *m*

boring *adj* fadalach, ràsanach, liosda,
màirnealach

born *past part v* beir

borrow *v* gabh/faigh *vt* air iasad o/bho

borrowed *adj & past part* air iasad *m*

borrowing *n* iasad *m*

bosom *n* **1** (*general*) uchd *m*, com *m*,
broilleach *m*; **2** (*woman's ~*) cìochan *fpl*

boss[1] *n* (*in woodwork etc*) cnap *m*

boss[2] *n* (*of firm etc*) ceannard *m*

botanical *adj* luibheach

botanist *n* luibh-eòlaiche *m*

botany *n* luibh-eòlas *m*

botcher *n* uaipear *m*, cearbair(e) *m*

both *adv & adj* **1** (*of things etc*) gach cuid
f, an dà chuid *f*; **2** (*of people*) le chèile, nan
dithis; **3** (*before adjs*) eadar; **4** (*as adj*)
gach

bother *n* dragh *m*

bother *v* **1** (*annoy*) cuir dragh air, bodraig
vt; **2** (*take trouble*) bodraig *vi*

bottle *n* botal *m*, buideal *m*

bottom *adj* as ìsle; ìochdair

bottom *n* **1** (*base*) bonn *m*, bun *m*;
2 (*lowest part*) an ceann as ìsle; **3** (*of river
etc*) grinneal *m*; **4** *in expr* ~ **of the sea**
grunnd *m* na mara; **5** (*backside*) màs *m*,
tòn *f*

bough *n* meang(l)an *m*, geug *f*

boulder *n* ulbhag *f*, ulpag *f*

boundary *n* crìoch *f*

bourgeois *adj & n* bùirdeasach *m*

bourgeoisie *n* bùirdeasachd *f*

bow[1] *n* (*before royalty etc*) ùmhlachd *f*

bow[2] *n* **1** (*of boat*) toiseach *m*; **2** (*weapon*)
bogha(-saighde) *m*; **3** (*for stringed
instrument*) bogha *m*

bow *v* **1** crom *vt*, lùb *vt*; **2** (*before royalty
etc*) dèan ùmhlachd *f*

bowed *adj* **1** lùbte; **2** (*of head*) crom

bowels *n* innidh *f*

bowl *n* cuach *f*, bobhla *m*

bow-legged *adj* camachasach, gòbbhlach

bowstring *n* taifeid *f*

box *n* bogsa *m*, bucas *m*

boxer *n* bogsair *m*

boxing *n* bogsadh/bogsaigeadh *m*

boy *n* gille *m*, balach *m*

boyfriend *n* car(a)bhaidh *m*, leannan *m*,
bràmair *m*

brace *n* (*pair*) càraid *f*, caigeann *f*
bracelet *n* bann-làimhe *m*
bracken *n* raineach *f*, roineach *f*
bracket *n* (*typog*) camag *f*
braid *v* fill *vt*, dualaich *vt*
braided *adj & past part* fillte
brain, **brains** *n* eanchainn *f*
brain *v* cuir an eanchainn à
brainless *adj* faoin, baoth
brainy *adj* inntinneach
brainteaser *n* tòimhseachan *m*
brake *n* (*on wheel etc*) brèig *f*, casgan *m*
bramble *n* **1** (*plant*) dris *f*; **2** (*fruit*) smeur *f*
bran *n* garbhan *m*
branch *n* **1** (*of organisation etc*) meur *f*;
  2 (*of tree*) geug *f*, meang(l)an *m*
branch *v* meuraich *vi*
brand *n* (*make*) seòrsa *m*
brand-new *adj* ùr-nodha
brandish *v* crath *vt*
brass *adj* pràiseach
brass *n* pràis *f*
brat *n* droch isean *m*, ablach *m*, peasan *m*
brave *adj* **1** (*phys*) gaisgeil, treun; **2** (*rashly* ~) dàna; **3** (*morally* ~) misneachail
bravery *n* **1** (*phys*) gaisge *f*, gaisgeachd *f*; **2** (*rash* ~) dànadas *m*; **3** (*moral* ~) misneach *f*, misneachd *f*
brawl *n* tuasaid *f*, sabaid *f*
brawl *v* sabaid *vi*, dèan sabaid ri
brawny *adj* (*person*) tomadach, calma
brazen *adj* ladarna, gun nàire
breach *n* **1** (*gap*) beàrn *mf*; **2** (*infraction*) briseadh *m*
breadth *n* farsaingeachd *f*, leud *m*
break *v* **1** bris(t) *vti*; **2** (~ *promise etc*) rach *vi* air ais air
break *n* **1** bris(t)eadh *m*; **2** (*pause*) stad (beag)
breast *n* **1** (*woman's* ~) cìoch *f*; **2** (*general*) uchd *m*, com *m*, broilleach *m*
breath *n* **1** anail *f*; **2** (~ *of life*) deò *f*; **3** *in expr* ~ **of wind** deò gaoithe, oiteag *f*, ospag *f*
breathalyser *n* poca-analach *m*
breathe *v* analaich *vi*
breather *n* stad (beag) *m*
breed *v* **1** (*plants, animals*) tàrmaich *vt*; **2** (*humans & animals*) gin *vti*
breeding *n* **1** (*humans & animals*) gineadh *m*, (*cattle*) dàir *f*; **2** (*manners*) modh *mf*
breeze *n* oiteag *f*, ospag *f*, osnadh *m*

Breton *n* (*lang*) Breatnais *f*
brewer *n* grùdair(e) *m*
brewery *n* taigh-grùide *m*
brewing *n* grùdaireachd *f*
bridge *n* **1** drochaid; **2** *in expr* ~ **of the nose** bràigh *m* na sròine
brief *adj* goirid
briefcase *n* màileid *f*
brier *n* dris *f*
bright *adj* **1** (*of light etc*) soilleir; **2** (*mentally*) toinisgeil, eirmseach
brilliance *n* (*of light*) lainnir *f*
brilliant *adj* **1** (*of light*) lainnireach; **2** (*intellectually*) sàr-thoinisgeil, air leth toinisgeil
brimstone *n* pronnasg *m*
brindled *adj* riabhach
bring down *v* (*cause to fall*) leag *vt*
bring *v* thoir *vt*
bristle *n* frioghan *m*, calg *m*
Britain *n* Breatann *mf*
Britanny *n* A' Bhreatann Bheag *f*
broad *adj* farsaing, leathann
broadcast *n* craoladh *m*, craobh-sgaoileadh *m*
broadcast *v* craoil *vti*, craobh-sgaoil *vti*
broadcaster *m* craoladair *m*
broadcasting *n* craoladh *m*, craobh-sgaoileadh *m*
broaden *v* leudaich *vti*
broadened *adj* leudaichte
broadly *adv*, *in expr* ~ **speaking** san/anns an fharsaingeachd *f*
broadsword *n* claidheamh *m* leathann
brochure *n* leabhrachan *m*, leabhran *m*
broke *adj* gun sgillinn *f* ruadh
broken *adj & past part* briste
bronze *n* umha *m*
broth *n* brot *m*, eanraich *f*
brothel *n* taigh-siùrsachd *m*
brother *n* bràthair *m*
brother-in-law *n* bràthair-cèile *m*
brow *n* mala *f*, bathais *f*, clàr *m* an aodainn, maoil *f*
brown *adj* donn
brown-haired *adj* donn
bubble *n* gucag *f*, builgean *m*
bucket *n* **1** bucaid *f*, peile *m*, cuinneag *f*; **2** (*milking*) cuman *m*
bucket *v*, *in expr* **it was** ~**ing down** bha dìle bhàthte ann
bud *n* gucag *f*

budget *n* buidseat *m*
buffoon *n* bumalair *m*, baothair *m*
buffoonery *n* bumalaireachd *f*, baothaireachd *f*
bugger *n* **1** bugair *m*; **2** *in expr* **don't give a ~** cha toir mi hòro-gheallaidh *m* air
bugle *n* dùdach *f*, dùdag *f*
build *n* (*physique*) dèanamh *m*
build *v* tog *vt*
builder *n* togalaiche *m*, neach-togail *m*
building *n* **1** (*abstr*) togail *f*; **2** (*con*) togalach *m*
built *adj & past part* air a (*etc*) thogail
bulb *n* (*plant/light*) bolgan *m*
bulge *n* bogha *m*
bulky *adj* tomadach
bull *n* tarbh *m*
bullet *n* peilear *m*
bulling *adj* (*of cattle*) fo dhàir *f*
bullock *n* damh *m*
bully *n* burraidh *m*, maoidhear *m*
bullying *n* burraidheachd *f*, maoidheadh *m*
bulwark *n* mùr *m*, dìdean *f*
bum *n* (*backside*) màs *m*
bundle *n* pasgadh *m*, pasgan *m*, ultach *m*
bundle *v* **1** ~ **up** tru(i)s *vt*; **2** (*push*) brùth *vt*, sàth *vt*
bungler *n* cearbair *m*, uaipear *m*
buoy *n* put(a) *m*
buoyancy *n* fleòdradh *m*
burden *n* eallach *m*, uallach *m*
burial *n* tiodhlacadh *m*
burial ground *n* cill *f*, cladh *m*
burly *adj* (*build*) tomadach, dèanta, leathann
burn[1] *n* (*injury*) losgadh *m*
burn[2] *n* (*stream*) allt *m*, sruth(an) *m*
burn *v* loisg *vti*, dàth *vt*
burnt *adj* loisgte
burst[1] *n* **1** (*onset*) brag *m*, (*laughter*) lasgan *m*; **2** (*energy etc*) sgairt *f*
burst[2] *n* (*pipe etc*) sgàineadh *m*
burst *v* **1** (*pipes etc*) sgàin *vti*, spreadh *vi*; **2** (*emerge*) brùchd *vi*
bury *v* (*dead*) tiodhlaic *vt*, adhlaic *vt*
bus *n* bus *m*
bush *n* dos *m*, preas *m*

business *n* **1** (*commercial* ~) gnothach *m*, gnìomhachas *m* ; **2** (*abstr*) malairt *f*; **3** (*affair*) nì *m*, gnothach *m*, cùis *f*
businessman *n* fear-gnothaich *m*, fear-malairt *m*, fear-gnìomhachais *m*
businesswoman *n* tè-ghnothaich *f*, tè-mhalairt *f*, tè-ghnìomhachais *f*
bus-stop *n* àite-stad bus *m*
bustle *n* drip *f*, sgairt *f*
busy *adj* **1** (*people*) trang; **2** (*situations*) dripeil
butcher *n* bùidsear *m*, feòladair *m*
butcher *v* casgair *vt*
butchering, **butchery** *n* spadadh *m*, casgairt *f*
butt **1** (*archery etc*) targaid *f*; **2** (*recipient etc*) cùis *f*, culaidh *f*
butter *n* ìm *m*
butter *v* **1** cuir ìm air; **2** *in expr* ~ **someone up** dèan miodal do chuideigin/ ri cuideigin
butterfly *n* dealan-dè *m*
buttock *n* màs *m*
button *n* putan *m*
buy *v* ceannaich *vti*
buyer *n* ceannaiche *m*
buying *n* ceannachd *nf*, ceannach *m*
buzzard *n* clamhan *m*
buzz *n* crònan *m*
buzz *v* dèan crònan
buzzer *n* (*alarm etc*) srannan *m*
buzzing *n* crònan *m*
by *adv*, *in exprs* **put ~** cuir mu seach, **pass ~ rach** seachad; ~ **and** ~ ri tìde *f*
by *prep* **1** le; **2** (*motion*) seachad air; **3** (*beside*) ri taobh *m*; **4** ~ **and large** san/ anns an fharsaingeachd *f*, ~ **the way/ in the ~-going** san dol-seachad, ~ **day and** ~ **night** a latha 's a dh'oidhche, **little** ~ **little** beag is beag, beag air bheag, mean air mhean, (*of time*) ~ **and** ~ mu dheireadh thall, ri tìde *f*, **close** ~ faisg air làimh, faisg air
bye-law *n* frith-lagh *m*
by-election *n* fo-thaghadh *m*
by-name *n* far-ainm *m*, frith-ainm *m*
bypass *n* seach-rathad *m*
byre *n* bàthach *f*, bàthaich *m*

C

cab *n* (*taxi*) tagsaidh *m*
cabbage *n* càl *m*
caber *n* cabar *m*
cabin *n* **1** bothan *m*; **2** (*on ship etc*) cèabain *m*
cabinet *n* (*pol*) caibineat *m*
cabinetmaker *n* saor-àirneis *m*
cable *n* càball *m*
cache *n* stòr *m* (falaichte)
cack *n* cac *m*
cackle *v* gloc *vi*
cackle, cackling *n* gloc *m*, glocail *f*, gogail *f*
cadence *n* dùnadh *m*
cadge *v* (~ *gifts*) dèan faoighe *f*
cadging *n* (*for gifts*) faoighe *f*
café *n* cafaidh *mf*, taigh-bìdh *m*
cage *n* cèidse *f*
cairn *n* càrn *m*
cake *n* cèic *f*
calamitous *adj* dosgainneach
calamity *n* dosgainn *f*
calculate *v* **1** (*distance etc*) tomhais *vt*; **2** (*sums etc*) àireamhaich *vti*, obraich *vt* a-mach
calculation *n* tomhas *m*, àireamhachadh *m*
calculator *n* àireamhair *m*
calendar *n* mìosachan *m*
calf *n* **1** (*animal*) laogh *m*; **2** (*of leg*) calpa *m*
calfskin *n* laoighcionn *m*
call *n* **1** (*cry*) gairm *f*, glaodh *m*, èigh *f*; **2** (*visit*) tadhal *m*, cèilidh *mf*
call *v* **1** (*cry*) gairm *vti*, glaodh *vi*, èigh *vi*; **2** (*visit*) tathaich *vti*, tadhail *vi*; **3** (*refer to as*) can *vi* ri
calling *n* **1** (*shouting etc*) gairm *f*, èigheachd *f*; **2** (*visiting*) tadhal *m*; **3** (*vocation*) gairm *f*
calm *adj* ciùin
calm *n* **1** (*temperament etc*) ciùineas *m*; **2** (*weather*) fèath *mf*
calm *v* ciùinich *vti*, tàlaidh *vti*
calorie *n* calaraidh *m*
calumny *n* **1** (*action*) cùl-chàineadh *m*; **2** (*words*) cùl-chainnt *f*
camel *n* càmhal *m*
camera *n* **1** camara *m*; **2** *in expr* **in ~** ann an dìomhaireachd

camouflage *n* breug-riochd *m*
camp *n* campa *m*
camp *v* campaich *vi*
campaign *n* iomairt *f*
campaign *v* dèan iomairt *f*
campaigner *n* neach-iomairt *m*
campaigning *n* iomairt *f*
camping *n* campachadh *m*
can *n* (*for drinks etc*) cana *m*, canastair *m*
can *v* **1** (*be permitted*) faod *vi def*; **2** (*may*) faod *vi def*; **3** (*ability*) urrainn *f*; **4** (*expr possibility etc*) gabh *vi*
Canada *nf* Canada
Canadian *n & adj* Canèidianach *m*
cancel *v* **1** (*function etc*) cuir *vt* dheth; **2** (*entry etc*) dubh *vt* a-mach
cancellation *n* **1** (*function etc*) cur *m* dheth; **2** (*entry etc*) dubhadh *m* a-mach
cancer *n* aillse *f*
candid *adj* fosgailte, faoilidh, fosgarra
candidate *n* tagraiche *m*, neach-tagraidh, neach-iarraidh *m*
candle *n* coinneal *f*
Candlemas *n* an Fhèill Brìde *f*
candlestick *n* coinnlear *m*
candour *n* fosgailteachd *f*, fosgarrachd *f*
cane *n* **1** (*material*) cuilc *f*; **2** (*stick*) bata (-cuilce) *m*
canine *adj* conail
canister *n* canastair *m*
cannabis *n* cainb *f*, (*plant*) cainb-lus *m*
canoe *n* curach *f* Innseanach
canteen *n* biadhlann *f*
canvas *n* cainb *f*, canabhas *m*
canvass *v* sir taic/bhòtaichean
cap *n* (*headgear*) ceap *m*, bonaid *mf*
cap *v* **1** (*limit*) cuibhrich *vt*
capability *n* comas *m*
capable *adj* comasach
capacious *adj* **1** (*premises etc*) farsaing; **2** (*vessel etc*) luchdmhor
capacity *n* **1** (*abstr*) tomhas-lìonaidh *m*; **2** (*ability*) comas *m*; **3** (*role*) dreuchd *f*
cape¹ *n* (*headland*) maol *m*, rubha *m*
cape² *n* (*garment*) cleòc(a) *m*, tonnag *f*
caper *v* leum *vi*

capercaillie, capercailzie *n* capall-coille *m*

capering *n* leumadaich *f*

capillary *n* cuisle chaol *f*

capital *n* 1 (*fin*) calpa *m*; 2 (*city*) ceanna-bhaile *m*, prìomh bhaile *m*; 3 (*orthog*) litir mhòr *f*

capital *adj* 1 (*fin*) calpach; 2 (*first rate*) anabarrach math, barraichte

capitalism *n* calpachas *m*

capitalist *n* calpaiche *m*

capitulate *v* strìochd *vi*

capitulation *n* strìochdadh *m*

capping *n* (*limiting*) cuibhreachadh *m*

caprice *n* baogaid *f*

capricious *adj* caochlaideach, baogaideach

capsize *v* 1 (*as vt*) cuir *vt* thairis; 2 (*as vi*) rach *vi* thairis

captain *n* caiptean *m*, sgiobair *m*

captivated *adj* fo gheasaibh

captivating *adj* meallach, tàlaidheach

captive *adj* an làimh

captive *n* prìosanach *m*, ciomach *m*, (*neach etc*) an làimh/an sàs

captivity *n* braighdeanas *m*, ciomachas *m*

capture *n* glacadh *m*, grèim *m*

capture *v* glac *vt*, cuir *vt* an làimh

captured *adj & past part* glacte, an làimh, an sàs

car *n* càr *m*, carbad *m*

carbon *n* gualan *m*

carbuncle *n* neasgaid *f*, guirean *m*

carcase *n* 1 corp (marbh) *m*; 2 (*not human*) closach *f*

card *n* cairt *f*

cardboard *n* cairt-bhòrd *m*

cardinal *adj* prìomh

cardinal *n* càirdineal *m*

care *n* 1 (*caution*) faiceall *f*, aire *f*; 2 (*responsibility*) cùram *m*; 3 (*worry*) cùram *m*, iomagain *f*

care *v* 1 (*tend*) altraim *vt*, eiridnich *vt*; 2 (*expr affection*) bi *v irreg* measail air

career *n* dreuchd *f*

careful *adj* cùramach, faiceallach

caress *v* cniadaich *vt*, brìodail *vt*

caressing *n* cniadachadh *m*

caretaker *n* neach-gleidhidh *m*

cargo *n* cargu & carago *m*, luchd *m*, eallach *m*

carnage *n* dòrtadh-fala *m*, bùidsearachd *f*, àr *m*

carnal *adj* feòlmhor, collaidh

carnation *n* càrnaid *f*

carnivore *n* feòil-itheadair *m*, ainmhidh feòil-itheach *m*

carnivorous *adj* feòil-itheach

carousal, carousing *n* pòitearachd *f*

carouse *v* pòit *vi*

carpenter *n* saor *m*

carpentry *n* saorsainneachd *f*

carpet *n* brat-ùrlair *m*, brat-làir *m*

carrageen *n* cairgein & carraigean *m*

carriage *n* 1 (*vehicle*) carbad *m*; 2 (*transportation*) giùlan *m*; 3 (*charges*) faradh *m*

carriageway *n* rathad *m*, slighe *f*

carrier *n* neach-giùlain *m*

carrion *n* 1 ablach *m*; 2 *in expr* ~ **crow** feannag dhubh *f*

carrot *n* curran *m*

carry *v* 1 giùlain *vt*, iomchair *vt*; 2 *in expr* ~ **out** (*task*) coilean *vt*, cuir *vt* an gnìomh, gnìomhaich *vt*; 3 *in expr* ~ **on** (*continue*) cùm air *vi*, lean air *vi*; 4 *in expr* ~ **on** (*behave*) giùlain f(h)èin

carry-on, carrying-on *n* (*behaviour*) dol-a-mach *m*

cart *n* cairt *f*

cartoon *n* dealbh-èibhinn *mf*, cartùn *m*

carve *v* 1 (*wood etc*) snaigh *vt*; 2 (*meat*) geàrr *vt*

carving *n* 1 (*wood etc: process*) snaigheadh *m*, (*product*) obair-shnaighte *f*; 2 (*meat*) gearradh *m*

cascade *n* (*waterfall*) eas *m*, leum-uisge *m*, spùt *m*

case *n* 1 (*luggage*) màileid *f*, ceas *m*; 2 (*legal*) cùis *f*, cùis-lagha *f*; 3 (*gram*) tuiseal *m*; 4 (*fact*) *in exprs* **in that** ~, mas ann mar sin a tha a' chùis; 5 *in expr* **in** ~ air eagal; 6 *in expr* **in any** ~ co-dhiù

cash *n* 1 airgead-làimhe/ullamh *m*

cask *n* baraille *m*

cassette *n* cèiseag *f*

cassock *n* casag *f*

cast[1] *n* (*play etc*) muinntir *f*, sgioba *mf*

cast[2] *n* (*throw*) tilgeadh *m*, tilgeil *f*, (*of weapon*) urchair *f*

cast *v* tilg *vt*, caith *vt*

castigate *v* cronaich *vt*

castle *n* caisteal *m*

castrate *v* spoth *vt*

castration *n* gearradh *m*, spothadh *m*

castrato n caillteanach m
casual adj (attitude) coma co-dhiù, mì-dhìcheallach; gun adhbhar; socrach
casualty n (accident etc) leòinteach m
cat n cat m
catastrophe n sgrios m
catch v 1 glac vt; 2 in expr ~ **(up with)** beir vi air; 3 (illness etc) gabh vt; 4 in expr ~ **sight** faigh sealladh air
catching adj (infectious) gabhaltach
catechise v ceasnaich vt
catechism n 1 (book) leabhar-cheist m; 2 (questioning) ceasnachadh m
catechist n ceistear m
categorical adj (firm) deimhinn(e)
categorically adv 1 (firmly) gu deimhinne, gun teagamh m; 2 (utterly) gu buileach, uile-gu-lèir
category n seòrsa m, gnè f
cater v 1 (restaurant etc) ullaich biadh m; 2 (supply) solair vti, solaraich vti; 3 (satisfy) coilean vt, leasaich vt
catering n ullachadh m bìdh
cathedral n cathair-eaglais f
Catholic n & adj Caitligeach m
cattle n crodh m
caught adj & past part an sàs, an làimh, glacte
cauldron n coire m
cauliflower n càl-colaig m
cause n 1 adhbhar m, fàth m, cùis f; 2 (principle) adhbhar m
cause v 1 is v irreg def adhbhar m; 2 in expr ~ **to be** v cuir vt air, fàg vt
causeway n cabhsair m
caustic adj geur, guineach, searbh
caution n 1 (prudence) faiceall f; 2 (warning) earalachadh m, rabhadh m
caution v 1 (legal) earalaich vt; 2 (general) thoir rabhadh do
cautious adj faiceallach
cavalry n eachraidh m
cave, cavern n ua(i)mh f
cavity n toll m
caw n gràg m, ròcail f
caw v dèan gràgail f
cawing n gràgail f, ròcail f
cease v 1 (end) thig vi gu crìch, sguir vi; 2 (desist) leig vt seachad, sguir vi (de)
ceaseless adj, **ceaselessly** adv, gun sgur
ceilidh n cèilidh mf
ceiling n mullach-seòmair m

celebrate v 1 (praise etc) mol vt, luaidh vt; 2 (observe) cùm vt, glèidh vt
celebrated adj (renowned) cliùiteach, iomraiteach
celebration n 1 (observance) cumail f, gleidheadh m; 2 (party) pàrtaidh m, hòro-gheallaidh m
celebrity n 1 (abstr) ainmealachd f; 2 (person) neach m ainmeil, neach iomraiteach
celery n soilire m
celestial adj nèamhaidh, speurach
celibacy n seachnadh feise m
cell n 1 (biol) cealla f; 2 (of saint etc) cill f
Celt n Ceilteach m
Celtic adj Ceilteach
cement n saimeant m, tàth m
cement v tàth vt
cemetery n cladh m, clachan m, cill f
censorious adj cronachail, coireachail
censure n cronachadh m
censure v cronaich vt
census n cunntas-sluaigh m
centilitre n ceudailiotair m
centimetre n ceudameatair m
centipede n ceud-chasach m
central adj meadhanach
centralisation n meadhanachadh m
centralise v meadhanaich vti
centre n 1 meadhan m; 2 (location) ionad m
centrifugal adj meadhan-sheachnach
century n linn mf
cereal n arbhar m, gràn m
ceremony n (event) deas-ghnàth m
certain adj 1 (sure) cinnteach, deimhinn(e); 2 sònraichte, àraidh
certainly adv gu dearbh
certainty n cinnt f
certificate n teisteanas m
certify v thoir teisteanas m
cessation n stad m
chafe v (skin) rùisg vt
chaff n càth f, moll m
chagrin n frionas m
chagrined adj frionasach
chain n cuibhreach m, slabhraidh f
chain (up) v cuibhrich vt, cuir vt air slabhraidh
chair n cathair f, sèithear m
chairman n cathraiche m, fear-cathrach m

chairperson *n* cathraiche *m*, neach-cathrach *m*

chalk *n* cailc *f*

challenge *n* dùbhlan *m*

challenge *v* **1** thoir dùbhlan do; **2** (*decision etc*) cuir *vi* an aghaidh

chamber *n* seòmar *m*

champion *n* curaidh *m*

chance *adj* tuiteamach

chance *n* **1** (*luck*) tuiteamas *m*; **2** (*opportunity*) cothrom *m*

chance *v* **1** tuit *vi* do; **2** *in expr* ~ **upon** tachair *vi* air, amais *vi* air

chancellor *n* seansailear *m*

change *n* **1** atharrachadh *m*, caochladh *m*, mùthadh *m*; **2** (*situation*) ùrachadh *m*; **3** (*money*) iomlaid *f*

change *v* atharraich *vti*, caochail *vi*, mùth *vi*

changeable *adj* caochlaideach

Channel Islands (the) *npl* Eileanan a' Chaolais *mpl*

chanter *n* (*bagpipe*) feadan *m*

chaos *n* **1** (*cosmology*) eu-cruth *m*; **2** (*untidiness*) *in expr* **in** ~ troimh-a-chèile

chapel *n* caibeal *m*

chapter *n* (*book*) caibideil *mf*

character *n* **1** nàdar *m*, (*humans*) mèinn *f*, (*hereditary*) dualchas *m*; **2** (*in play etc*) caractar *m*, pearsa *m*

characteristic *n* feart *m*

charcoal *n* gual-fiodha *m*

charge *n* **1** (*responsibility*) cùram *m*; **2** (*cost*) cosgais *f*; **3** (*fee etc*) tuarastal *m*; **4** (*legal*) casaid *f*; **5** (*attack*) ionnsaigh *f*

charge *v* **1** (*make responsible*) cuir uallach *m* air; **2** (*for goods etc*) iarr pàigheadh airson); **3** (*banking etc*) cuir *vt* ri cunntas; **4** (*attack*) thoir ionnsaigh air, rach *vi* sìos; **5** (*legal*) cuir casaid air, cuir fo chasaid

charitable *adj* **1** (*apt to give*) tabhairteach; **2** (*involved in charity*) carthannach; **3** (*kindly*) coibhneil

charity *n* **1** (*abstr*) carthannas *m*, carthannachd *f*; **2** (*organisation*) buidheann-carthannais, buidheann-carthannach *mf*; **3** (*alms*) dèirc *f*; **4** (*Bibl:*) gràdh *m*

charm *n* **1** (*magical*) geas *f*, seun *m*, ortha *f*; **2** (*personal*) taitneas *m*, ciatachd *f*

charming *adj* **1** (*person*) taitneach, ciatach, tlachdmhor; **2** (*person & place*) grinn

chart *n* **1** (*map etc*) cairt *f*; **2** (*table etc*) clàr *m*

charter *n* cairt *f*, cùmhnant *m* sgrìobhte

chase *n* **1** tòir *f*, ruaig *f*; **2** (*hunting*) ruaig *f*

chase *v* **1** rua(i)g *vt*, ruith *vi* às dèidh; **2** *in expr* ~ **away** rua(i)g *vt*, fuadaich *vt*

chaste *adj* geanmnaidh

chasten *v* ùmhlaich *vt*, nàraich *vt*

chastise *v* peanasaich *vt*

chastity *n* geanmnachd *f*

chat *n* còmhradh *m*

chat *v* dèan còmhradh

chattels *npl* **1** (*bits & pieces*) trealaich *f*; **2** (*possessions*) maoin *f*

chatter, chattering *n* cabadaich *f*, cabaireachd *f*, gobaireachd & gabaireachd *f*, goileam *m*

chatter *v* bleadraig *vi*

chatty *adj* còmhraideach, bruidhneach

cheap *adj* **1** (*in price*) saor, air bheag prìs *f*, air prìs ìseal; **2** (*petty*) suarach

cheat *n* cealgair(e) *m*, mealltair *m*, neach-foille *m*

cheat *v* **1** meall *vt*, thoir an car à, dèan foill air; **2** (*vi*) bi ri foill *f*

cheated *adj* air do (*etc*) m(h)ealladh

cheating *adj* meallta(ch)

cheating *n* foill *f*, mealladh *m*

check *v* **1** (*examine*) sgrùd *vt*, dèan ath-sgrùdadh air, thoir sùil air; **2** (*stop*) bac *vt*, cuir stad air, cuir bacadh air

check-out *n* àite-pàighidh *m*

check-up *n* àth-sgrùdadh *m*

cheek *n* **1** gruaidh *f*, pluic *f*; **2** (*insolence*) aghaidh *f*, bathais *f*

cheep, cheeping *n* bìd *m*, bìogail *f*

cheep *v* bìog *vi*

cheer *n* **1** (*approval*) iolach *f*; **2** (*mood*) misneachail

cheer *v* **1** dèan/tog iolach do; **2** *in expr* ~ **up!** tog ort!

cheerful *adj* greannmhor, aighearach, cridheil, sunndach

cheerfulness *n* aighear *m*, sunnd *m*

cheerio! *excl* tìoraidh!

cheery *adj* (*person*) aighearach, (*person, atmosphere etc*) cridheil

cheese *n* càise *mf*

chef *n* còcaire *m*

chemical *adj* ceimigeach

chemical *n* ceimig *f*

chemist *n* **1** ceimigear *m*; **2** (*pharmacist*) neach *m* chungaidhean

chemistry *n* ceimigeachd *f*

cheque *n* seic *f*

chequebook *n* seic-leabhar *m*

chess *n* tàileasg *m*

chest *n* **1** (*thorax*) cliabh *m*, broilleach *m*; **2** (*furniture*) ciste *f*

chew *v* **1** cnàmh *vti*, cagainn *vti*, cnuas & cnuasaich *vti*; **2** *in exprs* ~**ing the cud/ fat**, a' cnàmh na cìre

chick *n* isean *m*

chicken *n* (*young*) isean *m*, eireag *f*, (*mature*) cearc *f*

chide *v* cronaich *vt*, càin *vt*

chief *adj* prìomh, àrd

chief *n* **1** (*leader etc*) ceannard *m*; **2** (*of clan*) ceann-cinnidh *m*, ceann-feadhna *m*

chilblain *n* cusp *f*

child *n* **1** (*abstr & general*) duine cloinne *m*; **2** (*particular*) leanabh *m*, pàiste *m*, leanaban *m*, naoidhean *m*, (*boy*) balach *m* (beag), (*girl*) caileag *f* (bheag)

childhood *n* leanabas *m*

childish *adj* leanabail

childless *adj* gun chlann

children *n* clann *f*

chill *adj* fuaraidh, fionnar

chill *n* fionnarachd *f*, fuachd *f*

chill *v* fuaraich *vti*, meilich *vti*

chilly *adj* fuaraidh, fionnar

chimney *n* similear *m*, luidhear *m*

China *n* Sìona *f*

Chinese *adj* Sìonach

chip *n* (*wood etc*) sgealb *f*

chips *npl* sliseagan-buntàta *fpl*

chirp, chirping *n* bìd *m*, bìogail *f*

chirp *v* bìog *vi*

chisel *n* gilb *f*

chocolate *n & adj* seòclaid *f*

choice *adj* taghta

choice *n* **1** (*thing chosen*) roghainn *mf*; **2** (*alternative*) roghainn *mf*; **3** (*choosing*) taghadh *m*

choir *n* còisir *f*, còisir-chiùil *f*

choke mùch *vt*, tachd *vt*

choose *v* **1** (*select*) tagh *vt*, roghnaich *vti*; **2** (*single out*) sònraich *vt*

chop *v* **1** (*wood etc*) sgud *vti*; **2** *in exprs* ~ **off** sgath *vt* dheth

chopper *n* làmhthuagh *f*

chosen *adj & past part* **1** (*selected*) taghta; **2** (*singled out*) sònraichte

Christendom *n, used with art*, a' Chrìosdachd *f*

Christian *adj* Crìosdail

Christian *n* Crìosdaidh *m*

Christianity *n* **1** (*faith*) Crìosdaidheachd *f*; **2** (*conduct*) Crìosdalachd *f*

Christmas *n* Nollaig *f*, ~ **Day/Eve** Là/ Oidhche (na) Nollaig

chuffed *adj* toilichte

chunk *n* cnap *m*, geinn *m*

church *n* eaglais *f*

churchyard *n* cladh *m*, clachan *m*, cill *f*

churlish *adj* iargalt(a), droch-nàdarrach

churn *n* crannag *f*, muidhe *m*, crannachan *m*

cigarette *n* toitean *m*

cinder *n* èibhleag *f*

cinema *n* taigh-dhealbh *m*

cinnamon *n* caineal *m*

circle *n* cearcall *m*

circle *v* iadh & iath *vt*, cuartaich/cuairtich *vt*

circuit *n* cuairt *f*

circular *adj* cruinn, cearclach

circular *n* (*corres*) cuairt-litir *f*

circulate *v* **1** (*as vi*) rach *vi* timcheall, rach *vi* mun cuairt; **2** (*as vt*) cuir *vt* timcheall, cuir *vt* mun cuairt

circulation *n* cuartachadh *m*

circumspect *adj* aireach, faiceallach

circumspection *n* aire *f*, faiceall *f*

circumstance *n* **1** cùis *f*, suidheachadh *m*; **2** (*eventuality*) cor *m*

citizen *n* **1** (*general*) neach-àiteachaidh *m*; **2** (*of country*) saoranach *m*, neach-dùthcha

citizenship *n* **1** (*status*) saoranachd *f*, inbhe neach-dùthcha *f*; **2** (*rights etc*) còir dùthcha *m*

city *n* baile-mòr *m*, cathair *f*

civic *adj* catharra

civil *adj* **1** (*polite*) modhail, cùirteil; **2** (*relating to citizens*) sìobhalta, catharra

civilian *n* sìobhaltair *m*

civility *n* modh *mf*

civilisation *n* sìobhaltachd *f*

cladding *n* còmhdach *m*

claim *n* (*law etc*) tagairt *f*, tagradh *m*

claim *v* **1** (*rights etc*) tagair *vt*; **2** (*assert*) cùm a-mach *vi*

claimant neach-tagraidh *m*, tagraiche *m*
clamour *n* gleadhraich *f*
clamp *n* teanchair & teannachair *m*, glamradh *m*
clan *n* cinneadh *m*, clann *f*, fine *f*
clang *n* gliong *m*
clang *vt* dèan gliong *m*
clanging *n* gliongadaich *f*
clannish *adj* cinneadail
clansman *n* fear-cinnidh *m*
clanswoman *n* bean-chinnidh *f*
clap *v* buail basan
clapping *n* bas-bhualadh *m*, bois-bhualadh *m*
clarification *n* soilleireachadh *m*
clarify *v* soilleirich *vt*
clarity *n* soilleireachd *f*
clarsach *n* clàrsach *f*
clash *n* **1** (*noise*) gliongadaich *f*; **2** (*confrontation*) connsachadh *m*, connspaid *f*
clash *v* **1** (*make noise*) dèan gliongadaich; **2** (*disagree etc*) connsaich *vi* le
clasp *n* cromag *f*
class *n* **1** (*school*) clas *m*; **2** (*social*) seòrsa *m*
classical *adj* clasaigeach
classification *n* seòrsachadh *m*
classified *adj & past part* **1** seòrsaichte; **2** (*confidential*) dìomhair
classify *v* seòrsaich *vt*
clattering *n* glagadaich *f*
claw *n* ìne *f*
clay *n* crèadh *f*
claymore *n* claidheamh-mòr *m*, claidheamh leathann *m*, claidheamh dà-làimh *m*
clean *adj* glan
clean *v* glan *vt*
cleanse *v* glan *vt*
cleanliness *n* glaine *f*
clear *adj* **1** (*light etc*) soilleir; **2** (*audible, visible*) taisbeanach; **3** (*of ground etc*) rèidh; **4** (*evident etc*) follaiseach, lèir; **5** (*argument etc*) soilleir
clear *v* **1** (*population*) fàsaich *vt*, fuadaich *vt*; **2** (*of obstacles etc*) rèitich *vt*; **3** ~ **up** (*misunderstandings*) soilleirich *vt*; **4** ~ **off!** thoir do chasan leat!
clearance *n* (*population*) fàsachadh *m*, fuadach *m*, fuadachadh *m*

cleared *adj & past part* (*area of ground etc*) rèidh
cleg *n* creithleag *f*
clemency *n* iochd *f*, tròcair *f*
clement *adj* **1** (*weather*) ciùin, sèimh; **2** (*ruler etc*) iochdmhor, tròcaireach
clergy *n* clèir *f*
clergyman *n* ministear *m*, clèireach *m*, pears'-eaglais *m*
clerical *adj* **1** (*relig*) clèireachail; **2** (*secretarial etc*) clèireachail
clerk *n* **1** (*in office etc*) clèireach *m*, (*higher status*) clàrc *m*
clever *adj* **1** (*mentally*) glic, eirmseach; **2** (*practically*) tapaidh, gleusta, deas; **3** (*resourceful*) innleachdach
cleverness *n* **1** (*mental*) gliocas *m*; **2** (*practical*) tapachd *f*; **3** (*resourcefulness*) innleachd *f*
cliff *n* creag *f*, bearradh *m*, stalla *m*
climate *n* clìomaid *f*
climb *v* dìrich *vt*, s(t)reap *vti*
clinking *n* gliong *m*, gliongartaich *m*, clagarsaich *f*
clip *n* (*for fastening*) cromag *f*, ceangal *m*
clip *v* **1** (*cut*) geàrr *vt*; **2** (*shear*) lom *vt*, rùisg *vt*
cloak *n* cleòc(a) *m*
clock *n* gleoc *m*, cloc/cleoc *m*
clockwise *adj & adv* deiseil & deiseal
clod *n* (*of earth*) ploc *m*, fòid/fòd *f*
clog *v* stop *vt*
cloister *n* clabhstair *m*
close *adj* **1** (*near*) faisg air, dlùth air; **2** (*weather*) bruicheil, bruthainneach
close *n* (*tenement*) clobhsa *m*
close *n* crìoch *f*, **bring to a** ~ thoir *vt* gu crìch
close *v* **1** (*as vt*) dùin *vt*, thoir *vt* gu crìch; **2** (*as vi*) dùin *vi*
closed *adj & past part* dùinte
closeness *n* faisge *f*, dlùths *m*
closet *n* clòsaid *f*
closure *n* dùnadh *m*
cloth *n* **1** (*material*) clò *m*, aodach *m*; **2** (*dusting etc*) clùd *m*, clobhd *m*, brèid *m*
clothes, clothing *n* aodach *m*, trusgan *m*
cloud *n* neul *m*, sgòth *f*
cloud (over) *v* neulaich *vti*
cloudy *adj* neulach, sgòthach
clove *n* clòbha *f*
clover *n* clòbhar *m*, seamrag *f*

clown n 1 (*circus*) cleasaiche m, tuaistear m; 2 (*buffoon*) amadan m, bumailear m

club[1] n 1 (*weapon*) cuaille m; 2 (*sport*) caman m

club[2] n (*association*) comann m, club m

cluck v dèan gogail f

clucking n gogail f

clump n bad m

clumsy adj cearbach

cluster n 1 (*fruits etc*) bagaid f; 2 (*people*) grunnan m

co- prefix co-

coach[1] n (*transport*) coidse f

coach[2] n (*instructor etc*) neach-teagaisg m, neach-trèanaidh m

coach v 1 teagaisg vt; 2 (*sport etc*) trèan vt

coal n gual m

coalition n co-bhanntachd f

coalmine n mèinn(e)-guail f

coarse adj 1 (*to touch*) garbh; 2 (*uncouth*) garbh, borb; 3 (*crude*) drabasta, draosta

coarseness n 1 (*to touch*) gairbhe f, gairbhead m; 2 (*uncouthness*) gairbhe f, gairbhead m; 3 (*crudeness*) drabastachd f, draostachd f

coast n oirthir f, costa m

coastguard n 1 (*organisation*) maoras-cladaich m; 2 (*individual*) maor-cladaich m

coat n còta m

coat v còmhdaich vt, cuir brat air

coathanger crochadair-còta m

cobbler n greusaiche m

cobweb n lìon damhain-allaidh m

cock n 1 (*fowl*) coileach m; 2 (*penis*) slat f

cock v (*gun*) cuir vt air lagh

cock-crow n gairm-coilich f

cocked adj & past part (*of gun*) air lagh f

cockle n coilleag f, srùban m

cockroach n càrnan m

cocky adj bragail

cocoa n còco m

coconut n cnò-bhainne f, cnò-còco f

cod n trosg m, bodach-ruadh m

coddle v (*spoil*) mùirnich vt, maothaich vt

code n còd m

coffee n cofaidh mf

coffin n ciste-laighe f

cognate adj dàimheil

coin n bonn m airgid

coincide v co-thuit vi

coincidence n co-thuiteamas m

coincidental adj co-thuiteamach

coke n (*fuel*) còc m

cold adj fuar, fionnar

cold n 1 (*phys*) fuachd mf; 2 (*ailment: used with art*) an cnatan m, am fuachd m

coldly adv (*behaviour etc*) gu fionnar

coldness n (*phys*) fuachd mf, (*phys & emotional*) fionnarachd f

collaborate v co-obraich vi

collaboration n co-obrachadh m

collar n coilear m

collarbone n cnà(i)mh m an uga, cnà(i)mh a' choileir

colleague n co-obraiche m, companach m

collect v cruinnich vi, tionail vi

collection n cruinneachadh m

collective adj coitcheann

college n colaiste f

collide v co-bhuail vi

collision n co-bhualadh m

colon n 1 (*typog*) dà-phuing f, còilean m; 2 (*part of intestine*) an caolan mòr

colony n colonaidh m

colour n 1 dath m; 2 (*complexion*) tuar m, snuadh m

colour v dath vt, cuir dath air

colour-blind adj dath-dhall

coloured adj & past part dathte

column n colbh m

comb n 1 cìr f; 2 (*bird*) cìrean m

comb v cìr vt

combat n còmhrag f

combat v sabaid vi ri, strì vi ri

combine v measgaich vt, co-mheasgaich vti

combination n measgachadh m

come v thig vi irreg

comedian n cleasaiche m

comedy n 1 (*abstr*) àbhachd f; 2 (*play etc*) cleas-chluich f

comely adj ceanalta

comfort n cofhurtachd f, furtachd f

comfort v furtaich vi air, cofhurtaich vt

comfortable adj 1 (*phys*) cofhurtail, seasgair; 2 (*fin*) airgeadach, gu math dheth

comforting adj sòlasach

comic n (*comedian*) cleasaiche m

comic, comical adj èibhinn, àbhachdach

coming n teachd m

comma n cromag f

command n 1 (*abstr*) ceannas m; 2 (*instruction etc*) òrdugh m, reachd m

command v 1 (*order*) thoir òrdugh do;
2 (*be in command of*) bi vi irreg an ceann
commander n ceannard m
commanding adj (*personality etc*)
ceannsalach
commemorate v cuimhnich vt
commemoration n 1 (*abstr*) cuimhne
f, cuimhneachadh m; 2 (*monument etc*)
cuimhneachan m
commemorative adj cuimhneachaidh
commence v tòisich vti air/ri
commencement n tòiseachadh m
comment v thoir (seachad) beachd
commerce n ceannachd f, ceannach m,
malairt f
commercial adj malairteach
commercial n sanas-reic m
commission n 1 (*task etc*) teachdaireachd
f; 2 (*body*) coimisean m; 3 (*payment*)
tuarastal m; 4 (*in armed services*)
barantas-oifigich m; 5 (*for work*) òrdugh
m
commission v (*work*) òrdaich vt
commit v (*carry out*) dèan vt, gnìomhaich
vt
commitment n dealas m
committee n comataidh f
common adj 1 coitcheann; 2 in expr ~
sense toinisg f, ciall f; 4 (*frequently
met with*) cumanta; 5 (*uncouth etc*) mì-
mhodhail, garbh, borb
common n 1 (*land*) coitcheann m,
(*grazing*) am monadh
commonly adv gu tric, an cumantas m, am
bitheantas m
commonwealth n co-fhlaitheas m
commotion n ùpraid f
communal adj coitcheann
commune n co-chomann m
communicant n (*relig*) comanaiche m
communicate v 1 com-pàirtich vt;
2 (*express*) cuir vt an cèill; 4 (*relig*)
comanaich vi
communication n 1 (*abstr*) conaltradh
m, eadar-theachdaireachd f; 2 (*individual
message*) fios m, teachdaireachd f;
3 (*communicating*) com-pàirteachadh m
Communion n 1 (*relig*) comanachadh m,
òrdaighean mpl
communism n co-mhaoineas m
communist n & adj co-mhaoineach m

community n 1 (*people*) coimhearsnachd
f; 2 (*commune etc*) comann m, co-
chomann m
compact adj 1 (*dense etc*) dlùth, dòmhail &
dùmhail; 2 (*small*) mion, meanbh
compact n (*agreement*) co-chòrdadh m,
cùmhnant m
compact v teannaich vti
companion n companach m
companionable adj cèilidheach,
cuideachdail
companionship n companas m
company n 1 (*commerce etc*) companaidh
mf; 2 (*social*) cuideachd f, comann m;
3 (*troops etc*) còmhlan m
comparable adj coimeasach
comparative adj coimeasach
compare v dèan coimeas eadar, coltaich ri
vt, samhlaich ri vt
compared adj & past part, ~ **to/with** an
coimeas ri, an taca ri
comparison n 1 coimeas m; 2 in expr **in** ~
to an coimeas ri, an taca ri
compass n combaist f
compassion n iochd f, truas m, truacantas
m
compassionate adj 1 (*merciful*)
iochdmhor, truacanta; 2 (*sympathetic*)
co-fhulangach, co-mhothachail
compatibility n co-fhreagarrachd f,
(*people*) co-chòrdalachd f
compatible adj co-fhreagarrach,
freagarrach do/air
compel v thoir vi air, co-èignich vt
compensate v (*fin*) dìol vt, cuidhtich vi
compensation n (*fin*) dìoladh m,
cuidhteachadh m
compère n fear an taighe m
competence n comas m
competent adj comasach
competition n 1 co-fharpais f, farpais f;
2 (*rivalry*) còmhstri f
competitive adj farpaiseach
competitor n co-fharpaiseach m,
farpaiseach
compilation n co-chruinneachadh m
complain v 1 gearain vi, talaich vi
complaining adj gearanach
complaint n 1 (*grumble etc*) gearan m;
2 (*official*) casaid f; 3 (*ailment*) gearan m,
galar m, tinneas m

complete *adj* **1** (*entire*) iomlan, slàn, gu lèir *adv*; **2** (*finished*) deiseil, ullamh; **3** (*utter*) dearg (*precedes noun*), gu c(h)ùl *m*

complete *v* cuir *vt* crìoch air, thoir *vt* gu buil, thoir *vt* gu crìch, thoir *vt* gu ceann

completed *adj & past part* crìochnaichte

completely *adv* **1** (gu) buileach, gu h-iomlan, gu tur

complex *adj* **1** (*in structure etc*) iomadh-fhillte; **2** (*hard to understand*) deacair, amalach

complex *n* (*facilities*) ionad *m*

complexion *n* **1** (*features*) dreach *m*, tuar *m*; **2** (*appearance*) coltas *m*, cruth *m*

complexity *n* **1** (*in structure etc*) iomadh-fhillteachd *f*; **2** (*difficulty of understanding*) deacaireachd *f*; **3** (*problem*) duilgheadas *m*

compliance *n* gèilleadh *m*

compliant *adj* umha(i)l, macanta, strìochdach

complicated *adj* **1** (*in structure etc*) iomadh-fhillte; **2** (*hard to understand*) deacair, amalach

compliment *n* **1** moladh *m*; **2** (*in corres*) with ~s le deagh dhùrachd *f*

compliment *v* dèan moladh air

complimentary *adj* **1** luaidheach, molaidh air ; **2** (*free*) an-asgaidh

comply *v* **1** (*submit etc*) gèill *vi* do; **2** (*regulations*) cùm *vi* ri

comportment *n* giùlan *m*, iomchar *m*, dol-a-mach *m*

compose *v* **1** (*write etc*) dèan *vt* (suas), cuir *vt* ri chèile; **2** (*regain composure*) socraich *vt*

composed *adj & past part* **1** (*written etc*) dèanta; **2** (*calmed etc*) socraichte

composer *n* ùghdar *m*, sgrìobhadair *m*, (*mus*) ceòl-sgrìobhaiche *m*

compound *adj* fillte

comprehend *v* tuig *vti*, fidir *vt*

comprehension *n* tuigse *f*

compress *v* teannaich *vt*

compressed *adj & past part* teannaichte

compression *n* teannachadh *m*

compromise *n* co-rèiteachadh *m*, còrdadh *m*

compulsion *n* co-èigneachadh *m*

compulsory *adj* èigeantach, èigneachail, do-sheachainte

computation *n* tomhas *m*, àireamhachd *f*

compute *v* (*distance etc*) tomhais *vt*

computer *n* coimpiutair *m*

computerisation *n* coimpiutaireachadh *m*

computing *n* coimpiutaireachd *f*

comrade *n* companach *m*

con *prefix* co-

conceal *v* cuir *vt* am falach *m*, falaich *vt*, ceil *vt*

concealed *adj & past part* am falach, falaichte

concealment *n* ceileadh *m*, ceiltinn *f*, falach *m*, cleith *f*

concede *v* **1** (*relinquish*) gèill *vi*; **2** (*agree*) aidich *vi*

conceit *n* fèin-mholadh *m*, mòrchuis *f*, leòm *f*

conceited *adj* mòrchuiseach, mòr às (*etc*) fhèin

conceive *v* **1** (*become pregnant*) gin *vti*; **2** (*think up etc*) innlich *vt*

concentric *adj* co-mheadhanach

concept *n* bun-bheachd *m*

conception *n* **1** (*gynaecology etc*) gineamhainn *m*; **2** (*plan etc*) innleachadh *m*; **3** (*understanding*) fios *m*, tuigse *f*

concern *n* **1** (*interest*) aire *m*, for *m*; **2** (*worry*) iomagain *f*, dragh *m*; **3** (*for others*) co-fhulangas *m*, co-mhothachadh *m*; **4** (*business*) gnothach *m*

concern *v* **1** (*affect etc*) buin *vi* do/ri; **2** *in expr* ~ **oneself** gabh uallach; **3** *in expr* **as far as . . . is** ~**ed**, a thaobh

concerned *adj & past part* **1** (*worried*) fo uallach; **2** (*relevant*) buntainneach, an sàs

concerning *prep* a thaobh, mu dheidhinn

concert *n* cuirm-chiùil *f*

concierge *n* dorsair *m*

conciliate *v* thoir *vt* gu rèite

conciliation *n* rèiteachadh *m*

conciliator *n* neach-rèiteachaidh *m*

concise *adj* **1** (*to the point*) pongail; **2** (*short*) goirid

conclude *v* **1** (*come to conclusion*) co-dhùin *vi*; **2** (*bring to close*) thoir *vt* gu crìch, thoir *vt* gu ceann *m*, crìochnaich *vt*

conclusion *n* **1** (*meeting etc*) co-dhùnadh *m*; **2** *in expr* **bring to** ~ thoir *vt* gu buil *f*, thoir *vt* gu co-dhùnadh *m*

conclusive *adj* deimhinnte, dearbhte

concord *n* co-chòrdadh *m*

concrete[1] *adj* saimeant

concrete[2] *adj* **1** (*actual*) sònraichte

concubine n coimhleapach mf
condemn v 1 (criticise) cronaich vt;
2 (sentence etc) dìt vt
condemnation n dìteadh m
condensation n co-dhlùthachadh m
condense v 1 (abridge) giorraich vt; 2 (of vapour) co-dhlùthaich vti
condition n 1 (state) cor m, staid f;
2 (stipulation) cor m, cumha m, cùmhnant m
conditional adj 1 (gram) cumhach m;
2 (dependent) an crochadh air, a rèir
condom n casgan m
conduct n giùlan m, dol-a-mach m
conduct v 1 (argument) tagair vt; 2 (guide) treòraich; 3 (music) stiùir vti; 4 (behave) in expr ~ oneself giùlain; 5 (carry out) cuir vt an gnìomh; 6 (current) giùlain vt
conductor n 1 (orchestra) stiùireadair m;
2 (current etc) stuth-giùlain m
cone n 1 (geometry etc) còn m; 2 pine/fir ~ durcan m
confederation n (countries) co-fhlaitheas m
conference n co-labhairt f, còmhdhail f
confess v 1 (admit) aidich vti; 2 (relig) dèan faoisid, faoisidich vti
confession n 1 (relig) faoisid f; 2 (legal etc) aideachadh m
confessor n (relig) sagart-faoisid m
confidant n fear-rùin m
confide v leig do rùn
confidence n 1 (trust etc) earbsa f; 2 (in oneself) misneachd f; 3 (secret etc) rùn m
confident adj 1 (assured) misneachail;
2 (hopeful) dòchasach; 3 (certain) cinnteach
confidential adj dìomhair
confidentiality n dìomhaireachd f
confirm v 1 (prove) dearbh vt; 2 (assert) daingnich vt
conflict n còmhrag f, còmhstri f, strì f
confluence n comar m, inbhir m
confront v (oppose) seas vi ri
confuse v 1 (mix) measgaich vt suas;
2 (puzzle) breislich vt, cuir vt am breisleach, cuir vt troimh-a-chèile
confusion n 1 (different things) measgachadh m suas; 2 (disturbance etc) ùpraid f; 3 (mental) breisleach mf
congenial adj taitneach
congested adj dòmhail/dùmhail

congestion n dùmhlachd f
congratulate v cuir meal-a-naidheachd air
congratulations excl meal do naidheachd! f
congregate v tionail vi, thig vi còmhla, cruinnich vi
congregation n coitheanal m
congress n 1 (organisation) còmhdhail f;
2 (sexual) co-ghineadh m, cuplachadh m
conical adj cònach
coniferous adj cònach
conjectural adj tuaireamach, baralach
conjecture n tuaiream f, tuairmeas m
conjecture v thoir tuairmeas, beachdaich vi
conjunction n (gram) naisgear m
conjurer n cleasaiche m, caisreabhaiche m
conjuring n cleasachd f, caisreabhachd f
connect v ceangail vt, (together) co-cheangail vt
connected adj & past part ceangailte, co-cheangailte; 2 (associated) ~ with an lùib, an cois (both with gen)
connection n 1 ceangal m, co-cheangal m; 2 (link) ceangal m, gnothach m;
3 (familial) buinteanas m 4 in expr in ~ with a thaobh (with gen)
conquer v ceannsaich vt, thoir buaidh air
conqueror n ceannsaiche m
conquest n ceannsachadh m
conscience n cogais f
conscientious adj dìcheallach, cogaiseach
conscientiousness n dìcheall m, dìcheallachd f
conscious adj 1 (faculties) mothachail;
2 (aware) fiosrach, mothachail
consciousness n 1 (faculties) fiosrachd f;
2 (awareness) mothachadh m
consecrate v coisrig vt
consecrated adj & past part coisrigte
consecration n coisrigeadh m
consecutive adj an ceann m a chèile, an sreath mf a chèile, co-leanailteach
consensus m co-aontachd f
consent n aonta(dh) m, cead m
consent v aontaich vti, co-aontaich vti
consequence n (action etc) toradh m, buaidh f, buil f
conservancy n glèidhteachas m
conservation n glèidhteachas m
conservationist n neach-glèidhteachais m
conservative adj glèidhteach

Conservative adj (pol) Tòraidheach
Conservative n (pol) Tòraidh m
conserve v glèidh vt
conserved adj & past part glèidhte
consider v 1 (think) saoil vi, creid vi;
2 (think over) beachdaich vi, gabh beachd,
smaoin(t)ich vi, cnuasaich vi; 3 (observe)
beachdaich vt
consideration n 1 (care) co-fhulangas m;
2 (thinking over) beachdachadh m; 3 in
expr **take into** ~ cuir vt san àireimh f;
4 (fee etc) tuarastal m, duais f
consistent adj 1 (unvarying) seasmhach,
neo-chaochlaideach; 2 (tallying with)
co-chòrdail
consolation n furtachd f, cofhurtachd f
console v furtaich vi, cofhurtaich vt
consolidate v co-dhaingnich vt
consonant n (lang) co-fhoghar m, consan
m, connrag f
conspicuous adj faicsinneach, follaiseach,
suaicheanta
conspicuousness n faicsinneachd f
conspiracy n (plot) co-fheall f, cuilbheart f
conspire v dèan co-fheall f, innlich
cuilbheart f
constable n constabal m
constancy n 1 (durability etc)
maireannachd f, seasmhachd f; 2 (loyalty)
dìlseachd f, seasmhachd f
constant adj 1 (lasting) buan,
maireannach, seasmhach; 2 (unchanging)
neo-atharrachail; 3 (loyal) dìleas,
seasmhach; 4 (ceaseless) gun sgur adv
constantly adv gun sgur, daonnan
constellation n reul-bhad m
constituency n (pol) roinn-taghaidh f,
roinn-phàrlamaid f
constituent n 1 (part) pàirt mf, earrann f;
2 (pol) neach-taghaidh m
constitution n 1 (phys) dèanamh m;
2 (country etc) bun-reachd m, bonn-
stèidh f
constitutional adj 1 bun-reachdail;
2 co-chòrdail
constrict v teannaich vt, fàisg vt, tachd vt
constriction n teannachadh m
construct v 1 cum vt, dealbh vt, dèan vt;
2 (building etc) tog vt
consul n consal m
consular adj consalach

consult v sir beachd m, gabh comhairle o/
bho, cuir comhairle ri
consultation n co-chomhairle f, sireadh
beachd o/bho, gabhail comhairle
consume v caith vt
consumer n neach-caitheimh, caitheadair
m, neach-cleachdaidh m
consumption n 1 (fin etc) caitheamh f;
2 (illness: used with art) a' chaitheamh f
contact n 1 (phys) beantainn m, suathadh
m; 2 in expr **in (physical)** ~ **with** an
taice ri; 3 (relations etc) muinntireachd f,
conaltradh m
contact v cuir fios gu
contact lens n lionsa-suathaidh f
contagious adj gabhaltach
contain v gabh vt
contaminate v truaill vt
contamination n truailleadh m
contemplate v meòraich, cnuasaich,
beachdaich
contemporary adj co-aimsireil
contemporary n co-aois m, co-aoiseach m
contempt n tàir f, tarcais f, dìmeas m
contemptible adj tàireil, suarach
contemptuous adj tarcaiseach, tailceasach
content adj toileach, sona, riaraichte,
toilichte
content[1] n (book etc) susbaint f, brìgh f
content[2], **contentment** n toileachas m,
toil-inntinn f, toileachas-inntinn m
content v toilich vt, riaraich vt
contented adj toileach, sona
contention n connspaid f
contentious adj connspaideach
contents n, 1 na tha ann; 2 (list) clàr-innse
m; 3 (abstr) susbaint f, brìgh f
contest n strì f, farpais f
contestant n farpaiseach m
continent n 1 (general) roinn f, mòr-roinn
f, mòr-thìr f; 2 (local) tìr-mòr m
continental adj mòr-roinneach, mòr-
thìreach
contingency n tuiteamas m
contingent adj tuiteamach
contingent n (troops etc) buidheann f,
còmhlan m, cuideachd f
continue v lean vi
continuity n leantalachd f, leanailteachd f
continuous, **continual** adj leanailteach,
leantainneach, gun sgur

contraception, contraceptive n casg-gineamhainn m

contraceptive adj casg-gineamhainneach

contract n (official etc) cunnradh m, cùmhnant m

contract v (shrink) teannaich vti, lùghdaich vti, fàisg vt, rach vi a-steach

contradict v cuir vi an aghaidh

contraption n inneal m, innleachd f

contrast v cuir vt an aghaidh, dèan eadar-dhealachadh m

contribute v 1 (give) thoir vt seachad; 2 (assist) cuidich vti, cuir vti ri

contribution n 1 (gift) dèirc f; 2 (payment) tabhartas m; 3 (help) cuideachadh m

contrive v 1 (invent) innlich vt, dealbh vt; 2 (manage) rach vi aig air

contrived adj & past part fallsa, breugach

contrivance n 1 (abstr) innleachdadh m; 2 (con) inneal m, innleachd f

control v ceannsaich vt, cùm smachd air

controversial adj connspaideach

controversy n connspaid f

conundrum n tòimhseachan m

convene v gairm vt

convenience n goireas m

convenient adj goireasach, deiseil

convent n clochar m

convention n 1 (gathering) co-chruinneachadh m; 2 (agreement) cùmhnant m; 3 (practice) gnàth m, cleachdadh m

conventional adj gnàthach

converge v co-aom vi

convergence n co-aomadh m

conversant adj eòlach

conversation n agallamh m, còmhradh m, craic f

converse v dèan còmhradh, bruidhinn vi

conversion n 1 (esp relig) iompachadh m; 2 (dwelling etc) leasachadh m, atharrachadh m

convert n (relig) iompachan m, (person) neach fo chùram m

convert v 1 (relig) iompaich vt; 2 (dwelling etc) leasaich vt, atharraich vt

converted adj & past part 1 (relig) iompaichte, fo chùram m; 2 (dwelling etc) leasaichte

convey v 1 (transport) giùlain vt, iomchair vt; 2 (legal) thoir thairis còraichean fpl; 3 (make understood) cuir vt an cèill

conveyance n 1 (transport) carbad m, seòl-iomchair m; 2 (legal) toirt thairis chòraichean

conveyancing n toirt f thairis chòraichean

conviction n 1 (legal) dìteadh m; 2 (opinion) beachd

convivial adj 1 (person) cuideachdail, cèilidheach; 2 (gathering etc) làn cridhealais

conviviality n cridhealas m

coo v dèan dùrdail f

cooing n dùrdail f

cook n còcaire m

cooker n cucair m

cookery, cooking n còcaireachd f

cool adj fionnar, fuaraidh

cool, cool down v fionnraich vti, fuaraich vti

co-operate v co-obraich vi

co-operation n co-obrachadh m

co-operative adj co-obrachail

co-operative n co-chomann m

co-ordinate v co-òrdanaich vt

copious adj lìonmhor, pailt

copper n copar m

coppersmith n ceàrd-copair m

copulate v co-ghin vi, cuplaich vi, rach air muin

copulation n co-ghineadh m, cuplachadh m

copy n mac-samhail m, lethbhreac m

copy v (reproduce) dèan lethbhreac de

coquette n guanag f

coquettish adj guanach

coracle n curach f

cord n còrd m

core n eitean m, buillsgean m

cork n àrc f, (bottle) corcais f

corn[1] n (agric) arbhar m

corn[2] n (on foot) còrn m

corner n cùil f, còrnair m, oisean m, uilinn f

cornflakes npl bleideagan-coirce fpl

corn-yard n iodhlann f

coronation n crùnadh m

corporal adj corporra

corporal n corpailear m

corporate adj corporra

corpse n corp (marbh) m, marbhan m

corpulent adj sultmhor

correct adj ceart, cruinn

correct v ceartaich vt, cuir vt ceart

correction n ceartachadh m

correspond v 1 bi vi irreg co-fhreagarrach do; 2 (by letter etc) co-fhreagair vi, sgrìobh vi gu chèile

correspondence n 1 (abstr) co-fhreagairt f; 2 (con) post m, litrichean fpl

correspondent n 1 (by letter etc) co-sgrìobhadair m, co-sgrìobhaiche m; 2 (journalism) neach-naidheachd, naidheachdair m

corresponding adj co-fhreagarrach

corridor n trannsa f

corrie n coire m

corroborate v co-dhearbh vt

corrosion n 1 (abstr) meirgeadh m; 2 (con) meirg f

corrugate v preas

corrugated adj preasach

corrupt adj coirbte, truaillte

corrupt v coirb vt, truaill vt

corrupted adj & past part coirbte, truaillte

corruption n 1 (abstr) coirbteachd f, truaillidheachd f; 2 (action) coirbeadh m, truailleadh m

cosmonaut n speuradair m, speurair m

cost n cosgais f, cosg m

cost v cosg vt

costly adj cosgail, daor

costume n (stage etc) culaidh f

cosy adj seasgair, cofhurtail

cotton n cotan m, canach mf

couch n langasaid f

cough n casadaich f, casad m

cough v dèan casad m, casadaich vi

coughing n casadaich f

council n comhairle f

councillor n comhairliche m

counsel n 1 (advice) comhairle f; 2 (advocate) neach-tagraidh m

counsellor n neach-comhairle m

count v cunnt vti, cunntais vti

counter n (in shop etc) cuntair m

counter v rach vi an aghaidh

country n 1 dùthaich f, tìr f, rìoghachd f; 2 (group territory etc) dùthaich f; 3 (rural area) dùthaich f

county n siorrachd f, siorramachd f

couple n 1 (man & wife) càraid f; 2 (twosome) dithis f

couple v 1 (connect etc) co-cheangail vt; 2 (sexually) cuplaich vi

coupling n 1 (carriages etc) co-cheangal m; 2 (sexually) cuplachadh m, (cattle) dàir f

coupon n cùpon m

courage n 1 (phys) gaisge f, gaisgeachd f, dànadas m, braisead f; 2 (inner) misneach f, misneachd f, smior m

courageous adj 1 (phys) gaisgeil, dàna, bras; 2 (morally) misneachail

courier n teachdaire m

course n 1 (academic etc) cùrsa m; 2 (seafaring etc) cùrsa m, gabhail mf, seòl m; 3 in exprs **in due** ~, ri tìde; 4 (sports etc) raon m, cùrsa m

court n (royal etc) cùirt f

court v 1 (amorously) dèan suirghe air; 2 (through ambition etc) dèan miodal do, dèan sodal ri

courtesan n siùrsach f, strìopach f

courteous adj cùirteil, sìobhalta, modhail, suairc(e)

courtesy n modhalachd f, sìobhaltachd f, modh mf

courting n suirghe f, leannanachd f

courtly adj cùirteil

courtship n suirghe f, leannanachd f

cousin n co-ogha m

cove n geodha mf, camas m, bàgh m, òb m

covenant n (fin etc) cùmhnant m, cunnradh m

cover n còmhdach m

cover v còmhdaich vt

covered adj & past part còmhdaichte

covering n còmhdach m

coverlet n cuibhrig mf

covert adj falaichte, dìomhair

covertly adv os ìosal

covet v sanntaich vt, miannaich vt, togair vt

covetous adj sanntach

covetousness n sannt m

cow n bò f, for pl crodh m

cow v cuir vt fo eagal

cowed adj & past part fo eagal

coward n gealtaire m, cladhaire m

cowardice n gealtachd f, cladhaireachd f

cowardly adj gealtach, cladhaireach

coy adj màlda

crab n partan m, (large) crùbag f

crabbit adj greannach, cròst(a), dìombach

crack n 1 (noise) brag m, pleasg m; 2 (split etc) sgoltadh m; 3 (conversation) craic f

crack v **1** (*noise*) dèan brag *m*, dèan pleasg *m*; **2** (*split etc*) sgàin *vti*, sgoilt & sgolt *vti*

cracking n (*splitting etc*) sgoltadh *m*

cradle n creathail *f*

craft n ceàird *f*

craftsman n fear-ceàirde/-ciùird *m*

crafty adj carach, seòlta, fiar

crag n creag *f*, carraig *f*

craggy adj creagach

cramp n (*used with art*) an t-orc

crane n **1** (*device*) crann *m*; **2** (*bird*) corra-mhonaidh *f*

crannog n crannag *f*

crap n cac *m*

crash n **1** (*impact*) bualadh *m*; **2** (*noise*) stàirn *f*; **3** (*accident*) tubaist-rathaid *f*

crawl v snàig *vi*, crùb *vi*

creak, creaking n dìosgan *m*, dìosgail *f*

creak v dèan dìosgan *m*

cream n **1** (*of milk*) uachdar *m*, bàrr *m*; **2** (*cosmetic*) cè *m*

creamy adj uachdarach

crease n preasag *f*, filleadh *m*

crease v preas *vt*, fill *vt*

create v cruthaich *vt*, innlich *vt*

creation n **1** (*artistic etc*) cruthachadh *m*; **2** (*of plans etc*) innleachadh *m*; **3** (*relig*) cruitheachd *f*, used with art, **Creation** A' Chruitheachd

creative adj cruthachail; innleachdach, tionnsgalach

creativity n (*innovation*) tionnsgal *m*, tionnsgalachd *f*, innleachd *f*

creator n **1** (*relig*) **the Creator** An Cruthadair, An Cruthaidhear; **2** (*arts etc*) ùghdar *m*; **3** (*technical*) tionnsgalair *m*

creature n creutair *m*

credibility n creideas *m*

credible adj so-chreidsinn

credit n (*fin*) dàil *f*

creed n (*relig etc*) creud *f*, creideamh *m*

creel n cliabh *m*

creep v èalaidh *vi*, snàig *vi*

crescent n corran *m*

crest n **1** (*of cock*) cìrean *m*, (*other birds*) topan *m*; **2** (*hill*) mala *f* (cnuic *etc*)

crestfallen adj gun mhisneachd *f*

crevice n còs *m*, sgoltadh *m*

crime n eucoir *f*

criminal adj eucorach

criminal n eucorach *m*

crimson adj crò-dhearg

cringe v crùb *vi*, strìochd *vi*

cripple n crioplach *m*

crisis n èiginn *f*, cruaidh-chàs *m*, gàbhadh *m*

criterion n slat-thomhais *f*

critic n **1** (*faultfinder*) cronadair *m*; **2** (*arts etc*) neach-sgrùdaidh *m*, sgrùdair *m*, breithniche *m*

critical adj **1** (*finding fault*) càineach; **2** (*crucial*) deatamach, riatanach

criticise v **1** (*adversely*) càin *vti*, faigh cron do; **2** (*review*) sgrùd *vt*, breithnich *vt*

criticism n **1** (*adverse*) càineadh *m*, cronachadh *m*; **2** (*review*) sgrùdadh *m*, breithneachadh *m*, lèirmheas *m*

critique n sgrùdadh *m*, breithneachadh *m*, lèirmheas *m*

croak n ròcail *f*, gràg *m*

croak v dèan gràgail *f*

croaking n ròcail *f*, gràgail *f*

croft n croit/cruit *f*, lot *f*

crofter n croitear/cruitear *m*

crofting n croitearachd *f*

cromag n cromag *f*

crony n seana-charaid *m*

crook n **1** (*person*) eucorach *m*; **2** (*bend*) lùb *m*, caime *f*; **3** (*staff*) cromag *f*

crooked adj crom, fiar

crop[1] n (*agric ~ & ~s*) bàrr *m*, pòr *m*

crop[2] n (*of bird*) sgròban *m*

cross adj crost(a), feargach

cross n **1** crois ; **2** (*crucifix*) crann-ceusaidh *m*; **3** (*heraldry etc*) crann

cross v **1** rach *vi* tarsainn; **2** (*thwart etc*) rach *vi* an aghaidh; **3** (*relig*) *in expr* ~ **oneself** dèan comharradh na croise *m*

crossbar n crann-tarsainn *m*

cross-border adj tar-chrìochail

cross-examine v cruaidh-cheasnaich *vt*, mion-cheasnaich *vt*

cross-fertilise v tar-thoraich *vt*

crossing n (*water*) aiseag *mf*

cross-reference n tar-iomradh *m*

crosspiece n rong *f*, rongas *m*

crossroads n crois-rathaid *f*

crossword n tòimhseachan-tarsainn *m*

crotchet n (*mus*) dubh-nota *m*

crouch n crùban *m*, crùbagan *m*

crouch v dèan crùban, dèan crùbagan, rach *vi* nad *etc* chrùban/chrùbagan, crùb *vi*

crouched, crouching adj & adv nad chrùban/chrùbagan, nad ghurraban

crow¹ *n* feannag *f*, **carrion** ~ feannag dhubh, **hooded** ~ feannag ghlas

crow² *n* (*of cock*) gairm *f*

crow *v* (*cock etc*) gairm *vi*

crowd *n* **1** grunn *m*, sluagh *m*, (*derog*) gràisg *f*, prabar *m*; **2** (*gang*) treud *m*

crowd *v* **1** (*as vt*) lìon; **2** (*as vi*) rach/thig a-steach

crowded *adj* dòmhail/dùmhail, loma-làn

crowdie *n* gruth *m*, slaman *m*

crown *n* **1** (*for royalty etc*) crùn *m*; **2** (*of head*) mullach a' chinn

crown *v* crùn *vt*

crowning *n* crùnadh *m*

crucial *adj* deatamach

crucifix *n* crann-ceusaidh *m*, crois *f*

crucifixion *n* ceusadh *m*

crucify *v* ceus *vt*

crude *adj* **1** (*in unprocessed state*) amh; **2** (*uncouth*) gràisgeil; **3** (*obscene, coarse*) drabasta, draosta

cruel *adj* cruaidh, an-ìochdmhor

cruelty *n* an-iochd *f*

cruisie *n* crùisgean *m*

crumb *n* criomag *f*, sprùilleag *f*

crumble *v* **1** (*as vt*) criomagaich; **2** (*as vi*) rach *vi* ann an criomagan

crunch, crunching *n* cnagadh *m*

crunch *v* cnag *vi*

crusade *n* cogadh-croise *m*

crush *v* preas *vt*, pronn *vt*

crust *n* plaosg *m*, rùsg *m*

crutch *n* **1** (*of body*) gobhal *m*; **2** (*walking aid*) crasg *f*, croitse *f*

crux *n*, *in expr* **the ~ of the matter** cnag na cùise *f*

cry *n* **1** (*call*) gairm *f*, èigh *f*, glaodh *m*; **2** (*anguish etc*) gaoir *f*

cry *v* **1** (*call*) gairm *vi*, èigh & èibh *vi*, glaodh *vi*; **2** (*weep*) guil *vi*, gail *vi*, caoin *vi*, ràn *vi*

crying *n* **1** (*calling*) gairm *f*, èigheachd *f*; **2** (*weeping*) gul *m*, caoineadh *m*, rànail *m*, rànaich *mf*

crystal *n* criostal *m*

cub *n* cuilean *m*

cube *n* ciùb *m*

cubic *adj* ciùbach

cuckold *n* cèile meallta *m*

cuckold *v*, meall

cuckoo *n* cuthag *f*

cucumber *n* cularan *m*

cud *n* cìr *f*, **chewing the ~** a' cnàmh na cìre

cudgel *n* cuaille *m*

Culdee *n* Cèile-Dè *m*

cull *v* tanaich *vt*

cull, culling *n* tanachadh *m*

culpability *n* coireachd *f*

culpable *adj* coireach, ciontach

cultivate *v* (*land*) àitich *vt*, obraich *vt*

cultivated *adj* **1** (*land*) àitichte; **2** (*person*) cultarail

cultural *adj* cultarach

culture *n* cultar *m*

cultured *abj* (*of person*) cultarail

cumin *n* lus-MhicCuimein *m*

cumulative *adj* tionalach

cunning *adj* carach, seòlta, fiar, innleachdach

cunning *n* seòltachd *f*, innleachd *f*

cup *n* **1** cupa *m*, cùp *m*, cupan *m*, copan *m*; **2** (*trophy etc*) cuach *f*

cupboard *n* preas(a) *m*

curb *n* bacadh *m*

curb *v* bac *vt*, cuir bacadh air

curd(s) *n* gruth *m*, slaman *m*

cure *n* leigheas *m*, ìocshlaint *f*

cure *v* **1** (*malady*) leighis *vt*, slànaich *vi*, (*patient*) cuir *vt* am feabhas; **2** (*fish etc*) ciùraig *vt*

curious *adj* **1** (*strange*) neònach; **2** (*inquisitive*) ceasnachail, faighneach, faighneachail

curl *n* bachlag *f*, camag *f*, dual *m*

curl *v* (*hair*) bachlaich *vt*, dualaich *vt*

curled, curly *adj* (*hair*) bachlach, camagach, dualach

curlew *n* guilbneach *m*

curling *n* (*sport*) crolaidh *m*, curladh *m*

currency *n* (*con*) airgead *m*; **2** (*rates*) ruith-airgid *f*

current *adj* làithreach, an là an-diugh

current *n* sruth *m*

curriculum *n* clàr-oideachais *m*

curriculum vitae *n* cunntas-beatha *m*

curse *n* **1** (*malediction*) mallachd *f*; **2** (*swear*) mionn *mf*, mionnan *m*

curse *v* **1** (*as vt:* ~ *someone/something*) mallaich; **2** (*as vi: swear*) mionnaich, bòidich

cursed *adj* mallaichte

cursing *n* **1** (*malediction*) mallachadh *m*; **2** (*swearing*) mionnachadh *m*, speuradh *m*

cursor *n* cùrsair *m*

cursory *adj* aithghearr, cabhagach
curtail *v* **1** (*shorten*) giorraich *vt*; **2** (*cut short*) cuir stad air
curtailed *adj & past part* giorraichte
curtailment *n* giorrachadh *m*
curtain *n* cùirtean *m*, cùirtear *m*
curvature *n* caime *f*, lùbadh *m*
curve *n* **1** caime *f*, lùb *f*; **2** (*in river*) camas *m*
curve *v* crom *vti*, lùb *vti*
curved *adj* cam, lùbte, crom
cushion *n* pillean *m*, cuisean *m*
custard *n* ughagan *m*
custody *n* **1** (*care*) cùram *m*; **2 have ~ of** (*object*) glèidh *vt*; **3** (*prison etc*) *in expr* **in ~** an grèim, an làimh
custom *n* àbhaist *m*, cleachdadh *m*; dòigh *m*; gnàth *m*, gnàths *m*, nòs *m*

customary *adj* àbhaisteach, gnàthach, cumanta
customer *n* neach-ceannach(d) *m*; neach-dèilige
customs *n* cusbainn *f*
cut *n* gearradh *m*
cut *v* **1** geàrr *vt*; **2 ~ up** mion-gheàrr *vt*; **3** (*crops*) buain *vt*
cutting *adj* (*remarks etc*) geur, guineach
CV *n* cunntas-beatha *m*
cycle *n* **1** (*velocipede*) baidhsagal *m*, rothar *m*; **2** (*science etc*) cuairt *f*
cyclic, cyclical *adj* cuairteach
cycling *n* baidhsagalachd *f*, rothaireachd *f*
cyclist *n* baidhsagalair *m*
cymbal *n* tiompan *m*
Czech Republic (the) *n* An t-Seic *f*

D

dab *v* suath *vt*
Daddy *n* Dadaidh *m*
daddy-longlegs *n* breabadair *m*
daffodil *n* lus a' chrom-chinn *m*
daft *adj* gòrach, amaideach
dagger *n* biodag *f*
daily *adj* làitheil
daily *adv* gach là *m*, a h-uile là
dainty *adj* mìn
dairy *n* taigh-bainne *m*
daisy *n* neòinean *m*
dale *n* gleann *m*, gleannan *m*
dam *n* dam *m*
damage *v* mill *vt*, dochainn *vt*
damage *n* milleadh *m*, cron *m*, damaiste *m*
damaged *adj* millte
damn *n*, (*idiom*) **I don't give a ~ for** cha toir mi hòro-gheallaidh air, chan eil diù a' choin agam mu
damn *v* **1** dìt *vt*; **2** (*in excls*) **~ it!** mac an donais! taigh na galla dha!
damnation *n* dìteadh *m*
damned *adj* **1** mallaichte; **2** (*excl*) (*X*) na croiche!, na galla!
damp *adj* tais
damp *n* taiseachd *f*
dampen *v* taisich *vt*
dampness *n* taise *f*, taiseachd *f*, dampachd *f*
damp-proof *adj* taise-dhìonte, taise-dhìonach
dance *n* dannsa *m*
dance *v* danns *vti*
dancer *n* dannsair *m*
dancing *n* dannsadh *m*
dandelion *n* beàrnan-Brìde *m*
dandruff *n* càrr/càir *f*
danger *n* cunnart *m*, gàbhadh *m*
dangerous *adj* cunnartach, gàbhaidh
dangle *v* **1** (*vi*) bi *vi irreg* air bhodagan; **2** (*vt*) cuir air bhodagan
dank *adj* tungaidh
dare *v* **1** dùraig *vi*; **2** (*challenge*) thoir dùbhlan do
daring *adj* dàna, bras
daring *n* dànadas *m*, braisead *f*

dark *adj* **1** dorch(a), ciar; **2** (*qualifying colour*) dubh-
darken *v* **1** ciar *vi*, doilleirich *vti*; **2** (*make darker*) duibhrich *vt*
dark-haired *adj* dubh, dorcha
darkness *n* dorchadas *m*, duibhre *f*
darling *adj* gaolach
darling *n* **1** luaidh *m*; **2** (*expr*) **~!** a ghaoil!, a luaidh!
darn *v* càirich *vt*
dart *n* gath *m*, guin *m*
dash *n* **1** ruith *f*, dian-ruith & deann-ruith *f*; **2** (*typog*) sgrìob *f*
dash *v* ruith *vi*
data *n* dàta *m*, fiosrachadh *m*
database *n* stòr-dàta *m*
date[1] *n* (*calendar ~*) ceann-là & ceann-latha *m*; **2** *in expr* **bring up to ~** ùraich *vt*
date[2] *n* (*fruit*) deit *f*
date *v* **1** (*document etc*) cuir ceann-là air; **2** (*become outdated*) rach *vi irreg* às an fhasan
dated *adj* sean(n)-fhasanta, às an fhasan *m*
dative *adj* tabhartach
daub *v* smeur/smiùr *vt*
daughter *n* nighean *f*
daughter-in law *n* bana-chliamhainn *f*, bean-mhic *f*
daunt *v* cuir *vt* fo eagal *m*, cuir eagal (*with prep* air), geiltich *vt*
dawn *n* **1** camhana(i)ch an latha *f*, bris(t)eadh an latha *m*; **2** (*idiom*) **from ~ to dusk** o mhoch gu dubh
day *n* là & latha *m*
daybreak *n* bris(t)eadh an latha *m*
daylight *n* solas an latha *m*
dead *adj* **1** marbh; **2** (*exact*) *in expr* **in the ~ centre of** ann an teis-meadhan; **3** (*completely*) calg-dhìreach
deadline *n* ceann-ama *m*
deadly *adj* marbhtach, bàsmhor
deaf *adj* bodhar
deafen *v* bodhair *vt*
deafness *n* buidhre *f*
deal *n* **1** (*business*) cunnradh *m*; **2** (*arrangement*) cùmhnant *m*; **3** (*degree*) **a good deal more than** fada nas (*with comp adj*)

deal v 1 (*cards*) riaraich *vti*, roinn *vti*; 2 ~
with dèilig ri

dealer n (*commerce etc*) neach-dèiligidh *m*

dear *excl*, ~ **oh** ~ dhuine! dhuine!, obh!
obh!, ~ **me!** O mo chreach!

dear *adj* 1 (*expensive*) daor, cosgail;
2 (*person*) ionmhainn, gaolach, caomh;
3 (*affectionate address*) **my** ~ a ghràidh,
m' eudail; 4 (*in corres*) ~ **Sir** A Charaid,
~ **Sirs** A Chàirdean, ~ **Madam** A
Bhanacharaid

dearth n cion *m*, gainne *f*, dìth *m*

death n bàs *m*, caochladh *m*, eug *m*

death-bed n leabaidh bàis *f*

death-dealing *adj* marbhtach, bàsmhor

debase v 1 (*humiliate*) ìslich *vt*, maslaich
vt, dèan *vi irreg* dìmeas air, cuir *vt* (ann)
an suarachas *m*; 2 (*corrupt*) truaill *vt*;
3 (*currency*) dì-luachaich *vt*

debate n deasbad *mf*, connsachadh *m*

debate v deasbad *vti*, deasbair *vi*,
connsaich *vi*

debauch v claon *vt*, coirb *vt*, truaill *vt*

debauchery n 1 (*sexual*) mì-gheanmnachd
f, strìopachas *m*; 2 (*drinking*) pòitearachd
f

debilitate v lagaich *vti*, fannaich *vi*

debility n laigse *f*

debris n sprùilleach *m*

debt n fiach *m*

debtor n fèichear *m*

decade n deichead *m*

decadence n claonadh *m*

decadent *adj* air claonadh

decapitate v dì-cheannaich *vt*

decapitation n dì-cheannadh *m*

decay n lobhadh *m*, seargadh *m*

decay v lobh *vi*, caith *vi*, crìon *vi*

deceit n mealladh *m*, cealg *f*, foill *f*

deceitful *adj* mealltach, cealgach, fallsa,
foilleil

deceive v meall *vt*, cealg *vt*, dèan foill air

deceived *adj* meallta

deceiver n mealltair *m*, cealgair(e) *m*

December n an Dùbhlachd *f*

decency n beusachd *f*

decent *adj* 1 (*moral etc*) còir, beusach;
2 (*fair*) cothromach; 3 (*appropriate*)
cothromach, iomchaidh

deception n mealladh *m*, cealg *f*, foill *f*

deceptive *adj* mealltach

decide v 1 (*make decision*) co-dhùin *vi*,
thig *vi* gu co-dhùnadh; 2 *in expr* ~ **on**
(*appoint*) sònraich *vt*; 3 (*form intention*)
cuir *vt* romhad

deciduous *adj* seargach

decimal *adj* deicheach

decimal n deicheamh *m*

decipher v fuasgail *vt*

decision n co-dhùnadh *m*

decision-making n co-dhùnadh *m*

decisive *adj* 1 (*of persons*) duineil;
2 (*crucial*) prìomh

decisiveness n (*in character*) duinealas *m*

declare v 1 abair *vti irreg*, can *vti def*, cuir
vt an cèill

decline n lùghdachadh *m*, crìonadh *m*

decline v 1 (*deteriorate etc*) lùghdaich *vi*,
crìon *vi*, rach *vi* nas miosa; 2 (*refuse*) diùlt
vt; 3 (*gram*) claoin *vi*

decompose v lobh *vi*, bris *vi* sìos

decomposition n lobhadh *m*, bris(t)eadh
m sìos

decorate v maisich *vt*, sgeadaich *vt*

decoration n maiseachadh *m*,
sgeadachadh *m*

decorative *adj* sgeadachail

decorous *adj* 1 (*well-behaved*) beusach,
modhail; 2 (*proper*) cubhaidh, iomchaidh

decorum n stuaim *f*, deagh bheus *f*, modh
mf

decrease n lùghdachadh *m*

decrease v lùghdaich *vti*, (*as vi*) rach sìos

decree n òrdugh *m*

decree v òrdaich *vi*

decrepit *adj* (*people*) breòite, anfhann

decriminalise v dì-eucoirich *vt*

decriminalisation n dì-eucoireachadh *m*

dedicate v coisrig *vt*

dedication n coisrigeadh *m*

deduce v dèan *vt irreg* a-mach, obraich *vt*
a-mach, dèan *vt irreg* dheth

deduct v (*subtract*) thoir *vt* air falbh bho/o

deduction n 1 (*subtraction*) toirt *f* air falbh
bho/o; 2 (*intellectual*) dèanamh a-mach,
obrachadh a-mach *m*, dèanamh dheth

deed n 1 (*action*) gnìomh *m*; 2 (*feat*) euchd
m

deep *adj* 1 (*phys*) domhainn;
2 (*personality*) domhainn, dìomhair

deep freeze n reothadair *m*

deep n, *used with art*, **the** ~ an dubh-
aigeann *m*, an doimhne *f*

deepen *v* doimhnich *vti*

deer *n* **1** (*general*) fiadh *m*; **2** (*particular*) **red** ~ damh *m*, (*hind*) eilid *f*, **roe** ~ boc (-earba) *m*, (*female*) earb *f*

deface *v* mill *vt*

defamation *n* tuaileas *m*, mì-chliù *m*

defamatory *adj* tuaileasach

defame *v* cùl-chàin *vt*, mì-chliùitich *vt*

defeat *n* call *m*, (*military*) ruaig *f*

defeat *v* **1** faigh buaidh air, dèan an gnothach/a' chùis air, buadhaich *vi* air; **2** (*befail*) fairtlich air, faillich air

defecate *v* cac *vi*

defecation *m* cacadh *m*

defect *n* fàillinn *f*, meang *f*

defect *v* trèig *vi*

defective *adj* **1** (*having defect*) meangail; **2** (*incomplete*) neo-iomlan

defence *n* dìon *m*

defenceless *adj* gun dìon *m*

defend *v* dìon *vt*   .

defendant *n* neach-dìona *m*

defender *n* dìonadair *m*

defensible *adj* so-dhìonta

defer *v* **1** cuir *vt* air (an) ath là, cuir *vt* air dàil, cuir dàil ann an/air; **2** (*give way*) gèill *vi* do

deference *n* urram *m*, ùmhlachd *nf*

deferential *adj* umha(i)l

defiance *n* dùbhlan *m*

deficiency *n* **1** (*lack*) easbhaidh *f*, dìth *m*; **2** (*fault*) fàilligeadh *m*

deficient *adj* **1** (*missing*) easbhaidheach, a dhìth; **2** (*faulty*) easbhaidheach

deficit *n* **1** easbhaidh *f*, dìth *m*; **2** (*in balance sheet etc*) call *m*

defile *v* truaill *vt*, salaich *vt*

defilement *n* truailleadh *m*

define *v* mìnich *vt*, soilleirich *vt*

definite *adj* cinnteach, deimhinne/ deimhinnte

definitely *adv* gu dearbh, gun teagamh

definition *n* mìneachadh *m*

deflation *n* (*economics*) seargadh *m*

deforestation *n* dì-choilleachadh *m*

deform *v* cuir *vt* à cumadh

deformity *n* **1** (*abstr*) mì-chumadh *m*; **2** (*specific*) meang *f*

defraud *v* feallaich *vt*, dèan foill air

defrost *v* dì-reoth *vti*

deft *adj* deas, ealamh

defunct *adj* **1** (*persons*) marbh, nach maireann; **2** (*systems etc*) a chaidh à cleachdadh *m*

defy *v* thoir dùbhlan do

degeneracy *n* (*moral*) coirbteachd *f*

degenerate *adj* (*morally*) coirbte

degenerate *v* rach *vi* sìos, rach *vi irreg* am miosad

degradation *n* ìsleachadh *m*

degrade *v* ìslich *vt*

degree *n* **1** (*heat etc*) puing *f*; **2** (*progress etc*) ìre *f*; **3** (*academic*) ceum *m*

dehydrate *v* sgreubh *vt*, crìon *vti*, searg *vti*

dehydration *n* sgreubhadh *m*, crìonadh *m*, seargadh *m*

deity *n* **1** (*abstr*) diadhachd *f*; **2** (*god*) dia *m*

dejected *adj* fo bhròn, dubhach, smalanach, fo smalan *m*, sìos ann an inntinn *f*

dejection *n* bròn *m*, smalan *m*, smuairean *m*

delay *n* dàil *f*, maille *f*

delay *v* **1** (*hinder*) cuir maille air/ann, cuir dàil air/ann, cùm *vt* air ais; **2** (*drag one's heels*) màirnealaich *vi*, bi *vi irreg* màirnealach

delectable *adj* blasmhor

delegate *n* riochdaire *m*

delegate *v* tiomain *vt*

delegation *n* **1** (*abstr*) tiomnadh *m*; **2** (*con*) buidheann-riochdachaidh *mf*

delete *v* dubh *vt* às, dubh *vt* a-mach

deliberate *adj* a dh'aon ghnothach/rùn

deliberate *v* (*reflect, discuss*) beachdaich *vi*

deliberately *adv* a dh'aon ghnothach/rùn

deliberation *n* beachdachadh *m*

delicacy *n* **1** (*refinement*) fìnealtas *m*; **2** (*vulnerability*) maothachd *f*

delicate *adj* **1** (*refined*) fìnealta; **2** (*vulnerable*) maoth

delicious *adj* ana-bhlasta

delight *n* aighear *m*, aoibhneas *m*, sòlas *m*

delight *v* toilich *vt*, riaraich *vt*

delighted *adj & past part* làn-thoilichte, riaraichte, sòlasach

delightful *adj* taitneach, ciatach

delinquency *n* coire *f*, ciontachd *f*

delinquent *n* coireach *m*, ciontach *m*

delirious *adj* breisleachail

delirium *n* breisleach *mf*

deliver v **1** (*goods etc*) lìbhrig vt, liubhair vt; **2** (*liberate*) saor vt, fuasgail vt; **3** (*baby*) asaidich vt; **4** (*speech etc*) gabh vt, thoir vt seachad

deliverance n saorsa f, fuasgladh m

delivery n **1** (*goods etc*) lìbhrigeadh m, liubhairt m; **2** (*baby*) asaid f

delude v meall vt, dall vt

deluge n tuil f, dìle f (bhàthte)

delusion n mealladh m, dalladh m

delusory adj mealltach

delve v rannsaich vt, cladhaich vt

demand n **1** iarrtas m; **2** (*economics*) fèill f, margadh m

demand v iarr vt

demean v dìblich vt, ìslich vt

demented adj air bhoile, air chuthach, às do (*etc*) rian, às do chiall

demi- prefix leth-

democracy n deamocrasaidh m

democrat n deamocratach m

democratic adj deamocratach

demolish v leag vt, sgrios vt

demolition n leagail f, sgrios m

demon n deamhan m

demonstrate v **1** (*prove*) dearbh vt; **2** (*display*) taisbean vt; **3** (*pol*) tog vt fianais

demonstration n **1** (*proof*) dearbhadh m; **2** (*products etc*) taisbeanadh m; **3** (*pol*) fianais-dhùbhlain f, (*march*) caismeachd f

demoralize v mì-mhisnich vt

demote v ìslich vt

demure adj stuama

den n **1** (*topog*) lag mf; **2** (*animal etc*) garaidh m

denial n àicheadh m

denigrate v dèan dìmeas air

Denmark n An Danmhairg f

denounce v **1** (*betray*) brath vt; **2** (*oppose*) cuir vi an aghaidh, rach vi irreg an aghaidh

dense adj **1** (*trees etc*) dòmhail/dùmhail, dlùth, tiugh; **2** (*mentally*) maol, maol-aigneach, tiugh

density n dlùths m, tiughad m, tighead m

dent n beàrn m, tulg m

dental adj deudach, fiaclach

dentist n fiaclair(e) m

dentistry n fiaclaireachd f

dentures n fiaclan-fuadain fpl

denunciation n **1** (*betrayal*) brathadh m; **2** (*opposition*) cur m an aghaidh

deny v **1** (*accusation etc*) àicheidh vt; **2** (*reject*) diùlt vti, àicheidh vt; **3** (*deprive*) cùm vt air ais o/bho

depart v falbh vi, imich vi

department n roinn f

departmental adj roinneil

departure n falbh m

depend v **1** (*accept support*) cuir taic air/ri; **2** (*trust*) cuir creideas ann an, cuir earbsa ann an; **3** (*vary*) bi vi irreg an crochadh air

dependable adj urrasach

dependence n eisimeileachd f, eisimeil f

dependent adj **1** an eisimeil (*with gen*); **2** (*addicted*) an urra ri, na etc t(h)ràill aig

dependent n neach-eisimeil m

depict v dealbh

deplorable adj maslach, tàmailteach

deplore v is v irreg & def, is olc le

deploy v cuir vt an gnìomh

depopulate v fàsaich vt

depopulation n fàsachadh m

deport v fuadaich vt, fògair vt

deportment n giùlan m

deposit n **1** (*advance*) eàrlas m; **2** (*payment in account*) tasgadh m

deposit v taisg vt

depot n **1** (*store etc*) batharnach m; **2** (*base*) ionad m

deprecate v coirich vt

depress v **1** (*phys*) brùth vt sìos; **2** (*sadden etc*) cuir vt sìos, fàg vt dubhach, fàg vt fo smalan

depressed adj fo bhròn, dubhach, smalanach, fo smalan, sìos ann an inntinn, ìosal/ìseal

depression n **1** (*mood*) bròn m, smalan m, smuairean m, leann-dubh m; **2** (*mood/weather*) ìsleachadh m

deprivation n **1** (*action*) cumail f air ais; **2** (*poverty etc*) easbhaidh f

deprive v cùm vt air ais o/bho

depth n doimhneachd f

deputation n buidheann-tagraidh mf

depute, **deputy** adj iar-, leas-

deputy n neach-ionaid m

derelict adj trèigte

deride v mag vi, dèan fanaid air

derision n magadh m, fanaid f

derisive adj 1 (deriding) magail;
2 (inadequate) suarach

derivation n 1 (abstr) freumh-fhaclachd f,
freumhachadh m; 2 (con) freumh m, bun
m, tùs m

derivative adj iasadach

derive v (as vi) thig vi bho/o

derogatory adj cur-sìos

derrick n crann(-togail) m

descend v (phys) teirinn & teàrn vti à,
crom vi o/bho & le, thig vi sìos/a-nuas

descendant n fear m/tè f de shìol, fear/tè
de shliochd (both with gen)

descended (from) past part de shliochd
m, de shìol m (both with gen)

descent n 1 (phys) teàrnadh m, cromadh
m; 2 (ancestry) sinnsearachd f

describe v thoir tuairisgeul air

description n 1 (person/thing) tuairisgeul
m; 2 (events etc) cunntas m

descriptive adj dealbhach, tuairisgeulach

desert n fàsach mf, dìthreabh f

desert v 1 trèig vt, dìobair vt; 2 (soldiers
etc) teich vi

deserted adj & past part 1 (empty)
uaigneach, fàsaichte, fàs; 2 (abandoned)
trèigte

deserter n fear-teichidh m

desertification n fàsachadh m

desertion n trèigsinn m, (from army etc)
teicheadh m

deserve v bi vi irreg airidh air

deserving adj airidh, toillteanach air

desiccate v tiormaich vti

design n dealbh & deilbh mf

design v dealbh & deilbh vt, dealbhaich vt

designate v (specify) sònraich vt, (name)
ainmich vt

designer n dealbhaiche & deilbhiche m,
neach-deilbh m

designing n dealbhadh & deilbheadh m,
dealbhachadh m

desire n miann mf, rùn m, togradh m,
dèidh f

desire v miannaich vt rùnaich vt, togair vti

desist v leig vi, sguir vi de

desk n deasg m

desolate adj fàsail; 2 (person) trèigte,
truagh

despair n eu-dòchas m

despicable adj suarach, tàireil

despise v dèan tàir air, dèan tarcais air

despite prep a dh'aindeoin (with gen)

despised adj & past part fo dhìmeas

despondency n mì-mhisneachd f

despondent adj gun mhisneach f,
dubhach, smalanach

despot n aintighearna m, deachdaire m

despotism n aintighearnas m,
deachdaireachd f

dessert n mìlsean m

dessert-spoon n spàin-mìlsein f

destabilise v dì-dhaingnich vt

destination n ceann-uidhe m

destined adj & past part an dàn

destiny n dàn m, crannchur m

destitute adj airceach, ainniseach

destitution n airc f, ainnis f

destroy v mill vt, sgrios vt, cuir vi às do

destruction n milleadh m, sgrios m

destructive adj millteach, sgriosail

detach v dealaich vt

detached adj & past part 1 dealaichte;
2 (personality) fad' às, dùinte

detachment n 1 (abstr) dealachadh m;
2 (troops etc) buidheann mf, còmhlan m,
cuideachd f

detail n mion-phuing f

detailed adj mionaideach, mion-

detain v 1 (delay) cùm vt air ais; 2 (in
custody) cùm vt an làimh, cùm vt an
grèim/an sàs

detect v lorg vt, faigh lorg air

detection n lorg f

detector n lorgair m

detention n 1 (abstr) làmh f, grèim m, sàs
m; 2 (detaining) cumail f an làimh/an
grèim/an sàs

deter v bac vt, caisg vt

deteriorate v 1 mùth vi, rach vi am miosad
m; 2 (person) rach vi bhuaithe

deterioration n 1 mùthadh m, dol m am
miosad m, fàillinn f; 2 (person) dol m
bhuaithe

determination n daingneachd f, rùn
suidhichte

determine v 1 (form plan etc) cuir
romhad; 2 (discover) dearbh vt

determined adj & past part 1 (persistent)
daingeann, suidhichte; 2 (resolved)
mionnaichte, suidhichte

deterrent n bacadh m, seòl-bacaidh m,
casg m

detest *v* fuathaich *vt*, bi *vi irreg* gràin aig (*with prep* air)

detestable *adj* gràineil, fuathach

detour *n* bealach *m*

detrimental *adj* millteach

devalue *v* dì-luachaich *vti*

devaluation *n* dì-luachadh *m*

devastate *v* lèirsgrios *vt*

devastation *n* lèirsgrios *m*

develop *v* 1 (*as vt: improve*) leasaich *vt*; 2 (*as vi: make progress etc*) thig *vi* air adhart

developing *adj*, *in expr* ~ **country** tìr *mf* fo leasachadh *m*

development *n* 1 (*improvement*) leasachadh *m*; 2 (*persons, progress*) adhartas *m*, piseach *m*

deviate *v* saobh *vi*

deviation *n* saobhadh *m*

device *n* inneal *m*, innleachd *f*

devil *n* diabhal *m*

devilish *adj* diabhlaidh

devious *adj* 1 (*behaviour*) fiar, carach; 2 (*route etc*) cuairteach

devise *v* innlich *vt*, dealbh *vt*, tionnsgail/tionnsgain *vt*

devoid (of) *adj* às aonais, às eugmhais

devolution *n* tiomnadh chumhachdan *m*, sgaoileadh-cumhachd *m*

devolve *v* tiomnaich *vt*

devolved *adj & past part* tiomnaichte

devote *v* coisrig *vt*

devotion *n* 1 (*relig*) cràbhadh *m*, diadhachd *f*; 2 (*love*) teas-ghràdh *m*

devour *v* glam/glamh *vt*, sluig *vt*, ith *vt* gu glàmach

devout *adj* cràbhach, diadhaidh

devoutness *n* cràbhadh *m*, diadhachd *f*

dew *n* dealt *mf*, dr(i)ùchd *m*

dewy *adj* dealtach

dexterity *n* deas-làmhachd *f*

dexterous *adj* làmhach, deas-làmhach

diabetes *n* tinneas an t-siùcair *m*

diabolical *adj* diabhlaidh

diagonal *adj* trastanach

diagonal *n* trastan *m*

diagram *n* diagram *m*, dealbh-chumadh *mf*

dial *n* (*clock etc*) aodann *m*, aghaidh *f*

dial *v* fònaig

dialect *n* dualchainnt *f*

dialogue *n* co-chòmhradh *m*, còmhradh-dithis *m*

diamond *n* daoimean *m*

diaphragm *n* sgairt *f*

diarrhoea *n* buinneach *f*, sgàird *f*, spùt *m*

diary *n* leabhar-latha *m*

dictate *v* 1 (*letter etc*) deachd *vt*; 2 (*command etc*) òrdaich *vi*

dictation *n* (*letter etc*) deachdadh *m*

dictator *n* 1 (*pol etc*) deachdaire *m*; 2 (*letter etc*) neach-deachdaidh *m*

dictatorial *adj* deachdaireach, ceannsalach

dictatorship *n* deachdaireachd *f*

diction *n* labhradh *m*

dictionary *n* faclair *m*

dicy *adj* 1 (*dodgy*) cugallach; 2 (*risky*) cunnartach

didactic *adj* oideachail

die *v* caochail *vi*, siubhail *vi*, eug *vi*, bàsaich *vi*

die, *pl* **dice**, *n* dìsinn *m* & dìsne *mf*, *pl* dìsnean *m*

diesel *n* dìosail *m*

diet *n* riaghailt-bìdh *f*

difference *n* 1 diofar *m*, eadar-dhealachadh *m*

different *adj* diof(a)rach, diofraichte & deifrichte, eadar-dhealaichte

differentiate *v* eadar-dhealaich, dèan eadar-dhealachadh, dèan sgaradh eadar

differentiation *n* eadar-dhealachadh *m*

difficult *adj* 1 (*to do*) doirbh, duilich; 2 (*to understand*) deacair; 3 (*circumstances etc*) cruaidh, duilich

difficulty *n* 1 (*problem*) duilgheadas *m*; 2 (*predicament*) càs *m*, cruaidh-chàs *m*, èiginn *f*

diffident *adj* diùid, nàrach

diffuse *adj* sgaoilte, sgapte/sgapta

diffuse *v* craobh-sgaoil *vti*

diffusion *n* craobh-sgaoileadh *m*

dig *v* cladhaich *vti*, ruamhair *vi*

digest *v* 1 cnàmh *vti*; 2 (*mentally*) cnuasaich *vt*

digestion *n* cnàmh *m*

digging *n* cladhach *m*

digit *n* (*arith*) figear *m*

digital *adj* (*IT etc*) figearail, didseatach

dignified *adj* stàiteil, stòlda, stuama

dignify *v* àrdaich *vt*, urramaich *vt*

dignity *n* 1 (*rank*) urram *m*, inbhe *f*, mòralachd *f*; 2 (*manner*) stàitealachd *f*, stòldachd *f*

digs *n* lòistinn *m*, taigh-loidsidh *m*

dilatory *adj* màirnealach, slaodach

dilemma *n* imcheist *f*

diligence *n* dìcheall *m*

diligent *adj* dìcheallach

dilute *v* tanaich *vt*, lagaich *vt*

dilute *adj*, **diluted** *adj* & *past part*, tanaichte

dim *adj* 1 (*light etc*) doilleir; 2 (*unintelligent*) maol-aigneach, tiugh

dim *v* doilleirich *vti*

dimension *n* 1 (*size*) meud *m*, meudachd *f*; 2 (*measurement*) tomhas *m*

diminish *v* lùghdaich *vti*, beagaich *vti*

diminution *n* lùghdachadh *m*, beagachadh *m*

diminutive *adj* meanbh, bìodach, crìon

dimple *n* tibhre *m*

din ùpraid *f*, gleadhar *m*, othail *f*, iorghail *f*

dine *v* gabh dinnear *f*

dingy *adj* 1 (*dark*) doilleir; 2 (*grubby*) mosach, luideach

dining-room *n* seòmar-bìdh *m*, rùm-bìdh *m*

dinner *n* dinnear *f*, diathad *f*

diocese *n* sgìre-easbaig *f*, sgìreachd-easbaig *f*

dip *n* 1 (*action*) tumadh *m*, bogadh *m*; 2 (*liquid*) dup *m*

dip *v* 1 (*in liquid*) tum *vt*, bog *vt*; 2 (*sheep*) dup *vti*

diploma *n* teisteanas *m*

diplomacy *n* dioplòmasaidh *mf*

diplomat *n* rìochdaire dioplòmasach

diplomatic *adj* dioplòmasach

dipping *n* 1 (*in liquid*) tumadh *m*, bogadh *m*; 2 (*sheep*) dupadh *m*

dipsomania *n* tinneas na dibhe *m*

direct *adj* dìreach

direct *v* 1 (*conduct etc*) treòraich *vt*, stiùir *vt*; 2 (*manage*) stiùir *vt*

direction *n* 1 taobh *m*, rathad *m*; 2 (*compass*) àird *f*

directly *adv* 1 (*straight*) dìreach; 2 (*immediately*) gun dàil, air ball, anns a' bhad; 3 (*shortly*) a dh'aithghearr, an-ceartuair

director *n* neach-stiùiridh *m*

directory *n* leabhar-seòlaidh *m*

dirge *n* tuireadh *m*

dirk *n* biodag *f*

dirt *n* salchar *m*

dirty *adj* salach, rapach

dis- *prefix* 1 ana- ; 2 eas- ; 3 mì-

disability *n* ciorram *m*

disabled *adj* ciorramach

disadvantage *n* anacothrom *m*, mì-leas *m*

disadvantage *v* mì-leasaich *vt*

disadvantaged *adj* & *past part* 1 (*person*) fo anacothrom *m*; 2 (*region etc*) mì-leasaichte

disagree *v* rach *vi* an aghaidh, eas-aontaich *vi*

disagreeable *adj* neo-thaitneach

disagreement *n* 1 (*disagreeing*) dol *m* an aghaidh; 2 (*abstr & con*) eas-aonta *f*, mì-chòrdadh *m*

disallow *v* mì-cheadaich *vt*

disappear *v* rach *vi* à sealladh

disappoint *v* meall *vt*, leig *vt* sìos

disappointment *n* bris(t)eadh-dùil *m*, mealladh-dùil *m*

disapproval *n* coireachadh *m*, dol *m* an aghaidh

disapprove *v* coirich *vt*, rach *vi* an aghaidh

disarm *v* dì-armaich *vti*

disarmament *n* dì-armachadh *m*

disarray *n* mì-riaghailt *f*

disaster *n* tubaist *f*, mòr-thubaist *f*, calldachd *f*

disbelief *n* às-creideamh *m*

disc, disk *n* clàr *m*

discard *v* tilg *vt* air falbh

discernible *adj* follaiseach, so-fhaicinn

discerning *adj* tuigseach

discernment *n* tuigse *f*

discharge *v* 1 (*duties etc*) coilean *vt*; 2 (*debt*) ìoc *vt*, pàigh *vt*; 3 (*person*) saor *vt*; 4 (*gun*) loisg *vt*, tilg *vt*; 5 (*cargo etc*) dì-luchdaich *vti*

disciple *n* deisciobal *m*

discipline *n* 1 smachd *m*; 2 (*ed*) cuspair *m*

discipline *v* 1 (*assert authority*) smachdaich *vt*, cuir smachd air; 2 (*punish*) peanasaich *vt*

disclose *v* foillsich *vt*, leig *vt* ris

disclosure *n* (*abstr*) foillseachadh *m*, leigeil *m* ris

disco *n* diosgo *m*

discomfort *n* anshocair *f*

disconcert *v* buair *vt*

disconnect *v* neo-cheangail *vt*, sgaoil *vt*

disconsolate *adj* brònach, dubhach

discontent *n* mì-thoileachadh *m*, diomb *m*

discontented *adj* mì-thoilichte, diombach

discontinue v cuir stad air, leig vt seachad, sguir vi de

discord n **1** eas-aonta f, mì-chòrdadh m; **2** (music) dì-chòrda m

discount n lùghdachadh prìse/phrìsean m, ìsleachadh prìse/phrìsean m

discount v (trade etc) leag/lùghdaich/ìslich prìs(ean) f, reic vti air prìs(ean) ìsleachaidh

discourage v **1** mì-mhisnich vt; **2** (dissuade from) thoir comhairle gun

discouragement n **1** (action) mì-mhisneachadh m; **2** (state of mind) mì-mhisneachd f

discourteous adj mì-mhodhail

discourtesy n mì-mhodh m

discover v **1** (facts) faigh vt a-mach; **2** (objects) lorg vt

discredit n **1** (loss of trust) mì-chreideas m; **2** (loss of reputation) mì-chliù m

discreet adj **1** (keeping confidentiality) rùnach; **2** (tactful etc) tuigseach

discrepancy n eadar-dhealachadh m, diofar m

discretion n (tact) tuigse f, breithneachadh m

discriminate v **1** (unjustly) dèan lethbhreith an aghaidh; **2** (differentiate) eadar-dhealaich vi, dèan eadar-dhealachadh eadar

discrimination n **1** (bias) lethbhreith f; **2** (capacity) breithneachadh m; **3** (abstr) eadar-dhealachadh m

discriminatory adj (biased) lethbhreitheach

discuss v deasbair vi mu, deasbad vi, beachdaich vi

discussion n **1** (abstr) deasbaireachd f; **2** (con) deasbad mf

disdain n tarcais f, tailceas m, tàir f, dìmeas m

disdain v dèan tarcais air, dèan tàir air, dèan dìmeas air

disdainful adj tarcaiseach, tailceasach, tàireil

disease n tinneas m, galar m, (abstr) euslaint f

disembark v rach vi air tìr

disentangle v rèitich vt, fuasgail vt

disentangled adj & past part rèidh

disgrace n **1** (abstr) masladh m, tàmailt f; **2** (source of) cùis-mhaslaidh f

disgrace v nàraich vt, maslaich vt

disgraceful adj maslach, tàmailteach, nàr

disgruntled adj diombach, gruamach, mì-riaraichte

disguise n breug-riochd m

disgust n gràin f, sgreamh m

disgust v sgreamhaich vt, cuir sgreamh air

disgusting adj gràineil, sgreamhail

dish n soitheach m

dish-cloth n brèid-shoithichean m

dishonest adj eas-onarach, mì-onarach

dishonesty n mì-onair m

dishonour n eas-onair f, eas-urram m

dishonourable adj eas-urramach

dishwasher n nigheadair-shoithichean m

disillusion v bris(t) misneachd f

disillusionment call misneachd m

disinclined adj aindeonach, leisg

disingenuous adj cealgach, fallsa

disinherit v thoir/cùm oighreachd bho/o

disinterested adj neo-thaobhach

disjointed adj **1** (lit) às an alt m; **2** (discourse etc) briste

dislike n mì-thaitneamh m

dislike v, **I** ~ is beag orm, cha toigh leam

dislocate v (joint) cuir vt às an alt

disloyal adj mì-dhìleas, neo-dhìleas

disloyalty n mì-dhìlseachd f, neo-dhìlseachd f

dismal adj **1** (weather etc) doilleir; **2** (depressed) dubhach, sìos ann an inntinn f; **3** (condition etc) bochd, truagh

dismantle v thoir vt às a chèile

dismay n mì-mhisneach(d) f

dismay v **1** (discourage) mì-mhisnich vt; **2** (alarm) cuir eagal air

dismiss v **1** cuir vt air falbh; **2** (employee etc) cuir vt à dreuchd

dismissal n (employee etc) cur m à dreuchd

dismount v teirinn & teàrn vi bho/o

disobedience n eas-ùmhlachd f

disobedient adj eas-umhail

disobey v rach vi an aghaidh

disorder n **1** (unorderliness) mì-rian m, mì-riaghailt f; **2** (emotional) buaireas m; **3** (mental) mì-rian m; **4** (civil) aimhreit f, buaireas m

disorderly adj mì-rianail, mì-riaghailteach, buaireasach, aimhreiteach

disown v diùlt vt, àicheidh vt

disparage v dèan tàir air, cuir vt an suarachas

disparagement n **1** (*abstr*) tàir f; **2** (*action*) cur an suarachas m
disparaging adj tàireil
disparate adj (gu tur) eadar-dhealaichte
disparity n neo-ionannachd f
dispense v **1** (*supply*) solair vt, riaraich vt; **2** in expr ~ **with** dèan vi irreg às aonais
dispersal n sgaoileadh m, sgapadh m
disperse v sgaoil vti, sgap vti
display n (*art etc*) taisbeanadh m
display v **1** (*art etc*) taisbean & taisbein vt; **2** (*IT etc*) sealladh m, clàr-taisbeanaidh m
displease v mì-thoilich vt
displeasure n mì-thoileachas m; diomb m
disposal n **1** (*ridding*) faighinn f cuidhteas m; **2** (*sale*) reic m
dispose v (*place etc*) suidhich vt, socraich vt
disposition n (*temperament*) nàdar m, mèinn f, aigne f
dispossess v cuir vt à seilbh
disprove v breugnaich vt
disputatious adj connsachail, connspaideach
dispute n connsachadh m, connspaid f
dispute v **1** (*as vi*) connsaich vi; **2** (*as vt*) ceasnaich vt, cuir vt an ceist
disqualification n dì-cheadachadh m
disqualify v dì-cheadaich vt
disquiet n iomagain f, imcheist f
disregard n **1** (*lack of concern*) neo-chùram m; **2** (*lack of respect*) dìmeas m
disreputable adj **1** (*appearance*) cearbach, luideach, grodach; **2** (*character*) neo-mheasail, fiadhaich, tàmailteach, maslach
disrepute n mì-chliù m
disrespect n dìmeas m, eas-urram m
disrupt v buair vt, cuir vt troimh-a-chèile, cuir vt thar a chèile
disruption n **1** (*action*) buaireadh; **2** (*affairs*) aimhreit f
dissatisfaction n mì-thoileachadh m
dissatisfy v mì-thoilich vt
dissembler n cealgair(e) m
dissembling adj cealgach
disseminate v sgaoil vt, craobh-sgaoil vt
dissemination n sgaoileadh m, craobh-sgaoileadh m
dissent n eas-aonta f
dissent v eas-aontaich vi
dissenting adj eas-aontach
dissertation n tràchdas m

disservice n mì-sheirbheis f
dissident adj eas-aontach
dissident n eas-aontaiche m
dissimilar adj eu-coltach
dissimilarity n eu-coltas m
dissimulation n cealgaireachd f
dissipate v **1** (*wealth*) struidh vt, caith vt, ana-caith vt; **2** (*clouds etc*) sgaoil vi
dissipation n **1** (*wealth*) struidheadh m, ana-caitheamh f; **2** (*clouds etc*) sgaoileadh m
dissolve v leagh vti, sgaoil vti
dissuade v thoir comhairle air/do gun, thoir vt air gun
distance n astar m
distant adj **1** fad' air falbh, cèin, iomallach; **2** (*person*) fad' às
distaste n gràin f
distasteful adj gràineil, mì-chàilear
distend v at vi, sèid vi
distil v tarraing vti
distillation n tarraing f, grùdadh m
distiller n grùdair(e) m
distillery n taigh-staile m
distinct adj **1** (*sound etc*) taisbeanach; **2** (*different*) eadar-dhealaichte, air leth, fa leth, diof(a)rach
distinction n **1** (*difference*) eadar-dhealachadh m; **2** (*pre-eminence*) àrd-urram m, òirdheirceas m
distinctive adj air leth, àraidh
distinctly adv gu taisbeanach, gu soilleir
distinguish v eadar-dhealaich vt, dèan eadar-dhealachadh
distinguished adj (*pre-eminent*) barraichte, òirdheirc
distort v **1** (*phys*) cuir vt à cumadh; **2** misrepresent) dèan mì-aithris air, thoir claon-iomradh air
distortion n **1** (*phys*) ath-chumadh m; **2** (*misrepresentation*) mì-aithris m, claon-iomradh m
distract v tarraing aire f
distracted adj & past part **1** (*preoccupied*) fad' às; **2** (*intense*) às do rian
distraction n **1** (*pastime*) caitheamh-aimsir m, cur-seachad m; **2** (*lack of attention*) cion aire m; **3** (*mental state*) boile f
distress n èiginn f
distress v sàraich vt, cràidh vt, pian vt, tàmailtich vt

distressed *adj* nad (*etc*) èiginn *f*, cràidhte, air sàrachadh, air tàmailteachadh

distribute *v* roinn *vt*, riaraich *vt*, sgaoil *vt*

distribution *n* roinn *f*, riarachadh *m*, sgaoileadh *m*

district *n* ceàrn *m*, sgìre *f*, tìr *f*

distrust *n* mì-earbsa *m*, amharas *m*

distrustful *adj* mì-earbsach, amharasach

disturb *v* 1 (*bother*) cuir dragh air; 2 (*disrupt*) buair *vt*

disturbance *n* 1 (*action*) buaireadh *m*; 2 (*result*) aimhreit *f*, buaireas *m*, an-fhois *f*

disunity *n* eas-aonachd *f*

disuse *n* mì-chleachdadh *m*

ditch *n* clais *f*, dìg *f*

ditty *n* duanag *f*, luinneag *f*

dive *v* dàibh *vi*, dàibhig *vi*

diver *n* dàibhear *m*

diverge *v* dealaich *vi* ri chèile

diverse *adj* caochladh *n*

diversion *n* 1 (*fun*) dibhearsain *m*, spòrs *f*, fearas-chuideachd *f*; 2 (*traffic*) tionndadh slighe *m*

diversity *n* iomadachd *f*

divert *v* 1 (*phys*) tionndaidh *vt* a leth-taobh *m*; 2 (*amuse etc*) thoir dibhearsain do

divide *v* pàirtich *vt*, riaraich *vt*, roinn *vt*, sgar *vt*

divided *adj & past part* 1 roinnte, air sgaradh; 2 (*arith*) air a roinn

dividend *n* buannachd *f*; duais *f*

divine *adj* diadhaidh

diving *n* dàibheadh *m*, dàibhigeadh *m*

divinity *n* 1 (*abstr*) diadhachd *f*; 2 (*subject*) diadhaireachd *f*

division *n* 1 (*process*) pàirteacheadh *m*; 2 (*by force etc*) sgaradh *m*; 3 (*arith etc*) roinn *f*; 4 (*con*) roinn *f*

divorce *n* sgaradh-pòsaidh *m*

divorce *v* dealaich *vi* ri

divot *n* fàl *m*, ploc *m*, sgrath/sgroth *f*

divulge *v* foillsich *vt*, innis *vt*

dizziness *n* tuainealaich *f*, luasgan *m*

dizzy *adj* tuainealach

do *v* 1 dèan *vt irreg*

docile *adj* 1 sèimh, ciùin, sàmhach; 2 (*biddable*) macanta, umha(i)l

docility *n* 1 sèimhe *f*, ciùineas *m*; 2 (*obedience*) macantas *m*, ùmhlachd *f*

dock¹ *n* (*bot*) copag *f*

dock² *n* (*in seaport etc*) doca *m*

dock¹ *v* 1 (*cut*) giorraich *vt*, cut & cutaich *vt*; 2 (*reduce*) lùghdaich *vti*

dock² (*ship etc: as vt*) cuir *vt* san doca, (*as vi*) rach *vi* a-steach dhan doca

docken *n* (*bot*) copag *f*

docker *n* docair *m*

doctor *n* 1 (*medical*) do(c)tair *m*, lighiche *m*; 2 (*non-medical*) Dr *m*

doctorate *n* dotaireachd *f*

doctrine *n* teagasg *m*

document *n* sgrìobhainn *f*, pàipear *m*

documentary *adj* 1 sgrìobhte; 2 (*media etc*) aithriseach

documentary *n* (*media etc*) film *m*/ pròram *m* aithriseach

dodge *n* (*stratagem etc*) innleachd *f*, plòidh *f*

dodgy *adj* 1 (*dubious*) cugallach; 2 (*risky*) cunnartach

doff *v* cuir *vt* de

dog *n* cù *m*, madadh *m*

dogged *adj* 1 (*persistent etc*) leanailteach, dìorrasach; 2 (*stubborn*) dùr, rag, rag-mhuinealach

dogmatic *adj* (*intractable*) rag-bharaileach

dole *n* dòil *m*

dole out *v* riaraich *vt*

doleful *adj* brònach, smalanach

doll *n* liùdhag *f*, doileag *f*

dollar *n* dolair *m*

dolt *n* bumailear *m*, ùmaidh *m*, stalcaire *m*

domestic *adj* taigheil

domesticate *v* callaich *vt*

domesticated *adj* 1 (*animal*) calla/callda; 2 (*home-loving*) dachaigheil

domestication *n* callachadh *m*

domicile *n* àite-fuirich *m*, àite-còmhnaidh *m*, dachaigh *f*

dominance *n* smachd *m*, làmh-an-uachdair *f*

dominant *adj* 1 (*exerting power*) ceannsalach, smachdail; 2 (*principal*) prìomh

dominate *v* 1 (*achieve dominance*) ceannsaich *vt*, smachdaich *vt*, cuir *vt* fo smachd, faigh smachd air; 2 (*maintain dominance*) cùm *vt* fo smachd

domineering *adj* ceannsalach

donate *v* tiodhlaic *vt*, thoir *vt* (seachad)

donation *n* tabhartas *m*, tiodhlac *m*

done *adj & past part* 1 dèanta & dèante; 2 (*finished*) deiseil, ullamh; 3 *in expr* **well**

~! math fhèin!, math thu fhèin!, nach math a rinn thu!

donor *n* tabhartaiche *m*, tabhairteach *m*

doomsday *n* Là Luain *m*

door *n* **1** doras *m*; **2** (*idiom*) **at death's ~** ri uchd *m* a' bhàis

doorman *n* dorsair *m*, portair *m*

doorpost *n* ursainn *f*

doorstep *n* leac (an) dorais *f*

doorway *n* doras *m*

dormant *adj* nad (*etc*) chadal, nad thàmh

dormitory *n* seòmar-cadail *m*

dose *n* tomhas (ìocshlaint) *m*

double *adj* dùbailte

double *v* (*numbers etc*) dùblaich *vti*

double-barrelled *adj* dùbailte

doubt *n* **1** teagamh *m*; **2** (*perplexity*) imcheist *f*, iomadh-chomhairle *f*

doubt *v* cuir *vt* an teagamh, cuir *vt* an amharas, cuir teagamh ann

doubtful *adj* teagmhach

doubting *adj* teagmhach, amharasach

doubtless *adv* gun teagamh

dough *n* taois *f*

dour *adj* dùr

dove *n* calman *m*

dowdy *adj* cearbach, luideach, robach

down *adv* **1** (*movement*) sìos, a-nuas; **2** (*position*) shìos

downcast *adj* smalanach, fo smalan, dubhach, sìos ann an inntinn *f*, ìseal/ìosal

downhill *adv* leis a' bhruthaich

downpour *n* dìle *f*, dòrtadh *m*

downstairs *adj* **1** (*position*) shìos an staidhre; **2** (*movement*) sìos an staidhre

downstream *adv* (*movement*) leis an t-sruth

downwards *adv* sìos, a-nuas

dowry *n* tochradh *m*

doze *n* clò-chadal *m*, leth-chadal *m*, dùsal *m*, norrag *f*

doze *v* dèan dùsal *m*, dèan norrag (bheag)

dozen *n* dusan *m*

dozy *adj* **1** (*sleepy*) cadalach; **2** (*mentally*) maol-aigneach

drab *adj* (*colour*) lachdann, odhar, doilleir

draft *n* (*document*) dreachd *f*, dreachdadh *m*

drag *v* tarraing *vti*, slaod *vti*

dragonfly *n* tarbh-nathrach *m*

drain *n* **1** (*agric etc*) clais *f*, drèana *f*; **2** (*source*) traoghadh *m*

drain *v* **1** (*empty*) tràigh *vt*; **2** (*liquids*) taom *vt*

drainage *n* drèanadh *m*

drainpipe *n* pìob-drèanaidh *f*

drake *n* ràc *m*, dràc *m*

dram *n* drama *mf*, dram *mf*

drama dràma *mf*

dramatic *adj* dràmadach/dràmatach

dramatist *n* sgrìobhaiche *m* dràma, dràmaire *m*

draught *n* (*liquid*) tarraing *f*, balgam *m*, sgailc *f*, steallag *f*

draughtboard *n* bòrd-dàmais *m*

draughts *n* (*game*) dàmais *f i*

draw *n* (*match etc*) geama ionannach *m*

draw *v* **1** (*pull*) tarraing *vti*, slaod *vti*, dragh *vt*; **2** *in exprs* **~ lots** cuir croinn, tilg croinn; **3** *in expr* **~ near** dlùthaich *vi*, teann *vi*

drawing *n* dealbh *mf*

drawing-pin *n* tacaid *f*, tacaid-balla *f*

dread *n* uamhann *m*, oillt *f*, uabhas *m*

dreadful *adj* oillteil; eagalach, uabhasach, sgriosail

dreadfully *adv*, uabhasach, eagalach, garbh

dream *n* bruadar *m*, aisling *f*

dream *v* bruadair *vi*

dreamer *n* aislingiche *m*

dreary *adj* **1** (*mournful*) tiamhaidh; **2** (*tedious*) slaodach

dregs *n* (*liquids*) grùid *f*

drench *v* drùidh *vi* air

drenched *adj & past part* drùidhte, bog fliuch

dress *n* **1** (*woman's*) dreasa *f*; **2** (*mode*) èideadh *m*

dress *v* **1** (*oneself*) cuir *vti* umad (*etc*); **2** (*someone else*) cuir aodach air; **3** *in expr* **~ up** sgeadaich *vt*

dresser *n* (*furniture*) dreasair *m*

dressing-gown *n* còta-leapa *m*

dried *adj & past part* **1** tiormaichte; **2** *in expr* **~ up** crìon, seac

drift *n* (*snow*) cuithe *f*, cathadh *m*

drift *v* (*snow*) rach *vi irreg* na chuithe, cath *vi*

drifter *n* (*fishing*) drioftair *m*

drill[1] *n* (*tool*) drile *f*, snìomhaire *m*, tolladair *m*

drill[2] *n* (*army etc*) drile *f*

drill[1] *v* toll *vt*

drill[2] *v* (*army etc*) drilich *vi*, dèan drile *f*
drink *n* deoch *f*
drink *v* **1** òl *vti*, gabh *vt*
drinker *n* pòitear *m*, misgear *m*
drinking *n* **1** (*general*) òl *m*; **2** (*alcoholic*) pòitearachd *f*
drip, **dripping** *n* **1** (*abstr & con*) sileadh *m*, snighe *m*; **2** (*sound*) gliog *m*
drive *n* **1** (*engin*) iomain *f*; **2** (*trip*) cuairt; **3** (*energy etc*) dèanadas *m*
drive *v* **1** (*vehicle*) dràibh *vti*, dràibhig *vti*; **2** (*machinery etc*) iomain *vt*
drivel *n* **1** seile *m*, ronn *m*; **2** (*nonsense etc*) amaideas *m*, sgudal *m*
driver *n*, (*vehicle*) dràibhear *m*
driving *n* (*vehicle*) dràibheadh *m*
drizzle *n* ciùbhran/ciùthran *m*
drizzle *v* braon *vi*
droll *adj* èibhinn, ait
drone[1] *n* (*bagpipe*) dos *m*
drone[2] *n* **1** (*bee*) seillean dìomhain *m*; **2** (*sound*) torman *m*
droning *n* torman *m*
droop *v* searg *vi*
drop *n* **1** boinne *f*, braon *m*, drùdhag *f*, boinneag *f*
drop *v* **1** (*as vi*) tuit *vi*; **2** (*as vt*) leig *vt* às; **3** (*release*) leag *vt*
drought *n* tiormachd *f*, tart *f*
drove *n* (*cattle*) dròbh *m*
drover *n* (*livestock*) dròbhair *m*
drown *v* **1** bàth *vt*
drowsy *adj* cadalach
drudge *n* tràill *mf*, sgalag *f*
drudgery *n* tràilleachd *f*, obair sgalaig *f*
drug *n* **1** (*medical*) cungaidh *f*, cungaidh-leighis *f*; **2** (*medical & illicit*) droga *f*
druid *n* draoidh *m*
drum *n* (*mus*) druma *mf*
drunk *adj* **1** air mhisg *f*, air an daoraich (*dat of* daorach *f*), leis an daoraich
drunkard *n* pòitear *m*, misgear *m*
drunkenness *n* daorach *f*, misg *f*, smùid *f*
dry *adj* **1** tioram; **2** (*from thirst*) pàiteach, tartmhor, ìotmhor; **3** *in exprs* ~ **spell** turadh *m*; **4** (*animal*) seasg
dry *v* **1** tiormaich *vti*; **2** *in expr* ~ **up** (*wither*) crìon *vti*
dryer *n* tiormadair *m*
dryness *n* **1** tiormachd *f*; **2** (*thirst*) pathadh *m*, tart *m*, ìota *m*
dual *adj* dùbailte

dubious *adj* **1** (*having doubts*) teagmhach, amharasach; **2** (*unreliable*) neo-earbsach, cugallach
duchess *n* ban-diùc *f*
duck *n* tunnag *f*, (*wild*) lach *f*
duck *v* (*in liquid*) tum *vt*
ducking *n* (*in liquid*) tumadh *m*
due *adj* **1** (*fitting*) dligheach, cubhaidh, iomchaidh; **2** *in expr* **in** ~ **course** ri tìde
due *n* (*what one is entitled to*) dlighe *f*, dleas *m*
duel *n* còmhrag-dithis *f*
duet *n* òran-dithis *m*
duke *n* diùc *m*
dull *adj* **1** (*light etc*) doilleir, ciar; **2** (*tedious*) liosda, slaodach
dull *v* **1** (*light etc*) doilleirich *vti*; **2** (*pain etc*) faothaich *vti*, lasaich *vt*
dulse *n* duileasg *m*
duly *adv* gu dligheach
dumb *adj* balbh
dumbness *n* balbhachd *f*
dump *n* **1** (*rubbish heap etc*) òtrach *m*; **2** (*place*) àite *m* grodach, àite *m* gun fheum
dun *adj* odhar, ciar, lachdann, riabhach
dunce *n* bumailear *m*, ùmaidh *m*, stalcaire *m*
dung *n* (*manure*) innear/inneir *f*, todhar *m*, buachar *m*
dunghill *n* dùnan *m*, siteag & sitig *f*, òtrach *m*
duodenum *n* beul a' chaolain *m*
dupe *v* thoir an car à, dèan foill air, cealg *vt*
duplicate *n* **1** mac-samhail *m*, lethbhreac *m*
duplicate *v* dèan mac-samhail de, dèan lethbhreac de
duplicity *n* cealg *f*, foill *f*
durable *adj* buan, maireannach
duration *n* fad *m*
during *prep* ann an, fad, ri
dusk *n* **1** duibhre *f*, eadar-sholas *m*, camhanaich *f* na h-oidhche, beul *m* na h-oidhche; **2** (*idiom*) **from dawn to** ~ o mhoch gu dubh
dust *n* duslach *m*, dust *m*, stùr *m*
dust *v* dustaig *vti*
dustbin *n* biona-sgudail *m*
duster *n* dustair *m*
dusty *adj* dustach, stùrach
Dutch *adj* Duitseach
Dutchman *n* Duitseach *m*

dutiful *adj* dleastanach
duty *n* **1** dleastanas *m*, dleas *m*; **2** (*tax*) cìs *f*
dwang *n* rong *m*, rongas *f*
dwarf *n* luchraban *m*, troich *mf*
dwell *v* **1** (*live*) fuirich *vi*, tàmh *vi*;
  2 (*inhabit*) tuinich *vi*, àitich *vt*, gabh
  còmhnaidh
dweller *n* neach-còmhnaidh *m*, neach-
  àiteachaidh *m*, tuiniche *m*

dwelling *n* còmhnaidh *f*; àite-còmhnaidh
  m, àite-fuirich *m*, fàrdach *f*
dye *n* dath *m*
dye *v* dath *vt*, cuir dath air
dyed *adj* dathte
dyke *n* gàrradh *m*
dynamic *adj* innsgineach
dynasty *n* gineal *mf*, cineal *m*, sliochd *m*

E

each *adj* **1** gach; **2** *as pron in expr* ~ **other** a chèile, cach-a-chèile; **3** (*per capita*) an urra

eager *adj* **1** (*endeavour etc*) dian; **2** (*person*) dealasach, èasgaidh

eagerness *n* dealas *m*, èasgaidheachd *f*, dealasachd *f*

eagle *n* iolair(e) *f*

ear *n* **1** cluas *f*; **2** (*idiom*) **give** ~ dèan èisteachd; **3** (*corn*) dias *f*

earache *n* grèim-cluaise *m*

eardrum *n* druma *mf* (na) cluaise, faillean *m*

earl *n* iarla *m*

earldom *n* iarlachd *f*

early *adj* moch, tràth

early *adv* **1** moch, tràth; **2** (*before set time*) tràth *adv*, ron mhithich, ron àm

earmark *n* comharradh-cluaise *m*

earmark *v* **1** (*livestock*) cuir comharradh-cluaise air; **2** (*general*) comharraich *vt*

earn *v* coisinn *vt*, buannaich *vt*

earnest *adj* **1** (*personality*) dùrachdach, stòlda; **2** *in exprs* **in**~ ann an da-rìribh

earnings *n* cosnadh *m*, tuarastal *m*

ear-ring *n* cluas-fhail *f*

earth *n* **1** (*planet*) an cruinne *mf*, an cruinne-cè *mf*, an talamh *m*; **2** (*ground*) talamh *m*, (*soil*) ùir *f*

earthly *adj* **1** talmhaidh *adj*; **2** (*temporal*) saoghalta, talmhaidh

earthquake *n* crith-thalmhainn *f*

earthworm *n* cnuimh-thalmhainn *f*, boiteag *f*

ear-wax *n* cèir-cluaise *f*

earwig *n* gòbhlag *f*, fiolan *m*, fiolan-gòbhlach *m*

ease *n* **1** fois *f*, socair *f*, *in expr* **take your** ~ gabh fois; **2** (*mood*) **at** ~ socair, socrach

ease *v* **1** (*suffering etc*) faothaich *vti*, lasaich *vt*; **2** (*bonds etc*) fuasgail *vt*

easel *n* sorchan-dealbha *m*

easier *comp adj* nas fhasa

easiest *sup adj*, as fhasa

easing *n* **1** (*pain etc*) faothachadh *m*, furtachd *f*; **2** (*bonds etc*) fuasgladh *m*

east *adj* sear *adj*, an ear *f*

east *adv* an ear *f*, sear *adv*

east *n* ear *f*

Easter *n* a' Chàisg

easterly *adj* an ear *f*

eastern *adj* an ear *f*

East Indies (the) *npl* Na h-Innseachan an Ear *fpl*

eastwards *adv* an ear, chun an ear, chun na h-àirde an ear

easy *adj* **1** furasta, soirbh, sìmplidh; **2** (*financially* ~) seasgair; **3** (*idioms*) **take things** ~ gabh *vi* air do (*etc*) s(h)ocair *f*, **take it** ~! air do shocair!

easy-going *adj* **1** (*patient*) foighidneach; **2** (*not disciplinarian*) ceadach; **3** (*nonchalant*) coma co-dhiù

eat *v* ith *vti*

eatable *adj* ion-ithe

eating *n* ithe(adh) *m*

eaves *n* anainn *f*

eavesdrop *v* dèan farchluais

eavesdropping *n* farchluais *f*

ebb *n* (*tide*) tràghadh *m*, traoghadh *m*

ebb *v* (*tide*) tràigh *vi*, traogh *vi*

eccentric *adj* (*behaviour*) neònach, às a' chumantas, rudanach

ecclesiastic, ecclesiastical *adj* eaglaiseil

ecclesiastic *n* eaglaiseach *m*, pears-eaglais *m*

echo *n* mac-talla *m*, sgailc-creige *f*

echo *v* ath-ghairm *vi*

eclectic *adj* ioma-sheòrsach

eclipse *n* dubhadh *m*

eclipse *v* duibhrich *vti*

economic *adj* (*related to economics*) eaconamach

economical *adj* **1** (*thrifty*) cunntach, caomhantach; **2** (*cheap*) cothromach, dòigheil

economics *n* eaconamachd *f*, eaconamas *m*

economise *v* caomhain *vti*, glèidh *vt*, sàbhail *vt*

economist *n* eaconamair *m*

economy *n* **1** eaconamaidh *m*; **2** *in exprs* **domestic** ~ taigheadas *m*, banas-taighe *m*

ecstasy n **1** (*the state*) mire f, meadhail f, meadhradh m; **2** (*drug*) eacstasaidh m

ecstatic adj air mhire

eddy n cuairteag f

edge n **1** iomall m, oir f; **2** (*of blade etc*) faobhar m

edgy adj clisgeach

edible adj ion-ithe

edict n riaghailt f, reachd m

edit v deasaich vt

editing n deasachadh m

edition n **1** (*abstr*) deasachadh m; **2** (*con*) clò-bhualadh m eagran m

editor n deasaiche m, neach-deasachaidh m

educate v foghlaim vt, teagaisg vt, thoir sgoil do

educated adj foghlaimte, foghlamaichte, ionnsaichte

education n foghlam m, ionnsachadh m, oideachas m, sgoil f

educational adj **1** (*providing education*) oideachail; **2** (*to do with education*) foghlaim

eel n easgann f

eerie adj iargalta, uaigealta

effect n **1** (*of action etc*) toradh m, buil f, buaidh f, èifeachd f; **2** (*impression*) drùidheadh m; **3** in expr **put into** ~ cuir vt an gnìomh

effective adj èifeachdach

effectiveness n èifeachdachd f, èifeachdas m

effects npl (*belongings*) sealbh/seilbh f

effeminacy n boireanntachd f

effeminate adj boireannta

effervescence n (*personal*) beothalas m

effervescent adj **1** (*liquid*) builgeanach; **2** (*personal*) beothail

efficiency n èifeachdachd f, èifeachdas m

efficient adj èifeachdach

effigy n ìomhaigh f

effluent n às-shruthadh m

effort n **1** (*abstr*) saothair f; **2** (*con*) oidhirp f, spàirn f

effrontery n ladarnas m, aghaidh f, bathais f

egalitarian adj co-ionannachail

egg n ugh m

egg-cup n gucag-uighe f

egg-shaped adj ughach

egg-white n gealagan m

ego n, *used with art*, **the** ~ am fèin m

egoist, egotist n fèinear m

egoism, egotism n fèineachd f

egotistical adj fèineil

Egypt n An Èipheit f

Egyptian n & adj Èipheiteach m

eiderdown n clòimhteachan m

eight numeral & adj **1** ochd; **2** (*people*) ochdnar mf

eighteen numeral & adj ochd-deug

eighth adj ochdamh

eighth n ochdamh m

eightsome n ochdnar mf

eighty num and adj ceithir fichead, ochdad m

either adv **1** nas motha; **2** in expr ~ ... **or** an dara/dàrna cuid ... no

eject v tilg vt a-mach, cuir vt a-mach

elaborate adj **1** (*involving much work*) saothrach; **2** (*detailed*) mionaideach; **3** (*multi-faceted*) iomadh-fhillte

elaborate v **1** (*develop*) innlich vt, tionnsgail vt, obraich vt a-mach; **2** (*give more detail*) leudaich vi

elastic adj sùbailte

elastic n lastaig f

elasticity n sùbailteachd f

elated adj & past part aoibhneach

elbow n uileann/uilinn f

elbow v uillnich vti, thoir ùpag(an) f do

elder[1] n **1** (*religious*) èildear m, foirfeach m; **2** (*older*) am fear/an tè as sine

elder[2] n (*tree*) ruis f, droman m

elect v tagh vt

elected adj & past part taghte

election n taghadh m

elector n neach-taghaidh m

electoral adj taghaidh

electorate n luchd-bhòtaidh m

electric adj dealain

electrical adj **1** dealain

electrician n dealanair m

electricity n dealan m

electrify v **1** (*lit*) dealanaich vt; **2** (*fig*) cuir gaoir air

electronic adj eileagtronaigeach, dealanach

elegance n grinneas m, snas m

elegant adj grinn, fìnealta, eireachdail

elegiac adj tuireach

elegy n cumha m, marbhrann m, tuireadh m

element n eileamaid f

elementary *adj* **1** bunaiteach; **2** (*simple*) sìmplidh

elevate *v* àrdaich *vt*

elevator *n* àrdaichear *m*

eleven *n and num adj* aon-deug

eligibility *n* ion-roghnachd *f*, freagarrachd *f*

eligible *adj* **1** ion-roghnach, freagarrach; **2** (*qualified*) uidheamaichte

eliminate *v* **1** (*expel*) thoir *vt* à, cuir *vt* a-mach à, geàrr *vt* às; **2** (*destroy*) cuir *vi* às do

elimination *n* **1** (*removal*) toirt *f* à, cur *m* a-mach à, gearradh *m* às; **2** (*destruction*) cur *m* às; **3** (*expulsion*) tilgeadh *m*, tilgeil *f*, toirt *f* air falbh

elision *n* (*gram*) bàthadh *m*

elm *n* leamhan *m*

elongate *v* sìn *vti*, fadaich *vti*

elope *v* teich *vi*

elopement *n* teicheadh *m*

eloquence *n* fileantachd *f*, deas-bhriathrachd *f*

eloquent *adj* fileanta, deas-bhriathrach, deas-labhrach

else *adj* **1** eile; **2** *in exprs* **anything ~** an còrr *m*

elucidate *v* mìnich *vt*, soilleirich *vt*

elucidation *n* mìneachadh *m*, soilleireachadh *m*

elusive *adj* doirbh a ghlacadh, doirbh a lorg

emaciated *adj* seang, seargte

e-mail *n* post-dealain *m*

emanate *v* thig a-mach à

emancipate *v* saor *vt*, fuasgail *vt*

emancipation *n* **1** (*action*) saoradh *m*, fuasgladh *m*; **2** (*state*) saorsa

emasculate *v* (*castrate*) spoth *vt*, geàrr *vt*

embargo *n* bacadh *m*

embark *v* **1** (*as vi*) rach *vi* air bòrd; **2** (*as vt*) cuir *vt* air bòrd; **3** *in expr* **~ on** (*undertake*), tòisich *vi* air, rach *vi* an sàs ann an, gabh *vt* os làimh

embarrass *v* **1** (*shame*) nàraich *vt*, tàmailtich *vt*, maslaich *vt*; **2** (*make uneasy*) cuir *vt* troimh-a-chèile, buair *vt*

embarrassed *adj & past part* **1** (*shamed*) nàrach; **2** (*uneasy*) troimh-a-chèile, air do (*etc*) b(h)uaireadh; **3** (*shy*) diùid, nàrach, air do (*etc*) nàrachadh

embarrassment *n* **1** (*shame*) nàire *f*, tàmailt *f*, masladh *m*; **2** (*uneasiness*) buaireas *m*; **3** (*shyness*) diùide *f*, nàire *f*

embassy *n* **1** (*abstr*) tosgaireachd *f*; **2** (*institution*) ambasaid *f*

embellish *v* maisich *vt*, sgeadaich *vt*, snuadhaich *vt*

embellishment *n* maiseachadh *m*, sgeadachadh *m*, snuadhachadh *m*

ember *n* èibhleag *f*

embitter *v* searbhaich *vt*

embittered *adj & past part* searbhta

emblem *n* suaicheantas *m*

embrace *v* **1** teannaich *v*; **2** (*include*) gabh *vt* a-steach; **3** (*adopt*) gabh *vi* ri

embroidery *n* **1** (*activity*) grèis *f*; **2** (*product*) obair-ghrèis(e) *f*

embryo *n* cruth *m*

emerald *n* smàrag *f*

emerge *v* **1** (*from place*) thig *vi* a-mach à; **2** (*become known*) thig *vi* am follais; **3** (*come to fore*) thig *vi irreg* an uachdar

emergency *n* **1** (*situation*) cruaidh-chàs *m*; **2** (*abstr*) èiginn *f*

emigrant *n* eilthireach *m*

emigrate *v* fàg do dhùthaich fhèin, rach *vi irreg* a-null thairis

emigration *n* às-imrich *f*

émigré *n* eilthireach *m*

eminence *n* **1** (*rank*) mòr-inbhe *f*; **2** (*topog*) àird(e) *f*

eminent *adj* **1** (*most important etc*) prìomh ; **2** (*distinguished*) inbheil

emit *v* cuir *vt* (a-mach), leig *vt* a-mach

emotion *n* faireachdainn *f*

emotional *adj* **1** (*of person*) gluaiste, (*troubled*) buairte; **2** (*event*) gluasadach, drùidhteach, (*troubling*) buaireasach

emotive *adj* gluasadach, drùidhteach, (*troubling*) buaireasach

empathy *n* co-fhaireachdainn *f*

emperor *n* ìompaire *m*

emphasis *n* cudrom *m*

emphasise *v* cuir/leig cudrom air

emphatic *adj* deimhinn(e), deimhinnte, cinnteach, làidir

empire *n* ìompaireachd *f*

employ *v* **1** (*use*) cleachd *vt*, iomair *vt*; **2** (*workers*) fastaich/fastaidh, *vt*, thoir obair do

employee *n* neach-obrach *m*, obraiche *m*, cosnaiche *m*

employer *n* fastaidhear *m*, fastaiche *m*

employment *n* **1** (*abstr*) cosnadh *m*, obair *f*; **2** (*act of employing*) fastadh *m*

empower *v* thoir ùghdarras do, thoir cumhachd do

empowered *adj & past part* ùghdarraichte

empress *n* ban-ìompaire *f*

emptiness *n* fal(a)mhachd *f*

empty *adj* **1** falamh; **2** (*place*) falamh, fàs; **3** (*without substance*) dìomhain

empty *v* **1** falmhaich *vt*; **2** (*liquids*) tràigh/ traogh *vt*, taom *vt*; **3** (*population*) fàsaich *vt*

empty-headed *adj* faoin

enable *v* cuir an comas, cuir air chomas do, thoir comas/cothrom do

enamel *n* cruan *m*

enchant *v* cuir *vt* fo gheasaibh

enchanted *adj & past part* seunta, fo gheasaibh

enchantment *n* **1** (*abstr*) geasachd *f*; **2** (*spell*) geas *f*

encircle *v* cuartaich *vt*

enclose *v* **1** cuartaich *vt*, iath *vt*; **2** (*corres etc*) cuir *vt* an cois, cuir *vt* an lùib

enclosed *adj & past part* **1** cuartaichte; **2** (*corres etc*) an cois, an lùib

enclosure *n* **1** (*action*) cuartachadh *m*, iathadh *m*; **2** (*enclosed area*) lann *f*, crò *m*

encompass *v* **1** (*encircle*) cuairtich *vt*; **2** (*embrace*) gabh *vt* a-steach

encourage *v* **1** (*raise spirits etc*) misnich *vt*; **2** (*urge*) cuir impidh air, brosnaich *vt*, coitich *vt*

encouragement *n* **1** (*raising of spirits etc*) misneachadh *m*; **2** (*urging*) brosnachadh *m*, coiteachadh *m*

encouraging *adj* misneachail, brosnachail

encumber *v* uallaich *vt*

encumbrance *n* uallach *m*, eallach *m*

end *n* **1** (*phys*) ceann *m*; **2** (*abstr*) deireadh *m*, crìoch *f*; **3** *in expr* on ~ an ceann a chèile, a sreath a chèile

end *v* **1** (*complete*) cuir crìoch air, thoir *vt* gu crìch, crìochnaich *vt*; **2** (*meeting etc*) dùin *vti*

endanger *v* cuir *vt* an cunnart

endangered *adj & past part* an cunnart

endearments *npl* faclan *mpl* gaoil, briathran *mpl* gaoil

endeavour *n* iomairt *f*, oidhirp *f*

endeavour *v* feuch *vi*, dèan iomairt, dèan oidhirp

ending *n* (*meeting etc*) co-dhùnadh *m*, crìoch *f*, deireadh *m*

endless *adj* **1** (*continual*) gun sgur *m*; **2** (*eternal*) sìorraidh, bith-bhuan

endorse *v* **1** (*cheque etc*) cuir ainm ri; **2** (*support*) cuir aonta ri

endurance *n* cruas *m*, cruadal *m*, fulang *m*, fulangas *m*

endure *v* **1** fuiling *vti*; **2** (*persist*) lean *vi*

enduring *adj* **1** (*persisting*) leantainneach; **2** (*eternal*) maireannach, buan, bith-bhuan

enemy *n* nàmhaid *m*

energetic *adj* lùthmhor, brìoghmhor, sgairteil

energy *n* **1** lùth *m*; **2** (*individuals*) lùth(s) *m*, brìgh *f*, spionnadh *m*, sgairt *f*

enfeeble *v* lagaich *vti*, fannaich *vi*

enforce *v* cuir *vt* an gnìomh

engage *v* dèan *vt*, bi *vi irreg* an sàs

engaged *adj & past part*, **1** (*phone etc*) trang

engagement *n* **1** (*betrothal*) gealladh-pòsaidh *m*; **2** (*appointment etc*) coinneamh *f*

engine *n* einnsean *m*

engineer *n* einnseanair *m*, innleadair *m*

engineer *v* innlich *vt*

engineering *n* einnseanaireachd *f*, innleadaireachd *f*

English *adj* Sasannach

English *n* **1** (*lang*) Beurla *f*; **2** (*people*) the ~ na Sasannaich *mpl*

engrave *v* gràbhail *vt*

engraver *n* gràbhalaiche *m*

engraving *n* gràbhaladh *m*, gràbhalachd *f*

enhance *v* **1** (*increase*) meudaich *vt*; **2** (*improve*) leasaich *vt*

enhancement *n* **1** (*increase*) meudachadh *m*; **2** (*improvement*) leasachadh *m*

enigma *n* tòimhseachan *m*

enjoy *v* **1** gabh tlachd ann an, meal *vt*; còrd *vi* ri

enjoyable *adj* **1** tlachdmhor; **2** a chòrdas riut

enjoyment *n* tlachd *f*, toil-inntinn *f*, toileachas *m*

enlarge *v* **1** (*as vt*) meudaich *vt*, leudaich *vt*; **2** (*as vi*) rach *vi irreg* am meud, leudaich *vi*

enlarged *adj* meudaichte, leudaichte

enlargement *n* meudachadh *m*, leudachadh *m*

enlighten *v* soilleirich *vt*

enlightened *adj & past part* (*aware*)
tuigseach, toinisgeil, saor-inntinneach

enlightenment *n* soilleireachadh *m*,
soillseachadh *m*

enlist *v* (*in forces*) liostaig *vi*, gabh *vi* san
arm

enliven *v* beothaich *vt*, brosnaich *vt*, brod
vt

enmity *n* nàimhdeas *m*

ennoble *v* uaislich *vt*

enormous *adj* ro-mhòr, uabhasach mòr,
eagalach mòr

enough *n* **1** gu leòr *adv*, leòr *f*; **2** foghain *vi*

enquire *v* faighnich *vi* de/do

enquiry *n* **1** ceist *f*; **2** (*investigation*)
rannsachadh *m*, faighneachd *f*

enrage *v* cuir an fhearg air, feargaich *vt*

enraged *adj & past part* air bhoile, air
bhàinidh, air chuthach

enrich *v* **1** beartaich & beairtich *vi*,
saidhbhrich *vt*; **2** (*soil*) mathaich *vt*

enrol clàraich *vti*

enrolment *n* clàrachadh *m*

en route air an t-slighe

enslave *v* tràillich *vt*

enslavement *n* **1** (*abstr*) tràilleachd *f*;
2 (*enslaving*) tràilleachadh *m*

ensnare *v* rib *vt*, glac *vt* (ann an ribe)

entangle *v* amail *vt*, aimhreitich *vt*

enter *v* **1** rach/thig a-steach do, inntrig *vi*;
2 (*keyboard etc*) put *vt* ann an, cuir *vti*
a-steach

enterprise *n* iomairt *f*

enterprising *adj* iomairteach,
ionnsaigheach, gnìomhach

entertainment *n* **1** dìbhearsain *m*;
2 (*hospitality*) fèisteas *m*

enthusiasm *n* **1** (*general*) dealas *m*;
2 (*particular*) dèidhealachd *f*

enthusiastic *adj* **1** (*general*) dealasach;
2 (*particular*) dèidheil

entice *v* meall *vt*, tàlaidh *vt*, breug *vt*

enticement *n* mealladh *m*, tàladh *m*

enticing *adj* meallach, tàlaidheach

entire *adj* **1** (*undivided*) iomlan, slàn; **2** (*in
entirety*) gu lèir, air fad

entirely *adv* gu tur, gu buileach, gu
h-iomlan, uile-gu-lèir

entitled *adj & past part* airidh air

entitlement *n* **1** (*abstr*) dlighe *f*, dleas
m, còir *f*, airidheachd *f*; **2** (*amount*)
cuibhreann *mf*

entrails *n* **1** mionach *m*, innidh *f*;
2 (*animal*) greallach *f*

entrance *n* **1** (*abstr*) teachd-a-steach *m*,
inntrigeadh *m*; **2** (*con*) rathad-inntrigidh
m, slighe-inntrigidh *f*; **3** (*admission*)
inntrigeadh *m*

entrant *n* **1** (*competition*) farpaiseach *m*;
2 (*exam*) deuchainniche *m*

entreat *v* guidh *vi* air, iarr *vi* gu dian air,
cuir *vt* impidh air

entreaty *n* guidhe *mf*, impidh *f*

entrepreneur *n* neach-iomairt *m*

entrust *v* earb *vt* ri, cuir cùram air, leig
vt le

entry *n* **1** (*abstr*) inntrigeadh *m*, teachd-a-
steach *m*; **2** (*con*) doras/rathad-inntrigidh
m; **3** (*tenement*) clobhsa *m*

entwine *v* suain *vt*

entwined *adj & past part* air suaineadh,
fillte; air amaladh

enunciate *v* cuir *vt* an cèill

envelop *v* paisg *vt*, suain *vt*

envelope cèis-litreach

envious *adj* farmadach

environment *n* àrainneachd *f*

envoy *n* tosgaire *m*

envy *n* farmad *m*, tnù(th) *m*

envy *v* gabh farmad *m* ri

ephemeral *adj* diombuan, siùbhlach

epicentre *n* teis-meadhan *m*

epilogue *n* dùnadh *m*, faclan-dùnaidh *mpl*

episcopal *adj* easbaigeach

Episcopalian *nm & adj* Easbaigeach

episode *n* earrann *f*

epitaph *n* marbhrann *m*

equal *adj* co-ionann/co-ionnan

equal *n* coimeas *m*, mac-samhail *m*, seis(e)
m

equal *v* ionann is, co-ionann

equality *n* co-ionannachd *f*

equanimity *n* socair-inntinn *f*

equation *n* (*maths*) co-aontar *m*

equator *n* am meadhan-chearcall *m*

equidistant *adj* co-astarail

equilibrium *n* meidh *f*, cothrom *m*

equip *v* uidheamaich *vt*

equipment uidheam *f*, acainn *f*

equipped *adj* uidheamaichte, acainneach

equitable *adj* cothromach, dìreach, gun
chlaonadh *m*

equivalence *n* co-ionannachd *f*

equivalent *adj* co-ionann

equivocal *adj* dà-sheaghach
era *n* linn *f*
eradicate *v* cuir às do, spìon *vt* (às a (*etc*) b(h)un)
erase *v* dubh *vt* às
erect *adj* dìreach
erect *v* tog *vt*
erode *v* criom *vt*, cnàmh *vt*, bleith *vt*
erosion *n* criomadh *m*, cnàmhadh *m*, bleith *f*
err *v* rach *vi* air iomrall, rach *vi* air seachran, dèan mearachd
errand *n* teachdaireachd *f* gnothach *m*
erratic *adj* neo-chunbhalach, caochlaideach, carach, luasganach
erring *adj* seachranach
erroneous *adj* mearachdach, iomrallach
error *n* **1** (*abstr*) iomrall *m*; **2** (*con*) mearachd *f*
erudite *adj* foghlaimte, foghlamaichte
erudition *n* sgoilearachd *f*
erupt *v* **1** brùchd *vt*; **2** (*volcanic*) spreadh *vi*
eruption *n* **1** brùchdadh *m*; **2** (*of volcanic*) spreadhadh *m*
escape *n* **1** (*abstr*) teicheadh *m*, tàrradh/tàireadh *m* às; **2** (*means*) dol-às *m*
escape *v* teich *vi*, tàrr/tàir *vi* às
escort *n* (*guard etc*) coimheadach *m*, freiceadan *m*, faire *f*
escort *v* **1** (*accompany*) rach *vi* còmhla ri; **2** (*under supervision*) thoir *vt irreg* gu
especially *adv* **1** (*qualifying adj/adv*) air leth; **2** (*particular*) gu h-àraidh, gu sònraichte
espouse *v* taobh *vi* ri
essay *n* aiste *f*
essayist *n* aistear *m*
essence *n* brìgh *f*, sùgh *m*
essential *adj* **1** (*indispensable*) riatanach, deatamach, do-sheachainte; **2** (*fundamental*) bunaiteach
establish *v* **1** (*inaugurate*) stèidhich *vt*, cuir *vt* air b(h)onn, cuir *vt* air chois; **2** (*demonstrate*) dearbh *vt*
establishment *n* **1** (*abstr*) stèidheachadh *m*, cur *m* air b(h)onn, cur air chois; **2** (*con*) ionad *m*
estate *n* **1** (*landed*) oighreachd *f*; **2** (*housing*) ionad-thaighean *m* sgeamathaighean *m*
esteem *n* meas *m*, urram *m*, onair *f*
esteem *v* meas *vt*

esteemed, estimable *adj* measail, urramach, miadhail
estimate *n* meas *m*, tuaiream *f*, tuairmeas *m*, tuairmse *f*
estimate *v* **1** meas *vt*, thoir tuaiream air; **2** (*value*) cuir luach air
estuary *n* beul-aibhne *m*, inbhir *m*
eternal *adj* maireannach, sìorraidh, bith-bhuan, sìor-mhaireannach
eternity *n* sìorraidheachd *f*
ethereal *adj* adharail, spioradail, neo-chorporra
ethical *adj* beusail, eiticeil
ethics *n* beus-eòlas *m*, beusalachd *f*, eitic *f*
ethnic *adj* (*relating to ethnicity*) cinealach
ethnicity *n* cinealachd *f*
ethos *n* **1** (*essential feature(s)*) brìgh *f*, susbaint *f*; **2** (*rationale*) feallsanachd *f*
etymology *n* **1** (*discipline*) freumh-fhaclachd *f*; **2** (*particular*) freumh *m*, bun *m*, tùs *m*
eulogy *n* moladh
euro *n* euro *mf*
Europe *n* An Roinn Eòrpa *f*, Eòrpa *f*
European *adj & n* Eòrpach, na Roinn Eòrpa
evacuate *v* falmhaich *vt*, (*people*) fàsaich *vt*
evacuation *n* falmhachadh *m*, (*people*) fàsachadh *m*
evacuee *n* fògrach *m*, neach-fuadain *m*
evade *v*, siolp *vi* air falbh, èalaidh *vi* às, èalaidh *vi* air falbh
evaluate *v* **1** (*value*) luachaich *vt*, cuir luach air; **2** (*general*) meas *vt*
evaluation *n* **1** (*monetary*) luachachadh & luachadh *m*; **2** (*general*) measadh *m*
evaporate *v* deataich *vi*
evaporation *n* deatachadh *m*
evasive *adj* (*person*) mì-fhosgarra, fiar
eve *n* oidhche *f*
even *adj* **1** (*surface etc*) còmhnard, rèidh; **2** (*not odd*) cothrom; **3** (*steady*) cunbhalach, cothromach; **4** (*equal*) co-ionann
even *adv* eadhon, fiù is/agus, uiread is/agus
even-handed *adj* cothromach
evening *n* feasgar *m*, **good ~!** feasgar math!
event *n* **1** (*occurrence*) tachartas *m*, tuiteamas *m*; **2** (*sports etc*) co-fharpais *f*
eventful *adj* tachartach

eventuality n (*circumstance*) cor m
eventually adv aig a' cheann m thall, mu dheireadh thall, luath no mall
ever adv 1 (*with neg v*) gu bràth tuilleadh; 2 *in expr* **for** ~ gu bràth, gu sìorraidh, a-chaoidh
evergreen adj sìor-uaine
everlasting adj maireannach
every adj a h-uile, gach
everybody, **everyone** pron a h-uile duine m, na h-uile pron
everyday adj làitheil
everything n a h-uile càil, a h-uile sìon, gach (aon) rud, gach (aon) nì
evict v cuir vt a-mach (à)
evidence n 1 (*testimony*) fianais f, teisteanas m; 2 (*proof*) dearbhadh m
evident adj follaiseach, soilleir
evidentness n follais f
evil adj olc
evil n donas m, olc m
evil-natured, **evil-tempered** adj droch-nàdarrach
evolution n meanbh-chinneas m, mùthadh m
evolve v 1 (*life*) mùth vi; 2 (*develop*) atharraich vi (mean air mhean)
ewe n caora f
exact adj 1 (*accurate*) ceart, (*figures etc*) cruinn, grinn; 2 (*person*) pongail, mionaideach
exactly adv dìreach
exalt v àrdaich vt, cuir vt an àirde
examination n 1 (*educational etc*) deuchainn f; 2 (*medical etc*) sgrùdadh m
examine v 1 (*educational etc*) ceasnaich vt, thoir deuchainn do; 2 (*medical etc*) sgrùd vt, dèan sgrùdadh air
examinee n deuchainniche m
examiner n 1 sgrùdaiche m; 2 (*educational etc* ~) neach-ceasnachaidh m
example n eisimpleir m
exasperate v leamhaich vt
exasperated adj & past part frionasach, diombach, sàraichte
exasperating adj frionasach, leamh
exceed v rach vi irreg thairis, rach seachad air
exceedingly adv anabarrach, ro- *prefix*, uabhasach (fhèin), cianail fhèin
excellence n feabhas m, òirdheirceas m

excellent adj air leth, air leth math, math dha-rìribh, barrail, òirdheirc
exception n, *in expr* **with the** ~ **of** ach a-mhàin
exceptional adj air leth, às a' chumantas
excess n, cus m, tuilleadh 's a chòir
excessive adj 1 cus m; 2 ro- *prefix*
excessively adv ro
exchange n 1 (*general*) malairt f, iomlaid f; 2 (*currency*) iomlaid f
Exchequer, the n Roinn f an Ionmhais
excite 1 (*emotions*) tog vt; 2 (*people*) brod vt, gluais vt, spreòd vt, cuir vt air bhioran; 3 (*sexually*) brod vt
excited adj & past part air bhioran, togarrach, meanmnach
excitement n togarrachd f, meanmnachd f
exclamation n 1 clisgeadh m; 2 (*gram*) clisgear m
exclude v cùm vt bho/o, dùin vt a-mach (à)
exclusion n dùnadh m a-mach, às-dhùnadh m
excrement n cac m
excursion n cuairt f, sgrìob f
excuse n leisgeul m
excuse v 1 gabh leisgeul do, math vt do; 2 (*excl*) ~ **me!** gabh(aibh) mo leisgeul!; 3 (*allow*) thoir cead (do)
execute v 1 (*task etc*) thoir vt gu buil, gnìomhaich vt; 2 (*kill*) cuir vt gu bàs
executive adj gnìomhach
executive n 1 gnìomhaiche m; 2 **the** ~ an roinn-gnìomha f
exempt adj saor (bho/o), neo-bhuailteach (do)
exempt v saor vt (bho/o)
exemption n saoradh m (bho/o)
exercise n eacarsaich f
exercise v 1 (*make use of*) cleachd vt; 2 (*put into effect*) cuir vt an gnìomh; 3 (*take exercise*) bi vi irreg ag eacarsaich
exhaust n (*engine*) tràghadh/traoghadh m
exhaust v 1 (*person*) claoidh vt; 2 (*use up*) caith vt
exhausted adj & past part 1 (*person*) claoidhte; 2 (*resources etc*) caithte, cosgte
exhaustion n 1 (*people*) claoidheachd f; 2 (*resources etc*) caithteachd f caitheamh m
exhibit v 1 seall vt; 2 (*art etc*) taisbean/taisbein vt

exhibition n 1 (*art etc*) taisbeanadh m

exhilarate v cuir aoibhneas/sunnd air, sunndaich vt

exhort v brosnaich vt, earalaich vt

exhortation n brosnachadh m, earail f, earalachadh m

exile n 1 (*abstr*) eilthireachd f; 2 (*person*) neach-fuadain m, fòg(ar)rach m, eilthireach m

exile v fuadaich vt, fògair vt

exist v 1 bi vi irreg ann; 2 (*live*) mair vi beò, bi vi irreg beò

existence n 1 (*abstr*) bith f; 2 (*life*) beatha f

exit n doras dol a-mach m, slighe dol a-mach f

exonerate v saor vt o choire f

exotic adj allmharach, coigreach

expand v 1 leudaich vti, meudaich vti; 2 (*swell*) sèid vi, at vi

expanded adj 1 leudaichte, meudaichte; 2 (*swollen*) sèidte, air sèid(eadh)

expansion n 1 leudachadh m, meudachadh m; 2 (*swelling*) sèideadh m

expect v 1 (*anticipate*) coimhead vi ri; 2 (*suppose, await*) bi vi irreg an dùil

expectation n dùil f, fiughair f

expedient adj iomchaidh, freagarrach

expedient n innleachd f, seòl m

expedition n turas m

expel v fògair vt, cuir vt a-mach (à)

expenditure n teachd-a-mach m, caiteachas m

expense n cosgais f

expensive adj cosgail, daor

experience v 1 (*sensations etc*) mothaich vt; 2 (*know*) fiosraich vt

experience n eòlas m

experienced adj eòlach, fiosrach, cleachdte

experiment n deuchainn f, dearbhadh m

expert adj 1 (*knowledgeable*) eòlach; 2 (*at tasks etc*) teòma

expert n (*person*) eòlaiche m

expertise n 1 (*knowledge*) eòlas m; ealantachd f, teòmachd f

expiation n rèite f

expire v 1 (*breathe*) analaich vi; 2 (*die*) bàsaich vi, caochail vi

explain v mìnich vt, soilleirich vt

explanation n mìneachadh m, soilleireachadh m

explanatory adj mìneachail

explode v spreadh vti

exploit n euchd m, cleas m, plòidh f

exploit v 1 dèan feum m (de), thoir brìgh f (à); 2 (*unfairly*) gabh brath air, gabh fàth air

explore v rannsaich vt

explorer n rannsachair m

explosion n spreadhadh m

explosive adj (*short-tempered*) cas

explosive(s) n(pl) stuth-spreadhaidh m

export n 1 (*abstr*) às-mhalairt f; 2 (*con*) às-bhathar m

export v às-mhalairtich vti, reic vt an cèin

exporter n às-mhalairtear m

expose v leig vt (ris), thoir vt am follais, (*body*) rùisg vt

exposed adj ris, rùisgte, nochdte

exposition n cunntas m, mìneachadh m

exposure n 1 (*baring*) leigeil m ris, toirt f am follais, (*body*) rùsgadh m; 2 (*aspect*) sealladh-aghaidh m

express adj 1 (*rapid*) luath; 2 (*deliberate*) a dh'aon ghnothach, a dh'aon rùn

express n (*train*) luath-thrèana f

express v cuir vt an cèill

expression n 1 (*facial*) fiamh m, mèinn f, coltas m; gnùis f; 2 (*lang*) abairt f, dòigh-labhairt f; 3 (*expressing*) cur m an cèill

expressly adv a dh'aon ghnothach, a dh'aon rùn

extend v 1 (*increase*) leudaich vti; 2 (*stretch*) sìn (a-mach) vti

extended adj 1 (*increased*) leudaichte; 2 (*stretched out*) sìnte (a-mach)

extension n 1 (*increase*) leudachadh m; 2 (*stretching out*) sìneadh m

extensive adj 1 (*sizeable*) farsaing, leathann, mòr; 2 (*non-intensive*) sgaoilte

extent n 1 (*phys*) farsaingeachd f; 2 (*degree etc*) meud m

exterior n (an) taobh a-muigh

external adj (*phys*) an taoibh a-muigh

extinct adj marbh, à bith

extinguish smà(i)l vt (às), cuir vt às, mùch vt, tùch vt

extinguisher n smàladair m, mùchadair m

extract n earrann f

extract v thoir vt às, tarraing vt às

extraordinary adj às a' chumantas, air leth

extravagant adj caith(t)each

extreme *adj* **1** anabarrach, ro- ;
  2 (*exceptional*) air leth
extreme *n* (*eg of climate*) anabarr *m*
extremely *adv* anabarrach, air leth, ro-
extremity *n* **1** (*area*) iomall *m*, crìoch *f*;
  2 (*line*) ceann *m*; **3** (*crisis etc*) èiginn *f*
exuberance *n* suilbhireachd *f*
exuberant *adj* suilbhir

eye *n* **1** sùil *f*
eyeball *n* clach *f* na sùla
eyebrow *n* mala *f*
eyelash *n* fabhra *m*, rosg *m*
eyelid *n* fabhra *m*
eyesight *n* fradharc/radharc *m*, lèirsinn *f*
eyewitness *n* sùil-fhianais *f*

F

fable *n* uirsgeul *m*, fionnsgeul *m*
façade *n* **1** (*building etc*) aghaidh *f*;
  2 (*pretence*) sgàil *f*
face *n* (*person*) aodann *m*, aghaidh *f*, ~ **to**
  ~ aghaidh ri aghaidh
face *v* **1** (*turn towards*) cuir aghaidh ri;
  2 (*be orientated towards*) bi *vi irreg*
  mu choinneimh (*with gen*), bi *vi irreg* fa
  chomhair; **3** *in expr* ~ **up to** seas *vi* ri
facility *n* **1** goireas *m*; **2** (*flair*) alt *m*
facing *adv* mu choinneimh, fa chomhair
facsimile *n* mac-samhail *m*, lethbhreac *m*
fact *n* fìrinn *f*, rud *m*
factor[1] *n* (*estate etc*) bàillidh *m*, maor *m*
factor[2] *n* (*aspect*) adhbhar *m*, eileamaid *f*
faculty *n* comas *m*
fade *v* crìon *vti*
fail *v* **1** (*as vi*) fàillig *vi*, rach *vi* fodha; **2** (*as
  vt*) fàillig *vt*; **3** (*health*) rach *vi* bhuaithe
failing *n* fàilligeadh *m*, fàillinn *f*
failure *n* fàilligeadh *m*
faint *adj* fann, lag
faint *n* neul *m*, laigse *f*
faint *v* fannaich *vi*, fanntaig *vi*, rach *vi irreg*
  an laigse, rach *vi irreg* an neul
faint-hearted *adj* meata
fair *adj* **1** (*complexion*) bàn; **2** (*just*)
  cothromach, reusanta; **3** (*attractive*)
  bòidheach, maiseach
fair *n* (*market*) fèill *f*, faidhir *f*
fair-haired *adj* bàn
fairly *adv* **1** (*quite*) car *m*, caran *m*, an ìre
  mhath; **2** (*justly*) gu cothromach
fairy *n* sìthiche *m*, bean-sìth(e) *f*
faith *n* creideamh *m*
faithful *adj* dìleas
faithfulness *n* dìlseachd *f*
faithless *adj* mì-dhìleas
fake *adj* fuadain, brèige
fake *n* **1** (*dissembler etc*) mealltair *m*,
  cealgair(e) *m*; **2** (*object*) rud *m* brèige
fall[1] *n* tuiteam *m*
fall[2] *n* (*autumn*) foghar *m*
fall *v* **1** tuit *vi*,; **2** (*rest*) laigh *vi*; **3** *in exprs* ~
  into disuse rach *vi irreg* à cleachdadh, ~
  out (*ie quarrel*) rach *vi irreg* thar a chèile,
  rach *vi irreg* a-mach air a chèile

fallow *adj* bàn
falls *n* (*waterfall*) eas *m*, leum-uisge *m*,
  linne *f*, spùt *m*
false *adj* **1** (*deceitful etc*) meallta,
  mealltach, fallsa; **2** (*artificial*) fuadain,
  brèige; **3** (*wrong*) ceàrr
fame *n* cliù *m*, glòir *f*
familiar *adj* **1** (*knowledgeable*) eòlach;
  2 (*accustomed*) cleachdte; **3** (*frequently
  met with*) cumanta, gnàthach
familiarity *n* eòlas *m*
family *n* **1** (*immediate*) teaghlach *m*;
  2 (*extended*) càirdean (*pl of* caraid *m*),
  daoine (*pl of* duine *m*), cuideachd *f*
famine *n* gort(a) *f*
famous *adj* ainmeil, cliùiteach, iomraiteach
fan *m* (*for ventilation etc*) gaotharan *m*
fancy *v* bi *v irreg* airson, iarr *vt*
fancy dress *n* culaidh-choimheach *f*
fank *n* faing *f*, fang *m*
far *adj & adv* **1** (*distant*) fad(a); **2** (*time*)
  in expr **so** ~ gu ruige seo, chun a seo;
  3 (*intensifier*) fada
faraway *adj* fad' air falbh, cèin
fare[1] *n* (*charge*) faradh *m*
fare[2] *n* (*provisions*) biadh *m*, lòn *m*
farewell *n* **1** cead *m*; **2** (*as excl*) ~! soraidh
  f leat/leibh!, beannachd *f* leat/leibh!, slàn
  leat/leibh!
far-fetched *adj* (a thèid) thar na fìrinn
farm *n* tuathanas *m*
farmer *n* tuathanach *m*
farming *n* **1** (*activity*) tuathanachas *m*;
  2 (*subject*) àiteachas *m*
fascinated *adj* fo gheasaibh
fashion *n* fasan *m*
fashion *v* cum *vt*, dealbh *vt*
fashionable *adj* fasanta, san fhasan
fast *adj* luath
fast *n* trasg *f*, trasgadh *m*
fast *v* bi *vi irreg* na do thrasg, traisg *vi*
fasten *v* ceangail *vt*
fastening *n* ceangal *m*
fast-flowing *adj* cas, bras
fastidious *adj* òrraiseach
fat *adj* reamhar, sultmhor
fat *n* **1** crèis *f*, geir *f*, saill *f*; **2** (*body*) sult *m*

fatal *adj* marbhtach
fate *n* dàn *m*, crannchur *m*
fated *adj* an dàn
father *n* athair *m*
father-in-law *m* athair-cèile *m*
fatten *v* reamhraich *vti*
fatty *adj* crèiseach
faucet *n* goc *m*
fault *n* 1 (*person/object*) fàillinn *f*, gaoid *f*; 2 (*object*) easbhaidh *f*, cearb *f*; 3 (*moral*) meang *f*; 4 (*geological etc*) sgàineadh *m*; 5 (*action*) ciont(a) *m*; 6 *in exprs* **at ~** coireach, ciontach
favour *n* fàbhar *m*, seirbheis *f*, bàidh *f*
favour *v* 1 (*side with*) cùm taobh ri; 2 (*prefer*) is *v irreg & def* fheàrr le
favourable *adj* fàbharach
favourite *adj* as fheàrr le
fawn *adj* odhar
fawn *n* mang *f*
fawn *v* dèan miodal, dèan sodal
fawning *n* miodal *m*, sodal *m*
fax *n* facs *m*
fax *v* cuir *vti* mar fhacs
fear *n* 1 eagal/feagal *m*, fiamh *m*; 2 *in expr* **for ~ that** air eagal is, mus/mun *conj*
fearful *adj* eagalach
feasibility *n* ion-dhèantachd *f*
feasible *adj* ion-dhèanta
feast *n* 1 (*banquet*) cuirm *f*, fèisd *f*, fleadh *m*; 2 (*relig*) fèill *f*
feast-day *n* latha-fèille *m*
feat *n* euchd *m*, cleas *m*
feather *n* ite *f*
feathered *adj* iteach, iteagach
feature *n* (*characteristic*) feart *m*
February *n* an Gearran *m*
fecund *adj* torrach
fee *n* (*charge*) tuarastal *m*
feeble *adj* fann, lag, lapach, meata
feeble-minded *adj* lag san inntinn
feed *v* 1 (*give food*) biath *vt*, beathaich *vt*; 2 (*eat*) gabh *vt* biadh
feel *v* 1 fairich *vti*; 2 (*be conscious of*) mothaich *vt*; 3 (*touch etc*) làimhsich *vt*
feeling *adj* mothachail
feeling *n* 1 (*phys*) faireachdainn *f*; 2 (*abstr*) mothachadh *m*; 3 (*act*) faireachdainn, mothachadh *m*
fell *v* leag *vt* (gu làr *m*)
fellow *n* fear *m*, gille *m*, balach *m*, duine *m*, creutair *m*

fellow- *prefix* co-
fellowship *n* 1 (*friendship*) comann *m*, cuideachd *f*, caidreabh *m*, conaltradh *m*; 2 (*association etc*) comann *m*, caidreabh *m*
female *n* (*human*) boireannach *m*, tè *f*
female *adj* boireann
feminine *adj* 1 boireannta; 2 (*gram*) boireann
fence *n* feansa *f*, callaid *f*
fern(s) *n* raineach *f*
ferocious *adj* garg
ferocity *n* gairge *f*
ferret *n* feòcallan *m*
fertile *adj* torrach
fertilisation *n* torachadh *m*, sìolachadh *m*
fertilise *v* 1 (*ground*) leasaich *vt*, mathaich *vt*; 2 (*embryo*) toraich *vt*
fertilised *adj* torrach
fertiliser *n* leasachadh *m*, mathachadh *m*
fertility *n* torachas *m*
fervent *adj* (*person*) dùrachdach, (*person/emotions etc*) dian
fervour *n* dèine *f*
festival *n* 1 fèis; 2 (*relig*) fèill *f*
festive *adj* cuirmeach
fetch *v* faigh *vt*
fetter *n* geimheal *m*
fetter *v* geimhlich *vt*
fettle *n*, *in expr* **in fine ~** ann an deagh thriom, air a (*etc*) d(h)òigh
feud *n* falachd *f*, connsachadh *m*
fever *n* fiabhras *m*, teasach *m*
few *adj*, *in exprs* **very ~** glè bheag
few *n* beagan *m*, grunnan *m*
fickle *adj* caochlaideach, carach, luaineach
fiction *n* ficsean *m*, uirsgeul *m*
fictional, fictitious *adjs* uirsgeulach
fiddle *n* fidheall *f*
fiddler *n* fidhlear *m*
fidelity *n* dìlseachd *nf*
fidgety *adj* luasganach
field *n* 1 achadh *m*, pàirc(e) *f*, raon *m*; 3 (*area of knowledge etc*) raon *m*
field glasses prosbaig *f*
fiendish *adj* diabhlaidh
fierce *adj* 1 (*contest etc*) dian; 2 (*person*) garg, fiadhaich
fierceness *n* gairge *f*
fifteen *n and num adj* còig-deug
fifth *n* còigeamh
fifth *num adj* còigeamh

fifty *n and num adj* leth-cheud *m*, caogad *m*

fig *n* fìogais *f*, fìge *f*

fight *n* **1** (*phys*) sabaid *f*, còmhrag *f*, tuasaid *f*; **2** (*verbal*) trod *m*; **3** (*abstr*) strì *f*

fight *v* **1** sabaid *vi*, gleac *vi*; **2** (*verbally*) troid *vi*

fighting *n* sabaid *f*, còmhrag *f*

fig-tree *n* crann-fìogais *m*, crann-fìge *m*

figurative *adj* figearach

figure *n* **1** (*shape*) cruth *m*, dealbh *mf*; **2** (*physique*) dèanamh *m*; **3** (*arith etc*) àireamh *f*, figear *m*

file[1] *n* (*metalwork etc*) eighe *f*

file[2] *n* (*paperwork etc*) faidhle *m*

fill *n* làn *m*, leòr *f*

fill *v* lìon *vti*

filled *adj* lìonta

filler *n* lìonadair *m*

filly *n* loth *f*

film *n* **1** (*covering*) sgàil(e) *f*; **2** (*cinema etc*) film *m*

filter *n* sìol(t)achan *m*

filter *v* sìolaidh *vti*

filtering, filtration *n* sìoladh *m*

filth *n* salchar *m*

filthy *adj* salach

fin *n* ite *f*

final *adj* deireannach

finally *adv* **1** (*eventually*) aig deireadh an là, aig a' cheann thall; **2** (*at long last*) mu dheireadh thall

finance *n* ionmhas *m*

financial *adj* ionmhasail

find *v* **1** faigh *vt irreg*, lorg *vt*, faigh lorg air; **2** ~ **out** (*discover*) faigh *vt* a-mach

fine *adj* **1** (*texture etc*) mìn; **2** (*appearance etc*) gasta, àlainn, brèagha, grinn; **3** (*weather*) math, brèagha; **4** (*as excl*) ~! taghta!; **5** (*excellent*) glan, gasta; **6** (*health/ spirits*) air dòigh *f*, gu dòigheil

fine *n* unnlagh *m*, càin *f*

finger *n* corrag *f*, meur *f*

finger *v* làimhsich *vt*

fingerprint *n* meur-lorg *f*

finish *v* cuir crìoch air, crìochnaich *vt*

finished *adj & past part* **1** (*task etc*) coileanta, crìochnaichte; **2** (*person*) deiseil, ullamh

finite *adj* crìoch(n)ach

Finland *n* An Fhionnlainn *f*

fir *n* giuthas *m*, *in expr* ~ **cone** durcan *m*

fire *n* **1** teine *m*; **2** *in expr* ~ **engine** einnsean-smàlaidh *m*

fire *v* **1** (*firearm*) tilg *vt*, leig *vt*, loisg *vti*; **2** (*dismiss*) cuir *vt* à dreuchd

fire-extinguisher *n* inneal-smàlaidh *m*

fireplace *n* teallach *m*, teinntean *m*

fireside *n* cagailt *f*, taobh *m* an teine, teallach *m*

firm *adj* **1** (*constant*) cunbhalach; **2** (*solid*) teann, daingeann; **3** (*in character*) duineil

firm *n* companaidh *mf*

firmament *n* iarmailt, an *f*

first *adj* **1** ciad; **2** (*pol*) **the ~ Minister** am Prìomh Mhinistear *m*; **3** *in expr* **head ~** an comhair do chinn

first *adv* an toiseach

firstly *adv* sa chiad àite

firth *n* linne *f*

fish *n* iasg *m*

fish *v* iasgaich *vi*

fisher, fisherman *n* iasgair *m*

fishing *n* iasgach *m*

fishmeal *n* min-èisg *f*

fissure *n* sgoltadh *m*, sgàineadh *m*

fist *n* dòrn *m*, cròg *f*

fistful *n* làn *m* dùirn

fit *adj* **1** (*well*) slàn, fallain, ann an deagh thriom *mf*; **2** (*ready*) deiseil, ullamh; **3** (*phys*) air chothrom; **4** (*suitable*) freagarrach, cubhaidh

fit *n* **1** (*outburst etc*) lasgan *m*; **2** *in expr* **fainting** ~ neul *m*, laigse *f*

fit *v* **1** (*clothing*) thig *vi* do; **2** (*go into space*) teachd *vi*; **3** (*premises etc*) uidheamaich *vt*

fitted out *adj & past part* uidheamaichte, acainneach

fitting *adj* **1** freagarrach, cubhaidh, iomchaidh, **a ~ conclusion** co-dhùnadh freagarrach/cubhaidh; **2** *in exprs* **as is ~** mar as cubhaidh dhut (*etc*), mar as còir

fittings *npl* uidheam *f*, acainn *f*

five *n and num adj* **1** (a) còig; **2** (*people*) còignear *mf*

fivesome *n* còignear *mf*

fix *n* (*situation*) èiginn *f*, staing *f*, cruaidh-chas *m*

fix *v* **1** (*repair*) càirich *vt*, cuir *vt* ceart, cuir *vt* air dòigh; **2** (*sort out*) rèitich *vt*, socraich *vt*; **3** ~ **together** tàth *vt*, ceangail *vt* ri chèile

fixed *adj & past part* **1** (*firm*) teann, suidhichte; **2** (*put right*) rèidh, socraichte;

3 (*repaired*) càirichte; **4** (*settled*) seasmhach, suidhichte

fjord *n* loch-mara *m*

flabby *adj* (*body*) sultach, bog

flair *n* liut *f*

flame *n* lasair *f*

flame *v* las *vi*

flaming *adj* lasrach

flammable *adj* lasanta

flannel *n* flanainn *f*

flare *v*, ~ **up** *v* las *vi*

flash *n* **1** lasair *f*, drithleann *m*; **2** (*instant*) plathadh *m*

flash *v* deàlraich *vi*

flashing *adj* lasrach

flashy *adj* spaideil

flask *n* searrag *f*

flat *adj* còmhnard, rèidh

flat *n* (*dwelling*) lobht(a) *m*

flattened *adj* leudaichte

flatter *v* dèan miodal, dèan brìodal

flattery *n* miodal *m*, brìodal *m*

flatulence *n*, *used with art*, a' ghaoth

flatulent *adj* gaothach

flaw *n* **1** (*moral*) meang *f*; **2** (*object*) fàillinn *f*, easbhaidh *f*, gaoid *f*

flawless *adj* **1** (*person*) gun mheang; **2** (*object*) gun fhàillinn

flax *n* lìon *m*

flea *n* deargad *f*, deargann *f*

flee *v* tàrr/tàir *vi* às, teich *vi*

fleece *n* rùsg *m*

fleece *v* **1** (*sheep*) rùisg *vti*; **2** (*cheat*) spùill *vt* gu buileach

fleet *n* cabhlach *m*, (*ships*) loingeas/luingeas *m*

fleeting *adj* diombuan

flesh *n* feòil *f*

fleshly, fleshy *adj* feòlmhor

flex *n* (*elec*) fleisg *f*

flexibility *n* sùbailteachd *f*

flexible *adj* lùbach, sùbailte

flight *n* **1** (*bird etc*) iteag *f*; **2** (*journey*) turas-adhair *m*; **3** (*battle etc*) ruaig *f*, ruith *f*, teicheadh *m*

flimsy *adj* **1** (*material etc*) tana; **2** (*easily broken*) brisg

fling *v* tilg *vt*

flipper *n* clabar-snàimh *m*

flit (*Sc*) *v* imrich *vi*, dèan *vt* imrich

flitting *n* imrich *f*

float *v* **1** (*as vt:*) cuir *vt* air flod; **2** (*as vi*) bi *vi irreg* air fleòdradh

flock *n* **1** (*animals*) treud *m*, greigh *f*; **2** (*birds*) ealt(a) *f*

flock *v* cruinnich *vi*

flood *n* dìle *f*, tuil *f*

floor *n* ùrlar *m*, làr *m*

floppy *adj* sùbailte

flour *n* flùr *m*, min-flùir *f*

flow *v* dòirt *vi*, sruth *vi*, ruith *vi*, sil *vi*, taom *vi*

flow *n* sruth *m*

flower *n* dìthean *m*, flùr *m*, sìthean *m*

flowery *adj* (*covered in flowers*) flùranach

fluctuating *adj* caochlaideach, a' dol suas is sìos

fluency *n* (*speech*) fileantachd *f*

fluent *adj* (*lang*) fileanta, siùbhlach

flush *n* (*face*) rudhadh *m*, rudhadh-gruaidhe *m*

flushed *adj* (*complexion*) ruiteach

flute *n* cuisle-chiùil *f*

flutter *v* (*wings etc*) plap *vi*, plosg *vi*

fluttering *n* (*wings etc*) plap *m*, plosg *m*, plosgartaich *f*

fly *n* **1** cuileag *f*; **2** (*fishing*) maghar *m*

fly *v* itealaich *vi*, rach *vi irreg* air iteig, sgiathaich *vi*, stiùir (*plèana*) *vt*

flying *adj & pres part* air iteig

flying *n* **1** (*abstr*) iteag *f*; **2** (*action*) itealaich *f*

fly-over *n* (*road*) os-rathad *m*

foam cop *m*, cobhar *m*

foaming *adj* copach

fodder *n* connlach *f*, fodar *m*

foe *n* nàmhaid *m*, eascaraid *m*

fog *n* ceò *mf*

foggy *adj* ceòthach, ceòthar

fold[1] *n* (*livestock*) crò *m*, (*cattle*) buaile *f*

fold[2] *n* (*material etc*) filleadh *m*

fold *v* **1** fill *vt*, preas *vt*, *in expr* ~ **up** paisg *vt*; **2** (*fail*) rach *vi* fodha

folded *adj & past part* fillte

folder *n* pasgan *m*

foliage *n* duilleach *m*

folk *n* **1** (*people*) daoine *mpl*; **2** (*inhabitants*) muinntir *f*

folks *npl* (*relatives*) daoine *mpl*, cuideachd *f*, càirdean *mpl*

follow *v* lean *vti*

follower *n* neach-leanmhainn *m*

following n (*followers*) luchd-leanmhainn m

following adj **1** a leanas; **2** (*next*) ath

folly n gòraiche f

fond adj dèidheil, measail

fondle v cnèadaich/cniadaich vt

fondness n dèidh f

food n biadh m

fool n amadan m, òinseach f, bumailear m, ùmaidh m, stalcaire m

foolish adj gòrach, amaideach, faoin, baoth

foolishness n gòraiche f, amaideas m, faoineas m

foot n **1** (*part of body*) cas f, **on** ~ de chois; **2** (*base*) bun m, bonn m; **3** (*measurement*) troigh f

football n ball-coise m

footpath n frith-rathad m

footprint n lorg(-coise) f

footstep n ceum m

footwear n caisbheart f

for prep **1** do; **2** airson; **3** (*since*) o chionn/ bho chionn; **4** (*during*) fad

for conj (*because*) oir

forbid v toirmisg vt

forbidden adj toirmisgte

force n **1** (*pol etc*) cumhachd mf; **2** (*phys*) neart m, spionnadh m; **3** (*violence*) fòirneart m, ainneart m, èiginn f; **4** (*body*) feachd f

force v thoir vt air, co-èignich vt

fore- prefix ro-

forearm n ruighe mf

forecast n ro-aithris f

forecaster n tuairmsear m

forehead n bathais f, maoil f, clàr-aodainn m

foreign adj cèin, coimheach, thall thairis

foreigner n coigreach m, eilthireach m, coimheach m

foreleg n cas f toisich

foreman n maor m, maor-obrach m

foremost adj prìomh

foresee v ro-aithnich vt

foresight n ro-shealladh m

foreskin n ro-chraiceann m

forest n coille (mhòr) f

forester n forsair m, coilltear m

forestry n forsaireachd f

forewarn v cuir vt air earalas

foreword n ro-ràdh m

forge n ceàrdach f, teallach (ceàrdaich) m

forget v **1** dìochuimhnich vt; **2** (*exprs*) **I** ~ chan eil cuimhne agam

forgetful adj dìochuimhneach

forgetfulness n dìochuimhne f

forgive v thoir mathanas do, ma(i)th

forgiveness n mathanas m

forgotten adj & past part, air dìochuimhne

fork n **1** gobhal/gabhal m; **2** (*table*) forc(a) f, greimire m; **3** (*farm etc*) gòbhlag f, gràpa m

forked adj gòbhlach

form[1] n **1** (*shape*) cumadh m, cruth m, dealbh mf; **2** (*borrowed*) riochd m; **3** (*mood*) dòigh f, gleus mf

form[2] n (*seat*) furm m

form[3] n (*document*) foirm mf

form v cum vt, dealbh vt

formal adj foirmeil

former adj sean(n), a bha ann roimhe

forsake v trèig vt, cuir cùl ri

fort n **1** daingneach f; **2** (*hist*) dùn m

fortify v (*building etc*) daingnich vt

fortitude n misneach(d) f, cruadal m

fortnight n cola-deug mf

fortress n daingneach f

fortuitous adj tuiteamach

fortunate adj fortanach

fortune n **1** (*luck*) fortan m, sealbh m; **2** (*financial*) beartas m, ionmhas m, saidhbhreas m, stòras m

forty n and num adj dà fhichead, ceathrad m

forwards adv air adhart, air aghaidh

foster-brother/-sister n co-alta mf

foul, foul play n (*sport*) fealladh m

found v cuir vt air chois, cuir vt air b(h)onn

fountainhead n màthair-uisge f

four n and num adj **1** (*objects*) ceithir **2** (*people*) ceathrar mf; **3** in expr **on all** ~s air a (*etc*) m(h)àgan/air a m(h)àg(a)ran

four-legged adj ceithir-chasach

foursome n ceathrar mf

fourteen n and num adj ceithir-deug

fourth n ceathramh m

fourth num adj ceathramh

four-wheeled adj ceithir-chuibhleach

fox n sionnach m, madadh-ruadh m, balgair m

foyer n for-thalla m

fraction n bloigh f

fragment n bìdeag f, criomag f, bloigh f

fragment *v* (*vi*) rach ann am bìdeagan, (*vt*) cuir ann an bìdeagan

fragmented *adj* briste, ann am bìdeagan, ann an criomagan, pronn

fragrant *adj* cùbhraidh

frame *n* **1** cèis *f*, frèam *m*; **2** *in expr* ~ **of mind** fonn *m*, gean *m*, gleus *m*

framework *n* frèam *m*

France *n* An Fhraing *f*

frank *adj* fosgarra, fosgailte

fraud *n* foill *f*

fraudulent *adj* foilleil, fealltach

fraudulently *adv* le foill

free *adj* **1** (*at liberty*) saor, mu sgaoil, mu rèir; **2** (*without constraints*) saor; **3** (*at leisure*) saor; **4** (*gratis*) saor, saor 's an-asgaidh

free *v* fuasgail *vt*, cuir *vt* mu sgaoil, leig *vt* mu sgaoil, cuir/leig *vt* mu rèir

freedom *n* saorsa

free-standing *adj* neo-eisimeileach

freeze *v* reoth *vti*

freezer *n* reothadair *m*

freight *n* luchd *m*

French *adj* Frangach

French *n* (*lang*) Fraingis *f*

Frenchman *n* Frangach *m*

frequency *n* tricead *m*

frequent *adj* cumanta

frequent *v* tathaich *vi* air

frequently *adv* (gu) tric, gu bitheanta, gu minig

fresh[1] *adj* **i** ùr; **2** *in expr* ~ **water** fìor-uisge *m*

fresh[2] *adj* (*temperature*) fionnar

fretful *adj* frionasach

friction *n* **1** suathadh *m*; **2** (*between people*) mì-chòrdadh *m*

Friday *n* Dihaoine *m*

fridge *n* frids *m*, fuaradair *m*

fried *adj & past part* ròsta

friend *n* caraid *m*

friendly *adj* càirdeil

friendship *n* càirdeas *m*

fright *n* **1** (*abstr*) eagal/feagal *m*; **2** (*con*) clisgeadh *m*

frighten *v* cuir eagal air

frightful *adj* eagalach, uabhasach, oillteil

frightfully *adv* eagalach

frill *n* fraoidhneas *m*

fringe *n* **1** (*periphery*) iomall *m*, oir *f*; **2** (*material etc*) fraoidhneas *m*

frivolity *n* aotromas *m*, faoineas *m*

frivolous *adj* aotrom, faoin

frock *n* froca *m*

frog *n* losgann *m*

from *prep* **1** (*direction*) bho/o; **2** (*point of origin*) à; **3** (*sequence of time*) bho/o

front *adj* **1** toisich; **2** *in expr* ~ **door** doras mòr, doras-aghaidh *m*

front *n* **1** (*part*) toiseach *m*; **2** (*surface*) beulaibh *m*, aghaidh *f*, back to ~ cùlaibh air beulaibh; **3** *in expr* **in** ~ air thoiseach; **4** *in expr* **in** ~ (*opposite*) mu choinneimh, fa chomhair, ro; **5** (*weather*) aghaidh *f*

frontier *n* crìoch *f*

frontwards *adv* an comhair do thoisich, an comhair do chinn

frost *n* reothadh *m*

froth *n* cop *m*, cobhar *m*

frothy *adj* copach

frown *n* mùig *m*, gruaim *f*, sgraing *f*

frown *v* cuir mùig ort, cuir gruaim ort

frowning *adj* gruamach

frozen *adj* reòthta/reòthte

fruit *n* **1** meas *m*; **2** (*produce*) toradh *m*

fruitful *adj* tor(r)ach

fruitless *adj* **1** (*trees etc*) gun mheas *m*; **2** (*vain*) dìomhain, gun toradh

fruity *adj* measach

fry *v* frighig *vt*, ròist/ròst *vt*

fuck *v* rach *vi* air muin

fuel connadh *m*

fugitive *n* fògrach/fògarrach *m*

full *adj* **1** (*filled*) làn, lìonta; **2** (*complete*) làn, iomlan

full *v* luaidh *vt*

full-grown *adj* inbheach, foirfe, an ìre

fulling *n* luadhadh *m*

fully *adv* gu h-iomlan, uile-gu-lèir

fulmar *n* fulmair *m*

fulness *n* lànachd *nf*

fumes *n* deatach *f*

fun *n* **1** spòrs *f*, dibhearsain *m*; **2** *in expr* **make** ~ dèan fanaid, mag *vi*

function *n* **1** (*use*) gnìomh *m*, feum *m*; **2** (*post*) oifis *f*, dreuchd *f*, obair *f*; **3** (*action*) gnìomh *m*; **4** (*event*) cuirm *f*

function *v* obraich

fund *n* maoin *f*, stòr *m*

fund *v* maoinich *vt*

fundamental *adj* bunaiteach

funeral *n* tiodhlacadh *m*, adhlacadh *m*,
tòrradh *m*

funnel *n* **1** (*industrial*) luidhear *m*, similear
m; **2** (*pouring*) lìonadair *m*

funny *adj* **1** (*amusing*) èibhinn,
àbhachdach; **2** (*peculiar*) neònach, àraid

furious *adj* air chuthach, air bhoile, air
bhàinidh, fiadhaich

furlough *n* fòrladh *m*

furnace *n* fùirneis *f*

furnish *v* **1** (*fit out*) uidheamaich *vt*;
2 (*house etc*) cuir àirneis ann an;
3 (*supply*) solair *vt*

furnishings *npl* àirneis *f*, àirneis bhog

furrow *n* **1** (*ground*) clais *f*, sgrìob *f*;
2 (*brow*) preas *m*, preasan *m*

furrow *v* **1** (*ground*) sgrìob *vt*, claisich *vt*;
2 (*brow*) preas *vt*

furry *adj* molach

further *adj* (*additional*) a bharrachd,
tuilleadh, eile

furthermore *adv* a bharrachd air sin, a
thuilleadh air sin

fury *n* cuthach *m*, bàinidh *f*

fussy *adj* ro-chùramach, ro-phongail

futile *adj* faoin, dìomhain

futility *n* faoineas *m*

future *adj* **1** ri teachd; **2** (*gram*)
teachdail

future *n* **1** (*with art*), **the** ~ an t-àm ri
teachd; **2** *in expr* **in** ~ bho seo a-mach,
turas *m* eile

G

gable *n* stuadh *f*
Gael *n* Gàidheal *m*
Gaelic *n* Gàidhlig *f*
gaffer *n* maor *m*, maor-obrach *m*
gain *n* (*fin*) prothaid *f*, buannachd *f*
gain *v* coisinn *vt*, buannaich *vt*
gait *n* gluasad *m*, giùlan *m*
gale *n* gèile *m*
gallery *n* (*exhibitions etc*) taisbean-lann *f*, gailearaidh *m*
galling *adj* leamh, frionasach
gallon *n* galan *m*
gallows *n* croich *f*
gambler *n* ceàrraiche *m*
gambling *n* (*act*) ceàrrachadh *m*, (*abstr*) ceàrrachas *m*
game *n* **1** cluich(e) *m*, geam(a) *m*; **2** (*hunted creatures*) sitheann *f*
gamekeeper *n* geamair *m*
gang *n* buidheann *mf*, treud *m*
gannet *n* sùlaire *m*, (*young*) guga *m*
gap *n* beàrn *mf*, fosgladh *m*
garage *n* garaids *f*
garb *n* èideadh *m*
garden *n* gàrradh *m*, lios *mf*
gardener *n* gàirnealair *m*
gardening *n* gàirnealaireachd *f*
garlic *n* creamh *m*
garrison *n* gearastan *m*
garron *m* gearran *m*
garrulous *adj* beulach, cabach, gobach
garter *n* gartan *m*
gas *n* **1** deatach *f*; **2** (*domestic*) gas *m*
gasp, gasping *n* plosg *m*
gasp *v* plosg *vi*
gate *n* geata *m*
gather *v* **1** (*people*) cruinnich *vti*, tionail *vi*, thig còmhla; **2** (*livestock*) cruinnich *vt*, tionail *vt*, tru(i)s *vt*; **3** (*tuck*) tru(i)s *vt*
gathered *adj & past part* cruinn
gathering *n* cruinneachadh *m*, co-chruinneachadh *m*, tional *m*
gauge *n* (*measurer*) tomhas *m*, meidheadair *m*
gauge *v* tomhais *vt*
gear[1] *n* **1** (*possessions*) trealaich *f*; **2** (*equipment etc*) uidheam *f*, acainn *f*

gear[2] *n* (*engin*) gèar *f*, gìodhar *m*
gear up *v* uidheamaich *vt*
geared up *adj & past part* uidheamaichte, acainneach
gelding *m* gearran *m*
gender *n* gnè *f*
gene *n* gine *f*
general *adj* **1** coitcheann; **2** *in expr* **in ~** (*on the whole*) san fharsaingeachd; **3** *in expr* **in ~** (*normally*) an cumantas, am bitheantas, mar as trice
general *n* seanailear *m*
generally *adv* **1** (*on the whole*) san fharsaingeachd; **2** (*normally*) an cumantas, am bitheantas, mar as trice
generation *n* **1** (*time*) linn *m*; **2** (*people*) ginealach *m*
generator *n* gineadair *m*
generosity *n* fialaidheachd *f*
generous *adj* fialaidh, fial, faoilidh, tabhartach
genitals *n* buill-ghineamhainn *mpl*
genitive *adj* ginideach
genteel *adj* uasal
gentility *n* (*abstr*) uaisle *f*
gentle *adj* ciùin, sèimh
gentleman *n* duine-uasal *m*, uasal *m*
genuine *adj* **1** (*authentic*) fìor; **2** (*sincere*) neo-chealgach, dìreach
geography *n* cruinn-eòlas *m*, tìr-eòlas *m*
geology *n* geòlas *m*
germ *n* bitheag *f*
German *n & adj* **1** Gearmailteach *m*; **2** (*language*) a' Ghearmailtis *f*
Germany *n* A' Ghearmailt *f*
germinate *v* ginidich *vi*
germination *n* ginideachadh *m*
gesture *n* **1** gluasad *m*; **2** (*beckoning*) smèideadh *m*
gesture *v* (*greet*) smèid *vi*
get *v* **1** (*obtain*) faigh *vt irreg*; **2** (*become*) fàs *vi*
ghost *n* taibhse *mf*, tannasg *m*
giant *n* famhair *m*, fuamhaire *m*
gibbet *n* croich *f*
giddiness *n* **1** tuainealaich *f*, luasgan *m*; **2** (*character*) guanalas *m*

giddy *adj* tuainealach, guanach

gift *n* **1** tiodhlac *m*, gibht *f*, tabhartas *m*; **2** (*talent*) tàlann *m*

gift *v* tiodhlaic *vt*, thoir *vt* seachad

gill *n* (*fish*) giùran *m*

ginger *adj* ruadh

girl *n* **1** caileag *f*, nighean *f*

girlfriend *n* leannan *m*, bràmair *m*

give *v* **1** thoir *vt irreg*, thoir *vt* seachad, tiodhlaic *vt*; **2** (*deliver*) gabh *vt*

giver *n* tabhartaiche *m*, tabhairteach *m*

glad *adj* **1** (*pleased*) toilichte **2** (*willing*) toileach

gladness *n* gàirdeachas *m*, toileachas *m*, toil-inntinn *f*, toileachas-inntinn *m*

glance *n* plathadh *m*, sùil (aithghearr) *f*

glance *v* thoir *vt irreg* sùil (aithghearr)

gland *n* fàireag *f*

glass *n* glainne *f*

glasses *npl* (*spectacles*) glainneachan *fpl*, speuclairean *mpl*

glasshouse *n* taigh-glainne *m*

glen *n* gleann *m*

glimpse *n* aiteal *m*, plathadh *m*

glint *n* lainnir *f*, deàlradh *m*

glitter *n* lainnir *f*, deàlradh *m*

glitter *v* deàlraich *vi*

global *adj* cruinneil

globe *n* cruinne *mf*

gloom, gloominess *n* **1** (*light*) doilleireachd *f*; **2** (*mood etc*) gruaim *f*, smalan *m*

gloomy *adj* **1** (*setting etc*) ciar; **2** (*light*) doilleir; **3** (*mood etc*) doilleir, gruamach, mùgach

glorify *v* glòraich *vt*

glorious *adj* glòrmhor, òirdheirc

glory *n* **1** (*fame*) cliù *m*, glòir *f*; **2** (*spiritual*) glòir *f*

gloss *n* (*lustre*) lìomh *f*

glossy *adj* lìomharra

glove *n* làmhainn *f*, miotag *f*, meatag *f*

glue *n* glaodh *m*

glue *v* glaodh *vt*

glug *v* plubraich *vi*, plub *vt*

glutton *adj* geòcaire *m*, craosaire *m*

gluttonous *adj* geòcach, craosach

gluttony *n* geòcaireachd *f*, craos *m*

gnash *v* gìosg *vt*

gnaw *v* cagainn *vti*

go *v* **1** (*proceed*) rach *vi irreg*, falbh *vi*, gabh *vti*; **2** (*change*) rach *vi irreg*; **3** (*leave*) falbh *vi*

goal *n* **1** (*aim*) miann *mf*, rùn *m*; **2** (*sport*) tadhal *m*

goat *n* gobhar *mf*

gob *n* gob *m*, cab *m*

gobble *v* glam/glamh *vt*

God, god *m* Dia, dia *m*

goddess *n* ban-dia *f*

godfather *n* goistidh *m*

godhead *n* diadhachd *f*

godliness *n* diadhachd *f*

gold *n* òr *m*

gold, golden *adj* òir

goldsmith *n* òr-cheàrd *m*

golf *n* go(i)lf *m*

good *adj* **1** math; **2** deagh; **3** (*measure*) pailt; **4** (*exprs*) ~ grief! an dòlas!, O mo chreach!, mo chreach-s' a thàinig!, ~ heavens! a chiall!

good *n* feum *m*, math *m*

good- *prefix* deagh-

goodbye *excl* beannachd leat/leibh!, slàn leat/leibh!, mar sin leat/leibh!

goodness *n* **1** (*moral*) mathas *m*; **2** (*food etc*) brìgh *f*, susbaint *f*; **3** (*excl*) ~! a chiall!, (my) ~!, ~ me! obh! obh!

goods *n* **1** (*merchandise*) bathar *m*; **2** (*possessions*) maoin *f*

goodwill *n* deagh-thoil *f*, deagh-ghean *m*

goose *n* gèadh *mf*

gooseberry *n* gròiseid *f*

gore *n* fuil *f*

gorgeous *adj* greadhnach

gorse *n* conasg *m*

gory *adj* fuil(t)each

gossip *n* **1** (*abstr*) seanchas *m*; **2** (*person*) goistidh *m*

gossip *v* bi *vi irreg* ri seanchas

govern *v* riaghail *vti*, riaghlaich *vti*

government *n* **1** (*abstr*) riaghladh *m*; **2** (*con*) riaghaltas *m*

governor *n* riaghladair *m*

gown *n* gùn *m*

grab *v* gabh grèim air

grace *n* gràs *m*

graceful *adj* eireachdail, gràsmhor

gracefulness *n* gràsmhorachd *f*

graceless *adj* gun ghràs *m*

gracious *adj* gràsmhor

graciousness *n* gràsmhorachd *f*

grade *n* ìre *f*

gradient *n* **1** (*abstr*) caisead *m*; **2** (*con*) bruthach *mf*, leathad *m*

gradually *adv* mean air mhean, uidh air n-uidh, beag àir bheag

graduate *v* gabh ceum *m*, ceumnaich *vi*

graduation *n* ceumnachadh *m*

grain *n* **1** gràinnean *m*; **2** (*crops*) gràn *m*, (*single*) gràinne *f*

graip *n* gràpa *m*

gram(me) *n* gram *m*

grammar *n* gràmar *m*

grammatical *adj* gràmarach

grand *adj* **1** (*important*) mòr, mòr agad/asad (*etc*) fhèin; **2** (*great*) glan, gasta, sgoinneil, taghta

grandchild *n* ogha *m*

granddaughter *n* ban-ogha *f*

grandeur *n* mòrachd *f*

grandfather *n* seanair *m*

grandmother *n* seanmhair *f*, granaidh *f*

grandson *n* ogha *m*

granite clach-ghràin *f*, eibhir *f*

granny *n* granaidh *f*

grant *n* tabhartas *m*

grant *v* builich *vt* air

granular *adj* gràinneach

grape *n* fìon-dhearc *f*

graph *n* graf *m*

grasp *n* grèim *m*, glacadh *m*

grasp *v* **1** glac *vt*, gabh grèim air, greimich *vi* air/ri; **2** (*understand*) tuig *vt*

grass *n* feur *m*

grasshopper *n* fionnan-feòir *m*

grassy *adj* feurach

grate *n* grèata *m*

grate *v* sgrìob *vti*

grateful *adj* taingeil, buidheach

gratification *n* toileachadh *m*

grating[1] *n* (*scraping*) sgrìobadh *m*

grating[2] *n* (*grid etc*) cliath *f*

gratitude *n* taing *f*, taingealachd *f*, buidheachas *m*

grave[1] *adj* **1** (*character*) stòlda; **2** (*state*) fìor dhroch

grave[2] *adj* (*lang*) trom

grave *n* uaigh *f*

gravel *n* grinneal *m*, morghan *m*

gravestone *n* leac *f*, leac uaighe *f*, clach-chinn *f*

gravity *n* (*force*) iom-tharraing *f*

graze[1] *v* (*skin etc*) rùisg *vt*

graze[2] *v* (*livestock etc*) ionaltair *vi*

grazing *n* **1** (*abstr*) feurachadh *m*, ionaltradh *m*; **2** (*pasture*) feurach *m*, ionaltradh *m*, clua(i)n *f*

grease *n* crèis *f*

greasy *adv* crèiseach

great *adj* **1** mòr; **2** (*excellent*) gasta, taghta

great- *prefix* iar-

greatcoat *n* còta-mòr *m*

greater *comp adj* mò/motha

greatness *n* **1** (*size*) meudachd *f*; **2** (*reputation*) mòrachd *f*

Greece *n* A' Ghrèig *f*

greed *n* gionaiche *m*, sannt *m*, (*food*) geòcaireachd *f*

greedy *adj* gionach, sanntach, (*food*) geòcach

Greek *adj* Greugach

Greek *n* **1** (*person*) Greugach *m*; **2** (*language*), a' Ghreugais *f*

green *adj* uaine, gorm, glas

green *n* **1** uaine *m*; **2** (*expanse*) rèidhlean *m*

greenhouse *n* taigh-glainne *m*

greens *n* (*vegetables*) glasraich *f*

greet *v* fàiltich *vt*, cuir fàilte air

greeting *n* fàilte *f*, dùrachd *f*

gregarious *adj* greigheach, cèilidheach

grey *adj* **1** glas; **2** (*landscape, hair*) liath

greyhound *n* mial-chù *m*

grid *n* cliath *f*

griddle, **gridiron** *n* (*baking*) greideal *f*

grief *n* **1** mulad *f*, dòlas *m*, (*excl*) **good ~!** an dòlas!, O mo chreach!, mo chreach-s' a thàinig!

grievance *n* cùis-ghearain *f*

grieve *v* **1** caoidh *vti*; **2** (*mourn*) bi *vi irreg* ri bròn

grievous *adj* crài(dh)teach

grill *n* (*cooking*) grìos *m*

grill *v* **1** (*cookery*) grìosaich *vt*; **2** (*interrogate*) mion-cheasnaich *vt*

grind *v* **1** (*general*) pronn *vt*; **2** (*corn*) meil *vt*, bleith *vt*

grip *n* grèim *m*, glacadh *m*

grip *v* gabh grèim air

grizzled *adj* riabhach

groan *n* (*pain etc*) cnead *m*

groan *v* dèan cnead, leig cnead

grocer *n* grosair *m*

groove *n* clais *f*

grope *v* **1** (*search*) rùraich *vi*; **2** (*feel*) smeuraich *vi*

gross *adj* **1** (*character*) garbh, borb;
2 (*money*) iomlan, slàn

grotty *adj* mosach, dràbhail, grodach

grouchy *adj* crost(a), gruamach, fo
ghruaim *f*

ground *adj & past part* pronn

ground *n* **1** (*land*) talamh *m*, fearann *m*;
2 (*surface*) làr *m*; **3** (*music*) ùrlar *m*; **4** ~**s**
(*justification etc*) adhbhar *m*

groundless (*without justification*) gun
adhbhar

grounds² *npl* (*liquids*) grùid *f*

group *n* **1** (*people*) grunn *m*; **2** (*formed*)
còmhlan *m*, buidheann *mf*

grouse¹ *n* (*bird*) coileach-fraoich *m*

grouse² *n* (*grumble etc*) gearan *m*

grouse *v* gearain *vi*

grove *n* doire *mf*

grow *v* **1** fàs *vi*; **2** (*become*) fàs *vi* ; **3** ~ **up**
thig *vi irreg* gu inbhe

growl, growling *n* dranndan *m*, dranndail
f, grùnsgal *m*

growl *v* dèan drannndan

grown *adj & past part* dèanta/foirfe

grown-up *adj & n* inbheach *m*

growth *n* fàs *m*, cinneas *m*

grub¹ *n* (*insect*) cnuimh *f*

grub² *n* (*food*) biadh *m*

grumble *n* gearan *m*

grumble *v* gearain *vi*

grumbling *adj* gearanach

grumbling *n* gearan *m*

grumpiness *n* gruaim *f*

grumpy *adj* gruamach, fo ghruaim, crost(a)

grunt *n* **1** gnòsail *f*; **2** (*pig*) rùchd *m*

grunt *v* **1** dèan gnòsail *f*; **2** (*pig*) rùchd *vi*

guarantee *n* **1** (*general*) barantas *m*; **2** (*fin*)
urras *m*

guarantee *v* rach *vi* an urras

guard *n* **1** (*abstr*) faire *f*; **2** (*con*) faire *f*,
freiceadan *m*; **3** (*single*) neach-faire *m*

guess *n* tuaiream *f*, tuairmse *f*, tomhas *m*

guess *v* tomhais *vt*, thoir tuaiream

guest *n* aoigh *m*

guidance *n* **1** treòrachadh *m*, iùl *m*;
2 (*advice*) comhairle *f*

guide *n* **1** neach-iùil *m*, neach-treòrachaidh
m

guide *v* treòraich *vt*, seòl *vt*, stiùir *vt*

guideline(s) *n(pl)* stiùireadh *m*, seòladh *m*

guilt *n* ciont(a) *m*, coill *f*

guiltless *adj* neoichiontach

guilty *adj* ciontach, coireach

gull *n* faoileag *f*

gullet *n* slugan *m*

gulp, gulping *n* glug *m*, glugan *m*

gum *n* (*substance/adhesive*) bìth *f*,
(*adhesive*) glaodh *m*

gum(s) *n* (*mouth*) càireas *m*, càirean *m*

gumption *n* toinisg *f*, ciall *f*

gun *n* gunna *m*

gunner *n* gunnair *m*

gurgle, gurgling *n* **1** (*persons*) glug *m*;
2 (*liquids*) glugan *m*, plubraich *f*

gust *n* osag *f*, oiteag *f*

gut *n* **1** (*intestine*) caolan *m*, mionach *m*

gut *v* (*fish etc*) cut *vti*

gutter¹ *n* (*drainage*) guitear *m*

gutter² *n* (*fish etc*) cutair *m*

H

habit *n* cleachdadh *m*, àbhaist *f*, gnàth *m*
habitat *n* àrainn *f*
habitual *adj* àbhaisteach, gnàthach
hag *n* badhbh *f*, cailleach *f*
haggis *n* taigeis *f*
hail, hailstone *n* clach-mheallain *f*
hair *n* 1 (*human*) falt *m*, gruag *f sing coll*, (*single*) fuiltean *m*, ròineag *f*; 2 (*animal*) fionnadh *m*, gaoisid *f*; 3 (*idiom*) ~ **of the dog** leigheas na poit *m*
hairdresser *n* gruagaire *m*
hairdryer *n* tiormaichear-gruaig *m*
hairy *adj* fionnach, molach, robach, ròmach
half *adv* leth, leitheach
half *n* leth *f*, leth-chuid *f*
halfway *adv* leitheach-slighe, leitheach-rathaid
hall *n* talla *m*
Halloween *n* Oidhche Shamhna *f*
halo *n* fàinne-solais *f*
hamlet *n* clachan *m*
hammer *n* òrd *m*
hand *n* 1 làmh *f*; 2 *in expr* **on the other** ~ air mhodh eile, air an làimh eile
hand *v* 1 sìn *vt* gu; 2 *in exprs* ~ **over** thoir *vt* seachad
handbag *n* màileid-làimhe *f*
handball *n* ball-làimhe *m*
handcuffs *n* glasan-làimhe *fpl*
handful *n* làn *m* dùirn, dòrlach *m*
handgun *n* dag(a) *m*
handicap *n* 1 (*general*) bacadh *m*; 2 (*phys*) ciorram *m*
handicapped *adj* 1 (*disabled*) ciorramach; 2 (*economically etc*) ana-cothromach
handkerchief *n* neapaigear *m*
handle *n* 1 (*tool etc*) cas *f*; 2 (*jug etc*) cluas *f*
handle *v* 1 (*phys*) làimhsich *vt*, (*tool etc*) iomair *vt*; 2 (*situation etc*) dèilig *vi* ri, làimhsich *vt*
handlebar *n* crann-làmh *m*
handshake *n* crathadh-làimhe *m*
handsome *adj* gasta, eireachdail
handwriting *n* làmh-sgrìobhadh *m*
handy *adj* 1 (*convenient*) deiseil, ullamh, goireasach; 2 *in expr* **come in** ~ dèan

feum, bi *vi irreg* feumail; 3 (*person*) gleusta, deas-làmhach
hang *v* croch *vt*
hanged *adj & past part* crochte
hanging *adj & pres part* an crochadh *m*, crochte
hangman *n* crochadair *m*
hangover *n* ceann daoraich *m*
happen *v* 1 (*occur*) tachair *vi*; 2 (*become of*) èirich *vi*; 3 (*chance*) tachair *vi*, tuit *vi*; 4 *in expr* ~ **upon** (*come across*) tachair *vi* air, amais *vi* air
happening *n* tachartas *m*, tuiteamas *m*
happy *adj* toilichte, sona
happy-go-lucky *adj* guanach, coma co-dhiù
harass *v* claoidh *vt*, sàraich *vt*
harassment *n* sàrachadh *m*
harbour *n* port *m*, cala *m*
hard *adj* 1 cruaidh; 2 (*painful*) duilich; 3 (*taxing*) doirbh; 4 (*to understand*) deacair
harden *v* cruadhaich *vti*
hard-hearted *adj* cruaidh-chridheach
hardihood *n* cruadal *m*, cruas *m*
hardiness *n* cruas *m*, fulang *m*
hardness *n* cruas *m*
hardship *n* cruadal *m*
hardworking *adj* gnìomhach, dèanadach, dìcheallach, èasgaidh, cruaidh air an obair
hardy *adj* fulangach, cruadalach, cruaidh
hare *n* maigheach *f*, geàrr *f*
harm *n* 1 lochd *m*, milleadh *m*, beud *m*, cron *m*
harm *v* 1 goirtich *vt*, mill *vt*, dèan cron air
harmful *adj* lochdach, cronail, millteach, cunnartach
harmonious *adj* ceòlmhor
harmony *n* 1 (*music*) co-sheirm *f*; 2 (*agreement*) co-aontachadh *m*, co-chòrdadh *m*; 3 (*idiom*) **in** ~ rèidh *adj*
harness *n* uidheam *f*, acainn *f*
harp *n* clàrsach *f*, cruit *f*
harper *n* clàrsair *m*, cruitear *m*
harpsichord *n* cruit-chòrda *f*
harrow *n* cliath *f*

harrow *v* **1** (*agric*) cliath *vti*;
2 (*emotionally*) cràidh *vt*
harrowing *adj* crài(dh)teach, dòrainneach
harsh *adj* **1** (*person etc*) cruaidh, garbh;
2 (*sensation etc*) geur, searbh
harshness *n* cruas *m*, gèire *f*, searbhachd *f*
harvest *n* foghar *m*, buain *f*
haste *n* cabhag *f*, deann *f*
hasten *v* **1** (*as vi*) dèan cabhag *f*; **2** (*as vt*)
cuir cabhag air
hasty *adj* cabhagach
hatch *v* **1** (*eggs*) guir *vti*; **2** (*plot etc*) innlich
vt
hatchet *n* làmhthuagh *f*, làmhadh *m*,
làmhag *f*
hate *n* gràin *f*, fuath *m*
hate *v* fuathaich *vt*, bi *vi irreg* gràin agad
(*etc*) air
hateful *adj* gràineil, fuathach
hatred *n* gràin *f*, fuath *m*
haugh *n* innis *f*
haughtiness *n* àrdan *m*, uaibhreas *m*,
uabhar *m*
haughty *adj* uaibhreach, àrdanach
haul *v* tarraing *vti*, slaod *vti*
haulage *n* **1** giùlan *m*; **2** (*charge*) faradh *m*
haunt *v* (*visit*) tathaich *vi* air
have *v* **1** bi *vi irreg* aig; **2** gabh *vt*, thoir *vt*;
3 ~ **to** (*must*) feum *vi*, 's fheudar; **4** ~ **to**
(*be compelled*), thig *vi irreg* air
hay *n* tràthach *m*
hay-fork *n* gòbhlag *f*
hazardous *adj* cunnartach
haze *n* ceò *m*
hazel *n* calltainn *m*
hazelnut *n* cnò challtainn *f*
hazy *adj* ceòthach
he *pers pron* e
head *adj* prìomh
head *n* **1** ceann *m*; **2** (*of organisation etc*)
ceannard *m*; **3** *in expr* ~ **on** an comhair a
(*etc*) thoisich; **4** *in expr* **a** ~ (*each*) an urra
headache *n* ceann goirt *m*
headgear *n* ceannbheart *f*
heading *n* ceann *m*
headland *n* rubha *m*
headline *n* ceann-naidheachd *m*
headlong *adj* nad (*etc*) dheann-ruith, nad
dheann
headlong *adv* an comhair do (*etc*) chinn
headstrong *adj* **1** (*wilful*) ceann-làidir;
2 (*obstinate*) rag-mhuinealach

head-teacher *n* maighstir-sgoile *m*
heal *v* slànaich *vti*, leighis *vt*
healing *n* slànachadh *m*, leigheas *m*
health *n* slàinte *f*
healthy *adj* slàn, fallain
heap *n* tòrr *m*, cruach *f*
heap *v* cruach *vt*, càrn *vt*
hear *v* cluinn *vt irreg*
hearing *n* claisneachd/claisteachd *f*
heart *n* **1** cridhe *m*; **2** *in exprs* **in good** ~
misneachail
heartbeat *n* buille-cridhe *f*
heartbreak *n* bris(t)eadh-cridhe *m*
heartburn *n* losgadh-bràghad *m*
hearth *n* cagailt *f*, teallach *m*, teinntean *m*
hearthstone *n* leac-theallaich *f*
heartiness *n* cridhealas *m*
heart-rending *adj* dòrainneach
hearty *adj* cridheil
heat *n* teas *m*
heat, heat up, *v* teasaich *vti*
heater *n* uidheam-teasachaidh *f*
heath *n* **1** monadh *m*, sliabh *m*, mòinteach
f; **2** (*plant*) fraoch *m*
heathen *n* cinneach *m*
heather *n* fraoch *m*
heather-cock *n* coileach-fraoich *m*
heating *n* teasachadh *m*
heave *v* **1** (*throw*) tilg *vt*, caith *vt*; **2** (*haul*)
tarraing *vi*, slaod *vi*
heaven *n* **1** nèamh *m*, flaitheas *m*, pàrras
m; **2** *in expr* **the** ~**s** an iarmailt *f*; **3** (*excl*)
good ~**s!** obh! obh!, O mo chreach!
heavenly *adj* nèamhaidh
heaviness *n* truimead *m*
heavy *adj* trom, cudromach
Hebrew *adj & n* Eabhrach
Hebrew *n* (*lang*) Eabhra *f*
hectare *n* heactair *m*
hectic *adj* dripeil
hedge *n* callaid *f*, fàl *m*
hedgehog *n* gràineag *f*
heed *n* aire *f*, feart/feairt *f*
heel *n* sàil *f*, bonn-dubh *m*
height *n* àirde *f*
heir *n* oighre *m*
heiress *n* ban-oighre *f*
held *adj & past part* **1** glèidhte; **2** (*captive*)
an grèim, an sàs, an làimh
helicopter *n* heileacopta(i)r *m*
hell *n* ifrinn *f*, iutharn(a) *f*
hellish *adj* **1** ifrinneach; **2** (*fig*) sgriosail

hello *excl* halò
helm *n* falmadair *m*, ailm *f*
helmet *n* cloga(i)d *mf*
help *n* **1** (*relief*) cobhair *f*, (*as excl*)
~! (dèan) cobhair orm!, cuidich mi!;
2 (*general*) cuideachadh *m*; **3** (*person*)
cuidiche *f*
help *v* **1** cuidich *vti*, dèan cobhair air;
2 (*idiom*) **it can't be ~ed** chan eil
cothrom air
helper *n* cuidiche *m*
helpful *adj* cuideachail
hem *n* fàitheam *m*
hemisphere *n* leth-chruinne *mf*
hemp *n* cainb *f*
hen *n* cearc *f*
henceforth *adv* o seo a-mach
her *poss adj* a
her *pron* i
herb *n* luibh *mf*, lus *m*
herd *n* treud *m*, (*cattle*) buar *m*
herd *v* buachaillich *vi*
heritage *n* **1** dìleab *f*; **2** (*property etc*)
oighreachd *f*; **3** (*cultural*) dualchas *m*
hermaphrodite *adj* fireann-boireann
hermaphrodite *n* fireann-boireann *m*
hero *n* curaidh *m*, gaisgeach *m*, laoch *m*
heroic *adj* gaisgeil
heroism *n* gaisge *f*, gaisgeachd *f*
heron *n* corra-ghritheach *f*
herself *reflexive pron* i fhèin
hesitate *v* màirnealaich *vi*, bi *vi irreg* an
imcheist, bi eadar-dhà-lionn; bi *v irreg &*
def leisg le
hesitating *adj* (*undecided*) an imcheist,
eadar-dhà-lionn
heterogeneous *adj* ioma-sheòrsach
hibernation *n* cadal-geamhraidh *m*
hiccups *n* an aileag *f*
hidden *adj & past part* falaichte, am falach,
air falach
hide[1] *n* (*pelt*) seiche *f*, bian *m*
hide[2] *n* (*place*) àite-falaich *m*
hide *v* **1** (*as vt*) cuir *vt* am falach, ceil *vt*;
2 (*as vi*) rach *vi* am falach
hide-and-seek *n* falach-fead *m*
hide-out *n* àite-falaich *m*
hiding[1] *n* (*concealment*) falach *m*
hiding[2] *n* slacadh/slaiceadh *m*, pronnadh
m
high *adj* àrd
higher *adj* nas àirde

highland *adj* (*topog*) àrd-thìreach
highland *n* (*topog*) àrd-thìr *f*
Highland *adj* Gàidhealach
Highlander *n* Gàidheal *m*
Highlands *n* a' Ghàidhealtachd *f*
highlight *v* **1** soillsich *vt*; **2** (*emphasise etc*)
cuir cudrom air
high-ranking *adj* inbheil
highway *n* rathad-mòr *m*
high-yielding *adj* torrach
hilarity *n* cridhealas *m*
hill *n* cnoc *m*
hillock *n* cnoc *m*, cnocan *m*, toman *m*,
tulach *m*
hillside, hillslope *n* leathad *m*, ruighe *mf*
hilly *adj* cnocach, monadail
him *pron* e
himself *reflexive pron* e fhèin
hind *n* (*deer*) eilid *f*
hinge *n* lùdag *f*, banntach *f*
hip *n* cruachann *f*
hippopotamus *n* each-aibhne *m*
hire *v* (*workers*) fastaich, *also* fastaidh *vt*
hirsute *adj* ròmach
historian *n* eachdraiche *m*
historical *adj* eachdraidheil
history *n* eachdraidh *f*
hither *adv* an seo, a-bhos, an taobh seo, an
taobh a-bhos, a-nall
hitherto *adv* gu ruige seo
hoar frost *n* liath-reothadh *m*
hoard *n* tasgaidh *f*
hoard *v* taisg *vt*
hoarse *adj* tùchanach, garbh
hoarseness *n* tùchadh *m*
hobby *n* cur-seachad *m*
hobnail *n* tacaid *f*
hoe *n* todha *m*
hoe *v* todhaig *vt*
hoeing *n* obair-todha *f*
hog(g) *n* othaisg *f*
hoist *v* tog *vt*
hold *n* grèim *m*
hold *v* **1** (*take hold of*) gabh grèim (air),
(*keep*) cùm grèim (air); **2** (*contain*) cùm
vt, gabh *vt*; **3** *in expr* ~ **back** (*delay*) cùm
vt air ais, cuir maille air/ann an); **4** *in expr*
~ **on** (*save*) cùm *vt*, glèidh *vt*
holding *n* (*land*) lot *f*
hole *n* toll *m*
hole *v* toll *vt*

holiday n 1 (*vacation*) saor-latha m, ~s làithean-saora/saor-làithean mpl; 2 (*public*) latha-fèille m

holiness n naomhachd f

Holland n An Òlaind f

hollow adj còsach, falamh

hollow n 1 toll m; 2 (*topog*) còs m, glac f, lag f

holly n cuileann m

holy adj naomh

homage (*before royalty etc*) ùmhlachd f

home adv dhachaigh

home n 1 dachaigh f; 2 in exprs **at ~** aig an taigh

homeland n dùthaich f

homesick adj cianalach

homesickness n cianalas m

homewards adv dhachaigh

homogeneous adj aon-sheòrsach

homonym n co-ainmear m

homosexuality n fearas-feise f

honest adj onarach, ionraic

honesty n onair f, ionracas m

honey n mil f

honeycomb n cìr-mheala f

honeymoon n mìos nam pòg m

honeysuckle n iadh-shlat f, lus m na meala m

honorary adj onarach, urramach

honour n 1 (*personal*) onair f; 2 (*distinction*) urram m; 3 (*renown*) cliù m, glòir f

honour v 1 (*bestow*) onaraich vt, cuir/ builich urram air; 2 (*respect*) onaraich vt; 3 (*fulfil*) coilean vt

honourable adj onarach, urramach

hood n (*headgear*) cochall m

hoodie n feannag ghlas

hoof n ìne f, ladhar m

hook n (*for fastenings etc*) cromag f, dubhan m

hoolie n hòro-gheallaidh m

hooligan n glagaire m

hooliganism n miastachd f, glagaireachd f

hoop n (*wooden*) rong f

hooter n dùdach f, dùdag f

hope n 1 dòchas m; 2 (*expectation*) dùil f

hope v bi vi irreg an dòchas

hopeless adj gun dòchas

hopelessness n eu-dòchas m

horizon n fàire f

horizontal adj còmhnard

horn n 1 (*animal*) adharc f; 2 (*instrument/ drinking*) còrn m

hornless adj maol

horrible adj 1 uabhasach, oillteil, sgreamhail; 2 (*behaviour*) suarach

horrify v cuir oillt air, oilltich vt

horror n uamhann m, oillt f, uabhas m

horse n each m

horsefly n creithleag f

horsehair n gaoisid f

horseman n marcaiche m

horsemanship n marcachadh m, marcachd f

horseshoe n crudha m

horticulture n tuathanachas-gàrraidh m

hose¹ n (*water*) pìob-uisge f

hose² n (*stockings*) osain/osanan m, stocainnean f

hospitable adj fialaidh, fial, fàilteachail, fàilteach, faoilidh

hospital n ospadal m, taigh-eiridinn m

hospitality n aoigheachd f, furan m

host¹ n (*hotel*) òstair m, (*house*) fear (an) taighe m

host² n 1 (*body*) mòr-shluagh m; 2 (*army*) feachd mf

hostage n bràigh mf

hostel n ostail f

hostile adj nàimhdeil

hostility n nàimhdeas m

hot adj teth

hot-blooded adj lasanta

hotel n taigh-òsta m

hotelier n òstair m

hot-water-bottle n botal-teth m

hour n uair f

house n taigh m, fàrdach f

house v 1 (*people*) thoir taigh do, thoir lòistinn do; 2 (*objects*) glèidh vt

housecoat n còta-leapa m

house-fly n cuileag f

housewife n bean (an) taighe f

housework n obair-taighe f

housing n taigheadas m

how inter adv 1 ciamar; 2 dè cho

howe n (*topog*) lag m

however adv 1 ge-tà, co-dhiù, a dh'aindeoin; 2 (*concessive*) air cho

howl n (*dog*) ulfhart m, donnal m

howl v 1 (*animals*) nuallaich, (*dogs*) dèan ulfhart m; 2 (*humans*) ràn vi

howling n 1 (*animals*) nuallaich f, (*dogs*) donnalaich f; 2 (*humans*) rànail m, rànaich f

hubbub n ùpraid f, gleadhraich f, othail f, iorghail f, toirm f

hue n 1 (*colour*) dath m; 2 (*complexion*) fiamh m, neul m; 3 (*features*) tuar m

hug v fàisg vt

huge adj ro-mhòr, uabhasach mòr, eagalach mòr

hum n crònan m, torman m

hum v dèan crònan m, dèan torman m

human adj daonna

humane adj truacanta, iochdmhor, daonnach

humanity n 1 (*abst*) daonnachd f; 2 (*con*) an cinne-daonna m, mac an duine m

humble adj 1 (*status*) ìosal/ìseal, iriosal/iriseal; 2 (*self-effacing*) umha(i)l, iriosal/iriseal

humble v (*humiliate*) ùmhlaich vt, irioslaich/irislich vt, ìslich vt

humbleness ùmhlachd f, irioslachd/irisleachd f

humid adj tais

humidity n taise f, taisead m

humiliate v ùmhlaich vt, irioslaich/irislich vt, ìslich vt

humiliation n ùmhlachadh m, irioslachadh/irisleachadh m, ìsleachadh m

humility n irioslachd/irisleachd f

humming n crònan m, torman m

humorous adj èibhinn, àbhachdach

humour n 1 àbhachd f, àbhachdas m; 2 (*mood*) gleus mf, gean m

hump n (*on back*) croit/cruit f

hump-backed adj crotach

hundred n and num adj ceud m

hundredth n ceudamh m

hundredth num adj ceudamh m

hung adj & past part crochte

Hungarian n & adj Ungaireach m

Hungary n (*used with art*) An Ungair f

hungry adj acrach, acrasach, gionach

hunt n sealg f, ruaig f

hunt v sealg vti

hunter, huntsman n sealgair m

hunting n sealg f

hurricane n doineann f

hurried adj cabhagach

hurry n cabhag f

hurry v 1 (*as vi*) greas vi air, dèan cabhag, ~ (**up**)! greas ort! ; 2 (*as vt*) ~ **up** cuir cabhag air, luathaich vt

hurt adj & past part ciùrrte, leònta/leònte, air do (*etc*) ghoirteachadh

hurt n ciùrradh m, leòn m, goirteas m

hurt v 1 (*as vt*) goirtich vt, ciùrr vt, leòn vt; 2 (*as vi*) bi vi irreg goirt

hurtful adj 1 (*emotionally*) cronail; 2 (*remarks etc*) guineach

husband n duine m, cèile m, companach m

hush! excl ist!, pl istibh!, also eist!, pl eistibh!

hush v ciùinich vt, (*child*) tàlaidh vt

husk n cochall m, plaosg m

hydro-electricity n dealan-uisge m

hydrogen n hàidraidean m

hymn n laoidh mf, dàn spioradail m

hyphen n tàthan m

hypocrisy n cealg f

hypocrite n cealgair(e) m

hypocritical adj cealgach

hypothesis n beachd-bharail f

hypothetical adj baralach

I

I *pers pron* mi, mise

ice *n* eigh/eighre *f*, deigh *f*

iceberg *n* cnoc-eighre *m*, beinn-deighe *f*

ice cream *n* reòiteag *f*

Iceland *n* Innis Tìle *f*

Icelander *n* Tìleach *m*

Icelandic *adj* Tìleach

icicle *n* caisean reòthta *m*, stob reòthta *m*

icon *n* ìomhaigh cràbhaidh *f*

Id *n* (*psych*), *used with art*, **the ~** an t-Eadh *m*

idea *n* beachd *m*, beachd-smuain *f*, smuain *f*

identical *adj* co-ionann

idiom *n* (*lang*) gnàthas-cainnte *m*

idiomatic *adj* (*lang*) gnàthasach

idiot *n* amadan *m*, bumailear *m*, òinseach *f*

idle *adj* **1** (*unoccupied*) na do (*etc*) thàmh, dìomhain; **2** (*lazy*) leisg; **3** *in expr* ~ **talk** rabhd *m*, ràbhart *m*

idleness *n* **1** (*inactivity*) tàmh *m*; **2** (*laziness*) leisg(e) *f*

idol *n* ìomhaigh *f*, iodhal *m*

if *conj* **1** ma, (*neg*) mur(a); **2** (*hypothetical, past/conditional*) nan

ignite *v* **1** (*as vt*) cuir teine ri, las *v*; **2** (*as vi*) rach *vi* na t(h)eine

ignominy *n* nàire *f*, masladh *m*

ill *adj* **1** (*sick*) tinn, euslainteach, bochd; **2** *in expr* ~ **at ease** anshocrach; **3** (*bad*) droch; eu- *or* mì-

ill-bred *adj* mì-mhodhail

illegal *adj* mì-laghail

illegitimate *adj* **1** (*bastard*) dìolain; **2** (*morally etc*) neo-dhligheil

illegitimacy *n* (*bastardy*) dìolanas *m*

ill-health *n* tinneas *m*, euslainte *f*, anfhannachd *f*

ill-humour *n* gruaim *f*

ill-humoured *adj* gruamach

ill-mannered *adj* mì-mhodhail

illness *n* **1** (*abstr*) tinneas *m*, euslainte *f*; **2** (*con*) tinneas *m*, galar *m*

ill-tempered *adj* **1** crost(a), diombach, gruamach, greannach; droch-nàdarrach

ill-timed *adj* mì-thràthail

ill-treatment *n* droch-làimhseachadh *m*

illuminate *v* soilleirich *vt*

illumination *n* soilleireachadh *m*

illustrate *v* dealbhaich *vt*

illustrious *adj* ainmeil, cliùiteach, iomraiteach, òirdheirc

ill-will *n* gamhlas *m*, mì-rùn *m*

im- *neg prefix* do-, mì-, eu-

image *n* **1** (*art etc*) ìomhaigh *f*; **2** (*likeness*) mac-samhail *m*

imagery *n* ìomhaigheachd *f*

imaginary *adj* mac-meanmnach

imagination *n* mac-meanmna *m*

imaginative *adj* mac-meanmnach, tionnsgalach

imagine *v* dealbh *vt*

immature *adj* an-abaich

immeasurable *adj* gun tomhas

immerse *v* bog *vt*, tum *vt*

immersion *n* bogadh *m*, tumadh *m*

immigrant *n*, neach-imrich *m*, in-imriche *m*

immigration *n* imrich a-steach *f*, in-imrich *f*

imminent *adj* a tha a' tighinn

immoral *adj* mì-bheusach

immorality *n* mì-bheus *f*

immune *adj* saor, dìonta

impact *n* **1** (*phys*) co-bhualadh *m*; **2** (*effect*) buaidh *f*; **3** (*impression*) drùidheadh *m*

impartial *adj* cothromach, gun lethbhreith *f*

impatience *n* **1** mì-fhoighidinn *f*; **2** (*longing*) fadachd *f*, fadal *m*

impatient *adj* mì-fhoighidneach

impede *v* cuir bacadh air, cuir maille air/ann

imperative *adj* **1** (*essential*) riatanach, deatamach; **2** (*gram*) àithneach

imperfect *adj* neo-choileanta

imperial *adj* ìompaireil

impermeable *adj* neo-dhrùidhteach

impersonal *adj* **1** neo-phearsanta; **2** (*person etc*) fuar, fad'-às, dùinte

impersonate *v* pearsanaich *vt*, riochdaich *vt*

impertinence *n* mì-mhodh *mf*, beadaidheachd *f*, dànadas *m*

impertinent *adj* mì-mhodhail, beadaidh, dàna, bathaiseach

impetuous *adj* bras, cas

impetus *n* deann *f*, dèine *f*

implacable *adj* neo-thruacanta

implement *n* inneal *m*, acainn *f*

implement *v* cuir *vt* an gnìomh, thoir *vt* gu buil

implicated *adj & past part* an lùib, an sàs

impolite *adj* mì-mhodhail

import[1] *n* (*trade*) bathar a-steach *m*, in-mhalairt *f*

import[2] *n* (*meaning*) seagh *m*, brìgh *f*

import *v* thoir *vt* a-steach

importance *n* diofar *m*, deifir *f*, cudrom *m*

important *adj* cudromach, trom

impossible, **impracticable** *adjs* do-dhèanta

impractical *adj* do-dhèanta

impression *n* 1 (*mark*) comharradh *m*, lorg *f*; 2 (*impact*) drùidheadh *m*; 3 (*printing*) clò-bhualadh *m*

impressive *adj* drùidhteach

imprint *n* 1 (*phys*) lorg *f*; 2 (*publishing*) clò *m*

imprisonment *n* braighdeanas *m*, daorsa *f*, ciomachas *m*

improbable *adj* eu-coltach

impromptu *adj* gun ullachadh *m*

improper *adj* 1 (*unsuitable*) mì-iomchaidh; 2 (*indecent etc*) mì-bheusach, drabasta

improve *v* 1 (*as vt*) leasaich *vt*; 2 (*as vi*) rach *vi* am feabhas

improvement *n* 1 leasachadh *m*; 2 (*in skill etc*) piseach *m*

impudence *n* beadaidheachd *f*, dànadas *m*

impudent *adj* beadaidh, dàna, bathaiseach

impulsive *adj* bras

in *prep* 1 (*position, situation*) ann an; (*movement*) a-steach, a-staigh

in- *neg prefix* mì-, do-, an-, eu/ao-, neo-

inaccurate *adj* mearachdach

inactivity *n* tàmh *m*

inadequacy *n* uireasbhaidh *f*

inadequate *adj* uireasbhach

inadvertent neo-aireach

inappropriate *adj* neo-iomchaidh

incalculable *adj* gun tomhas *m*

incantation *n* ortha *f*

incapable *adj* neo-chomasach

incessant *adj* leanailteach

incest *n* col *m*

incestuous *adj* colach

inch *n* òirleach *mf*

incident *n* tachartas *m*, tuiteamas *m*

incidental *adj* tuiteamach

incisor *n* (*tooth*) clàr-fhiacail *f*

inclination *n* 1 (*desire*) togradh *m*; 2 (*tendency*) aomadh *m*

incline *n* 1 claonadh *m*; 2 (*topog*) leathad *m*, bruthach *mf*

incline *v* 1 crom *vti*, claon *vt*; 2 (*tend*) aom *vi*

inclined *adj* dual(t)ach, buailteach

include *v* gabh *vt* a-steach

income *n* teachd-a-steach *m*

incomer *n* coigreach *m*, srainnsear *m*

incoming *adj* a thig *vi* a-steach

incompetence *n* neo-chomasachd *f*

incompetent *adj* neo-chomasach

incomplete *adj* neo-iomlan

inconsistent *adj* 1 (*variable*) caochlaideach, neo-sheasmhach; 2 (*contradictory etc*) neo-chòrdail

inconvenience *n* dragh *m*

inconvenience *v* cuir dragh air, bodraig *vt*

incorrect *adj* mearachdach, ceàrr

increase *n* 1 meudachadh *m*, àrdachadh *m*

increase *v* meudaich *vti*, cinn *vi*, rach *vi* am meud

incumbent *adj* mar fhiachaibh air

indebted *adj & past part* (*fin*) fo fhiachaibh

indecent *adj* mì-bheusach, drabasta

indecency *n* mì-bheusachd *f*, drabastachd *f*

indeed *adv* 1 gu dearbh; 2 (*as intensifier*) gu dearbh fhèin, uabhasach fhèin, cianail (fhèin)

indefinite *adj* neo-chinnteach

indentation *n* eag *f*

independence *n* neo-eisimeileachd *f*

independent *adj* neo-eisimeileach

index *n* 1 (*contents*) clàr-amais *m*; 2 (*scale*) clàr-innse *m*

India *n* na h-Innseachan *fpl*

Indian *n & adj* Innseanach *m*

indicate *v* comharraich *vt*

indicative *adj* taisbeanach

indicator *n* taisbeanair *m*

Indies, the *npl*, **the East** ~ na h-Innseachan an Ear *fpl*, **the West** ~ na h-Innseachan an Iar *fpl*

indifference *n* (*attitude*) neo-shuim *f*

indifferent *adj* 1 coma; 2 (*quality*) meadhanach
indigence *n* uireasbhaidh *f*, ainniseachd *f*
indigenous *adj* dùthchasach, tùsanach
indigent *adj* uireasbhach
indignant *adj* diombach
indignation *n* diomb *m*
indignity *n* tàmailt *f*
indirect *adj* neo-dhìreach
indispensable *adj* riatanach
indissoluble *adj* do-sgaoilte
individual *adj* 1 (*personal*) pearsanta; 2 (*separate*) fa leth
individual *n* neach *m*, duine *m*, urra *m*
individually *adv* fa leth
Indo-European *adj & n* Indo-Eòrpach *m*
indolence *n* leisg(e) *f*
indolent *adj* leisg
industrial *adj* gnìomhachail, tionnsgalach
industrious *adj* dèanadach, gnìomhach, dìcheallach
industriousness *n* dèanadas *m*, gnìomhachas *m*
industry *n* 1 (*abstr*) dèanadas *m*; 2 (*manufacturing etc*) gnìomhachas *m*
inebriate *v* cuir *vt* air mhisg
inebriated *v* misgeach, air mhisg
inefficiency *n* neo-èifeachdas *m*
inefficient *adj* neo-èifeachdach
inequality *n* eas-aontarachd *f*, neo-ionannachd *f*
infant *n* leanabh *m*, leanaban *m*, pàiste *m*
infantile *adj* leanabail
infatuate *v* dall *vt*, cuir *vt* fo gheasaibh
infectious *adj* gabhaltach
inferior *adj* 1 (*in rank*) ìochd(a)rach, (n)as ìsle; 2 (*in quality*) (n)as miosa
inferior *n* ìochdaran *m*
inferiority *n* ìochdaranachd *f*
infernal *adj* ifrinneach
infertile *adj* neo-thorrach
infertility *n* neo-thorrachas *m*
infestation *n* plàigh *f*
infinite *adj* neo-chrìochnach
infinitive *adj* neo-chrìochnach
infinity *n* neo-chrìochnachd *f*
infirm *adj* euslainteach, anfhann
infirmary *n* taigh-eiridinn *m*
infirmity *n* 1 euslainte *f*, anfhannachd *f*, laigse *f*
inflame *v* cuir lasair ri
inflammable *adj* lasanta

inflate *v* sèid *vt* (suas)
inflation *n* 1 (*lit*) sèideadh *m*; 2 (*fin*) atmhorachd *f*
inflexible *adj* rag
influence *n* 1 (*personal etc*) cumhachd *mf*, buaidh *f*; 2 *in expr* **under the ~ of** an lùib *f*, fo bhuaidh *f* (*both with gen*)
influence *v* thoir buaidh air
influential *adj* buadhach, cumhachdach
inform *v* 1 thoir fios gu, cuir fios gu, cuir brath gu, innis do
informal *adj* neo-fhoirmeil
informality *n* neo-fhoirmealachd *f*
information *n* fiosrachadh *m*, fios *m*
informed *adj* fiosrach, fiosraichte
infra- *prefix*, fo-, bun-
ingenious *adj* innleachdach, teòma, tionnsgalach
ingenuity *n* innleachd *f*, tionnsgal *m*
ingredient *n* tàthchuid *f*, cungaidh *f*
inhabit *v* còmhnaich *vi* ann an, fuirich *vi* ann an, àitich *vt*
inhabitant *n* neach-àiteachaidh *m*, neach-còmhnaidh *m*
inherent *adj* 1 (*in person*) dual(t)ach; 2 (*in situation etc*) bunaiteach, bunasach, gnèitheach
inherit *v* sealbhaich *vt* (mar oighreachd), faigh *vt* mar oighreachd
inheritance *n* 1 (*material*) oighreachd *f*; 2 (*cultural*) dualchas *m*
inheritor *n* oighre *m*
inimical *adj* nàimhdeil
initial *adj* ciad
initially *adv* an toiseach(-tòiseachaidh), sa chiad dol-a-mach, sa chiad àite
injure *v* 1 (*phys*) goirtich *vt*, (*phys/emotionally*) leòn *vt*, ciùrr *vt*; 2 (*emotionally*) dèan cron air
injured *adj* leònta/leònte, ciùrrte
injurious *adj* cronail, lochdach, millteach
injury *n* 1 (*phys/emotional*) leòn *m*; 2 (*emotional*) cron *m*
injustice *n* mì-cheartas *m*
ink *n* inc *m*, dubh *m*
inn *n* taigh-òsta *m*
innards *n* innidh *f*, mionach *m*, (*animals*) greallach *f*
innate *adj* 1 (*in person*) dual(t)ach; 2 (*in object*) gnèitheach
innkeeper *n* òstair *m*, fear (an) taighe *m*
innocence *n* neoichiontachd *f*

innocent *adj* neoichiontach, neoichionta
innuendo *n* leth-fhacal *m*
innumerable *adj* do-àireamh
input *n* cur-a-steach *m*
input *v* cuir *vt* ann an
inquiry *n* rannsachadh *m*
inquisitive *adj* ceasnachail, faighneachail
insane *adj* air chuthach, air bhàinidh, air bhoile, às do (*etc*) chiall, às do rian
insanity *n* cuthach *m*, bàinidh *f*, boile *f*
insect *n* frìde *f*, meanbh-fhrìde *f*
inseparable *adj* do-sgaradh
inside *adv* 1 (*position*) a-staigh;
  2 (*movement*) a-steach
inside *n* 1 taobh a-staigh *m*, (*building etc*) broinn *f*; 2 (*in expr*) ~ **out** caoin air ascaoin
inside *prep* 1 (*position*) a-staigh ann an, am broinn; 2 (*movement*) a-steach do
insight *n* 1 (*abstr*) tuigse *f*, lèirsinn *f*;
  2 (*con*) geur-bheachd *m*
insignificant *adj* crìon, suarach
insipid *adj* leamhach
inspect *v* sgrùd *vt*
inspection *n* sgrùdadh *m*
inspector *n* neach-sgrùdaidh *m*
inspire *v* misnich *vt*
instalment *n* earrann *f*
instance *n* 1 (*example*) eisimpleir *m*, **for** ~ mar eisimpleir; 2 *in expr* **in the first** ~ an toiseach, anns a' chiad dol-a-mach
instant *adj* grad-
instant *n* 1 mòmaid *f*, plathadh *m*, tiota *m*;
  2 (*idiom*) **in an** ~ ann am priobadh (na sùla)
instruct *v* 1 (*educate etc*) teagaisg *vt*, oileanaich *vt*; 2 (*command etc*) òrdaich *vt*
instruction *n* 1 (*ed*) foghlam *m*, teagasg *m*, oileanachadh *m*; 2 (*command etc*) òrdugh *m*; 3 ~**s** (*for use etc*) seòladh *m*
instrument *n* 1 (*device etc*) inneal *m*, ball-acainn *m*; 2 (*musical*) ionnsramaid *f*, inneal-ciùil *m*
insubordinate *adj* eas-umhail
insulate *v* dealaich *vt*
insulating *adj* (*non-conductive*) do-ghiùlan
insult *n* tàmailt *f*, tàir *f*
insult *v* dèan tàir air, tàmailtich *vt*
insulting *adj* tàmailteach, tàireil
insurance *n* àrachas *m*, urras *m*
integrity *n* ionracas *m*

intellect *n* inntinn *f*
intellectual *adj* inntinneach
intelligence *n* inntinn *f*, tuigse *f*
intelligent *adj* toinisgeil, tuigseach, eirmseach
intend *v* bi *vi irreg* airson, cuir *vt* romhad (*etc*), rùnaich *vi*
intense *adj* 1 (*persons etc*) dian; 2 (*heat etc*) anabarrach
intensity *n* dèine *f*
intensive *adj* dian, dlùth
intent, intention *n* rùn *m*
intentionally *adv* a dh'aon rùn, a dh'aon ghnothach
inter- *prefix* eadar-
inter *v* tiodhlaic *vt*, adhlaic *vt*
interact *v* eadar-obraich *vi*
intercourse *n* 1 (*social*) conaltradh *m*, caidreabh *m*; 2 (*sexual*) cleamhnas *m*, feis(e) *f*, co-ghineadh *m*, cuplachadh *m*
interest *n* 1 ùidh *f*; 2 (*fin*) riadh *m*
interesting *adj* inntinneach, ùidheil
interface *n* eadar-aghaidh *f*
interfere *v* gabh gnothach ri, buin *vi* do/ri
interim *adj* eadar-amail
interior *n* taobh a-staigh *m*, (*building etc*) broinn *f*
interlude *n* eadar-ùine *f*
intermarriage *n* eadar-phòsadh *m*
intermediate *adj* eadar-mheadhanach
intermingle, intermix *v* co-mheasgaich, coimeasgaich *vti*
international *adj* eadar-nàiseanta
internet *n* eadar-lìon *m*
interpret *v* 1 (*explain etc*) mìnich *vt*;
  2 (*lang*) eadar-theangaich *vti*
interpretation *n* 1 mìneachadh *m*;
  2 (*lang*) eadar-theangachadh *m*
interpreter *n* (*lang*) eadar-theangaiche *m*
interrogate *v* ceasnaich *vt*
interrogation *n* ceasnachadh *m*
interrogative *adj* ceisteach
interrogator *n* neach-ceasnachaidh *m*
interrupt *v* (*halt*) caisg *vt*, (*intrude etc*) bris(t) *vi* a-steach air
interruption *n* (*halting*) casgadh *m*, (*intrusion etc*) bristeadh a-steach *m*
interval *n* 1 (*space*) beàrn *mf*; 2 (*time*) eadar-ùine *f*
interview *n* agallamh *m*
intestine *n* 1 caolan *m*; 2 ~**s** innidh *f*, (*animals*) greallach *f*

intimate *adj* dlùth, dlùth-chàirdeil
into *prep* do, a-steach do
intoxicating *adj* daorachail
intoxication *n* daorach *f*, misg *f*
intrepid *adj* dàna, cruadalach
intrepidity *n* dànadas *m*, cruadal *m*
introduce *v* (*people*) cuir *vt* an aithne
introduction *n* **1** (*people*) cur an aithne;
  2 (*book etc*) ro-ràdh *m*
introvert *adj* dùinte
intuition *n* imfhios *m*
intuitive *adj* imfhiosach
inured *adj* dèanta (**to** ri)
invalid *adj* (*documents etc*) neo-dhligheach
invalid *n* euslainteach *m*
invent *v* innlich *vt*, tionnsgail/tionnsgain
  vt
invention *n* innleachd *f*, tionnsgal *m*
inventive *adj* innleachdach, tionnsgalach
inventiveness *n* innleachd *f*, tionnsgal *m*
inventor *n* tionnsgalair *m*, innliche *m*
invert *v* **1** (*turn over*) cuir *vt* bun-os-cionn;
  2 (*maths etc*) cuir *vt* an àite a chèile
inverted *adj & past part* **1** (*turned over*)
  bun-os-cionn; **2** (*typog*) ~ **commas**
  cromagan turrach *fpl*
invest *v* (*fin*) cuir *vt* an seilbh
investigate *v* rannsaich *vt*
investigation *n* rannsachadh *m*
investment *n* **1** (*abstr, activity*) cur an
  seilbh *m*, tasgadh *m*; **2** (*funds*) airgead an
  seilbh *m*, airgead-tasgaidh *m*
investor *n* neach-tasgaidh *m*
invigorate *v* neartaich *vt*
invitation *n* cuireadh *m*, fiathachadh *m*
invite *v* fiathaich *vt*, iarr *vt*
invoice *n* cunntas *m*
involved *adj & past part* **1** an sàs ann
  an; **2** *in expr* **get** ~ gabh gnothach ri;
  3 (*attached to*) an lùib (*with gen*)
ir- *neg prefix* mì-, neo-, eas-
Ireland *n* Èirinn (*gen* na h-Èireann) *f*
Irish *adj* Èireannach, na h-Èireann
Irishman *n* Èireannach *m*

Irish Republic (the) *n* Poblachd na
  h-Èireann *f*
iron *n* iarann *m*
iron *v* (*clothes etc*) iarnaich & iarnaig *vti*
iron filings min-iarainn *f*
ironic(al) *adj* ìoranta
ironing *n* (*activity/items*) iarnachadh &
  iarnaigeadh *m*
irony *n* ìoran(t)as *m*
irreconcilable *adj* do-rèiteachail
irregular *adj* **1** mì-riaghailteach, mì-òrdail;
  2 (*gram*) neo-riaghailteach
irrelevant *adj* nach buin ris a' chùis/ris
  a' ghnothach, gun bhuntainneas, nach eil
  buntainneach
irresponsible *adj* neo-chùramach
irreverent *adj* eas-umhail, eas-urramach
irrigate *v* uisgich *vti*
irrigation *n* uisgeachadh *m*
irritable *adj* crost(a), dranndanach,
  frionasach, cas
irritate *v* cuir greann air, cuir an fhearg air
irritating *adj* (*situations etc*) leamh
Islamic *adj* Ioslamach
island *n* eilean *m*, innis *f*
islander *n* eileanach *m*
isle *n* eilean *m*
Isle of Man Eilean Mhanainn *m*
isolated *adj* iomallach
Israel *n* Iosarail/Israel *f*
Israeli *n* Iosaraileach/Israeleach *m*
Israelite *n & adj* Iosaraileach/Israelach *m*
issue *n* **1** (*matter etc*) ceist *f*, cùis *f*,
  gnothach *m*; **2** (*outcome*) toradh *f*, buil *f*
  3 (*progeny*) gineal *mf*, sìol *m*, sliochd *m*
issue *v* cuir *vt* a-mach
it *pron* (*f*) i, (*m*) e
Italian *adj & n* **1** Eadailteach *m*; **2** (*lang*) an
  Eadailtis *f*
italics *npl* clò eadailteach *m*
Italy *n* An Eadailt *f*
itch *n* tachas *m*
itch *v* tachais *vi*
ivy *n* eidheann *f*

J

jab *n* (*elbow etc*) ùpag *f*
jab *v* (*with elbow etc*) uillnich *vti*, thoir ùpag do
jackdaw *n* cathag *f*
jagged *adj* eagach
jam *n* silidh *m*
jamb *n* ursainn *f*
janitor *n* dorsair *m*
January *n* am Faoilteach/Faoilleach *m*
Japan *n* an t-Seapan *f*, Iapan *f*
Japanese *n* (*lang*) Seapanais *f*, Iapanais *f*
jaundice *n* a' bhuidheach *f*
jaw *n* giall *f*, peirceall *m*
jawbone *n* peirceall *m*
javelin *n* gath *m*, sleagh *f*
jealous *adj* 1 (*esp sexually*) eudach, eudmhor; 2 (*envious*) farmadach
jealousy *n* 1 (*esp sexual*) eud *m*, eudach *m*; 2 (*envy*) farmad *m*
jeans *n* dinichean *fpl*
jeer *v* mag *vi* air
jeering *adj* magail
jeering *n* magadh *m*
jelly *m* silidh *m*
jersey *n* geansaidh *m*
jest *n* fealla-dhà *f*
Jew *n* Iùdhach *m*
jewel *n* seud *m*, àilleag *f*, leug *f*, (*ornamental*) usgar *m*
jeweller *n* seudaire *m*
Jewish *adj* Iùdhach
jiffy *n* (*instant*) priobadh (na sùla) *m*, tiota *m*
jingle *v* dèan gliong
jingling *n* gliong *m*, gliongartaich *f*
job *n* obair *f*, cosnadh *m*, dreuchd *f*
Jock and Doris *n* deoch-an-dorais *f*
jog *n* (*with elbow etc*) ùpag *f*
jog *v* (*with elbow etc*) put *vt*, thoir ùpag do
join *v* 1 (*fix*) ceangail *vt*, tàth *vt*; 2 (*enlist etc*) gabh *vi* ann an
joint *adj* co- *prefix*
joint *n* (*anat*) alt *m*
jointed *adj* altach

joke *n* 1 fealla-dhà *f*, abhcaid *f*; 2 (*story*) naidheachd *f*; 3 (*practical*) cleas *m*, car *m*
joke *v* bi *vi irreg* ri fealla-dhà
joking *n* fealla-dhà *f*
jollity *n* cridhealas *m*
jostle *n* ùpag *f*
jostle *v* uillnich *vti*, put *vti*
journal *n* 1 (*diary*) leabhar-latha *m*; 2 (*periodical*) iris *f*, ràitheachan *m*
journalist *n* neach-naidheachd *m*, naidheachdair *m*
journey *n* turas *m*
journey *v* siubhail *vi*, imich *vi*, triall *vi*
jovial *adj* cridheil
joy *n* gàirdeachas *m*, àgh *m*
joyful *adj* aighearach, greannmhor, àghmhor
judge *v* breithnich *vti*, thoir breith air
judg(e)ment *n* 1 (*capacity*) tuigse *f*, toinisg *f*; 2 (*legal*) breith *f*, binn *f*, breithneachadh *m*
juggler *n* cleasaiche *m*
juggling *n* cleasachd *f*
juice *n* sùgh *m*
juicy *adj* sùghmhor
July *n* an t-Iuchar *m*
jumble *n* 1 (*collection*) trealaich *f*, truileis *f*, sgudal *m*; 2 (*disorder*) bùrach *m*
jump *n* leum *m*, sùrdag *f*
jump *v* 1 leum *vti*; 2 (*fright*) clisg *vi*
jumper *n* geansaidh *m*
jumpy *adj* (*nervous etc*) clisgeach
June *n* an t-Ògmhios *m*
junk *n* 1 (*objects*) trealaich *f*, truileis *f*; 2 (*rubbish*) sgudal *m*
jury *n* diùraidh *m*
just *adj* (*upright*) dìreach, ceart
just *adv* 1 (*simply, altogether*) dìreach!; 2 (*moment ago*) dìreach; 3 (*expr agreement*) ~ **so!** dìreach (sin)!; 4 *in expr* ~ **about** (*practically*) cha mhòr, an ìre mhath; 5 (*in comparisons*) a cheart
justice *n* ceartas *m*, còir *f*, ionracas *m*
juvenile *adj* leanabail

K

kail *n* càl *m*

keel *n* **1** (*boat*) druim *m*; **2** *in expr* **put on an even** ~ rèitich *vt*

keen *adj* **1** èasgaidh, dùrachdach, dian; **2** *in expr* ~ **on** dèidheil air

keenness *n* dèine *f*

keep *v* **1** cùm *vt*; **2** (*store*) glèidh *vt*

keepsake *n* cuimhneachan *m*

kelp *n* ceilp *f*

kelpie *n* each-uisge *m*

kennel *n* taigh *m* chon

kept *adj & past part* glèidhte

kerb *n* (*pavement*) iomall-cabhsair *m*

kernel *n* eitean *m*

kestrel *n* clamhan-ruadh *m*

kettle *n* coire *m*

key *n* **1** (*for locking etc*) iuchair; **2** (*music*) gleus *m*

keyboard *n* meur-chlàr *m*

khaki *adj* lachdann

kid *n* **1** (*goat*) meann *m*; **2** (*child*) pàiste *m*

kid *v* tarraing *vi* à

kidney *n* dubhag *f*, àra *f*, àirne *f*

kill *v* marbh *vt*

killer *n* marbhaiche *m*, murtair *m*

killing *n* marbhadh *m*

kiln *n* àth *f*

kilo, kilogram *n* cilo *m*, cileagram *m*

kilometre *n* cilemeatair *m*

kilt *n* fèile(adh) beag, èile(adh) beag

kilt *v* tru(i)s *vt*

kin *adj* càirdeach do

kind *adj* coibhneil, laghach

kind *n* seòrsa *m*, gnè *f*

kindle *v* **1** (*as vt*) las *vt*; **2** (*as vi*) gabh *vi*

kindliness *n* coibhneas *m*

kindly *adj* coibhneil, còir, bàidheil

kindness *n* **1** (*abstr*) coibhneas *m*; **2** (*con*) bàidh *f*

king *n* rìgh *m*

kingdom *n* rìoghachd *f*

kingly *adj* rìoghail

kinship *n* càirdeas *m*

kirkton *n* clachan *m*

kirkyard *n* cladh *m*, clachan *m*, cill *f*

kiss *n* pòg *f*

kiss *v* pòg *vt*

kitchen *n* cidsin *m*

kite *n* **1** (*structure*) iteileag *f*; **2** (*bird*) clamhan-gòbhlach *m*

kitten *n* piseag *f*, isean-cait *m*

knack *n* liut *f*

knead *v* (*dough*) fuin *vt*

knee *n* glùn *f*

kneecap *n* failmean/falman *m*

knees-up *n* hòro-gheallaidh *m*

knickers *n* drathais/drathars *f*

knight *n* ridire *m*

knit *v* figh *vti*

knitted *adj & past part* fighte

knitter *n* figheadair *m*

knitting *n* fighe *f*

knob *n* cnap *m*, cnag *f*

knobby, knobbly *adj* cnapach

knock *n* **1** (*sound*) cnag *f*; **2** (*on door etc*) gnogadh *m*; **3** (*blow*) buille *f*, bualadh *m*

knock *v* **1** (*as vi*) cnag *vi*; **2** (*as vt*) gnog *vt*; **3** (*strike*) buail *vt*; **4** *in expr* ~ **down** *v* leag *vt*

knocking *n* (*noise, on door etc*) gnogadh *m*

knoll *n* tom *m*, cnoc *m*, tulach *m*, tolm *m*

know *v* **1** (*esp people*) bi *vi irreg* eòlach air; **2** (*facts*) bi *vi irreg* fios agad

knowe *n* tom *m*, cnoc *m*, tulach *m*, tolm *m*

knowledge *n* **1** (*information*) fios *m*; **2** (*learned*) eòlas *m*

knowledgeable *adj* eòlach, fiosrach

knuckle *n* rùdan *m*

kyle(s) *n* caol *m*, caolas *m*

L

label *n* bileag *f*

label *v* cuir bileag air, bileagaich *vt*

laboratory *n* obair-lann *f*, deuchainn-lann *f*

labour *n* 1 saothair *f*, obair *f*; 2 (*pol*) **Labour** na Làbaraich *mpl*, am Pàrtaidh Làbarach

labour *v* saothraich *vi*, obraich *vi*

labourer *n* obraiche *m*

lace *n* (*shoe*) barrall *m*, iall-bròige *f*

lacerate *v* reub *vt*

lack *n* dìth *m*, cion *m*, easbhaidh *f*

lack *v* 1 bi *vi irreg* às aonais, bi gun; 2 (*be absent*) bi a dhìth, bi a dh'easbhaidh

lacking *adj & pres part* 1 a dhìth, a dh'easbhaidh; 2 gun, às aonais

lad, laddie *n* gille *m*, balach *m*

ladle *n* ladar *m*, liagh *f*

lady *n* 1 (*woman*) bean-uasal *f*; 2 (*female lord*) baintighearna *f*, leadaidh *f*

ladybird *n* daolag-bhreac-dhearg *f*

lag (behind) *v* bi *vi irreg* air dheireadh

lair *n* garaidh *m*

laird *n* uachdaran *m*, tighearna *m*

lake *n* loch *m*

lamb *n* 1 (*animal*) uan *m*; 2 (*meat*) uainfheòil *f*

lame *adj* crùbach, bacach, cuagach

lament *n* tuireadh *m*, cumha *m*

lament *v* caoidh *vti*, caoin *vi*, dèan tuireadh

lamentation *n* caoidh *f*, tuireadh *m*

lamp *n* lampa *mf*, lòchran *m*

land *n* 1 (*territory*) dùthaich *f*, tìr *f*; 2 (*earth*) talamh *m*, fearann *m*; 3 **on** ~ air tìr

land *v* laigh *vi*

landing-place *n* 1 (*boats*) laimrig *f*, cidhe *m*; 2 (*aircraft*) raon-laighe *m*

landlady *n* (*boarding house etc*) bean-taighe *f*

landlord *n* (*pub etc*) fear-taighe *m*, òstair *m*

landmark *n* (*navigational*) comharradh-stiùiridh *m*, iùl *m*

landowner *n* 1 neach-fearainn *m*; 2 (*landed*) tighearna *m*, uachdaran *m*

landscape *n* 1 (*phys*) cruth-tìre *m*; 2 (*art etc*) dealbh-tìre *mf*, sealladh-tìre *m*

lane *n* caol-shràid *f*, lònaid *f*

language *n* 1 (*general*) cainnt *f*; 2 (*national etc*) cànan *m*, cànain *f*

lanky *adj* caol, seang

lantern *n* lanntair *m*, lainntear *m*, lòchran *m*

lap² *n* (*part of body*) uchd *m*

lap² *n* (*race*) cuairt *f*

lap *v* imlich *vt*

lapwing *n* curracag *f*

large *adj* 1 mòr, (*burly*) tomadach; 2 *in expr* **by and** ~ san fharsaingeachd

larger *comp adj* mò/motha

lark *n* 1 (*bird*) uiseag *f*, topag *f*; 2 (*fun*) plòidh *f*, spòrs *f*; 3 (*trick etc*) car *m*, cleas *m*

laser *n* leusair *m*

lass, lassie *n* caileag *f*, nighean *f*

last *adj* mu dheireadh, deireannach

last *adv* 1 (*position*) air deireadh; 2 (*time*) *in expr* **at (long)** ~ mu dheireadh (thall)

last *v* 1 (*survive*) mair *vi*; 2 (*continue*) lean *vi*

lasting *adj* maireannach, leantainneach

latch *n* clàimhean *m*

late *adj & adv* 1 (*after time etc*) air deireadh, fadalach; 2 (*advanced hour*) anmoch; 3 (*deceased*) nach maireann

Latin *adj* Laidinneach

Latin *n* (*lang*) Laideann *f*

latter *adj* deireannach

lattice cliath-uinneig *f*

laugh *n* gàire *mf*

laugh *v* dèan gàire, gàir *vi*

laughing *n* gàireachdainn *f*, gàireachdaich *f*

laughing-stock *n* cùis-mhagaidh *f*, adhbhar-gàire *m*

laughter *n* gàire *mf*, gàireachdainn *f*

launch *v* 1 (*boat*) cuir *vt* air flod, cuir *vt* air bhog *f*; 2 (*company etc*) cuir *vt* air chois, cuir *vt* air b(h)onn

laundry *n* taigh-nighe *m*

law *n* lagh *m*

lawful *adj* 1 (*legal*) laghail; 2 (*legitimate*) dligheach

lawn *n* faiche *f*, rèidhlean *m*
lawsuit *n* cùis *f*, cùis-lagha *f*
lawyer *n* neach-lagha *m*
lay *n* (*poem*) laoidh *mf*
lay *v* **1** (*floortiles etc*) leag *vt*; **2** (*egg*) beir *vt*
laziness *n* leisg(e) *f*
lazy *adj* leisg
lazy-bed *n* feannag *f*
lazybones *n* leisgeadair *m*
lead *adj* (*principal etc*) prìomh
lead *n* **1** (*example*) stiùir *f*; **2** (*position*) *in expr* **in the ~** air thoiseach; **3** (*canine*) iall *f*
lead *n* (*metal*) luaidhe *mf*
lead *v* **1** treòraich *vt*, stiùir *vt*; **2** (*as vi*) bi *vi irreg* air thoiseach; **3** *in expr* **~ astray** claon *vt*, cuir *vt* air seachran, cuir *vt* air iomrall
leader *n* ceannard *m*
leadership *n* **1** (*abstr*) ceannardas *m*; **2** (*con*) luchd-ceannais *m*
leaf *n* duilleag *f*
leaflet *n* (*publication*) duilleachan *m*, bileag *f*
leak *n* aoidion *m*
leaking *adj* aoidionach
leakproof *adj* dìonach, uisge-dhìonach
leaky *adj* aoidionach
lean *adj* **1** (*person*) tana, seang; **2** (*meat*) gun saill *f*, neo-shultmhor
lean *v* **1** (*incline*) bi *vi irreg* air fhiaradh; **2** (*for support*) cuir/leig do thaic, cuir/leig do chudrom
leaning *adj* **1** (*not vertical*) claon, air fhiaradh *m*; **2** (*supported*) an taic, an tacsa
leap *n* leum *m*, sùrdag *f*
leap *v* leum *vti*
leap year *n* bliadhna-lèim *f*
learn *v* ionnsaich *vti*, tog *vt*
learned *adj* foghlaimte, foghlamaichte
learner *n* neach-ionnsachaidh *m*
learning *n* ionnsachadh *m*, foghlam *m*, oideachas *m*
lease *n* gabhail *mf*
lease *v* **1** (*~ out*) thoir *vt* (seachad) air gabhail/air mhàl; **2** (*rent*) gabh *vt* air mhàl
leash *n* iall *f*
least 1 *comp adj* lugha; **2** *in expr* **at ~** co-dhiù; **3** *in expr* **at the very ~** aig a' char as lugha
leather *adj* leathair
leather *n* leathar *m*

leave *n* **1** (*permission*) cead *m*; **2** (*parting*) cead *m*, *in expr* **take ~** gabh cead de; **3** (*furlough etc*) fòrladh *m*
leave *v* **1** (*depart*) falbh *vi*; **2** (*depart from*) fàg *vt*; **3** (*put behind*) fàg *vt*; **4** (*cause to be left*) fàg *vt*; **5** (*desert*) trèig *vt*
leavings *n* fuidheall *m*
lecher *n* drùisear *m*
lecherous *adj* drùiseach
lechery *n* drùis *f*
lecture *n* òraid *f*
lecturer *n* òraidiche *m*
ledge *n* leac *f*, oir *f*
leek *n* creamh-gàrraidh *m*
lees *n* grùid *f*
left *adj* clì, ceàrr
left-handed *adj* ciotach
leg *n* cas *f*
legacy *n* dìleab *f*
legal *adj* **1** laghail; **2** (*legitimate etc*) dligheach
legend *n* uirsgeul *m*, fionnsgeul *m*, faoinsgeul *m*
legendary *adj* uirsgeulach
legible *adj* so-leughte
legislate *v* reachdaich *vi*
legislation *n* **1** (*action*) reachdachadh *m*; **2** (*laws etc*) reachdas *m*
legislature *n* reachdaireachd *f*
legitimate *adj* dligheach
leisure *n* saor-ùine *f*
leisurely *adj* socrach
lemon *n* liomaid *f*
lend *v* thoir *vt* air iasad *m*, thoir iasad de
length *n* fad *m*
lengthen *v* **1** (*as vt*) cuir *vt* am fad; **2** (*as vi*) rach *vi* am fad
lenite *v* sèimhich *vt*
lenition *n* sèimheachadh *m*
lens *n* lionsa *f*
leopard *n* liopard *m*
leper *n* lobhar *m*
leprosy *n* luibhre *f*
lesbian *adj & n* leasbach *f*
-less *suffix* mì-, eu/ao-
lesser *adj* **1** as lugha; **2** mion- *prefix*; **3** (*taxonomy*) beag
lesson *n* leasan *m*
lest *conj* air eagal is gu, gun fhios nach, mus
let *v* **1** (*permit*) leig *vt* le; **2** *in expr* **~ go** (*release*) leig às *vt*, saor *vt*, fuasgail *vt*, leig *vt* mu sgaoil, cuir *vt* mu sgaoil; **3** *in expr* **~**

off (*emit etc*) leig *vt* (às); **4** *in expr* ~ **on**
leig *vi* ort (*etc*); **5** *in expr* ~ **down** (*lower*)
leag *vt*; **6** *in expr* ~ **down** (*disappoint
etc*) leig *vt* sìos; **7** (~ *property etc*) thoir *vt*
(seachad) air mhàl
lethargic *adj* mall, slaodach, marbhanta,
trom
letter *n* litir *f*
lettuce *n* leiteis *f*
level *adj* **1** (*horizontal*) rèidh, còmhnard;
2 (*election etc*) co-ionann
level *n* **1** (*of progress etc*) ìre *f*; **2** (*of rank
etc*) inbhe *f*; **3** (*of height etc*) àirde *f*
lever *n* luamhan *m*
lewd *adj* drabasta, draosta, collaidh
lewdness *n* drabastachd *f*, draostachd *f*
lexicography *n* faclaireachd *f*
liable *adj* buailteach
liar *n* breugaire *m*
libel *n* tuaileas *m*
libel *v* cuir tuaileas air
liberal *adj* **1** (*generous*) fialaidh, fial,
tabhartach; **2** (*permissive etc*) ceadach,
ceadachail; **3** (*pol*) libearalach (*m & adj*),
~ **Democrat** Libearalach Deamocratach
liberate *v* saor *vt*, cuir/leig *vt* mu sgaoil,
fuasgail *vt*
library *n* leabharlann *mf*
licence *n* cead *m*
license *v* ceadaich *vt*, ùghdarraich *vt*
licensee *n* (*hotel etc*) òstair *m*, fear (an)
taighe *m*
licensing *n* ceadachadh *m*, ùghdarrachadh
m
lichen *n* crotal *m*
licit *adj* ceadaichte, laghail
lick *n* imlich *f*
lick *v* imlich *vti*
lie *n* (*untruth*) breug *f*
lie¹ *v* laigh *vi*
lie² *v* (*tell untruths*) innis/dèan breug(an)
life *n* **1** beatha *f*, saoghal *m*; **2** (*breath*) deò
f, rong *m*; **3** (*span*) maireann *m*, beò *m*, là
m; **4** *in exprs* **for dear** ~mar do bheatha,
aig peilear do bheatha
life-belt *n* crios-sàbhalaidh *m*, crios-
teasairginn *m*
lifeboat *n* bata-teasairginn *m*, bàta-coibhre
m
life-jacket *n* seacaid-teasairginn *f*
lifelong *adj* fad-beatha
lifestyle *n* dòigh-beatha *f*

lifetime *n* maireann *m*, beò *m*, là *m*, rè *f*,
linn *mf*, saoghal *m*
lift *n* (*elevator*) àrdaichear *m*
lift *v* tog *vt*
light *adj* aotrom
light *n* solas *m*
light *v* **1** las *vti*; **2** (*ignite*) cuir *vt* air
light upon *v* **1** (*rest*) laigh *vi* air; **2** (*chance*)
amais *vi* air
light-heartedness *n* mire *f*, sunnd *m*,
aighearachd *f*
lightning *n* dealanach *m*
like *adj* **1** (*similar*) coltach ri; **2** (*exactly*)
ionann agus
like *n* leithid *f*, coimeas *m*, samhail *m*
like *v* **1** is *vi irreg def* toigh le, bi *vi irreg*
dèidheil air; **2** (*wish*) togair *vti*; **3** *in expr*
what would you ~? dè (a) tha a dhìth
oirbh?
likeable *adj* tlachdmhor, taitneach, ciatach
likelihood *n* coltas *m*
likely *adj* coltach
liken *v* coimeas *vt*, dèan coimeas eadar
likeness *n* **1** (*abstr*) coltas *m*; **2** (*con*)
ìomhaigh *f*; **3** (*shape etc*) riochd *m*
likewise *adv* cuideachd, mar an ceudna
liking *n* **1** (*affection*) tlachd *f*, spèis *f*, bàidh
f, dèidh *f*
lily *n* lili(dh) *f*
limit *n* **1** (*maximum*) crìoch *f*; **2** (*edge*)
crìoch *f*, iomall *m*
limit *v* cuingealaich *vt*, cuir crìoch ri
limited *adj* **1** (*attitudes*) cumhang;
2 (*business*) earranta
limp *adj* bog
limp *n* ceum *m*
limp *v* bi *vi irreg* cuagach, bi bacach, bi
crùbach
limping *adj* cuagach, bacach, crùbach
line *n* **1** loidhne *f*; **2** (*verse/objects etc*)
sreath *mf*
line *v* (*curtains etc*) lìnig *vt*
linen *n* anart *m*
ling¹ *n* (*fish*) langa *f*
ling² *n* (*plant*) fraoch *m*
linguist *n* cànanaiche *m*
linguistic *adj* cànanach
linguistics *n* cànanachas *m*
lining *n* (*material*) lìnigeadh *m*
link *n* **1** (*con*) tinne *f*, ceangal *m*; **2** (*abstr*)
ceangal *m*; **3** (*relationship*) dàimh *mf*;
4 (*familial*) buinteanas *m*

link *v* ceangail *vt*, co-cheangail *vt*

linkage *n* ceangal *m*

linked *adj & past part* co-cheangailte

linn *n* linne *f*

lint *n* lìon *m*

lion *n* leòmhann *m*

lip *n* **1** (*mouth*) bile *f*, li(o)p *f*; **2** (*jug etc*) bile *f*, oir *f*, iomall *m*

lipstick *n* dath-lipean *m*

liquid *adj* sruthach

liquid *n* lionn *m*

liquidate *v* **1** (*company etc*) leagh *vt*; **2** (*kill*) cuir *vi* às do

liquidation *n* (*company etc*) leaghadh *m*

lisp, lisping *n* liotachas *m*

lisp *v* bi *vi irreg* liotach

lisping *adj* liotach

list *n* **1** (*general*) liosta *f*; **2** (*publication*) clàr *m*

list *v* dèan liosta de

listen *v* èist

listener *n* neach-èisteachd *m*

literal *adj* litireil

literary *adj* litreachail

literate *adj* litireach

literature *n* litreachas *m*

litigious *adj* connspaideach, agartach

litre *n* liotair *m*

litter¹ *n* (*rubbish*) truileis *f*, sgudal *m*

litter² *n* (*young*) cuain *f*, àl *m*

little *adj* beag

little *n* (*amount*) beagan *m* (*with gen*), a bheag (de)

littoral *n* oirthir *f*, costa *m*

live *adj* beò

live *v* **1** (*be alive*) bi *vi irreg* beò, mair *vi* beò; **2** (*dwell etc*) fuirich *vi*, còmhnaich *vi*, fan *vi*; **3** (*survive*) thig *vi* beò

livelihood *n* teachd-an-tìr *m*, beòshlaint *f*, bith-beò *f*

lively *adj* **1** beothail; **2** (*idioms*) **look ~!** tog *vi* ort!, crath dhìot an cadal!

liver *n* adha *m*, (*animal*) grùthan *m*

livestock *n* stoc *m*, (*cattle*) crodh *m*, sprèidh *f*

living *adj* beò

living *n* **1** (*abstr*) bith-beò *f*; **2** (*livelihood*) teachd-an-tìr *m*, beòshlaint *f*; **3** (*income*) teachd-a-steach *m*

lizard *n* laghairt *mf*

load *n* **1** (*burden*) eallach *m*, uallach *m*, ultach *m*; **2** (*cargo*) luchd *m*; **3** (*in pl*) ~s (*many*) tòrr *m*

loading *n* luchdachadh *m*

loaf *n* lof *mf*, buileann *f*

loan *n* iasad *m*

loanword *n* facal-iasaid *m*

loathe *v* fuathaich *vt*

loathing *n* gràin *f*, fuath *m*

loathsome *adj* gràineil, fuathach

lobster *n* giomach *m*

lobsterpot *n* cliabh ghiomach *m*

local *adj* ionadail

locate *v* (*find*) faigh lorg air

location *n* (*position etc*) suidheachadh *m*, àite *m*

loch *n* loch *m*

lochan *n* lochan *m*

lock¹ *n* (*door etc*) glas *f*

lock² (*hair*) dual *m*

lock *v* glais/glas *vt*

locked *adj & past part* glaiste

locum *n* neach-ionaid *m*

locust *n* lòcast *m*

lodge *v* **1** (*as vi*) fan *vi*, fuirich *vi*; **2** (*as vt*) thoir taigh/lòistinn do; **3** (*deposit*) taisg *vt*

lodger *n* lòistear *m*

lodging(s) *n* lòistinn *m*, fàrdach *f*

loft *n* lobht(a) *m*

loggerheads *n*, **at ~** thar a chèile, troimh-a-chèile

lonely, lonesome *adj* aonaranach, uaigneach

long *adj* **1** (*time/dimension*) fad(a); **2** (*weary*) cian; **3** *in expr* ~ **drawn out** fadalach, màirnealach; **4** (*idioms*) ~ **time no see!** 's fhada o nach fhaca mi thu!

long *adv* **1** (*dimension*) de dh'fhad/a dh'fhad; **2** (*of time*) fada; **3** (*exprs*) **at ~ last** mu dheireadh thall, ~ **ago** o chionn fada nan cian, fada fada ron a seo

long- *prefix* fad-

long *v* **1** *in expr* ~ **for** (*desire*) miannaich *vt*; **2** *in expr* ~ **for** (*nostalgically*) ionndrainn *vt*

longing *n* **1** (*desire*) miann *mf*; **2** (*nostalgic*) cianalas *m*; **3** (*impatience*) fadachd *f*

look *n* **1** sùil *f*; **2** (*aspect*) dreach *m*; **3** (*features*) tuar *m*; **4** (*transient*) fiamh *m*; **5** (*resemblance*) coltas *m*

look *v* **1** coimhead *vi*, thoir sùil air; **2** *in expr* ~ **for** sir *vt*, lorg *vt*, bì *vi irreg* an tòir air

loom *n* (*weaving*) beart-fhighe *f*
loop *n* lùb *f*
loose *adj* 1 fuasgailte, sgaoilte, neo-cheangailte; 2 (*behaviour*) mì-bheusach
loose *v* leig (às) *vt*
loosen *v* fuasgail *vt*, sgaoil *vt*, lasaich *vt*
lord *n* 1 (*ruler etc*) tighearna *m*; 2 (*peer etc*) morair *m*; 3 (*excl*) **Good ~!** a Thighearna!
lorry *n* làraidh *f*
lose *v* caill *vti*
loss *n* call *m*
lost *adj & past part* air chall, caillte
lot[1] *n* 1 (*fate*) crannchur *m*; 2 *in exprs* **draw ~s** cuir crainn, tilg crainn, cuir crannchur
lot[2] *n* 1 (*quantity*) mòran *m*, grunn *m*, tòrr *m* (*all with gen*), gu leòr *adv* ; 2 (*exprs*) **thanks a ~!** mòran taing!, ceud taing!, **a ~ better** fada/mòran nas fheàrr
loth *adj* leisg, aindeonach
lottery *n* crannchur *m*
loud *adj* 1 (*high*) àrd; 2 (*noisy*) faramach, fuaimneach; 3 (*style*) spaideil
loudspeaker *n* glaodhaire *m*
louse *n* mial *f*
lout *n* duine borb
loutish *adj* gràisgeil
loutishness *n* gràisgealachd *f*
love *n* 1 (*intimate ~*) gaol *m*, (*affection*) gràdh *m*, **in ~** ann an gaol; 2 (*beloved*) leannan *m*; 3 (*address*) **(my) ~!** a ghaoil!, a luaidh!, a ghràidh!, m' eudail!
love *v* 1 (*intimately*) bi *vi irreg* gaol agad air, (*general*) bi *vi irreg* gràdh agad air; 2 (*enjoy*) is *vi irreg & def* toigh le
loveliness *n* bòidhchead *f*, maise *f*
lovely *adj* brèagha, bòidheach, maiseach
lover *n* leannan *m*
loving *adj* gaolach, gràdhach, maoth
low *adj* 1 (*position etc*) ìosal/ìseal; 2 (*depressed*) smalanach, sìos anns an inntinn; 3 (*morale*) gun mhisneach(d)
low *v* (*cattle*) geum *vi*, (*deer*) langanaich *vi*

lower *adj* 1 (*position etc*) ìochd(a)rach; 2 *in expr* ~ **lip** beul-ìochdair *m*; 3 (*comp adj*) (n)as ìsle
lower *v* ìslich *vt*, (*phys*) leag *vt*
lowing *n* (*cattle*) geumnaich *f*, (*deer*) langanaich *f*
Lowland *adj* Gallta, (*lang*) ~ **Scots** a' Bheurla Ghallta
Lowlander *n* Gall *m*
Lowlands *n* 1 **the** ~ A' Ghalltachd *f*, A' Mhachair(e) Ghallta, Machair na h-Alba; 2 (*general*) còmhnardan *mpl*
lowliness *n* ùmhlachd *f*, irioslachd/ irisleachd *f*
lowly *adj* umha(i)l, ìosal/ìseal, iriosal/ iriseal
loyal *adj* dìleas
loyalty *n* dìlseachd *f*, dìlse *m*
lubricate *v* ùillich *vt*
lubrication *n* ùilleachadh *m*
luck *n* fortan *m*, sealbh *m*
lucky *adj* fortanach, sealbhach
luggage *n* trealaichean *fpl*, bagaichean *mpl*
lukewarm *adj* leth-fhuar, fionnar
lullaby *n* tàladh *m*, òran-tàlaidh *m*
lumber *n* trealaich *f*
lump *n* ceap *m*, cnap *m*, meall *m*
lumpy *adj* cnapach
lunch *n* 1 biadh meadhan-là *m* ruisean *m*; 2 (*packed*) pìos *m*
lung *n* sgamhan *m*
lurch *v* tulg *vi*, luaisg *vi*
lurching *n* tulgadh *m*
lure *v* tàlaidh *vt*, meall *vt*
lust *n* drùis *f*, ana-miann *fm*
lust *v* miannaich *vi*
lustful *adj* drùiseach, drùiseil
Luxemburg *n* Lucsamburg *f*
Luxemburger *n & adj* Lucsamburgach *m*
luxurious *adj* sòghail
luxury *n* sògh *m*
lying *adj* (*mendacious*) breugach

M

machair *n* machair(e) *mf*
machine *n* inneal *m*
mackerel *n* rionnach *m*
mad *adj* air chuthach, air bhàinidh, air bhoile
Madam *n* Bean-uasal *f*
madness *n* boile *f*, cuthach *m*
magazine *n* 1 (*publishing*) iris *f*, ràitheachan *m*; 2 (*gun*) cèis-bhiadhaich *f*; 3 (*armoury*) armlann *mf*
maggot *n* cnuimh *f*, cnuimheag *f*
magic *adj* draoidheil, seunta
magic *n* draoidheachd *f*
magical *adj* draoidheil
magician *n* draoidh *m*
magistrate *n* maighstir lagha *m*
magnanimity *n* mòr-mheanmna *m*, àrd-aigne *m*
magnanimous *adj* mòr-mheanmnach
magnet *n* clach-iùil *f*, magnait *f*
magnetic *adj* iùil-tharraingeach, magnaiteach
magnetism *n* iùil-tharraing *f*
magnificent *adj* greadhnach, glòrmhor, òirdheirc
magnify *v* meudaich *vt*
magnitude *n* meudachd *f*
maid *n* 1 (*servant*) searbhanta *f*; 2 (*woman*) maighdeann *f*; 3 (*virgin*) maighdeann *f*, òigh *f*, ainnir *f*
maidenhead, **maidenhood** *n* maighdeannas *m*
mail *n* post *m*
main *adj* prìomh
mainland *n* tìr-mòr
mains *n* (*agric*) mànas *m*
maintain *v* 1 (*assert*) cùm *vt* a-mach; 2 (*support*) cùm *vt* suas; 3 (*machinery etc*) gleus *vt*, càirich *vt*
maintenance *n* 1 (*abst*) cumail suas *m*; 2 (*keep*) beathachadh *m*; 3 (*machinery etc*) gleusadh *m*, càradh *m*
majestic *adj* 1 greadhnach, glòrmhor; 2 (*monarchic*) rìoghail
majesty *n* 1 (*abstr*) rìoghalachd *f*; 2 (*grandeur*) mòrachd *f*, greadhnachas *m*

major *adj* 1 (*principal*) prìomh; 2 (*important*) mòr, glè chudromach
major *n* (*rank*) màidsear *m*
majority *n* mòr-chuid *f*
make *v* 1 dèan *vt irreg*; 2 (*create*) dealbh *vt*; 3 (*force*) thoir *vt* air; 4 (*arouse*) cuir *vt* air; 5 (*cause*) fàg *vti*
maladministration *n* mì-rianachd *f*
malady *n* tinneas *m*, galar *m*
male *adj* fireann, fireannta
male *n* fireannach *m*
malevolence *n* gamhlas *m*, mì-rùn *m*
malevolent *adj* gamhlasach
malice *n* gamhlas *m*, mì-rùn *m*, nimh/neimh *m*
malicious *adj* gamhlasach, nimheil
mallet *n* fairche *m*
malnutrition *n* dìth beathachaidh *m*
malpractice *n* mì-chleachdadh *m*
Mammy *n* Mamaidh *f*
man *n* 1 (*gender*) fear *m*, fireannach *m*; 2 duine *m*; 3 (*mankind*) mac-an-duine *m*, an cinne-daonna *m*
manage *v* 1 (*organisation etc*) stiùir *vt*, riaghail *vt*; 2 (*handle*) dèilig *vi* ri, làimhsich *vt*; 3 (*succeed*) faigh *vi* air, rach *vi* agad (*etc*) air, dèan a' chùis air; 4 (*live*) thig *vi irreg* beò, thig suas
management 1 (*abstr*) stiùireadh *m*, riaghladh *m*; 2 (*con*) luchd-stiùiridh *m*, luchd-riaghlaidh *m*
manager *n* manaidsear *m*, neach-stiùiridh *m*, neach-riaghlaidh *m*
manageress *n* bana-mhanaidsear *f*
mane *n* muing *f*
mangle *v* reub *vt*
manhandle *v* 1 (*struggle*) slaod *vi*, tarraing *vi*; 2 (*handle*) droch-làimhsich *vt*
manifest *v* 1 (*show*) taisbein *vt*, nochd *vt*; 2 *in expr* ~ **itself** thig *vi* an uachdar, thig *vi* am follais, nochd *vt*
manifold *adj* iomadh-fhillte
mankind *n* mac-an-duine *m*, an cinne-daonna *m*
manliness *n* duinealas *m*, fearalachd *f*
manly *adj* duineil, fearail

man-made adj 1 (*manufactured*)
saothraichte; 2 (*substitute*) fuadain, brèige

manner n 1 (*doing*) dòigh m, modh mf, nòs
m; 2 (*behaving*) dol-a-mach m

manners n beus f, modh mf

mannish adj duineil, fireannta

manpower n 1 luchd-obrach m ; 2 (*abstr*)
sgiobachd f

manslaughter n duine-mharbhadh m,
murt m

manual n leabhrachan m, leabhran m,
(*instruction*) leabhar-mìneachaidh m

manufacture n saothrachadh m

manufacture v saothraich vt, dèan vt

manufacturing n saothrachadh m

manure n mathachadh m, leasachadh m,
innear/inneir f

manure v mathaich vt, leasaich vt

manuscript n làmh-sgrìobhainn mf

Manx adj Manainneach

Manxman n Manainneach m

many adj 1 mòran m; 2 in expr **so** ~
uimhir f, uiread m; 3 in expr **how** ~ cia
mheud

many n mòran m

map n clàr-dùthcha m, mapa m

mar v mill vt

marble n màrmor m

March n am Màrt m

march[1] n (*boundary*) crìoch f

march[2] n 1 (*soldiers etc*) màrsail f,
mèarrsadh m; 2 (*music*) caismeachd f

marching n màrsail f, mèarrsadh m

mare n làir f

margarine n margarain m

margin n iomall m, oir f

marginal adj iomallach, air an iomall m

mariner n maraiche m, seòladair m

mark n comharra(dh) m

mark v 1 (*leave*) fàg lorg air, fàg
comharradh air; 2 (*stain*) fàg spot m air,
fàg smal air; 3 (*education*) ceartaich vt,
comharraich vt; 4 (*celebrate*) comharraich
vt

market n margadh mf, margaid f, fèill f

marketing n margaideachd f

market-place n ionad-margaidh m

marking n (*education*) ceartachadh m,
comharrachadh m

marquee n puball/pùball m

marriage n pòsadh m

married adj & past part pòsta

marry v pòs vti

Mars n Màrt m

marsh n fèith(e) f, boglach f

mart[1] n (*animal*) mart m

mart[2] n (*market*) margadh mf, fèill f

marvel n iongnadh m, mìorbhail f

marvellous adj iongantach, mìorbhaileach

masculine adj 1 fireann, fireannta;
2 (*gram*) fireann

mash v pronn

mashed adj & past part pronn

mask n 1 masg m; 2 (*disguise*) aghaidh-
choimheach f, aodannan m

mason n clachair m

mass adj mòr-

mass[1] n 1 (*abstr*) tomad m; 2 (*quantity*)
meud mòr, uimhir f, uiread m; 3 (*people*)
sluagh mòr, meud mòr dhaoine

mass[2] n (*relig*) aifreann mf

massacre n casgairt f, murt m

massacre v casgair vt

massage n suathadh m, suathadh bodhaig

massage v suath vt

mast n (*ship etc*) crann m

master n 1 (*authority*) maighstir m,
uachdaran m; 2 (*boat etc*) caiptean m,
sgiobair m; 3 in expr ~ **of ceremonies**
fear an taighe m

master v 1 (*people etc*) ceannsaich vt, faigh
làmh-an-uachdair air; 2 (*topic etc*) faigh
eòlas air

masterful adj ceannsalach, smachdail

masterly adj ealanta, barraichte

masterwork n sàr-obair f

masticate cnàmh vt, cnuas vti, cagainn vti

masturbate v brod vt, fèin-bhrod vi

masturbation n brodadh m, fèin-
bhrodadh m

match[1] n (*lighting*) maids(e) m, lasadair m

match[2] n (*opponent*) seis(e) m

match v freagair vi, co-fhreagair vi

matching adj co-fhreagarrach

mate n 1 (*pal*) companach m, caraid m;
2 (*ship*) meite m

mate v co-ghin vi, cuplaich vi

material adj 1 corpora, stuthail, nitheil,
rudail; 2 (*significant*) cudromach,
seaghach; 3 (*real*) fìor

material n 1 (*fabric etc*) stuth m;
2 (*general*) stuth m, adhbhar m

materialism n saoghaltachd f

materialist n duine saoghalta

materialistic *adj* saoghalta

materially *adv* **1** (*financially*) a thaobh airgid, a thaobh beartais; **2** (*significantly*) gu mòr, gu ìre mhòir

maternal *adj* màthaireil; **2** (*relationships*) màthar

maternity *n* màthaireachd *f*

mathematics, maths *n* matamataig *m*

mating *n* co-ghineadh *m*, cuplachadh *m*

matter *n* **1** (*substance*) stuth *m*; **2** (*affair etc*) cùis *f*, gnothach *m*; **3** (*subject*) cuspair *m*; **4** (*wrong*) what's the ~? dè a tha ceàrr?, **what's the ~ with you?** dè a tha a' cur ort?; **5** (*pus*) brachadh *m*, iongar *m*

matter *v* bi *vi irreg* gu diofar

mature *adj* **1** (*person*) inbheach, abaich; **2** (*fruits etc*) abaich

mature *v* abaich *vi*, thig *vi* gu inbhe, thig *vi* gu ìre

maturity *n* **1** (*adulthood*) inbhe *f*, ìre *f*; **2** (*fruits etc*) abaichead *m*

maul *v* **1** (*manually*) garbh-làimhsich *vt*; **2** (*defeat*) pronn *vt*, dochainn *vt*

maw *n* **1** (*mouth*) craos *m*; **2** (*craw*) sgròban *m*; **3** (*stomach*) maodal *f*, mionach *m*

maximum *adj* as motha

May *n* an Cèitean *m*, a' Mhàigh *f*

may *v* **1** (*permitted*) faod *vi def*; **2** (*possibility*) faod *vi def*; **3** (*wish*) gum(a) *conj*

maybe *adv & conj*, is dòcha, (is) ma(th) dh'fhaodte/'s mathaid

mayor *n* mèar *m*

MC *n* fear an taighe *m*

me *pers pron* mì, mise

meadow, meadowland *n* clua(i)n *f*, dail *f*, faiche *f*, lèana *f*

meal¹ *n* (*cereals etc*) min *f*

meal² *n* biadh *m*, diathad *f*, lòn *m*

mealtime *n* tràth-bìdh *m*

mean *adj* **1** (*petty*) crìon, suarach; **2** (*stingy*) spìocach, mosach

mean *n* meadhan *m*

mean *v* **1** ciallaich *vt*, minig *vt*; **2** (*be serious*) bi *v irreg* ann an da-rìribh; **3** (*intend*) bi *vi irreg* airson dh'aon ghnothach *m*

meander *v* lùb *vi*

meandering *adj* lùbach

meaning *n* ciall *f*, (*sense*) brìgh *f*, seagh *m*

meaningful *adj* brìoghmhor

meaningless *adj* gun chiall

means *n* **1** dòigh *f*, meadhan *m*; **2** *in expr* **by ~ of** tro mheadhan; **3** (*wealth etc*) beartas *m*, saidhbhreas *m*

meantime *n* eadar-àm *m*

meanwhile *adv* rè na h-ùine seo/sin

measles *n* a' ghriù(th)lach *f*

measure *n* **1** (*abstr/tool*) tomhas *m*; **2** (*amount*) na h-uimhir *f*, na h-uiread *m*; **3** (*expedient*) ceum *m*

measure *v* (*dimensions etc*) tomhais *vt*

measurement *n* tomhas *m*

measuring *adj* tomhais

meat *n* feòil *f*

mechanic *n* meacanaig *m*, innleadair *m*

mechanical *adj* innealach

mechanism *n* **1** (*con/mechanical*) inneal *m*; **2** (*mean*) meadhan *m*

meddle *v* gabh gnothach ri, buin *vi* do/ri

media *npl* na meadhanan *mpl*

medical *adj* lèigheil, meidigeach

medicine *n* **1** (*abstr*) eòlas-leighis *m*; **2** (*medication*) leigheas *m*, ìocshlaint *f*, cungaidh *f*, cungaidh-leighis *f*

medieval *adj* meadhan-aoiseil

meditate *v* meòraich *vi*

meditation *n* meòrachadh

Mediterranean *adj* Meadhan-thìreach

Mediterranean *n*, **the ~** A' Mhuir Mheadhan-thìreach *f*

medium *adj* meadhanach

medium *n* meadhan *m*

meek *adj* umha(i)l, macanta

meekness ùmhlachd *f*

meet *v* **1** (*congregate*) cruinnich *vi*, coinnich *vi*, thig *vi* còmhla, tionail *vi*; **2** (*encounter*) coinnich *vi*, tachair *vi*

meeting *n* **1** (*business etc*) coinneamh *f*; **2** (*encounter*) coinneachadh *m*

melancholy *adj* **1** (*mood etc*) gruamach, dubhach, fo ghruaim; **2** (*atmosphere etc*) tiamhaidh

melancholy *n* gruaim *f*, mulad *m*

melodious *adj* ceòlmhor, fonnmhor, binn

melody *n* port *m*, fonn *m*

melon *n* meal-bhucan *m*

melt *v* leagh *vti*

member *n* ball *m*

membership *n* ballrachd *f*

memorandum *n* cuimhneachan *m*, meòrachan *m*

memorial *adj* cuimhneachaidh

memorial n 1 cuimhneachan m;
2 (*monument*) clach-chuimhne f, clach-chuimhneachain f, clach-chuimhneachaidh f

memorise v meòraich vt, cùm vt air mheomhair, cùm vt air chuimhne f

memory n 1 (*faculty*) meomhair f, cuimhne f; 2 (*impression*) cuimhne f

menace v maoidh vi, bagair vi air

menace n maoidheadh m

mend v 1 (*repair*) càirich vt, càir vt;
2 (*improve*) leasaich vt

mendacious adj breugach

menstruation n fuil-mìosa f

mental adj inntinn, inntinneach, inntinneil

mention n iomradh m, guth m, tarraing f

mention v 1 thoir iomradh, thoir guth air;
2 in expr **not to ~** gun ghuth air

menu n 1 (*café etc*) clàr-bìdh m; 2 (*IT*) clàr-iùil m

merchant n ceannaiche m, marsanta m

merciful adj iochdmhor, tròcaireach

mercury n airgead-beò m

mercy n iochd f, tròcair f, truas m

merge v co-mheasgaich vti, co-aonaich vti

merit n 1 (*worth*) luach m, fiù m, (*person*) airidheachd f; 2 (*honour*) cliù m

merit v toill vt

meritorious adj airidh

mermaid n maighdeann-mhara f

merriment n cridhealas m, mire f

merry adj 1 aighearach, in expr **Merry Christmas/Xmas!** Nollaig Chridheil!;
2 (*tipsy*) air leth-mhisg

mess n 1 (*litter*) truileis f; 2 (*state*) bùrach m

message n fios m, teachdaireachd f

messenger n teachdaire m

metal adj meatailt, de mheatailt

metal n meatailt f

metallic adj meatailteach

metamorphosis n cruth-atharrachadh m

meteor n dreag f

meteorology n eòlas-sìde m

meter n meidheadair m

method n 1 (*abstr*) òrdugh m, riaghailt f, rian m; 2 (*way*) dòigh f, seòl m, alt m

methodical adj òrdail, riaghailteach, rianail

methodicalness n òrdugh m, riaghailt f, rian m

methodology n dòigh-obrach f

meticulous adj mionaideach, mion-chùiseach, pongail

metre n 1 (*unit*) meatair m; 2 (*rhythm*) meadrachd f, rannaigheachd f

metric adj meatrach

metrical adj meadrachail

mew v dèan mialaich/miamhail

mewing, miaowing, n mialaich f, miamhail f

microwave n meanbh-thonn f

midday n meadhan-là m

midden n siteag f, òtrach m, dùnan m

middle n meadhan m

middling adj & adv meadhanach

midge n meanbh-chuileag f

midget n luchraban m

midnight n meadhan-oidhche m

midsummer n leth an t-samhraidh m

midwife n bean-ghlùine f

midwinter n leth a' gheamhraidh m

mien n mèinn f, dreach m, snuadh m

might n 1 (*abstr*) cumhachd mf; 2 (*phys*) neart m

might v 1 (*possibility*) faod vi def;
2 (*permission*) faod

mighty adj 1 cumhachdach; 2 (*phys*) neartmhor

migrant n neach-imrich m

migration n imrich f

mild adj 1 (*weather etc*) ciùin, sèimh;
2 (*illness etc*) beag

mile n mìle mf

militant adj mìleanta

militant n mìleantach m

military adj armailteach

milk n bainne m

milk v bleoghain vti

milking n bleoghann f

mill n muileann mf, muilinn f

mill v (*corn etc*) meil vt, bleith vt

miller n muillear m

million n millean m

millstone n clach-mhuilinn f

mimic v atharrais vt

mimicry n atharrais f

mind n 1 inntinn f; 2 (*preoccupation etc*) cùram m, aire f; 3 (*intention*) in expr **make up one's ~** cuir romhad (*etc*);
4 (*memory*) cuimhne f; 5 (*sanity etc*) ciall f, rian m, reusan m

mind v (*care*) in exprs **I don't ~!** tha mi coma!, **never ~!** coma leat!, dad ort!

mine *poss pron* leam(sa)
mine *n* mèinn(e) *f*
miner *n* mèinnear *m*
mineral *adj* mèinneach/mèinneil
mineral *n* mèinnear *m*, mèinnearach *m*
mineralogy *n* mèinn-eòlas *m*, mèinnearachd *f*
mingle *v* measgaich *vt*, co-mheasgaich, coimeasgaich *vti*
minimum *adj* as lugha
mining *n* mèinnearachd *f*
minister *n* ministear *m*
ministry *n* ministrealachd *f*
minor[1] *adj* 1 (*lesser*) mion- *prefix*, beag; 2 (*slight*) beag
minor[2] *adj* (*under-age*) mion-aoiseach
minor *n* (*person*) mion-aoiseach *m*
minority *n* mion-chuid *f*, beag-chuid *f*
minute *adj* 1 (*small*) crìon; 2 (*detailed*) mion-, mionaideach
minute *n* mionaid *f*
miracle *n* mìorbhail *f*
miraculous *adj* mìorbhaileach
mire *n* eabar *m*, poll *m*
mirth *n* mire *f*
mis- *prefix* mì-
miscarriage *n* breith an-abaich *f*
miscellaneous *adj* measgaichte, de gach seòrsa
miscellany *n* measgachadh *m*
mischance *n* 1 (*abstr*) mì-shealbh *m*; 2 (*con*) tubaist *f*
mischief *n* donas *m*
misconduct *n* mì-ghiùlan *m*
miserable *adj* truagh, brònach
misery *n* truaighe *f*
misfortune *n* (*abstr*) mì-shealbh *m*, (*abstr & con*) dosgainn *f*, driod-fhortan *m*
mishap *n* tubaist *f*, driod-fhortan *m*
misinterpret *v* mì-mhìnich *vt*
misjudge *v* mì-thuig *vt*
mislead *v* meall *vt*
misleading *adj* meallta
mismanagement *n* mì-rianachd *f*
misprint *n* clò-mhearachd *f*
Miss *n* A' Mhaighdeann(-uasal) *f*
miss *v* 1 (*fail*) caill *vt*; 2 (*pine for*) ionndrainn *vt*, bi *vi irreg* fadachd ort
missile *n* urchair *f*
missing *adj* a dhìth, a dh'easbhaidh
mission *n* teachdaireachd *f*, rùn *m*

missionary *n* teachdaire *m*, miseanaraidh *m*
mist *n* ceò *m*, ceathach *m*
mistake *n* mearachd *f*, iomrall *m*
mistaken *adj* mearachdach, iomrallach, ceàrr
Mister *n* Maighstir *m*
mistress *n* 1 (*superior*) bana-mhaighstir *f*; 2 (*partner*) coimhleapach *f*
mistrust *n* mì-earbsa *m*
misty *adj* fo cheò *m*, ceòthach
mitigate *v* maothaich *vt*
mitten *n* miotag *f*
mix *v* measgaich *vt*, coimeasgaich *vt*
mixed *adj & past part* measgaichte
mixer *n* measgaichear *m*
mixing, mixture *n* measgachadh *m*, coimeasgachadh *m*
moan *v* 1 (*grief etc*) caoin *vi*; 2 (*complain*) gearain *vi*
mob *n* gràisg *f*, prabar *m*
mobile *adj* 1 (*moving*) gluasadach; 2 air chrothrom; 3 (*portable*) so-ghiùlain, *in expr* ~ **phone** fòn-làimhe *mf*
mobility *n* (*abstr*) gluasadachd *f*, (*ability*) cothrom gluasaid *m*, comas gluasaid *m*
mock *v* mag *vi*, dèan fanaid air
mockery *n* fanaid *f*, magadh *m*
mocking *adj* magail
Mod *n* Mòd *m*
mode *n* (*doing*) dòigh *f*, (*abstr*) modh *mf*
model *n* mac-samhail *m*
moderate *adj* 1 (*average*) meadhanach; 2 (*temperate*) measarra, stuama
modern *adj* ùr, ùr-nodha
modernisation *n* ùrachadh *m*
modernise *v* ùraich
modest *adj* 1 (*shy*) diùid, màlda; 2 (*temperate*) measarra; 3 (*average*) meadhanach
modicum *n* na h-uimhir *f*
modish *adj* fasanta
Mohammedan *n & adj* Mohamadanach *m*
moist *adj* tais
moisten *v* taisich *vt*
moistness, moisture *n* taise *f*, taiseachd *f*
molar *n* (*tooth*) fiacail-chùil *f*
mole *n* 1 (*animal*) famh *f*; 2 (*spot*) ball-dòrain *m*
moment *n* 1 mòmaid *f*, tiota *m*; 2 *in expr* **the** ~ *conj* (*as soon as*), cho luath agus/is
monastery *n* manachainn *f*

Monday *n* Diluain *m*
money *n* airgead *m*
monitor *n* (*IT*) foillsear *m*
monitor *vt* cùm sùil air
monk *n* manach *m*
monkey *n* muncaidh *m*
monolith *n* tursa *m*
monster *n* uilebheist *mf*
month *n* mìos *mf*
monthly *adj* mìosach, mìosail
monument *n* clach-chuimhne *f*
moo *v* geum *vi*
mood *n* **1** gean *m*, gleus *m*, fonn *m*; **2** (*gram*) modh *mf*
moody *adj* **1** (*changeable*) caochlaideach; **2** (*temporary*) dubhach, diombach
mooing *n* geumnaich *f*
moon *n* gealach *f*
moonshine *n* (*whisky*) poitean *m*
moor, moorland *n* mòinteach *f*, monadh *m*, sliabh *m*, aonach *m*
moral *adj* beusach, moralta
morale *n* misneach(d) *f*
morality *n* moraltachd *f*
morals *n* beusan *fpl*
more *adv, pron & n* **1** tuilleadh *m*, barrachd *f*; **2** *in expr* ~ **than** barrachd air, còrr is, ~ **than enough** tuilleadh 's a' chòir; **3** (**else**) a bharrachd; **4** (*additional*) a bharrachd; **5** *in expr* ~ **or less** an ìre mhath
morning *n* madainn *f*
morose *adj* gruamach, mùgach
morrow, the *n, in expr* **on the** ~ làrna-mhàireach *adv*
morsel *n* grèim *m*
mortal *adj* **1** (*not immortal*) bàsmhor; **2** (*deadly*) marbhtach, bàsmhor
mortgage *n* morgaidse *m*
mortification *n* **1** (*humiliation*) ìsleachadh *m*, ùmhlachadh *m*; **2** (*shaming*) nàrachadh *m*
mortify *v* **1** (*humiliate*) ìslich *vt*, ùmhlaich *vt*; **2** (*shame*) nàraich *vt*
mosque *n* mosg *m*
moss *n* (*bot*) còinneach *f*
most *n* **1** a' mhòr-chuid *f*, a' chuid-mhòr, a' chuid as mò/as motha; **2** *in expr* **at** ~ aig a' char as mò
most *sup adj* **1** as ; **2** (*very*) anabarrach, glè
mostly *adv* mar as trice

moth *n* leòman *m*
mother *n* màthair *f*
motherhood *n* màthaireachd *f*
mother-in law *n* màthair-chèile *f*
motherly *adj* màthaireil, màithreil
motion *n* gluasad *m*
motionless *adj* gun ghluasad
motive *n* adhbhar *m*
motor *n* motair *m*
motor-bike *n* motair-baidhc *m*, motair-rothar *m*
motorcar *n* càr *m*, carbad *m*
mould[1] *n* (*growth*) clòimh liath *f*
mould[2] *n* (*template*) molldair *m*
mound *n* tom *m*, tolman *m*, tòrr *m*
mount *n* (*horse*) each(-dìollaid) *m*
mount *v* **1** leum *vi* air muin; **2** (*copulate*) rach *vi* air muin; **3** (*organise*) cuir *vt* air chois
mountain *n* beinn *f*, sliabh *m*
mountain ash *n* caorann *mf*
mountainous *adj* beanntach, sliabhach, monadail
mourn *v* **1** (*as vi*) bi *vi irreg* ri bròn, caoidh *vi*, caoin *vi*, dèan tuireadh; **2** (*as vt*) caoidh *vt*
mourning *n* bròn *m*
mouse *n* luch *f*, luchag *f*
mouth *n* beul *m*, cab *f*, gob *m*, craos *m*, **shut your** ~! dùin do bheul!, dùin do chab!
mouth music *n* port-à-beul *m*
mouthful *n* làn beòil *m*
move *n* **1** (*flitting*) imrich *f*; **2** *in expr* **get a** ~ **on** dèan cabhag!, tog ort!
move *v* **1** (*phys*) gluais *vti*, caraich *vti*, cuir car dìot; **2** (*emotionally*) gluais *vti*, drùidh *vi* air **4** (*flit*) imrich *vi*, dèan imrich
movement *n* **1** gluasad *m*; **2** (*faculty*) lùth *m*, lùths *m*
moving *adj* **1** (*in motion*) gluasadach, siùbhlach; **2** (*emotionally*) gluasadach, drùidhteach
moving *n* **1** (*phys*) gluasad *m*; **2** (*flitting*) imrich *f*
mow *v* lom *vt*, geàrr *vt*
much *adj, adv, n,* **1** (*quantity*) mòran *m*; **2** *in expr* **too** ~ cus *m*; **3** mòran, fada, fiù is/agus, uimhir, uiread; **4** *in expr* **how** ~ dè
mucus *n* ronn *m*
mud *n* poll *m*, eabar *m*

mug *n* (*drinking*) muga *f*
mugging *n* brath-ghoid *f*
muggy *adj* (*weather*) bruthainneach
mull over *v* cnuasaich *vi*, meòraich *vi* air
multi- *prefix* ioma-
multiplication *n* iomadachadh *m*
multiply *v* 1 (*increase*) cinn *vi*, meudaich *vi*; 2 (*as vt*) iomadaich *vt*
Mummy *n* Mamaidh *f*
munitions *n* connadh-làmhaich *m*
murder *n* murt *m*
murder *v* murt *vt*
murderer *n* murtair *m*, marbhaiche *m*
murmur, murmuring *n* crònan *m*, monmhar *m*, (*water*) torman *m*
muscle *n* fèith *f*
muscular *adj* fèitheach
muse *v* meòraich *vi*, cnuasaich *vi*
museum *n* taigh-tasgaidh *m*

music *n* ceòl *m*
musical *adj* ceòlmhor, fonnmhor
musician *n* neach-ciùil *m*
Muslim *n & adj* Muslamach *m*, Mohamadanach *m*
mussel *n* feusgan *m*
must *v* feum *vi*, is/'s fheudar dhut (*etc*)
mutate *v* mùth *vi*
mutation *n* mùthadh *m*
mutton *n* muilt-fheoil *f*, feòil-caorach *f*
mutual *adj* 1 a chèile; 2 co-
my *poss adj* mo, agam
myself *reflexive pron* mi fhìn
mysterious *adj* dìomhair
mystery *n* 1 (*abstr*) dìomhaireachd *f*; 2 (*enigma*) tòimhseachan *m*
myth *n* uirsgeul *m*, fionnsgeul *m*, faoinsgeul *m*, miotas *m*

N

nail[1] *n* (*finger etc*) ìne *f*

nail[2] *n* (*joinery*) tarrang *f*, tarrag *f*

naked *adj* lomnochd, rùisgte, lom

nakedness *n* luime *f*

name *n* 1 ainm *m*, **what's your ~?** dè an t-ainm a th' ort/oirbh?; 2 (*reputation*) cliù *m*

name *v* ainmich *vt*, thoir ainm air

namely *adv* is/'s e sin

nap *n* norrag(-chadail) *f*, dùsal *m*, norradaich *f*

napkin *n* neapaigin *f*

nappy *n* badan *m*

narration *n* aithris *f*, (*con*) cunntas *m*

narrow *adj* caol, cumhang

narrow, narrows *n* caol *m*, caolas *m*

narrow *v* 1 (*as vi*) fàs *vi* caol; 2 (*as vt*) cuingealaich *vt*

narrow-minded *adj* cumhang

nasty *adj* 1 (*appearance*) mosach; 2 (*behaviour*) suarach

nation *n* nàisean *m*

national *adj* nàiseanta

nationalism *n* nàiseantachas *m*

nationalist *n & adj* nàiseantach *m*

nationality *n* nàiseantachd *f*

nationhood *n* nàiseantachas *m*

native *adj* dùthchasach

native *n* dùthchasach *m*

natural *adj* 1 (*of Nature*) nàdarra(ch); 2 (*human*) dual(t)ach

naturally *adv* 1 (*manner*) gu nàdarra(ch); 2 (*of course*) tha f(h)ios *m*

nature *n* 1 (*natural world*) nàdar *m*; 2 (*character*) nàdar *m*, aigne *f*, mèinn *f*; 3 (*hereditary*) dualchas *m*

naughty *adj* crost(a), dona, mì-mhodhail

navel *n* imleag *f*

navy *n* 1 (*institution*) nèibhi(dh) *mf*; 2 (*vessels*) cabhlach *m*, loingeas *m*

Nazi *adj & n* Nàsach *m*

neap-tide *n* conntraigh *f*

near *adj* 1 faisg

near *prep* faisg air, dlùth do/air, an còir

near *v* dlùthaich *vi* ri, teann *vi* ri/air

nearly *adv* 1 faisg air, teann air; 2 cha mhòr *adv*, theab *vi*; 3 *conj* gu bhith

nearness *n* faisge *f*

neat *adj* (*person*) grinn, cuimir, (*person/ object*) sgiobalta, (*objects*) snasail, snasmhor

neatness *n* grinneas *m*, sgiobaltachd *f*

necessary *adj* deatamach, riatanach, feumail

neck *n* 1 amha(i)ch *f*, muineal *m*

neckband, necklace *n* crios-muineil *m*

nectar *n* neactair *m*

need *n* 1 feum *m*, easbhaidh *f*; 2 *in expr* **in ~** feumach, easbhaidheach, air; 3 (*indigence*) airc *f*, uireasbhaidh *f*

need *v* feum *vti def*, bi *vi irreg* feum agad, bi *vi irreg* a dhìth/a dh'easbhaidh ort, bi *vi irreg* feumach air; 2 chan fhuilear *adv*

needed *adj* (*lacking*) a dhìth

needle *n* snàthad *f*

needlework *n* 1 (*activity*) grèis *f*; 2 (*product*) obair-ghrèis *f*

needy *adj* feumach, easbhaidheach, uireasbhach

negative *adj* àicheil

neglect *n* dearmad *m*

neglect *v* 1 (*fail*) dearmaid *vi*, cuir *vt* air dhearmad; 2 (*forget*) dearmaid *vt*, leig *vt* air dhearmad

neglectful *adj* dearmadach

negligence *n* dearmad *m*, dearmadachd *f*

negligent *adj* dearmadach

neigh *n* sitir *f*

neigh *v* sitrich *vi*

neighing *n* sitir *f*

neighbour *n* nàbaidh *m*, coimhearsnach *m*

neighbourhood *n* coimhearsnachd *f*, nàbaidheachd *f*

neighbourly *adj* nàbaidheil

neither *adv* 1 nas motha; 2 *in constr* **~ . . . nor . . .** (*followed by nouns or proper nouns*) aon chuid *f* . . . no . . . , ; 3 (*idiom*) **~ one thing nor another** eadar-dhà-lionn

neither *conj* cha mhotha (a)

neither *pron* aon seach aon

neologism *n* nuadh-fhacal *m*

neophyte *n* iompachan *m*

nephew n (*brother's son*) mac bràthar m, (*sister's son*) mac peathar m

nerve n 1 (*anat*) lèith f, nèarbh f; 2 (*cheek*) bathais f, aghaidh f, (*idioms*) **what a ~!** abair bathais/aghaidh!

nervous, nervy adj clisgeach, nèarbhach, frionasach

nest n nead m

net adj lom

net n lìon m

nether adj ìochd(a)rach

netting n lìon m

nettle n feanntag f, deanntag f

network n lìonra m

neuk n cùil f

neuter adj neodrach

neuter v spoth vt, geàrr vt

neutral adj neo-phàirteach

neutrality n neo-phàirteachd f

never adv 1 (*for past time, with a v in the neg*) a-riamh; 2 (*for future time, with a v in the neg*) a-chaoidh, gu bràth, gu sìorraidh (tuilleadh); 3 ~ **mind!** coma leat!, dad ort!, **the twelfth of ~** Là-Luain m

nevertheless adv, *also* **nonetheless** adv, a dh'aindeoin cùise f, a dh'aindeoin sin, an dèidh sin

new adj ùr, nuadh

newly adv ùr, nuadh

news n naidheachd f, fios m, guth m, (*TV etc*) **the ~** na naidheachdan

newsman n fear-naidheachd m, neach-naidheachd m, naidheachdair m

newspaper n pàipear-naidheachd m

next adj 1 ath; 2 in expr ~ **to** (*phys*) ri taobh (*with gen*), làmh ri

next adv an dèidh sin

nibble v creim vt, pioc vt

nice adj (*people, objects etc*) snog, (*people*) laghach

nick n 1 (*indentation etc*) eag f; 2 (*condition*) gleus mf; 3 (*jail*) prìosan m

nickname n far-ainm m, frith-ainm m

niece n (*brother's daughter*) nighean bràthar f, (*sister's daughter*) nighean peathar f

niggardly adj spìocach, mosach

niggling adj frionasach

night n oidhche f

nightmare n trom-laighe mf

nil n neoni f

nimble adj clis, deas, ealamh; 2 (*athletic*) lùthmhor

nimbleness n 1 cliseachd f; 2 (*agility*) lùth/lùths m

nine n and num adj 1 naoi/naodh; 2 (*people*) naoinear/naodhmar mf

nineteen num naoi-deug/naodh-deug

ninety n and num adj ceithir fichead 's a deich m, naochad m

ninth n naoidheamh/naodhamh m

ninth num adj naoidheamh/naodhamh

no adj 1 expr by neg forms of the verb chan eil; 2 (*expr prohibition*) chan fhaodar (*present passive of* faod vi) *followed by the appropriate verbal noun,* ~ **smoking** chan fhaodar smocadh m

no adv, chan e, chan eil, chan ann, chan eadh *etc*

nobbly adj cnapach

nobility n 1 (*abstr*) uaisle f; 2 (*con*) **the ~** na h-uaislean mpl

noble adj uasal, flathail

noble, nobleman n duine-uasal m, flath m, mòr-uasal m

nobody, no-one n duine m (*after neg v*)

no-claims discount n lùghdachadh neo-thagraidh m

nod n gnogadh-cinn m

nod v 1 gnog do cheann; 2 in expr ~ **off** rach vi/tuit vi na do chlò-chadal, norradaich vi

noise n fuaim mf, toirm f, faram m

noisy adj fuaimneach, faramach

nomad n iniltear m

nominate v ainmich vt

nomination n ainmeachadh m

non- prefix neo-

non-commital adj neo-cheangaltach, leam-leat

none pron 1 (*objects*) gin pron; 2 (*people*) aon duine (*with reg v*)

nook n cùil f

noon n meadhan-là m

noose n lùb f, dul m

nor conj cha mhotha (a)

normal adj cumanta, àbhaisteach

normality n cumantas m

normally adv 1 (*habitually*) am bitheantas, an cumantas, mar as trice; 2 (*usually*) mar as àbhaist; 3 (*correctly*) mar as còir

Norse adj Lochlannach

Norseman n Lochlannach m

north adj tuath

north n **1** tuath f; **2** (point) an àird(e) tuath f
northerly adj mu thuath
northern adj **1** tuath; **2 the Northern Lights** Na Fir Chlis mpl
Norway n Nirribhidh f, Lochlann f
Norwegian n & adj Lochlannach m
nose n sròn f
nostalgia n cianalas m, fadachd f, fadal m
nostalgic adj cianalach
nostril n cuinnean m
not adv, **1** expressed by pre-verbal particles cha, chan, cha do, nach, nach do, mur(a), na etc; **2** rendered by gun followed by infinitive
notch n eag f
note n **1** nota f; **2** (music) pong m
note v **1** (acknowledge) thoir fa-near do; **2** (mentally) meòraich vt
nothing n **1** (zero) neoni f; **2** (in neg exprs) càil (sam bith), rud m sam bith; **3** (idioms) **have ~ to do with!** na gabh gnothach ri
notice n **1** (attention) aire f, feart f, for m, sùim f; **2** (information) sanas m; **3** (warning) brath f
notice v thoir an aire, thoir fa-near do, mothaich vt
notorious adj suaicheanta
nought n neoni f
noun n ainmear m
nourishment n lòn m, beathachadh m
novel adj **1** (new) ùr, nuadh; **2** (odd) annasach

novel n nobhail f
novelist n nobhailiche mf
novelty n **1** (abstr) ùrachd fr; **2** (object etc) annas m
November n an t-Samhain f
now adv **1** a-nis(e), an-dràsta, an-ceartuair; **2** (excl) ~ ~! ud! ud!
nub n, in expr ~ **of the matter** cnag f na cùise
nuclear adj niùclasach
nude adj lomnochd
nude n lom-neach m
nudity n luime f
nuisance plàigh f, dragh m
numb adj lapach, meilichte
numb v meilich vt
number n àireamh f, figear m
numeral n figear m
numerous adj lìonmhor
nun n cailleach-dhubh f
nurse n nurs f, banaltram f, bean-eiridinn f
nurse v eiridnich vt, altraim vt
nursery n **1** (room) seòmar-cloinne m; **2** (ed) sgoil f àraich; **3** (gardening) lios-àraich m
nursing n eiridinn m, banaltramachd f
nut n (bot/engin) cnò f
nutrients npl beathachadh m
nuts, nutty adj às do chiall
nutty adj (taste) cnòthach
nylon n nàidhlean m, (as adj) nàidhlein

O

oak n darach m
oar n ràmh m
oath n (swear) mionn mf, mionnan m, bòid f
oatmeal n min-choirce f
oats n coirce m
obedience n ùmhlachd f
obedient adj umha(i)l
obeisance n (before royalty etc) ùmhlachd f
obey v bi vi irreg umhail do
object n 1 rud m, nì m; 2 (butt) cùis f, culaidh f, fàth m, cuspair m; 3 (reason) adhbhar; 4 (gram) cuspair m
object v cuir vi an aghaidh
objection n 1 gearan m
objective adj cothromach, neo-phàirteach
objective n rùn m, amas m
objectivity n cothromachd f, neo-phàirteachd f
obligation n comain f
oblige v 1 (compel) cuir vi mar fhiachaibh air; 2 (accommodate) dèan fàbhar/bàidh/ seirbheis do
obliged adj & past part 1 (compelled) mar fhiachaibh ort (etc); 2 (grateful) an comain, fo fhiachaibh do
obliging adj (person) èasgaidh, deònach
oblique adj claon, fiar
obliqueness n claonadh m
oblivion n dìochuimhne f
obscene adj drabasta, draosta
obscenity n drabastachd f, draostachd f
obscure adj 1 (dim) doilleir; 2 (abstruse) deacair; 3 (unknown) neo-ainmeil, neo-aithnichte
obscure v 1 (darken) doilleirich vt, neulaich vt; 2 (conceal) ceil vt, falaich vt
obsequious adj umha(i)l
obsequiousness ùmhlachd f
observance n (keeping) gleidheadh m
observant adj mothachail, furachail
observe v 1 (notice) mothaich vt; 2 (keep) glèidh vt; 3 (celebrate) cùm vt
obsession n beò-ghlacadh m
obsolete adj à cleachdadh m

obstacle n bacadh m, cnap-starra m
obstinacy n raige f
obstinate adj rag, dùr, rag-mhuinealach
obstruct v bac vt
obstruction n bacadh m, cnap-starra m
obtain v faigh vt
obvious adj follaiseach, soilleir, am follais
obviously adv 1 tha f(h)ios; 2 follaiseach/ soilleir
obviousness n follais f
occasion n 1 uair f, turas m; 2 (cause) adhbhar m; 3 (event) tachartas m
occasional adj corra
occasionally adv bho àm gu àm, an-dràsta 's a-rithist, uaireannan, air uairean, air uairibh
occupant n (inhabitant) neach-còmhnaidh m, (owner) seilbheadair m
occupation n obair f, dreuchd f
occur v 1 (happen) tachair vi; 2 (come to mind etc) thig vi a-steach ort (etc)
occurrence n tachartas m, tuiteamas m
ocean n cuan m, fairge f
o'clock adv uair f, uairean fpl
octave n (music) gàmag f
October n an Dàmhair f
odd adj 1 (not even) còrr; 2 (occasional) corra; 3 (strange) neònach, annasach
odds npl in expr fair ~ cothrom m na Fèinne
odds and ends criomagan fpl, trealaich f
odour n boladh m
oesophagus n slugan m
of prep de
of course adv tha f(h)ios m
off adv 1 dheth; 2 (exprs) far ~ fad' air falbh, make ~ tàrr vi às, put ~ (till another day) cuir air ath là, go ~ (deteriorate) rach vi bhuaithe, take ~ cuir vt dhìot
off prep bhàrr, far
offence n 1 oilbheum m; 2 (illegality) coire f, eucoir f
offend v 1 (insult) thoir oilbheum do; 2 (law) dèan coire, ciontaich vi
offender n (law) ciontach m, coireach m

offensive *adj* **1** (*action etc*) oilbheumach, tàmailteach; **2** (*smell etc*) sgreamhail, sgreataidh

offer *n* tairgse *f*

offer *v* **1** tairg *vt*, tabhainn *vt*; **2** (*relig*) ìobair *vt*

offering *n* **1** tabhartas *m*; **2** (*relig*) ìobairt *f*

off-hand *adj* fionnar, coma co-dhiù, fad' às

office *n* oifig *f*, oifis *f*

officer *n* oifigear *m*, oifigeach *m*

official *adj* oifigeil

official *n* oifigeach *m*

offspring *n* clann *f*, gineal *mf*, sìol *m*, sliochd *m*

often *adv* (gu) tric, iomadach uair *f*, iomadh uair, gu minig

oil *n* ola *f*, ùilleadh *m*

oily *adj* ùilleach

ointment *n* ungadh *m*

OK, okay *adj, adv & excl* ceart gu leòr

old *adj* sean, seann

omen *n* manadh *m*

omission *n* dearmad *m*

omit *v* **1** (*exclude*) fàg às; **2** (*neglect*) dearmaid *vi*, cuir *vt* air dhearmad

omni- *prefix* uile-

on *prep* air

on *adv* air adhart

once *adv* **1** (*past*) uair, uaireigin; **2** (*occasion*) aon uair, aon turas; **3** *in exprs* ~ **upon a time** fada, fada ro seo, uaireigin den t-saoghal

once *conj* (*as soon as*) aon uair is/'s/agus

one *adj* **1** *n and num adj* aon *m*, aonan *m*; **2** (*contrast to another*) an dara/an dàrna; **3** (*of pair*) leth-

one *n* **1** (*masc*) fear *m*; **2** (*fem*) tè *f*; **3** ~**s** (*people/objects*) feadhainn *f*; **4** (*in succession*) ~ **after another** an ceann a chèile, aon an dèidh aoin; **5** (*in turn*) ~ **after the other/~ by** ~ fear *m*/tè *f* mu seach, fear seach fear, tè seach tè

one *pron* duine *m*, neach *m*

onerous *adj* trom

one-way *adj* aon-sligheach

onion *n* uinnean *m*

on-line *adj* air-loidhne

onlooker *n* neach-coimhid *m*

onslaught *n* ionnsaigh *mf*

onus *n* uallach *m*

open *adj* **1** fosgailte; **2** (*frank/approachable etc*) fosgailte, fosgarra,

faoilidh; **3** *in exprs* **bring into the** ~ thoir *vt* am follais

open *v* fosgail *vti*

opened *adj & past part* fosgailte

open-handed *adj* fialaidh, fial

opener *n* fosglair *m*

opening *n* **1** (*aperture*) fosgladh *m*, beàrn *mf*; **2** (*opportunity*) cothrom *m*

openness *n* fosgailteachd *f*, fosgarrachd *f*

operate *v* obraich *vt*

operation *n* **1** (*abstr*) gnìomh *m*; **2** (*con*) gnothach *m*; **3** (*medical*) opairèisean *mf*

opponent *n* **1** (*competition*) farpaiseach *m*; **2** (*politics*) neach-dùbhlain *m*

opportune *adj* **1** (*timeous*) mithich, tràthail; **2** (*appropriate*) fàbharach, freagarrach

opportunity *n* cothrom *m*, fosgladh *m*, fàth *m*

opposed *adj* an aghaidh (*with gen*)

opposite *adv & prep*, mu choinneimh, fa chomhair (*with gen*)

opposite *n* ceart-aghaidh *f*

opposition *n* **1** (*abstr*) cur *m* an aghaidh, dùbhlan *m*; **2** (*con*) dùbhlanaich *mpl*

oppression *n* fòirneart *m*

oppressor *n* neach-fòirneirt *m*

optic, optical *adj* fradharcach

option *n* roghainn *mf*

or *conj* **1** no; **2** *in expr* ~ **else** air neo

oral *adj* beòil

orange *adj* orains, dearg-bhuidhe

orange *n* **1** (*fruit*) orainsear *m*; **2** (*colour*) orains *f*, dearg-bhuidhe *m*

oration *n* òraid *f*

orbit *n* cuairt *f*, reul-chuairt *f*

orchard *n* ubhalghort *m*

ordain *v* **1** (*order*) òrdaich *vt*; **2** (*appoint*) suidhich *vt*

ordained *adj & past part* **1** (*prescribed*) òrdaichte; **2** (*fated*) an dàn

ordeal *n* deuchainn *f*

order *n* **1** (*command*) òrdugh *m*; **2** (*sequence*) òrdugh *m*; **3** (*orderliness*) òrdugh *m*, rian *m*; **4** (*working condition*) dòigh *f*, gleus *mf*, òrdugh *m*; **5** *in expr* **in** ~ **to** *conj* gus

order *v* òrdaich *vti*

ordered *adj* òrdail, riaghailteach, rianail

orderliness *n* òrdugh *m*, riaghailteachd *f*, rian *m*

orderly *adj* òrdail, riaghailteach, rianail

ordinal *adj* òrdail

ordinance *n* riaghailt *f*, reachd *m*

ordinary *adj* àbhaisteach, cumanta, gnàthach

ore *n* mèinn(e) *f*

organ[1] *n* (*bodily*) ball *m*

organ[2] *n* (*mus*) òrgan *m*

organisation *n* 1 (*abstr*) òrdugh *m*, riaghailt *f*, rian *m*; 2 (*organising*) òrdachadh *m*, cur an òrdugh *m*; 3 (*body*) buidheann *mf*

organise *v* 1 (*arrange*) cuir *vt* an òrdugh, òrdaich *vt*, cuir rian air; 2 (*establish*) cuir *vt* air chois, cuir *vt* air b(h)onn

origin *n* tùs *m*

original *adj* 1 (*innovative*) ùr; 2 (*first*) tùsail

originally *adv* o/bho thùs, an toiseach, an toiseach-tòiseachaidh, sa chiad àite

originate *v* tàrmaich *vt*

ornament *n* ball-maise *m*

ornithology *n* eun-eòlas *m*

oscillate *v* luaisg *vi*

oscillation *n* 1 (*abstr*) luasgadh *m*; 2 (*con*) luasgan *m*

other *adj* eile

otherwise *adv* air neo

otter *n* dòbhran *m*, biast-dhubh/bèist-dhubh *f*

ought *auxiliary v* bu (*past/conditional of* is *v irreg def*) chòir dhut

ounce *n* unnsa *m*

ourselves *reflexive pron* sinn fhèin/fhìn

out *adv & prep* 1 (*motion*) a-mach; 2 (*outside*) a-muigh

outburst *n* lasgan *m*

outcome *n* toradh *m*, buil *f*

outgoing *adj* (*sociable*) faoilidh, cuideachdail, fàilteach

outlaw *n* neach-cùirn *m*

outlaw *v* cuir *vt* fon choill

outlawed *adj & past part* 1 (*person*) fon choill; 2 (*substances etc*) mì-laghail, toirmisgte, fo thoirmeasg *m*, neo-cheadaichte

output *n* toradh *m*

outrageous *adj* uabhasach, (*scandalous*) tàmailteach, (*offensive*) oilbheumach

outside *adv* 1 (*movement*) a-mach; 2 (*position*) a-muigh

outside *n* taobh a-muigh *m*

outside *prep* air (an) taobh a-muigh

outskirts *n* iomall *m*

outstanding *adj* 1 (*excellent*) air leth (math); 2 (*unpaid*) gun phàigheadh

outwith *prep* 1 (*beyond*) thar; 2 (*outside*) air taobh a-muigh

oval *adj* ughach

oval *n* ughach *m*

ovary *n* ughlann *f*

over *adv* 1 (*movement*) thairis; 2 (*exprs*) ~ **and** ~ **again** (*expr repetition*) uair *f* is uair, **all** ~ (*finished*) seachad

over *prep* 1 (*position/movement*) thar; 2 (*movement*) tarsainn air, thairis air; 3 (*above*) os cionn; 4 (*time*) rè; 5 *in expr* **all** ~ (*everywhere*) air feadh

overcoat *n* còta-mòr *m*

overcome *v* 1 (*quell*) ceannsaich *vt*; 2 (*vanquish*) thoir buaidh air, dèan a' chùis/dèan an gnothach air

overflow *v* cuir *vi* thairis

overhead *adv* os do (*etc*) chionn

overseas *adv* 1 (*movement*) a-null thairis; 2 (*position*) thall thairis

oversight *n* (*omission*) dearmad *m*

overt *adj* follaiseach

overtime *n* còrr-ùine *f*, seach-thìm *f*

overturn *v* 1 (*as vt*) cuir bun-os-cionn, cuir car de, cuir thairis; 2 (*as vi*) rach car de, rach thairis

owe *v* bi *vi irreg* fo fhiachaibh do

owl *n* cailleach-oidhche *f*

own *adj* 1 (*possessing*) agad; 2 (*using poss pron*) fhèin

owner *n* sealbhadair *m*

ox *n* damh *m*

ox-tail *n* earball-daimh *m*

oxygen *n* ogsaidean *m*

oystercatcher *n* gille-brì(gh)de *m*, trilleachan *f*

P

pace n 1 (*stride*) ceum m; 2 (*speed*) astar m; 3 in expr **keep** ~ cùm ruith

pace v ceumnaich vi

Pacific, n the An Cuan Sèimh m

pacify v 1 (*calm etc*) ciùinich vt, sìthich vt, sèimhich vt, socraich vt; 2 (*subdue*) ceannsaich vt

pack[1] n paca m

pack[2] n (*people*) gràisg f

pack v 1 (*parcel etc*) paisg vt; 2 in exprs ~ **up** (*break down*) bris vi

package parsail m, pasgadh m, pasgan m

packed adj & past part 1 (*places etc*) loma-làn, dòmhail & dùmhail; 2 (*objects etc*) **closely** ~ dlùth

packed lunch n pìos m

packet n pacaid f

packing n pasgadh m

pact n còrdadh m

paddle n pleadhag f

paddle v pleadhagaich vti

pagan n & adj pàganach m

page n (*book etc*) duilleag f, taobh-duilleig(e) m

pail n peile m, bucaid f, (*milking*) cuman m, cuinneag f

pain n pian mf, cràdh m

pain v pian vt, cràidh vt, ciùrr vt

pained adj dòrainneach

painful adj goirt, dòrainneach, pianail, crài(dh)teach

painstaking adj mion-chùiseach, ro-phongail, ro-mhionaideach

paint n peant(a) m

paint v peant vti

painter n peantair m

pair n 1 dithis f; 2 (*objects*) paidhir mf

Pakistan n Pagastan f

pal n companach m, caraid m

palace n pàileis f, lùchairt f

palate n càirean m

pale-faced adj glaisneulach

palm[1] n (*hand*) bas f, bois f, glac f

palm[2] n (*tree*) pailm f, craobh-phailm f

palpitate v plosg vi, plap vi

palpitation n plosg m, plosgadh m, plosgartaich f

pamphlet n leabhrachan m, leabhran m

pan n pana m

pancake n foileag f

pane n lòsan m

panel n pannal m

pang n guin m

pannier n cliabh m

pant n plosg m

pant v plosg vi

panting n plosg m, plosgadh m, plosgartaich f

pants n 1 (*underwear*) drathais & drathars f; 2 (*trousers*) briogais f, triubhas m

paper n pàipear m

papist adj pàpanach

Papist n Pàpanach m

parable n cosamhlachd f

Paradise n Pàrras m, Flaitheas m

paraffin n paireafain m

parallel adj co-shìnte

parcel n parsail m, pasgan m

parched adj 1 (*person*) ìotmhor; 2 (*ground etc*) tioram

pardon n mathanas m

pardon v 1 ma(i)th vt, thoir mathanas do; 2 in exprs (*as apology*) ~ **me!** gabh(aibh) mo leisgeul m!, (*what did you say?*) ~? b' àill leibh?

parent n pàrant m

parenthesis n eadar-ràdh m

parish n sgìre f, sgìreachd f, paraiste f

parity n ionannachd f, co-ionannachd f

park n pàirc(e) f, raon m

parliament n pàrlamaid f

parliamentary adj pàrlamaideach

parrot n pearraid f

part n 1 (*proportion*) cuid f, pàirt m; 2 (*section*) earrann f; 3 (*share*) cuid f, roinn f; 4 (*side*) taobh m

part v dealaich vti

participant n com-pàirtiche m, (*competitor*) farpaiseach m

participate v gabh pàirt m, gabh com-pàirt f, com-pàirtich vi

participation n com-pàirt f

particle n 1 mìr m, mìrean m; 2 (*gram*) mion-fhacal m

particular adj **1** àraidh, sònraichte; **2** (precise) mion-chùiseach, pongail

parting n dealachadh m

partition n pàirteacheadh m

partition v pàirtich vt, roinn vt

partner n **1** pàirtiche m, com-pàirtiche m; **2** (sexual) coimhleapach mf, companach mf

party n **1** pàrtaidh m; **2** (gathering) pàrtaidh m, hòro-gheallaidh m

pass n **1** (topog) bealach m; **2** (games) pas m; **3** (document) cead-inntrigidh m, pas m

pass v **1** rach vi seachad air; **2** (spend) cuir vt seachad, caith vt; **3** (exprs) ~ **away** (ie die) caochail vi, siubhail vi, ~ **water** dèan mùn m, mùin vi

passage n **1** (building) trannsa f; **2** (book) earrann f; **3** (topog) bealach m; **4** (voyage) aiseag mf, (maritime) turas-mara m

passenger n neach-siubhail m

passionate adj lasanta, dìoghrasach

passive adj fulangach

passport n cead-siubhail m, cead dol thairis m

past adj & adv **1** seachad; **2** in expr ~ **it** tha e air a dhol dheth, air a dhol bhuaithe; **3** (gram) caithte

past, the n an t-àm a chaidh seachad, an t-àm a dh'fhalbh

paste n glaodhan m

pastime n cur-seachad m

pastry n pastra f

pasture n clua(i)n f, ionaltradh m

pasture v feuraich vt

patch n (material etc) tuthag f, brèid m

Paternoster n paidir f

path n frith-rathad m, slighe f

patience n foighidinn f

patient adj foighidneach

patient n euslainteach m

patron n neach-taice m, goistidh m

patronage n taic(e) f, goistidheachd f

patronymic n sloinneadh m

pattern n pàtran m

paunch n maodal f, mionach m

pavement n cabhsair m

pavilion n pàillean m

paving stone (floor) leac-ùrlair f, (pavement) leac-cabhsair f

paw n cròg f, spòg f, màg f

paw v (handle) (droch-)làimhsich vt

pay n pàigh m, pàigheadh m, tuarastal m

pay v **1** pàigh vti; **2** (exprs) ~ **attention** thoir an aire, thoir fea(i)rt, ~ **a compliment** dèan moladh, ~ **a visit** rach vi air chèilidh, dèan cèilidh, tadhail vi, ~ **back** dìoghail & dìol vt

payment n **1** pàigheadh m, dìoladh m; **2** (reparation) èirig f

paypoint n àite-pàighidh m

pea n peasair f

peace n **1** sìth f; **2** (tranquillity) fois f, sìth f; **3** in expr ~ **of mind** toil-inntinn f

peaceful adj **1** sìtheil; **2** (calm, tranquil) sàmhach

peach n peitseag f

peak n (mountaintop) stùc f, binnean m

peal n (bells) seirm f, bualadh m

peanut n cnò-thalmhainn f

pear n peur f

peasantry n tuath f

peat n **1** (coll) mòine f; **2** (single) fòid f, fàd

pebble n dèideag f, molag f

peck v pioc vti

pedal n troighean m

pedestrian n coisiche m

pee n mùn m

pee v dèan mùn m, mùin vi

peel n (vegetables etc) rùsg m, plaosg m

peel v (vegetables etc) rùisg vt, plaoisg vt

peeled adj & past part rùisgte

peer n **1** (lord) morair m; **2** (equal) seise m

peevish adj frithearra, crost(a)

peewit n curracag f

peg n cnag f

pellet n peilear m

pelt v tilg vt, caith vt

pen[1] n (writing) peann m

pen[2] n (livestock) buaile f, crò m

penal adj peanasach

penalise v peanasaich

penalty n peanas m

pencil n peansail m

penetrate v **1** (make one's way into) rach vi a-steach, bris vi a-steach; **2** (pierce) toll vt; **3** (pass) thig vi, rach vi, bris vi; **4** (water) drùidh vi

penis n bod m, slat f

penny n **1** sgillinn f; **2** **Scots** ~ peighinn f

pension n peinnsean m

pensioner n neach-peinnsein m

people n **1** (humans) daoine mpl; **2** (populace) sluagh m, tuath f; **3** (locals)

muinntir *f*, poball *m*; **4** (*relatives*)
càirdean *mpl*, daoine *mpl*; **5** (*associates*)
muinntir *f*, cuideachd *f*; **6** (*tribe, etc*)
cinneadh *m*
pep up *v* piobraich *vt*
pepper *n* piobar *m*
pepper *v* piobraich *vt*
per capita *adv* an urra *f*
perceive *v* faic *vt*, mothaich *vt*
per cent *adv* sa cheud
perception *n* **1** (*capacity*) tuigse *f*, lèirsinn
f; **2** (*sight*) fradharc/radharc *m*, lèirsinn *f*;
3 (*idea*) beachd *m*
perceptive *adj* geurchuiseach, tuigseach,
mothachail
perch *v* laigh *vi*
perfect *adj* **1** coileanta; **2** (*morally*) foirfe;
3 (*expr*) ~! taghta!
perfection *n* coileantachd *f*, (*moral*)
foirfeachd *f*
perforate *v* toll *vt*
perform *v* **1** (*fulfil*) coilean *vt*, thoir *vt* gu
buil *f*; **2** (*theatre etc*) cluich *vi*, cleasaich
vi; **3** (*music etc*) gabh *vt*; **4** (*acquit*) dèan
vt
performance *n* (*fulfilment*) coileanadh *m*,
toirt *f* gu buil
perfume *n* cùbhrachd *f*
perhaps *adv & conj* **1** is/'s dòcha, (is)
ma(th) dh'fhaodte/is mathaid, theagamh;
2 (*as conj*) is/'s dòcha, (is) ma(th)
dh'fhaodte, theagamh, faodaidh
peril *n* gàbhadh *m*, cunnart *m*
perilous *adj* gàbhaidh, cunnartach
period *n* **1** (*time*) greis *f*, treis *f*;
2 (*educational*) tràth
(-teagaisg) *m*; **3** (*menstrual*) fuil-mìosa *f*
periodical *n* iris *f*, (*quarterly*) ràitheachan
m
peripheral *adj* iomallach
periphery *n* iomall *m*
permanent *adj* maireannach, buan
permeable *adj* so-dhrùidhteach
permissible *adj* ceadaichte
permission *n* cead *m*
permissive *adj* ceadachail
permit *n* cead *m*
permit *v* leig *vi* le/do), ceadaich *vt*
permitted *adj & past part* ceadaichte
perplex *v* cuir *vt* an imcheist
perplexed *adj* an/fo imcheist *f*,
imcheisteach

perplexing *adj* imcheisteach
perplexity *n* imcheist *f*
persevere *v* cùm *vi* (ri), lean *vi* air
persevering *adj* leantainneach
persistent *adj* **1** (*person*) gramail &
greimeil; **2** (*situation*) leanailteach
person *n* neach *m*, pearsa *m*, duine *m*
personal *adj* pearsanta
personality *n* pearsantachd *f*
personnel *n* sgiobachd *f*, luchd-obrach *m*
perspiration *n* fallas *m*
perspire *v* bi *vi irreg* fallas ort (*etc*), cuir
fallas, bi *vi irreg* nad (*etc*) fhallas
persuade *v* cuir ìmpidh air, iompaich *vt*
persuasion *n* ìmpidh *f*
persuasive *adj* ìmpidheach
perverse *adj* **1** (*obstinate*) rag, dùr, rag-
mhuinealach; **2** (*morally*) claon
perversion *n* claonadh *m*
perversity *n* (*obstinacy*) raige *f*
pervert *v* truaill *vt*, (*justice*) claon *vt*
pest *n* plàigh *f*
pestiferous *adj* plàigheil
pestilence *n* plàigh *f*
pestilential *adj* plàigheil
pet *n* peata *m*
peter out *v* sìolaidh *vi* às
petition *n* tagradh *m*
petrol *n* peatroil/peatrail *m*
petticoat *n* còta-bàn *m*
petty *adj* **1** (*small*) mion- *prefix*; **2** (*small-
minded etc*) crìon, suarach
pharmacist *n* neach-chungaidhean *m*
pharmacy *n* **1** (*premises*) bùth-
chungaidh(ean) *f*; **2** (*profession*) eòlas
leigheasan *m*, eòlas chungaidhean *m*
pheasant *n* easag *f*
phenomenal *adj* iongantach
phenomenon *n* **1** (*science*) sìon *m*;
2 (*wonder*) iongantas *m*, mìorbhail *f*,
suaicheantas *m*
philosopher *n* feallsanach *m*
philosophy *n* feallsanachd *f*
phlegm *n* ronn *m*
phone *n* fòn *mf*
phone *v* cuir fòn *mf*, fòn *vi*, fònaig *vi* gu
photograph *n* dealbh *mf*
physical *adj* corporra
physique *n* dèanamh *m*
piano *n* piàna/piàno *m*
pibroch *n* ceòl-mòr *m*, pìobaireachd *f*
pick[1] *n* (*tool*) pic *m*, piocaid *f*

pick² *n* (*choice*) roghainn *f*
pick *v* **1** (*select*) tagh *vt*, roghnaich *vt*;
  2 (*flowers etc*) cruinnich *vt*; **3** (*at food*)
  pioc *vi*, creim *vi*; **4** ~ **up** tog *vt*
pickaxe *n* pic *m*, piocaid *f*
pickle *n* picil *f*
picnic *n* cuirm-chnuic *f*
Pict *n* Cruithneach *m*
Pictish *adj* Cruithneach
picture *n* dealbh *mf*
picture *v* dealbh *vt*
piece *n* **1** (*bit*) criomag *f*, bloigh *f*, mìr
  m; **2** (*component*) pìos *m*, earrann *f*;
  3 (*sandwich*) pìos *m*; **4** (*exprs*) **in one** ~
  slàn is fallain, **bits and** ~**s** trealaich *f*
pierce *v* toll *vt*
piercing *n* tolladh *m*
piety *n* cràbhadh *m*, diadhachd *f*
pig *n* muc *f*
pigeon *n* calman *m*
piggy-back *n* gioma-goc *m*
pig-headed *adj* rag-mhuinealach
piglet *n* uircean/oircean *m*
pigsty *n* fail-mhuc *f*
pigtail *n* figheachan *m*
pile *n* cruach *f*, tòrr *m*, dùn *m*
pile, **pile up** *v* càrn *vt*, cruach *vt*
pilfer *v* dèan mion-bhraide *f*
pilfering *n* mion-bhraide *f*
pilgrim *n* taistealach *m*
pilgrimage *n* taisteal *f*
pill *n* pile *f*
pillar *n* **1** (*architecture etc*) colbh *m*;
  2 (*rock*) carragh *f*
pillion *n* pillean *m*
pillow *n* cluasag *f*
pilot *n* pìleat/paidhleat *m*
pimple *n* plucan *m*, guirean *m*
pin *n* prìne *m*, dealg *f*
pincers *n* teanchair/teannachair *m*
pinch *n* (*with fingernails etc*) gòmag *f*,
  pioc *m*
pinch *v* **1** (*with fingernails etc*) pioc *vt*;
  2 (*steal*) goid *vti*, dèan braid *f*
pinching *n* **1** (*with fingernails etc*) piocadh
  m; **2** (*stealing*) goid *f*, braid *f*
pine *n* giuthas *m*, *in exprs* ~ **wood/forest**
  giùthsach *f*, ~ **cone** durcan *m*
pinhead *n* ploc-prìne *m*
pink *adj* pinc
pink *n* pinc *m*
pinkie (*Sc*) *n* lùdag *f*

pinnacle *n* binnean *m*
pins and needles an cadal-deilgneach *m*
pint *n* pinnt *m*
pipe *n* **1** pìob *f*, feadan *m*; **2** (*smoking*)
  pìob(-thombaca); **3** (*instrument*) cuisle *f*,
  cuislean *m*; **4** (*bag~*) pìob *f*, pìob mhòr
piper *n* pìobaire *m*
piping *n* pìobaireachd *f*
piss *n* mùn *m*
piss *v* dèan mùn *m*, mùin *vi*, caill mùn
pistol *n* daga & dag *m*
pit *n* **1** (*hollow*) lag *mf*, glac *f*, sloc *m*;
  2 (*mining*) mèinn(e) *f*
pitch¹ *n* (*tar*) bìth *f*, tèarr/teàrr *f*
pitch² *n* (*playing*) raon-cluiche *m*
pitch³ *n* (*musical*) àirde (san sgàla) *f*
pitch *v* **1** (*throw*) tilg, sad *vt*; **2** (*movement*)
  tulg *vi*
pitch-fork *n* gòbhlag *f*
piteous *adj* truagh, suarach
pith *n* glaodhan *m*
pitiable, **pitiful** *adj* truagh, suarach
pitiless *adj* neo-thruacanta, an-iochdmhor
pity *n* **1** iochd *f*, truas *m*, truacantas *m*; **2** *in*
  expr **that's a** ~! tha sin duilich!, is duilich
  sin!, is truagh sin!, b' olc an airidh (e)!
pitying *adj* truasail
place *n* **1** (*general*) àite *m*; **2** ionad *m*
place *v* cuir *vt*, socraich *vt*, suidhich *vt*
placename *n* ainm-àite *m*
plague *n* plàigh *f*
plague *v* (*exasperate*) leamhaich *vt*, sàraich
  vt
plaid *n* **1** breacan *m*; **2** (*blanket*) plaide *f*
plain *adj* **1** (*evident*) soilleir, follaiseach,
  lèir; **2** (*simple*) sìmplidh, aon-fhillte;
  3 (*unpretentious*) sìmplidh, lom
plain *n* (*topog*) còmhnard *m*, machair *mf*
plaintive *adj* tiamhaidh
plait *n* dual *m*, filleadh *m*
plait *v* (*rope etc*) dualaich *vt*, fill *vt*
plaited *adj & past part* fillte
plan *n* **1** plana *m*; **2** (*strategy*) innleachd *f*;
  3 (*drawing*) dealbh-chumadh *m*
plan *v* **1** (*general*) planaig *vti*; **2** (*technical*
  etc) dealbh/deilbh *vt*; **3** (*strategy etc*)
  innlich *vt*
plane¹ *n* (*carpentry*) locair *f*, locar *m*
plane² *n* (*aircraft*) plèana *mf*, itealan *m*
plane³ *n* (*geometry etc*) raon *m*
plane *v* locair *vti*
planet *n* planaid *f*

plank n dèile f, clàr m
planner n neach-dealbhaidh m
planning n dealbhadh m, planaigeadh m
plant¹ n (botanical) luibh mf, lus m
plant² n (manufacturing etc) **1** (equipment etc) uidheam f; **2** (factory) factaraidh f
plant v cuir vt
plaster n **1** (building etc) sglàib f; **2** (sticking) plàsd & plàst m
plastic n & adj plastaig f
plate n **1** (tableware) truinnsear m; **2** (metal etc) lann f
platform n **1** (builiding) àrd-ùrlar m; **2** (railway etc) àrd-chabhsair m, còmhnard m; **3** (oil) clàr m
platter n mias f
plausible adj beulach, beulchair
play n **1** (activity) cluich & cluiche m, cleas m; **2** (con) dealbh-chluich mf
play v cluich vti
player n cluicheadair m
playground n raon-cluiche m
playgroup n cròileagan m
playing n cluich/cluiche m, cleas m
plea n **1** (request) guidhe mf; **2** (legal) tagradh m, tagairt f
plead v **1** guidh vi; **2** (legal) tagair vti
pleasant adj tlachdmhor, taitneach, ciatach
pleasantness n taitneas m
please v **1** (content) còrd vi riut (etc), toilich vt, riaraich vt, taitinn vi ri; **2** (wish) togair vi; **3** (request) mas e do thoil f/ur toil e
pleased adj & past part **1** (satisfied) toilichte, riaraichte, air do dhòigh; **2** (proud) moiteil
pleasing adj tlachdmhor, taitneach
pleasurable adj tlachdmhor
pleasure n tlachd f, taitneas m, toileachadh m
pleat n filleadh m
pleat v fill vt
pleated adj & past part fillte
pledge n gealladh m, geall m
pledge v geall vti, thoir gealladh, rach vi an geall
Pleiades, the n An Grioglachan m
plentiful adj pailt, lìonmhor
plenty n **1** (sufficiency) pailteas m; **2** in expr ~ **of** gu leòr
pliable adj sùbailte, so-lùbte, so-lùbadh
pliant adj lùbach

pliers npl greimire m
plop n plub m
plop v plubraich vi, plub vi
plot¹ n **1** (conspiracy) cuilbheart f, innleachd f; **2** (lit) sgeul m
plot² n **1** (ground) pìos-fearainn m, pìos-talmhainn m; **2** (bed) ceapach mf
plot v innlich vt, dèan co-fheall
plough n **1** (agric) crann m; **2** (astronomy) **The Plough** An Crann-arain
plough v treabh vti
ploughing n treabhadh m
plover n feadag f
ploy n **1** (activity) plòidh f; **2** (stratagem) innleachd f
pluck n (courage etc) smior m, misneach(d) f
pluck v (flower etc) spìon vt
plug n cnag f, plucan m
plumage n iteach m
plumber n plumair m
plunder n cobhartach mf, creach f
plunder v creach vti, spùill/spùinn vti
plunge n tumadh m
plunge v tum vt
plural adj (gram) iolra
plural n (gram) iolra m
pm adv feasgar
poacher n poitsear m
pocket n pòcaid f
pod n (shell) plaosg m
pod v (vegetables etc) plaoisg/plaosg vt
poem n dàn m, duan m, laoidh mf, bàrdachd f
poet n bàrd m, filidh m
poetic adj bàrdail
poetry n bàrdachd f, rann m, dànachd f
poignant adj tiamhaidh
point n **1** (pin etc) bior m, gob m, rinn m; **2** (topog) àird f, rubha m, sròn f, rinn m; **3** (argument etc) puing f; **4** (issue) ceist f, cùis f, rud m
point v **1** (with finger etc) tomh vi; **2** in expr ~ **out** sònraich vt
pointed adj **1** (sharp) biorach; **2** (to the point) pongail
pointless adj dìomhain, faoin, gun fheum
poison n puinnsean m, nimh/neimh m
poison v puinnseanaich vt
poisonous adj puinnseanach, nimheil
poke v brodaich vt
poker n pòcair m

Poland n A' Phòlainn f
polar bear n mathan-bàn m
pole n **1** (*joinery etc*) cabar m, pòla m;
  2 (*geog*) pòla m
Pole n Pòlach m
police n poileas m
policeman n poileasman m, poileas m
policewoman n ban-phoileas f
policing n obair poileis f
policy n poileasaidh m
Polish adj Pòlach
polish n lìomh f
polish v lìomh vt
polished adj lìomharra
polite adj modhail, cùirteil
politeness n modhalachd f
political adj poilitigeach
politician n neach-poilitigs m
politics n poilitigs f
poll n **1** (*vote*) taghadh m; **2** (*head*) ceann m
pollutant n stuth-truaillidh m
pollute v truaill vt, salaich vt
polluted adj & past part truaillte
pollution n truailleadh m
poly- prefix ioma-
polygamy n ioma-phòsadh m
polyglot adj ioma-chànanach
polygon n ioma-cheàrnag f
pompous adj mòrchuiseach
pond n lochan m, lòn m, glumag f
ponder v cnuas/cnuasaich, meòraich/
  meamhraich vi
ponderous adj **1** (*heavy*) trom;
  2 (*lumbering etc*) slaodach
pony n pònaidh m
pony-tail n figheachan m
pool n lòn m, glumag f
poor adj **1** (*indigent*) bochd;
  2 (*unfortunate*) truagh, bochd;
  3 (*inadequate*) droch, suarach
poor n (*indigent*), **the ~** am bochd m, na
  daoine bochda mpl
poorly adv **1** gu dona; **2** (*unwell*) bochd
Pope n Pàpa m
popish adj pàpanach
populace n sluagh m, muinntir f, poball m
popular adj **1** mòr-chòrdte; **2** (*public*)
  poibleach
population n **1** (*con*) sluagh m, muinntir f,
  poball m; **2** (*abstr*) àireamh-sluaigh f
pork n feòil-muice f, muic-fheòil f
porpoise n pèileag f

porridge n lite f, brochan m
port[1] m (*harbour*) port m
port[2] n (*wine*) fion-poirt m
portable adj so-ghiùlan
porter n **1** portair m; **2** (*doorkeeper*)
  dorsair m
portion n cuid f, cuibhreann mf, roinn f
portray v **1** (*acting etc*) riochdaich vt;
  2 (*drawing etc*) dealbh vt, tarraing vt
portrayal n riochdachadh m; (*drawing
  etc*) dealbhadh m, tarraing f
Portugal n, used with art, A' Phortagail f
Portuguese n & adj Portagaileach m
position n **1** (*job*) oifis f, dreuchd f;
  2 (*phys*) suidheachadh m
possession(s) n seilbh f, maoin f
possessive adj seilbheach
possessor n seilbheadair/sealbhadair m
possible adj ion-dhèanta
post[1] n (*mail*) post m
post[2] (*wooden*) post m, stob m
post- prefix iar-
postal adj tron phost
postcard n cairt-phuist f
postcode n còd-puist m
postie, postman n post(a) m
postpone v cuir vt dheth, cuir vt air an ath
  là, cuir vt air ais
postscript n fo-sgrìobhadh m
posture n giùlan m
pot n poit f
potato, potatoes n & npl buntàta m
poteen n poitean m
potent adj **1** (*ruler etc*) cumhachdach;
  2 (*drink etc*) làidir; **3** (*remedy etc*)
  èifeachdach, buadhmhor
potential n comas m
potter n crèadhadair m
pottery n crèadhadaireachd f
pound[1] n **1** (*money*) not(a) m; **2** (*weight*)
  punnd m
pound[2] n (*enclosure*) punnd m
pound v pronn
pounded adj pronn
pounding n pronnadh m
pour v dòirt vti, sil vti, ruith vti
powder n pùdar/fùdar m
powder v pùdaraich/fùdaraich vt, cuir
  pùdar/fùdar air
power n **1** (*might*) cumhachd mf, neart m;
  2 (*pol etc*) cumhachd mf, ùghdarras m,
  smachd m, reachd m; **3** (*vigour*) neart

m; **4** (*electric*) cumhachd *mf*, dealan *m*;
5 (*capability*) comas *m*

powerful *adj* **1** (*phys*) làidir, neartmhor,
lùthmhor; **2** (*pol etc*) cumhachdach

practicable *adj* ion-dhèanta, a ghabhas
dèanamh

practically *adv* an ìre mhath

practice *n* **1** (*music etc*) cleachdadh *m*;
2 (*custom*) cleachdadh *m*, àbhaist *f*

praise *n* moladh *m*, luaidh *m*

praise *v* mol *vt*, luaidh *vt*, dèan moladh air,
dèan luaidh air

praiseworthy *adj* ionmholta

prattle *n* goileam *m*, gobaireachd/
gabaireachd *f*

prattling *adj* gobach

pray *v* **1** (*beseech etc*) guidh *vi* air; **2** (*relig*)
dèan ùrnaigh

prayer *n* **1** (*entreaty*) guidhe *mf*; **2** (*relig*)
ùrnaigh *f*, guidhe *mf*

pre- *prefix* ro-

preamble *n* ro-ràdh *m*

precarious *adj* **1** (*unreliable*) cugallach;
2 (*risky*) cunnartach

precious *adj* luachmhor, prìseil

precipice *n* bearradh *m*, stalla *m*

precipitate *adj* **1** (*actions etc*) cabhagach,
bras; **2** (*stream etc*) cas, bras

precipitation *n* (*liquids*) sileadh *m*

précis *n* geàrr-chunntas *m*

precise *adj* **1** (*person*) pongail,
mionaideach; **2** (*accurate*) grinn, pongail

precision *n* (*accuracy*) pongalachd *f*

precocious *adj* luathaireach

predator *n* sealgair *m*

predestination *n* ro-òrdachadh *m*

predicament *n* **1** (*situation*) càs *m*, cùil-
chumhang *f*; **2** (*indecision*) ioma(dh)-
chomhairle *f*, imcheist *f*

predict *v* ro-innis *vt*

predictable *adj* ro-innseach

preface *n* ro-ràdh *m*

prefer *v* is *v irreg def* fheàrr

preference *n* roghainn *mf*

prefix *n* ro-leasachan *m*

pregnancy *n* leatrom *m*

pregnant *adj* torrach, trom

prejudice *n* claon-bhàidh *f*, claon-bhreith *f*

prejudice *v* (*situation etc*) dèan dochann
air, dèan cron air

premature *adj* **1** ron àm *m*, ron mhithich *f*;
2 (*birth*) an-abaich

prematurely *adv* ron àm *m*, ron mhithich *f*

premier *n* prìomhaire *m*

preoccupation *n* cùram *m*

preoccupied *adj* **1** (*anxious*) fo chùram;
2 (*distracted*) fad' às

preparation *n* deasachadh *m*,
uidheamachadh *m*, ullachadh *m*

prepare *v* **1** deasaich *vt*, ullaich *vt*;
2 (*adjust etc*) gleus *vt*; **3** (*equip etc*)
uidheamaich *vt*

prepared *adj & past part* **1** deiseil,
ullamh, deas; **2** (*engine etc*) air ghleus
mf; **3** (*equipped etc*) uidheamaichte;
4 (*willing*) deònach

pre-payment *n* ro-phàigheadh *m*

preponderance *n* tromalach *f*

preposition *n* roimhear *m*

Presbyterian *n & adj* Clèireach *m*

Presbyterianism *n* Clèireachd *f*

presbytery *n* clèir *f*

pre-school *adj* fo-sgoile

prescribe *v* òrdaich *vt*

prescription *n* (*med*) òrdugh-cungaidh *m*

pre-selection *n* ro-thaghadh *m*

presence *n* **1** làthair *f*; **2** (*abstr*)
làthaireachd *f*

present *adj* **1** an làthair *f*, ann *adv*;
2 (*current*) *in exprs* **at ~** aig an àm *m* seo,
an-dràsta

present[1] *n* tiodhlac *m*, gibht *f*

present[2] *n* (*time*) *in exprs* **the ~** an t-àm
a tha an làthair, **at ~** aig an àm seo, a-nis,
an-dràsta, (*general*) san latha an-diugh *m*

present *v* **1** (*products etc*) taisbean/
taisbein *vt*; **2** (*gift*) thoir (seachad) *vt*,
tiodhlaic *vt*

presentation *n* **1** (*techniques etc*)
taisbeanadh *m*; **2** (*formal*) tabhartas *m*

preserve *v* glèidh *vt*

preserved *adj & past part* glèidhte

president *n* ceann-suidhe *m*

press *n* **1** (*publishing*) clò *m*; **2** *in expr* **the
~** (*media*) na pàipearan(-naidheachd) *mpl*

press *v* **1** (*phys*) fàisg *vt*, teannaich *vt*;
2 (*urge*) coitich *vt*, brosnaich *vt*; **3** (*hurry*)
cuir cabhag air, greas *vt*

pressing *adj* (*urgent*) cabhagach,
èiginneach, cudromach

pressure *n* **1** (*phys*) cudrom/cuideam *m*;
2 (*stress*) uallach *m*

pretend *v* leig *vi* ort (*etc*)

pretext *n* leisgeul *m*

pretty *adj* grinn, bòidheach, ceanalta

pretty *adv* gu math, an ìre mhath

prevent *v* bac *vt*, cuir bacadh air, caisg *vt*, cuir casg air

prevention *n* casg *m*, casgadh *m*

preventive *adj* casgach

prey *n* cobhartach *mf*, creach *f*

price *n* prìs *f*

prick *v* cuir bior ann an

prickle *n* bior *m*, calg *m*, dealg *f*

pride *n* 1 (*legitimate*) pròis *f*, moit *f*; 2 (*excessive*) àrdan, mòrchuis *f*, uabhar *m*, uaibhreas *m*

prime *adj* 1 prìomh; 2 (*of high quality*) fìor mhath

prime *n* treun *f* do neirt

prince *n* prionnsa *m*

princely *adj* flathail

princess *n* bana-phrionnsa *f*

principal *n* (*institution etc*) prionnsapal *m*, ceannard *m*

principal *adj* prìomh

principle *n* prionnsapal *m*

print *n* 1 (*publications*) clò; 2 (*trace*) lorg *f*, làrach *f*

print *v* (*publish*) clò-bhuail *vt*, cuir *vt* an clò

printed *adj & past part* clò-bhuailte

printer *n* clò-bhualadair *m*

printing *n* clò-bhualadh *m*

prison *n* prìosan *m*

prisoner *n* prìosanach *m*, ciomach *m*

private *adj* 1 (*secret*) uaigneach, dìomhair; 2 (*confidential*) dìomhair, pearsanta; 3 (*place*) prìobhaideach

privately *adv* (*in confidence etc*) os ìosal/ os ìseal, gu dìomhair

prize *n* duais *f*

probability *n* coltachd *f*

probable *adj* coltach

probably *adv* tha coltach

probity *n* ionracas *m*

problem *n* 1 (*question*) ceist *f*, cùis; 2 (*difficulty*) duilgheadas *m*, trioblaid *f*

proceed *v* rach *vi* air adhart

process *n* gnìomh *m*; modh *m*

process *v* 1 (*prepare etc*) giullaich *vt*, gnìomhaich *vt*, saothraich *vt*; 2 (*information*) làimhsich *vt*, cuir *vt* an eagar

processing *n* (*industry etc*) giullachadh *m*, gnìomhachadh *m*, saothrachadh *m*

processor *n* (*IT*) gnìomh-inneal *m*

proclamation *n* gairm *f*

procrastinate *v* màirnealaich *vi*, maillich *vi*

prodigal *adj* stròdhail/struidheil

produce *n* toradh *m*

produce *v* 1 (*industry etc*) saothraich *vt*, dèan *vt*, tàrmaich *vt*; 2 (*cinema etc*) riochdaich *vt*

producer *n* 1 (*goods etc*) neach-dèanaidh *m*; 2 (*film etc*) riochdaire *m*

product *n* 1 toradh *m*; 2 ~s (*goods*) bathar *m*

productive *adj* torrach

profane *v* truaill *vt*

profession *n* (*occupation*) dreuchd *f*

professional *adj* dreuchdail, proifeiseanta

professor *n* proifeasair *m*, ollamh *m*

proficiency *n* comas *m*

proficient *adj* comasach

profile *n* 1 (*phys*) leth-aghaidh *f*; 2 (*account*) cunntas *m*; 3 (*publicity etc*) ìomhaigh *f*

profit *n* 1 (*fin*) prothaid *f*, buannachd *f*; 2 (*general*) buannachd *f*, tairbhe *f*

profit *v* tairbhich/tarbhaich *vi*

profitable *adj* tairbheach/tarbhach, buannachdail

profound *adj* domhainn

progeny *n* 1 (*humans*) gineal *mf*, sìol *m sing coll*, sliochd *m sing coll*; 2 (*animals*) àl *m*

program, programme *n* prògram *m*

programming *n* prògramadh *m*

progress *n* 1 (*abstr*) adhartas *m*; 2 (*activity etc*) piseach *m*, adhartas *m*

progressive *adj* adhartach

prohibit *v* toirmisg *vt*

prohibited *adj & past part* toirmisgte, fo thoirmeasg

prohibition *n* toirmeasg *m*

prohibitive *adj* toirmeasgach

project *n* pròiseact *mf*, plana *m*

prologue *n* ro-ràdh *m*

prolong *v* sìn *vt* a-mach

promise *n* gealladh *m*, geall *m*

promise *v* geall *vti*, thoir gealladh *m*

promised *adj & past part* 1 geallta; 2 *in expr* **the ~ land** tìr a' gheallaidh *mf*

promising *adj* gealltanach

promontory *n* rubha *m*

promote *v* àrdaich *vt*

prompt *adj* 1 (*timeous*) an deagh àm *m*, mithich *adj*; 2 (*person*) deas, èasgaidh, ealamh

promptly *adv* gu deas e, (*timeously*) an deagh àm

prone *adj* 1 (*position*) air do (*etc*) bheul fodhad, air do bheul sìos, sìnte; 2 (*tending*) buailteach do

pronoun *n* riochdair *m*

pronounce *v* (*lang*) fuaimnich *vt*

pronunciation *n* (*lang*) fuaimneachadh *m*

proof *n* dearbhadh *m*

prop *n* taic(e) *f*

propagate *v* tàrmaich *vt*

propel *v* iomain *vt*

propellant *n* stuth-iomain *m*

proper *adj* 1 (*suitable*) dòigheil, iomchaidh, cothromach, cubhaidh; 2 (*decent*) beusach; 3 (*real*) fìor

properly *adv* gu dòigheil

property *n* 1 (*possessions*) sealbh *m*, seilbh *f*; 2 (*characteristic*) buadh *f*, feart *m*

prophecy *n* fàidheadaireachd *f*, fàisneachd *f*

prophesy *v* fàisnich *vti*

prophet *n* fàidh *m*, fiosaiche *m*

propitious *adj* fàbharach

proportionately *adv* a rèir

proposal *n* moladh *m*

propose *v* 1 (*intend*) cuir *vi* romhad, rùnaich *vi*; 2 (*offer*) tairg *vi*; 3 (*recommend*) mol *vti*

propped *adj & past part* an taic, an tacsa

proprietor *n* seilbheadair/sealbhadair *m*

prose *n* rosg *m*

prospective *adj* san t-sealladh, san amharc

prosper *v* soirbhich *vi*

prosperity *n* soirbheachas *m*, soirbheachadh *m*

protection *n* 1 tèarmann *m*, dìon *m*; 2 (*con*) fasgadh *m*

protest *n* 1 (*general*) gearan *m*; 2 (*demonstration etc*) fianais-dhùbhlain *f*

protest *v* 1 (*general*) gearain *vi*; 2 (*demonstrate etc*) tog fianais

protester *n* (*pol etc*) neach-togail-fianais *m*

Protestant *n & adj* Pròstanach *m*

proud *adj* 1 (*legitimately*) pròiseil, moiteil; 2 (*excessively*) uaibhreach, àrdanach, mòrchuiseach

prove *v* dearbh *vt*

proved, **proven** *adj & past part* dearbhte

proverb *n* seanfhacal *m*, ràdh *m*

provide *v* 1 (*general*) thoir *vt* seachad; 2 (*supply*) solair *vt*; 3 (*fin etc*) ullaich *vt*

provided *conj* air chumha is, cho fad' is

providence *n* sealbh *m*, freastal *m*

provision *n* ullachadh *m*

provisional *adj* sealach

provisions *n* lòn *m*

provost *n* pròbhaist *m*

prow *n* toiseach *m*

proximity *n* faisge *f*

prudence *n* faiceall *f*, earalas *m*

prudent *adj* faiceallach

psychiatrist *n* lighiche-inntinn *m*

psychiatry *n* leigheas-inntinn *m*

psychologist *n* inntinn-eòlaiche *m*

psychology *n* eòlas-inntinn *m*

puberty *n* inbhidheachd *f*

pubes *n*, **pubic hair** *n* ròm *mf*, gaoisid/gaosaid *f*

public *adj* 1 (*communal*) coitcheann, poblach; 2 (*opposite of* private) follaiseach, poblach

publication *n* 1 (*abstr*) foillseachadh *m*; 2 (*abstr & con*) clò-bhualadh *m*; 3 (*periodical*) iris *f*, ràitheachan *m*

publicise *v* cuir *vt* am follais, thoir *vt* am follais, foillsich *vt*

publicity *n* 1 (*abstr*) follaiseachd *f*, sanasachd *f*; 2 (*con*) sanas(an) *m*(*pl*)

publish *v* foillsich *vt*, cuir *vt* an clò

publisher *n* foillsichear *m*

publishing *n* foillseachadh *m*

pudding *n* 1 mìlsean *m*; 2 (*savoury*) marag *f*

puddle *n* glumag *f*, lòn *m*

pull *n* tarraing *f*, slaodadh *m*

pull *v* 1 tarraing *vti*, slaod *vti*

pullet *n* eireag *f*

pulley *n* ulag *f*

pullover *n* geansaidh *m*

pulp *n* glaodhan *m*, pronnadh *m*

pulpit *n* cùbaid *f*, crannag *f*

pulverise *v* pronn *vt*

pulverised *adj & past part* pronn, air a (*etc*) p(h)ronnadh

pump *n* pumpa *m*

punctilious *adj* mionchuiseach, pongail, mionaideach

punctual *adj* pongail

puncture *n* toll *m*

puncture *v* toll *vt*

punish *v* peanasaich *vt*, smachdaich *vt*
punishment *n* peanas *m*
punitive *adj* peanasach
pup *n* cuilean *m*
pupil *n* **1** (*ed*) sgoilear *m*; **2** (*eye*) dubh (na sùla) *m*
puppet *n* fear-brèige *m*, pupaid *f*
puppy *n* cuilean *m*
purchaser *n* neach-ceannach *m*
purchasing *n* ceannach *m*
purgatory *n* purgadair *m*
purling *n* (*of stream*) crònan *m*, torman *m*
purple *adj* corcair, purpaidh
purple *n* purpar *m*, purpaidh *f*
purpose *n* rùn *m*; **2** *in expr* **on** ~ a dh'aon rùn, a dh'aon ghnothach

purring *n* crònan *m*
pursue *v* rua(i)g *vt*, lean *vt* (gu dian)
pursuit *n* **1** tòir *f*, ruaig *f*; **2** (*military*) ruith *f*; **3** (*hobby etc*) cur-seachad *m*
pus *n* brachadh *m*, iongar *m*
push *v* put *vt*, brùth *vt*, sàth *vt*
pustule *n* guirean *m*
put *v* cuir *vt*
putrefaction *n* grodadh *m*, lobhadh *m*, brèine *f*
putrefy *v* grod *vi*, lobh *vi*
putrid *adj* grod, lobhte
puzzle *n* tòimhseachan *m*
puzzle *v* cuir *vt* an imcheist
puzzled *adj* & *past part* an/fo imcheist
puzzling *adj* imcheisteach

Q

quadrangle *n* ceithir-cheàrnag *f*
quadrilateral *adj* ceithir-cheàrnach
quadruped *adj & n* ceithir-chasach *m*
quagmire *n* sùil-chritheach *f*, bog *m*,
  boglach *f*, fèith(e) *f*
quaich *n* cuach *f*
quaint *adj* neònach, annasach, seann-
  fhasanta
quake *n* crith *f*
quake *v* bi *vi irreg* air chrith *f*, crith *vi*
qualification *n* **1** (*study etc*)
  uidheamachadh *m*; **2** (*written*) teisteanas
  m, barantas *m*; **3** (*modification*)
  lùghdachadh *m*, maothachadh *m*
qualified *adj & past part* **1** (*formally*)
  uidheamaichte, barantaichte; **2** (*with
  reservations*) le cumha, le teagamh, le
  cùl-earbsa
qualify *v* **1** (*be up to*) bi *vi* aig ìre;
  2 (*formally*) bi *vi* uidheamaichte;
  3 (*modify*) lùghdaich *vt*, maothaich *vt*
quality *n* **1** (*attribute etc*) buadh *f*, feart *m*,
  beus *f*; **2** (*degree*) mathas *m*
quandary *n* ioma(dh)-chomhairle *f*,
  imcheist *f*
quantity *n* uimhir *f*, uiread *m*, meud *m*
quarrel *n* **1** (*verbal*) trod *m*, argamaid *f*
  eatarra (*etc*); **2** (*verbal/phys*) tuasaid *f*;
  3 (*phys*) sabaid *f*
quarrel *v* **1** (*verbally*) troid *vi*, connsaich
  vi; **2** (*phys*) sabaid *vi*; **3** (*fall out*) rach *vi*
  thar a chèile
quarrelling *n* trod *m*
quarrelsome *adj* connspaideach,
  connsachail, aimhreiteach
quarry[1] *n* (*stone etc*) cuaraidh *m*
quarry[2] *n* (*hunters etc*) creach *f*
quart *n* cairteal *m*
quarter *n* **1** ceathramh *m*; **2** (*time*) cairteal
  m, ceathramh *m*; **3** (*of year*) ràith *f*
quarterly *n* (*periodical*) ràitheachan *m*
quarters *n* **1** (*military*) taigh-feachd *m*,
  gearastan *m*, cairtealan *mpl*; **2** (*non-
  military*) àite-fuirich *m*, lòistinn *m*,
quaver *v* crith *vi*
quay *n* cidhe *m*, laimrig *f*

queen *n* banrigh *f*, banrighinn *f*
queer *adj* neònach
quell *v* ceannsaich *vt*, mùch *vt*
quelling *n* ceannsachadh *m*
quench *v* **1** (*thirst*) bàth *vt*; **2** (*fire etc*)
  mùch *vt*
querulous *adj* gearanach
query *n* ceist *f*
question *n* **1** ceist *f*; **2** (*point*) ceist *f*, cùis *f*
question *v* **1** (*put questions*) ceasnaich
  vt, cuir ceist(ean) *f*; **2** (*doubt*) cuir *vt* an
  teagamh *m*, cuir teagamh ann an
questionable *adj* amharasach
questioner *n* ceistear *m*
questioning *n* ceasnachadh *m*
questionnaire *n* ceisteachan *m*
queue *n* ciudha *mf*
quick *adj* **1** (*moving*) luath, astarach;
  2 (*performing*) clis, deas, tapaidh,
  ealamh; **3** (*mentally*) luath san inntinn,
  geurchuiseach, geur san inntinn;
  4 (*hurried*) aithghearr
quicken *v* luathaich *vti*
quickly *adv* gu luath
quickness *n* **1** (*performing*) luas *m*,
  cliseachd *f*; **2** (*mental/phys*) graide *f*
quick-tempered *adj* aithghearr, cas
quiet *adj* **1** ciùin, sàmhach, sèimh;
  2 (*persons*) tostach; **3** *in expr* **be** ~! tost!,
  ist(ibh)!/eist(ibh)!
quiet(ness) *n* **1** (*silence*) tost *m*; **2** (*calm*)
  ciùineas *m*, sàmhchair *f*
quieten *v* **1** (*make silent*) tostaich *vt*;
  2 (*make calm*) ciùinich *vti*, sìthich *vti*,
  socraich *vti*, tàlaidh *vt*
quietly *adv* os ìosal/os ìseal
quilt *n* cuibhrig *mf*
quit *adj* saor *adj* is, cuidhteas *m* de
quit *v* fàg *vt*, trèig *vt*
quite *adv* **1** (*completely*) (gu) buileach, gu
  tur, gu h-iomlan, gu leòr; **2** (*somewhat*) gu
  math; **3** (*agreement*) dìreach (sin)!
quiver *v* bi *vi irreg* air chrith *f*, crith *vi*
quiz *n* ceasnachadh *m*
quota *n* cuid *f*, cuibhreann *mf*, cuota *m*

R

rabbit _n_ rabaid _f_, coineanach _m_
rabble _n_ prabar _m_, gràisg _f_
race[1] _n_ **1** (_ethnicity_) cineal _m_; **2** (_tribe etc_)
  sìol _m_, cinneadh _m_, gineal _mf_; **3** _in expr_
  the human ~ an cinne-daonna _m_
race[2] _n_ (_sports etc_) rèis _f_
racial _adj_ cinneadail, cinealtais
racialism, **racism** _n_ cinealtas _m_, gràin-
  cinnidh _f_
racialist, **racist** _adj_ cinealtach
racist _n_ neach cinealtach
racket[1] _n_ (_noise_) gleadhraich _f_, ùpraid _f_,
  othail _f_
racket[2] (_sport_) racaid _f_
racket[3] (_practice_) feall-ghnìomh _m_, foill _f_,
  malairt fhoilleil _f_
radiance _n_ deàlradh _m_, lainnir _f_
radiant _adj_ deàlrach, lainnireach,
  boillsgeach
radiate _v_ **1** (_shine_) deàlraich _vi_; **2** (_emit_)
  sgaoil _vt_
radio _n_ rèidio _m_
radioactive _adj_ rèidio-bheò
raffle _n_ crannchur-gill _m_
rafter _n_ cabar _m_
rag _n_ luideag _f_, clùd & clobhd _m_
rage _n_ cuthach _m_, bàinidh _f_, boile _f_
ragged _adj_ cearbach, luideach
raging _adj_ **1** (_person_) air chuthach, air
  bhàinidh, air bhoile; **2** (_sea_) doineannach
raid _n_ creach _f_
rail _n_ rèile _f_
railings _n_ rèilichean _fpl_
rain _n_ uisge _m_
rain _v_ **1** bi _vi irreg_ an t-uisge ann, sil _vi_;
  2 (_idiom_) ~**ing cats and dogs** dìle
  bhàthte
rainbow _n_ bogha-frois(e) _m_
raincoat _n_ còta-frois(e) _m_
rainfall _n_ sileadh _m_
rainforest _n_ coille-uisge _f_
rainproof _adj_ uisge-dhìonach
raise _v_ tog _vt_
rake _n_ (_tool_) ràcan _m_, ràc _m_
rally _n_ tional _m_, cruinneachadh _m_
rally _v_ (_encourage_) misnich _vt_, ath-
  mhisnich _vt_

ram _n_ (_tup_) rùda _m_, reithe _m_
rampart _n_ mùr _m_
random _adj_ **1** tuaireamach; **2** _in expr_ **at** ~
  air thuaiream _f_
randy _adj_ drùiseach, drùiseil
range _n_ **1** (_series_) raon _m_, sreath
  _mf_; **2** (_artillery_) raon-bualaidh _m_;
  3 (_mountains_) sreath _mf_
ranger _n_ maor _m_
rank _n_ (_degree_) inbhe _f_
ransack _v_ rannsaich _vt_
ransom _n_ èirig _f_
ransom _v_ fuasgail _vt_ le èirig _f_, saor/
  saoraich _vt_ le èirig
rape _n_ èigneachadh _m_
rape _v_ èignich _vt_
rapid _adj_ **1** (_general_) luath;
  2 (_watercourse_) bras, cas; **3** (_person_)
  grad, aithghearr
rapier _n_ claidheamh-caol _m_
rapist _n_ èigneachair _m_
rare _adj_ **1** (_scarce_) gann, tearc, ainneamh;
  2 (_unusual_) annasach
rarely _adv_ gu tearc, is _v irreg def_ gann
rarity _n_ **1** (_abstr_) gainne _f_, gainnead _m_,
  teirce _f_; **2** (_con_) annas _m_, suaicheantas _m_
rat _n_ radan/rodan _m_
rate _n_ **1** (_speed_) astar _m_, luas _m_;
  2 (_progress etc_) ruith _f_; **3** (_fin_) luach _m_, ìre
  _f_; **4** (_taxes_) ~**s** reataichean _mpl_
rate _v_ (_evaluate_) meas _vt_, cuir luach air,
  luachaich _vt_
rather _adv_ **1** (_somewhat_) car, caran,
  beagan, rudeigin, rud beag; **2** (_expr
  preference_) b' fheàrr leam (_etc_); **3** _in expr_
  ~ **than** seach _prep_
ratify _v_ daingnich _vt_
ration _n_ cuibhreann _mf_
rational _adj_ reusanta
rationale _n_ feallsanachd _f_
rattle[1] _n_ (_toy etc_) clach-bhalg _f_
rattle[2] _n_ (_noise_), **rattling** _n_ clagarsaich _f_,
  glagadaich _f_, gleadhraich _f_
rattle _v_ dèan glagadaich, dèan gleadhraich
raven _n_ fitheach _m_
ravish _v_ (_rape_) èignich _vt_
ravisher _n_ èigneachair _m_

raw *adj* (*unprocessed*) amh

ray *n* gath *m*, leus *m*

raze *v*, *in expr* ~ **to the ground**, leag *vt* gu làr

razor *n* ealtainn *f*, ràsair *m*

re(-) *prefix* ath-

reach *v* 1 (*arrive*) ruig *vti*; 2 (*abstr*) thig *vi* gu; 3 (*attain*) ruig *vi* air; 4 (*pass*) sìn *vt*

read *v* leugh *vti*

reader *n* leughadair *m*

reading *n* leughadh *m*

ready *adj* 1 (*prepared etc*) deiseil, ullamh, deas; 2 (*keen*) èasgaidh, deònach; 3 (*convenient*) ullamh

real *adj* 1 (*actual*) nitheil, fìor, rudail; 2 (*genuine*) fìor ; 3 (*out & out*) fìor, dearg, gu c(h)ùl

realise *v* 1 (*comprehend*) tuig *vti*, fidir *vti*; 2 (*become aware*) tuig *vti*, thig *vi* a-steach ort

realism *n* fìorachas *m*

reality *n* fìorachd *f*

really *adv* fìor, uabhasach fhèin, gu dearbh

re-animate *v* ath-bheothaich *vt*

re-appraisal *n* ath-bheachdachadh *m*

re-appraise *v* ath-bheachdaich *vi*

rear *n* 1 (*group etc*) deireadh *m*; 2 (*building etc*), cùl *m*, cùlaibh *m*, tòn *f*; 3 (*backside*) tòn *f*, màs *m*

rear *v* 1 (*children etc*) tog *vt*; 2 *in expr* ~ **up** èirich *vi* (suas)

reason[1] *n* 1 (*faculty*) reusan *m*; 2 (*sanity*) ciall *f*, rian *m*, reusan *m*

reason[2] *n* (*cause*) adhbhar *m*, cùis *f*, fàth *m*

reason *v* reusanaich *vi*

reasoning *n* reusanachadh *m*

reasonable *adj* 1 (*logical*) reusanta, ciallach; 2 (*appropriate*) cothromach, reusanta; 3 (*sensible*) toinisgeil, ciallach

re-assess *v* ath-mheas *vt*

re-assessment *n* ath-mheasadh *m*

rebel *n* reubalach *m*

rebel *v* dèan ar-a-mach *m*, èirich *vi* (suas)

rebellion *n* ar-a-mach *m*

rebuke *n* achmhasan *m*

rebuke *v* cronaich *vt*, thoir achmhasan do

recall *v* 1 (*remember*) cuimhnich *vi* air, meòraich *vti*; 2 (*call back*) gairm *vt* air ais

receipt *n* (*money etc*) cuidhteas *m*

recent *adj* ùr

recently *adv* (bh)o chionn ghoirid

reception *n* 1 (*welcome*) fàilte *f*; 2 (*desk*) ionad-fàilte *m*; 3 (*function*) cuirm *f*

receptionist *n* (*hotel etc*) fàiltiche *m*

recession *n* seacadh *m*, crìonadh *m*

recitation *n* aithris *f*

recite *v* aithris *vti*

reckon *v* 1 (*arithmetic etc*) cunnt *vti*; 2 (*consider*) saoil *vi*, meas *vi*; 3 (*in expr*) **what do you ~?** dè do bheachd (air)?

reckoning *n* 1 (*arithmetic etc*) cunntas *m*, cunntadh *m*; 2 (*sum*) cunntas *m*

recline *v* 1 (*movement*) laigh *vi* (sìos); 2 (*position*) bi *v irreg* nad (*etc*) laighe

recognised *adj & past part* aithnichte

recollect *v* cuimhnich *vi* air

recollection *n* cuimhne *f*

recommend *v* mol *vt*

recommendation *n* moladh *m*

reconcile *v* rèitich *vt*

reconciliation *n* rèite *f*

record *n* 1 (*events etc*) cunntas *m*, clàr *m*; 2 (*sound*) clàr *m*

record *v* 1 (*events etc*) clàraich *vt*, sgrìobh cunntas air/de; 2 (*sound*) clàraich *vt*

recording *n* 1 (*abstr*) clàrachadh *m*; 2 (*con*) clàr *m*

recount *v* 1 (*relate*) thoir cunntas de/air, innis *vt*

re-count *n* ath-chunntadh *m*

re-count *v* ath-chunnt *vti*, cunnt *vt* a-rithist

recover *v* 1 (*improve*) rach *vi* am feabhas, thig *vi* bhuaithe, fàs nas fheàrr; 2 (*retrieve*) faigh *vt* air ais

re-create *v* ath-chruthaich *vt*

recreation *n* (*pastime etc*) cur-seachad *m*

recruit *v* 1 fastaich *vt*

rectangle *n* ceart-cheàrnach *m*, ceart-cheàrnag *f*

rectangular *adj* ceart-cheàrnach

rectify *v* ceartaich *vt*, cuir *vt* ceart, leasaich *vt*

rectum *n* tòn *f*

recycle *v* ath-chuartaich *vt*

red *adj* ruadh, dearg

red *n* dearg *m*

redcoat *n* saighdear-dearg

redcurrant *n* dearc-dhearg

redden *v* 1 (*as vt*) deargaich *vt*; 2 (*as vi*) fàs *vi* dearg

reddish- *adj prefix* dearg-

reduce *v* lùghdaich *vti*, ìslich *vt*

reduction *n* lùghdachadh *m*

reed *n* 1 cuilc *f*; 2 (*instrument*) ribheid *f*

reel n **1** (*thread etc*) iteachan m, piorna mf;
2 (*dance*) ruidhle m, ridhil m
redundant adj (*surplus*) anbharra
re-election n ath-thaghadh m
refectory n biadh-lann f
refer v **1** (*admin etc*) cuir vt gu;
2 (*mention*) thoir iomradh, thoir tarraing,
thoir guth air
referee n (*sport*) rèitear m
reference n **1** (*character*) teisteanas m;
2 (*mention*) iomradh m, tarraing f, guth m
reflect v **1** (*think*) cnuas vi, cnuasaich vi,
meòraich vi; **2** (*mirror etc*) tilg vt air ais,
ath-thilg vt
reflection n **1** (*contemplation etc*)
cnuasachadh m, meòrachadh m; **2** (*image*)
faileas m, ath-ìomhaigh f
reformation n ath-leasachadh m
reform v **1** (*reshape*) ath-chruthaich vt;
2 (*improve*) leasaich vt, ath-leasaich vt
refrain n (*music etc*) sèist mf
refrain v cùm vi bho/o, seachain vt
refresh v ùraich vt
refreshment n **1** (*abstr*) ùrachadh m;
2 (*con*) biadh m (is deoch f), lòn m,
beathachadh m
refrigerate v fionnraich vt
refrigeration n fionnrachadh m
refrigerator n frids m, fuaradair m
refuge n tèarmann m, comraich f, dìon m,
fasgadh m
refugee n fògrach/fògarrach m
refusal n diùltadh m
refuse n sgudal m, fuidhleach m
refuse v diùlt vti
refute v breugnaich vt
regal adj rìoghail
regard n **1** (*respect*) meas m, urram m;
2 (*affection*) spèis f; **3** (*concern*) for m,
sùim f; **4** (*corres etc*) **kind ~s** leis gach
deagh dhùrachd; **5** in expr **with ~ to**
thaobh/a thaobh
regarding prep thaobh/a thaobh
regiment n rèiseamaid f
region n **1** ceàrn m, sgìre f, tìr mf;
2 (*admin*) roinn f
register v clàraich vti
register n clàr m
registration n clàrachadh m
regret n aithreachas m
regret v bi vi irreg duilich, bi vi irreg an
t-aithreachas ort (*etc*)

regular adj **1** (*orderly*) riaghailteach,
òrdail; **2** (*consistent*) cunbhalach
regularise v riaghailtich vt
regularity n riaghailteachd f
regulate v riaghlaich vt, riaghailtich vt,
riaghail vt
regulation n **1** (*abstr*) riaghladh m; **2** (*con*)
riaghailt f
rehearsal n aithris f
rehearse v aithris vti
reign n rìoghachadh m
reign v rìoghaich vi
reject v diùlt vt
rejection n diùltadh m
rejoice v dèan gàirdeachas
rejoicing n gàirdeachas m
relate v **1** (*recount*) innis vt, aithris v; **2** (*be
connected*) bi vi irreg co-cheangailte ri
related adj **1** (*kinship*) càirdeach;
2 (*linked*) co-cheangailte
relation[1] n (*kin*) caraid m, pl càirdean,
neach-dàimh m
relation[2] **1** (*relevance*) buinteanas m; **2** in
expr **in ~ to** an coimeas ri
relationship n **1** (*kinship*) càirdeas
m; **2** (*general*) càirdeas m, dàimh mf;
3 ceangal m, co-cheangal m
relative adj **1** (*dependent on
circumstances*) a rèir; **2** (*gram*)
dàimheach
relax v **1** (*rest*) gabh fois f, bi vi irreg
nad thàmh m; **2** gabh vi air do shocair f;
3 (*calm*) socraich vti, as excl **~!** socair!, air
do shocair!; **4** (*free*) fuasgail vt
relaxation n fois f, socair f
relaxed adj socair, socrach
release v **1** (*free*) fuasgail vt, cuir/leig vt
mu sgaoil, saor vt; **2** (*fire*) leig vt; **3** (*let
out*) leig vt à; **4** (*bring out*) cuir vt a-mach
relevance n buinteanas m
relevant adj **1** a bhuineas ri/do
reliable adj **1** (*morally*) earbsach,
urrasach; **2** (*practically*) seasmhach,
cunbhalach
reliance n earbsa f, creideas m
relic n **1** (*residue*) fuidheall m, iarmad m;
2 (*keepsake*) cuimhneachan m
relief n furtachd f, faothachadh/faochadh
m
relieve v faothaich vti, furtaich vi
religion n creideamh m
religious n diadhaidh, cràbhach

relinquish *v* leig *vt* de, leig *vt* seachad, trèig *vt*

relinquishment *n* leigeil seachad *f*, trèigsinn *m*

reluctance *n* leisg(e) *f*

reluctant *adj* leisg, aindeonach, *in expr* **be** ~ is *v irreg* & *def* leisg le, bi *vi irreg* leisg(e) ort

rely *v* cuir earbsa ann an, earb thu fhèin ri

remain *v* fuirich *vi*, fan *v*

remainder *n* **1** (*residue*) fuidheall *m*, iarmad *m*

remark *n* facal *m*

remark *v* thoir *vt* iomradh air

remarkable *adj* air leth, sònraichte

remedial *adj* leasachaidh

remedy *n* **1** (*cure*) leigheas *m*, ìocshlaint *f*; **2** (*solution*) leasachadh *m*, fuasgladh *m*

remedy *v* (*situation*) leasaich *vt*, cuir *vt* am feabhas, cuir *vt* ceart

remember *v* cuimhnich *vti*, meòraich *vi* air

remembrance *n* cuimhne *f*

remind *v* **1** (*recall*) cuir *vt* ann an cuimhne; **2** (*jog memory*) cuimhnich *vi* do, cuir *vt* na do (*etc*) chuimhne

reminisce *v* cuimhnich *vi*, meòraich *vi*

remnant, remnants *n* fuidheall *m*, iarmad *m*

remote *adj* **1** (*peripheral*) iomallach, cèin; **2** (*time/space*) cian; **3** (*isolated*) uaigneach; **4** (*withdrawn*) fad' às, dùinte

remoteness *n* (*time/space*) cian *m*

removal *n* **1** toirt air falbh, toirt às; **2** (*flitting*) imrich *f*

remove *v* thoir *vt* air falbh, thoir *vt* às

remuneration *n* pàigh *m*, pàigheadh *m*, tuarastal *m*, cosnadh *m*

rend *v* reub *vt*, srac *vt*

renew *v* **1** (*renovate*) ùraich *vt*, ath-nuadhaich *vt*; **2** (*replace*) ath-nuadhaich *vt*; **3** (*reaffirm*) ath-nuadhaich *vt*

renewal *n* ùrachadh *m*, ath-nuadhachadh *m*

renovate *v* ùraich *vt*, nuadhaich *vt*, ath-nuadhaich *vt*, cuir *vt* air dòigh *f*

renovation *n* ùrachadh *m*, nuadhachadh *m*, ath-nuadhachadh *m*, cur air dòigh *m*

renown *n* cliù *m*, glòir *f*

renowned *adj* ainmeil, iomraiteach, cliùiteach

rent¹ *n* (*property etc*) màl *m*

rent² *n* (*rip*) reubadh *m*, sracadh *m*

rent *v* **1** (*as vt*) gabh *vt* air mhàl; **2** (*as vi*) thoir *vt* seachad air mhàl

rented *adj* & *past part* air mhàl

repair *n* càradh *m*

repair *v* càirich *vt*

repairer *n* neach-càraidh *m*

repay *v* dìoghail/dìol *vt*

repayment *n* dìo(gh)ladh *m*

repeat *v* **1** (*verbally*) can *vt def* a-rithist, can *vt* turas eile; **2** (*actions etc*) dèan *vt* a-rithist/turas eile

replace *v* **1** (*return*) cuir *vt* air ais na àite; **2** (*substitute*) cuir *vt* an àite

replacement *n* (*stand-in*) neach-ionaid *m*

replica *n* mac-samhail *m*, lethbhreac *m*

reply *n* freagairt *f*

reply *v* freagair *vi*, thoir freagairt

report¹ *n* **1** (*newspaper etc*) iomradh *m*, aithisg *f*, cunntas *m*; **2** (*formal*) aithisg *f*

report² *n* (*gunfire*) urchair *f*

repository *n* ionad-tasgaidh *m*

represent *v* (*lawyer etc*) riochdaich *vt*

representation *n* riochdachadh *m*

representative *n* riochdaire *m*

repress *v* ceannsaich *vt*, mùch *vt*

repression *n* ceannsachadh *m*, mùchadh *m*

repressive *adj* ceannsachail

reproach *n* tarcais *f*, tailceas *m*

reproach *v* cronaich *vt*, càin *vt*; **2** (*accuse*) tilg *vt* air

reproachful *adj* tarcaiseach, tailceasach

reproduce *v* **1** (*breed*) gin *vti*, tàrmaich *vti*; **2** (*copy etc*) dèan lethbhreac/mac-samhail

reproduction *n* **1** (*breeding*) gineadh *m*, gineamhainn *m*; **2** (*copying*) mac-samhlachadh *m*, (*con*) lethbhreac *m*, mac-samhail *m*

reproductive *adj* gineamhainn *m*

reptile *n* pèist *f*

republic *n* poblachd *f*

republican *adj* & *n* poblachdach *m*

republicanism *n* poblachdas *m*

reputation *n* ainm *m*, cliù *m*

request *n* iarrtas *m*, iarraidh *m*

request *v* iarr *vt*

rescue *n* sàbhaladh *m*

rescue *v* teasairg/teasraig *vt*, sàbhail *vt*

research *v* rannsaich, dèan rannsachadh

research *n* rannsachadh *m*, sgrùdadh *m*

resemblance *n* samhladh *m*, coltas *m*, coimeas *m*

resemble *v* bi *vi irreg* coltach ri, bi *vi irreg* coltas ort

resembling *adj* coltach ri

reservation *n* **1** (*booking*) gleidheadh *m*; **2** (*place*) tèarmann *m*; **3** (*doubt*) teagamh *m*, amharas *m*

reserve *n* **1** (*money etc*) stòr *m*, stòras *m*; **2** (*place*) tèarmann *m*; **3** (*reticence*) diùide *f*, dùinteachd *f*

reserve *v* (*book*) glèidh *vt*

reserved *adj & past part* **1** glèidhte; **2** (*reticent*) diùid, sàmhach, fad' às, dùinte

reservoir *n* loch-tasgaidh *m*

reside *v* còmhnaich *vi*, fuirich *vi*

residence *n* **1** (*abstr*) còmhnaidh *f*; **2** (*con*) àite-còmhnaidh *m*, àite-fuirich *m*, dachaigh *f*

resident *n* neach-còmhnaidh *m*

residue *n* fuidheall *m*, iarmad *m*

resolute *adj* **1** (*determined*) gramail/ greimeil, misneachail, suidhichte; **2** (*bold*) dàna

resolution *n* **1** (*character*) misneach(d) *f*; **2** (*solution*) fuasgladh *m*; **3** (*aim*) rùn *m*

resolve *n* rùn suidhichte *m*

resolve *v* **1** (*as vt*) cuir *vt* romhad, rùnaich *vi*; **2** (*solve*) fuasgail *vt*, rèitich *vt*

resource *n* **1** (*materials*) goireas *m*, stòras *m*; **2** (*admin*) ionmhas *m*

resourceful *adj* innleachdach, tionnsgalach

resourcefulness *n* innleachd *f*, tionnsgal *m*, tionnsgalachd *f*

respect *n* meas *m*, urram *m*

respect *v* thoir urram, thoir meas (do)

respectable, **respected** *adj* measail

respectful *adj* modhail, cùirteil, sìobhalta

respiration *m* analachadh *m*

respite *n* faothachadh/faochadh *m*

respond *v* freagair *vt*

response *n* freagairt *f*

responsibility *n* uallach *m*, cùram *m*, dleastanas *m*

responsible *adj* **1** (*in charge*) an urra ri; **2** (*cause*) coireach ri

rest[1] *n* fois *f*, tàmh *m*; **2** *in expr* **come to ~** laigh *vi*; **3** (*music*) tost *m*

rest[2] *n* **1** (*other people*) càch *pron*, an fheadhainn *f* eile; **2** (*other things*) an còrr *m*; **3** (*remainder*) fuidheall *m*

rest *v* gabh fois *f*, leig d' anail

restaurant *n* taigh-bìdh *m*

restless *adj* luaisgeach

restrain *v* caisg *vt*, bac *vt*, cuir casg air, ceannsaich *vt*

restraint *n* bacadh *m*, casg *m*, casgadh *m*

restrict *v* (*limit*) cuingealaich *vt*, cuibhrich *vt*

result *n* (*consequence*) toradh *m*, buil *f*, èifeachd *f*

retailing *n* meanbh-reic *m*

retain *v* glèidh *vt*, cùm *vt* (air ais)

retard *v* cuir maille air/ann, maillich *vt*

retch *v* rùchd *vi*

retching *n* rùchd *m*, rùchdail *f*

retire *v* **1** (*for night*) rach *vi* a laighe, rach *vi* don leabaidh *f*; **2** (*from work*) leig dhìot obair *f*/dreuchd *f*

retirement *n* cluaineas *m*

retract *v* thoir *vt* air ais, tarraing *vti* air ais

retrospect *n* ath-bheachd *m*

return *n* tilleadh *m*

return *v* **1** (*as vi*) till *vi*; **2** (*as vt*) cuir *vt* air ais, thoir *vt* air ais

reveal *v* **1** (*objects*) leig *vt* ris, nochd *vt*, seall *vt*; **2** (*facts*) foillsich *vt*

revelation *n* (*facts*) foillseachadh *m*

revenge *n* dìoghaltas *m*

revenue *n* teachd-a-steach *m*

reverence *n* urram *m*

reverend *adj* urramach

review *n* **1** (*critique*) lèirmheas *m*; **2** (*study*) sgrùdadh *m*, rannsachadh *m*; **3** (*reappraisal*) ath-sgrùdadh *m*, ath-bheachdachadh *m*

review *v* **1** (*book etc*) dèan lèirmheas air; **2** (*study*) sgrùd *vt*, rannsaich *vt*; **3** (*reappraise etc*) ath-bheachdaich *vi* air, ath-sgrùd *vt*

revile *v* màb *vt*, càin *vt*

revise *n* **1** (*exam etc*) ath-sgrùd *vt*; **2** (*go back on*) atharraich *vt*

revival *n* **1** (*general*) ath-bheothachadh *m*; **2** (*relig ~*) dùsgadh *m*

revive *v* ath-bheothaich *vt*

revolt *n* ar-a-mach *m*

revolt *v* èirich *vi* (suas), dèan ar-a-mach

revolver *n* daga/dag *m*

reward *n* duais *f*

rheumatism *n* an lòinidh *mf*

rhyme *n* co-fhuaim *m*

rhyme *v* dèan co-fhuaim

ribbon *n* rioban *m*

rice *n* rus *m*

rich *adj* **1** (*wealthy*) beartach, saidhbhir;
2 (*soil*) torrach

riches *n* beartas *m*, saidhbhreas *m*,
ionmhas *m*, stòras *m*, maoin *f*

rick *n* cruach *f*, coc/goc *m*, ruc(a) *m*

rid *adj & adv* **1** saor, cuidhteas, clìoras

rid *v, in expr* ~ **oneself** (*etc*) faigh
cuidhteas (de), faigh clìor is

riddle *n* (*puzzle etc*) tòimhseachan *m*

riddle *v* (*grain etc*) criathraich *vt*

ride *n* (*vehicle*) cuairt *f*

ride *v* **1** (*horse*) marcaich *vi*; **2** (*vehicle*)
siubhail *vi*

rider *n* marcaiche *m*

ridge *n* **1** (*topog*) druim *m*; **2** (*agric*)
iomair(e) *f*, imire *m*

ridge-pole *n* maide-droma *m*, maide-
mullaich *m*

ridicule *n* fanaid *f*, bùrt *m*

ridicule *v* dèan fanaid air

ridiculous *adj* amaideach, gun chiall *f*

riding *n* (*horse*) marcachadh *m*, marcachd *f*

rifle *n* raidhfil *f*

rifle *v* rannsaich *vt*

rig¹ *n* (*agric*) iomair(e) *f*, imire *m*

rig² *n* **1** (*equipment etc*) uidheam *f*, acainn *f*

rigging *n* uidheam *f*, acainn *f*

right *adj* **1** (*dexter*) deas, ceart; **2** (*correct*)
ceart

right *n* **1** (*hand*) an làmh dheas;
2 (*justice etc*) còir *f*, ceartas *m*, ceart *m*;
3 (*entitlement*) còir *f*, dlighe *f*, dleas *m*

righteous *adj* ionraic, dìreach

righteousness *n* ionracas *m*

rightful *adj* dligheach

rightly *adv* **1** (*morally etc*) mar bu chòir;
2 *in expr* **if I remember** ~ mas math mo
chuimhne *f*

rigid *adj* **1** rag, cruaidh; **2** (*person*) rag-
bharaileach, rag-mhuinealach

rigidity *n* raige *f*

rig out *v* (*equip*) uidheamaich *vt*, beartaich
vt

rig up *v* tog *vt*

rim *n* oir *f*, bile *f*, iomall *m*

ring *n* **1** cearcall *m*; **2** (*finger*) fàinne *mf*

ringlet *n* dual *m*, bachlag *f*, camag *f*

ring-road *n* cuairt-rathad *m*

rinse *v* sgol *vt*

rip *n* reubadh *m*

rip *v* reub *vt*, srac *vt*

ripe *adj* abaich

ripen *v* abaich *vti*

ripeness *n* abaichead *m*

rise *n* **1** (*slope*) leathad *m*, bruthach *mf*;
2 (*increment*) àrdachadh *m*; **3** *in expr*
take a ~ **out of** farranaich *vt*, tarraing
vi à

rise *v* **1** (*phys*) èirich *vi*; **2** (*become higher*)
rach *vi* an-àird *f*; **3** (*rebel*) ~ **(up)** èirich
suas, dèan ar-a-mach

risk *n* cunnart *m*

risky *adj* **1** cunnartach, gàbhaidh;
2 (*precarious*) cugallach

rival *n* farpaiseach *m*

rivalry *n* còmhstri *f*, farpais *f*

road *n* rathad *m*

roar *n* beuc *m*, ràn *m*

roar *v* beuc *vi*, ràn *vi*, (*animals*) nuallaich
vi

roaring *n* beucadh *m*, rànail *m*, rànaich *f*

roast *adj & past part* ròsta

roast *v* ròist *vt*

roast, roasted *adj & past part* ròsta

rob *v* creach *vti*, spùill/spùinn *vti*

robber *n* mèirleach *m*, spùinneadair *m*,
gadaiche *m*

robe *n* èideadh *m*

robin *n* brù-dhearg *m*

robust *adj* (*person*) calma, tapaidh,
rùdanach

rock *n* **1** creag *f*; **2** (*pillar*) carragh *f*

rock *v* **1** (*as vi*) tulg *vi*, luaisg *vi*; **2** (*as vt*)
tulg *vt*

rocket *n* rocaid *f*

rocking *n* luasgan *m*, tulgadh *m*

rocking-chair *n* sèithear-tulgaidh *m*

rocky *adj* creagach

roe-buck *n* boc-earba *m*

roe-deer *n* earb *f*

roll *v* **1** (*seas etc*) tulg *vi*, luaisg *vi*; **2** (*ball
etc*) roilig *vi*; **3** *as vt* (*pastry etc*) roilig
vti; **4** (*material*) ~ **(up)** paisg *vt*, fill *vt*;
5 (*sleeves etc*) ~ **up** tru(i)s *vt*

Roman *adj & n* Ròmanach *m*

romance *n* **1** (*novel*) ròlaist *m*, nobhail
romansach *f*; **2** (*affair*) leannanachd *f*

Romania *n* Romàinia *f*

Romanian *n & adj* Romàinianach *m*

Rome *n* An Ròimh *f*

roof *n* mullach *m*, ceann *m*

roof-tree *n* maide-droma *m*, maide-
mullaich *m*

rook *n* ròcais *f*

room *n* **1** (*space*) rùm *m*; **2** (*apartment*) seòmar *m*, rùm *m*

root *n* freumh *m*

rope *n* ròp(a) *m*

rosary *n* conaire *f*, paidirean *m*

rose *n* ròs *m*

rot *n* grodadh *m*, lobhadh *m*

rot *v* grod *vi*, lobh *vi*

rotate *v* **1** (*as vi*) rach *vi irreg* mun cuairt; **2** (*as vt*) cuir *vt* mun cuairt, cuir car ort; **3** (*crops etc*) cuartaich *vt*

rotted, rotten *adj* grod, lobhte

rottenness *n* lobhadh *m*

rough *adj* **1** garbh; **2** (*hairy*) molach, fionnach; **3** (*uncouth etc*) borb, garg

roughness *n* gairbhe *f*, gairbhead *m*

round *adj* cruinn

round *adv* timcheall, mun cuairt/mu chuairt

round *n* cuairt *f*

round *prep* **1** timcheall (air), mun cuairt air; mu

round up *v* (*livestock etc*) cruinnich *vt*, tionail *vt*, tru(i)s *vt*

roundabout *n* timcheallan *m*

roundness *n* cruinne *mf*, cruinnead *m*

rouse *v* **1** (*wake*) dùisg *vti*, mosgail *vti*; **2** (*encourage etc*) brod *vt*, brosnaich *vt*, misnich *vt*

rout *n* rua(i)g *f*, ruith *f*

route *n* rathad *m*, slighe *f*

routine *adj* gnàthach

routine *n* gnàth-chùrsa *m*

row[1] *n* **1** (*din*) gleadhraich *f*, othail *f*, faram *m*; **2** (*quarrel*) trod *m*, tuasaid *f*

row[2] *n* **1** (*line etc*) sreath *mf*; **2** *in expr* **in a ~** an sreath a chèile, an ceann a chèile, an dèidh a chèile

row[1] *v* (*boat*) iomair *vti*

row[2] *v* (*quarrel*) connsaich *vi*, troid *vi*

rowan *n* caorann *mf*

rowdy *adj* ùpraideach, gleadhrach

rowing *n* (*boat*) iomradh *m*

royal *adj* rìoghail

royalties *npl* dleas-ùghdair *m*

royalty *n* **1** rìoghalachd *f*

rubber *n* rubair *m*

rubbish *n* **1** (*refuse*) sgudal *m*, fuidhleach *m*; **2** (*objects*) sgudal *m*, truileis *f*, trealaich *f*; **3** (*possessions*) trealaich *f*

rucksack *n* màileid-droma *f*, poca-droma *m*

ruddy *adj* ruiteach

rude *adj* mì-mhodhail, mì-shìobhalta

rugged *adj* garbh

ruin *n* **1** (*building*) tobhta *f*, làrach *f*; **2** (*fin*) bris(t)eadh *m*

ruin *v* **1** creach *vt*, sgrios *vt*, mill *vt*; **2** (*child etc*) mill *vt*; **3** (*fin*) bris(t) *vt*

ruination *n* **1** creach *f*, sgrios *m*, milleadh *m*; **2** (*fin*) bris(t)eadh *m*

ruinous *adj* **1** (*causing ruin*) sgriosail, millteach; **2** (*building*) a' tuiteam sìos, a' tuiteam às a chèile

rule[1] *n* **1** (*authority*) ceannsal *m*, smachd *m*, reachd *m*; **2** (*ordinance etc*) riaghailt *f*, reachd *m*

rule[2] *n* (*measurer*) rùilear *m*

rule *v* **1** (*govern*) riaghail *vti*; **2** (*ordain*) reachdaich *vi*, òrdaich *vi*

ruler[1] *n* (*head*) riaghladair *m*

ruler[2] *n* (*measurer*) rùilear *m*

rum *n* ruma *m*

rumble, rumbling *n* **1** torman *m*; **2** (*eructation*) rùchdail *f*

ruminate *v* **1** (*cows etc*) cnàmh a' chìr; **2** (*human*) cnuas/cnuasaich *vi*

rummage *v* ruamhair *vi*, rùraich *vi*, rannsaich *vi*, sporghail *vi*

rumour *n* fathann *m*

run *n* **1** ruith *f*; **2** *in exprs* **on the ~** fon choill

run *v* **1** ruith *vti*; **2** (*misc exprs*) **~ out** ruith *vi* a-mach, **~ away** (*flee*) teich *vi*, tàrr às, **~ over** (*overflow*) cuir *vi* thairis

rung *n* rong *f*, rongas *m*

running *n* ruith *f*

runny *adj* (*thin*) tana

runway *n* raon-laighe *m*

rural *adj* dùthchail

rush, rushes *n(pl)* (*plant*) luachair *f*

rush *n* **1** (*haste*) cabhag *f*; **2** (*gait*) dian-ruith/deann-ruith *f*

rush *v* (*as vt*) cuir cabhag air

Russia *n* Ruisia *f*, an Ruis *f*

Russian[1] *n & adj* Ruiseanach *m*

Russian[2] *n* (*lang*) Ruiseanais *f*

rust *n* meirg *f*

rust *v* meirg *vti*, meirgich *vti*

rustproof *adj* meirg-dhìonach

rusty *adj* meirgeach

rut *n* (*furrow*) clais *f*, sgrìob *f*

rut, rutting (*deer*) dàmhair *f*

rutting *adj* (*deer*) dàireach

rye *n* seagal *m*

S

sack *n* poca *m*, sac *m*
sack *v* 1 (*ransack etc*) rannsaich *vt*, creach *vt*; 2 (*dismiss*) cuir *vt* à dreuchd
sacred *adj* naomh, coisrigte
sacrifice *n* (*relig*) ìobairt *f*
sacrifice *v* (*relig*) ìobair *vt*
sad *adj* brònach, muladach, truagh, dubhach, cianail
saddle *n* dìollaid/diallaid *f*
sadness *n* bròn *m*, mulad *m*, cianalas *m*
safe *adj* 1 (*building etc*) dìonach, tèarainte; 2 (*person*) sàbhailte; 3 *in expr* ~ **and sound** slàn is fallain, gu slàn fallain
safeguard *n* tèarmann *m*, dìon *m*
safeguard *v* dìon *vt*
safety *n* tèarainteachd *f*, sàbhailteachd *f*
sailor *n* seòladair *m*, maraiche *m*
saint *n* naomh *m*
saintliness *n* naomhachd *f*
saintly *adj* naomh
salary *n* tuarastal *mf*
sale *n* 1 reic *m* 2 (*livestock*) fèill *f*
salesperson neach-reic *m*
saliva *n* seile *m*
sallow *adj* odhar, lachdann
salmon *n* bradan *m*
salt *n* salann *m*
saltire *n* crann *m*
salutation *n* fàilte *f*
salute *n* fàilte *f*
salute *v* fàiltich *vt*
same *adj* 1 ceart, ceudna, dearbh
same *n* 1 (*similar*) ionann, co-ionann; 2 *in expr* **the ~ again** uimhir eile, uiread eile
sample *n* eisimpleir *mf*, taghadh *m*, samhla *m*
sanctity *n* naomhachd *f*
sanctuary *n* tèarmann *m*, comraich *f*
sand *n* gainmheach *f*
sandal *n* cuaran *m*
sandpaper *n* pàipear-gainmhich *m*
sandwich *n* pìos *m*, ceapaire *m*
sandy *adj* gainmheil
sane *adj* ciallach
sanity *n* ciall *f*, rian *m*, reusan *m*
sap *n* 1 (*juice*) snodhach *m*, sùgh *m*; 2 (*essence*) brìgh *f*

sarcasm *n* gearradh *m*, searbhas *m*, beum *m*
sarcastic *adj* geur, searbh, beumach
sardonic *adj* searbh
satchel *n* màileid *f*
satellite *n* saideal *m*
satire *n* aoir *f*
satirical *adj* aoireil
satisfaction *n* toileachadh *m*, sàsachadh *m*.
satisfied *adj & past part* riaraichte, sàsaichte, toilichte
satisfy *v* riaraich *vt*, sàsaich *vt*, toilich *vt*
Saturday *n* Disathairne *m*
sauce *n* 1 (*dressing*) leannra *m*, sabhs *m*; 2 (*cheek*) aghaidh *f*, bathais *f*
saucer *n* sàsar *m*, flat *m*
saunter *v* sràidearaich *vi*
sausage *n* isbean *m*
savant *n* eòlaiche *m*, saoi *m*
save *v* 1 sàbhail *vt*, teasairg/teasraig *vt*; 2 (*convert*) tèarainn *vt*, sàbhail *vt*; 3 (*preserve*) glèidh *vt*; 4 (*money*) sàbhail *vt*, glèidh *vt*, cuir *vt* mu seach; 5 (*reserve money*) caomhain *vt*
saved *adj & past part* sàbhailte
savings *n* sàbhaladh *m*, tasgadh *m*
sawdust *n* min-sàibh *f*
say *v* abair *vti irreg*, can *vti def*
saying *n* seanfhacal *m*, facal *m*, ràdh *m*
scab *n* sgreab *f*, càrr *f*
scale[1] *n* (*of fish, reptile etc*) lann *f*
scale[2] *n* 1 (*range*) raon *m*, sreath *mf*; 2 (*mus*) sgàla *f*; 3 (*proportion*) sgèile *f*, tomhas *m*
scales *n* (*balance*) meidh *f*, cothrom *m*
scallop *n* creachan *m*
scalpel *n* sgian lèigh *f*
scandalous *adj* tàmailteach, maslach
Scandinavia *n* Lochlann *mf*
Scandinavian *n & adj* Lochlannach *m*
scant *adj* gann, tearc
scantness *n* gainne *f*, gainnead *m*, teirce *f*
scanty *adj* 1 gann, tearc; 2 (*hair etc*) gann, tana; 3 (*garment*) goirid, geàrr, gann
scar *n* làrach *f*
scarce *adj* gann, tearc

scarceness, **scarcity** *n* gainne *f*, gainnead *m*, teirce *f*

scarecrow *n* bodach-ròcais *m*

scare *n* eagal *m*, clisgeadh *m*

scare *v* cuir an t-eagal (air)

scared *adj & past part* fo eagal

scarlet *adj* 1 sgàrlaid; 2 *in expr* ~ **fever** am fiabhras dearg *m*

scarlet *n* sgàrlaid *f*

scary *adj* critheanach

scatter *v* sgap *vti*, sgaoil *vti*

scatter-brained *adj* guanach

scattered *adj & past part* sgapte

scenery *n* sealladh-dùthcha *m*

scent *n* fàileadh *m*, àile *m*, boladh *m*

sceptical *adj* teagmhach

schedule *n* clàr-tìde *m*, clàr-obrach *m*

scheme *n* 1 sgeama *m*; 2 (*plot etc*) innleachd *f*, cuilbheart *f*

scheme *v* dèan innleachd(an)

scholar *n* (*pupil*) sgoilear *m*, (*authority*) eòlaiche *m*

scholarly *adj* sgoilearach

scholarship *n* sgoilearachd *f*

school *n* sgoil *f*

schooling *n* sgoil *f*, foghlam *m*

schoolmaster *n* maighstir-sgoile *m*

schoolmistress *n* ban(a)-mhaighstir-sgoile *f*

schoolteacher *n* tidsear *m*, fear-teagaisg *m*, neach-teagaisg *m*, bean-teagaisg *f*, maighstir-sgoile *m*, ban(a)-mhaighstir-sgoile *f*, ban-sgoilear *f*

science *n* saidheans *m*, eòlas *m*

scientific *adj* saidheansail

scientist *n* neach-saidheans *m*, eòlaiche *m*

scoff[1] *v* (*mock*) mag *vi*, dèan fanaid (air)

scoff[2] *v* (*devour*) glàm/glamh *vt*

scoffing *adj* (*mocking*) magail

scoffing[1] *n* (*mockery*) magadh *m*

scoffing[2] *n* (*devouring*) glàmadh, glamhadh *m*

scold *v* càin *vt*, cronaich *vt*

scolding *n* càineadh *m*, cronachadh *m*

scoop *n* ladar *m*, liagh *f*, taoman *m*

scorch *v* dòth *vt*

score[1] *n* (*notch*) sgrìob *f*

score[2] *n and num adj* (*twenty*) fichead *m*

score[3] *n* (*sport*) sgòr *m*, cunntas *m*

scorn *n* tarcais *f*, tailceas *m*, tàir *f*, dìmeas *m*

scorn *v* dèan tarcais, dèan tàir, dèan dìmeas (air)

scorned *adj & past part* fo dhìmeas

scornful *adj* tarcaiseach, tailceasach, tàireil, dìmeasach

Scot *n* Albannach *m*

Scotland *n* Alba *f*

Scots *n* (*lang*) (a') B(h)eurla Ghallta *f*, Albais *f*

Scotsman *n* Albannach *m*

Scots pine *n* giuthas *m*

Scotswoman *n* ban-Albannach *f*

Scottish *adj* Albannach

scoundrel *n* slaightire *m*, balgair *m*

scourge *n* 1 sgiùrs(air) *m*; 2 (*event*) sgrios *m*, plàigh *f*

scourge *v* sgiùrs *vt*

scowl *n* drèin *f*, gruaim *f*, mùig *m*, sgraing *f*

scowl *v* cuir drèin, cuir gruaim, cuir mùig (ort) (*etc*)

scowling *adj* gruamach

scrap[1] *n* 1 (*piece*) mìr *m*, bìdeag *f*, criomag *f*; 2 (*remnant*) fuidheall *m*

scrap[2] *n* (*fight*) tuasaid *f*, sabaid *f*

scrap[1] *v* (*fight*) bi *vi irreg* ri tuasaid

scrap[2] *v* (*discard*) bris(t) *vt* suas, cuir *vi* às (do)

scrape *n* 1 (*scratch etc*) sgrìob *f*; 2 (*situation etc*) (droch) staing *f*, cùil-chumhang *f*

scrape *v* 1 (*general*) sgrìob *vti*; 2 (*involuntarily*) rùisg *vt*

scratch *n* sgrìob *f*, sgròb *m*

scratch *v* 1 (*damage*) sgrìob *vt*; 2 (*relieve*) tachais *vt*, sgròb *vt*, sgrìob *vt*

sratchy *adj* sgrìobach

scream *n* sgreuch *m*, sgread *m*, sgiamh *m*

scream *v* leig sgread, sgreuch *vi*, sgread *vi*, sgiamh *vi*

screech *n* sgread *m*, sgreuch *m*

screech *v* sgread *vi*, sgreuch *vi*

screen *n* sgàilean *m*

screen *v* sgàil *vt*, sgàilich *vt*, falaich *vt*, ceil *vt*

screw *n* sgriubha *mf*, bithis *f*

screwdriver *n* sgriubhaire *m*

scripture *n* sgriobtar *m*

scrotum *n* clach-bhalg *m*

scrub *v* sgùr *vt*

scruffy *adj* luideach, robach

scruple *n* imcheist *f*, teagamh *m*

scrupulous *adj* **1** (*morally*) ionraic, onarach, cogaiseach; **2** (*punctilious*) mion-chùiseach, mionaideach, pongail, cùramach

scrutineer *n* sgrùdair *m*

scrutinise *v* sgrùd *vt*, rannsaich *vt*

scrutiny *n* sgrùdadh *m*, rannsachadh *m*

scullery *n* cùlaist *f*

sculpture *n* **1** (*action*) snaigheadh *m*; **2** (*product*) ìomhaigh (shnaighte)

scurf *n* càrr *f*

scurrilous *adj* tuaileasach, sgainnealach, maslach

scythe *n* speal *f*

sea *n* **1** muir *mf*, cuan *m*, fairge *f*; **2** *in expr* (*fig*) **all at** ~ troimh-a-chèile, am breisleach

sea-bed *n* grunnd na mara *m*, grinneal *m*

seaboard *n* oirthir *f*

sea-chart cairt-iùil *f*

seafarer *n* maraiche *m*

seagull *n* faoileag *f*

seal[1] *n* (*creature*) ròn *m*

seal[2] *n* (*image*) seula *m*

seam *n* fuaigheal *m*

seam *v* fuaigh *vt*, fuaigheil *vt*

seaman *n* maraiche *m*, seòladair *m*

search *n* tòir *f*, lorg *f*

search *v* **1** rannsaich *vt*; **2** ~ **for** lorg *vt*, sir *vt*

seashore *n* tràigh *f*, cladach *m*

sea-sickness *n* cur *m* na mara, tinneas *m* (na) mara

season *n* **1** ràith *f*; **2** (*general*) tràth *m*

sea-spray *n* cathadh-mara *m*

seat *n* **1** (*phys*) suidheachan *m*; **2** (*abstr*) àite-suidhe *m*; **3** *in expr* **take a** ~! dèan suidhe *m*!; **4** (*site*) ionad *m*; **5** (*backside*) màs *m*, tòn *f*

sea-trout *n* bànag *f*

sea-voyage *n* turas-mara *m*

seaweed *n* feamainn *f*

secluded *adj* falaichte, uaigneach

second *adj* dara/dàrna

second *n* (*time*) diog *m*, tiota *m*

second *v* (*support*) cuir taic *f* (ri)

secondary *adj* **1** (*subsidiary*) fo-

second-hand *adj* cleachdte

secrecy *n* dìomhaireachd *f*

secret *adj* **1** (*place*) uaigneach; **2** (*fact etc*) dìomhair

secret *n* cagar *m*, rùn (dìomhair) *m*

secretarial *adj* clèireach

secretary *n* **1** (*clerk*) clèireach *m*; **2** (*PA, political etc*) rùnaire *m*

secrete[1] *v* (*conceal*) cuir *vt* am falach, falaich *vt*

secrete[2] *v* (*ooze*) sil *vti*, snigh *vti*

secretly *adv* os ìosal/os ìseal

section *n* **1** (*objects*) earrann *f*, pàirt *mf*; **2** (*group*) roinn *f*, buidheann *mf*

sector *n* roinn *f*

secular *adj* saoghalta, talmhaidh

secure *adj* **1** (*safe*) tèarainte, dìonach; **2** (*fin*) urrasach

security *n* tèarainteachd *f*

sediment *n* grùid *f*

see *v* **1** faic *vti irreg*, seall *vti*, amhairc *vti*

seed *n* sìol *m*, fras *f*

seek *v* sir *vt*, lorg *vt*

seem *v* bi *vi irreg* coltas (air)

seemingly *adv* a rèir c(h)oltais

seer *n* fiosaiche *m*, fàidh *m*

seethe *v* **1** (*liquids*) goil *vi*; **2** (*person*) bi *vi irreg* air bhoile, bi *vi irreg* air bhàinidh

segregate *v* dealaich *vt*

segregation *n* dealachadh *m*

seize *v* glac *vt*, beir *vi*, gabh grèim (air), greimich *vt*

seized *adj & past part* glacte

seizure *n* glacadh *m*

seldom *adv* is gann, is ainneamh

select *v* tagh *vt*, roghnaich *vt*

selected *adj & past part* air do (*etc*) thaghadh, taghta

selection *n* taghadh *m*, roghainn *m*

-self *reflexive suffix* fhìn, fhèin

self- *reflexive prefix* fèin-

selfish *adj* fèineil, fèin-chùiseach

selfishness *n* fèinealachd *f*

selfless *adj* neo-fhèineil

sell *v* reic *vti*

seller *n* reiceadair *m*

semen *n* sìol *m*

semi(-) *prefix* leth-

seminar *n* seiminear *m*, co-labhairt *f*

senate *n* seanadh *m*

senator *n* seanadair *m*

send *v* cuir *vt*

senior *adj* **1** (*first*) prìomh; **2** (*oldest*) as sine

sense *n* (*intelligence*) tuigse *f*, ciall *f*

senseless *adj* **1** (*foolish*) gun chiall, dìomhain, faoin; **2** (*stunned*) gun mhothachadh

sensibility *n* mothachadh *m*

sensible *adj* ciallach, tuigseach, toinisgeil

sensitive *adj* **1** mothachail; **2** (*touchy*) frionasach

sensitivity *n* mothachadh *m*

sensual *adj* feòlmhor, collaidh

sensuality *n* feòlmhorachd *f*

sentence *n* **1** (*legal*) binn *f*, breith *f*; **2** (*gram*) seantans *mf*, rosg-rann *f*

sentence *v* **1** thoir a-mach binn, thoir breith (air)

sentiment *n* **1** (*feeling*) mothachadh *m*; **2** (*opinion*) beachd *m*, smuain *f*

sentimental *adj* maoth-inntinneach

sentinel, **sentry** *n* neach-faire *m*

separate *adj* air leth, fa leth, eile, eadar-dhealaichte

separate *v* dealaich *vti*, roinn *vt*

separation *n* dealachadh *m*

September *n* an t-Sultain *f*

sequence *n* sreath *mf*, ruith *f*

serene *adj* ciùin, socair, suaimhneach

series *n* sreath *mf*

serious *adj* **1** (*important*) trom, cudromach; **2** (*severe*) droch; **3** (*earnest*) dùrachdach, (*sober*) stòlda; **4** ann an da-rìribh

serpent *n* nathair *f*

serve *v* **1** fritheil *vi* (air), freastail; **2** (*dish*) riaraich *vt*, thoir *vt* seachad; **3** (*mate*) rach *vi irreg* air muin

service *n* **1** freastal *m*, frithealadh *m*; **2** (*help*) seirbheis *f*

service *v* **1** (*machinery etc*) gleus *vt*, cùm *vt* air dòigh; **2** (*support*) fritheil *vi* (air)

servile *adj* tràilleil

session *n* seisean *m*

set *adj & past part* suidhichte, stèidhichte

set *n* seat(a) *m*

set *v* suidhich *vt*, socraich *vt*, cuir *vt*

setback *n* duilgheadas *m*, bacadh *m*

settee *n* sòfa *f*, langasaid *f*

setting *n* suidheachadh *m*

settle *v* socraich *vti*

settled *adj & past part* suidhichte, seasmhach

settlement *n* **1** (*habitational*) tuineachadh *m*; **2** (*solution*) rèiteachadh *m*

settler *n* neach-tuineachaidh *m*

seven *n and num adj* **1** seachd; **2** (*people*) seachd(n)ar *nf*

seventeen *n and num adj* seachd-deug

seventh *n* seachdamh *m*

seventh *num adj* seachdamh

seventy *n and num adj* trì fichead 's a deich, seachdad *m*

sever *v* **1** (*excise*) geàrr *vt* dheth; **2** (*part*) dealaich *vti*, sgar *vti*

several *adj* beagan *m*, grunnan *m*

severe *adj* **1** (*person etc*) cruaidh, teann; **2** (*unbearable*) goirt; **3** (*extreme*) droch

sew *v* fuaigh *vti*, fuaigheil *vti*

sewage *n* òtrachas *m*

sewer *n* sàibhear *m*, giodar *m*

sewing *n* fuaigheal *m*

sewn *adj & past part* fuaighte

sex *n* **1** (*gender*) gnè *f*; **2** (*lovemaking*) feis(e) *f*, sùgradh *m*

sexist *adj* gnèitheil

sexual *adj* gnèitheach, gnèitheasach

shabby *adj* luideach, cearbach, robach; (*of conduct*) tàireil

shackle *n* geimheal *m*

shackle *v* geimhlich *vt*

shade *v* duibhrich *vti*

shadow *n* dubhar *m*, sgàil(e) *f*, dubharachd *f*, faileas *m*

shadowy *adj* faileasach

shady *adj* dubharach

shaft *n* **1** (*ray*) gath *m*; **2** (*engin*) crann *m*; **3** (*handle*) cas *f*

shaggy *adj* molach, ròmach, fionnach, robach

shake *n* crith *f*

shake *v* **1** (*deliberately*) crath *vti*; **2** (*involuntarily*) bi *vi irreg* air chrith

shaking *adj* air chrith

shaking *n* luasgan *m*

shaky *adj* (*lit*) cugallach, critheanach, tulgach

shallow *adj* eu-domhainn, tana

shambles *n* bùrach *m*

shame *n* nàire *f*, masladh *m*, tàmailt *f*

shame *v* nàraich *vt*, maslaich *vt*

shame-faced *adj* nàrach

shameful *adj* nàr, maslach, tàmailteach

shameless *adj* gun nàire, ladarna

shaming *n* nàrachadh *m*, maslachadh *m*

shamrock *n* seamrag *f*

shape *n* cruth *m*, cumadh *m*, dealbh/deilbh *mf*

shape *v* cum *vt*, dealbh *vt*

shapely *adj* cuimir

share *n* **1** cuid *f*, cuibhreann *m*, roinn *f*

share *v* co-roinn *vt*; pàirtich *vt*, roinn *vt*, riaraich *vt*

shared *adj & past part* **1** roinnte; **2** (*common*) coitcheann

sharp *adj* geur

sharpen *v* faobharaich *vt*, geuraich *vt*

sharpness *n* gèire *f*

shatter *v* **1** (*as vi*) rach *vi irreg* ann am bloighdean

shave *v* beàrr *vt*, lom *vt*

she *pers pron* i, (*emph*) ise

sheaf *n* sguab *f*

shear *v* rùisg *vt*, lom *vt*

shearing *n* rùsgadh *m*, lomadh *m*

shears *n* deamhais *mf*

shebeen *n* taigh-dubh *m*, bothan *m*

shed *n* seada *mf*, bothan *m*

shed *v* dòirt *vt*

sheep *n* caora *f*, (*pl*) caoraich *fpl*

sheepdog *n* cù-chaorach *m*

sheepfank faing *f*, fang *m*

sheepfold *n* crò(-chaorach) *m*, faing *f*, fang *m*

sheepish *adj* nàrach, air do nàrachadh

sheep-shearer *n* lomadair *m*

sheep-tick *n* mial-chaorach *f*

sheet *n* **1** (*bed*) siota *m*; **2** (*paper*) duilleag *f*

shelf *n* **1** sgeilp *f*; **2** (*topog*) leac *f*

shell *n* plaosg *m*, slige *f*

shell[1] *v* rùisg *vt*, plaoisg

shell[2] *v* (*bombard*) tilg slige(ach)an (air)

shellfish *n* maorach *m*

shelter *n* fasgadh *m*, dìon *m*

shelter *v* **1** (*as vi*) gabh fasgadh; **2** (*as vt*) thoir fasgadh (do)

sheltered *adj* fasgach, dìonach

sheltering *adj* fasgach, dìonach

shepherd *n* cìobair *m*

sheriff *n* siorram *m*

shield *n* sgiath *f*, targaid *f*

shield *v* dìon *vt*

shieling *n* àirigh *f*, ruighe *mf*

shift *v* caraich *vt*, gluais *vti*, cuir car (de)

shifting *adj* **1** (*moving*) gluasadach; **2** (*inconstant*) caochlaideach, carach, luaineach

shifty *adj* fiar, carach

shilling *n* tastan *m*

shin *n* lurgann *f*, faobhar na lurgainn *m*

shine *n* (*polish*) lìomh *f*

shine *v* **1** (*as vi*) deàlraich *vi*, deàrrs *vi*; **2** (*as vt*) lìomh *vt*

shingle *n* mol *m*, morghan *m*

shining *adj* **1** deàlrach; **2** (*polished*) lìomharra

shinty *n* iomain *f*, camanachd *f*

ship *n* long *f*, soitheach *m*, bàta (mòr) *m*

shipping *n* loingeas/luingeas *m*, luingearachd *f*

shipwreck *n* long-bhris(t)eadh *m*

shirt *n* lèine *f*

shit *v* cac *vi*

shit(e) *n* cac *m*

shiver *n* crith *f*

shiver *v* crith *vi*, bi *vi irreg* air chrith

shivering *adj* air chrith

shivering *n* crith *f*

shock *n* clisgeadh *m*

shocking *adj* oillteil, uabhasach

shoddy *adj* **1** luideach, cearbach, robach; **2** (*careless*) dearmadach, coma co-dhiù

shoe *n* bròg *f*

shoe *v* (*horse*) crudhaich *vt*, cuir crudha (air)

shoe-lace *n* iall-bròige *f*, barrall *m*

shoemaker, shoe-repairer *n* greusaiche *m*

shoot *n* (*plant*) ògan *m*, gas *f*, bachlag *f*

shoot *v* **1** (*discharge*) loisg *vti*, tilg *vti* (air); **2** (*hit*) tilg *vi* ann an, leig peilear ann an

shooting *n* losgadh *m*, tilgeil *f*

shop *n* bùth *f*

shopkeeper *n* neach-bùtha *m*

shore *n* tràigh *f*, cladach *m*

short *adj* goirid, geàrr, aithghearr

shortage *n* cion *m*, dìth *m*, gainne *f*, uireasbhaidh *f*

shortcoming *n* fàillinn *f*, meang *m*

shorten *v* **1** (*as vt*) giorraich *vt*; **2** (*as vi*) rach *vi* an giorrad

shortly *adv* a dh'aithghearr, an ceann goirid, (ann) an ùine gheàrr

shortness *n* giorrad *m*

shorts *n* briogais ghoirid

shot *n* **1** (*discharge*) urchair *f*; **2** (*attempt*) oidhirp *f*, ionnsaigh *f*

should *auxiliary v* bu (*past/conditional of* is *v irreg def*) chòir *f*

shoulder *n* **1** gualann/gualainn *f*

shout *n* glaodh *m*, iolach *f*, èigh *f*

shout *v* glaodh *vi*, dèan/tog iolach *f*, èigh *vi*

shove *v* put *vt*; sàth *vt*, spàrr *vt*

shovel *n* sluasaid *f*

show *n* **1** (*exhibition*) taisbeanadh *m*; **2** (*ostentation*) spaide *f* show *v* seall *vt*, nochd *vt*, taisbean/taisbein *vt*

shower *n* 1 (*rain*) fras *f*; 2 (*equipment*) frasair *m*

showery *adj* frasach

showing *adv* ris

showy *adj* spaideil, basdalach

shrewd *adj* geurchuiseach, tuigseach, seòlta

shriek *n* sgread *m*, sgreuch *m*

shriek *v* sgread *vi*, sgreuch *vi*

shrill *adj* sgalanta

shrimp *n* carran *m*

shrink *v* lùghdaich *vti*, teannaich *vti*

shrinkage *n* lùghdachadh *m*, teannachadh *m*

shrivel *v* searg *vi*, crìon *vi*

shroud *n* marbhphaisg *f*

shrub *n* preas *m*, dos *m*

shrunken *adj & past part* crìon, seargte

shun *v* 1 (*avoid*) seachain *vt*, cùm *vi* (obho); 2 (*ostracise*) cuir cùl (ri)

shut *adj & past part* dùinte

shut *v* dùin *vti*

shy *adj* diùid

shy *v* (*horse etc*) thoir uspag

shyness *n* diùide *f*, diùideachd *f*

sick *adj* 1 (*ill etc*) tinn, euslainteach, anfhann, bochd; 2 (*fed up*) seac searbh sgìth

sick *n* (*vomit*) dìobhairt *m*

sicken *v* 1 (*as vi*) fàs *vi* tinn; 2 (*disgust*) cuir sgreamh (air), sgreataich *vt*

sickle *n* corran *m*

sickness *n* tinneas *m*, gearan *m*, galar *m*

side *n* taobh *m*

sideways *adv* an comhair do (*etc*) thaoibh

siege *n* sèist *mf*

siesta *n* dùsal-feasgair *m*

sieve *n* criathar *m*

sieve, sift *v* criathraich *vt*

sigh *n* osna *f*, osnadh *m*, osann *m*, ospag *f*

sigh *v* leig/dèan osna, osnaich *vi*

sighing *n* osnaich *f*, osnachadh *m*

sight *n* amharc *m*, sealladh *m*, (f)radharc *m*, fianais *f*, lèirsinn *f*

sign *n* comharra(dh) *m*, samhla(dh) *m*

sign *v* (*documents etc*) cuir d' ainm ri

signal *n* sanas *m*, comharra(dh) *m*

signature *n* ainm (sgrìobhte) *m*

significance *n* brìgh *f*, ciall *f*

significant *adj* 1 (*important*) cudromach; 2 (*meaningful*) brìgheil

signify *v* ciallaich *vt*

signpost *n* clàr-seòlaidh *m*, post-seòlaidh *m*, soidhne *m*

silence *n* tost *m*, sàmhchair *f*

silent *adj* sàmhach, nad (*etc*) thost

silk *n* sìoda *m*

silky *adj* sìodach

silliness *n* gòraiche *f*, amaideas *m*, faoineas *m*

silly *adj* gòrach, faoin, baoth

silt *n* eabar *m*, poll *m*

silver *n* airgead *m*

similar *adj* coltach

similarity *n* coltas *m*

simile *n* samhla(dh) *m*

simple *adj* sìmplidh

simplicity *n* sìmplidheachd *f*

simplify *n* sìmplich *vt*

simultaneous *adj* co-amail

sin *n* peacadh *m*

sin *v* peacaich *vi*

since *conj* 1 (*causal*) on/bhon, a chionn is; 2 (*time*) o/bho

since *prep* (*temporal*) o chionn/bho chionn

sincere *adj* dùrachdach, fosgarra

sincerity *n* dùrachd *mf*, treibhdhireas *m*

sincerely *adv* (*corres*) **yours** ~ le dùrachd, is mise le meas

sinew *n* fèith *f*

sinewy *adj* fèitheach

sinful *adj* peacach

sing *v* seinn *vti*, gabh *vt*

singe *v* dòth *vt*

singer *n* seinneadair *m*

single *adj* 1 sìngilte; 2 (*unmarried*) gun phòsadh

singular *adj* sònraichte

sink *n* (*kitchen etc*) sinc(e) *mf*

sink *v* 1 (*as vi*) tràigh *vi*, traogh *vi*, sìolaidh *vi*; cuir *vt* fodha

sinner *n* peacach *m*

sip *n* drùdhag *f*, balgam *m*

siren *n* dùdach *mf*, dùdag *f*

sister *n* piuthar *f*

sit *v* suidh *vi*, dèan suidhe

site *n* 1 làrach *f*, ionad *m*

sitting *n* suidhe *m*

situation *n* suidheachadh *m*

six *n and num adj* 1 sia; 2 (*people*) sianar *mf*

sixth *n* siathamh *m*

sixth *num adj* siathamh

sixty *n and num adj* trì fichead *m*, seasgad *m*

sixteen *n and num adj* sia-deug

size *n* meud *m*, meudachd *f*
sizeable *adj* tomadach
skeleton *n* cnàimhneach *m*
skelp *n* dèiseag *f*, sgailc *f*
skelp *v* thoir *vt* sgailc (do)
sketch *n* sgeidse *f*
ski *n* sgì *f*
ski *v* sgithich *vi*
skiing *n* sgitheadh *m*
skilful, skilled *adj* gleusta, sgileil, teòma
skill *n* sgil *m*
skin *n* **1** (*human*) craiceann *m*; **2** (*animal*) seiche *f*, bian *m*; **3** (*fruit etc*) plaosg *m*, rùsg *m*
skin *v* **1** (*fruit etc*) rùisg *vt*, plaoisg *vt*; **2** (*animal*) thoir an craiceann de; **3** (*graze etc*) rùisg
skinny *adj* caol, tana, seang
skip *n* leum *m*, sùrdag *f*
skip *v* (*jump*) leum *vi*, dèan sùrdag
skipper *n* sgiobair *m*
skirt *n* sgiort *f*
skittish *adj* **1** guanach, luaineach, tuainealach; **2** (*mettlesome*) clisgeach, sgeunach
skivvy *n* sgalag *f*
skull *n* claigeann *m*
sky *n* speur *m*, adhar *m*, iarmailt *f*
skylark *n* uiseag *f*, topag *f*
slab *n* leac *f*
slacken *v* fuasgail *vt*, lasaich *vt*
slander *n* cùl-chàineadh *m*
slander *v* cùl-chàin *vt*, càin *vt*
slanderous *adj* cùl-chainnteach
slant *n* fiaradh *m*, claonadh *m*
slanting *adj* air fhiaradh, fiar
slap *n* sgailc *f*, sgealp *f*, sgleog *f*, dèiseag *f*
slap *v* sgealp *vt*
slate *n* sglèat *mf*
slaughter *n* casgairt *f*
slaughter *v* casgair *vt*
slaughterhouse *n* taigh-spadaidh *m*
slave *n* tràill *mf*
slaver *n* ronn *m*, seile *m*
slavery *n* tràilleachd *f*
slay *v* casgair *vt*, murt *vt*, marbh *vt*
sledge *n* slaodan *m*
sleek *adj* slìom
sleep *n* cadal *m*
sleep *v* dèan cadal, caidil *vi*
sleeping-bag *n* poca-cadail *m*
sleepy *adj* cadalach

sleet *n* flinne *m*
sleeve *n* muin(i)chill/muil(i)cheann *m*
sleigh *n* slaodan *m*
slender *adj* caol, seang
slice *n* sliseag *f*
slide *n* (*structure*) sleamhnag *f*, sleamhnan *m*
slide *v* sleamhnaich *vi*
slight *adj* beag
slight *v* cuir *vt* an suarachas, cuir *vt* air dìmeas, cuir *vt* air bheag sùim, dèan dìmeas (air)
slightly *adv* beagan
slim *adj* caol, tana, seang
slim *v* seangaich *vt*
slime *n* clàbar *m*
slink *v* èalaidh *vi*, siolp *vi*
slip *n* **1** (*stumble*) tuisleadh *m*; **2** (*error*) mearachd *f*, iomrall *m*; **3** *in expr* ~ **of the tongue** tapag *f*
slip *v* **1** (*stumble*) tuislich *vi*, (*slide*) sleamhnaich *vi*; **2** (*movement*) siolp *vi*, èalaidh *vi*
slipper *n* slapag *f*
slippery *adj* sleamhainn
slipshod *adj* dearmadach, coma co-dhiù
slippy *adj* sleamhainn
slip-up *n* mearachd *f*
slit *n* sgoltadh *m*
slit *v* sgoilt *vt*
sliver *n* sgealbag *f*
slogan *n* sluagh-ghairm *f*
slop *v* dòirt *vt*
slope *n* leathad *m*, bruthach *mf*, aodann *m*
slope *v* **1** claon *vti*
sloping *adj* claon
sloppy *adj* **1** (*food etc*) tana; **2** (*careless*) dearmadach, coma co-dhiù; **3** (*appearance*) cearbach, luideach, robach
slosh *v* plubraich *vi*, plub *vi*
sloth *n* leisg(e) *f*
slothful *adj* leisg, dìomhain
slovenly *adj* luideach, rapach, robach
slow *adj* mall, slaodach, màirnealach
slow, slow down *v* **1** (*as vi*) rach *vi irreg* am maille; **2** (*as vt*) cuir maille (air/ann an)
slowness *n* maille *f*
sludge *n* eabar *m*, poll *m*
slug *n* **1** (*creature*) seilcheag *f*; **2** (*bullet*) peilear *m*
sluggish *adj* slaodach

slum *n* slum(a) *m*

slumber *n* suain *f*

slurry *n* giodar *m*

slut *n* luid *f*, sgliùrach *f*, breunag *f*

sly *adj* carach, fiar

smack *n* sgailc *f*, sgealp *f*, dèiseag *f*

smack *v* sgealp *vt*

small *adj* **1** beag, mion-

smart *adj* **1** (*neat*) grinn, cuimir, snasail; **2** (*quick*) geur/luath nad (*etc*) inntinn, eirmseach, geurchuiseach, toinisgeil

smash *v* smuais *vt*, smùid *vt*, spealg *vt*, bris(t) *vt* ann an spealgan

smashed *adj & past part* **1** smuaiste, briste, ann an spealgan *fpl*; **2** (*drunk*) air do (*etc*) phronnadh

smashing *adj* (*great*) sgoinneil, taghta, math dha-rìribh

smear *v* smiùr *vt*, smeur *vt*

smell *n* àile(adh)/fàile(adh) *m*, boladh *m*

smell *v* (*as vt*) fairich *vt*, feuch *vt*

smiddy *n* ceàrdach *f*

smile *n* faite-gàire *f*, fiamh a' ghàire *m*, snodha-gàire *m*

smile *v* dèan faite-gàire, dèan fiamh a' ghàire, dèan snodha-gàire

smirk *n* mìog *f*

smite *v* buail *vt*

smith *n* **1** ceàrd/cèard *m*

smithy *n* ceàrdach *f*

smoke *n* smùid *f*, ceò *m*, toit *f*

smoke *v* **1** (*fire etc*) cuir smùid *f*, smùid *vi*; **2** (*tobacco*) smoc *vti*

smoking *n* (*tobacco etc*) smocadh *m*

smoky *adj* ceòthach, toiteach

smooth *adj* mìn, rèidh

smoothe *v* dèan *vt* rèidh, dèan *vt* mìn

smother (*fire etc*) mùch *vt*, tùch *vt*, (*person*) tachd *vt*

smoulder *v* cnàmh-loisg *vi*

smudge *n* smal *m*

smudge *v* smeur *vt*

smuggler *n* cùl-mhùtaire *m*

smuggling *n* cùl-mhùtaireachd *f*

smut *n* **1** (*spot*) smal *m*, spot *m*; **2** (*suggestiveness*) drabastachd *f*, draostachd *f*, rabhd *m*

smutty *adj* (*suggestive*) drabasta, draosta

snack *n* srùbag *f*, pìos *m*

snag *n* duilgheadas *m*

snail *n* seilcheag *f*

snake *n* nathair *f*

snappy *adj* aithghearr

snare *n* ribe *mf*

snarl *v* dèan dranndan

snarl, snarling *n* dranndan *m*, dranndail *f*

snatch *v* glac *vt*, beir *vi irreg* (air)

sneak *v* èalaidh *vi*, snàig *vi*, siolp *vi*

sneer *v* dèan fanaid *f* (air)

sneering *n* fanaid *f*

sneeze *n* sreothart *m*

sneeze *v* dèan sreothart *m*

sneezing, sneezing fit *n* sreothartaich *f*

sniff *n* boladh *m*

sniff *v* gabh boladh (de)

snivel *v* smùch *vi*

snooze *n* dùsal *m*, norrag *f*

snooze *v* dèan dùsal *m*, gabh norrag *f*

snore *n* srann *f*

snore *v* srann *vi*

snoring *n* srannail *f*

snout *n* soc *m*

snow *n* sneachda *m*

snow *v* cuir (sneachda *m*)

snowdrift *n* cathadh *m*

snowflake *n* bleideag *f*, pleòideag *f*

snowman *n* bodach-sneachda *m*

snowplough *n* crann-sneachda *m*

snub *v* cuir do chùl ri

snug *adj* seasgair

so *adv* **1** (*before an adj*) cho; **2** mar sin

so *conj* **1** (*therefore*) mar sin; **2** (*in order that*) gus an

soak *v* **1** drùidh *vi* (air), fliuch *vt*; **2** (*steep*) cuir *vt* am bogadh

soaked, soaking *adj* bog fliuch

soap *n* siabann *m*

soapy *adj* siabannach

sob *n* glug-caoinidh *m*

sob *v* dèan glug-caoinidh

sober *adj* measarra, stuama, stòlda

sobriety *n* stuaim *f*

soccer *n* ball-coise *m*

sociability *n* conaltradh *m*

sociable *adj* cuideachdail, conaltrach, cèilidheach

social *adj* **1** (*person*) conaltrach; **2** sòisealta

socialism *n* sòisealachd *f*

socialist *adj* sòisealach

socialist *n* sòisealach *m*

society *n* comann *m*, sòisealtas *m*

sock *n* socais *f*

socket *n* (*electric*) bun-dealain *m*

sod *n* **1** fòid/fòd *f*, fàl *m*; **2** (*person*) trustar *m*

sofa *n* langasaid *f*

soft *adj* bog

soften *v* maothaich *vti*, bogaich *vti*

software *n* bathar bog

soggy *adj* bog fliuch

soil *n* talamh *m*, ùir *f*

soil *v* salaich *vt*

solace *n* furtachd *f*, sòlas *m*

solder *v* tàth *vt*

soldier *n* saighdear *m*

sole *n* bonn *m*

solemn *adj* sòlaimte

solicitor *n* neach-lagha *m*

solicitude *n* iomagain *f*

solid *adj* teann

solitary *adj* uaigneach, aonaranach

solitude *n* uaigneas *m*, aonaranachd *f*

solution *n* **1** (*melting*) leaghadh *m*, eadar-sgaoileadh *m*; **2** (*answer*) fuasgladh *m*

solve *v* (*resolve*) fuasgail *vt*

some *pron* feadhainn *f*, cuid *f*

somebody, someone *pron* cuideigin *mf*

somersault *n* car a' mhuiltein *m*

something *pron* rudeigin *m*

sometimes *adv* uaireannan *adv*, air uairean

somewhat *adv* rudeigin, rud beag, car

somnolent *adj* cadalach

son *n* mac *m*

song *n* òran/amhran *m*

son-in-law *n* cliamhainn *m*

soon *adv* a dh'aithghearr

soot *n* sùith(e) *mf*

soothe *v* ciùinich *vt*, tàlaidh *vt*

soothsayer *n* fiosaiche *m*

sorcerer *n* draoidh *m*

sorcery *n* draoidheachd *f*

sordid *adj* **1** (*morally*) suarach, truaillidh, coirbte; **2** (*phys*) dràbhail, salach, grod, mosach

sore *adj* goirt

sorrow *adj* bròn *m*, mulad *m*, tùirse/tùrsa *f*

sorrowful *adj* brònach, muladach, tùrsach

sorry *adj* duilich

sort *n* seòrsa *m*, gnè *f*

sort *v* seòrsaich *vt*

soul *n* anam *m*

sound *adj* fallain

sound *n* fuaim *mf*

soup *n* brot *m*, eanraich *f*

sour *adj* goirt, searbh, geur

source *n* bun *m*, tùs *m*

south *n & adj* **1** deas *f*

southerly *adj* mu dheas

southern *adj* deas, mu dheas

souvenir *n* cuimhneachan *m*

sovereign *n* rìgh *m*

sow *n* cràin *f*, muc *f*

sow *v* cuir *vt*

sowing *n* cur *m*

space *n* **1** (*room*) rùm *m*; **2** (*opening*) beàrn *mf*; **3** (*extra-terrestrial*) fànas *m*

spade *n* spaid *f*, caibe *m*

Spain *n* An Spàinn *f*

spanner *n* spanair *m*

spar *n* (*bar*) rong *f*, rongas *m*

spare *adj* **1** (*free*) saor; **2** (*surplus*) a bharrachd

spare *v* caomhainn *vt*

spark *n* sradag *f*

sparkle *n* drithleann *m*, lainnir *f*

sparkle *v* lainnrich *vi*

sparkling *adj* lainnireach

sparrow *n* gealbhonn *m*

sparse *adj* gann, tana

speak *v* bruidhinn *vti*, labhair *vi*

speaker *n* (*lecturer etc*) òraidiche *m*, neach-labhairt *m*

spear *n* gath *m*, sleagh *f*

special *adj* àraidh, sònraichte, air leth

specialist *n* speisealaiche

species *n* gnè *f*, cineal *m*, seòrsa *m*

specific *adj* àraidh, sònraichte

specifically *adv* a dh'aon ghnothach, a dh'aon rùn

specify *v* sònraich *vt*, comharraich *vt*

specimen *n* sampall *m*

speck *n* smal *m*

speckled *adj* ballach, breac

spectacle *n* sealladh *m*

spectacles *npl* speuclairean *mpl*, glainneachan *fpl*

spectacular *adj* drùidhteach

spectator *n* neach-coimhid *m*

spectre *n* bòcan *m*, taibhse *mf*

speculate *v* **1** (*mentally*) beachdaich *vi* (air); **2** (*fin*) dèan tuairmeas

speculation *n* **1** (*mental*) beachdachadh *m*; **2** (*fin*) tuairmeas *m*

speculative *adj* **1** (*mentally*) beachdachail, baralach; **2** (*fin*) tuairmseach

speech *n* **1** (*general*) cainnt *f*, labhairt *f*;
2 (*oration*) òraid *f*; **3** (*lang*) còmhradh *m*

speechless *adj* balbh

speed *n* luas *m*, astar *m*

speedy *adj* luath, cabhagach

spell[1] *n* (*enchantment*) geas *f*, seun *m*,
ortha *f*

spell[2] *n* (*time*) greis *f*

spell *v* litrich *vt*

spellbound *adj & past part* fo gheasaibh

spelling *n* litreachadh *m*

spend *v* **1** (*money*) cosg *vt*, caith *vt*;
2 (*time*) cuir *vt* seachad

spendthrift *adj* caith(t)each, struidheil &
stròdhail

spendthrift *n* struidhear *m*

spent *adj & past part* **1** (*money*) cosgte,
caithte; **2** (*energy etc*) caithte

sperm *n* sìol(-ginidh) *m*

spew *v* cuir *vti* a-mach, sgeith *vi*

sphere *n* cruinne *mf*

spherical *adj* cruinn

spice *n* spìosradh *m*

spice *v* spìosraich *vt*

spicy *adj* spìosrach

spider *n* damhan-allaidh *m*

spike *n* spìc *f*, bior *m*

spill *v* dòirt *vti*

spin *n* **1** (*revolution*) car *m*; **2** (*trip*) cuairt

spin *v* cuir car de

spine *n* **1** (*backbone*) cnà(i)mh (an) droma
m; **2** (*thorn*) bior *m*

spinster *n* boireannach gun phòsadh *m*

spirit *n* **1** (*relig*) spiorad *m*; **2** (*ghost*)
taibhse *mf*; **3** (*courage*) misneach(d) *f*,
smior *m*; **4** (*alcoholic*) ~s deoch-làidir *f*

spirited *adj* misneachail, smiorail/smearail

spiritual *adj* (*relig*) spioradail

spirituality *n* spioradalachd *f*

spirtle *n* maide-poite *m*

spit[1] *n* (*saliva*) smugaid *f*

spit[2] *n* (*rod*) bior-ròstaidh *m*

spit *v* tilg smugaid *f*

spite *n* gamhlas *m*, tarcais *f*, tailceas *m*

spite *v* dèan tarcais *f* (air)

spiteful *adj* gamhlasach, tarcaiseach,
tailceasach

spittle *n* smugaid *f*

splash *n* plubraich *f*, plub *m*

splash *v* plubraich *vi*, dèan plubraich, plub
vi

splendid *adj* gasta, greadhnach, àlainn

splendour *n* greadhnachas *m*

split *adj & past part* **1** sgoilte; **2** *in phr*
split-new ùr-nodha

split *n* sgàineadh *m*, sgoltadh *m*

split *v* **1** sgoilt & sgolt *vti*; **2** ~ (**up**) (*divide*)
roinn *vt* (suas); **3** *in expr* ~ **up** (*separate*)
dealaich *vi*

splosh *v* plubraich *vi*, plub *vi*

splutter *v* dèan plubraich *f*

spoil *v* **1** (*as vi*) rach *vi irreg* bhuaithe;
2 (*as vt*) mill *vt*

spoil, spoils *n* cobhartach *mf*, spùilleadh &
spùinneadh *m*, creach *f*

spoilt *adj & past part* millte

spoke *n* spòg *f*

spokesman *n* fear-labhairt *m*

spokesperson *n* neach-labhairt *m*

sponsor *n* goistidh *m*

sponsorship *n* goistidheachd *f*

spool *n* iteachan *m*

spoon *n* spàin *f*

sport *n* spòrs *f*

sporting *adj* (*fair*) cothromach

sporty *adj* spòrsail

spot *n* **1** (*pimple etc*) guirean *m*, plucan *m*;
2 (*place*) bad *m*, àite *m*; **3** (*spot*) smal *m*,
spot *m*

spot *v* (*see*) faigh fàire (air)

spouse *n* cèile *m*

spout *n* **1** (*tube*) feadan *m*; **2** (*jet*) spùt *m*,
steall *f*; **3** (*waterfall*) spùt *m*

sprain *n* sgochadh *m*, siachadh *m*

sprain *v* sgoch *vt*, siach *vt*

spray *n* **1** (*device*) steallaire *m*; **2** (*cloud*)
cathadh-mara *m*

spray *v* steall *vti*

spree *n* (*bout*) daorach *f*

spread *v* sgaoil *vti*

sprightly *adj* lùthmhor, clis, sgairteil,
brìoghmhor

spring *n* **1** (*leap*) leum *m*; **2** (*well*) fuaran
m, tobar *mf*; **3** (*season*) earrach *m*; **4** *in
expr* ~ **tide** reothart *mf*

spring *v* **1** (*leap*) leum *vi*; **2** (*appear*) nochd
vi

sprinkle *v* crath *vt*

sprint *n* deann-ruith/dian-ruith *f*

sprout *n* **1** (*plant*) bachlag *f*

sprout *v* (*plant*) cuir a-mach bachlagan

spruce *adj* cuimir, snasail, sgiobalta

spruce *n* giuthas *m*

spry *adj* beothail, clis

spur v 1 (*encourage*) brosnaich vt, spreig vt, stuig vt, piobraich vt; 2 (*hurry*) cuir cabhag (air), greas vt, brod vt

spurt n 1 (*liquid*) steall f, stealladh m, spùt m; 2 (*acceleration*) briosgadh m, cabhag f

spurt v (*liquid*) steall vti, spùt vti

spy n 1 brathadair m, neach-brathaidh m

spying n (*espionage*) brathadh m

spy v brath vi

squabble n connsachadh m, tuasaid f, trod m

squabble v connsaich vi, troid vi

squabbling n trod m

squad n buidheann mf, sguad m

squalid adj 1 dràbhail, robach, grod, mosach; (*of behaviour*) suarach, tàireil

squall n sgal m, meall m

squalor n mosaiche f

squander v caith vt

square adj ceàrnach

square n (*shape*) ceàrnag f

squash v 1 (*press*) brùth vt, preas vt; 2 (*quell*) ceannsaich vt, mùch vt

squat n crùban m

squat v dèan crùban, crùb vi

squeak, squeaking n 1 (*rubbing*) dìosgan m, dìosgail f, gìosg m

squeak v 1 (*rubbing*) gìosg vi

squeal n sgiamh m, sgal m

squeal v sgiamh vi, sgal vi

squeamish adj òrraiseach

squeeze n teannachadh m, fàsgadh m

squeeze v teannaich vt, fàisg vt, preas vt

squint adj (*aslant*) claon, fiar, air fhiaradh

squint n claonadh m, fiaradh m, spleuchd m

squint v seall vi claon, seall vi fiar, spleuchd vi

squirrel n feòrag f

squirt n steall f, stealladh m

squirt v steall vti

stab n 1 sàthadh m; 2 (*try*) oidhirp f, ionnsaigh mf

stab v sàth vti

stabilise v 1 (*as vt*) bunailtich vt; 2 (*as vi*) fàs vi bunailteach

stability n bunailteachd f, seasmhachd f

stable adj seasmhach, bunailteach

stable n stàball m

stack n cruach f, mulan m, coc/goc m

stack v cruach vt, càrn vt

stackyard n iodhlann f

staff¹ n (*employees*) luchd-obrach m

staff² n 1 (*stick*) bachall m; 2 (*music*) cliath f

stag n damh m

stage¹ n (*level*) ìre f

stage² n (*structure*) àrd-ùrlar m

stagger v 1 tuimhsich vi, tuislich vi; 2 (*surprise*) cuir mòr-iongnadh air

stagnant adj marbh

staid adj stòlda

stain n smal m, spot m, sal m

stain v 1 dath vt; fàg smal, fàg spot (air)

stained adj & past part dathte

stair n 1 (*step*) ceum m; 2 (*staircase*) staidhre f, staidhir f

staircase, stairs n staidhir f, staidhre f

stake¹ n (*post*) post m, stob m, cipean m

stake² n (*wager*) geall m

stalk n gas f

stallion n àigeach m

stalwart adj 1 (*sturdy*) calma, tapaidh, smiorail, treun; 2 (*loyal*) seasmhach, daingeann, dìleas

stalwart n curaidh m, gaisgeach m

stamina n 1 (*strength*) neart m, spionnadh m; 2 (*resilience*) cumail-ris f, fulang m,

stamp n (*postage*) stamp(a) f

stamp v 1 (*letter*) cuir stamp(a) (air); 2 (*trample*) breab vt, stamp vti

stance n (*phys, moral, philo etc*) seasamh m

stand v 1 (*rise*) seas vi, èirich vi; 2 (*bear*) fuiling/fulaing vti, cuir vi suas ri

standard adj 1 (*usual*) suidhichte, cumanta, gnàthach; 2 (*common*) coitcheann

standard n 1 (*criterion*) slat-thomhais f; 2 (*level*) ìre f, inbhe f

standing n (*rank*) seasamh m, inbhe f

stanza n rann mf

star n reul f, rionnag f

starch n stalc m

stare n spleuchd m

stare v spleuchd vi

starfish n crasgag/crosgag f

stark adj garbh, cruaidh

starling n druid f, druideag f

start n 1 (*beginning*) toiseach m, tùs m, tòiseachadh m; 2 (*shock*) clisgeadh m, uspag f

start v 1 tòisich vi (air/ri), teann vi (ri); 2 (*fright*) clisg vi, thoir uspag f

startle v cuir clisgeadh air, clisg vt

starvation n gort/goirt f

starve *v* **1** (*as vi*) caochail *vi* leis a' ghoirt;
2 (*as vt*) cuir trasg, leig goirt (*air*)

state *n* **1** (*condition*) cor *m*, staid *f*; **2** (*pol*)
stàit

state *v* cuir *vt* an cèill; thoir *vt* (seachad)

stately *adj* stàiteil

statement *n* **1** (*abstr*) cur *m* an cèill *f*;
2 (*account*) aithris *f*, aithisg *f*, (*legal*)
teisteanas *m*

statesman *n* stàitire *m*

station *n* stèisean *m*

stationary *adj* na stad *m*, gun ghluasad *m*

stationery *n* pàipearachd *f*, stuth-
sgrìobhaidh *m*

statue *n* ìomhaigh *f*

stature *n* **1** (*height*) àirde *f*; **2** (*rank*) inbhe *f*

status *n* inbhe *f*, seasamh *m*

statute *n* reachd *m*, riaghailt *f*

statutory *adj* reachdail, dligheach

staunch *adj* seasmhach, daingeann, dìleas,
treun, làidir

staunch *v* caisg *vt*

stave *n* (*music*) cliabh *m*

stay *v* **1** (*remain*) fuirich *vi*, fan *vi*; **2** (*dwell*)
fuirich *vi*, fan *vi*, gabh còmhnaidh

steadfast *adj* **1** (*loyal*) dìleas; **2** (*enduring*)
daingeann, seasmhach

steady *adj* **1** (*firm*) cunbhalach,
bunai(l)teach, seasmhach, daingeann,
teann; **2** (*person*) stòlda, suidhichte; **3** *as
adv in exprs* ~!, ~ **on!**, socair!

steady *v* daingnich *vt*

steak *n* staoig *f*

steal *v* goid *vt*, dèan mèirle

stealing *n* goid *f*, mèirle *f*, braid *f*

steam *n* toit *f*, smùid *f*, deatach *f*

steam *v* cuir toit

steel *n* stàilinn *f*, cruaidh *f*

steep *adj* cas

steep *v* tum *vt*, cuir *vt* am bogadh

steeple *n* stìopall *m*

steer *v* stiùir *vt*

stem *n* **1** (*plant*) gas *f*; **2** (*boat*) toiseach *m*

stench *n* tòchd *m*

step *n* ceum *m*

step *v* gabh ceum *m*, thoir ceum

step-brother *n* leas-bhràthair *m*

step-child *n* dalta *mf*

step-father *n* oide *m*

step-mother *n* muime *f*

stepping-stone *n* sìnteag *f*

step-sister *n* leas-phiuthar *f*

sterile *adj* **1** (*barren*) seasg, neo-thorrach;
2 (*fruitless*) gun toradh, gun fheum,
dìomhain

stern *n* (*boat*) deireadh *m*

stern *adj* **1** (*hard*) cruaidh, teann;
2 (*unsmiling*) dùr, gruamach, gnù,
mùgach

sternum *n* cliathan *m*

stew *n* stiubha *f*

steward *n* maor *m*; (*on boat*) stiùbhard *m*

stick *n* bata *m*, maide *m*

stick *v* **1** (*adhere*) lean *vi* (ri); **2** (*catch*) rach
vi an sàs; **3** (*thrust*) sàth *vt*

stiff *adj* **1** rag; **2** (*difficult*) doirbh, cruaidh

stiffen *v* ragaich *vti*

stiffness *n* raige *f*

stifle *v* **1** (*fire etc*) smà(i)l *vt*, mùch *vt*, tùch
vt; **2** (*life*) mùch *vt*, tachd *vt*; **3** (*uprising
etc*) mùch *vt*, ceannsaich *vt*

still *adj* **1** (*weather*) ciùin, sàmhach, sèimh;
2 (*motionless*) gun ghluasad *m*, nad thàmh

still *adv* **1** fhathast; **2** (*nevertheless*) a
dh'aindeoin sin, a dh'aindeoin cùise, air a
shon sin

still *n* (*apparatus*) poit-dhubh *f*

still *v* ciùinich *vti*, sìthich *vti*, socraich *vti*

stimulate *v* **1** (*phys*) brod *vt*, (*emotionally*)
brosnaich *vt*; **2** (*revive*) beothaich *vt*

sting *n* guin *m*, gath *m*

sting *v* guin *vt*, cuir gath ann an

stinginess *n* spìocaireachd *f*

stinging *adj* geur, goirt; (*remarks*)
guineach

stingy *adj* spìocach, mosach

stink *n* tòchd *m*

stint *n* greis *f*, treis *f*

stipend *n* tuarastal *f*

stipulate *v* sònraich *vt*

stipulation *n* **1** (*abstr*) sònrachadh *m*;
2 (*con*) cumha *f*, cùmhnant *m*

stir *v* **1** (*phys*) gluais *vi*, caraich *vi*;
2 (*emotionally*) gluais *vt*, drùidh *vi* (air);
3 (*liquids etc*) cuir car de

stirk *n* gamhainn *m*

stitch *n* **1** (*needlework*) grèim *m*; **2** (*pain*)
acaid *f*

stitch *v* fuaigh *vt*, fuaigheil *vt*

stoat *n* neas *f*

stob *n* stob *m*, post *m*

stock *n* **1** (*livestock*) stoc *m*, (*cattle*) sprèidh
f, crodh *m*; **2** (*goods*) bathar *m*; **3** (*fin*)
sèaraichean *mpl*, earrannan *fpl*

stocking *n* stocainn *f*, osan *m*
stolid *adj* stòlda, dùr
stomach *n* stamag *f*, goile *f*, balg *m*, broinn *f*, brù *f*, mionach *m*, maodal *f*
stone *n* clach *f*
stone *v* clach *vt*, tilg clachan air
stonemason *n* clachair *m*
stony *adj* clachach
stool *n* stòl *m*, furm *m*, creapan *m*
stoop *v* crùb *vi*
stop *n* **1** (*abstr*) stad *f*; **2** (*typog*) puing *f*
stop *v* **1** (*as vi*) stad *vi*, thig *vi* gu stad, sguir *vi*; **2** (*as vt*) stad *vt*, thoir *vt* gu stad, cuir stad air; **3** (*prevent*) cuir bacadh air, caisg *vt*, cuir casg air; **4** (*abandon*) leig *vt* de, leig *vt* seachad, sguir *vi* de
stopcock *n* goc *m*
storage *n* stòradh *m*
store *n* **1** (*repository*) ionad-tasgaidh *m*, tasgaidh *f*, stòr *m*; **2** (*shop*) bùth *mf*
store *v* stò(i)r *vt*, taisg *vt*
storey *n* lobht(a) *m*
storm *n* stoirm *f*, doineann *f*, gailleann *f*
stormy *adj* stoirmeil, doineannach, gailleannach, gailbheach
story *n* sgeulachd *f*, sgeul *m*, stòiridh *m*, naidheachd *f*
stout *adj* **1** (*brave*) treun; **2** (*plump*) reamhar, sultmhor
stove *n* stòbh(a) *mf*
stow *v* **1** (*store*) taisg *vt*, glèidh *vt*; **2** (*put away*) cuir *vt* (air falbh)
straddle *v* rach *vi irreg* casa-gòbhlach, rach *vi irreg* gòbhlachan (air)
straggle *v* bi *vi irreg* air dheireadh
straggler *n* slaodaire *m*
straight *adj* dìreach
straighten *v* dìrich *vti*
strain *n* **1** (*tension*) teannachadh *m*; **2** (*phys*) spàirn *f*; **3** (*psych*) uallach *m*
strain[1] *v* **1** (*tension*) teannaich *vt*; **2** (*phys*) dèan spàirn
strain[2] *v* (*liquids*) sìolaidh *vt*
strainer *n* **1** (*liquids*) sìol(t)achan *m*; **2** (*tensioner*) teannaire *m*
strait *n* caol *m*, caolas *m*
strand[1] *n* (*seashore*) tràigh *f*
strand[2] *n* (*material etc*) dual *m*
strange *adj* **1** (*odd*) neònach, annasach, iongantach; **2** (*unfamiliar*) coimheach
stranger *n* coigreach *m*, srainnsear *m*, coimheach *m*

strangle mùch *vt*, tachd *vt*
strangulation *n* mùchadh *m*, tachdadh *m*
strap *n* iall *f*
strapping *adj* tomadach, calma
stratagem *n* cuilbheart *f*, innleachd *f*
strategy *n* ro-innleachd *f*
strath *n* srath *m*
straw *n* **1** connlach *f*; **2** (*drinking*) sràbh *m*
stray *adj* (*lost*) air seachran, air iomrall
stray *v* rach *vi* air seachran, rach *vi* air iomrall
streak *n* stiall *f*, srian *f*
streak *v* stiall *vt*
stream *n* (*watercourse*) sruth *m*, allt *m*
stream *v* ruith *vi*, sruth *vi*, sil *vi*
street *n* sràid *f*
strength *n* **1** (*phys*) neart *m*, spionnadh *m*, lùth/lùths *m*, brìgh *f*; **2** (*pol etc*) cumhachd *mf*, neart *m*
strengthen *v* neartaich *vt*, daingnich *vt*
strenuous *adj* saothrachail
stress *n* **1** (*emphasis*) cudrom/cuideam *m*; **2** (*psych* ~) uallach *m*; **3** (*lang*) buille *f*, cudrom/cuideam *m*
stress *v* (*emphasise*) leig cudrom (air)
stretch *n* (*phys*) sìneadh *m*
stretch *v* sìn *vti*
stretched *adj & past part* sìnte
strew *v* sgaoil *vt*, sgap *vt*
strict *adj* cruaidh, teann
stride *n* **1** sìnteag *f*; **2** (*pace*) ceum *m*
strife *n* strì *f*, còmhstri *f*
strike *n* (*industrial etc*) stailc *f*
strike *v* **1** (*hit*) buail *vt*; **2** (*industry etc*) rach *vi irreg* air stailc; **3** (*impress*) drùidh air; **4** (*occur*) thig *vi* a-steach ort (*etc*)
striking *adj* drùidhteach
string *n* **1** sreang *f*; **2** (*musical*) teud *m*
string *v* **1** (*instrument*) cuir teud air
stringency *n* teanntachd *f*
stringent *adj* teann
strip *n* (*material etc*) stiall *f*
strip *v* (*body etc*) rùisg *vt*, lom *vt*
stripe *n* stiall *f*
stripe *v* stiall *vt*
striped *adj* stiallach
stripling *n* òganach *m*, òigear *m*
stripped *adj & past part* rùisgte
strive *v* **1** (*contend etc*) strì *vi*; **2** (*try*) dèan spàirn
stroke *n* **1** (*blow*) buille *f*, beum *m*; **2** (*sport*) buille *f*; **3** (*med*) stròc *m*

stroke *v* 1 (*dog etc*) slìob/slìog *vt*;
2 (*person*) cnèadaich/cniadaich *vt*

stroll *n* cuairt *f*, car *m*

stroll *v* coisich *vi* gu socrach, coisich air
ceum socrach

strong *adj* 1 làidir, neartmhor, lùthmhor,
treun

stronghold *n* daingneach *f*

strop *n* iall *f*

structural *adj* structarail

structure *n* structair *m*

struggle *n* 1 strì *f*, spàirn *f*, (*con*) gleac *m*;
2 (*campaign*) iomairt *f*

struggle *v* strì *vi*, gleac *vi*

strut *v* spai(s)dirich *vi*

strutting *adj* spai(s)direach

stubborn *adj* 1 (*obstinate*) rag, dùr, rag-
mhuinealach; 2 (*tenacious*) dìorrasach

stuck *adj & past part* an sàs

stud *n* (*horses*) greigh *f*

student *n* oileanach *m*

study *n* 1 (*learning*) ionnsachadh *m*;
2 (*investigation*) rannsachadh *m*, sgrùdadh
m; 3 (*room*) seòmar-leughaidh *m*

study *v* 1 (*learn*) ionnsaich *vt*; 2 (*research*)
rannsaich *vt*, sgrùd *vt*, dèan rannsachadh/
sgrùdadh air

stuff *n* 1 (*material*) stuth *m*, cungaidh *f*;
2 (*possessions*) trealaich *f*

stuff *v* 1 (*fill*) lìon *vt*; 2 (*push*) sàth *vt*, dinn
vti

stumble *n* tuisleadh *m*

stumble *v* tuislich *vi*

stumbling-block *n* cnap-starra(dh) *m*

stump *n* ploc *m*, stoc *m*

stun *v* cuir *vt* ann an tuaineal

stunt *n* cleas *m*

stupid *adj* 1 (*unintelligent*) gòrach, tiugh;
2 (*silly*) gòrach, amaideach, baoth, faoin

stupidity *n* 1 (*unintelligence*) gòraiche
f; 2 (*silliness*) gòraiche *f*, amaideas *m*,
faoineas *m*

stupor *n* tuaineal *m*

sturdiness *n* tapachd *f*

sturdy *adj* calma, tapaidh

sty *n* (*agric*) fail *f*

style *n* 1 stoidhle *f*; 2 (*mode*) modh *mf*,
nòs *m*

sub(-) *prefix*, fo-

subconscious *adj* 1 fo-mhothachail; 2 (*in
Freudian sense*) fo-inntinneil

subconscious *n* fo-inntinn *f*

subdue *v* 1 (*people*) ceannsaich *vt*, cuir *vt*
fo smachd; 2 (*spirit etc*) mùch *vt*,

subject *n* 1 (*matter*) cuspair *m*;
2 (*subservient*) ìochdaran *m*; 3 (*gram*)
cùisear *m*, suibseig *f*

subjection *n* 1 (*abstr*) ceannsal *m*, smachd
m; 2 (*con*) ceannsachadh *m*

subjugate *v* cuir *vt* fo smachd, smachdaich
vt, ceannsaich *vt*

subjugation *n* 1 (*abstr*) ceannsal *m*,
smachd *m*; 2 (*con*) ceannsachadh *m*

submerge *v* tum *vt*, cuir *vt* fodha

submission *n* gèilleadh *m*, strìochdadh *m*,
gèill *f*

submissive *adj* macanta, umha(i)l

submissiveness *n* ùmhlachd *f*

submit *v* 1 (*as vi*) gèill *vi*, strìochd *vi*; 2 (*as
vt*) cuir *vt* a-steach

subordinate *adj* ìochdarach *m*

subordinate *n* ìochdaran *m*

subscription *n* (*magazine etc*) fo-
sgrìobhadh *m*

subside *v* laigh *vi*, lùghdaich *vi*, rach *vi*
sìos, socraich *vi*, sìolaidh *vi*

subsidy *n* tabhartas *m*, subsadaidh *m*

subsistence *n* teachd-an-tìr *m*, bith-beò *mf*

substance *n* 1 (*abstr*) brìgh *f*, susbaint;
2 (*material*) stuth *m*

substantial *adj* tàbhachdach, tomadach

substantiate *v* dearbh *vt*

substitute *n* (*sport etc*) neach-ionaid *m*

substitute *v* cuir *vt* an àite

subterfuge *f* cuilbheart *f*, innleachd *f*

subterranean *adj* fon talamh

subtle *adj* (*mentally*) geurchuiseach,
innleachdach

subtract *v* thoir *vt* air falbh (*bho*)

suburb *n* iomall baile *m*

subway *n* fo-rathad *m*, fo-shlighe *f*

succeed *v* 1 (*follow*) lean *vt*, thig *vi* an
dèidh; 2 (*thrive etc*) soirbhich *vi*

success *n* 1 buaidh *f*; 2 (*material*)
soirbheachas *m*

successful *adj* soirbheachail

succession *n* (*sequence etc*) sreath *mf*

succinct *adj* cuimir

such *adj* de leithid *f*, den t-seòrsa *m*

such *adv in expr* ~ **a lot** na h-uimhir, na
h-uiread

suck *v* deothail *vti*, sùgh *vti*

suction *n* deothal *m*, sùghadh *m*

sudden *adj* grad, obann, gun fhiosta

suddenness *n* graide *f*, graidead *m*
suet *n* geir *f*
suffer *v* fuiling *vti*
suffering *n* cràdh *m*, fulang *m*, fulangas *m*
suffice *v* foghain *vi*
sufficiency *n* leòr *f*, fòghnadh *m*
sufficient *adj* & *n* gu leòr, na dh'fhòghnas
suffocate mùch *vt*
suffocation *n* mùchadh *m*
suffrage *n* còir-bhòtaidh *f*, guth-bhòtaidh *m*
sugar *n* siùcar *m*
suggest *v* mol *vt*
suggestion *n* moladh *m*
suicide *n* fèin-mhurt *m*
suit *n* (*apparel*) deise *f*, culaidh(-aodaich) *f*, trusgan *m*
suit *v* freagair *vi* (air/do), thig *vi* (do/ri)
suitable *adj* freagarrach, iomchaidh
sulk *n* gruaim *f*, mùig *m*
sulk *v* cuir gruaim/mùig ort
sulkiness *n* gruaim *f*, mùig *m*
sulking, **sulky**, **sullen** *adj* gruamach, mùgach
sully *v* truaill *vt*, salaich *vt*, cuir smal air
sulphur *n* pronnasg *m*
sulphurous *adj* pronnasgail
sultry *adj* (*weather*) bruthainneach, bruicheil
sum *n* sùim *f*
summarise *v* thoir geàrr-chunntas (air)
summary *adj* aithghearr, bras
summary *n* geàrr-chunntas *m*
summer *n* samhradh *m*
summit *n* mullach *m*, bàrr *m*
summon *v* gairm *vt*, cuir *vi* a' dh'iarraidh, cuir fios (air)
summons *n* **1** gairm *f*; **2** (*legal*) sumanadh *m*, bàirlinn *f*
summons *v* (*legal*) sumain *vt*
sumptuous *adj* sòghail
sun *n* grian *f*
sunbathe *v* gabh a' ghrian
sunbeam *n* gath-grèine *f*
sunburn *n* losgadh-grèine *m*
Sunday *n* Didòmhnaich *m*, Latha na Sàbaid *m*
sunder *v* **1** (*separate*) dealaich *vt*; **2** (*split*) sgàin *vti*
sundial *n* uaireadair-grèine *m*
sundry *adj* **1** (*assorted*) de gach seòrsa *m*, de dh'iomadach seòrsa, measgaichte *adj*; **2** (*various*) caochladh *m* (*with gen*)

sunny *adj* grianach
sunrise *n* èirigh *f* (na) grèine
sunset *n* dol-fodha *m* (na) grèine, laighe *mf* (na) grèine
sunshade *n* sgàilean-grèine *m*
sunstroke *n* beum-grèine *m*
sunwise *adj* & *adv* deiseal
superannuation *n* **1** (*abstr*) peinnseanachadh *m*; **2** (*con*) peinnsean *m*
supercilious *adj* àrdanach
superficial *adj* uachdarach, eu-domhainn
superfluous *adj* thar a' chòrr, iomarcach
superior *adj* **1** (*rank*) uachdarach; **2** (*in quality*) (n)as fheàrr
superior *n* (*rank*) uachdaran *m*
supernatural *adj* os-nàdarra(ch)
superstition *n* saobh-chràbhadh *m*
superstitious *adj* saobh-chràbhach
supervise *v* cùm sùil air, stiùir *vt*
supper *n* suipear *f*
supple *adj* sùbailte, lùbach
supplier *n* solaraiche *m*
supplies *n* lòn *m*
supply *n* **1** (*abstr*) solar *m*; **2** (*con*) pailteas *m*, leòr *f*
supply *v* solaraich *vt*
support *n* taic(e) *f*, tacsa *m*
support *v* **1** (*assist*) cùm taic ri, thoir taic do, seas *vt*; **2** (*side*) cùm taobh ri, gabh taobh; **3** (*maintain*) cùm *vt* suas
supporter *n* neach-taice *m*
supporting, **supportive** *adj* taiceil
suppose *v* saoil *vi*
suppress *v* mùch *vt*, ceannsaich *vt*, cùm *vt* fodha
suppurate *v* iongraich *vi*
supreme *adj* (*highest*) àrd-, sàr-
sure *adj* **1** cinnteach, deimhinn(e); **2** (*reliable*) earbsach, seasmhach
surety *n* urras *m*
surface *n* uachdar *m*, bàrr *m*
surface *v* thig *vi* an uachdar
surfeit *n* sàth *m*, leòr *f*, cus *m*
surge *v* brùchd *vi*
surgeon *n* làmh-lèigh *m*, lannsair *m*
surgery *n* **1** (*discipline*) làmh-leigheas *m*; **2** (*intervention*) obair-lèigh *f*; **3** (*place*) lèigh-lann *m*
surly *adj* gruamach, mùgach, gnù, iargalt(a)
surname *n* sloinneadh *m*, cinneadh *m*
surplus *n* còrr *m*, cus *m*
surprise *n* iongnadh *m*

surprise *v* cuir iongnadh air
surprising *adj* iongantach
surrender *n* gèilleadh *m*, strìochdadh *m*
surrender *v* gèill *vi*, strìochd *vi*
surround *v* cuartaich *vt*, iadh & iath *vt*
survey *n* 1 (*land etc*) tomhas *m*, suirbhidh *m*; 2 (*investigation*) sgrùdadh *m*, rannsachadh *m*
survey *v* 1 (*land etc*) tomhais *vt*; 2 (*study etc*) sgrùd *vt*, rannsaich *vt*, dèan sgrùdadh/rannsachadh air
surveyor *n* neach-tomhais *m*
survive *v* thig *vi* beò, mair *vi* beò
suspect *adj* fo amharas *m*
suspect *n* neach fo amharas *m*
suspect *v* bi *vi irreg* amharas agad
suspend *v* 1 (*phys*) croch *vt*; 2 (*delay*) cuir dàil air; 3 (*debar*) cuir *vt* à dreuchd
suspension *n* 1 crochadh *m*; 2 (*debarment*) cur à dreuchd *m*
suspicion *n* amharas *m*
suspicious *adj* amharasach
sustain *v* (*feed*) cùm *vt* suas, beathaich *vt*
sustenance *n* lòn *m*, beathachadh *m*
swagger *v* spai(s)dirich *vi*
swallow[1] *n* balgam *m*, steallag *f*
swallow[2] *n* (*bird*) gòbhlan-gaoithe *m*
swallow *v* sluig/slug *vti*
swallowing *n* slugadh *m*
swamp *n* boglach *f*, fèith(e) *f*, bog *m*
swan *n* eala *f*
swarm *n* sgaoth *m*
swarm *v* sgaothaich *vi*
swarthy *adj* ciar, lachdann
sway *v* luaisg *vi*, tulg *vi*
swear *n* mionn *mf*, bòid *f*
swear *v* mionnaich *vti*
swearing *n* 1 (*oath*) mionnachadh *m*; 2 (*cursing*) droch-chainnt *f*, mionnachadh *m*, guidheachan *mpl*
sweat *n* fallas *m*
sweat *v* bi *v irreg* fallas (ort), cuir fallas
sweaty *adj* fallasach
Sweden *n* An t-Suain *f*
sweep *v* sguab *vti*
sweet *adj* 1 (*taste*) milis; 2 (*smell*) cùbhraidh; 3 (*sound*) binn
sweet *n* 1 (*dessert*) mìlsean *m*; 2 (*sweetie*) suiteas *m*
sweeten *v* mìlsich *vt*

sweetheart *n* leannan *m*
sweetness *n* mìlseachd *f*
swell *v* at *vi*, sèid *vi*, bòc *vi*
swelling *v* at *m*, bòcadh *m*
swift *adj* (*movement*) luath, siùbhlach; (*performing tasks etc*) clis, deas, ealamh; (*sudden*) grad
swim *v* snàmh *vi*
swimmer *n* snàmhaiche *m*
swimming *n* snàmh *m*
swing *n* 1 (*structure*) dreallag *f*; 2 (*movement*) gluasad *m*
swing *v* luaisg *vi*, tulg *vi*
Swiss *adj* Eilbheiseach
switch[1] *n* (*elec*) suidse *f*
switch[2] *n* (*stick*) gad *m*
switch *v* 1 (*lights etc*) cuir *vt* air; 2 (*exchange*) cuir *vt* an àite a chèile
Switzerland *n* An Eilbheis *f*
swoon *n* neul *m*, laigse *f*
swoon *v* rach *vi* an neul, rach *vi* an laigse, fannaich *vi*, fanntaich *vi*
sword *n* claidheamh *m*
swordsman *n* claidheamhair *m*
syllable *n* lide *m*; bìog *f*, bìd *m*, smid *f*
syllabus *n* clàr-oideachais *m*, clàr-oideachaidh *m*
symbol *n* comharra(dh) *m*, samhla(dh) *m*
symbolic, symbolical *adj* samhlachail
symbolise *v* riochdaich *vt*, samhlaich *vt*
symbolism *n* samhlachas *m*
symmetrical *adj* cothromaichte
symmetry *n* co-chothromachd *f*
sympathetic *adj* co-fhulangach, mothachail, co-mhothachail, tuigseach
sympathise *v* co-fhuiling *vi*, co-mhothaich *vi*
sympathy *n* co-fhulangas *m*, co-mhothachadh *m*, tuigse *f*
symposium *n* co-labhairt *f*
symptom *n* comharra(dh) *m*
synopsis *n* giorrachadh *m*, geàrr-chunntas *m*
synthetic *adj* fuadain
syphon *n* lìonadair *m*
syringe *n* steallair(e) *m*
system *n* 1 (*order*) riaghailt *f*, rian *m*; 2 (*procedure*) siostam *m*, modh *mf*, dòigh *f*
systematic(al) *adj* riaghailteach, òrdail

T

table *n* **1** bòrd *m*; **2** (*in book etc*) clàr *m*

tacit *adj* tostach

taciturn *adj* tostach, dùinte, diùid

tack¹ *n* (*sailing*) gabhail *mf*, taca *f*

tack² *n* (*nail*) tacaid *f*

tacket *n* tacaid *f*

tackle *n* (*gear*) uidheam *f*, acainn *f*

tackle *v* thoir ionnsaigh, thoir oidhirp (air), rach *vi* an sàs (ann an)

tactic *n* innleachd *f*

tactical *adj* innleachdach

tadpole *n* ceann-pholan *m*, ceann-simid *m*

tail *n* earball *m*

tailor *n* tàillear *m*

taint *v* **1** (*sully*) truaill *vt*, salaich *vt*; **2** (*flavour*) thoir droch bhlas do

take *v* gabh *vti*, thoir *vt*

taken in *adj & past part* (*deceived*) meallta

tale *n* sgeulachd *f*, sgeul *m*

talent *n* tàlann *m*

talented *adj* tàlantach, ealanta

talk *n* **1** (*abstr*) bruidhinn *f*; **2** (*conversation*) còmhradh *m*; **3** (*speech*) òraid *f*

talk *v* **1** bruidhinn *vi*, labhair *vi*; **2** (*converse*) dèan còmhradh *m*

talkative *adj* còmhraideach, bruidhneach, beulach, cabach, gabach

talking *n* bruidhinn *f*, labhairt *f*

tall *adj* àrd

talon *n* spu(i)r *m*, ìne *f*

tame *adj* **1** (*animal etc*) call(t)a, solta; **2** (*insipid*) gun bhrìgh, gun smior

tame *v* callaich *vt*, ceannsaich *vt*

tamper *v* **1** bean *vi*, buin *vi*; **2** (*with malice*) mill *vt*

tan *v* **1** (*leather*) cairt *vt*; **2** (*sunbathe*) gabh a' ghrian

tangible *adj* beanailteach

tank¹ *n* (*water etc*) amar *m*

tank² *n* (*warfare*) tanca *f*

tanker *n* tancair *m*

tanning *n* (*leather*) cartadh *m*

tannoy *n* glaodhaire *m*

tap¹ *n* (*plumbing*) tap *mf*, goc *m*

tap² *n* (*blow*) cnag *f*

tape *n* teip *f*

tar *n* teàrr *f*, bìth *f*

tardy *adj* **1** (*late*) fadalach; **2** (*slow*) mall, màirnealach, athaiseach

targe, target *n* targaid *f*

target *n* targaid *f*, cuspair *m*

tariff *n* clàr-phrìsean *m*

tarnish *v* smalaich *vt*, dubhaich *vt*, cuir smal, cuir sgleò (air)

tart *adj* **1** (*taste*) geur, searbh; **2** (*remarks etc*) geur, searbh, guineach

tart *n* (*pastry*) pithean *m*

tartan *n* breacan *m*

tartan *adj* breacanach, tartanach

task *n* obair *f*, pìos obrach *m*, gnìomh *m*, gnothach *m*

taste *m* **1** (*flavour*) blas *m*; **2** (*quantity*) blasad *m*; **3** (*discernment*) tuigse *f*

taste *v* (*as vt*) blais *vt*, feuch *vt*

tasteless *adj* mì-bhlasta, gun bhlas *m*

tasty *adj* blasta, blasmhor

tatter *n* luideag *f*, cearb *f*

tattered *adj & past part* luideach, cearbach, ann an luideagan, reubte

tatty *adj* luideach, cearbach

taunt *n* beum *m*, magadh *m*

taunt *v* mag *vi* (air)

taut *adj* teann

tavern *n* taigh-òsta *m*

tawdry *adj* suarach, grodach, dràbhail

tawny *adj* lachdann, odhar, ciar

tax *n* cìs *f*, càin *f*

tax *v* **1** (*charge*) cuir/leag càin (air); **2** (*levy*) cuir cìs (air)

taxable *adj* cìs-bhuailteach

taxation *n* cìs *f*, càin *f*

taxi *n* tagsaidh *m*

tea *n* **1** (*drink*) tì *f*, teatha *f*; **2** (*meal*) biadh-feasgair *m*

teach *v* teagaisg *vti*, ionnsaich *vti*

teacher *n* fear-teagaisg *m*, neach-teagaisg *m*, bean-teagaisg *f*, tidsear *m*, maighstir-sgoile *m*, ban(a)-mhaighstir-sgoile *f*

teaching *n* teagasg *m*, oileanachadh *m*

team *n* buidheann *mf*, sgioba *mf*

tear¹ *n* (*rip*) reubadh *m*, sracadh *m*

tear², teardrop *n* deur *m*

tear v 1 (*rip*) reub vt, srac vt; 2 (*snatch*) spìon vt; 3 (*rush etc*) falbh nad dhian-ruith

tearful adj deurach

tease v tarraing vi (à), farranaich vt

teat n sine f

tea-towel n tubhailte-shoithichean f

technical adj teicnigeach

technician n teicneòlaiche m

technique n dòigh(-obrach) f, alt m

technological adj teicneòlach

technologist n teicneòlaiche m

technology n teicneòlas m

tedious adj fadalach, liosta, màirnealach

tedium n fadachd f, fadal m, fadalachd f, liostachd f

teem v cuir vi thairis

teenager n deugaire m

telephone n fòn mf

telephone v cuir fòn mf, fòn vi, fònaig vi (gu)

telescope n prosbaig mf

television n telebhisean m

tell v 1 (*command*) òrdaich vi; 2 (*recount*) innis vti

temper n nàdar m

temperament n mèinn f, nàdar m

temperance n stuamachd f

temperate adj 1 (*weather*) sèimh; 2 (*people*) measarra, stuama

temperature n teòthachd f

tempest n doineann f, gailleann f

tempestuous adj gailbheach, doineannach

temple[1] n (*relig*) teampall m

temple[2] n (*anat*) lethcheann m

temporal adj aimsireil, talmhaidh, saoghalta

temporary adj sealach

tempt v buair vt, meall vt, tàlaidh vt

temptation n buaireadh m, mealladh m

ten n and num adj 1 deich; 2 (*people*) deichnear mf

tenacious adj dìorrasach

tenacity n dìorrasachd f

tenancy n gabhaltas m

tenant n màladair m

tend[1] v (*care*) eiridnich vt

tend[2] v (*be liable to*) bi vi irreg buailteach, bi dual(t)ach

tendency n 1 (*trend*) aomadh m; 2 (*propensity*) buailteachd nf

tender adj maoth, (*emotionally*) bog

tender n (*offer*) tairgse f

tender v (*offer*) tairg vti

tendril n ògan m

tense n (*gram*) tràth m

tense adj 1 (*phys*) teann, rag; 2 (*emotionally*) nèarbhach, clisgeach, frionasach

tense v teannaich vti

tension n 1 (*phys*) teannachadh m; 2 (*emotional*) frionas m

tent n teanta f, pàillean m, puball/pùball m

tenterhooks npl, in expr **on ~** air bhioran mpl

tenth n deicheamh m

tenth num adj deicheamh

tenure n gabhaltas m

tepid adj leth-fhuar, flodach

term[1] n 1 (*condition*) cumha f; 2 (*terminology*) briathar m; 3 in exprs **on good ~s with** rèidh ri

term[2] n (*period*) teirm f

terminal n (*IT*) ceann-obrach m

terminate v cuir crìoch air, thoir vt gu crìch

terminology n 1 (*abstr*) briathrachas m; 2 (*lexicon*) briathrachan m

terminus n ceann-uidhe m

terra firma n tìr mf, talamh tioram m

terrible adj eagalach, uabhasach, sgriosail

terribly adv uabhasach, anabarrach, eagalach

terrier n abhag f

terrify v cuir oillt, cuir eagal mòr (air), oilltich vt

territory n dùthaich f, tìr mf

terror n uamhann m, oillt f, uabhas m

terse adj aithghearr

test n dearbhadh m, deuchainn f

test v cuir vt gu deuchainn, dearbh vt

testament n (*legal etc*) tiomnadh m

testicle n magairle mf, clach f

testify v thoir fianais f

testimonial n teisteanas m

testimony n fianais f, teisteanas m, dearbhadh m

testy, tetchy adj frionasach, cas

tether n feist(e) f, teadhair f

text n 1 teacsa f; 2 (*sermon etc*) ceann-teagaisg m

textual adj teacsail

than conj na

thank *v* **1** thoir taing *f* (do); **2** *in exprs* ~ **you!** tapadh leat/leibh!, taing dhut/dhuibh!

thankful *adj* taingeil, buidheach

thanks *n* taing *f*, **many** ~!, ~ **a lot!** mòran taing!

that *adj* sin, a tha 'n sin, ud

that *rel pron* a, (*neg*) nach

that *pron* sin, siud

that *conj* gu, gun, gum, (*neg*) nach

thatch *n* tughadh *m*

thatch *v* tugh *vt*

thaw *n* aiteamh *m*

thaw *v* leagh *vti*

the *definite art* an etc

theatre *n* taigh-cluiche *m*

theft *n* goid *f*, mèirle *f*

them *pron mpl & fpl* iad, (*emph*) iadsan

theme *n* cuspair *m*

themselves *reflexive pron* iad fhèin

then *adv* **1** (*time*) aig an àm sin; **2** (*next*) an uair sin; **3** (*so*) ma-thà/ma-tà

theologian *n* diadhaire *m*

theology *n* diadhachd *f*

theory *n* **1** (*surmise*) beachd *m*, beachd-smuain *m*; **2** (*hypothesis*) teòiridh *f*

therapist *n* leasaiche *m*, teiripiche *m*

there *adv* **1** an sin, sin, an siud; **2** (**over**) ~ thall (an sin); **3** (*present*) ann, an làthair

there *pron* **1** (*expressed by the v irreg* bi, *& a prep phrase*); **2** (*expressed by the v irreg* bi *& a prep pron*); **3** (*expressed by the v irreg* bi *& a verbal expr*)

therefore *adv* a chionn sin, air sgàth sin, mar sin, do bhrìgh sin, uime sin

thereupon *adv* le sin, leis a sin

thermometer *n* teas-mheidh *f*, tomhas-teas *m*

these *pron*, *see* **this**

thesis *n* tràchdas *m*

they *pron mpl & fpl* iad, (*emph*) iadsan, iad fhèin

thick *adj* **1** (*phys*) tiugh; **2** (*trees etc*) dlùth, dùmhail; **3** (*mentally*) tiugh, maol

thicket *n* doire *mf*, bad *m*

thickness *n* tighead *m*

thickset *adj* tomadach

thief *n* gadaiche *m*, mèirleach *m*

thieve *v* goid *vti*, dèan mèirle, dèan braid

thieving *n* goid *f*, mèirle *f*, braid *f*

thigh *n* sliasaid *f*, leis *f*

thimble *n* meuran *m*

thin *adj* **1** (*person*) caol, tana, seang; **2** (*substance*) lom, tana; **3** (*sparse*) tana, gann, lom

thin *v* (*crops etc*) tanaich *vt*

thing *n* rud *m*, nì *m*

think *v* **1** (*consider*) beachd-smaoin(t)ich *vi*, beachdaich *vi*, smaoin(t)ich *vi*, cnuas(aich) *vi*, meòraich *vi* (air); **2** (*believe*) creid *vi*, saoil *vi*, bi *vi irreg* den bheachd

thinking *n* **1** (*activity*) smaoin(t)eachadh *m*, beachdachadh *m*; **2** (*rationale*) feallsanachd *f*

think-tank *n* buidheann-beachdachaidh *mf*

thinning *adj* tana

third *n* trian *m*

third *n and num adj* treas

thirst *n* pathadh *m*, tart *m*, ìota(dh) *m*

thirsty *adj* pàiteach, tartmhor, ìotmhor

thirteen *n and num adj* trì-deug

thirty *n and num adj* deich ar fhichead, fichead 's a deich, trithead *m*

this, **these** *pron* seo

thistle *n* cluaran *m*, fòghnan *m*, gìogan *m*

thither *adv* **1** ann, a-null; **2** *in expr* **hither and** ~ thall 's a-bhos, a-null 's a nall

thong *n* iall *f*

thorax *n* cliabh *m*

thorn *n* **1** (*plant*) droigheann *m*; **2** (*prickle*) dealg *f*, bior *m*

thorny *adj* **1** droighneach; **2** (*tricky etc*) duilich. doirbh

thorough *adj* **1** (*person*) pongail, dìcheallach, dealasach; **2** (*job etc*) mionaideach; **3** (*utter*) dearg, gu c(h)ùl

thoroughfare *n* tro-shlighe *f*

though *adv* ge-tà

though *conj* ged

thought *n* **1** (*activity*) smaointeachadh *m*, beachdachadh *m*; **2** (*a*) smuain/smaoin *f*, beachd *m*, beachd-smuain *m*; **3** (*concern*) for *m*

thoughtful *adj* **1** (*pensive etc*) smuainteachail; **2** (*considerate*) tuigseach, suimeil

thousand *n and num adj* mìle *m*

thrash *v* slaic *vt*

thrashing *n* slaiceadh *m*

thrawn *adj* rag, dùr, rag-mhuinealach

thread *n* **1** (*single*) snàthainn *m*; **2** (*coll*) snàth *m*

threadbare *adj* lom

threat *n* maoidheadh *m*, bagairt *f*, bagradh *m*

threaten *v* maoidh *vi*, bagair *vi* (air)

three *n and num adj* **1** trì; **2** (*people*) triùir *mf*

threefold, **three-ply** *adj* trì-fillte

threesome *n* triùir *mf*

thresh *v* buail *vti*

threshold *n* stairsneach *f*

thrifty *adj* cùramach (a thaobh airgid), glèidhteach

thrill *n* gaoir *f*

thrill *v* cuir gaoir *f* (air)

thrilling *adj* gaoireil

thrive *v* soirbhich *vi*

throat *n* amha(i)ch *f*, sgòrnan *m*

throb *n* plosg *m*

throb *v* plosg *vi*, dèan plosgartaich

throbbing *n* plosgadh *m*, plosgartaich *f*

throne *n* rìgh-chathair *f*

throng *n* sluagh mòr, mòr-shluagh *m*

throng *v* rach ann an ceudan, ann am mìltean, ann an dròbh(an)

throttle *v* mùch *vt*, tachd *vt*

through *adv* **1** (*finished etc*) deiseil, ullamh, deas; **2** *in expr* ~ **and** ~ gu c(h)ùl

through *prep* tro

throw *n* tilgeadh *m*

throw *v* **1** tilg *vt*, caith *vt*; **2** *in exprs* ~ **up** tilg (suas) *vti*, dìobhair *vti*, sgeith *vti*, cuir *vti* a-mach

thrush *n* (*bird*) smeòrach *f*

thrust *n* **1** sàthadh *m*; **2** (*essence*) brìgh *f*, comhair *m*

thrust *v* sàth *vti*, spàrr *vt*

thumb *n* òrdag *f*

thump *n* buille *f*, buille-dùirn *f*

thump *v* dòrn *vt*, slaic *vt*

thunder *v* tàirneanaich *vi*

thunder *n* tàirneanach *m*

Thursday *n* Diardaoin *m*

thus *adv* air an dòigh seo, air an dòigh a leanas, mar seo

thwart *v* cuir bacadh, cuir stad (air)

tick[1] *n* (*marking etc*) strìochag *f*

tick[2] *n* diog *m*, tiota *m*

tick[3] *n* (*parasite*) mial *f*

ticket *n* tiogaid *f*, tigeard *f*

tickle *v* diogail *vti*

ticklish *adj* diogalach, ciogailteach

tide *n* seòl-mara *m*, làn-(mara) *m*, tìde-mhara *mf*

tidings *n* naidheachdan *fpl*, sgeul *m*, guth *m*

tidy *adj* **1** (*trim etc*) cuimir, grinn, sgiobalta, snasail, snasmhor; **2** (*neat*) sgiobalta, cunbhalach

tidy *v* sgioblaich *vt*, òrdaich *vt*, cuir *vt* an òrdugh, cuir *vt* air dòigh, rèitich *vt*

tie *n* **1** (*necktie*) taidh *f*; **2** (*bind*) ceangal *m*, bann *m*; **3** (*link*) dàimh *mf*, càirdeas *m*

tie *v* ceangail *vt*

tier *n* sreath *mf*

tight *adj* **1** teann; **2** (*scarce*) gann

tighten *v* teannaich *vti*

tightening *n* teannachadh *m*

tile *n* leac *f*

till *n* (*register*) cobhan(-airgid) *m*, (*checkout*) àite-pàighidh *m*

till *v* àitich *vt*, obraich *vt*

tiller *n* **1** (*boat*) failm *f*, ailm *f*; **2** (*agriculturalist*) fear-àitich *m*

tilt[1] *n* (*slant*) claonadh *m*, fiaradh *m*

tilt[2] *n*, *in expr* **at full** ~ nad (*etc*) dhian-ruith, aig peilear do (*etc*) bheatha

tilt *v* claon *vi*, aom *vi*, rach *vi* air fhiaradh

tilted, **tilting** *adjs* air fhiaradh

timber *n* fiodh *m*

time *n* **1** (*abstr*) tìm *f*; **2** (*clock*) uair *f*; **3** (*experienced*) tìde *f*, ùine *f*; **4** (*historical*) àm *m*, linn *mf*, rè *f*; **5** (*appointed*) àm *m*, tràth *m*; **6** (*period*) ùine *f*, greis *f*, treis *f*, tamall *m*; **7** (*occasion*) uair *f*, turas *m*; **8** *in exprs* **some** ~ uaireigin *adv*

timely, **timeous** *adj* mithich, an deagh àm, tràthail

timepiece *n* uaireadair *m*

times *adv* (*arith etc*) uiread *m*, air iomadachadh (le)

timescale *n* raon-ama *m*

timetable *n* clàr-tìde *m*, clàr-ama *m*

timid *adj* **1** (*shy*) diùid, nàrach, màlda; **2** (*nervous*) clisgeach; **3** (*fearful*) meata, gealtach

timidity *n* **1** (*shyness*) diùide *f*, nàire *f*; **2** (*fearfulness*) meatachd *f*, gealtachd *f*

tin *n* **1** (*metal*) staoin *f*; **2** (*can*) cana *m*, canastair *m*

tinge *n* **1** fiamh *m*, dath *m*; **2** (*complexion*) fiamh *m*, tuar *m*

tinker *n* ceàrd *m*

tinkle *v* dèan gliong, dèan gliongartaich

tinkling *n* gliong *m*, gliongartaich *f*

tint *n* **1** fiamh *m*, dath *m*; **2** (*complexion*) fiamh *m*, tuar *m*

tiny *adj* crìon, meanbh, mion

tip *n* (*end*) bàrr *m*

tippler *n* pòitear *m*, misgear *m*

tippling *n* pòitearachd *f*

tipsy *adj* air leth-mhisg

tiptoe *n* corra-biod *m*

tire *v* **1** sgìthich *vti*; **2** (*as vi*) fàs *vi* sgìth; **3** *in expr* ~ **out** claoidh *vt*

tired *adj & past part* **1** sgìth; **2** *in exprs* ~ **out** claoidhte

tiresome *adj* draghail, sàrachail

tissue *n* stuth *m*

title *n* tiotal *m*

tittle-tattle *n* goileam *m*, cabaireachd *f*

tizzy *n*, *in expr* **in a** ~ troimh-a-chèile, am breisleach

to *conj* gus, airson

to *prep* **1** gu & gus; **2** do; **3** (*directions*) mu; **4** (*needing to be done*) ri

toad *n* muile-mhàg *f*

toast[1] *n* (*drink*) deoch-slàinte *f*

toast[2] *n* (*bread etc*) tost *m*

tobacco *n* tombaca *m*

today *adv* an-diugh

toe *n* òrdag *f*, òrdag-choise *f*

together *adv* còmhla, le chèile

toil *n* saothair *f*, obair chruaidh

toil *v* saothraich *vi*, bi *vi irreg* ag obair gu cruaidh

toilet *n*, taigh-beag *m*, (*public*) goireasan *mpl*

tolerable *adj* meadhanach math

tolerably *adv* meadhanach math

tolerance *n* ceadachas *m*

tolerant *adj* ceadach

tolerate *v* fuiling *vt*, cuir *vi* suas (le/ri)

tomb *n* uaigh *f*, tuam *m*

tombstone *n* leac-uaighe *f*

tomcat *n* cat fireann *m*

ton *n* tunna *m*

tongs *n* (*pair*) clobha *m*

tongue *n* **1** teanga *f*; **2** (*language*) cànain *f*, cànan *m*

tonne *n* tunna *m*

too[1] *adv* (*also*) cuideachd, mar an ceudna

too[2] *adv* **1** (*excessively*) ro; **2** *in expr* ~ **much** cus, tuilleadh 's a' chòir

tool *n* inneal *m*, ball-acfhainn *m*

tooth *n* fiacail *f*

toothache *n* dèideadh *m*

toothbrush *n* bruis-fhiaclan *f*

toothed *adj* fiaclach

toothpaste *n* uachdar-fhiaclan *m*

toothy *adj* fiaclach

top *adj* **1** (*phys*) as àirde; **2** (*best*) prìomh

top *n* **1** bàrr *m*, mullach *m*, ceann *m* as àirde; **2** (*in exprs*) **on** ~ **of** air muin

top *v* (*beat*) thoir bàrr *m* (air)

topic *n* cuspair *m*

topography *n* cumadh-tìre *m*

topsy-turvy *adj* bun-os-cionn, troimh-a-chèile

torch *n* leus *m*, lòchran *m*

torment *n* dòrainn *f*, cràdh *m*

torment *v* cràidh *vt*, sàraich *vt*, pian *vt*

torrent *n* **1** (*watercourse etc*) bras-shruth *m*, dòrtadh *m*; **2** (*downpour*) dìle *f*, dìle bhàthte

torso *n* com *m*

tortuous *adj* lùbach

torture *n* cràdh *m*, pianadh *m*

torture *v* cuir *vt* an cràdh, ciùrr *vt*, cràidh *vt*, pian *vt*

Tory *adj* Tòraidheach

Tory *n* Tòraidh *m*

toss *n* **1** (*throw*) tilgeadh *m*; **2** *in expr* **I don't give a** ~ cha toir mi hòro-gheallaidh

toss *v* **1** (*as vi*) tulg *vi*, luaisg *vi*; **2** (*as vt*) tilg *vt*; **3** *in expr* ~ **a coin** cuir crainn

total *adj* **1** iomlan, uile-gu-lèir; **2** (*utter*) dearg, gu c(h)ùl

total *n* sùim *f*, iomlan *m*

totally *adv* gu tur, (gu) buileach, gu h-iomlan, uile-gu-lèir

touch *v* **1** (*phys*) bean *vi* (ri/do), làimhsich *vt*; **2** (*fig, have to do with etc*) bean *vi* (ri), buin *vi* (do/ri), gabh gnothach (ri); **3** (*emotionally*) gluais *vti*, drùidh *vt* (air); **4** *in expr* ~ **on** (*mention*) thoir iomradh, thoir tarraing (air)

touching *adj* (*affecting*) gluasadach, drùidhteach

touchy *adj* frionasach

tough *adj* **1** (*person*) cruaidh, fulangach, buan; **2** (*material etc*) righinn

toughen *v* rìghnich *vti*

toughness *n* **1** (*person*) cruas *m*, fulang *m*, fulangas *m*; **2** (*material etc*) rìghnead *m*

tour *n* cuairt *f*, turas *m*

tourism *n* turasachd *f*

tourist *n* neach-turais *m*

towards *prep* a dh'ionnsaigh, chun
towel *n* tubhailte *f*, searbhadair *m*
tower *n* tùr *m*, turaid *f*
town *n* baile *m*
toy *n* dèideag *f*
trace *n* lorg *f*, làrach *f*, sgeul *m*
trace *v* faigh lorg *f* (air), lorg *vt*
track *n* **1** (*path*) ceum *m*, frith-rathad *m*, ùtraid *f*; **2** (*abstr*) slighe *f*; **3** (*trace*) lorg *f*
track, track down *v* faigh lorg *f* (air)
tract *n* (*pamphlet etc*) tràchd *mf*
tractable *adj* soitheamh, socharach
tractor *n* tractar *m*
trade *n* **1** (*craft*) ceàird *f*; **2** (*exchange*) malairt *f*, ceannachd *f*
trade *v* dèan malairt *f*, malairtich *vi*
trader *n* neach-malairt *m*, marsanta *m*, ceannaiche *m*
tradesman *n* **1** (*practitioner of trade*) fear-ceàirde *m*; **2** (*retailer etc*) marsanta *m*, ceannaiche *m*
trading *n* ceannachd *f*, ceannach *m*, malairt *f*
tradition *n* dualchas *m*, dùthchas *m*
traditional *adj* traidiseanta, dualchasach
tradition-bearer *n* seanchaidh *m*
traffic *n* **1** (*transport*) trafaig *f*; **2** (*trade*) malairt (mhì-laghail) *f*
traffic *v* dèan malairt (mhì-laghail) *f*
tragic *adj* dòrainneach, mìcheanta
trail *n* (*trace*) lorg *f*
trailer *n* (*transport*) slaodair *m*
train *n* (*rail*) trèan(a) *f*
train *v* **1** (*sport etc*) trèan *vti*; **2** (*teach*) teagaisg *vt*, oileanaich *vt*
trained *adj* ionnsaichte, uidheamaichte
training *n* **1** (*sport etc*) trèanadh *m*; **2** (*ed*) teagasg *m*, oileanachadh *m*, uidheamachadh *m*
trait *n* (*character*) fea(i)rt *m*
traitor *n* brathadair *m*
trample *v* saltair *vt*
trance *n* neul *m*
tranquil *adj* ciùin, sàmhach, sìtheil, sèimh
tranquillity *n* ciùineas *m*, sàmhchair *f*, sìth *f*, fois *f*
tranquillizer *n* tàmhadair *m*
transact *v* dèan *vt*
transaction *n* (*business*) gnothach *m*
transgress *v* **1** ciontaich *vi*; **2** (*relig*) peacaich *vi*

transgression *n* **1** ciont(a) *m*; **2** (*relig*) peacachadh *m*, peacadh *m*
transient, transitory *adj* diombuan, siùbhlach
translate *v* eadar-theangaich *vti*
translation *n* eadar-theangachadh *m*
translator *n* eadar-theangair *m*
transmission *n* **1** (*broadcasting*) craobh-sgaoileadh *m*, craoladh *m*; **2** (*abstr*) iomain *f*
translucent *adj* trìd-shoillseach
transmit *v* craobh-sgaoil *vti*
transmitter *n* crann-sgaoilidh *m*
transparent *adj* trìd-shoilleir
transport *n* **1** (*general*) còmhdhail *f*; **2** (*con*) siubhal *m*; **3** (*carriage*) giùlan *m*, iomchar *m*
transport *v* giùlain *vt*, iomchair *vt*
trap *n* ribe *mf*
trap *v* rib *vt*, glac *vt*
trapped *adj & past part* glacte, an sàs
trappings *n* uidheam *f*, acainn *f*
trash *n* trealaich *f*, truileis *f*, sgudal *m*
travel *n* siubhal *m*
travel *v* siubhail *vi*, triall *vi*
traveller *n* neach-siubhail *m*
travelling *adj* siubhail
trawler *n* tràlair *m*
tray *n* sgàl *m*
treacherous *adj* **1** (*person*) foilleil, cealgach; **2** (*situation*) cunnartach, cugallach
treachery *n* brathadh *m*, cealgaireachd *f*, foill *f*
tread *v* (*grapes etc*) saltair *vt*
treason *n* brathadh *m*
treasure *n* ionmhas *m*, ulaidh *f*, tasgaidh *m*
treasurer *n* ionmhasair *m*
treasury *n* (*department*) roinn an ionmhais *f*
treat *n* cuirm *f*
treat *v* **1** (*handle*) làimhsich *vt*, gnàthaich *vt*, dèilig *vi* (ri); **2** (*med*) leighis *vt*
treatise *n* tràchd *mf*, tràchdas *m*
treatment *n* **1** (*behaving*) làimhseachadh *m*, gnàthachadh *m*; **2** (*med*) leigheas *m*
treaty *n* co-chòrdadh *m*, cunnradh *m*
treble *adj* trìbilte
tree *n* craobh *f*, crann *m*
tremble *n* crith *f*
tremble *v* bi *vi irreg* air chrith *f*, crith *vi*
trembling *adj* air chrith *f*

tremendous adj 1 (size) uabhasach mòr;
2 (quality) uabhasach (fhèin) math, taghta

tremor n crith f

trench n clais f, trainnse f

trend n aomadh m

trendy adj fasanta

trespass n (land) bris(t)eadh m chrìochan

trespass v 1 (land) bris(t) crìochan fpl;
2 (relig) peacaich vi, ciontaich vi

trespassing n (land) bris(t)eadh chrìochan

trews n triubhas m

tri(-) prefix trì(-)

trial n 1 dearbhadh m; 2 (ordeal)
deuchainn f

triangle n trì-cheàrnag f, triantan m

triangular adj trì-cheàrnach, triantanach

tribe n treubh f, cinneadh m, fine f

tribulation n trioblaid f, deuchainn f

tribute n moladh m

trick n 1 cleas m, car m; 2 in expr **that'll
do the ~!** nì sin an gnothach!, nì sin a'
chùis!

trick v meall vt, thoir an car à

trickle n sileadh (beag)

trickle v sil vi

trifling adj crìon, suarach

trilingual adj trì-chànanach

trim adj cuimir, sgiobalta, snasail,
snasmhor

trim n gleus mf

trip¹ n (journey) turas m, cuairt f, sgrìob f

trip² n (stumble) tuisleadh m

trip v 1 (stumble) tuislich vi; 2 (as vt) cuir
camacag air

tripartite adj trì-phàirteach

triple adj trì-fillte, trìbilte

triumph n buaidh f

triumphant adj buadhmhor

trivial adj 1 (empty) faoin, dìomhain;
2 (insignificant) crìon, suarach

troop n 1 (military etc) buidheann mf,
cuideachd f; 2 (actors) còmhlan m

Tropic of Cancer n Tropaig Chansar f

Tropic of Capricorn n Tropaig
Chapricorn f

tropical adj tropaigeach

trot n trotan m

trot v dèan trotan m

trotting n trotan m

trouble n 1 (inconvenience) dragh m;
2 (misfortune) trioblaid f, duilgheadasan
mpl, (droch) staing f, èiginn f; 3 (effort)

saothair f; 4 (disturbance) aimhreit f,
buaireas m

trouble v 1 (inconvenience) cuir dragh
(air), bodraig vt; 2 (harass) sàraich vt;
3 (disturb) buair vt

troubled adj 1 (anxious) fo iomagain, fo
chùram; 2 (vexed) air do (etc) shàrachadh;
3 (upset) air do (etc) bhuaireadh, air do
thàmailteachadh

troublesome adj draghail, buaireasach

trounce v 1 (thrash) slaic vt; 2 (defeat)
dèan an gnothach/a' chùis air

troupe n còmhlan m

trousers n briogais f, triubhas m

trout n breac m

truce n fosadh m

truck¹ n (transport) làraidh f

truck² n (dealings), **have ~** bean vi (ri),
buin vi (do/ri), gabh gnothach (ri)

true adj 1 (factual) fìor, fìrinneach;
2 (genuine) fìor; 3 (loyal) dìleas

truly adv fìor

trumpet n trombaid f

trunk n 1 (body) com m; 2 (proboscis)
sròn f; 3 (luggage) ciste f; 4 (tree) stoc m,
bun craoibhe m

trust n 1 earbsa f, creideas m; 2 (legal etc)
urras m

trust v 1 thoir creideas m (do), earb vti (à);
2 in expr **~ in** cuir earbsa (ann an)

trusting adj earbsach

trustworthy adj earbsach

trusty adj dìleas

truth n fìrinn f

truthful adj fìrinneach

try n (attempt) oidhirp f

try v 1 feuch vti (ri); 2 (test) cuir vt gu
deuchainn, dearbh vt; 3 (vex etc) cuir vt
gu deuchainn

trying adj (vexing etc) deuchainneach

tub n ballan m, tuba mf

tube n feadan m, pìob f

tuberculosis n a' chaitheamh f

tuck up v (garment) tru(i)s vt

Tuesday n Dimàirt m

tug n tarraing f

tug v tarraing vti

tuition n teagasg m, oideachas m

tumble n tuiteam m

tumble v 1 (as vi) tuit vi; 2 (as vt) leag vt

tumour n at m

tumult n ùpraid f, iorghail f, othail f

tumultuous *adj* ùpraideach, iorghaileach
tune *n* **1** (*melody*) port *m*, fonn *m*;
2 (*tuning*) gleus *mf*, **in** ~ air ghleus
tune *v* (*instrument etc*) gleus *vt*, cuir *vt* air
ghleus
tuned *adj & past part* air ghleus
tuneful *adj* ceòlmhor, fonnmhor, binn
tuning *n* (*pitch*) gleus *mf*, (*action*) cur *m*
air ghleus
tuning-fork *n* gobhal-gleusaidh *m*
tup *n* reithe *m*, rùda *m*
turbulence *n* **1** (*unruliness*) gairge
f, aimhreit *f*, buaireas *m*; **2** (*sea etc*)
luaisgeachd *f*, tulgadh *m*
turbulent *adj* **1** (*unruly*) garg,
aimhreiteach, buaireasach; **2** (*sea etc*)
luaisgeach, tulgach
turd *n* tudan/tùdan *m*
turf *n* **1** (*single*) fàl *m*, sgrath *f*, ceap *m*, ploc
m; **2** (*coll/individual*) fòid/fòd *f*
Turk *n* Turcach *m*
Turkey *n* An Tuirc *f*
turkey *n* eun-Frangach *m*, cearc-Fhrangach
f
Turkish *adj* Turcach
turn *n* **1** (*movement*) car *m*, tionndadh *m*;
2 (*stroll*) car *m*, cuairt *f*; **3** (*queue etc*)
cuairt *f*; **4** (*deviation*) tionndadh *m*; **5** *in*
expr **in** ~ mu seach, fear *m* mu seach, tè *f*
mu seach
turn *v* tionndaidh *vti*
turret *n* turaid *f*
tussle *n* tuasaid *f*
tut tut! *excl* ud, ud!
tweed *n* clò *m*, **Harris** ~ An Clò Mòr, An
Clò Hearach
tweezers *n* greimiche *m*
twelfth *num adj* dara-deug

twelve *n and num adj* d(h)à-dheug, dusan *m*
twentieth *n* ficheadamh
twentieth *num adj* ficheadamh
twenty *n and num adj* fichead *m*
twice *adv* **1** (*repetitions*) dà uair, dà thuras;
2 (*quantity*) ~ **as much** a dhà uiread
twig *v* (*understand*) tuig *vti*
twilight *n* eadar-sholas *m*, camhana(i)ch *f*,
morning ~ camhana(i)ch an latha,
bris(t)eadh *m* an latha, **evening** ~ ciaradh
m, camhana(i)ch na h-oidhche, duibhre *f*
twin *n* leth-aon *m*, leth-chàraid *f*
twine *v* toinn *vti*
twinkle *v* priob *vi*
twinkling *n* priobadh *m*
twist *n* car *m*, snìomh *m*, toinneamh *m*
twist *v* snìomh *vt*, dualaich *vt*, toinn *vti*
twisted *adj & past part* snìomhte, toinnte
twitter *v* ceilearaich *vi*
two *n and num adj* **1** a dhà, dà; **2** (*people*)
dithis *f*; **3** (*as prefix*) **two-** dà(-)
two-eyed *adj* dà-shùileach
two-legged *adj* dà-chasach
twosome *n* dithis *f*
two-tier *adj* dà-shreathach
type[1] *n* (*kind*) seòrsa *m*, gnè *f*
type[2] *n* (*print*) clò *m*
type *v* clò-sgrìobh *vti*
typed *adj & past part* clò-sgrìobhte
typescript *n* clò-sgrìobhainn *f*
typewriter *n* clò-sgrìobhadair *m*
typical *adj* **1** (*representative*) samhlachail,
àbhaisteach; **2** (*characteristic*) dual(t)ach
typist *n* clò-sgrìobhaiche *m*
tyrannical *adj* aintighearnail
tyranny *n* aintighearnas *m*
tyrant *n* aintighearna *m*
tyre *n* taidhr *f*

U

udder *n* ùth *m*
ugliness *n* gràndachd *f*
ugly *adj* grànda
uileann pipes *n* pìob-uilne *f*
ulcer *n* neasgaid *f*
ultimate *adj* **1** (*final*) deireannach, mu
dheireadh; **2** (*best*), brod *m*, gun samhail,
gun choimeas, barraichte *adj*
ultimately *adv* aig a' cheann thall
umbilical *adj* imleagach
umbilicus *n* imleag *f*
umbrage *n*, (*idiom*) **take ~ at** gabh anns
an t-sròin
umbrella *n* sgàilean-uisge *m*
un(-) *prefix* **1** eu- *prefix*; **2** mì- *prefix*;
3 neo- *prefix*; **4** ain- *prefix*; **5** ana- *prefix*;
6 gun; **7** do- *prefix*
unable *adj* eu-comasach
unaccustomed *adj* neo-chleachdte
unadventurous *adj* lagchuiseach
unanimity *n* aon-inntinn *f*
unanimous *adj* aon-inntinneach, aon-
ghuthach, aon-toileach
unasked *adj* gun iarraidh
unassuming *adj* iriosal/iriseil
unattainable *adj* do-ruigsinn
unavoidable *adj* do-sheachanta
unceasing *adj*, unceasingly *adv* gun sgur
uncertain *adj* mì-chinnteach
uncertainty *n* teagamh *m*, mì-chinnt *f*
uncivil *adj* mì-shìobhalta
uncle *n* bràthair-màthar *m*, bràthair-athar
m
unclothed *adj* lomnochd, rùisgte, lom
uncommon *adj* neo-chumanta, tearc
unconcerned *adj* (*indifferent etc*) coma
unconditional *adj* gun chumhachan
unconscious *adj* gun mhothachadh
uncountable *adj* do-àireamh
uncouth *adj* borb, garbh, gràisgeil
uncouthness *n* gràisgealachd *f*
uncultivated *adj* fàs, bàn
undecided *adj* & *past part* ann an iomadh-
chomhairle, eadar-dhà-lionn
under(-) *prefix* **1** (*lower*) fo-;
2 (*subordinate*) fo-, iar-
under *prep* **1** fo; **2** (*adv*) fodha

under-clerk iar-chlèireach *m*
underclothes *npl* fo-aodach *m*
underdeveloped *adj* dì-leasaichte
under-gamekeeper iar-gheamair *m*
undergo *v* fuiling *vt*
undergraduate *n* fo-cheumnaiche *m*
underground *adj* fo-thalamh
undergrowth *n* fo-fhàs *m*
underhand *adj* cealgach, os ìosal/os ìseal
underline *v* **1** cuir loidhne fo;
2 (*emphasise*) comharraich *vt*, leig
cudrom air, daingnich *vt*
underling *n* ìochdaran *m*
underpants *n* drathais/drathars *f*
underpass *n* fo-rathad *m*, fo-shlighe *f*
understand *v* tuig *vti*, lean *vti*
understanding *adj* tuigseach, mothachail
understanding *n* **1** (*faculty*) tuigse *f*;
2 (*intelligence*) ciall *f*, toinisg *f*, tùr *m*;
2 (*guarantee*) geall *vi*
undertaker *n* neach-adhlacaidh *m*
undertaking *n* **1** (*project etc*) gnothach *m*;
2 (*assurance etc*) gealladh *m*
underwear *n* fo-aodach *m*
undo *v* **1** neo-dhèan *vt*; **2** (*untie etc*)
fuasgail *vt*, lasaich *vt*
undoubtedly *adv* gun teagamh
undress *v* **1** (*as vt*) rùisg *vt*; **2** (*as vi*) cuir
dhìot do chuid aodaich
undressed *adj* lomnochd, rùisgte
unease *n* an-shocair *f*, imcheist *f*
uneasy *adj* anshocrach, an-fhoiseil, fo
imcheist
unemployed *adj* gun obair, gun chosnadh
unemployment *n* cion-cosnaidh *m*
unenterprising *adj* lagchuiseach
unequal *adj* neo-ionann
unexpected *adj*, unexpectedly *adv*, gun
dùil ri, gun sùil ri, gun fhiosta
unfair *adj* mì-chothromach
unfairness *n* ana-cothrom *m*, mì-
chothrom *m*
unfaithful *adj* neo-dhìleas
unfamiliar *adj* coimheach
unfashionable *adj* neo-fhasanta
unfavourable *adj* neo-fhàbharach
unfeeling *adj* fuar, neo-mhothachail

unfeigned *adj* fìor, neo-chealgach

unfit *adj* (*health*) euslainteach, anfhann

unfold *v* sgaoil *vti*, fosgail *vti*

unforeseen *adj* gun dùil, gun sùil

unfortunate *adj* mì-fhortanach, mì-shealbhach

unfounded *adj* (*claim etc*) gun bhunait

unfriendly *adj* neo-chàirdeil

unfruitful *adj* neo-tharbhach, neo-thorrach

unfurl *v* sgaoil *vti*, fosgail *vti*

ungainly *adj* cearbach

ungodly *adj* neo-dhiadhaidh

ungovernable *adj* do-riaghlaidh

ungrateful *adj* mì-thaingeil, mì-bhuidheach

unhappiness *n* mì-shonas *m*

unhappy *adj* mì-shona, mì-thoilichte

unhealthy *adj* **1** (*in poor health*) tinn, euslainteach, anfhann; **2** (*bad for health*) mì-fhallain, dona dhut (*etc*)

unholy *adj* mì-naomh

unhurt *adj* slàn

unification *n* co-aonachadh *m*

unified *adj* & *past part* (co-)aonaichte

uniform *adj* cunbhalach, aon-fhillte

uniform *n* èideadh *m*, deise *f*

unify *v* co-aonaich *vt*

unilateral *adj* aon-taobhach

unimportant *adj* gun chudrom, gun bhrìgh, neo-chudromach

uninjured *adj* slàn

unintelligent *adj* neo-thoinisgeil

unintelligible *adj* do-thuigsinn

uninteresting *adj* liosta, tioram, neo-inntinneach

uninterrupted *adj* gun stad, gun sgur, leanailteach, leantainneach

uninvited *adj* & *adv* gun iarraidh

union *n* aonadh *m*

unique *adj* gun samhail, gun seis(e), air leth

unit *n* aonad *m*

unitary *adj* aonadach *m*

unite *v* **1** (*join*) ceangail *vt*, co-cheangail *vt*, aonaich *vti*; **2** (*cooperate*) thig *vi* còmhla

united *adj* & *past part* aonaichte, **the United Nations** Na Dùthchannan Aonaichte, **the United States** Na Stàitean Aonaichte

unity *n* aonachd *f*

universal *adj* (*common*) coitcheann, uile-choitcheann

universe *n* an domhan *m*, an cruinne-cè *mf*, A' Chruitheachd *f*

university *n* oilthigh *m*

unjust *adj* mì-cheart, ana-ceart

unkempt *adj* luideach, cearbach, robach

unkind *adj* neo-choibhneil

unkindness *n* neo-choibhneas *m*

unknowable *adj* do-aithnichte

unknown *adj* **1** neo-aithnichte; **2** *in exprs* ~ **to** (*ie without someone's knowledge*) gun fhios do

unlawful *adj* mì-laghail

unless *conj* ach, mur(a)

unlicensed *adj* gun cheadachd

unlike, unlikely *adj* eu-coltach

unlimited *adj* neo-chrìochnach

unload *v* falmhaich *vt*, aotromaich *vt*

unlucky *adj* mì-shealbhach, mì-fhortanach

unmanageable *adj* do-stiùiridh, do-cheannsachaidh

unmanly *adj* neo-fhearail

unnecessary *adj* neo-riatanach

unobtrusive *adj* neo-fhollaiseach

unoccupied *adj* **1** (*land etc*) fàs, falamh; **2** (*person*) nad (*etc*) thàmh, dìomhain

unofficial *adj* neo-oifigeil

unpaid *adj* **1** (*bill etc*) neo-dhìolta; **2** (*worker etc*) gun phàigheadh, gun tuarastal

unparalleled *adj* gun choimeas

unpleasant *adj* mì-thaitneach, mì-chàilear

unpolluted *adj* neo-thruaillidh

unprepared *adj* neo-ullamh, gun ullachadh

unproductive *adj* neo-tharbhach

unprofitable *adj* neo-bhuannachdail, neo-tharbhach

unprotected *adj* neo-thèarainte

unrecognised *adj* neo-aithnichte

unreasonable *adj* mì-reusanta

unreliable *adj* neo-earbsach, cugallach

unresolved *adj* gun fhuasgladh

unripe *adj* an-abaich

unrivalled *adj* gun seis(e), gun choimeas

unruliness *n* gairge *f*, aimhreit *f*, buaireas *m*

unruly *adj* garg, aimhreiteach, buaireasach, ùpraideach

unsafe *adj* mì-shàbhailte

unsaleable *adj* do-reicte**

unsavoury adj 1 (*lit*) mì-bhlasta; 2 (*in bad taste etc*) mì-chiatach
unselfish adj neo-fhèineil
unsettled adj neo-shuidhichte
unsheathe v rùisg vt
unskilled adj neo-ealanta, neo-uidheamaichte
unsociable adj neo-chuideachdail
unsolved adj gun fhuasgladh
unsound adj 1 (*health*) neo-fhallain; 2 (*unreliable*) neo-earbsach
unsparingly adv gun chaomhnadh
unspeakable adj do-labhairt
unstable adj neo-sheasmhach, critheanach, cugallach
unsteady adj critheanach, cugallach, tulgach
unsuitable adj mì-fhreagarrach, neo-iomchaidh
untidy adj mì-sgiobalta, troimh-a-chèile, cearbach, luideach, robach
untie v fuasgail vt
until conj gus
until prep 1 gu/gus; 2 (*up ~*) gu ruige
untimely adj neo-thràthail
untruth n breug f
untruthful adj breugach
unusual adj 1 neo-àbhaisteach, neo-chumanta; 2 (*novel*) annasach
unwell adj tinn, bochd
unwilling adj leisg, aindeonach
unwillingly adv an aghaidh do (*etc*) thoil
up adv & prep 1 (*position*) shuas; 2 (*to*) suas; 3 (*from*) a-nìos
up to prep (*movement/time*) chun
upkeep n 1 cumail suas f; 2 (*livestock etc*) beathachadh m
uphill adv ris a' bhruthaich
uphold v cùm vt suas
upland n aonach m, monadh m, bràigh m, uachdar m
uplifting adj brosnachail, a thogas an cridhe
upon prep 1 air; 2 (*in addition to*) thar
upper adj uachdrach
upright adj dìreach, onarach, ceart, ionraic
uproar n ùpraid f, gleadhar m, othail f, iorghail f
uproarious adj ùpraideach

upset v 1 (*overturn*) leag vt, cuir vt bun-os-cionn; 2 (*disarray*) cuir vt troimh-a-chèile; 3 (*disturb*) buair vt, cuir vt troimh-a-chèile
upsetting adj buaireasach, frionasach
upside down adj bun-os-cionn
upstairs adv 1 (*motion*) suas an staidhre ; 2 (*position*) shuas an staidhre
upstream adv (*motion*) ris an t-sruth
up-to-date adj ùr-nodha
upturn n (*improvement*) car math m
urban adj bailteil
urbane adj suairc(e)
urbanity n suairceas m
urge v 1 (*incite*) cuir ìmpidh air, spreig vt, stuig vt, coitich vt; 2 ~ **on** (*encourage*) brosnaich vt, piobraich vt, greas vt, iomain vt
urgency n deifir f, cabhag f
urgent adj deifireach, cabhagach
urging n impidh m & ìmpidh f, spreigeadh m
urinate v dèan mùn m, mùin vi
urination n mùn m, dèanamh mùin m
urine n mùn m, fual m
usage n cleachdadh m, àbhaist f, nòs m, gnàth(s) m
use n 1 (*utilisation*) feum m; 2 (*value*) feum m, math m
use v 1 cleachd vt, dèan feum de; 2 (*situation*) cleachd vi
used adj & past part cleachdte
useful adj feumail
useless adj gun fheum
user n neach-cleachdaidh m
usual adj àbhaisteach, cumanta, gnàthach
usually adv mar as trice, an cumantas, am bitheantas
uterus n machlag f
utilise v cleachd vt, cuir vt gu feum, dèan feum de
utility n 1 (*abstr*) feum m, feumalachd f; 2 (*con*) seirbheis f
utter adj dearg, gu c(h)ùl
utter v abair vt irreg, can vt def, cuir vt an cèill
utterly adv gu tur, gu h-iomlan, gu buileach, uile-gu-lèir, air fad
u-turn n car iomlan m
uvula n cìoch an t-slugain f

V

vacancy *n* dreuchd *f*/àite *m* ri lìonadh
vacant *adj* 1 (*site*) falamh, bàn; 2 (*post etc*)
  ri lìonadh
vacuous *adj* faoin
vacuum *n* fal(a)mhachd *f*
vagina *n* faighean *m*, pit *f*
vague *adj* (*imprecise*) neo-phongail,
  (*unclear*) neo-shoilleir
vain *adj* 1 (*futile*) faoin, dìomhain;
  2 (*conceited*) mòr asad fhèin,
  mòrchuiseach
valid *adj* èifeachdach, tàbhachdach
validate *v* dearbh *vt*
valley *n* gleann *m*
valour *n* gaisge *f*, gaisgeachd *f*
valuable *adj* luachmhor, prìseil
valuation *n* luachachadh *m*, meas *m*
value *n* luach *m*, fiach *m*, fiù *m*
value *v* 1 (*estimate*) luachaich *vt*, meas *vt*;
  2 (*prize*) cuir luach air
valued *adj* measail
valueless *adj* gun fhiù, gun luach
valve *n* cìochag *f*
vandal *n* milltear *m*
vanguard *n* toiseach *m*
vanity *n* 1 (*futility*) faoineas *m*, dìomhanas
  m; 2 (*conceit*) mòrchuis *f*
vapour *n* deatach *f*, smùid *f*
variable *adj* caochlaideach
variation *n* atharrachadh *m*
variety *n* 1 (*abstr*) caochladh *m*; 2 (*sort*)
  seòrsa *m*, gnè *f*
various *adj* caochladh *m*
varnish *n* falaid *m*
varnish *v* falaidich *vt*
vary *v* atharraich *vti*
vat *n* dabhach *f*
vault *n* (*architecture etc*) crùisle *m*,
  (*underground*) seilear-làir *m*, (*arched*)
  druim-bogha *m*
veal *n* laoigh-fheòil *f*
veer *v* claon *vi*
vegetable, vegetables *n* glasraich *f*
vehemence *n* dèineas *m*
vehement *adj* dian
vehicle *n* carbad *m*
vein *n* cuisle *f*, fèith *f*

velocity *n* luaths *m*, astar *m*
velvet *n* meileabhaid *f*
vendor *n* reiceadair *m*
venerable *adj* urramach
vengeance *n* dìoghaltas *m*
vennel *n* caol-shràid *f*
venom *n* nimh/neimh *m*, puinnsean *m*
venomous *adj* nimheil, puinnseanach,
  puinnseanta
venture *n* iomairt *f*
verb *n* gnìomhair *m*
verbal *adj* beòil
verbatim *adj & adv* facal air an fhacal
verbose *adj* faclach, briathrach
verdict *n* breith *f*
verge *n* 1 oir *f*, iomall *m*, crìoch *f*;
  2 (*roadside*) fàl *f*
verify *v* dearbh *vt*
vernacular *n* cainnt (na) dùthcha *f*, cainnt
  dhùthchasach *f*
vernacular *adj* dùthchasach
versatile *adj* iol-chomasach
versatility *n* iol-chomas *m*
verse *n* bàrdachd *f*, rann *m*, dànachd *f*
versification *n* rannaigheachd *f*
vertical *adj* dìreach
very *adv* 1 glè, fìor, ro; 2 cianail fhèin,
  uabhasach fhèin; 3 (*identical*) dearbh,
  ceart, ceudna, fhèin; 4 (*even*) fhèin
vessel *n* 1 (*sailing*) soitheach *m*, long *f*, bàta
  m; 2 (*dish*) soitheach *m*
vest *n* fo-lèine *f*, peitean *m*
vestige *n* lorg *f*
vet *n* bheat *m*, lighiche-bheathaichean *m*,
  lighiche-sprèidh *m*
vet *v* sgrùd *vt*
veto *n* bhìoto *m*
veto *v* dèan bhìoto air
vex *v* sàraich *vt*, claoidh *vt*, farranaich *vt*
vexing *adj* frionasach, leamh
vice¹ *n* 1 (*wickedness*) aingidheachd *f*;
  2 (*trait*) droch-ghnàths *m*, droch-bheus *f*,
  droch-bheart *f*
vice² *n* (*clamp*) teanchair/teannachair *m*
vice- *prefix* iar-
vice versa *adv*, (and) ~ agus a chaochladh

vicious *adj* 1 aingidh; 2 (*hurtful etc*) guineach, nimheil; 3 (*phys*) brùideil
victim *n* 1 (*accident*) leòinteach *m*; 2 (*injustice etc*) fulangaiche *m*
victor *n* buadhaiche *m*, buadhair *m*
victory *n* buaidh *f*
video *n* bhidio *mf*
view *n* 1 (*scenery*) sealladh *m*, sealladh-dùthcha *m* ; 2 (*vision*) fradharc, sealladh *m*, fianais *f*; 3 (*opinion*) beachd *m*
viewer *n* (*TV etc*) neach-coimhid *m*
vigilance *n* furachas *m*
vigilant *adj* furachail
vigorous *adj* lùthmhor, brìoghmhor, sgairteil
vigour *n* 1 (*phys*) lùth & lùths *m*, neart *m*, sgairt *f*; 2 (*intellectual*) sgairt *f*
vile *adj* 1 (*disgusting etc*) gràineil, grànda; 2 (*abject*) dìblidh
vilify *v* màb *vt*, dubh-chàin *vt*
vine *n* crann-fìona *m*, fìonan *m*
vinegar *n* fìon-geur *m*
violence *n* fòirneart *m*, ainneart *m*
violent *adj* brùideil, fòirneartach
violin *n* fidheall *f*
violinist *n* fìdhlear *m*
viper *n* nathair-nimhe *f*
virgin *n* òigh *f*, ainnir *f*, maighdeann *f*
virginal *adj* òigheil
virginity *n* maighdeannas *m*
virility *n* fearachas *m*
virtue *n* 1 (*conduct*) subhailc *f*, deagh-bheus *f*; 2 (*value*) brìgh *f*; 3 *in expr* **by ~ of** do bhrìgh, air sgàth, a chionn
virtuous *adj* (*conduct*) subhailceach, deagh-bheusach
virulent *adj* nimheil
visible *adj* ri f(h)aicinn, ris, faicsinneach, lèirsinneach
vision *n* 1 (*eyesight*) fradharc *m*, lèirsinn *f*; 2 (*foresight etc*) lèirsinn *f*; 3 (*dream etc*) aisling *f*
visit *n* 1 (*to person*) tadhal *m*, cèilidh *mf*, **pay X a ~** dèan cèilidh air X, *also* tadhail *vi* air; 2 (*to place*) turas *m*, sgrìob *f*
visit *v* 1 (*people*) tadhail *vi*, rach *vi* a chèilidh, rach air chèilidh air; 2 (*places*) rach *vi* air turas gu
visitor *n* 1 neach-tadhail *m*; 2 (*holidaymaker etc*) neach-turais *m*

vital *adj* 1 (*lively etc*) beothail, brìoghmhor, lùthmhor; 2 *in expr* **~ spark** rong *f*; 3 (*indispensable*) riatanach, deatamach, ro chudromach
vitality *n* beothalachd *f*
vivacious *adj* beothail, meanmnach
vivacity *n* beothalachd *f*, meanmna *m*
vocabulary *n* 1 (*abstr*) faclan *mpl*, briathran *mpl*; 2 (*con*) faclair *m*, briathrachan *m*
vocation *n* 1 (*calling*) gairm *f*; 2 (*occupation*) dreuchd *f*
vocational *adj* dreuchdail
vocative *adj* gairmeach
voice *n* guth *m*
voice *v* cuir *vt* an cèill
void *n* fal(a)mhachd *f*, fànas *m*, fàsalachd *f*
volatile *adj* caochlaideach
volcanic *adj*, bholcànach
volcano *n* bholcàno *m*, beinn-theine *f*
volume[1] *n* 1 (*capacity*) tomhas-lìonaidh *m*; 2 (*loudness*) àirde-fuaime *f*
volume[2] (*book*) leabhar *m*
voluntary *adj* saor-thoileach
volunteer *n* saor-thoileach *m*
vomit *n* dìobhairt *mf*
vomit *v* dìobhair *vti*, sgeith *vti*, cuir *vti* a-mach
vomiting *n* dìobhairt *mf*, sgeith *m*
voracious *adj* craosach, geòcach, gionach
vote *n* bhòt(a) *f*
vote *v* bhòt *vi*
voter *n* neach-bhòtaidh *m*
voting *n* bhòtadh *m*
vouch *v* rach *vi* an urras
voucher *n* cùpon *m*
vow *n* gealladh *m*, bòid *f*
vow *v* geall *vti*, thoir gealladh, gabh bòid, bòidich *vi*
vowel *n* fuaimreag *f*
voyage *n* turas-mara *m*, bhòids(e) *f*
vulgar *adj* 1 (*uncouth etc*) gràisgeil, garbh, borb; 2 (*indecent*) draosta, drabasta; 3 (*common*) coitcheann, cumanta
vulgarity *n* 1 (*uncouthness*) gràisgealachd *f*; 2 (*indecency*) draostachd *f*, drabastachd *f*
vulnerable *adj* so-leònte
vulva pit *f*

W

wafer *n* (*food*) sliseag *f*; **2** (*relig*) abhlan *m*

wag *v* **1** (*as vi*) bog *vi*; **2** (*as vt*) crath *vt*

wage, wages *n* tuarastal *m*, pàigheadh *m*, duais *f*, cosnadh *m*

wage *v* dèan *vt*

wager *n* geall *m*

wager *v* cuir geall; rach *vi irreg* an urras

wail *v* caoin *vi*, guil *vi*

waist *n* meadhan *m*

waistcoat *n* peitean *m*

wait *v* **1** fuirich *vi*, feith *vi* (ri); **2** (*serve*) fritheil *vi* (air)

waiter *n* gille-frithealaidh *m*

waiting list *n* liosta-feitheimh *f*

waitress *n* caileag-fhrithealaidh *f*

wake, waken *v* **1** dùisg *vti*; **2** *in excl* ~ **up!** dùisg!/dùisgibh!

wakened *adj & past part* na do dhùisg, na do (*etc*) dhùsgadh

Wales *n* A' Chuimrigh *f*

walk *n* cuairt *f*

walk *v* coisich *vi*, rach *vi irreg* de chois

walker *n* coisiche *m*

walking *n* coiseachd *f*

wall *n* **1** (*fortified*) mùr *m*; **2** balla *m*; **3** (*freestanding*) gàrradh *m*

wallpaper *n* pàipear-balla *m*

walnut *n* **1** cnò Fhrangach *f*, gall-chnò *f*

walrus *n* each-mara *m*

wan *adj* glaisneulach

wand *n* slat *f*, slatag *f*

wander *v* **1** (*travel*) rach *vi irreg* air fhuadan, bi *vi irreg* air fhuadan, rach/ bi air allaban; **2** (*stray*) rach *vi irreg* air seachran, rach *vi* air iomrall

wandering *adj* **1** (*astray*) air iomrall, air seachran; **2** (*exiled*) air fhuadan, air allaban

wandering *n* **1** (*astray*) seachran *m*, iomrall *m*; **2** (*exiled*) fuadan *m*, allaban *m*

want *n* **1** (*lack*) dìth *m*, cion *m*, uireasbhaidh *f*, easbhaidh *f*; **2** (*poverty*) bochdainn *f*, ainnis *f*

want *v* **1** (*require*) iarr *vt*, bi *vi* airson; **2** (*require*) sir *vt*; **3** (**what do you ~?**) dè tha a dhìth *m* oirbh?; **4** (*lack*) bi *vi irreg*

a dhìth, bi a dh'easbhaidh (air); **5** (*wish*) togair *vi*

wanting *adj* a dhìth, a dh'easbhaidh, easbhaidheach

war *n* cogadh *m*

warble *v* ceileir *vi*

warcry *n* gairm-cogaidh *f*, sluagh-ghairm *f*

wardrobe *n* preas-aodaich *m*

warehouse *n* batharnach *m*

wares *n* bathar *m*

warfare *n* cogadh *m*

warlike *adj* cathach, cogach

warm *adj* **1** (*weather etc*) blàth; **2** (*people etc*) blàth, cridheil, càirdeil

warm *v* teasaich *vt*, teòth *vt*, blàthaich *vt*

warm-hearted *adj* blàth-chridheach

warming *n* teasachadh *m*, blàthachadh *m*, teòthadh *m*

warmth *n* **1** blàths *m*; **2** (*people etc*) blàths *m*, cridhealas *m*

warn *v* thoir rabhadh do, earalaich *vt*

warning *n* rabhadh *m*, earalachadh *m*

warrant *n* bar(r)antas *m*

warranty *n* bar(r)antas *m*, urras *m*

warrior *n* fear-cogaidh *m*, gaisgeach *m*, laoch *m*, curaidh *m*

warship *n* long-chogaidh *f*

wart *n* foinne *m*

wary *adj* **1** (*alert*) faiceallach, cùramach; **2** (*mistrustful*) amharasach, teagmhach

wash *v* nigh *vt*, ionnlaid *vt*

washbasin *n* mias-ionnlaid *f*

washer[1] *n* (*ring*) cearclan *m*

washer[2] *n* (*machine*) nigheadair *m*

washing *n* (*abstr*) nighe *m*, ionnlad *m*, (*con*) nigheadaireachd *f*

washing-machine *n* nigheadair *m*, inneal-nigheadaireachd *m*

wasp *n* speach *f*

waste *adj* fàs

waste *n* **1** call *m*, cosg *m*; **2** (*refuse*) sgudal *m*

waste *v* caith *vt*, cosg *vt*, struidh *vt*

wasteful *adj* caith(t)each, struidheil

waster *n* struidhear *m*

watch[1] *n* **1** (*abstr*) faire *f*, caithris *f*; **2** (*con*) luchd-faire *m*, freiceadan *m*

watch[2] *n* (*timepiece*) uaireadair *m*
watch *v* coimhead *vt*
watcher *n* neach-coimhid *m*
watchful *adj* furachail
watchfulness *n* furachas *m*
watchman *n* fear-faire *m*, fear-coimhid *m*
water *n* uisge *m*, bùrn *m*
water *v* uisgich *vt*
waterfall *n* eas *m*, leum-uisge *m*, linne *f*, spùt *m*
waterfowl *n* & *npl* eun-uisge *m*
watering can *n* peile-frasaidh *m*
waterproof *adj* dìonach, uisge-dhìonach
watershed *n* **1** (*topog*) druim-uisge *m*; **2** (*defining stage etc*) sgarachdainn *f*
watertight *adj* (*house etc*) uisge-dhìonach
waterway *n* slighe-uisge *f*
watery *adj* uisgeach
waulk *v* luaidh *vti*
waulking *n* luadhadh *m*
wave *n* (*sea etc*) tonn *mf*
wave *v* **1** (*oscillate etc*) luaisg *vi*, tulg *vi*; **2** (*signal*) smèid *vi*, crath do làmh(an)
wax *n* cèir *f*
waxen, waxy *adj* cèireach
way *n* **1** (*road*) rathad *m*, slighe *f*; **2** (*direction*) taobh *m*, rathad *m*; **3** (*distance*) astar *m*; **4** (*method*) dòigh *f*, modh *mf*, seòl *m*; **5** (*custom etc*) dòigh *f*; **6** *in exprs* ~ **out** (*escape*) dol-às *m*
weak *adj* **1** (*phys*) lag, (*faint*) fann, lapach; **2** (*emotionally*) bog, meata, maoth, gun smior
weaken *v* lagaich *vti*, fannaich *vti*
weakening *n* lagachadh *m*, fàillinn *f*
weak-minded *adj* lag nad (*etc*) inntinn
weakness *n* laigse *f*
wealth *n* beartas/beairteas *m*, saidhbhreas *m*, ionmhas *m*, stòras *m*, maoin *f*
wealthy *adj* beartach/beairteach, saidhbhir
weapon *n* ball-airm *m*
wear *n* **1** (*abstr*) caitheamh *f*; **2** (*con*) aodach *m*
wear *v* (*clothes*) cuir *vt* ort/umad
wear out *v* **1** (*clothing etc*) caith *vt*; **2** (*exhaust*) claoidh *vt*, sgìthich *vt*
weariness *n* **1** (*fatigue*) sgìths *f*, claoidheadh *m*, claoidh *f*; **2** (*tedium etc*) fadachd *f*, fadal *m*
weary *adj* **1** (*fatigued*) sgìth, claoidhte, (*stressed*) sàraichte; **2** (*wearisome*) cian
weary *v* claoidh *vt*, sgìthich *vt*, sàraich *vt*
wearying *adj* sgìtheil

weasel *n* neas (bheag) *f*
weather *n* aimsir *f*, sìde/tìde *f*
weathercock *n* coileach-gaoithe *m*
weave *v* figh *vti*
weaver *n* breabadair *m*, figheadair *m*
weaving *n* fighe *mf*, breabadaireachd *f*
web *n* lìon *m*
wed *adj* & *past part* pòsta
wedder *n* mult/molt *m*
wedding *n* banais *f*
wedge *n* geinn *m*
wedlock *n* pòsadh *m*
Wednesday *n* Diciadain
wee *adj* **1** beag; **2** *in expr* **a** ~ **bit** (*adv*) caran *m*, rud beag *m*
weed *n* luibh *mf*, lus *m*
week *n* seachdain *f*
weekend *n* deireadh-seachdain *m*
weekly *adj* seachdaineach, seachdaineil, (*adv*) a h-uile seachdain
weep *v* caoin *vi*, guil *vi*, gail *vi*, ràn *vi*
weeping *n* caoineadh *m*, gul *m*, gal *m*, rànail *m*, rànaich *f*
weigh *v* **1** (*as vt*) cothromaich *vt*, cuideamaich *vt*; **2** (*mentally*) ~ **(up)** beachdaich *vi*, gabh beachd air
weight *n* cudrom *m*
weighty *adj* cudromach, trom
weir *n* cairidh/caraidh *f*
weird *adj* neònach
welcome *adj* **1** (*as excl*) ~! fàilte *f* oirbh/ort!; **2 you're** ~ is/'s e do bheatha *f*, is/'s e ur beatha
welcome *n* fàilte *f*, gabhail *mf*
welcome *v* cuir fàilte air, fàiltich *vt*
welcoming *adj* fàilteachail, fàilteach
weld *v* tàth *vt*
welfare *n* **1** (*circumstances*) cor *m*; **2** (*benefits etc*) sochair *f*
well *adj* gu math, fallain, slàn
well *adv* **1** gu math; **2** (*passive*) air *plus* deagh *adv*; **3** (*exprs*) ~ **done!** math thu fhèin!, nach math a rinn thu!, ~ **off** glè mhath dheth
well *n* tobar *mf*, fuaran *m*
well-behaved *adj* beusach, modhail, sìobhalta
wellbeing *n* (*circumstances}* cor *m*, math *m*
well(-)built *adj* **1** (*sturdy etc*) tomadach, tapaidh, calma; **2** (*building etc*) air a dheagh thogail
well-informed *adj* fiosrach

wellington (boot) n bòtann mf
well-known adj ainmeil, (persons) iomraiteach
well-liked adj mòr-thaitneach, mòr-chòrdte
well-mannered adj modhail
well-ordered adj dòigheil, òrdail, riaghailteach
well-timed adj an deagh àm m
Welsh adj Cuimreach
Welshman n Cuimreach m
west adj siar adj, an iar
west adv an iar f
west n iar f, (point) an àird an iar f, (location) an taobh an iar, an taobh siar
westerly adj 1 (from) on iar f; 2 (towards) (chun) an iar
western adj siar adj, an iar adv
West Indies (the) npl Na h-Innseachan an Iar fpl
westward(s) adv an iar, chun an iar, chun na h-àirde an iar
wet adj fliuch
wet v 1 fliuch vt; 2 in expr **wet yourself** caill do mhùn
wether n mult/molt m
whale n muc-mhara f
what inter pron dè
what rel pron na
whatever pron 1 (possibility) ge b' e; 2 (object) càil sam bith f, rud sam bith m, nì sam bith m; 3 (emph for **what**) dè fon ghrèin, dè air an t-saoghal
wheat n cruithneachd m
wheel n cuibhle f, roth mf
wheelchair n cathair-cuibhle f, sèithear-cuibhle m
wheeled adj rothach
wheesht! excl ist! (pl istibh!) & eist! (pl eistibh!), tost!
whelk n faochag f
whelp n cuilean m
when adv (inter) cuine
when conj (non-inter) nuair a
whenever pron 1 ge b' e cuin(e); 2 uair sam bith
where adv 1 (inter) càite; 2 in expr ~ ... **from?** cò às ...
where conj (non-inter) far a
wherever pron 1 ge b' e càit(e); 2 àite sam bith m; 3 (emph for **where**) càit air bith
whereupon adv (is) leis (a) sin

whether conj co-aca, co-dhiù
which pron cò
while conj fhad 's a
while n greis f, treis f, tamall m, tràth m
while v in expr ~ **away** cuir seachad
whim n saobh-smuain f
whimper n sgiùgan m
whimper v dèan sgiùgan m
whinny n sitir f
whinny v dèan sitir f
whin(s) n conasg m
whip n cuip f
whip v cuip vt, sgiùrs vt
whipping n cuipeadh m
whisky n uisge-beatha m, mac-na-bracha m
whisper n cagar m
whisper v cagair vti
whispering n cagar m, cagarsaich f
whistle n 1 (noise) fead f; 2 (instrument) feadag f, fìdeag f
whistle v 1 (single) dèan fead, leig fead (à); 2 (continuous) feadaireachd vi
whistling n 1 fead f; 2 (continuous) feadaireachd f, feadalaich f, feadarsaich f
white adj 1 (general) geal; 2 (hair etc) bàn, fionn
white n 1 geal m
whiten v gealaich vti
whiteness n gile f, gilead m
whiting n cuidhteag f
who inter pron cò
who rel pron a, (neg) nach
whoever pron 1 ge b' e cò; 2 duine m sam bith; 3 (who) cò air bith, cò fon ghrèin
whole adj 1 (entire) gu lèir, air fad, uile; 2 (intact) slàn, iomlan; 3 (time) fad
whole n 1 an t-iomlan m; 2 in expr **on the** ~ san fharsaingeachd f
wholeness n slàine f
wholesome adj slàn, fallain
whooping-cough n an triuthach f
why inter adv carson
wicked adj olc, aingidh
wickedness n olc m, donas m, aingidheachd f
widdershins adj tuathal
wide adj farsaing, leathann
widen v leudaich vti
widened adj leudaichte
widow n banntrach f
widower n banntrach f
widowhood n banntrachas m

width *n* farsaingeachd *f*, leud *m*
wield *v* làimhsich *vt*, iomair *vt*
wife *n* bean *f*, bean-phòsta *f*
wifie *n* cailleach *f*
wig *n* gruag-bhrèige *f*
wild *adj* **1** (*non-domesticated*) fiadhaich;
  2 (*weather etc*) garbh; **3** (*unruly,*
  turbulent) garbh, garg, borb; **4** (*angry*)
  fiadhaich; **5** (*hard-living etc*) fiadhaich,
  garbh; **6** *in expr* ~ **and woolly** molach
wildcat *n* cat-fiadhaich *m*
wilderness *n* fàsach *mf*, dìthreabh *f*
wildness *n* gairbhe *f*, gairbhead *m*, gairge
  f, buirbe *f*
wile *n* cuilbheart *f*, innleachd *f*, car *m*
wilful *adj* ceann-làidir, rag, rag-
  mhuinealach, dùr
will *n* **1** toil *f*; **2** (*document*) tiomnadh *m*
willing *adj* deònach, èasgaidh, toileach
willingly *adv* a dheòin
willingness *n* deòin *f*
willow *n* seileach *m*
willy-nilly *adv* a dheòin no a dh'aindeoin
wily *adj* carach, fiar, seòlta, caon
win *v* **1** (*as vt*) coisinn *vt*, faigh *vt*,
  buannaich *vt*; **2** (*as vi*) buannaich *vi*,
  buinnig *vi*
wind *n* **1** gaoth *f*; **2** (*intestinal*) a' ghaoth
wind *v* toinn *vt*
windfall *n* turchairt *f*
winding *adj* lùbach
winding-sheet *n* marbhphaisg *f*
windmill *n* muileann-gaoithe *mf*
window *n* uinneag *f*
windowsill *n* oir (na h-)uinneige *f*
windsock *n* muincheann-gaoithe *m*
windy *adj* gaothach
wine *n* fìon *m*
wing *n* **1** sgiath *f*; **2** *in expr* **on the** ~ air
  iteig
wink *n* norrag *f*, priobadh (na sùla) *m*
wink *v* priob *vi*, caog *vi*
winkle *n* faochag *f*
winner *n* buannaiche *m*
winter *n* geamhradh *m*
wintry *adj* geamhrachail
wipe *v* suath *vt*, siab *vt*
wiper *n* siabair *m*
wire *n* uèir *f*
wisdom *n* **1** gliocas *m*; **2** *in expr* ~ **tooth**
  fiacail-forais *f*
wise *adj* glic

wish *n* **1** (*desire*) miann *mf*, rùn *m*, togradh
  m, dèidh *f*; **2** (*expression*) guidhe *mf*,
  (*greeting*) dùrachd *m*, (*corres etc*) **with**
  best ~**es** leis gach deagh dhùrachd
wish *v* **1** (*desire*) miannaich *vt*, rùnaich
  vt; **2** is miann leam; **3** (*as vi*) togair *vi*;
  4 (*express*) guidh *vt*
wishing well *n* tobar m(h)iann *mf*
wisp *n* (*straw etc*) sop *m*
wit *n* **1** (*humour*) eirmse *f*; **2** (*sense*) toinisg
  f, ciall *f*; **3** (*sanity*) ciall *f*, rian *m*, reusan *m*
witch *n* bana-bhuidseach *f*
witchcraft *n* buidseachd *f*
with *prep* **1** (*accompanying*) còmhla ri,
  cuide ri, mar ri, maille ri; **2** (*by means of*)
  le; **3** (*as consequence of*) leis
withdraw *v* tarraing *vti* air ais, thoir *vt*
  air ais
withdrawn *adj* (*person*) fad' às, dùinte
wither *v* crìon *vti*, searg *vti*
withered *adj & past part* crìon, seargte
withhold *v* cùm *vt* air ais
without *prep* gun
withstand *v* **1** (*resist*) seas *vi* ri; **2** (*bear*)
  fuiling *vt*
witness *n* **1** (*abstr*) fianais *f*; **2** (*con*) neach-
  fianais *m*
witness *v* **1** faic *vt*, bi *vi irreg* nad (*etc*)
  neach-fianais *m*; **2** (*legal*) dèan fianais do
witty *adj* eirmseach
wizard *n* buidseach *m*, draoidh *m*
wizardry *n* draoidheachd *f*
wizened *adj* crìon
wobbly *adj* cugallach
woe *n* bròn *m*, mulad *f*, dòlas *m*, truaighe *f*
woeful *adj* brònach, muladach, truagh
wolf *n* madadh-allaidh *m*, faol *m*
woman *n* boireannach *m*, tè *f*, bean *f*
womanly *adj* banail
womb *n* machlag *f*, brù *f*, broinn *f*
wonder *n* iongnadh *m*, iongantas *m*,
  mìorbhail *f*
wonderful *adj* iongantach, mìorbhaileach
wood *n* **1** (*material*) fiodh *m*; **2** (*worked*)
  maide *m*; **3** (*trees*) coille *f*
woodcock *n* coileach-coille *m*
woodcutter *n* coillear *m*, gearradair-fiodha
  m
wooden *adj* fiodha
wood-louse *n* reudan *m*
wool *n* clòimh *f*, olann *f*
woollen *adj* de chlòimh *f*

woolly adj **1** (*lit*) clòimheach, ollach; **2** (*unkempt*) (**wild and**) ~ molach, ròmach; **3** (*thinking etc*) ceòthach

word n **1** facal *m*; **2** (*pronouncement etc*) briathar *m*; **3** (*promise*) facal *m*; **4** (*information*) fios *m*, guth *m*, sgeul *m*; **5** (*neg: syllable etc*) bìd *f*, bìog *f*, smid *f*

wordy adj faclach, briathrach

work n **1** (*abstr & con*) obair *f*, (*abstr*) cosnadh *m*

work v obraich *vti*

worker n **1** neach-obrach *m*, obraiche *m*

workforce n luchd-obrach *m*

workhorse n each-obrach *m*

working party n buidheann-obrach *mf*

workman n obraiche *m*, fear-obrach *m*

workshop n bùth-obrach *mf*

world n **1** (*abode*) saoghal *m*; **2** (*globe*) cruinne *mf*; **3** (*sphere*) saoghal *m*

worldly adj saoghalta, talmhaidh

worm n boiteag *f*, cnuimh *f*

worn adj & past part **1** caithte; **2** (*threadbare*) lom; **3** in expr ~ **out** (*objects*) caithte, (*exhausted etc*) claoidhte

worried adj **1** fo chùram *m*, draghail, fo iomagain, iomagaineach, fo uallach; **2** (*nervy*) frionasach

worry n dragh *m*, uallach *m*

worry v **1** (*as vi*) gabh dragh, gabh uallach; **2** (*as vt*) cuir dragh air, dèan dragh do

worrying adj draghail, iomagaineach, imcheisteach

worse comp adj **1** nas miosa; **2** in expr **you'd be none the** ~ ... cha bu mhiste sibh ...

worship n adhradh *m*

worship v dèan/thoir adhradh do

worst superlative adj **1** as miosa; **2** in exprs ~ **of** diù *m*

worth fiach *m*, luach *m*

worth n fiach *m*, **give me two pounds'** ~ **of it** thoir dhomh fiach dà nota dheth

worthless adj **1** (*valueless*) gun fhiù, gun luach; **2** (*useless*) gun fheum

worthwhile adj fiach adj

worthy adj **1** airidh, toillteanach (air); **2** (*decent*) còir

wound n leòn *m*, lot *m*, creuchd *f*

wound v leòn *vt*, lot *vt*, creuchd *vt*

wounded adj leònta/leònte

wounding adj (*remarks etc*) guineach, beumnach

woven adj & past part fighte

wrangle n conas *m*

wrangle v connsaich *vi*, connspaid *vi*

wrangling n connspaid *f*

wrangling adj connspaideach

wrap v **1** (*envelop etc*) suain *vt*; **2** ~ (**up**) (*parcel etc*) paisg *vt*, fill *vt*

wrapping n pasgadh *m*

wrath n fearg *f*

wrathful adj feargach

wreathe v toinn *vt*

wreck n (*ship*) long-bhris(t)eadh *m*

wreck v sgrios *vt*, mill *vt*

wren n dreathan-donn *m*

wrestle v gleac *vi*

wretch n **1** (*unfortunate etc person*) truaghan *m*; **2** (*despicable etc person*) duine suarach, duine tàireil

wretched adj **1** (*pitiable*) truagh; **2** (*despicable etc*) suarach, tàireil

wring v fàisg *vt*

wrinkle n preas *m*, preasag *f*, roc *f*

wrinkle v preas *vt*

wrinkled, wrinkly adj preasach

wrist n caol an dùirn *m*

writ n sgrìobhainn-cùirte *f*

write v **1** sgrìobh *vti*; **2** in expr ~ **off** cuir às a' chunntas

writer n sgrìobhadair *m*, sgrìobhaiche *m*

writing n sgrìobhadh *m*

wrong adj **1** (*incorrect*) ceàrr, mearachdach, iomrallach; **2** (*morally*) eucorach, olc

wrong adv **1** (*awry*) ceàrr, tuathal; **2** in expr **what's** ~ **with you**? dè a tha a' gabhail riut?, dè a tha thu a' gearan?; **3** in expr **go** ~ (*err*) rach *vi* air iomrall; **4** in expr **go** ~ (*morally*) rach *vi* air iomrall, rach *vi* air seachran

wrong n eucoir *f*, coire *f*

wrong v dèan eucoir air

wrongful adj eucorach

wynd n caol-shràid *f*

X

xenophobia *n* gall-ghamhlas *m*
Xmas *n* An Nollaig *f*

x-ray *n* x-ghath *m*, gath-x *m*
xylophone *n* saidhleafòn *m*

Y

yacht *n* sgoth-long *f*, gheat *f*
yard¹ *n* **1** (*enclosure*) cùirt *f*; **2** (*school etc*) raon-cluiche *m*; **3** (*agric*) iodhlann *f*
yard² *n* (*measurement*) slat *f*
yardstick *n* slat-thomhais *f*
yawl *n* geòla *f*
yawn *n* mèaran/mèanan *m*
yawn *v* dèan mèaranaich/mèananaich
yawning *n* mèaranaich/mèananaich
year *n* bliadhna *f*
yearling *adj* bliadhnach
yearling *n* bliadhnach *m*
yearly *adj* bliadhnail
yearning *n* fadachd *f*, fadal *m*
yeast *n* beirm *f*
yell *n* sgairt *f*, glaodh *m*, ràn *m*, sgal *m*, sgiamh *m*
yell *v* dèan sgairt, glaodh *vi*, ràn *vi*, sgal *vi*, sgiamh *vi*
yelling *n* sgreuchail *f*, rànail *m*, rànaich *f*, sgaladh *m*
yellow *adj* buidhe
yes *adv* **1** (*affirmative*) *rendered by repetition of verb in question*; **2** (*non-affirmative*) seadh *adv*
yesterday *adv* an-dè
yet *adv* fhathast
yet *conj* ge-tà, air a shon sin, ach
yew *n* iubhar *m*, (*tree*) craobh-iubhair *f*
yield *n* toradh *m*
yield *v* **1** (*submit*) gèill *vi*, strìochd *vi* (**to**) (do); **2** (*as vt*) thoir *vt* suas do; **3** (*provide*) thoir *vt* seachad

yielding *adj* (*ground etc*) bog, tais; (*person*) sochar, meata
yielding *n* gèilleadh *m*, strìochdadh *m*
yobbish *adj* gràisgeil
yobbishness *n* gràisgealachd *f*
yoke *n* cuing *f*
yolk *n* buidheagan *m*
yon, yonder *adj* ud, ann an siud
yonder *adv* **1** an siud, ann an siud; **2** *in expr* **over** ~ thall, thall an siud
you *pers pron* (*sing fam*) thu, (*pl & formal sing*) sibh, (*emph*) thusa, sibhse & thu fhèin, sibh fhèin
young *adj* òg
young *n* **1** (*animals*) àl *m*; **2** *in expr* **the** ~ na daoine òga
youngster *n* (*male*) òganach *m*, òigear *m*
your *poss adj* **1** (*sing, fam*) do (*lenites following cons where possible*), (*pl & formal sing*) ur, bhur; **2** *also expressed by prep prons* agad (*sing, fam*) & agaibh (*pl & formal sing*)
yours *poss pron* **1** (*sing, fam*) leat(sa), (*pl & formal sing*) leibh(se); **2** (*in corres*) ~**s sincerely** le dùrachd, is mise le meas
yourself, yourselves *reflexive pron* (*sing, fam*) thu fhèin, (*pl & formal sing*) sibh fhèin
youth *n* (*abstr*) **1** òige *f*; **2** (*person*) òigear *m*, òganach *m*; **3** (*coll*) òigridh *f*

Z

zeal *n* dìoghras *m*, dealas *m*, eud *m*

zealous *adj* dealasach, dùrachdach, dìcheallach

zero *n* neoni *f*

zestful *adj* brìoghmhor

zinc *n* sinc *m*

zone *n* sòn *m*

zoo *n* sutha *mf*

The Forms of the Gaelic Article

		Singular		Plural
		Masculine	**Feminine**	**Both Genders**
Nom & Acc		**an** (*before consonants, exc b,f, m, p*) **am** (*before b, f, m, p*) **an t-** (*before a vowel*)	**a'** (*before b, c, g, m, pl, which are lenited*) **an t-** (*before s followed by l, n or r, or by a vowel*) **an** (*before all other letters; f is lenited*)	**na** **na h-** (*before a vowel*)
	e.g.	an taigh, **an** sìol, **an** sruth **am** bodach, **am** fraoch, **am** mol **an t-**eilean	**a'** chraobh, **a'** ghaoth, **a'** phìob **an t-**sìde, **an t-**sròn **an** ite, **an** fhras	**na** caileagan, **na** rudan **na h-**òrain, **na** h-uairean
Gen		**a'** (*before b, c, g, m, p, which are lenited*) **an t-** (*before s followed by l, n or r, or by a vowel*) **an** (*before all other letters; f is lenited*)	**na** (**na h-** *before a vowel*)	**nan** (**nam** *before b, f, m, p*)
	e.g.	**a'** bhodaich, **a'** ghliocais, **a'** mhadaidh **an t-**sìl, **an t-**sruith **an** eilein, **an** taighe, **an** fhraoich	**na** gaoithe, **na** craoibhe, **na** sròine **na h-**ite	**nan** taighean, **nan** òran **nam** bodach, **nam** fìgean
Dat		**a'** (*before b, c, g, m, p, which are all lenited*) **an t-** (*before s followed by l, n, r, or by a vowel*) **an** (*before all other letters; f is lenited*)	**a'** (*before b, c, g, m, p, which are lenited*) **an t-** (*before s followed by l, n, r, or by a vowel*) **an** (*before all other letters; f is lenited*)	**na** (**na h-** *before a vowel*)
	e.g.	**a'** bhodach, **a'** chù, **a'** gheall **an t-**sìol, **an t-**sruth, **an t-**salann **an** eilean, **an** taigh, **an** fhraoch	**a'** ghaoith, **a'** chraoibh **an t-**sùil, **an t-**slàit, **an t-**sròin **an** tràigh, **an** fhàire	**na** caileagan, **na** h-òrain

Note: In the Dative Singular, for both genders, after a preposition ending in a vowel the article is shortened to 'n or 'n t-, and combined with the preposition. E.g. don bhùth, on taigh, on taigh, bhon t-sìol, tron choille, fon t-sruth, mun bhòrd.

265

The More Common Forms of the Gaelic Irregular and Defective Verbs

ABAIR

abair say (*pres part* **ag ràdh** saying, *infin* **a ràdh** to say)

Important Note: It is very common for the forms of this verb, except for the Past (Preterite), to be supplied by the defective verb **can** (see p268, 269 below).

IMPERATIVE

abram let me say	**na h-abram** let me not say
abair (*sing*) say	**na h-abair** (*sing*) don't say
abradh e/i let him/her say	**na h-abradh e/i** let him/her not say
abramaid let us say	**na h-abramaid** let us not say
abraibh (*pl*) say	**na h-abraibh** (*pl*) don't say
abradh iad let them say	**na h-abradh iad** let them not say

FUTURE (AND HABITUAL PRESENT)

their mi I will say, I say	**chan abair mi** I won't say, I don't say
an abair mi? will I say? do I say?	**nach abair mi?** won't I say? don't I say?

RELATIVE FUTURE
dè a their mi? what will I say?

PAST (PRETERITE)

thuirt mi I said	**cha tuirt mi** I didn't say
an tuirt mi did I say?	**nach tuirt mi?** didn't I say?

Note: **thuirt** also occurs as **thubhairt** (for emphasis); **tuirt** occurs as **tubhairt**

PERFECT AND PLUPERFECT

tha mi air ràdh I have said	**bha mi air ràdh** I had said
tha mi air a ràdh I have said it (*m or f*)	**bha mi air a ràdh** I had said it (*m or f*)

Note: In the Future, Relative Future, Past, Perfect and Pluperfect tenses, the same forms of the verb are used for all persons.

CONDITIONAL

theirinn I would say

theireadh* tu you would say

theireamaid we would say

an abrainn? would I say?

an abradh* tu? would you say?

an abramaid? would we say?

chan abrainn I wouldn't say

chan abradh* tu you wouldn't say

chan abramaid we wouldn't say

nach abrainn? wouldn't I say?

nach abradh* tu? wouldn't you say?

nach abramaid? wouldn't we say?

The forms marked * are used for all persons except the first singular, I. The forms in **-maid** are alternative forms for the first person plural, we.

BEIR

beir bear, catch (*pres part* **a' breith** bearing/catching, *infin* **a bhreith** to bear/catch)

IMPERATIVE

beiream let me bear

beir (*sing*) bear

beireadh e/i let him/her bear

beireamaid let us bear

beiribh (*pl*) bear

beireadh iad let them bear

na beiream let me not bear

na beir (*sing*) don't bear

na beireadh e/i let him/her not bear

na beireamaid let us not bear

na beiribh (*pl*) don't bear

na beireadh iad let them not bear

FUTURE (AND HABITUAL PRESENT)

beiridh mi I will bear, I bear

am beir mi? will I bear? do I bear?

cha bheir mi I won't bear, I don't bear

nach beir mi? won't I bear? don't I bear?

RELATIVE FUTURE

dè a bheir/bheireas mi? what will I bear?

PAST (PRETERITE)

rug mi I bore

an do rug mi did I bear?

cha do rug mi I didn't bear

nach do rug mi? didn't I bear?

PERFECT AND PLUPERFECT

tha mi air breith I have borne

tha mi air a bhreith I have borne it (*m*)

bha mi air breith I had borne

bha mi air a bhreith I had borne it (*m*)

CONDITIONAL

bheirinn I would bear

bheireadh* tu you would bear

bheireamaid we would bear

am beirinn? would I bear?

am beireadh* tu? would you bear?

am beireamaid? would we bear?

cha bheirinn I wouldn't bear

cha bheireadh* tu you wouldn't bear

cha bheireamaid we wouldn't bear

nach beirinn? wouldn't I bear?

nach beireadh* tu? wouldn't you bear?

nach beireamaid? wouldn't we bear?

The forms marked * are used for all persons except the first singular, I. The forms in -**maid** are alternative forms for the first person plural, we.

PAST PASSIVE

rugadh e he was born

an do rugadh e? was he born?

cha do rugadh e he wasn't born

nach do rugadh e? wasn't he born?

Note: In the Future, Relative Future, Past, Perfect, Pluperfect and Past Passive, the same forms of the verb are used for all persons.

CAN

can say (*pres part* **a' cantainn** saying, *infin* **a chantainn** to say)
Note: The following forms of this defective verb are very commonly used instead of the corresponding forms of **abair** (see p266, 267).

IMPERATIVE

canam let me say

can (*sing*) say

canadh e/i let him/her say

canamaid let us say

canaibh (*pl*) say

canadh iad let them say

na canam let me not say

na can (*sing*) don't say

na canadh e/i let him/her not say

na canamaid let us not say

na canaibh (*pl*) don't say

na canadh iad let them not say

FUTURE AND HABITUAL PRESENT

canaidh mi I will say, I say

an can mi? will I say? do I say?

cha chan mi I won't say, I don't say

nach can mi? won't I say? don't I say?

RELATIVE FUTURE

dè a chanas mi? what will I say?

PERFECT AND PLUPERFECT
tha mi air cantainn I have said
tha mi air a chantainn I have
  said it (*m*)

bha mi air cantainn I had said
bha mi air a chantainn I had said it
  (*m*)

Note: In the Future, Relative Future, Perfect and Pluperfect, the same forms of
the verb are used for all persons.

CONDITIONAL
chanainn I would say
chanadh* tu you would say
chanamaid we would say
an canainn? would I say?
an canadh* tu? would you say?
an canamaid? would we say?

cha chanainn I wouldn't say
cha chanadh* tu you wouldn't say
cha chanamaid we wouldn't say
nach canainn? wouldn't I say?
nach canadh* tu? wouldn't you say?
nach canamaid? wouldn't we say?

The forms marked * are used for all persons except the first singular, I. The
forms in -**maid** are alternative forms for the first person plural, we.

CLUINN

cluinn hear (*pres part* **a' cluinntinn** hearing, *infin* **a chluinntinn** to hear)

IMPERATIVE
cluinneam let me hear
cluinn (*sing*) hear
cluinneadh e/i let him/her hear

na cluinneam let me not hear
na cluinn (*sing*) don't hear
na cluinneadh e/i let him/her not
  hear

cluinneamaid let us hear
cluinnibh (*pl*) hear
cluinneadh iad let them hear

na cluinneamaid let us not hear
na cluinnibh (*pl*) don't hear
na cluinneadh iad let them not hear

FUTURE AND HABITUAL PRESENT
cluinnidh mi I will hear, I hear

an cluinn mi? will I hear? do
  I hear?

cha chluinn mi I won't hear, I don't
  hear
nach cluinn mi? won't I hear? don't I
  hear?

RELATIVE FUTURE
dè a chluinneas mi? what will I hear?

PAST (PRETERITE)
chuala mi I heard
an cuala mi? did I hear?

cha chuala mi I didn't hear
nach cuala mi? didn't I hear?

PERFECT AND PLUPERFECT

tha mi air cluinntinn
I have heard
tha mi air a chluinntinn (*m*)
I have heard it (*m*)

bha mi air cluinntinn
I had heard
bha mi air a chluinntinn
I had heard it (*m*)

Note: In the Future, Relative Future, Past, Perfect and Pluperfect, the same forms of the verb are used for all persons.

CONDITIONAL

chluinninn I would hear
chluinneadh* tu you would hear
chluinneamaid we would hear

cha chluinninn I wouldn't hear
cha chluinneadh* tu you wouldn't hear
cha chluinneamaid we wouldn't hear

an cluinninn? would I hear?
an cluinneadh* tu? would you hear?
an cluinneamaid? would we hear?

nach cluinninn? wouldn't I hear?
nach cluinneadh* tu? wouldn't you hear?
nach cluinneamaid? wouldn't we hear?

The forms marked * are used for all persons except the first singular, I. The forms in -**maid** are alternative forms for the first person plural, we.

DEAN

dèan do/make (*pres part* **a' dèanamh** doing/making, *infin* **a dhèanamh** to do/make)

IMPERATIVE

dèanam let me do
dèan (*sing*) do
dèanadh e/i let him/her do
dèanamaid let us do
dèanaibh (*pl*) do
dèanadh iad let them do

na dèanam let me not do
na dèan (*sing*) don't do
na dèanadh e/i let him/her not do
na dèanamaid let us not do
na dèanaibh (*pl*) don't do
na dèanadh iad let them not do

FUTURE AND HABITUAL PRESENT

nì mi I will do, I do
an dèan mi? will I do? do I do?

cha dèan mi I won't do, I don't do
nach dèan mi? won't I do? don't I do?

RELATIVE FUTURE

dè a nì mi? what will I do?

PAST (PRETERITE)

rinn mi I did
an do rinn mi? did I do?

cha do rinn mi I didn't do
nach do rinn mi? didn't I do?

PERFECT AND PLUPERFECT
tha mi air dèanamh I have done   **bha mi air dèanamh** I had done
tha mi air a dhèanamh   **bha mi air a dhèanamh**
  I have done it (*m*)   I had done it (*m*)

Note: In the Future, Relative Future, Past, Perfect and Pluperfect, the same forms of the verb are used for all persons.

CONDITIONAL
dhèanainn I would do   **cha dèanainn** I wouldn't do
dhèanadh* tu you would do   **cha dèanadh* tu** you wouldn't do
dhèanamaid we would do   **cha dèanamaid** we wouldn't do
an dèanainn? would I do?   **nach dèanainn?** wouldn't I do?
an dèanadh* tu? would you do?   **nach dèanadh* tu?** wouldn't you do?
an dèanamaid? would we do?   **nach dèanamaid?** wouldn't we do?

The forms marked * are used for all persons except the first singular, I. The forms in -**maid** are alternative forms for the first person plural, we.

FAIC

faic see (*pres part* **a' faicinn** seeing, *infin* **a dh'fhaicinn** to see)

IMPERATIVE
faiceam let me see   **na faiceam** let me not see
faic (*sing*) see   **na faic** (*sing*) don't see
faiceadh e/i let him/her see   **na faiceadh e/i** let him/her not see
faiceamaid let us see   **na faiceamaid** let us not see
faicibh (*pl*) see   **na faicibh** (*pl*) don't see
faiceadh iad let them see   **na faiceadh iad** let them not see

FUTURE AND HABITUAL PRESENT
chì mi I will see, I see   **chan fhaic mi** I won't see, I don't see
am faic mi? will I see? do I see? **nach f(h)aic mi?** won't I see? don't I see?

RELATIVE FUTURE
dè a chì mi? what will I see?

PAST (PRETERITE)
chunnaic/chunna mi I saw   **chan fhaca mi** I didn't see
am faca mi? did I see?   **nach f(h)aca mi?** didn't I see?

PERFECT AND PLUPERFECT
tha mi air faicinn I have seen   **bha mi air faicinn** I had seen
tha mi air fhaicinn I have seen **bha mi air fhaicinn** I had seen it (*m*)
it (*m*)

Note: In the Future, Relative Future, Past, Perfect and Pluperfect, the same forms of the verb are used for all persons.

CONDITIONAL

chithinn I would see

chitheadh* tu you would see

chitheamaid we would see

am faicinn? would I see?

am faiceadh* tu? would you see?

am faiceamaid? would we see?

chan fhaicinn I wouldn't see

chan fhaiceadh* tu you wouldn't see

chan fhaiceamaid we wouldn't see

nach f(h)aicinn? wouldn't I see?

nach f(h)aiceadh* tu? wouldn't you see?

nach f(h)aiceamaid? wouldn't we see?

The forms marked * are used for all persons except the first singular, I. The forms in **-maid** are alternative forms for the first person plural, we.

FAIGH

faigh get (*pres part* **a' faighinn** getting, *infin* **a dh'fhaighinn** to get)

IMPERATIVE

faigheam let me get

faigh (*sing*) get

faigheadh e/i let him/her get

faigheamaid let us get

faighibh (*pl*) get

faigheadh iad let them get

na faigheam let me not get

na faigh (*sing*) don't get

na faigheadh e/i let him/her not get

na faigheamaid let us not get

na faighibh (*pl*) don't get

na faigheadh iad let them not get

FUTURE AND HABITUAL PRESENT

gheibh mi I will get, I get

am faigh mi? will I get? do I get?

chan fhaigh mi I won't get, I don't get

nach f(h)aigh mi? won't I get? don't I get?

RELATIVE FUTURE

dè a gheibh mi? what will I get?

PAST (PRETERITE)

fhuair mi I got

an d' fhuair mi? did I get?

cha d' fhuair mi I didn't get

nach d' fhuair mi? didn't I get?

PERFECT AND PLUPERFECT

tha mi air faighinn I have got

tha mi air fhaighinn I have got it (*m*)

bha mi air faighinn I had got

bha mi air fhaighinn I had got it (*m*)

Note: In the Future, Relative Future, Past, Perfect and Pluperfect, the same forms of the verb are used for all persons.

CONDITIONAL

gheibhinn I would get	**chan fhaighinn** I wouldn't get
gheibheadh* tu you would get	**chan fhaigheadh* tu** you wouldn't get
gheibheamaid we would get	**chan fhaigheamaid** we wouldn't get
am faighinn? would I get?	**nach f(h)aighinn?** wouldn't I get?
am faigheadh* tu? would you get?	**nach f(h)aigheadh* tu?** wouldn't you get?
am faigheamaid? would we get?	**nach f(h)aigheamaid?** wouldn't we get?

The forms marked * are used for all persons except the first singular, I. The forms in -**maid** are alternative forms for the first person plural, we.

RACH

rach go (*pres part* **a' dol** going, *infin* **a dhol** to go)

IMPERATIVE

racham let me go	**na racham** let me not go
rach (*sing*) go	**na rach** (*sing*) don't go
rachadh e/i let him/her go	**na rachadh e/i** let him/her not go
rachamaid let us go	**na rachamaid** let us not go
rachaibh (*pl*) go	**na rachaibh** (*pl*) don't go
rachadh iad let them go	**na rachadh iad** let them not go

FUTURE AND HABITUAL PRESENT

thèid mi I will go, I go	**cha tèid mi** I won't go, I don't go
an tèid mi? will I go? do I go?	**nach tèid mi?** won't I go? don't I go?

RELATIVE FUTURE
cuin a thèid mi? when will I go?

PAST (PRETERITE)

chaidh mi I went	**cha deach(aidh) mi** I didn't go
an deach(aidh) mi? did I go?	**nach deach(aidh) mi?** didn't I go?

PERFECT AND PLUPERFECT
tha mi air dol/air a dhol, bha mi air dol/air a dhol I have gone, I had gone

Note: In the Future, Relative Future, Past, Perfect and Pluperfect, the same forms of the verb are used for all persons.

CONDITIONAL

rachainn I would go	**cha rachainn** I wouldn't go
rachadh* tu you would go	**cha rachadh* tu** you wouldn't go
rachamaid we would go	**cha rachamaid** we wouldn't go
an rachainn? would I go?	**nach rachainn?** wouldn't I go?
an rachadh* tu? would you go?	**nach rachadh* tu?** wouldn't you go?
an rachamaid? would we go?	**nach rachamaid?** wouldn't we go?

The forms marked * are used for all persons except the first singular, I. The forms in -**maid** are alternative forms for the first person plural, we.

RUIG

ruig *as vi* arrive, *as vt* reach (*pres part* **a' ruigsinn** arriving *etc, infin* **a ruigsinn** to arrive *etc*)

IMPERATIVE
ruigeam let me arrive   **na ruigeam** let me not arrive
ruig (*sing*) arrive   **na ruig** (*sing*) don't arrive
ruigeadh e/i let him/her arrive   **na ruigeadh e/i** let him/her not arrive
ruigeamaid let us arrive   **na ruigeamaid** let us not arrive
ruigibh (*pl*) arrive   **na ruigibh** (*pl*) don't arrive
ruigeadh iad let them arrive   **na ruigeadh iad** let them not arrive

FUTURE AND HABITUAL PRESENT
ruigidh mi I will arrive, I arrive   **cha ruig mi** I won't arrive, I don't arrive
an ruig mi? will I arrive? do I arrive?   **nach ruig mi?** won't I arrive? don't I arrive?

RELATIVE FUTURE
cuin a ruigeas mi? when will I arrive?

PAST (PRETERITE)
ràinig mi I arrived   **cha do ràinig mi** I didn't arrive
an do ràinig mi? did I arrive?   **nach do ràinig mi?** didn't I arrive?

PERFECT AND PLUPERFECT
tha mi air ruigsinn I have arrived   **bha mi air ruigsinn** I had arrived
tha mi air a ruigsinn I have reached it (*m or f*)   **bha mi air a ruigsinn** I had reached it (*m or f*)

Note: In the Future, Relative Future, Past, Perfect and Pluperfect, the same forms of the verb are used for all persons.

CONDITIONAL
ruiginn I would arrive   **cha ruiginn** I wouldn't arrive
ruigeadh* tu you would arrive   **cha ruigeadh* tu** you wouldn't arrive
ruigeamaid we would arrive   **cha ruigeamaid** we wouldn't arrive
an ruiginn? would I arrive?   **nach ruiginn?** wouldn't I arrive?
an ruigeadh* tu? would you arrive?   **nach ruigeadh* tu?** wouldn't you arrive?
an ruigeamaid? would we arrive?   **nach ruigeamaid?** wouldn't we arrive?

The forms marked * are used for all persons except the first singular, I. The forms in -**maid** are alternative forms for the first person plural, we.

thig come (*pres part* **a' tighinn** coming, *infin* **a thighinn** to come)

IMPERATIVE

thigeam let me come	**na tigeam** let me not come
thig (*sing*) come	**na tig** (*sing*) don't come
thigeadh e/i let him/her come	**na tigeadh e/i** let him/her not come
thigeamaid let us come	**na tigeamaid** let us not come
thigibh (*pl*) come	**na tigibh** (*pl*) don't come
thigeadh iad let them come	**na tigeadh iad** let them not come

FUTURE AND HABITUAL PRESENT

thig mi I will come, I come	**cha tig mi** I won't come, I don't come
an tig mi? will I come? do I come?	**nach tig mi?** won't I come? don't I come?

RELATIVE FUTURE
cuin a thig mi? when will I come?

PAST (PRETERITE)

thàinig mi I came	**cha tàinig mi** I didn't come
an tàinig mi? did I come?	**nach tàinig mi?** didn't I come?

PERFECT AND PLUPERFECT
tha mi air tighinn/a thighinn, bha mi air tighinn/a thighinn I have come, I had come

Note: In the Future, Relative Future, Past, Perfect and Pluperfect, the same forms of the verb are used for all persons.

CONDITIONAL

thiginn I would come	**cha tiginn** I wouldn't come
thigeadh* tu you would come	**cha tigeadh* tu** you wouldn't come
thigeamaid we would come	**cha tigeamaid** we wouldn't come
an tiginn? would I come?	**nach tiginn?** wouldn't I come?
an tigeadh* tu? would you come?	**nach tigeadh* tu?** wouldn't you come?
an tigeamaid? would we come?	**nach tigeamaid?** wouldn't we come?

The forms marked * are used for all persons except the first singular, I. The forms in -**maid** are alternative forms for the first person plural, we.

THOIR

thoir give/take/bring (*pres part* **a' toirt** giving *etc*, *infin* **a thoirt** to give *etc*)

IMPERATIVE

thoiream let me give	**na toiream** let me not give
thoir (*sing*) give	**na toir** (*sing*) don't give
thoireadh e/i let him/her give	**na toireadh e/i** let him/her not give
thoireamaid let us give	**na toireamaid** let us not give
thoiribh (*pl*) give	**na toiribh** (*pl*) don't give
thoireadh iad let them give	**na toireadh iad** let them not give

Note: In the first person sing and pl imperative **t(h)ugam** and **t(h)ugamaid** are also found, and in the third person sing and pl **t(h)ugadh**

FUTURE AND HABITUAL PRESENT

bheir mi I will give, I give	**cha toir mi** I won't give, I don't give
an toir mi? will I give? do I give?	**nach toir mi?** won't I give? don't I give?

RELATIVE FUTURE
dè a bheir mi? what will I give?

PAST (PRETERITE)

thug mi I gave	**cha tug mi** I didn't give
an tug mi? did I give?	**nach tug mi?** didn't I give?

PERFECT AND PLUPERFECT

tha mi air toirt I have given	**bha mi air toirt** I had given
tha mi air a thoirt I have given it (*m*)	**bha mi air a thoirt** I had given it (*m*)

Note: In the Future, Relative Future, Past, Perfect and Pluperfect, the same forms of the verb are used for all persons.

CONDITIONAL

bheirinn I would give	**cha toirinn** I wouldn't give
bheireadh* tu you would give	**cha toireadh* tu** you wouldn't give
bheireamaid we would give	**cha toireamaid** we wouldn't give
an toirinn? would I give?	**nach toirinn?** wouldn't I give?
an toireadh* tu? would you give?	**nach toireadh* tu?** wouldn't you give?
an toireamaid? would we give?	**nach toireamaid?** wouldn't we give?

The forms marked * are used for all persons except the first singular, I. The forms in -**maid** are alternative forms for the first person plural, we.

Note: **toir**, **thoir** and **toirt** are occasionally found as **tabhair**, **thabhair** and **tabhairt**.

bi be (*infin* **a bhith** to be)

IMPERATIVE
bitheam let me be
bi (*sing*) be
biodh/bitheadh e/i let him/
 her be
biomaid/bitheamaid let us be
bithibh (*pl*) be
biodh, bitheadh iad let them be

na bitheam let me not be
na bi (*sing*) don't be
na biodh/bitheadh e/i let him/her
 not be
na biomaid/bitheamaid let us not be
na bithibh (*pl*) don't be
na biodh, bitheadh iad let them not be

PRESENT
tha mi I am
a bheil mi? am I?

chan eil mi I am not
nach eil mi am I not?

FUTURE AND HABITUAL PRESENT
bidh/bithidh mi I will be, I am
am bi mi? will I be? am I?

cha bhi mi I won't be, I'm not
nach bi mi? won't I be? am I not?

RELATIVE FUTURE
ma bhios, ma bhitheas mi if I will be, if I am

PAST (PRETERITE)
bha mi I was
an robh mi? was I?

cha robh mi I wasn't
nach robh mi? wasn't I?

PERFECT AND PLUPERFECT
tha mi air a bhith I have been

bha mi air a bhith I had been

Note: In the Future, Relative Future, Past, Perfect, and Pluperfect, the same forms of the verb are used for all persons.

CONDITIONAL
bhithinn I would be
bhiodh*/bhitheadh tu you
would be
bhiomaid/bhitheamaid
we would be
am bithinn? would I be?
am biodh*/bitheadh tu?
would you be?
am biomaid/bitheamaid?
would we be?

cha bhithinn I wouldn't be
cha bhiodh*/bhitheadh tu you
wouldn't be
cha bhiomaid/bhitheamaid
we wouldn't be
nach bithinn? wouldn't I be?
nach biodh*/bitheadh tu?
wouldn't you be?
nach biomaid/bitheamaid?
wouldn't we be?

The forms marked * are used for all persons except the first singular, I. The forms in -**maid** are alternative forms for the first person plural, we. *See also following page.*

Constructions Using Bi as
an Auxiliary Verb

PRESENT AND PAST CONTINUOUS (ACTIVE, REFLEXIVE AND PASSIVE)
tha/bha e a' bualadh he is/was striking
tha/bha e gam bualadh he is/was striking them
tha/bha e ga bhualadh fhèin he is/was striking himself
tha/bha e ga bhualadh he is/was being struck (*also* he is/was striking him
   or it *m*)

PERFECT TENSES (PRESENT, PLUPERFECT, FUTURE AND
CONDITIONAL), ACTIVE AND PASSIVE
tha/bha e air bualadh he has/had struck
tha/bha e air am bualadh he has/had struck them
tha/bha e air a bhualadh he has/had been struck (*also* he has/had struck
   him *or* it *m*)
bidh e air bualadh he will have struck
bidh e air am bualadh he will have struck them
bidh e air a bhualadh he will have been struck (*also* he will have struck him
   or it *m*)
bhiodh e air bualadh he would have struck
bhiodh e air am bualadh he would have struck them
bhiodh e air a bhualadh he would have been struck (*also* he would have
   struck him *or* it *m*)

IMPERSONAL PASSIVE
thathar ag ràdh it is said *and* it is being said
bhathar ag ràdh it was said *and* it was being said
bithear ag ràdh it is said *and* it will be said
bhite/bhithist ag ràdh it would be said *and* it used to be said

The Gaelic Prepositional Pronouns

Below are given the principal Gaelic pronouns, followed by the forms of the prepositional pronouns to which they give rise. These are formed by combining a given preposition with each of the personal pronouns (*eg* **aig** combined with **mi** gives **agam**, **ri** combined with **sinn** gives **rinn**). The emphatic/reflexive particles **-sa**, **-se** *etc* (*as in* **agadsa** 'at yourself' *or* **dhìse** 'to *or* for herself') are shown in brackets.

à, **às**, from, out of: **asam(sa), asad(sa), às(-san), aiste(se), asainn(e), asaibh(se), asta(san),** from me, you *etc*

aig, at: **agam(sa), agad(sa), aige(san), aice(se), againn(e), agaibh(se), aca(san),** at me, you *etc*; *also* my *etc*, *as in* **an cù agam** my dog

air, on: **orm(sa), ort(sa), air(san), oirre(se), oirnn(e), oirbh(se), orra(san),** on me, you *etc*

an, **ann an/am**, in: **annam(sa), annad(sa), ann(san), innte(se), annainn(e), annaibh(se), annta(san),** in me, you *etc*

bho, from: **bhuam(sa), bhuat(sa), bhuaithe(san), bhuaipe(se), bhuainn(e), bhuaibh(se), bhuapa(san),** from me, you *etc*

chun, to: **chugam(sa), chugad(sa), chuige(san), chuice(se), chugainn(e), chugaibh(se), chuca(san),** to me, you *etc*

de & **dhe**, of, from: **dhìom(sa), dhìot(sa), dheth(san), dhith(se), dhinn(e), dhibh(se), dhiubh(san),** of/from me, you *etc*

do, to, for: **dhòmh(sa), dhut(sa), dhà(san), dhì(se), dhuinn(e), dhuibh(se), dhaibh(san),** to/for me, you *etc*

eadar, between: *combines with the pl pers prons* **sinn, sibh, iad** *to give the prep prons* **eadarainn, eadaraibh, eatarra**, between us, you, them

fo, under, beneath: **fodham(sa), fodhad(sa), fodha(san), fòidhpe(se), fodhainn(e), fodhaibh(se), fòdhpa(san),** under/beneath me, you *etc*

gu, to: **thugam(sa), thugad(sa), thuige(san), thuice(se), thugainn(e), thugaibh(se), thuca(san),** to me, you *etc*

le, with: **leam(sa), leat(sa), leis(-san), leatha(se), leinn(e), leibh(se), leotha(san),** with me, you *etc*, *also* 'mine', 'yours' *etc*, *as in* **is ann leamsa a tha e** it's mine, it belongs to me

mu, about, around; concerning: **umam(sa), umad(sa), uime(san), uimpe(se), umainn(e), umaibh(se), umpa(san)**, around/concerning me, you *etc*

o, from: **uam(sa), uat(sa), uaithe(san), uaipe(se), uainn(e), uaibh(se), uapa(san)**, from me, you *etc*

ri, to; against: **rium(sa), riut(sa), ris(-san), rithe(se), rinn(e), ribh(se), riutha(san)**, to/against me, you *etc*

ro, before: **romham(sa), romhad(sa), roimhe(san), roimhpe(se), romhainn(e), romhaibh(se), romhpa(san)**, before me, you *etc*

thar, across, over: **tharam(sa), tharad(sa), thairis(san), thairte(se), tharainn(e), tharaibh(se), tharta(san)**, across/over me, you *etc*

tro, through: **tromham(sa), tromhad(sa), troimhe(san), troimhpe(se), tromhainn(e), tromhaibh(se), tromhpa(san)**, through me, you *etc*